THE LIBRARY
CENTRAL COLLEGE OF COMMERCE
300 CATHEDRAL STREET
GLASGOW
G1 2TA

Preface

Cognitive Psychology and Instruction, Second Edition, is a revision of the book *Cognitive Psychology for Teachers,* first published in 1990. The original edition was aimed at giving educators a solid grounding in cognitive psychology and at helping them link the important findings of cognitive psychology to instruction. These goals remain the primary aims of the second edition. Like the first edition, the current text is directed at *all* educators and others who are interested in understanding the principles of cognitive psychology and in applying them to instruction and curriculum design.

The original book was organized into two major parts, the first laying out the basic principles of cognitive psychology, and the second concentrating on applications of a cognitive approach in the schools. The second edition retains this basic applied research distinction, but adds two major new sections, one outlining new research on the importance of beliefs in cognition, and a second that describes current approaches to problem solving, critical thinking, and reflective thought.

Cognitive Psychology and Instruction begins with Chapter 1, an introduction to cognitive psychology and how it developed into its current position of dominance in American psychology. Part I, "Information Processing Theory," then describes key elements of a cognitive model. Chapter 2, "Sensory Memory," begins this section, emphasizing the processes of perception and attention. Chapter 3, "Memory: Structures and Models," presents the modal model of memory and outlines key concepts that have guided cognitive research in the past two decades. Chapters 4 and 5, "Encoding Processes" and "Retrieval Processes," round out Part I by providing detailed accounts of how encoding and retrieval affect the nature and quality of cognitive processes.

As cognitive psychology matures, it is moving rapidly toward an increased emphasis on the role of beliefs in guiding and motivating cognitive processes. Part II, "Beliefs and Cognition," is an entirely new section, added to reflect these developments. Chapter 6, "Beliefs About Self," examines motivational issues of special importance to educators, including Bandura's social cognitive theory, attribution theory, and issues of student autonomy and control. Chapter 7, "Beliefs About Intelligence and Knowledge," is another entirely new chapter. It shows how beliefs about ability and the nature of knowledge are critical determinants of what students choose to do and what they achieve.

Part III, "Fostering Cognitive Growth," likewise contains two new chapters. Chapter 8, "Problem Solving and Critical Thinking," translates research from these two vital areas into practical applications in classrooms and other educational settings. Chapter 9, "Building Knowledge and Reflective Thought," provides an integrated view of how educators can build an environment based on cognitive principles that will stimulate cognitive growth, reflection, and self-regulation.

Part IV, the final section of the text, is entitled "Cognition in the Classroom." In general, the research presented in this section shows how greatly cognitive perspectives have affected our views of schooling. Three chapters in this section deal with dimensions of literacy. Chapter 10, "Learning to Read," and Chapter 11, "Reading to Learn," describe detailed accounts of linguistic and cognitive processes in beginning and later reading. Chapter 12, "Writing," illustrates how cognitive analyses have been applied to writing and have created new perspectives on writing instruction. Chapter 13, "Cognitive Processes in Mathematics," and Chapter 14, "Cognitive Processes in Science," show how cognitive theory has created fundamentally new conceptions of learning and teaching in math and science.

We do not think that cognitive psychology is the only approach to psychology that can inform education. We are, however, strongly committed to a view that principles drawn from cognitive psychology can greatly enrich our understanding of educational processes and goals. We also do not see cognitive psychology as a static body of knowledge. In the relatively short time since publication of the first edition, for example, we have seen tremendous movement in the field and we fully expect it to continue to evolve rapidly into the future.

Many, many individuals have been involved in making this second edition a reality. We wish to thank Chris Jennison, who encouraged our author group when we first began this project some years ago. For this second edition, our journey began with Robert Miller, then Education Editor for Macmillan, and has continued under the extraordinarily able guidance of Kevin M. Davis, Senior Education Editor at Merrill. We are also grateful to a particularly capable group of reviewers of this edition. These include Linda D. Chrosniak, George Mason University; Mary Lou Koran, University of Florida; Raymond W. Kulhavy, Arizona State University; Michael S. Meloth, University of Colorado; S. J. Samuels, The University of Minnesota; Robert Tennyson, The University of Minnesota; Charles K. West, University of Illinois at Urbana-Champaign; Frank W. Wicker, University of Texas at Austin; and Karen Zabrucky, Georgia State University. Their insights and suggestions have contributed measurably to our ability to create a useful account of cognitive psychology and its applications to education. We especially wish to thank Mary Irvin, who served as production editor for this edition, and our copyeditor, Linda Poderski: our interactions with them about this text and its features have filled us with admiration for their

25.99

R 370.152

THE LIBRARY
CENTRAL COLLEGE OF COMMERCE
300 CATHEDRAL STREET
GLASGOW
G1 2TA

This book is due for return on or before the last date shown below.

– 8 NOV 2016

/ 9 JAN 2017

WITHDRAWN

REFERENCE ONLY

WITHDRAWN

Don Gresswell Ltd., London, N.21   Cat. No. 1208

DG 02242/71

Cognitive Psychology and Instruction

Merrill, *an imprint of*
Prentice Hall
Englewood Cliffs

3230138239

Library of Congress Cataloging-in-Publication Data
Bruning, Roger H.
    Cognitive psychology and instruction / Roger Bruning, Gregg Schraw, Royce Ronning.—2nd ed.
      p. cm.
    Rev. ed. of: Cognitive psychology for teachers / John A. Glover, Royce R. Ronning,
    Roger H. Bruning. © 1990.
    Includes bibliographical references and index.
    ISBN 0-02-315911-1
    1. Learning. 2. Cognitive psychology. 3. Cognitive learning.   I. Schraw, Gregg. II. Ronning,
    Royce R. III. Glover, John A. Cognitive psychology for teachers. IV. Title.
  LB1060.B786   1995
  370.15'2—dc20   94-31791
                                                  CIP

Cover photo: David Tillinghast/The Image Bank
Editor: Kevin M. Davis
Production Editor: Mary Irvin
Text Designer: Kip Shaw
Cover Designer: Proof Positive/Farrowlyne Assoc., Inc.
Production Buyer: Pamela A. Bennett
Electronic Text Management: Marilyn Wilson Phelps, Matthew Williams, Jane Lopez, Karen L. Bretz

This book was set in Garamond ITC by Prentice Hall and was printed and bound
by R. R. Donnelley/Virginia. The cover was printed by Phoenix Color Corp.

 © 1995 by Prentice-Hall, Inc.
A Simon & Schuster Company
Englewood Cliffs, New Jersey 07632

All rights reserved. No part of this book may be reproduced, in any form or
by any means, without permission in writing from the publisher.

Earlier edition, entitled *Cognitive Psychology for Teachers*, © 1990 by Macmillan Publishing Company.

Printed in the United States of America

10 9 8 7 6 5 4 3 2

ISBN: 0-02-315911-1

Prentice-Hall International (UK) Limited, *London*
Prentice-Hall of Australia Pty. Limited, *Sydney*
Prentice-Hall of Canada, Inc., *Toronto*
Prentice-Hall Hispanoamericana, S. A., *Mexico*
Prentice-Hall of India Private Limited, *New Delhi*
Prentice-Hall of Japan, Inc., *Tokyo*
Simon & Schuster Asia Pte. Ltd., *Singapore*
Editora Prentice-Hall do Brasil, Ltda., *Rio de Janeiro*

skills and dedication. Finally, we offer our special thanks to our families, whose support and patience have sustained us through this effort.

We dedicate this edition to Royce R. Ronning, whose wonderful personal qualities and excellence of scholarship placed their mark on the original text and continue to shape this edition. As we worked on this revision and read what Royce had written, we were often reminded of how his intelligence and character helped form not only our perspective of cognitive psychology, but also the thoughts and values of a generation of students and colleagues at the University of Nebraska-Lincoln. Thoughts of Royce also brought to mind how the counsel, support, and friendship of his wife Ruth have been a source of comfort and pleasure for both of us. We are deeply grateful to both Royce and Ruth, and hope that what we have produced in this second edition remains true to their ideals.

R. B.
G. S.

Contents

Chapter 3
Memory: Structures and Models   47

Chapter 4
Encoding Processes   81

Chapter 11
Reading to Learn   263

Chapter 12
Writing   295

Chapter 13
Cognitive Approaches to Mathematics   319

Chapter 14
Cognitive Approaches to Science   343

CHAPTER 1

Introduction to Cognitive Psychology

A Brief History

Cognitive Themes for Education

Summary

Suggested Readings

This book is about cognitive psychology and its implications for education. *Cognitive psychology* is a theoretical perspective that focuses on the realms of human perception, thought, and memory. It portrays learners as active processors of information—a metaphor borrowed from the computer world—and assigns critical roles to the knowledge and perspective students bring to their learning. What learners do to enrich information, in the view of cognitive psychology, determines the level of understanding they ultimately achieve.

The cognitive psychology we describe now is the major force in American psychology. The past twenty years have witnessed its rise from relative obscurity to today, where advertisements for new faculty members in "cognitive psychology" and "cognitive science" outnumber those for "human learning" and "educational psychology." A number of powerful concepts have arisen within cognitive psychology, each with considerable explanatory power in education. Among these concepts are *schemata* (sing., *schema*), the idea that there are mental frameworks for comprehension; *constructive memory*, the view that knowledge is created by learners as they confront new situations; and *levels of processing*, the notion that memory is a by-product of the kind of processing that information receives. Now, as cognitive psychology evolves into a more mature form, it has begun to include social influences on cognitive development, the connections between cognition and motivation, self-awareness and cognitive strategies, and the development of subject matter expertise in such areas as mathematics and science. A major emphasis of this book is description and elaboration of these concepts and themes of cognitive psychology.

A BRIEF HISTORY

The Associationist Era

Each of us has his or her own view of the world, a "world hypothesis" (Pepper, 1942/1961) that guides our observations, our actions, and our understanding of our experience. Any theoretical perspective in psychology similarly rests on a particular view of the world; it counts some things as evidence and not others, organizes that evidence, and makes hypotheses about what the evidence means and how it is inter-related. Cognitive psychology is one such theoretical perspective; it makes the claim that the purpose of scientific psychology is to observe behavior—the observable responses of individuals—in order to make inferences about unobservable, underly-ing factors that can explain the actions we see. In cognitive psychology, observations are used to generate inferences about such factors as thought, language, meaning, and imagery. The field of cognitive psychology seeks to construct formal, systematic explanations about the nature and functions of our mental processes.

From about 1920 to about 1970, however, the world of psychology in the United States was dominated by a theoretical perspective of an entirely different sort—*asso-ciationism* (Dellarosa, 1988). The general goal of this stimulus-response paradigm of psychology was the derivation of elementary laws of behavior and learning and their extension to more complex settings. Inferences about these laws were tied closely to observed behavior. Animals, as well as humans, were suitable objects of study; inves-tigations of learning and memory in "lower organisms" were fueled by a faith that the laws of learning were universal and that work with animals in the laboratory could be extrapolated to humans. As Glover and Ronning (1987) stated, associationism was *the* American psychology during this fifty-year period; there was no real alternative in the United States.

Perhaps the clearest formulations of associationistic principles of learning were made by Clark Hull (1934, 1952) and his colleague Kenneth Spence (1936, 1956). Reasoning from the data of numerous experiments with laboratory animals, Hull and Spence derived equations based on hypothesized variables, such as strength of habits, drive, and inhibition, that enabled predictions to be made about behavior in laboratory settings. As Hull (1952) was able to demonstrate, the elementary laws of learning captured in equations such as these could account for many phenomena of trial-and-error learning and simple discrimination learning in animals.

The use of an associationistic theoretical framework was by no means limited only to those psychologists interested in simple learning phenomena in animals, how-ever. Especially in the United States the associationistic paradigm also dominated the study of memory, of thinking, and of problem solving (Dellarosa, 1988). The focus of study for the vast majority of research in memory during this period was so-called rote or nonmeaningful learning. Following a tradition begun by Hermann Ebbinghaus well before the turn of the century, researchers studied memory for individual items, most commonly nonsense syllables and individual words. The assumption underly-ing these investigations was that understanding simpler forms of learning and mem-ory would lead to understanding complex learning and memory phenomena.

The preferred research methods were those of *serial list learning,* in which one item cues the next item in the list, and *paired associate learning,* in which a "response" must be linked with a "stimulus." These methods allowed the development of associations to be most clearly predicted and studied. As this research was refined further, tables of norms were developed in which nonsense syllables and words were calibrated for their "meaningfulness"; that is, they were rated for the likelihood that they could "generate associates"—elicit responses from learners. Knowing these characteristics of words and syllables permitted researchers to manipulate "associative strength" of materials with precision (see Glaze, 1928; Noble, 1952; and Underwood & Schultz, 1960, for examples of these materials). Like the aims of Hull's and Spence's work with animals, the goal of this research was to develop a basic set of principles derived from the study of learning in its "pure" form that would apply to such broader contexts as learning and recall of materials in school.

A fundamental difficulty, however, was that as experimental psychologists made finer and finer distinctions within the confines of their research on animal "trial-and-error" learning and their studies of rote memory, their findings seemed to become less and less relevant for education and, for that matter, for anything but very limited aspects of human functioning. The search for general laws of learning that crossed all species and settings was failing. As experimental methodologies for studying learning and memory were refined and experiments became more valid internally (Campbell & Stanley, 1963), they were becoming less valid externally. As elucidated by experimental psychology in the United States, the "laws of learning" seemed to be described more properly as the "laws of animal learning," the "laws of animals learning to make choices in mazes," or the "laws of human rote memory" than the universal principles that the associationists sought.

Not all associationistic psychologies were leading to theoretical and applied dead ends, however. The so-called radical behaviorists, led by scientist-philosopher B. F. Skinner, made a strong impact on both psychology and education near the end of this period. Skinner's views were strongly environmental, in the tradition of the early behaviorist John B. Watson. Learners were seen as coming to learning *tabula rasa,* subject to conditioning by their environment. Like Watson, Skinner rejected the idea that the purpose of psychology was to study consciousness; the goal of psychology, he asserted, was to predict and control behavior. What organisms do, Skinner contended, is largely a function of the environment in which they are placed and their learning histories (Skinner, 1938, 1953). By controlling the antecedents and consequences for behavior, prediction and control can be achieved. Consequences for behavior are particularly critical, he argued. By providing positive consequences for behavior and by controlling the schedule by which these consequences were delivered, behavior could be controlled and shaped. In his research, Skinner demonstrated that his laboratory animals indeed were exquisitely sensitive to manipulations of both antecedents and consequences of their actions. Simple responses, such as bar pressing or pecking, were shown to have highly predictable characteristics linked with the patterns by which they produced consequences, such as food or drink (see Ferster & Skinner, 1957). Skinner also demonstrated that by working backward from consequences to the behaviors that preceded them, very complex sequences or chains of behaviors could be developed.

By the mid-1960s, behaviorism as guided by Skinner's views had become such a potent force in American psychology that, in many settings, consciousness was discredited as a respectable topic for research and theory (Baars, 1986). Part of the reason for behaviorism's extraordinary influence was that Skinner and his students had recognized the potential utility of behavioral principles in human learning and had begun to apply them successfully in a variety of settings. Initial applications were in residential treatment facilities for persons with mental illness and mental retardation; careful specification of behavioral goals and standardization of the environment were shown to be very useful for treating a wide range of problems. Extensions of behavioral principles to education soon followed, incorporated into such technologies as classroom management (e.g., Baer, Wolf, & Risley, 1968; Homme, Csanyi, Gonzales, & Rechs, 1968) and teaching machines (Holland & Skinner, 1961; Skinner, 1968). Teaching machines, Skinner contended, could provide the key elements of learning: frequent responding, progress in small steps, shaping, and positive reinforcement. By the early 1970s, as the cognitive movement was just beginning to emerge in American psychology, a range of applications of behavioral principles already were being used in therapeutic and educational settings.

Much of what we do today in education, in fact, reflects behaviorism's continuing influence. For instance, one can readily recognize behavioral features in familiar educational approaches such as instructional objectives, task analysis, and the use of positive reinforcers. All evolved out of a behavioral philosophy of learning specifying that responses must be sequenced appropriately, made overtly, and rewarded. Many of these derivations from behavioral psychology have helped make education more effective, more accountable, and more humane. In special education settings, especially, behavioral principles have provided an effective set of technologies for teaching that simply did not exist before.

At just about the time Skinner's behaviorism was becoming widely applied to education, however, the American psychological community was growing dissatisfied with the ability of stimulus-response psychologies to provide an adequate account of human thought and memory. For instance, the behaviorists' preoccupation with observable activity was considered by many to be much too limiting, even by those who considered careful observation the *sine qua non* of any scientific enterprise. Others decried what they saw as behaviorism's mechanistic view of human beings as controlled by their environments. A few feared that behavioral principles would be misused and worried about the possibility of a highly effective technology that could be used by those with totalitarian goals.

At the same time, many psychologists who were interested in mental processes seemed to be engaging in a futile exercise as they attempted to use associationist theoretical frameworks and behavioral concepts to describe the complexity of human thinking, memory, problem solving, decision making, and creativity. To try to explain this vast array of mental processes as a series of stimulus-response connections (see Goss, 1961) seemed neither to satisfy nor contribute greatly to our understanding of human cognition. As an explanatory system, associationism seemed to have reached its limits and to fail as a scientific, yet generalizable, psychology.

Adding to the growing perception of the narrowness of the prevailing associationism were voices from outside psychology that were raised when some psychologists tried to explain language development from a behavioral perspective. For instance, the publication of Skinner's *Verbal Behavior* in 1957 prompted strong reactions from linguists and set off a general debate about the adequacy of behavioral explanations of language development. In Skinner's judgment, language was acquired largely through processes of imitation, shaping, and reinforcement. These assertions were countered by linguists, however, who produced strong theoretical and empirical arguments against them. Rapid developments in linguistic theory (e.g., Chomsky, 1957, 1965) and research that showed qualitative differences in child and adult speech and less-than-theoretically-expected levels of imitation (see Brown, Cazden, & Bellugi, 1968; Ervin, 1964) did much to weaken behaviorism as a generally applicable theory of language development.

The Cognitive Era

No single event signaled an end to the associationistic era and the beginning of the cognitive revolution in American psychology. Early on, the cognitive revolution was a quiet one. Certainly, the "time was right," as American psychologists were becoming increasingly frustrated with limitations in behavioral theory and methods. As mentioned, research by linguists on the nature of language development supplied evidence against the radical environmentalist perspective offered by the behaviorists. Another prominent factor was the emergence of computers (Baars, 1986), which provided both a credible metaphor for human information processing and a significant tool for modeling and exploring human cognitive processes.

Beyond these general trends, the work of a number of individuals clearly was pivotal in creating a cognitive revolution. For instance, some point to the publication of Ulrich Neisser's *Cognitive Psychology* in 1967, which provided early definition to the new area of cognitive psychology, or even earlier, to the work of Jerome Bruner (Bruner, Goodnow, & Austin, 1956) or David Ausubel (Ausubel, 1960; Ausubel & Youssef, 1963), which emphasized mental structures and organizational frameworks. Others would nominate G. A. Miller's frequently cited article "The Magical Number Seven, Plus-or-Minus Two: Some Limits on Our Capacity for Processing Information" (1956b) or his founding, with Jerome Bruner, of the Center for Cognitive Studies at Harvard in 1960 (Baars, 1986). Many cite J. J. Jenkins's 1974 *American Psychologist* article, in which the fundamental differences between the mass of rote learning research he and others had done for a generation and their work within the new cognitive paradigm were contrasted. Still others would cite Marvin Minsky's 1975 "frames" paper, which outlined the necessary features of a vision system that could recognize simple objects. This paper highlighted the critical role of mental structures in human thinking and decision making, a theme echoed by others in the related concepts of *scripts* (Schank & Abelson, 1977) and *schemata* (Rumelhart, 1975).

Today, cognitive psychology is mainstream American psychology, and the cognitive perspective no longer is considered revolutionary. In education, however, its applications are only now being fully explored (DiVesta, 1989). This text presents many of the important concepts and points of view of cognitive psychology. We do this by organizing our thinking around several key themes in cognitive psychology that we see as most potent for educational practice.

COGNITIVE THEMES FOR EDUCATION

Cognitive psychology now encompasses an enormous body of research on a wide range of topics (see Eysenck & Keane, 1990). Not all of these have relevance for education, of course, and our strategy in this text is to organize the information we present around a few powerful themes. We hope that presenting these themes will help you judge the relevance of what you learn about cognitive psychology for teaching and learning.

1. *Cognitive psychology helps us see learning as a constructive, not a receptive, process.* In the view of most cognitive psychologists, learning is a product of the interaction among what learners already know, the information they encounter, and what they do as they learn. In a sense, learning can be thought of as created out of learners' points of view, their knowledge, their approaches to learning, and the information they encounter. It is not so much knowledge and skill acquisition as it is the *construction* of meaning by the learner (Jonassen, 1991). Knowledge is created, not simply acquired, and the engine that drives learning is the "search for meaning."

The old adage "You get out of it only what you put into it" aptly describes a cognitive perspective. Some students approach learning in passive and "shallow" ways, either failing to engage fully or relying heavily on rote memorization. Both cognitive research and our experience as educators tell us the resultant learning is likely to be both superficial and transitory. In contrast, other students' attempts at learning clearly are aimed at understanding; they relate new information to what they already know, organize it, and regularly check their comprehension.

2. *Cognitive psychology emphasizes the importance of structuring knowledge.* Among the most potent concepts of cognitive psychology is that of the *schema*. Schemata are mental frameworks we use to organize knowledge. They, in turn, direct perception, and attention, permit comprehension, and guide recall. This general concept appeared under a number of labels about twenty years ago in the work of several theorists, including Minsky (1975), Rumelhart (1975), Schank and Abelson (1977), and Winograd (1975); clever experimental demonstrations soon showed how powerfully these mental structures affected perception, learning, and memory.

Pichert and Anderson (1977), for example, asked individuals to read a passage describing a house either from the perspective of (1) a prospective home buyer or (2) a burglar. They hypothesized that these perspectives would activate different frameworks for comprehending the passage (would activate different schemata) and result in different recall patterns. As predicted, their readers did recall significantly more information relevant to their own perspective (e.g., "home buyers" were more likely to recall a leaking roof, for instance, information important to a prospective home buyer) than information relevant to the other perspective (e.g., remembering three parked ten-speed bikes, a detail the "burglars" noticed).

Experiments like these shifted many researchers' attention away from the abstract phenomenon of learning to *learners themselves*—to their prior knowledge and frames of reference, to the activities they undertook and the strategies they used as they learned, and to their role in creating new knowledge. Soon cognitive psychologists (e.g., Anderson & Pearson, 1984; Brown & Palincsar, 1982) suggested approaches to instruction based on these ideas—methods in which students were encouraged to describe what they already knew and how they felt about it, to link new information with old, to use analogies and metaphors as tools for understanding, and to create their own structures for organizing new information. As we see later, concepts like these have had a profound impact on thinking about instruction in virtually every area of the curriculum.

3. *Cognitive psychology emphasizes self-awareness and self-regulation of cognition.* One of the major effects of cognitive psychology on education has been to advance the idea of self-directed, strategic, reflective learning. Collectively, these ideas have been supported by a very large body of research in *metacognition,* which generally refers to two dimensions of thinking: (1) the *knowledge* people have about their own thinking and (2) their ability to use this awareness to *regulate* their own cognitive processes. As students progress through their school years, they typically develop along both dimensions, becoming (1) *more aware* of their own abilities to remember, learn, and solve problems and (2) *more strategic* in their learning, better able to manage their cognitive activities in learning, thinking, and problem solving. For instance, younger students often have little sense of their own cognitive activity and tend not to use such cognitive strategies as rehearsing or organizing information to help them remember. Older students, however, typically will try at least some study and rehearsal strategies to assist them in comprehension and recall.

One of the most important educational implications of research on metacognition has been the growing awareness that knowledge and skill acquisition are only a part of the picture of cognitive growth. Although knowledge and skills are important, students' learning strategies and their ability to reflect on what they have learned—to "think critically"—may be even more important. Without strategies, knowledge is "brittle" (Salomon & Perkins, 1989); that is, unless learners monitor and direct their cognitive processes, they are unlikely to be either effective learners or flexible, effective problem solvers. Students need to acquire not only knowledge but also "ways of knowing."

As cognitive psychology has matured, its scope has expanded greatly. Early cognitive research tended to stress memory, thinking, and problem-solving processes and their applications to instruction. Newer conceptions of cognitive psychology, however, include not only the "purely cognitive" variables of memory and thought but also the motivational and belief systems of learners. How confident, for instance, are students in their ability to perform certain actions, and what outcomes do they believe will result if they are successful? What reasons do they give for their successful and unsuccessful performances? What kinds of goals do learners typically seek? What beliefs do they hold about the nature of knowledge, their own abilities, their intelligence?

Research on such questions as these has emphasized the importance of learners' overall cognitive frameworks for motivating and regulating learning. For instance, theory and research focusing on such constructs as self-efficacy, outcome expectancy, and self-regulated learning (see Bandura, 1986; Schunk, 1989; Zimmerman, 1990) have shown that individuals constantly judge their own performances and relate them to desired outcomes; these judgments are an integral part of whether activities are attempted, completed, and repeated. Similarly, cognitive researchers have shown that the reasons individuals supply for their successes and failures—their attributions (S. Graham, 1991; Weiner, 1985)—also have important consequences for learning, as do the kinds of goals they seek (Ames & Archer, 1988). Still other researchers have stressed beliefs that people hold about the nature of knowledge (e.g., Schommer, 1990) and intelligence (e.g., Dweck & Leggett, 1988).

This growing area of research demonstrates that both cognitive and motivational variables need to be considered in accounting for student learning. Successful learning involves not only comprehension but also an active, motivated, self-regulated, and reflective learner. Cognitive activity occurs within a framework of learners' goals, expectancies, and beliefs. All have important consequences for determining what students choose to engage in, how persistent they are, and how much success they enjoy.

4. *Cognitive psychology stresses the role of social interaction in cognitive development.* The evolution of cognitive psychology is leading to another important understanding—the role of social interaction and discourse in cognitive development. Like many other traits, "ways of thinking" and "ways of knowing" need to be nurtured in a supportive social context (Bruning, in press).

Educators traditionally have stressed individual study as the route to cognitive growth. Recent cognitive research, however, has shown that social-cognitive activities, such as well-managed cooperative learning and classroom discussions, are particularly helpful in stimulating learners to clarify, elaborate, reorganize, and reconceptualize information (e.g., Calfee, Dunlap, & Wat, 1994; Dansereau, 1988; King, 1991). Peer interaction provides a forum for students encountering ideas and perceptions that differ from their own; new knowledge can be constructed out of these exchanges. Shared work on "real" tasks seems to be particularly rich in its potential for cognitive development; students can observe teachers and advanced peers, express their ideas, get feedback, and justify their claims. The goal is to help students participate in tasks at the outer reaches of their ability, but with social interaction providing the "scaffolding" for ways of thinking and doing that gradually are internalized (Hull, Rose, Fraser, & Castellano, 1991).

5. *Cognitive psychology stresses the contextual nature of knowledge, strategies, and expertise.* Throughout its history, the dominant metaphor of cognitive psy-

chology has been that of the computer. The human being is portrayed in this metaphor as a processor of information in which information enters into a system, is processed and stored, and can be recalled. In short, the mind is machinelike.

From cognitive psychology's earliest beginnings, however, another worldview—contextualism—was strongly voiced. The root metaphor of a contextualist perspective in cognitive psychology is not mind as machine, but rather the event, which emphasizes history and situation (Gillespie, 1992). Events are inherently situational, occurring in a context that includes other events and taking some or even much of its meaning from that context.

Contextualist views underlie many of the most fertile ideas of cognitive psychology. In early experimental demonstrations, for instance, Bransford and his colleagues (e.g., Bransford, Barclay, & Franks, 1972; Bransford & Franks, 1971) clearly showed that memory was strongly affected not only by the manipulations of the experiment but also by participants' knowledge of relations and events. Similarly, other work (Hyde & Jenkins, 1969; Jenkins, 1974; Tulving & Thompson, 1973) showed that memory was strongly influenced by learners' actions as they attempted to encode information. Learning and memory are not, it seems, so much a product of machinelike input and output, as they are something learners construct from their prior knowledge, intentions, and the strategies they use.

Today, this viewpoint is coming to fruition in the strong current interest in cognitive strategy instruction (e.g., see King, 1991; Pressley, El-Dinary et al., 1992; Pressley, Harris, & Marks, 1992). The goal is to help students manage their own learning. One of the findings of research in this area is that successful cognitive strategy training requires attention not only to the strategy itself but also to metacognitive knowledge—especially knowledge about how, when, and why to use particular strategies (Pressley, El-Dinary et al., 1992). Effective strategy use, in short, is thoroughly contextual.

In sum, our experience tells us that if we describe the concepts of cognitive psychology well and elaborate on these themes, you will see their considerable power for education. They not only can help you conceptualize your goals for education in cognitive terms but also should aid you in developing highly motivated students who can reason well, reflect on their thinking, and articulate what they know.

The cognitive concepts and principles we describe in this book fit well with many of our beliefs as educators: our sense of students as whole human beings; our advocacy of active, not passive, learning; and our valuing of individual differences. We believe you will find yourself drawn to this perspective; the "cognitive view" will begin to affect your thinking about your students and your beliefs about how they should be taught.

An Example

To help you get a better sense of the direction cognitive psychology will likely take you, think for a moment about one student—Kari, a fifteen-year-old girl in her first year at Southeast High School. It is now midway through the fall semester, and, all in all, Kari has made a reasonably good transition from junior to senior high school. Her grades are holding up fairly well, with one exception—a history class with the dreaded Mr. Bergstrom. But then, at this point, no one in the class has higher than a B anyway. Kari's immediate concern, however, is with an assignment for Ms. Lawrence's Citizenship Issues class. Printed on a half-sheet of ditto paper, here is how the assignment reads:

> Produce a first draft of a two-page paper on the issue YOU consider to be the most critical issue facing American youth today. Please type your draft and double space it. As we have done in the past, you need to make four copies. As usual, plan to read it in your small group and to get written comments from each of them. This draft is due Friday, the 17th. Final drafts are due a week from Friday, the 24th. P.S. Papers with lines shorter than four inches in length are NOT acceptable. This means you, Bobby!

We next see Kari the following Thursday in the school computer lab, where she has signed up for an hour's time before school. She pulls the assignment from her notebook. "Hmmm. . . . A two-pager. . . . Problems facing youth. Let's see, what should I pick? Jobs? Stress and suicide? Drugs? AIDS? Gangs?

"Jobs . . . much too dull," she thinks. "Stress and suicide? I've been reading about that, but writing about that would be so depressing. Drugs? Maybe. . . . AIDS? It'd be good, but I'm not going to write about it for Lawrence. Gangs, well . . . maybe. Hey, there were articles about drugs in the paper last Sunday; I could go look at those." She smiles at Ms. Lawrence's instructions to Bobby.

Twenty minutes later, Kari has yet to type a word, but by the half-hour, she is typing busily, occasionally looking at a copy of a newspaper article and into two books she has obtained from the school library. Ten minutes before the hour ends, we see success: The printer is clattering away well into the second page, and with six-inch lines, no less.

In many ways, Kari's assignment is a straightforward one, not much different from those given hundreds of thousands of times every day by teachers in schools across the United States and around the world. In each of them, a directive motivates a set of actions—the need to recall earlier events, to make decisions, to gather and use information, and to create a product. Most are simple assignments, yet all are very rich from a cognitive perspective. For Kari to be successful (and we presume she will be), she needs to engage in and guide herself in cognitive operations as diverse as extracting meaning from written instructions, translating thoughts into plans of action, combining stored and newly acquired information into words and sentences, and, of course, just making the word processor and printer work. When all of these dimensions are considered, the array of cognitive functions required seems almost so complex as to defy understanding.

In Kari's sequence of activities, however, we can see certain basic elements. To succeed, she must draw on a body of knowledge in memory. She must guide her mental activities by directing her attention toward some things and away from others. She must make sense of the details she encounters and get information in and out of memory. She must use language to express this information and, to finish the assignment successfully, make appropriate decisions about whether the emerging document "solves the problem"—that is, meets the criteria of the assignment.

We chose Kari as an example not because she is unique, but because the cognitive resources she must draw on and the actions she takes show many critical features of cognitive psychology. Her actions, though thoroughly familiar, illustrate key elements of human cognitive functioning: perception, attention, short- and long-term memory, associative processes, and problem solving and decision making. They represent motivated and self-directed cognitive activity. At the same time, they raise important questions about our information-processing capabilities—questions we address in the following chapters. These questions are:

1. How do learners focus their attention on certain elements in the world "out there" while ignoring others, and what are the limits of learners' capacities for "paying attention"?

2. How do learners acquire information, make sense of it, store it in memory, and retrieve it? Then, once information is stored, how is it organized, and what makes it more or less available when it is needed? In other words, why do we sometimes remember and sometimes forget? And perhaps most important, what role does our knowledge play in cognitive processes?

3. How important are the beliefs that students hold about their capabilities and the nature of intelligence? What role do learners' goals play in cognition? How do students learn to become autonomous, self-regulated learners?

4. How do learners use their cognitive processes in solving problems, and what kind of educational practices are likely to foster reflective thought?

In the chapters that follow in Part I, "Information-Processing Theory," we examine these questions. Chapter 2, "Sensory Memory," describes the critical cognitive operations of perception and attention and relates them to educational processes. Chapter 3, "Memory: Structures and Models," is an introduction to a topic of concern to all educators—memory. In this chapter, we open with a discussion of the topic of memory by examining the research and theory on the nature and organization of memory. Chapter 4, "Encoding Processes," expands our discussion of memory. It describes how the nature of activities that take place during learning affects memory. Finally, in the last chapter of this first part, Chapter 5, "Retrieval Processes," we explore factors that control recognition and recall as we retrieve information from memory.

By the time you have completed the first part of this text, then, you should have a clear sense of cognitive psychology's basic concepts and perspectives and some feeling for what it has to offer education. Part II, "Beliefs and Cognition," tracks the evolution of cognitive psychology into important new areas. It provides an important expansion of basic cognitive concepts into such areas as motivation, self-regulated learning, and the role of beliefs in learning. Part III, "Fostering Cognitive Growth," links cognitive psychology with the set of processes that many educators would place highest among their goals for students—the ability to think critically about issues, to reflect wisely on them, and to choose effective solutions for problems. Part IV, "Cognition in the Classroom," explores the utility of cognitive perspectives in understanding the fundamental skills that thread across all subject areas—language use, reading, and writing—and examines the growing number of applications of cognitive psychology to mathematics and science instruction.

SUMMARY

For most of this century, associationism was *the* American psychology. Working within this tradition, American psychologists attempted to derive basic laws governing learning and memory by studying these phenomena in simplified, rigorously controlled experimental settings. As this research became more and more focused, however, much of it seemed to become less and less relevant. Researchers could not find the general laws they were seeking. Nonetheless, one branch of stimulus-response psychology—radical behaviorism, which stressed objective observation of responses and environmental design—had a powerful impact on education that continues today. Radical behaviorism eschewed the "life of the mind" and instead focused on objective observation of responses and the environmental effects on them.

In psychology itself, however, was a growing dissatisfaction with stimulus-response theories, which increasingly were judged deficient for understanding complex mental events. Memory researchers experienced greater and greater frustration as they attempted to use associationistic theory and experimental studies of rote learning to explain human memory. The behavioral perspective also was attacked by linguists, who questioned its accounts of language development, and by others who criticized the idea of behavioral control and feared a technology of behavior management.

Now, American psychology is cognitive. Cognitive psychology portrays humans as information processors. The computer metaphor is reflected in both the theorizing and methods of many cognitive psychologists. Drawing on contextualist, as well as mechanist, philosophy, cognitive psychology also stresses the importance of learners' activities and mental structures in comprehension and in creating meaning. As cognitive psychology matures, it increasingly is focusing on how cognition develops in a social context and on the interaction between beliefs and cognition.

Although cognitive views have long since become dominant in psychology, only now are they beginning to have a significant impact on education. Our goal, therefore, is to present the concepts, principles, and perspectives of current cognitive psychology in detail and to help you explore their implications for educational practice.

SUGGESTED READINGS

Eysenck, M. W., & Keane, M. K. (1990). *Cognitive psychology: A student's handbook*. Hillsdale, NJ: Lawrence Erlbaum.

This text is an overview of the important areas of cognitive research. It was written as a sourcebook for undergraduates but is substantial enough to provide a useful summary of the field of cognitive psychology.

Gillespie, D. (1992). *The mind's we: Contextualism in cognitive psychology*. Carbondale: Southern Illinois University Press.

This scholarly book explores the emergence of contextualism as one of the two main metaphors underlying cognitive psychology. It provides a useful contrast of contextualist ways of thinking about cognition with mechanistic perspectives on cognition.

Mayer, R. E. (1992). *Thinking, problem solving, cognition* (2nd ed.). San Francisco: Freeman.

As its title implies, this book emphasizes the cognitive processes of reasoning and problem solving. It provides a summary of research developments in cognitive psychology, as well as gives an overview of classic theories of problem solving.

PART ONE

Information-Processing Theory

CHAPTER 2

Sensory Memory

Understanding the value of knowledge and the context in which it is used is an important step in learning about human cognition. Nowhere are the roles of knowledge and context clearer than in human perception, the topic of this chapter. Consider the following phrases:

THE CAT

OPEN DOOR

Although the print was somewhat unusual, you no doubt had little trouble reading THE CAT and OPEN DOOR. If you glance back at the phrases, though, you will see that something fairly remarkable occurred. The same printed symbol **A** worked as an *H* in THE and as an *A* in CAT. Similarly, one printed symbol was a *C* in CAT and an *O* in OPEN and DOOR. Somehow, the context in which these symbols appear influenced how you interpreted them. The context, of course, was provided by you; your knowledge of three-letter words beginning with *C* and ending with *T*, for example, allowed the **A** symbol to be read as an *A* instead of an *H* or something else.

The process by which stimuli are perceived, recognized, and understood (such as the **A** in CAT above) is referred to as **perception**. Perception is critical to all aspects of cognition and is itself directly influenced by the student's knowledge and the context of events created by his or her knowledge. Closely related to perception is **attention**, the allocation of a person's cognitive abilities. As you read this page, you also may be listening to the radio or snacking on some popcorn. What you perceive at any given moment depends on how your attention is divided among various tasks. On the one hand, if most of it is devoted to a weather forecast on the radio, you may not correctly perceive the meaning of some of what you are reading. On the other hand, if you are immersed in this chapter, you may not hear your name when the radio announcer calls it and says that you have five minutes to phone to collect a $1,000 prize. This chapter deals with perception and attention and their implications for the classroom teacher. It begins with an overview of the process of perception and then examines different models of attention.

PERCEPTION

Let's think for a moment about what is required for perception to occur. First, some aspect of the environment—some stimulus—has to be detected by the person (e.g., has to be seen or heard, but not necessarily understood). That stimulus then somehow must be transformed and held. This process usually is referred to as **storage**. Next, a body of knowledge has to be available and brought to bear on the stimulus (e.g., *cat, cut,* and *cot* are the three-letter words beginning with *c* and ending with *t*). This process usually is referred to as **pattern recognition**. Finally, some decision has to be made regarding its meaning (e.g., "It's an *a*"). This process is referred to as **assignment of meaning**.

The very common phenomenon of identifying the letter *a* seems far more complex when we consider what may happen during the process of perception. One important observation is the fact that perception takes time; identifying the **A** figure (or any other stimulus, for that matter) is not instantaneous. (Recall that the stimulus must be picked up and transformed, memory must be called up, the stimulus must be compared with what is in memory, and a decision must be made.) The fact that perception requires time and effort leads to a problem of sorts. Because environments may change rapidly (e.g., when watching a film or driving a car), a stimulus could stop being available before a meaning was assigned. (Imagine seeing **DCCR** projected by a slide projector for, say, one-tenth of a second.) Unless we can "hold" that stimulus for a while, our perceptual processes would stop in midstream (Fisher, Duffy, Young, & Pollatsek, 1988). The experience of watching a movie, for example, would be terribly frustrating if stimulus after stimulus disappeared before we could interpret their meanings. Our experience, however, tells us that such breakdowns in our perceptual processes occur infrequently. This is because our cognitive systems are equipped to register sensory information.

Sensory Registers

One of the capabilities of our cognitive system is that it can temporarily retain environmental information after it has disappeared (DiLollo & Dixon, 1988). Apparently, each of our senses has this ability—a **sensory register**—but research has focused almost entirely on vision and hearing. Here, we discuss the visual and auditory sensory registers in turn, emphasizing evidence for their existence and research on their characteristics.

Visual Registers.   The classic work on the visual registers was performed more than thirty years ago by George Sperling (1960). Sperling was engaged in basic perception research, attempting to identify the nature of the visual registers. As a part of his study, he showed subjects slides depicting arrays of letters, such as the one shown in Figure 2-1.

Sperling noted that when subjects were shown such an array of letters for less than 500 milliseconds (1 second consists of 1,000 milliseconds), they could recall about four of the letters. This number did not change, regardless of whether Sperling altered the length of time subjects saw the array (from 15 msec to 500 msec) or altered the number of letters they saw from four to twelve. He developed three hypotheses that could account for his results. First, it was possible that only the four letters reported by subjects were registered; that is, subjects saw only four letters and could not recall any more because they had never registered. Second, it might have been that all twelve letters were registered but that the letters somehow were lost before they could be reported. Third, it was possible that all twelve letters had been registered and were in memory but that somehow only the four reported were accessible at the time of recall.

To test these hypotheses, Sperling developed what has come to be called the *partial report method.* He reasoned that if subjects had more information available than they could report, he could sample their knowledge. So, rather than ask subjects to report all they saw, he asked them to recall only one of the rows of letters in the matrices they were shown (see Figure 2-1).

Sperling's partial-report procedure was very clever. Participants were told that after the array of letters disappeared from the screen, they would hear a tone. If the tone was of high pitch, subjects were to recall the top row. If the tone was of middle-range pitch, they were to recall the middle row. If the tone was of low pitch, they were to report the bottom row. Because the subjects had no way of knowing which

Figure 2-1
Stimulus array similar to that used by Sperling.

C	Z	K	L
D	P	M	B
R	L	X	N

row they would be asked to recall until after the array disappeared from view, the number of letters they recalled could be used as an estimate of the total number of letters they actually had available when they began their recalls. By varying the delay between the disappearance of the array and the tone, Sperling was able to estimate how long such information was retained.

The results of Sperling's study are summarized in Figure 2-2. As you can see, when the tone occurred immediately after the array was terminated, the subjects were able to remember about three of the four letters in the row for which they were cued. The value of 9 in Sperling's chart in Figure 2-2 is obtained by multiplying the average number of letters recalled in a row by the number of rows (3) to obtain an estimate of the total number of available letters. The longer the tone was delayed, however, the fewer letters were recalled. This decrease was very rapid. After only a 0.5-second delay, subjects recalled an average of slightly more than one letter per row overall, indicating that about four letters were available.

The data thus supported Sperling's second hypothesis; that is, all or most of the letters in the arrays were registered, but most were lost before they could be reported. Apparently, Sperling's subjects were able to hold visual information for about 0.5 second. After that time, it no longer was available, having decayed in sensory memory.

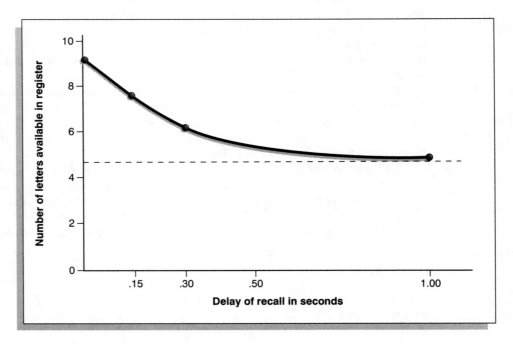

Figure 2-2
Results of Sperling's 1960 experiment. This graph is modeled after that presented by Sperling (1960). The dashed line represents recall without sampling.

The answer to Sperling's question was clear. People register a great deal of the information they see in brief presentations. After the information is removed from sight, however, it is available only briefly—about 0.5 second in Sperling's study. By the time Sperling's subjects could say the letters from one row (e.g., *c, z, k*), the rest of the information was gone.

Another question Sperling addressed in his 1960 paper was whether meaning had been assigned to information in the visual sensory register (or *icon,* as it has been called). To examine this question, Sperling (see also Sperling, 1983; Von Wright, 1972) presented arrays, such as the one in Figure 2-1, that contained both numbers and letters. Participants in the study then were given cues indicating that they were to recall either numbers or letters. Such cues would work only if meaning (number or letter) had been assigned to the information in the array. The results indicated that unlike the location cues we described earlier, number/letter cues were ineffective. This outcome strongly suggests that the information in the icon is held with limited processing. Had the arrays been processed (if meaning had been assigned), then the number/letter cues would have made a difference.

Our purpose here is not to detail all that is known about the icon (for excellent reviews see Chase, 1987; Sperling & Dosher, 1986). Rather, it is to point out that people do possess capabilities permitting visual information to be held for a time after it is no longer physically available. We also want to show the rather severe limits of our ability to perceive visual information (see Mewhort, Butler, Feldman-Stewart, & Tramer, 1988). A similar capability limits our ability to perceive auditory information.

Auditory Registers.   Although a majority of research on sensory registers has centered on the icon, considerable work also has been devoted to understanding the auditory register (the echo) (see Deutsch, 1987; Handel, 1988; Hawkins & Presson, 1987; Scharf & Buss, 1986; Scharf & Houtsma, 1986; Schwab & Nusbaum, 1986, for reviews). A particularly helpful study in the area is one by Darwin, Turvey, and Crowder (1972), using auditorially presented information, which replicated Sperling's work on the icon.

Darwin et al. presented the participants in their study with three brief lists containing numbers and letters. The lists were presented simultaneously over headphones so that it seemed one list came from the right, a second list from the left, and a third list from behind. After hearing the lists, subjects were given position cues to remember one of the lists. Darwin et al. delayed these cues from 0 to 4 seconds after the lists were presented.

The results closely resembled those reported by Sperling for the icon; that is, as the cue delay increased, recall performance decreased, until at about three seconds after the presentation, subjects' recall with cues was no better than without cues. When Darwin et al. contrasted number/letter cues with position cues, they found the number/letter cues to be relatively ineffective. So, much like the icon, it appears that an echo exists that holds relatively unprocessed information while perceptual processing begins. For example, a sixth-grader's echo will hold the first part of the words *direct object* (the sound of *dir*) until the rest of the sound has appeared (*ect*) so that meaning may be assigned to the phrase.

Comparisons of the visual and auditory sensory stores indicate some interesting differences (see Handel, 1988). The most obvious is the length of time information is stored in the registers: less than 0.5 second in the icon and slightly more than 3 seconds in the echo (see Chase, 1987; Hawkins & Presson, 1987). This greater ability of the echo to retain information seems related to the processing of language (see Schwab & Nusbaum, 1986).

One interesting phenomenon related to differences in the icon and the echo is the *modality effect* (Pisoni & Luce, 1986). This effect is seen when subjects are given lists of seven or eight items to remember. It turns out that subjects remember items better if they are presented auditorily, rather than visually—the modality effect. Careful analyses of this phenomenon (see Crowder, 1976; Darwin & Baddeley, 1974; Grossberg, 1986) have shown that the difference in memory for visually and auditorially presented information can be traced to recall of the last few items; that is, people who are given auditory information (a list of seven or eight things) make fewer errors at the end of the list than people who receive the same information visually.

Early commentaries on the modality effect suggested that this ability to recall more of the items at the end of a list when information is presented auditorily was due to the fact that the echo is larger than the icon (Crowder, 1976). More recently, however, researchers have shown that the modality effect does not occur equally for vowels and consonants (Deutsch, 1987) and that vowels and consonants are processed differently (Jusczyk, 1987). These differences (see Schwab & Nusbaum, 1986, for a review) have suggested to many researchers that the echo evolved as a component of our cognitive system specifically adopted for language processing. Certainly work demonstrating that more information in spoken language is carried by vowels than consonants supports this idea (Scharf & Buss, 1986; Scharf & Houtsma, 1986). In any event, both the icon and the echo are critical to the process of perception, for it is here that the initial processing of information begins.

Implications of Research on the Sensory Registers

Our brief review of research on the icon and the echo suggests some very direct implications for teaching. First, there are limits to the amount of information that can be perceived at any one time. The short duration of memory in the sensory registers should remind us of the need for teachers to pace carefully the delivery of information. Further, some work on developmental differences in cognition (e.g., Case, 1985) suggests that the size of the sensory registers increases with age. Children's sensory registers have more stringent constraints than those of adults. Especially with early elementary-age children, teachers must be aware of the need to manage the amount of information that children are expected to perceive at any one time.

Second, there may be real benefits to presenting information both visually and auditorily. Given the limits of students' ability to hold information in their sensory registers, we would expect that information presented both visually and auditorily would have a higher likelihood of being perceived than information presented only in one format. Using visual aids for auditory presentations and discussing visual materials seem to be reasonable approaches to increasing the likelihood that instructional materials will be perceived. It also is reasonable to assume that tactile, gustatory, and olfactory stimulation may enhance learning.

The sensory registers are crucial to perception, but becoming aware of the nature of the icon and the echo explains only the initial stages of perceptual processing. Further processing is needed to recognize patterns and to assign meaning. This processing usually is done on the basis of existing background knowledge and is the topic of the next major section of the chapter.

PATTERN RECOGNITION AND THE ASSIGNMENT OF MEANING

The assignment of meaning to incoming stimuli is such a common occurrence that we often take it for granted. Only when we face uncommon or unusual stimuli do we notice ourselves actively trying to assign meaning. Most psychologists argue, however, that the same processes occur in the nearly automatic assignment of meaning (e.g., reading the word *cheese*) and in our efforts to puzzle-out obscure meanings (e.g., deciphering a scribbled note) (Roth & Frisby, 1986).

The assignment of meaning to incoming stimuli depends on two things: the nature of the stimuli and our background knowledge (Marr, 1982, 1985). Clearly, visual perception cannot occur if nothing is seen. Not as obvious, however, is the fact that perception—which culminates in the assignment of meaning—also could not occur if no knowledge were available. Consider, for example, the differences in the assignment of meaning to a large plant with a tall, central trunk. One student, who has lived all of his life in the city, looks at the object and announces to us that he sees a tree. In contrast, a second person, who spent her childhood in the countryside and plans to go to college and major in forestry, indicates that she sees a hybrid American elm grafted onto a Chinese elm stock. Further, she states that it is an Ann Arbor variety and. . . . Although we left the second person before she could tell us all she saw, it is clear that the relative levels of knowledge these two persons have about trees determine, in part, what they perceive.

A second constraint on pattern recognition and the assignment of meaning is the context in which a stimulus occurs. Many words in the English language, such as *bank, tape,* and *progress,* are ambiguous or polysemous. Each of these words can be used as either a noun or a verb. Many words, including *bank,* are ambiguous even when used as nouns. Yet we rarely have any difficulty perceiving, recognizing, and assigning meaning to these words, provided we encounter them in a meaningful context. One reason is that contextual information helps us search our background knowledge more efficiently (Meyer & Schvaneveldt, 1976).

A third facet of the assignment of meaning is that various subprocesses must be involved (see Brown, McDonald, Brown, & Carr, 1988). A person's sense receptors must be oriented toward the source of the stimulation (the tree must be looked at), elements of the environmental stimulation must be extracted, and these elements must be compared with what is in memory. Staying with the tree example, such elements as the texture of the bark; the shape of the crown; the shape, texture, and color of the leaves; and the overall shape of the tree must be noted and compared with existing knowledge in order to make a correct identification.

Recognition occurs when elements match what is in memory ("Hmmm. Elms do have leaves with serrated edges."). Recognition can occur based on one cycle of information (orientation to the stimulus, feature extraction, comparison with memory, decision), or it can require considerable recycling as a person struggles to assign the correct meaning to an ambiguous stimulus.

In the remainder of the chapter, we examine each part of the perception cycle. We begin by reviewing the process of feature extraction or, as it is usually called, pattern recognition.

Pattern Recognition

Pattern recognition refers to how stimuli in the environment are recognized as something stored in memory (Goldstein, 1988). Although there are different ways of conceiving of the pattern recognition process, each presumes that stimuli are picked up by the sense receptors and held in the sensory registers while analyses of meaning are carried out. Incoming information is compared with knowledge stored in memory so that a decision can be made ("It's a frebus!").

Although there has been little argument about the general nature of pattern recognition (however, see Gibson & Spelke, 1983), there has been considerable debate about exactly how the analyses in pattern recognition occur. In particular, disagreements center on how the knowledge necessary to recognize stimuli is represented in memory. In general, psychologists studying pattern recognition have put forward four positions on how knowledge is maintained for perception: (1) templates, (2) prototypes, (3) feature analysis, and (4) structural descriptions. In the following sections, we examine each of these positions.

Templates. The simplest perspective on pattern recognition is that we store templates or exact mental copies of environmental objects in memory (Bruce & Green, 1985). In this view, incoming patterns of stimuli are compared with a person's existing templates. If the incoming pattern fits a template (e.g., **N**, the template for the letter *N*), the person then categorizes the stimulus pattern as being a part of the thing represented by the template. For example, when the pattern N is picked up, it is matched with a person's template **N**, and the pattern then is perceived as the letter *N*.

As Bruce and Green point out, however, this seemingly reasonable hypothesis starts to break down when we consider stimulus patterns that vary from the template. Consider the following: N Z z ⁊ ∽ 𝑛. Deciding whether all of these patterns are *N*s would seem to require a different template for each. In fact, a template would be needed for every possible variation of *N*.

Templates could be made to work with letters if we presumed they could be rotated to align with incoming stimuli (however, is ∨ a *Z* or an *N*?), but they do not fit real-life objects well or the ways pattern matching can work on shapes that are almost totally hidden from view (see Shimojo & Richards, 1986). Still, templates can be modified (see Caelli & Moraglia, 1986; Posner & Keele, 1968, 1970) so that they are more general and less tied to specific patterns. This variation of the template is referred to as a prototype.

Prototypes.   Prototypes differ from templates in that they are hypothesized to represent "best instances" of an object-category, such as *cup,* rather than being representations of specific objects (Caelli & Moraglia, 1986). An example of a prototype will help clarify the idea. Think about playground swings. There are many kinds of swings, but if we ask you to draw a picture of a swing, you probably would produce something like the object in Figure 2-3. Our swing is not a special make or model; it is a typical, ordinary swing. It has the basic elements of a swing: large A-shaped ends joined by a solid bar across the top and pairs of chains hanging down with seats attached to them. This "average" playground swing demonstrates the idea of prototype. It is a form representing the critical features of a set of objects we call swings. It is not, though, a representation of any specific swing.

The prototype perspective on pattern recognition holds that pattern recognition amounts to deciding whether or not a stimulus pattern matches the basic form of a prototype. If it does, the stimulus pattern is identified. Returning to our playground swing example, if you see a large object in a schoolyard that matches your prototype of swing, then you call it a swing.

People employ prototypes in many aspects of perception (see Roth & Frisby, 1986). Perception of faces (Reed, 1972) and problem types, for instance, seems consistent with the use of prototypes. Still, human perception is far more flexible than even prototypes would allow. For example, humans often can recognize brief, fragmentary glimpses of hidden objects (see Figure 2-4) and sometimes can recognize specific songs on the basis of very limited input (e.g., two or three notes). Perceptions based on such limited information would seem to indicate that prototypes alone could not be responsible for pattern recognition (Caelli & Moraglia, 1986; Shimojo & Richards, 1986). The ability to account for how people can recognize objects on the basis of very limited information is one of the strengths of the feature analysis model.

Figure 2-3
A typical playground swing.

Figure 2-4
Perception from limited input. What animal is outside the window?

Feature Analysis.   Most people who see Figure 2-4 decide that a cat is outside the window. They make this decision because some critical features distinguish cats from other animals. In particular, cats have triangular ears on a rounded head. Similarly, other objects are identified easily if their critical features are picked up (e.g., a Mercedes can be recognized by its distinctive hood emblem; oak trees have acorns and may be identified readily regardless of how unusual their bark or leaves may be).

Several feature analysis models were developed in the early years of cognitive psychology, the most famous being Selfridge's pandemonium model (1959). Feature analysis models continued to be popular because they seemed to be consistent with the neurophysiology of the visual cortex; that is, various cells in the cortex of the brain respond differently to different kinds of visual stimulation, roughly like certain aspects of Selfridge's model. More recent work, however, has suggested that the match to human neurophysiology is not as good as once thought (see Bruce & Green, 1985, for a detailed critique). Further, feature analysis models depend on sets of features in memory (e.g., the cat's ears), which are themselves no more than miniature templates (Bruce & Green, 1985).

Some pattern recognition processes indeed are governed by the analysis of distinctive features (Kellas, Ferraro, & Simpson, 1988). Still, human perception is more flexible yet. If pattern recognition depended solely on distinctive features, we could not identify a lop-eared manx (a tailless cat) as a cat; that is, this animal does not possess the distinctive features normally associated with cats, but it is still a cat. Similarly, to return to the playground swing example we used earlier, many contemporary swing sets have almost no features in common with typical swings except that they can be used by children to swing suspended above the ground. A still more flexible approach is needed to describe human pattern recognition.

Structural Descriptions.   Based largely on the work of the late David Marr (e.g., 1982, 1985) is the idea of pattern recognition occurring as a result of structural descriptions. As Marr (1985) pointed out, the idea of structural descriptions offers a highly flexible way of thinking about the use of knowledge in perception. Rather than imagining that knowledge is stored as templates, prototypes, or the minitemplates of distinctive features, a structural description approach argues that knowledge is stored as a set of statements about a particular object or class of objects.

In the structural description view, people construct "models" of objects with a set of relevant statements. Incoming information then is matched against these models. The models focus on necessary features but are less particular about other details. To use the example offered by Bruce and Green (1985, p. 175), a model for the letter *T* would likely be described as a vertical line bisecting a horizontal line, with the bisection occurring more than halfway up the vertical line and away from the ends of the horizontal line. This structural description, then, could identify +, ⊤, ≁, ⊤, and ⊤ as *T*s. The *T*s with slanted lines are allowed because the top lines do not diverge very far from horizontal. However, the figures ⌐, ⌐, +, and ∨ would not be identified as *T*s on the basis of the structural description. Structural descriptions also allow for pattern recognition based on fragmentary evidence, as when only part of a *T* is seen (Caelli & Moraglia, 1986).

An example drawn from school is the structural description of a "strait" in geography. A *strait* is described as a narrow body of water separating two land areas. This structural description allows a student to recognize the illustrations in Figure 2-5 as straits or bodies of water that are not straits. Similarly, structural descriptions are devised readily for other school-related concepts, such as *alliteration, literary style, form of historical event,* and so on.

Thinking of a structural description basis for pattern recognition is helpful to teachers because it suggests that perception can be guided by teaching students the proper knowledge needed for an accurate structural description. The structural description of a strait, for example, can be taught readily. Students quickly master the ability to identify straits, given practice with feedback in tasks such as the one shown in Figure 2-5. Similar instructional processes can be used to teach students to recognize specific problem types in mathematics, science, and social studies, as well as in industrial arts, business, and home economics. It is important to keep in mind, however, that teaching concepts should include the presentation of prototypes (e.g., "One of the things that sets democracies apart from other forms of government is . . .") in addition to structural descriptions.

THE ROLE OF KNOWLEDGE IN PERCEPTION AND MEANING

Knowledge directly influences perception, pattern recognition, and the assignment of meaning. Knowing what we see (or hear) and even how to look (or listen) depends on the knowledge we have (see McCann, Besner, & Davelaar, 1988). An expert chess player, for example, perceives midgame chessboards very differently

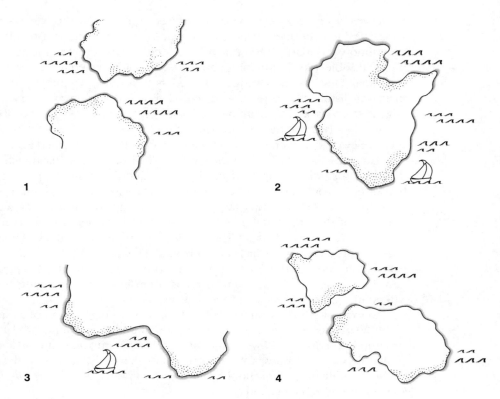

Figure 2-5
Structural descriptions in perception. Structural descriptions, such as that for a "strait" in geography, allow for flexible recognition. Most students can easily identify drawings 1 and 4 depicting "straits."

from a person who has never played the game. The expert sees that a king is in check, that a certain style of defense is being played, and so on, whereas a nonplayer merely perceives pieces he or she may not even be able to name on a checkerboard playing surface.

Knowledge also influences how we look for things to perceive. For example, an accomplished baseball fan knows the need to watch the shortstop's behavior to determine whether the pitcher is going to throw a fastball, curveball, or slider. A nonfan may have no inkling why the shortstop takes steps right or left as soon as the pitcher releases the ball. Similarly, an accomplished debater understands what to look for in evaluating other debaters, much as an expert welder knows what to examine in judging another welder's work.

It is clear, then, that knowledge permits perception to occur and guides our perception of new information (see Mandler, 1984). As we see in Chapter 3, one compelling way to envision our knowledge is by means of **schemata** (sing., *schema*).

Schemata are domain-organized knowledge structures in permanent memory that contain elements of related information and provide plans for gathering additional information (R. C. Anderson, 1984; Mandler, 1984; Rumelhart, 1980). Schemata incorporate the prototypes, feature analysis, and structural descriptions we described earlier. For example, a person's schema for "tree" will contain not only its structural description but also information about the nature of trees (they take in carbon dioxide and give off oxygen), where trees are found (not above certain elevations or in areas that are too dry or cold), and the care of trees (they must be pruned and watered).

Schemata are complex representations of knowledge. For example, a student may have a schema for "average speed" problems (e.g., Mr. Smith drives 530 miles from Lincoln, Nebraska, to Chicago, and then 90 miles to Milwaukee. If his trip took 9 hours and 15 minutes, what was his average speed?). Beyond the minimal structural description necessary to recognize the type of problem (a distance is given, a time is given, and the questioner wants to know an average speed), the student's schema may include procedures for solving some kinds of "average speed" problems (add up the total distance; convert driving time to minutes; etc.) and a rough idea of what a reasonable answer would look like. For complex problems like these, well-developed schemata are necessary to guide the student's perception in looking for additional information relevant to solving the problem (R. C. Anderson, 1984; Sternberg & Detterman, 1986). A more detailed discussion of schemata appears in Chapter 3.

Perception and Context

In some situations, appropriate schemata seem to be activated because of the results of pattern recognition processes. For example, if you are sitting quietly in your office and smell smoke, schemata for reacting to that situation are activated by the data. The activation of the schemata results primarily from the analysis of an environmental event. In such instances, schemata allow us to make sense of what we encounter and prepare us for continued analyses of the environment. Because schemata are activated by the data in the environment in such situations, this type of processing has been referred to as **data-driven** or "bottom-up" processing.

In contrast to data-driven processing is **conceptually driven** processing (see Norman, 1976; Norman & Bobrow, 1976; Roth & Frisby, 1986; Solso, 1988). In conceptually driven or "top-down" processing, schemata are activated by instructions (e.g., "First, look for the main idea") or related schemata (e.g., thinking about how early memories are stored may activate your schemata for the first memories you have). Here, the schemata are not activated primarily by some item being perceived. Instead, schema activation results from the context in which an item is encountered (as, say, making an A+ on your first cognitive psychology test causes you to interpret much of what your instructor says as "brilliant").

As intuitively appealing as the distinction between conceptually driven and data-driven perception has been, this view has become increasingly difficult to support. Simply, the line between conceptually and data-driven processes is too fuzzy to be of much help. Rather than being concerned with whether the context of percep-

Figure 2-6
Simple line drawings.

tion is top-down or bottom-up, it seems better to emphasize the quality of context for learning.

As we alluded earlier, context is created by both knowledge and surroundings. Without knowledge, surroundings may be difficult or impossible to interpret. Without surroundings, there is nothing to analyze for context. Although several studies have been made on the influence of context on perception, perhaps the clearest way to demonstrate the phenomenon is with some simple exercises. Look at Figure 2-6, in which several line drawings are presented, and take a moment to label each. After you have finished, look at Figure 2-7 and locate the line drawings. Now label them once again.

Most people have difficulty labeling the drawings shown in Figure 2-6. However, few people have any trouble identifying these fragments when presented in a meaningful context, as in Figure 2-7.

Examples of context are not limited to line drawings. Consider the following sentences:

The man walked into the quiet *wood.*

The man threw the *wood* into the fire.

The man got good *wood* on the ball.

The man was made of *wood.*

In each instance, the word *wood* is perceived differently because of the sentence context.

Figure 2-7
Simple lines in context.

Now consider, if you will, the game of baseball: sparkling diamonds, the old horsehide, the good lumber, the hit and run, stealing. Ah, springtime! Stop thinking about baseball now and think instead of, say, crimes: the hit and run, stealing, sparkling diamonds. Now think about home building and the good lumber. After you have finished that, think about the worn, horsehide jacket your friend wears.

If everything worked as we intended, we should have been able to invoke your "baseball" schema with the sentence asking you to consider baseball. In this context, "hit and run" refers to the batter hitting the ball while the base runner sprints from first base. A very different meaning for "hit and run" is constructed when your "crime" schema is activated. Finally, the schemata of "home building" and "worn jackets" also shape your perceptions.

Setting a context for perception is a critical element of effective teaching. Given an improper, confusing, or poorly organized context, students may never really understand what a teacher is trying to get across. With a clear context, perception and learning are far more likely.

As we have seen, context depends both on the students' knowledge and on the external environment. The ways teachers structure their classrooms and choose materials are important components in setting a context for learning. Teachers can help set an appropriate context by giving instructions (e.g., "Remember, you will be looking for bodies of water that separate areas of land") or activating students' schemata (e.g., "Recall that we heard how people in southern China have developed an agriculture based on the climate. When we think about northern China, what kinds of crops do you suppose are grown?"). Context also can be created by the activities and materials teachers employ (e.g., field trips, keeping journals, bulletin boards). Beyond the importance of context, though, is a set of important "laws of perceptual organization" that seem to govern why some perceptions are more likely to occur than others. We examine these "laws" in the next section.

The Gestalt Laws

Gestalt psychology was an important school of thought on which much of contemporary cognitive psychology is based. Leaders in this movement, which developed around the time of World War I, included Max Wertheimer, Kurt Koffka (1933), and Wolfgang Köhler (1929). Their primary focus was the study of perception; as a part of their research, they formulated a set of principles or laws that seemed to govern how people assign meanings to visual stimuli. These laws are helpful to teachers in understanding why students respond to information as they do and in predicting how students will react to novel information.

The law of **continuity** holds that perceptual organization tends to preserve smooth continuities, rather than abrupt changes. For example, the zigzag line in the top part of Figure 2-8 usually is perceived as a continuous line, rather than as separate lines making up the sides of triangles. Similarly, the bottom part of Figure 2-8 typically is seen as two smooth lines crossing at A, rather than as a pair of "V-like" shapes touching at A.

Figure 2-8
**The law of continuity. Perceptual
organization tends to preserve
smooth continuities, rather than
abrupt changes.**

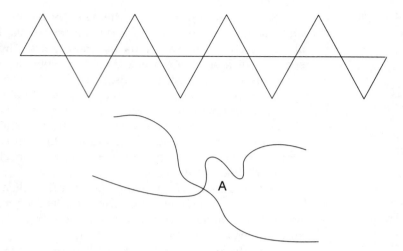

The law of **closure** states that incomplete figures tend to be seen as complete. Consider, for instance, the two drawings in Figure 2-9. Both figures are incomplete, but most people see them as a rectangle and a circle, respectively. Another example of the law of closure happens when we look up at a crescent moon and "see" the rest of the moon's disk finishing out the circle. The unlit part of the moon is, in fact, invisible, and the dark part of the circle we "see" is finished by our perception.

The law of **proximity** holds that things close together are grouped together in perception. Figure 2-10 shows two rows of eight vertical lines each. Looking at the top row only, most people see the lines as four pairs of vertical lines because of the proximity of the lines in each pair. In contrast, the vertical lines in the bottom row tend to be seen as three pairs (each pair surrounds a building), with an extra at each end of the row. Similarly, the dots in Figure 2-11a are seen as columns because they are closer together vertically than horizontally, while the dots in Figure 2-11b tend to be seen as rows.

The law of **similarity** refers to the phenomenon of similar objects tending to be perceived as related. Figure 2-12 demonstrates the law of similarity with a set of letters. In this case, the horizontal and vertical distances among the letters are the same, but most people perceive rows, rather than columns, because the same letter is repeated in rows.

Figure 2-9
**The law of closure. Incomplete
figures tend to be seen as
complete.**

Figure 2-10
The law of proximity. Things close together are grouped together in perception.

The Gestalt laws appeared in several works by Gestalt psychologists from the mid-1910s into the 1930s. By 1933, Koffka (1933) described the **Law of Prägnanz** as an overarching principle of perception from which each of the separate laws of perception stemmed. In short, the Law of Prägnanz holds that of all the possible organizations that could be perceived in a stimulus array, the one that actually will occur will be the one that possesses the best, simplest, and most stable form. In these terms, Koffka would have argued that the rows of letters in Figure 2-12, the three pairs of columns in Figure 2-11a, and so on are perceived, rather than their alternatives, because they are the "best" forms.

Figure 2-11
Columns and rows created by proximity.

a.

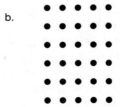

b.

Figure 2-12
The law of similarity. Similar objects tend to be perceived as related.

A	A	A	A	A
C	C	C	C	C
F	F	F	F	F
G	G	G	G	G
Z	Z	Z	Z	Z
A	C	F	G	Z
A	C	F	G	Z
A	C	F	G	Z
A	C	F	G	Z
A	C	F	G	Z

The logic behind the Law of Prägnanz (as well as its subordinate laws) has been disputed (see Roth & Frisby, 1986), but the general validity of these perceptual laws remains unaltered. More recent views of organization in perception, however, allow us to speculate more directly about why these Gestalt laws are valid. In the next section, we examine some of these views, but first it is appropriate to describe briefly work done on the Gestalt principles by Jean Piaget.

Piaget and Perception

As a by-product of his work on cognitive development, Piaget also focused on perceptual development (Piaget, 1969; see also Daehler & Bukatko, 1985). He did not argue that a one-to-one correspondence exists between cognitive and perceptual development, but he did propose that the two were closely linked. One of his primary examples of this linkage was the way children's perceptions tend to become less centered as they develop.

For Piaget, **cognitive centration** referred to the tendency to focus attention and thinking on a single dimension of a problem or situation. Cognitive centration is seen clearly in Piaget's conservation tasks, such as the one pictured in Figure 2-13. Here, children under about the age of six or so are asked whether there are more wrapped candies (Row A) than lemon drops (Row B). Typically, children of this age state there are the same number of the two types of candies. However, when we ask these children whether more wrapped candies are in the first row or lemon drops in the third row (Row C), most respond there are more lemon drops. From Piaget's perspective, these children are focusing only on a single dimension of the problem—the length of the rows. Because they are centered on length, the children cannot coordinate two sources of information—length and number of items.

Similar to cognitive centration, **perceptual centration** is the tendency to focus on only one aspect of a stimulus array. Piaget postulated that children who showed

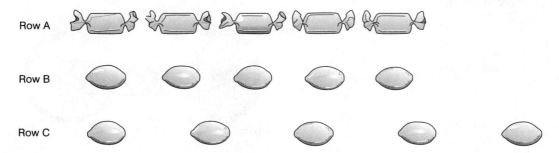

Figure 2-13
Cognitive centration.

cognitive centration would be more likely than other people to show perceptual centration, especially that described by the Gestalt rules. Indeed, Piaget's research demonstrated that young children are especially susceptible to the laws of continuity, closure, proximity, and similarity. Children find it difficult to see the zigzag lines in Figure 2-8 as a series of triangles even when they are guided to this by adults. Similarly, children seem more prone than adults to see incomplete figures as complete. Further, they have great difficulty not centering on the kinds of proximity shown in Figures 2-10 and 2-11.

Children's perceptual centration is important to teachers, especially to those who work with early elementary-age children. Besides setting a context for learning, teachers also must be aware of the Gestalt rules and how centration is likely to occur. Simply, young children tend to center on single aspects of their perceptions and need guidance in developing perceptual flexibility.

Recent Conceptions of Organization in Perception

As helpful as the Gestalt laws are for describing perceptual phenomena, they have had limited value in explaining why the phenomena work (Roth & Frisby, 1986). The Gestalt approach cannot, for example, explain why the shape in Figure 2-14a is seen as a circle in Figure 2-14b. Recent research, as might be expected, has examined such problems with an emphasis on the role of context in perception (e.g., Pomerantz, 1985; Roth & Frisby, 1986). The oval shape in Figure 2-14a is seen as a circle in Figure 2-14b because observers' "bicycle" schemata contain information telling them that bicycles have two round wheels. When the bicycle is identified, the front wheel (the shape from Figure 2-14a) is perceived as being turned at an angle, and so a different perspective of the circle is seen.

Roth and Frisby (1986) argue that the Gestalt laws operate on the basis of context. For example, the law of closure allows us to see the middle shape in the left side of Figure 2-15 as a letter *B*. However, the law of closure does not seem to oper-

Figure 2-14
A figure in two contexts.

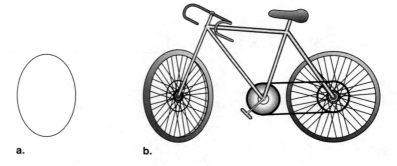

a.   b.

ate on this same shape in the right side of Figure 2-15. In this context, most people see the shape as the number 13, rather than as the letter *B*. These differences in perception clearly are due to context effects. The shape is embedded in familiar contexts (the reader's schemata for either letters or numbers are activated), and the law of closure operates in the A-B-C row, but it does not operate in the equally familiar 12-13-14 row. In this schema theory perspective, then, the Gestalt laws are seen as manifestations of the impact of context on perception.

Implications of Research on Organization in Perception

Important age-related changes in perception were highlighted in our discussion of the Gestalt laws of perception and how they described perceptual phenomena. In particular, we saw that young children have trouble decentering on perceptual input. Instead, they tend to focus on just one aspect of environmental information. These age-related differences also are reflective of knowledge-based differences; that is, older, better-versed students are more likely to attend to multiple aspects of environmental information than less-knowledgeable students. For example, third-year students in high school French are far better able to attend to pronunciation, dialect, grammar, and proper usage in critiquing a speech than students in beginning French.

Especially with beginning or less-knowledgeable students, teachers must carefully focus students' perceptions on critical information (J. S. Brown et al., 1988). For example, if a language teacher is working on dialogue with students, the teacher will need to guide students' attention to relevant aspects of the discourse being taught, including inflections and intonation. Without such guidance, the appropriate perceptions will not take place.

Figure 2-15
Context effects in perception.   A B C   12 13 14

ATTENTION

Interwoven with perception is *attention,* a person's allocation of cognitive resources to the tasks at hand. In general, the research on attention shows that human beings are severely limited in the number of things they can pay attention to simultaneously (e.g., Friedman, Polson, & Dafoe, 1988; Halpain, Glover, & Harvey, 1985). Although there are individual differences in this regard (see Friedman et al., 1988), most people cannot do more than one or two things at the same time; even the most able person can perform only a limited number of tasks simultaneously. This limitation makes what students attend to a significant part of instructional effectiveness.

Because students must learn a large amount of information in school, they need to select what they attend to. A sixth-grader might begin to pay careful attention to her teacher's explanation of an arithmetic problem but then shift her attention to a whispered conversation across the aisle. Her attention then might wander to the aroma drifting into the room from the cafeteria and later to sight of the snow falling outside. Hence, the explanation for how to work the new set of problems may not be remembered. At any given moment, of course, considerable other environmental information is not being selected, such as the papers posted on the bulletin boards, the materials at a reading center, and the comments of two boys behind her about a recent football game.

How does attention operate? Does the selection of what to attend to happen very early, before much processing of information has occurred, or does it happen later, after a great deal of information has been obtained? To help answer this question, we review three models of attention, examine the kinds of tasks students are asked to perform, describe cognitive skills that reduce the demands on students' attention, and then review the implications for teachers of research on attention. Research on this question sheds considerable light on how students allocate attention.

Broadbent's Early Selection Model.   The first theories of attention proposed that selection occurred very early in the analysis of information (see Nusbaum & Schwab, 1986). Characteristic of early selection models was Broadbent's (1958). Broadbent proposed that only a very limited processing capacity was available for dealing with information in the sensory registers. Because little capacity was available, he reasoned that selective attention was caused by the limited available resources being expended on some small component of environmental information. He further argued that any information not attended to would go unprocessed and be totally lost by means of decay.

Broadbent speculated that predetermined physical characteristics of environmental stimuli are the basis for the selection process. In this view, students might process sounds from a specific voice (the teacher's) or attend to certain aspects of material on the chalkboard, but not both. Although contemporary research has shown early selection models to be somewhat simplistic, Broadbent's model generated a great deal of work in the 1950s and 1960s. Most of this research employed what are referred to as **dichotic listening tasks**. These tasks are still important in attention research and mirror many classroom situations.

Dichotic listening tasks take advantage of multiple channel-recording possibilities. A tape is prepared so that it carries two messages, one to be delivered through each channel. Then, experimental subjects listen to the tape through headphones. One message comes to one ear, the second to the other ear. Typically, subjects are asked to shadow (repeat) the message being presented to only *one* of the two ears. This shadowing is used to ensure that the subjects indeed are attending to one of the messages and not the other.

Dichotic listening tasks are roughly comparable to what happens in a classroom when, say, a student listens to what a classmate has to say, and not the teacher's explanation. Studies employing dichotic listening tasks have found almost uniformly that subjects can remember very little of the information presented to their unshadowed ear except for some very basic properties of the unshadowed signal, such as whether the voice was male or female, the general pitch of the voice, and so on (Nusbaum & Schwab, 1986). Attention seems highly focused.

When people encounter too much information to process with their limited resources, Broadbent postulated, their processing is directed to parts of the environmental input. Unprocessed information, from this perspective, is lost. Broadbent also argued that people possess a "switching mechanism" that allows them to switch quickly from one source of environmental input to another and thereby *seem* to be able to process two sources of information at the same time. This would be equivalent to "jumping" very quickly between two television channels. "Switching ability" is limited, however, and becomes less functional as the information in any channel becomes more complex. In other words, switching might explain how people seem to be able to listen to the radio and work a crossword puzzle at the same time, but if the complexity of one of these tasks is increased (a lecture on perception, rather than music from a radio), switching back and forth would be far more difficult and ultimately would break down altogether.

Despite the general relevance of Broadbent's ideas, our everyday experiences and recent research both suggest that early selection models present an incomplete picture of attention. Consider, for example, the well-known "cocktail party" phenomenon. In this instance, a person may have all of her attention focused on an intense conversation with someone—cognitively shadowing the other person's arguments, as it were—but still may look around when she hears her name mentioned across the room. Similarly, think about the undergraduate immersed in his studies who hears the word *pizza* spoken by someone in the next room.

Anne Triesman performed a study in 1964 in which she employed the traditional dichotic listening task. Her study differed from previous work in that she switched messages from ear to ear in midexperiment. Subjects were asked to shadow their right ears. Rather than present a consistent message, though, she switched messages on the subjects so that the message into the left ear now was appearing in the right ear and vice versa. The subjects were not informed that this would happen and instead merely were instructed to shadow one ear.

If Broadbent's model was correct, not much should have happened; that is, subjects who shadowed their right ears simply should have continued to repeat what they heard without missing a beat. In fact, Triesman found that subjects occasionally switched the ear they shadowed when the message shifted; that is, they followed the meaning of the material, rather than its source. The inescapable conclusion from this outcome is that the subjects had to be processing at least a little bit of the meaning of the message coming to the unshadowed ear. Because they could do this, Broadbent's model could not be correct in all circumstances. Not surprisingly, one of the two major alternatives to Broadbent's model has been offered by Triesman.

Triesman's Attenuated Processing Model.   Triesman and her colleagues (Triesman, 1964, 1969; Triesman & Geffen, 1967; Triesman & Gelade, 1980; Triesman & Riley, 1969; Triesman & Schmidt, 1982; Triesman, Squire, & Green, 1974) created a model of attention allocation that has come to be known as an **attenuated processing model**. Similar to Broadbent, Triesman argued there is a limited capacity for processing incoming information. However, she hypothesized that different channels of information may use this capacity simultaneously. Because capacity is limited, though, some channels receive fairly complete processing, and others get only reduced or attenuated processing. This attenuated processing is enough to account for the cocktail party phenomenon and for the results of dichotic listening studies in which messages are shifted from ear to ear.

To test her model, Triesman (Triesman & Geffen, 1967; Triesman et al., 1974) performed a clever set of experiments. In one, subjects performed a dichotic listening task in which they shadowed one ear and signaled when they heard certain key words in either ear. If the subjects could recognize none of the key words in the unshadowed ear, the results would support Broadbent's model. If subjects did equally well in identifying the key words in both ears, however, a full processing model (see below) would be supported. To confirm the attenuated processing model, subjects would have to identify most of the key words in the shadowed ear and a smaller portion of them in the unshadowed ear.

The results strongly supported the attenuated processing model. Nearly 90 percent of the key words in the shadowed ear were identified, and almost 10 percent of the key words in the unshadowed ear were identified. More recent work (see Nusbaum & Schwab, 1986) also indicates that the pattern observed by Triesman and her associates is reliable. These data ruled out the early selection model and seemed to dismiss the full processing model. However, a closer examination of research on the full processing model revealed some unresolved issues.

Shiffrin's Full Processing Model.   R. M. Shiffrin, working from the base provided by Atkinson and Shiffrin's model of human information processing (Atkinson & Shiffrin, 1968), has developed what may be referred to as the **full processing model** of attention (Shiffrin, 1976; Shiffrin & Schneider, 1977). In this model, the selection of which stimulus to attend does not occur until after the pattern recognition processes have been completed. Further, Shiffrin presumed that pattern recognition processes occur automatically and without conscious attention (unless, of course, the person is trying to puzzle through an ambiguous stimulus array). These processes go to completion when either the pattern is recognized or no recognition is possible. The results of pattern recognition then are passed on to working memory. In the full processing model, the limitation on attention occurs in *memory,* not in the perceptual processes. It is the inability to retain all of the perceptual analyses we perform that limits our attention.

Interestingly, the full processing model is supported by research results that seem just as compelling as those that support the attenuated processing model (see Nusbaum & Schwab, 1986). For example, Shiffrin, Pisoni, and Castaneda-Mendez (1974) presented their subjects with white noise (random background noise) over their headphones. Embedded in the white noise were consonants (e.g., *k, d*) that the subjects were asked to recognize. As one element of the study, conditions in the experiment were varied so that subjects either (1) knew which ear the consonants would be heard in or (2) did not know. If subjects' performance in recognizing the consonants was poorer when they did not know which ear the consonants were coming to, the results would support the attenuation model; that is, the attenuation model would predict that knowing which ear the consonants were coming to would allow subjects to focus their attention on the relevant ear and thereby improve their performance. In contrast, if no difference was found between the two conditions (if knowing which ear the consonants were coming to made no difference), the results would support the full processing model.

The results of the Shiffrin et al. (1974) study supported the full processing model: The rate at which subjects could detect consonants was independent of the amount of information (one channel or two) they were monitoring. Other studies have confirmed these results (see Posner & Boies, 1971; Shiffrin & Gardner, 1972; Shiffrin & Schneider 1977; Sorkin & Pohlman, 1973; Wickens, 1980). The fact that strong evidence seems to support both the attenuated and the full processing models is a problem. Can both theories be correct? Are both wrong in some way? It turns out that this problem is resolved by examining the kinds of tasks people perform in studies of attention.

Cognitive Tasks: Resource-Limited and Data-Limited Processing

The problem of different studies supporting the attenuated processing and full processing models of attention can be resolved if we make a distinction in the kinds of cognitive tasks people perform (Fisher et al., 1988). We may refer to some tasks as data limited and others as resource limited (see Norman & Bobrow, 1976; Nusbaum & Schwab, 1986). In this perspective, a learner's cognitive resources are those things that may be used to complete a task: memory capacity, number of channels of input, cognitive effort, and so on. As we have seen, our cognitive resources are limited; only so much effort and memory capacity are available at any given time. For example, recall that visual sensory memory holds about seven pieces of information at a time. When all a person's cognitive resources are being devoted to one task (e.g., driving on a busy freeway), no resources may be left for other tasks (e.g., listening to the car radio).

In this context, then, **resource-limited** tasks are those in which performance will improve if more resources are shifted to them (Chandler & Sweller, 1990). To return to the example in the previous paragraph, your performance while driving in congested traffic depends on your ability to focus all of your resources on that task. Similarly, performance in reading this chapter will be poor if most cognitive resources are devoted to watching television, worrying about other classes, or thinking about lunch. If these resources are reallocated to reading, however, reading comprehension will improve.

Data-limited tasks are those in which performance is limited by the quality of data available in the task. Above some minimal amount of resources needed to perform the task in the first place, allocating more resources to a data-limited task will not improve performance. Trying to make sense of a poor-quality tape recording is an example of a data-limited task. If the tape is bad, after a certain amount of resources have been assigned to the task no amount of additional effort will help. For many students, following complicated instructions or "analyzing" Shakespearean sonnets may fit into the category of data-limited tasks; no matter how many resources they assign to the job, performance will not improve. Most serious, however, is when the data to complete a task do not exist—for example, when the first-semester calculus student has no prior knowledge of math concepts such as *algebra* and *trigonometry*.

Besides helping us think about instructional events, the distinction between resource-limited and data-limited tasks also helps us make sense of the conflicting results of studies on the allocation of attention. Indeed, the results of various studies in the area have depended less on their theoretical assumptions than on the type of tasks they employed (Nusbaum & Schwab, 1986). Triesman and Geffen (1967), for example, employed a resource-limited task, whereas Shiffrin et al. (1974) used a data-limited task.

In Triesman and Geffen's study (1967), subjects shadowed the message coming to one ear (a task requiring many resources) and simultaneously listened for target words in one ear or the other (a task that also requires many resources). Basically, Triesman and Geffen's results were due to the fact that most of their subjects' resources were devoted to the shadowing task. In other words, the demands of the task exceeded the participants' cognitive resources. Very few resources remained available for the monitoring task, and so performance was poor. If more resources could have been devoted to monitoring key words (by, say, eliminating the need to shadow the message), participants' performance would have improved. Overall, then, we may conclude that Triesman and Geffen found support for the attenuated processing model because they used a resource-limited task in their study. A similar argument can be made for support of Broadbent's full processing model.

In contrast, Shiffrin et al. (1974) employed a data-limited task. Recall that Shiffrin et al. had subjects listen for consonants against a background of white noise. Because the subjects in this study only had to identify the sound of consonants, rather than to deal with meaning (as was the case in Triesman and Geffen's study), relatively few resources were necessary. When subjects had to listen in both ears for the consonants, rather than in just one ear, they still had considerable resources left.

Assigning more resources could not improve performance. So, Shiffrin et al.'s results support the full processing model because of the type of task they used: a data-limited task.

From the perspective of resource- and data-limited tasks, we see that students have limited resources to allocate to tasks (Fisher et al., 1988; Reynolds, 1993). As long as the tasks leave some unused resources, students can take on additional tasks and can process information in parallel (two channels). If students are engaged in a resource-limited task, their performance may improve by shifting more resources to it. Thus, when students perform tasks that do not use all of their resources (e.g., listening to a teacher read the correct answers on a quiz, doodling on a note pad, and monitoring a nearby conversation in case baseball comes up), they appear to possess all of the available information before selection decisions are required. In contrast, when we involve students in tasks that require more resources than they have available (e.g., taking a difficult test in less than fifteen minutes), performance will suffer as students reach the limits of their cognitive resources.

Automatic Processes

Automatic cognitive processes require few resources (see Stanovich, 1990, for a review). The notion of automatic processes, or **automaticity**, was first conceived of by Neisser (1967) and has been elaborated by Laberge and Samuels (1974), Shiffrin and Schneider (1977), Neves and Anderson (1981), and Nusbaum and Schwab (1986). Although there are differences of opinion concerning the specifics of automatic processes, it is generally agreed that they (1) require little or no attention for their execution and (2) are acquired only through extended practice.

The existence of automatic processes helps us explain why people can perform different tasks simultaneously. Examples of automatic processes are decoding by good readers, shifting gears by accomplished drivers, punctuation of sentences by skilled writers, and finger movements by expert typists and piano players. Each of these processes appears to require few cognitive resources (e.g., being able to downshift into second while also talking to your passenger, watching traffic, and making a turn) and no conscious attention (e.g., how often have you thought about the process of shifting gears while doing it?).

It is easy to see how automatic processes are related to how students allocate their attention to tasks. For example, if a student could not perform most of the processes of division automatically, resources could not be devoted to making estimates and evaluating. Similarly, good readers can devote their attention to reading for meaning because decoding the words no longer requires much in the way of cognitive resources. Poor readers, in contrast, may have trouble with meaning because so many of their resources have to be used for decoding words, not because they lack poor comprehension skills (Laberge & Samuels, 1974; Samuels, 1988). Perhaps you have experienced this yourself when reading in a foreign language.

The research on automaticity implies that, in the beginning, performance on any cognitive activity will be awkward and slow. As learning proceeds, however, knowledge of facts can become knowledge of how to use those facts. This "proceduralized knowledge" is much more readily and quickly available for use and greatly reduces the demands on our limited processing resources during routine tasks such as reading.

In fact, there is a startling consistency in the research findings on skill acquisition in a wide range of tasks. Although performance initially may be halting, it soon improves to a reasonable level of competence. In most areas in which "expertise" has been investigated, however, performance continues to improve even after hundreds and even thousands of hours of practice! Such findings have been shown in studies as diverse as Crossman's (1959) classic investigation of cigar rolling (in which performance continued to improve over almost three million trials and two years!), the reading of inverted text after hundreds of pages (Kolers, 1975), and the continued learning of a card game after hundreds of hands (Neves & Anderson, 1981). Consider, for example, students' efforts to learn to ski, to ride a bicycle, or to develop mastery of a foreign language. Careful examination of their performance, even after many hours of practice, reveals substantial skill improvement.

One reason for continued improvement over long periods is that the amount of knowledge required for high-level performance in any field is immense. In chess, estimates of the amount of time spent learning by master chess players are on the order of 50,000 hours (Chase & Simon, 1973a, 1973b). From this tremendous investment of time (as much as many adults have spent reading in their entire lives), the chess master has acquired an enormous amount of knowledge about chess positions, organized into meaningful groupings that almost instantly can be recognized and acted on (Chase & Simon, 1973a, 1973b; DeGroot, 1965). Similarly, it seems reasonable to expect that to read well, to write well, to reason well, and to perform well in music, dance, or athletic competition, students must acquire and use large amounts of knowledge. Such abilities do not develop in a matter of hours, days, or even weeks; years of effort may be needed to acquire necessary knowledge and skills. Thus, our fifteen-year-old, Kari, is unlikely to be an expert either on the topic she has written about or in writing itself. Yet, our discussion to this point suggests that she already has acquired large amounts of knowledge and that this information is organized in very complex and varied ways.

IMPLICATIONS FOR INSTRUCTION: GUIDING AND DIRECTING ATTENTION

To many readers, the information presented in this chapter, given its highly theoretical nature, may seem unrelated to educational practice. There are a number of very important implications for learning and instruction, however. We now present six of these that we consider to be the most important.

1. *Information processing is constrained by a natural "bottleneck" in sensory memory.* Information processing is constrained by *limited processing capacity*. Because of this, it is essential that students allocate their resources to important information as selectively as possible. Indeed, students who selectively focus their

attention remember more important information without spending more time or effort studying (Reynolds, 1993). One way to help students focus their attention is to inform them prior to study what information is most important. Another powerful constraint on selective attention is prior knowledge. Students who know more about a topic find it easier to identify and focus on important information. For this reason, choosing a text wisely may greatly facilitate learning.

2. *Automaticity facilitates learning by reducing resource limitations.* Automatic processes allow students to use fewer cognitive resources in completing the same task. Teachers need to remember that cognitive processes become automatic only after extensive practice. Practice should be regular and varied; for example, you would not want to practice driving only in your driveway under ideal conditions. True automatic processing even on simple skills requires hundreds of hours of practice.

3. *Perception and attention are guided by prior knowledge.* What we already know profoundly affects the stimuli we perceive, how easily we recognize these stimuli, and even what meaning we give them. Students should be encouraged to use what they know to help them process new information. One way to do so is for teachers to provide preteaching "organizers" that activate existing knowledge (see Chapter 4). Another approach is to allow students to share knowledge in small group discussions prior to beginning a new, and possibly unfamiliar, task.

Moreover, teachers should carefully match instructional activities with students' current levels of knowledge. Instruction in, say, algebra is hardly likely to be perceived accurately if the students have not yet mastered the necessary prerequisites that make a lesson meaningful. In those cases in which sophisticated perceptions are the goal (e.g., noting different textures in chemicals, hearing when a clarinet is slightly out of tune), an extensive knowledge base is critical.

4. *Perception and attention are flexible processes.* Our ability to process new information is not as fixed as it might appear. Although it is true that everyone shares similar physical information-processing limitations, we are able to "cheat" in a number of ways. One way is to be automatic at a task. Automaticity *increases the rate* at which information is processed because perception and attention require fewer cognitive resources. In a sense, automaticity is equivalent to increasing the flow of water through a garden hose of fixed capacity; we cannot increase the diameter of the hose (processing capacity), but we can accelerate the flow of water (information). A second way to enhance processing flexibility is to attend selectively to what is important. This is exactly what happened in both Broadbent's and Triesman's studies. The key is to understand that perception and attention are under the partial control of learners, rather than the other way around. Any way that a teacher helps a student control these processes is a big step forward to independent learning.

5. *Resource and data limitations constrain learning.* Not all learning tasks are the same. Sometimes we are limited by our resources. Trying to monitor two conversations while driving in heavy traffic is simply impossible for most drivers. Teachers should recall that some tasks are too demanding for some students to master all at once; that is, students may lack the cognitive resources to process the amount of information they are expected to learn. If you suspect that a student lacks

the necessary resources for a learning task, break the task into smaller, manageable parts, provide an easier task, or make some kind of peer-tutor assistance available to the student. Expecting students to perform beyond their limitations undoubtedly will have negative effects on learning.

Sometimes learning is limited by the information to be learned. One example is when a student is asked to learn just too much information in too short a time. In this case, selectively attending to what is most important is an excellent strategy. But what about when there is too little information? For instance, textbooks often omit information that is important or even essential. When this happens, students are forced to provide this information themselves by checking other sources, asking for information, or making their own inferences (which consume precious resources). Unfortunately, many students simply give up because they cannot cross the gulf created by insufficient data. We encourage teachers to examine carefully the information students are expected to learn to ensure that too much or too little information does not create a problem.

6. *All students should be encouraged to "manage their resources."* Teachers should remember that students have limited attentional resources. This limitation makes teachers' choice of tasks for children and the management of their attention critical. Many school-related tasks demand all of a student's attention. Students cannot listen to the stereo, watch television, talk on the telephone, and do their homework simultaneously without the homework suffering as a result. One challenge is to structure the classroom environment so that students' attention is focused on important tasks. A second challenge is to encourage students to be strategic consumers of their limited processing resources. For example, evidence suggests that even college students fail to select appropriate study strategies (Wade, Trathen, & Schraw, 1990). In our opinion, helping students be more strategic, identify important information, and use prior knowledge is an essential part of teaching.

SUMMARY

In this chapter, we reviewed the processes of perception and attention. *Perception* is the assignment of meaning to incoming stimuli; *attention* is the allocation of cognitive resources to the tasks at hand.

Perception begins with the sense receptors. Each of our senses apparently has a sensory register. However, the majority of research has focused on the visual sensory register (icon) and the auditory sensory register (echo). The sensory registers are brief repositories of unprocessed information. They allow analyses of incoming stimuli to occur at the outset of the perception process.

Perception involves pattern recognition processes in which a person's knowledge is used to make decisions about the meaning of the stimuli. The exact mechanisms of pattern recognition are not clear, but many aspects of perception conform to the use of prototypes, distinctive features, and structural descriptions.

What is certain is that knowledge plays a powerful role in perception. Expectations and context affect perception. In addition, our perceptions seem to be governed by a set of laws first derived by the Gestalt psychologists.

There are several views of how attention is directed. The frame of reference of data-limited and resource-limited tasks lets us see that both the attenuated processing and the full processing models have explanatory strengths, depending on the kinds of tasks students are required to perform.

Accurate perception, however, is not our ultimate goal as teachers. A next step is helping students remember what is perceived and build more complex understandings. In the next chapter, we focus on the structure of human memory.

SUGGESTED READINGS

Chandler, P., & Sweller, J. (1990). *Cognition and Instruction, 8,* 293–332.

The article provides a detailed overview and experimental test of "cognitive load theory."

Reynolds, R. E. (1993). Selective attention and prose learning: Theoretical and empirical research. *Educational Psychology Review, 4,* 345–391.

This article provides a comprehensive review of research on attention during the past two decades.

Stanovich, K. E. (1990). Concepts in developmental theories of reading skill: Cognitive resources, automaticity, and modularity. *Developmental Review, 10,* 72–100.

This article considers the effects of resource limitations and automaticity on information processing.

CHAPTER 3

Memory: Structures and Models

For as long as we have thought about "human nature," that aspect called "memory" has intrigued us. The scientific study of memory is a recent matter, tracing back only a little more than a century to the beginnings of psychology as a systematic, experimental science. Most remarkable among the early studies of memory were those of Hermann Ebbinghaus (1850–1909), the first of which was published in 1885. Ebbinghaus's genius was to reduce the study of memory to its most elementary forms. Ebbinghaus studied rote memory, and the materials he used were the simplest of all possible units: lists of nonmeaningful syllables, so-called nonsense syllables (e.g., FOH, TAF). "Savings" in relearning was the measure of memory. A list was learned to a criterion of errorless recall. Later, after the list was relearned, the fewer the repetitions needed to achieve errorless recall, the greater the level of memory inferred. Ebbinghaus was particularly interested in how memory decreased over time. To explore this variable, he attempted relearning after intervals ranging from twenty minutes to one month.

The tradition of memory research begun by Ebbinghaus dominated the study of memory for nearly a century (see Chapters 1 and 2; also see MacLeod, 1988). In general, this research was based on the following assumptions (Jenkins, 1974): (1) Words were the primary mental units of language, (2) when units were used together, they became linked and were chained into larger units, (3) complex behaviors and patterns of thought were assembled from simple units, and (4) the mechanisms that produced learning and memory were primarily automatic.

Today, our conception of what constitutes the valid study of memory has broadened considerably. Memory theories based on rote memorization and extrapolation of basic principles from simple to complex behavior have been supplanted largely by those that describe complex, meaningful cognitive processes more directly and that have much more utility for education.

In this chapter, we introduce current conceptualizations of memory. We begin by presenting a model that portrays how information enters memory, is stored, and is retrieved. We describe several units that cognitive theorists have proposed as "building blocks of cognition." We explore the levels of processing model, which focuses on learners' activities as they try to understand and remember information. We then describe several key distinctions memory theorists have made that highlight important categories of memory and follow with a discussion of newer memory models, each highlighting significant qualities of human memory. In a final section, we lay out implications of memory research for education.

THE MODAL MODEL

Traditionally, memory researchers have understood the utility of dividing an examination of memory into stages of acquisition, storage, and retrieval. For a memory to be made, new information somehow must be acquired and brought into the system. Information also must be stored within the system and retrieved when it is needed. In the 1950s, cognitive scientists began creating models that acknowledged these stages; their models also clearly reflected the increasing influence of the computer as a metaphor for human cognition. The models came to be known collectively as **information processing models** (e.g., Atkinson & Shiffrin, 1968; Waugh & Norman, 1965) and their common features as the **modal model**. Although new memory models continue to evolve, the modal model (see Figure 3-1) provides a useful organizer for thinking about memory.

The modal model divides memory into three major categories: (1) sensory memory, (2) short-term (working) memory, and (3) long-term memory. As can be seen, information entering the system through sense receptors (e.g., eyes, ears) is registered first in sensory memory. In Chapter 2, "Sensory Memory," we described a number of major features of sensory memory, particularly the sensory registers for visual and auditory information (the *icon* and the *echo*) and the role of perception and attention in selecting information for further processing. In this chapter, we add basic information about short-term and long-term memory. Then, in Chapters 4 and 5, "Encoding Processes" and "Retrieval Processes," we discuss interactions among all three components of the system. Understanding the distinctive features of each dimension of the model is important to a full understanding of memory.

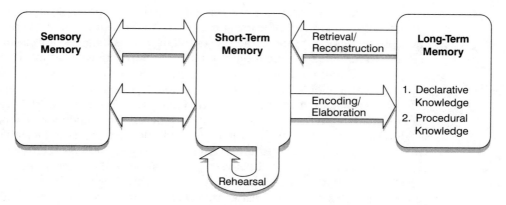

Figure 3-1
The modal model.

Sensory Memory

As we saw in Chapter 2, humans possess holding systems that maintain stimuli briefly so that perceptual analyses can occur. These systems—our **sensory memory**—allow us to hold on to information that no longer is in our environment. Information coming to us through our senses constantly changes; without some sort of "holding mechanism," it would be lost immediately as it is replaced by new sights, sounds, and sensations. Perception is rapid, but it does require time; our sensory memory provides this time.

Evidence based on the partial report method, such as that provided by Sperling (1960) on iconic memory and later by others on echoic memory (e.g., Darwin et al., 1972), gave early, strong evidence that sensory memory, though fleeting, is a real phenomenon. As illustrated in Chapter 2, information in this initial register must be "rescued" by further processing, recoded from the short-lived visual or auditory representation into more enduring forms or codes (Greene, 1992).

Short-Term Memory

At about the time that Sperling was conducting his investigations of sensory memory, research journals in learning and memory became filled with articles on how memory operates over spans of seconds or minutes. The name given to this type of memory was **short-term memory,** or simply **STM** (Broadbent, 1958; J. A. Brown, 1958; Melton, 1963; Peterson & Peterson, 1959).

Perhaps the most striking feature of STM is its limitations, especially its fragility and capacity. For instance, whenever attention is diverted from what is to be remembered, STM decays rapidly. Also, the capacity of STM typically is limited to only a few "chunks" of information (see discussion that follows). We know these features intuitively, of course. For instance, we generally need to continue paying close attention to new information and rehearsing it in order to "keep it in mind." Remembering a new phone number or the names of several new acquaintances, for instance, usually requires attention and repetition. Even a brief interruption or distraction may cause us to lose the fragile memory entirely, especially on first encounter.

The features of STM have been documented extensively in the research literature. For instance, in a groundbreaking early study, Peterson and Peterson (1959) demonstrated that STM was dependent on rehearsal and repetition. They presented their research participants with three-letter syllables (e.g., XJM) and tested their recall over intervals ranging from three to eighteen seconds. This task seems almost ridiculously simple. In the interval between presentation of the syllable and the signal to recall, however, the participants were given a three-digit number and, to prevent them from rehearsing the syllable, they were required to count backward from this number by threes immediately after having been given the syllable. Thus, the sequence on each trial was that individuals were given a syllable, next a three-digit number, and then were required to count backward by threes from the number until they were signaled to attempt recall. Under these conditions, recall deteriorated rapidly to the extent that after just eighteen seconds, recall was only about 10 percent. A large body of later research has verified the finding of a limited-capacity STM and shown that a particularly critical variable in what can be recalled in STM is the number of "chunks" of information (Murdock, 1961) the individual has to remember.

Chunks.   "If you throw a handful of marbles on the floor," wrote the Scottish metaphysician Sir William Hamilton, "you will find it difficult to view at once more than six, or seven at most without confusion." With this pronouncement, according to George A. Miller (1956a), Hamilton became the first person to propose an experimental test of how much can be mentally grasped at a given time. Later experimental work, in fact, did confirm Hamilton's conjecture: The limit on the number of units we can perceive accurately without counting is close to six; beyond this number, errors occur.

A related and probably better measure of mental capacity, however, is the ability to remember symbols in sequence. One example of this, called the **digit span**, is the number of digits individuals can recall when given a sequence of them. In general, when presented with a series of numbers one at a time, the maximum number that normal adults can recall is about seven or eight. Digit span has been of considerable interest to psychologists because it has a relationship to intelligence (an unusually short span often is associated with low intelligence) and because digit span increases with development (Dempster, 1981; Hunt, 1987; Miller, 1956a).

An individual who can recall eight numbers usually can manage about seven letters or six words. However, six randomly chosen words contain far more information than seven letters or eight digits. How is it that we can recall so much more information in word form than in numerical form? Miller (1956a) responded to this question by proposing an analogy. In terms of what we can "keep in mind," we seem to be in a position analogous to carrying a purse that will hold no more than seven coins, whether they are pennies or dollars. Obviously, we can carry far more in our memory if we stock it with information-rich "dollars" such as words, rather than "pennies" such as single letters or digits. The more information can be combined or unitized, the greater the amount of information we can hold in memory even though the number of units remains invariant.

In a landmark paper published in 1956 (Miller, 1956b) titled "The Magical Number Seven, Plus-or-Minus Two: Some Limits on Our Capacity for Processing Information," Miller not only presented considerable evidence regarding the limits of short-term memory but also introduced a unit against which this limit could be calibrated—the chunk. A **chunk** is any stimulus (e.g., letter, number, word, phrase) that has become unitized through previous experience (Simon, 1986). For example, the sequence of letters *X-J-M* consists of three chunks of information, as do the word sequence *cat-dog-fin* and the number sequence *7-1-9*. With learning, however, comes recoding and an increase in the amount of information included in a chunk. For most people, the units *IBM, 911,* and *a fat cat* each are one chunk. Thus, the immediate memory limits of "seven plus or minus two" should be measured in chunks, Miller argued, not the absolute amount of information being encoded.

Ericsson, Chase, and Faloon (1980) have provided us with a striking demonstration of the benefits of recoding information into ever-larger chunks. Their study had but a single participant—a college undergraduate—who had a simple task to perform: After being read a sequence of random digits at the rate of one per second, he was to recall that sequence. If he succeeded, the length of the sequence was increased by one. If he failed, it was reduced by one. Practice on the task continued one hour per day, three to five days per week, for more than a year and a half! At the end of each practice session, he recalled as many digits as he could.

The remarkable result of this study was that the subject's digit span improved from seven (recall this number?) to nearly eighty digits (see Figure 3-2)! His ability to recall digits at the conclusions of his sessions also improved dramatically. At the beginning, he had virtually no recall of the sequences he had heard that day. After twenty months of practice, however, his recall was more than 80 percent, with even higher recognition scores.

As Ericsson et al. pointed out, this extraordinary performance was not a feat of a memory wizard. Instead, it was achieved through the student's learning by extended practice to recode and recategorize information into meaningful chunks. Thus, the four-digit sequence *3-4-9-2* became "3 minutes 49 point 2 seconds, near world-record mile time" (the subject was a good long-distance runner). But this simple recoding was only the beginning. Soon he adopted the strategy of recoding the first six digits as two running times while rehearsing the most recently presented digits. After he reached the limits of this strategy and his performance plateaued (at about eighteen digits), he began to segment his groups into subgroups: He used two four-digit groups followed by two three-digit groups and the rehearsal group. After he reached yet another plateau, he introduced another level of organization, ending up with a retrieval organization consisting of three levels in a hierarchy that enabled him to store an average of nearly eighty digits. By imposing increasingly sophisticated hierarchical structures on what he was learning and by practicing them extensively, he was able to chunk more and more information.

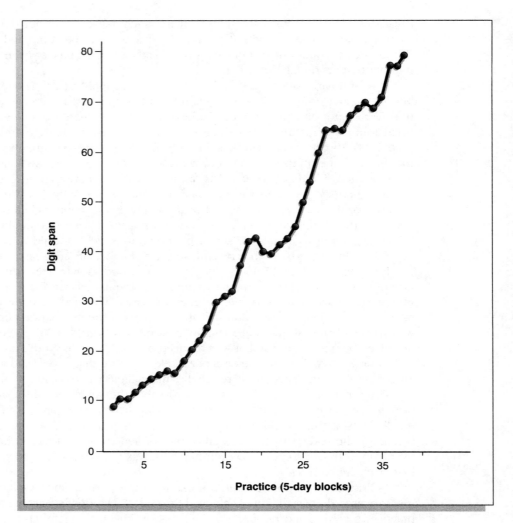

Figure 3-2
Results of Ericsson, Chase, and Faloon's (1980) study. This graph shows the change in
average digit span for the person who participated in the Ericsson et al. study. Each day
represents about one hour of practice. As you can see, the person's digit span increased
enormously.   (Reprinted by permission from Ericsson, K. A., Chase, W. G., & Faloon, S. [1980].
Acquisition of a memory skill. *Science, 208,* 1181. Copyright 1980 by the AAAS.)

The special significance of the concept of *chunk* is that it emphasizes the importance of prior knowledge in facilitating memory. The difficulty of recalling the letter string OSNIWTOTPODN certainly is different from remembering the sequence SON WIT TOP NOD. The primary determiner of whether the limits of immediate memory are reached is how easily and rapidly information can be recoded—that is, perceived as meaningful. As we saw in Chapter 2, rapid perceptual coding depends on the extent of prior experience and learning. The more expert the individual, the more easily this coding will occur (DeGroot, 1965; Chase & Simon, 1973a; Simon, 1986), a factor critical in cognitive processes as diverse as simple pattern recognition and high-level problem solving.

Long-Term Memory

Whereas sensory memory and STM involve events recently experienced, a third major system exists for memory traces developed over periods of days, weeks, months, and years. In the modal model, this aspect of memory is called **long-term memory**, or **LTM**. LTM is the permanent repository of the information we have accumulated.

Rehearsal and repetition, so crucial for STM, seem much less critical for LTM. For instance, we can state our uncles' names, recall large cities on the East Coast, or easily give examples of large, hairy animals without having to rehearse any of this information—despite the fact that we may not have thought of these topics for months or even years. Likewise, the implicit memory (Schachter, 1993) that lets us drive a car, brush our teeth, or type a letter comes from LTM.

Types of Knowledge in LTM.   Cognitive psychologists have found it useful to distinguish between the types of knowledge in memory. One major distinction is between declarative knowledge and procedural knowledge (J. R. Anderson, 1983a, 1993; Squire, 1987; Woltz, 1988). **Declarative knowledge** is factual knowledge: "knowing what." Examples of declarative memory are recalling that Sakhalin is an island off the coast of Siberia, that Ebbinghaus studied memory by using nonsense syllables, and that we had Oat Squares for breakfast. **Procedural knowledge**, in contrast, is "knowing how" to perform certain activities. Our procedural memory includes knowing how to drive a car, use a computer, or play the piano.

One important use for the declarative-procedural distinction has been to describe the kinds of learning that students may achieve. Novice students in a teacher education program, for instance, may memorize principles of classroom management (e.g, "Allow students to make value judgments") as declarative knowledge but may have little or no notion of how actually to use these principles in effective teaching (procedural knowledge).

Of course, not all procedural knowledge is "higher-order" knowledge based on more basic declarative knowledge. Procedural knowledge can be quite simple and only loosely linked with declarative knowledge. A young child, for instance, who has learned how to unlock a door, turn off a faucet, brush her teeth, and open a book is demonstrating her recall of procedural knowledge.

Also, procedural knowledge often is "automatized"; we often do things without any conscious attention to what we are doing or why we are doing it. In a university lecture class, for example, most students enter the room, find a seat, take out a notebook, and begin taking notes with little or no conscious attention to what they are doing. Similarly, decoding words and comprehending the meaning of what we are reading typically occurs quite automatically.

In most learning, of course, is an interplay between declarative and procedural knowledge, often guided by metamemory. Sometimes, for instance, our searches of declarative knowledge come at least partially under conscious control ("Who IS the author of *The Polar Express*? Let's see, wasn't that book a Caldecott Medal winner? That guy also wrote *Jumanji*. Just give me a minute; I'll think of his name!"). Similarly, a concert pianist learning a new song by Domenico Scarlatti, for instance, may search her memory for declarative knowledge about that composer's preferred method of executing certain embellishments such as the appoggiatura, mordent, and trill—declarative knowledge that will be used in the development of procedural knowledge. Conversely, the procedural knowledge involved in her performance gives substance to the declarative knowledge she possesses (e.g., "Scarlatti intended for the mordents to be played according to the basic tempo of the passage. That would mean that they should be thirty-second notes here.").

One important goal of education is the development of relatively large, stable, and interrelated sets of declarative knowledge. As educators, we expect students to be "knowledgeable." There is more, however; we also place a considerable premium on knowing "how to." Much important school learning combines declarative and procedural knowledge. We typically hope that knowledge is useful for doing something. For the practitioner in applied programs such as journalism, architecture, teaching, business, and medicine, procedural knowledge is a critical outcome of the educational process.

Within the category of declarative memory, Tulving (1972) and others (e.g., Squire, 1987) have distinguished further between memory for personal experience and memory for general knowledge. These categories have been labeled, respectively, **episodic memory** and **semantic memory**. Episodic memory refers to storage and retrieval of personally dated, autobiographical experiences (Tulving, 1983, 1985). Recall of childhood experiences, recollection of the details of a conversation with a friend, and remembering what you had for breakfast all fall within the realm of episodic memory. Episodic memories have "personal tags," and the basis for retrieval is an association with a particular time or place. Obviously, a great deal of what we must recall in order to function effectively in our personal lives is episodic.

Semantic memory, in contrast, refers to memory of general concepts and principles and their associations. Unlike episodic memory, semantic memory is not linked with a particular time and place. It contains such information as the facts that lemons are yellow and that computers contain chips. The organized knowledge we have about words and concepts and how they are associated also is in semantic memory. For instance, areas such as English literature and American history represent a vast network of semantic information that we (as we become more expert in the area) encode, organize, and have available for retrieval. Recalling word meanings, geographic locations, and chemical formulas requires searches of semantic memory.

Although the psychological validity of the episodic-semantic distinction has been criticized (e.g., McKoon & Ratcliff, 1986), it is useful for helping us think about the types of information we and our students must remember. On the one hand, our episodic memory must function well enough for us to locate ourselves in time and space and to have a reasonably accurate picture of our experiences. On the other hand, we need a broad knowledge base to think and reason effectively. Although some (e.g., Squire, 1987) see the distinction as reflecting separate systems in the brain, others (e.g., Roediger, 1990) argue that the important thing is the cognitive procedures that learners use. As we see later, recent work on the topic of **implicit memory** (an unintentional, nonconscious form of retention, such as that underlying tying one's shoes or playing a piece on the piano; see Roediger, 1990; Schacter, 1993; Schacter & Cooper, 1993) has rekindled strong interest in studying episodic memory processes.

Verbal and Imaginal Representation in Memory.   "A picture is worth a thousand words." Although the validity of this aphorism may be debatable, there is little doubt that we humans have extraordinary capabilities for remembering visual information. For example, Standing, Conezio, and Haber (1970), in an early study of visual recognition memory, showed subjects 2,500 slides for ten seconds each. Recognition, estimated from a test on a subset of these slides, was over 90 percent! In another study by Standing (1973), participants viewed an even larger number of pictures—10,000—over a five-day period. From their test performance, Standing estimated subjects' memory at 6,600 pictures, remembered in at least enough detail to distinguish these pictures from ones they had not seen before. Given evidence such as this, there is little doubt that pictorial information can be represented in our memories quite well. Most of us can easily conjure up images of a book, a soaring bird, a train wreck, or a walk in the woods.

One of the main contributions of cognitive psychology has been a revitalization of interest in mental imagery. Once largely banished from experimental psychology as subjective, mentalistic, and therefore unscientific (Watson, 1924), imagery has become a significant feature of the work of a number of cognitive psychologists.

Alan Paivio (1971, 1986a) has proposed that information is represented in two fundamentally distinct systems: one suited to verbal information and the other to images. The verbal coding system is adapted for linguistically based information and emphasizes verbal associations. According to Paivio, words, sentences, the content of conversations, and stories are coded within this system. In contrast, nonverbal information, such as pictures, sensations, and sound, are stored within the imaginal coding system (Paivio, Clark, & Lambert, 1988).

Paivio's theory has been called a **dual coding theory**, in that incoming information can be coded within one or both of the systems. To the extent that information can be coded into both systems, memory will be enhanced, whereas information coded only in the verbal system or only in the imaginal system will be less well recalled. In Paivio's view, the verbal and nonverbal codes are functionally independent and "contribute additively to memory performance" (1986a, p. 226). Paivio also has hypothesized that nonverbal components of memory traces generally are stronger than verbal memories.

Much of Paivio's early work demonstrated the effects of the abstractness of materials on their memorability and relating these results to dual coding theory. For instance, some words (e.g., *bird, star, ball, desk*) have concrete referents and presumably are highly imaginable. When presented with such words, both the verbal (e.g., the linguistic representation of the word *bird*, its pronunciation, its meaning) and the imaginal (e.g., an image of a bird soaring) representations are activated simultaneously. Other more abstract words, however, are far less readily imaginable (e.g., *aspect, value, unable*), and although they activate the verbal coding system, they activate the nonverbal system only minimally. In Paivio's view, memory for abstract materials should be poorer because such materials are represented only within a single system. Pictures, because they tend to be labeled automatically, should be more memorable than words (Paivio, 1986a) because, although pictures are labeled automatically (and hence dual coded), words, even concrete ones, are not necessarily automatically imaged (see also Svengas & Johnson, 1988).

In many studies, Paivio and his associates (e.g., Paivio, 1971; Paivio & Csapo, 1975; Paivio, Yuille, & Madigan, 1968) demonstrated the beneficial effects of imagery on learning and memory, consistent with his predictions. Words rated high in imagery have been shown to be better remembered in free recall, in serial learning (in which a series of words must be recalled in order), and in paired-associate learning (in which the "associate" of a word must be recalled when the word is presented). Instructions to subjects to "form images" also enhance memory.

Although there has been considerable debate about the exact mechanisms by which imagery functions (e.g., Intons-Peterson, 1993; Kosslyn, 1987; Pylyshyn, 1981), there is little doubt that imagery plays an important role in memory and cognition. A large body of evidence shows that materials high in imagery are more memorable and that learners instructed to create images will enhance their learning. The distinction between verbal and imaginal information reminds us that we often are biased as educators toward verbal instruction and rely heavily, perhaps even excessively, on verbal communication. Spoken and written words dominate our classrooms, whereas the potential roles of visual, auditory, and kinesthetic images often seem to be neglected.

THE BUILDING BLOCKS OF COGNITION

One challenge for a science of cognition is to find the most meaningful "units" for describing cognitive operations. In the preceding sections, we described an overall model for memory and some ways its contents can be described. In the following section, we present four concepts proposed by theorists as "building blocks of cognition." These concepts have common features, but each represents a somewhat different view of how best to conceptualize memory. The four concepts are *concepts, propositions, productions,* and *schemata.* Each continues to be important in thinking about memory.

Concepts

One of the major ways we deal with the bewildering array of information in the world is to form categories. Our language mirrors these categories; the words *grandfather, data, bird, psychology, red, dog,* and *hair* each represent a category meaningful to most of us. **Concepts** are the mental structures by which we represent meaningful categories. Particular objects or events are grouped together on the basis of perceived similarities; those that "fit" the category are *examples* or instances of the concept; those that do not are *nonexamples.* The similar features across examples of a concept (e.g., all oceans contain water and are large) are called **attributes**; features essential to defining the concept are called **defining attributes**. Learning concepts involves discovering the defining attributes, along with discovering the rule or rules that relate the attributes to one another.

Rule-Governed Theories of Conceptual Structure.   There is a rich tradition of psychological research on how we identify and acquire concepts. One such tradition, exemplified by the early work of Bruner et al. (1956), focused on *concept identification.* Bruner et al. presented students with an array of simple stimuli, such as triangles and squares, for which there were only four defining features: number, size, color, and form. The task was to discover the unknown concept. The experimenters determined the rules defining the concepts, which could be either relatively simple (e.g., "All green objects are examples") or quite complex (e.g., "Either green patterns or large patterns are examples"). A single stimulus (e.g., a green triangle) within the array was specified as a positive instance of the unknown concept to be discovered. On the basis of that example, the subjects were asked to formulate their best guesses—their hypotheses—about the unknown concept. They then were allowed to pick another stimulus from the array and to ask whether it was a positive or negative example of the concept, to which the experimenter responded truthfully. The procedure continued until subjects were confident they could identify the concept.

Bruner et al.'s work showed quite clearly that most individuals quickly formulate hypotheses about relevant attributes and choose stimuli accordingly. A sizable number of individuals adopt what is called a **conservative focusing strategy** to test their hypotheses (Bruner et al., 1956). Their first hypothesis is quite global. A protocol follows:

> This is a single large, green triangle. I can't rule out any of these things. But I can rule out examples with two and three objects, small- and medium-sized objects, red and blue objects, and circles and squares. Now, I'll pick a new example that differs in one and only one attribute from the first; in that way, I'm guaranteed to get new information.

Others adopt a strategy called **focus gambling**, in which they vary more than one attribute of a stimulus at once. In this strategy, subjects may shortcut the methodical steps of conservative focusing but also run the risk of getting no information at all by their selection. Still others use **scanning strategies,** in which they attempt to test several hypotheses at once, a technique that puts some strain on subjects' ability to remember and process information.

The work of Bruner et al. (1956) and others (e.g., Haygood & Bourne, 1965; E. M. Levin, 1966; Neisser & Weene, 1962) showed that individuals typically solve concept identification problems by trying to discover the rules relating the concept attributes. In general, concepts with more difficult rules are more difficult to learn. The simplest rules involve *affirmation* (e.g., any green object) and *negation* (e.g., any object that is not green), which apply if only one attribute is being considered. Most concepts, however, involve more than one relevant attribute and hence more complex rules. Among the most common are **conjunctive rules,** in which two or more attributes must be present (e.g., any triangle that is green), and **disjunctive rules,** in which an object is an example of a concept if it has one or the other attribute (e.g., either a triangle or a green object).

More recently, Bourne's work (Bourne, 1970, 1982) has represented the clearest statement of rule-governed conceptual structure. In his view, concepts are differentiated from one another on the basis of rules such as the above. These rules provide the means for classifying new instances as either linked with a concept or not. According to Bourne, membership in a conceptual class (e.g., grandfathers, data, birds) is determined by applying a set of rules. These rules can be learned either through instruction or through experience with instances that either are members of the class (positive instances) or are not (negative instances). Thus, one learns to classify a set of animals as birds or nonbirds by acquiring rules for combining characteristic attributes of birds (e.g., wings, bills, feathers). Instruction, according to Bourne, should involve presentation of both positive and negative instances (e.g., for birds, pigeons vs. bats) so that critical attributes clearly can be linked with the concept. Presumably, use of these rules unambiguously classifies a new instance as either a bird or a nonbird. Note, however, that this classification is a very simple one: A new instance either is a bird or is something else not a bird!

A rule-based conceptual system is not always adequate, however. Most natural or real-world concepts are "fuzzier" and differ qualitatively from those studied in the laboratory. For instance, consider the concept of *furniture.* We would all quickly agree that tables, chairs, sofas, and floor lamps are furniture. Furthermore, we can describe many rules that differentiate articles of furniture from other objects. But some of our attempts at rule formation quickly run into trouble. Presence of legs? But what about some floor lamps? A seating surface? But what about tables or a desk? Is a rug furniture? Some would say it is but would wish to include a qualifying statement or **hedge**—it is like furniture, but not *exactly* like it. What is the set of rules that unambiguously determine which objects are members of the concept class *furniture*? Logical efforts to determine such sets of rules mostly have been unsuccessful, especially with ambiguous examples such as *rug.* Rosch and Mervis (1975), dissatisfied both with the artificiality of laboratory work on concept formation and with the difficulties of classifying concepts with rule-governed approaches, proposed an alternative view based on "degree of family resemblance" to a highly typical instance of the concept, a **prototype.**

Prototype Theories of Conceptual Structure. Prototype theories of concepts, in contrast with rule-governed theories, do not assume an either-or, member-nonmember process of concept identification. Instead, prototype theorists (Rosch, 1978; Rosch & Mervis, 1975) have argued that conceptual class membership is determined by the degree to which an example is similar to a known instance in memory—one that seems to exemplify the concept best. As stated in Chapter 2, this line of reasoning is similar to that employed by perception theorists in accounting for pattern recognition in perception. Wattenmaker, Dewey, Murphy, and Medin (1986) suggest that the majority of "natural" or real-world concepts are structured in terms of sets of typical features. Particular instances of concepts in the real world do not have all of the defining features, but rather have a family resemblance. Thus, for North Americans, robins or bluejays often are prototypes of birds. We also might classify animals such as emus or penguins as "birds," but with less assurance. With instances like the latter ones, we frequently hedge; that is, we qualify our judgments with a statement such as, "Well, they are birds, but not the best examples of birds." The hedge is necessary because the emu and penguin do not exhibit a particularly strong family resemblance to robins or bluejays, yet they do have some resemblance. Table 3-1 shows examples of the typicality of members of certain superordinate categories. Rosch (1978), Anglin (1977), and others have provided evidence that young children learn category memberships for prototypical and near-prototypical instances before they learn the less typical ones.

Both rule-governed and prototype conceptual theories correctly classify many simple, naturally occurring phenomena, but both have difficulty developing clear categorizations for abstract concepts, such as *wisdom, justice,* and *equality.* What are the rules for defining a particular act as "wise" or "just"? Most of us find making such distinctions quite difficult because, in most cases, we can only categorize whether an act fits these categories if we understand the context in which the act occurred. As a result, a number of theorists have suggested that both rule-governed and prototype theories of concepts are inadequate. They propose a *probabilistic* view, in which a sufficient number of attributes must be present to reach a "critical mass"—the number sufficient to make a category judgment. This view incorporates some of the characteristics of rule-governed approaches but retains the "naturalness" of prototype views.

Probabilistic Theories of Conceptual Structure. Some theorists (e.g., Tversky, 1977; Wattenmaker et al., 1986) suggest that concept learning involves weighing probabilities. When faced with a new instance, the learner searches it for characteristic, but not necessarily defining, attributes (e.g., flying and singing in an animal that looks like a bird). Categorization as a bird, however, is determined by the summing of evidence for category membership against criteria stored in memory. If a particular instance reaches a critical sum of properties consistent with category membership, it is classed as an example of that concept. Thus, the emu, although it does not fly or sing melodiously, does lay and hatch eggs, feed its young in "birdlike" ways, and, in general, looks like a bird. Thus, it exhibits enough characteristics to be classified as a bird.

In general, the greater the sum beyond the critical value, the quicker the classification. On the one hand, robins and bluejays are identified quickly as birds and not

Table 3-1

Typicality of Members in Six Superordinate Categories. (From "Family Resemblance: Studies in the Internal Structure of Categories," by E. Rosch and C. B. Mervis, 1975, *Cognitive Psychology, 7,* pp. 573–605. Copyright 1975 by Academic Press, Inc. Reprinted by permission.)

Item	Furniture	Vehicle	Fruit	Weapons	Vegetable	Clothing
1	Chair	Car	Orange	Gun	Peas	Pants
2	Sofa	Truck	Apple	Knife	Carrots	Shirt
3	Table	Bus	Banana	Sword	String beans	Dress
4	Dresser	Motorcycle	Peach	Bomb	Spinach	Skirt
5	Desk	Train	Pear	Hand grenade	Broccoli	Jacket
6	Bed	Trolley car	Apricot	Spear	Asparagus	Coat
7	Bookcase	Bicycle	Plum	Cannon	Corn	Sweater
8	Footstool	Airplane	Grapes	Bow and arrow	Cauliflower	Underpants
9	Lamp	Boat	Strawberry	Club	Brussels sprouts	Socks
10	Piano	Tractor	Grapefruit	Tank	Lettuce	Pajamas
11	Cushion	Cart	Pineapple	Teargas	Beets	Bathing suit
12	Mirror	Wheelchair	Blueberry	Whip	Tomato	Shoes
13	Rug	Tank	Lemon	Icepick	Lima beans	Vest
14	Radio	Raft	Watermelon	Fists	Eggplant	Tie
15	Stove	Sled	Honeydew	Rocket	Onion	Mittens
16	Clock	Horse	Pomegranate	Poison	Potato	Hat
17	Picture	Blimp	Date	Scissors	Yam	Apron
18	Closet	Skates	Coconut	Words	Mushroom	Purse
19	Vase	Wheelbarrow	Tomato	Foot	Pumpkin	Wristwatch
20	Telephone	Elevator	Olive	Screwdriver	Rice	Necklace

mammals because they have many characteristics of birds and relatively few of mammals. On the other hand, emus and penguins have comparatively fewer bird characteristics (compared, say, with robins) and consequently are less likely to be identified quickly as birds. These expectations are similar to those of prototype theory. Note that the "critical sum" approach also has some characteristics of rule-governed conceptual behavior because the learner must have a "rule" for determining when a set of features reaches the critical value.

We should emphasize that the greater difficulty of categorizing emus and penguins as birds is probably, at least in part, because of our lack of familiarity with these animals. Nevertheless, probabilistic models emphasize that those exotic birds exhibit sufficient attributes common to birds that they are so classified. In the same way, a rug, though not exactly like "a piece of furniture," often is classified as furniture by virtue of its being used as furniture, its presence in homes, and so on.

Summary of Concepts.   Whether concepts are conceived of in terms of rules, prototypes, or probabilistic judgments, each of the theories of concept learning suggests that different cultures may define concepts in different ways, depending on the set of properties the culture uses to characterize the concept. For instance, Schwanen-flugel and Rey (1986) compared Spanish- and English-speaking individuals on proto-type tasks similar to those Rosch had used and found clear cultural differences even in such simple tasks as determining prototypical birds. One would expect even greater difference in classifying abstract concepts, in which the relevant attributes are much less obvious. Thus, classifications of abstract concepts such as *just* (or *unjust*) or *wise* (or *unwise*) could be expected to reflect strongly the cultural context in which they are used.

Medin, Wattenmaker, and Hampson (1987) suggest that simple rule-governed or prototype conceptual sortings are common in memory and are used widely when conceptual categorizations are easy to make. When objects contain attributes from multiple categories, however, or are influenced heavily by the context within which they occur (e.g., "ethical behavior"), people make categorizations probabilistically. It should be clear from the above that no unambiguous evidence exists supporting a single view of the nature of concepts. Some consensus, however, appears to be emerging concerning a probabilistic view.

Propositions

Suppose you read the following sentence:

> The trainer of the Kentucky Derby winner Alysheba was Jack Van Berg, who always wore a brown suit.

How can its meaning be represented in LTM? In general, the most common way cognitive psychologists have used to represent declarative knowledge, especially linguistic information, is by propositions (J. R. Anderson, 1976; Frederiksen, 1975; Kintsch, 1974; Rumelhart & Norman, 1978). A **proposition** is the smallest unit of knowledge that can stand as a separate assertion. Propositions are more complex than the concepts they include. Where concepts are the relatively elemental categories, propositions can be thought of as the mental equivalent of statements or assertions about observed experience and about the relationships among concepts. Propositions can be judged to be true or false (J. R. Anderson, 1985).

Propositional analysis has been used extensively in analyzing semantic units such as sentences or paragraphs. When we analyze the example sentence above, for instance, we can see that it can be broken into the following simpler sentences or "idea units":

1. Jack Van Berg was the trainer of Alysheba.
2. Alysheba won the Kentucky Derby.
3. Jack Van Berg always wore a brown suit.

These simple sentences are closely related to the three propositions underlying the complex sentence above. Each represents a unit of meaning about which a judgment of truth or falsity can be made. If any of these units of meaning are false, then of course the complex sentence is false. Propositions are not the sentences themselves; they are the meanings of the sentences. Memory contains the *meaning* of information, not its exact form.

Now examine the following two sentences without looking back. Have you seen either of them before?

1.   The Kentucky Derby was won by Alysheba.
2.   Jack Van Berg always wore a blue suit.

Most individuals readily will reject having seen sentence 2; after all, we have just read that Jack Van Berg always wore a brown, not blue, suit. Many will "recognize" sentence 1, however, even though they have not seen it. We remember the sense of oral and written statements; the *meaning* of propositions is what is preserved. In contrast, the surface structure of the information (e.g., whether the first sentence above read *Alysheba won the Kentucky Derby* or *The Kentucky Derby was won by Alysheba*) ordinarily is lost quickly unless we make a special effort to attend to it.

Propositions usually do not stand alone; they are connected with one another and may be embedded within one another. Kintsch (1986, 1988) has shown that texts can be viewed as ordered lists of propositions. In Kintsch's formal system of analysis, each proposition consists of a *predicate* and one or more *arguments*. Several examples are written below, using Kintsch's notation, in which predicates always are written first and propositions are enclosed by parentheses.

1.   John sleeps.   (SLEEP, JOHN)
2.   A bird has feathers.   (HAVE, BIRD, FEATHERS)
3.   If Mary trusts John, she is a fool.   IF, (TRUST, MARY, JOHN)(FOOL, MARY)

Kintsch and others have done propositional analyses of many texts, transforming them into **text bases**, which are ordered lists of propositions. Using such propositional analyses, Kintsch has shown that the reading rates in expository texts are directly related to the number of propositions in the texts. Moreover, Kintsch and others (e.g., Kintsch, 1988; Meyer & Rice, 1984) also have demonstrated experimentally that free recall patterns reflect the hierarchical propositional structure of the text.

As discussed below, cognitive theorists, such as J. R. Anderson, have hypothesized that propositions sharing one or more elements are linked with one another in **propositional networks**. As we will see, the notion that ideas are linked in large networks is very useful for thinking about the way information is stored in and retrieved from memory. Students' ability to comprehend information and to use it effectively in cognitive operations such as problem solving hinges on the quality of the networks they are able to create.

Productions

Whereas propositions can be seen as the basic units of declarative knowledge, **productions** are a way of representing procedural knowledge. Productions can be thought of as condition-action rules—IF/THEN rules that state an action to be performed and the conditions under which that action should be taken (J. R. Anderson,

1983a; Just & Carpenter, 1987). The idea of productions can be illustrated by the following set of instructions and actions for unlocking one's car:

Production A: If car is locked, then insert key in lock.

Production B: If key is inserted in lock, then turn key.

Production C: If door unlocks, then return the key to vertical.

Production D: If key is vertical, then withdraw key.

In general, productions are seen as having the capability of "firing" automatically: If the conditions specified exist, then the action will occur. Memory for productions ordinarily is implicit. Conscious thought typically is not involved. Outcomes of productions supply the conditions, as in the example above, to fire other productions in a sequence of cognitive processes and actions.

The idea of productions has been a useful one. It not only captures the automatic nature of much of cognition but also lends itself to modeling many cognitive processes on the computer. Productions can be specified formally as instructions in computer programs that operate on data and simulate cognitive processes. In reading, for example, Just and Carpenter (1987) incorporated the idea of production systems in an elaborate computer model (READER) to simulate various aspects of reading. In this model are productions such as:

If the word *the* occurs, assume a noun phrase is starting.

Thus, if READER encountered the word *the* in a text it was analyzing, this production would fire (an instruction is triggered in READER), leading READER to "infer" that it currently was processing a noun phrase.

Like propositions, productions are organized in networks called **production systems**. In a production system, multiple productions may be active at a given time. The outcomes of the productions modify memory and activate knowledge, which in turn may activate new productions and new knowledge. Cognition moves ahead from state to state until its ultimate goal is accomplished.

Production systems enable us to represent the dynamic, changing aspects of cognitive processes. For instance, Just and Carpenter pointed out that, in reading, one of the strengths of conceptualizing certain cognitive processes as production systems is that they nicely capture the "automatic side" of reading. In reading, as in many of our cognitive functions, we do not necessarily think about what we are doing—we simply do it. Similarly, J. R. Anderson (1987, 1993) has used the concept of *production systems* in modeling the many automatic processes of problem solving (see Chapter 8). Knowledge, once in production form, is seen as applying much more rapidly and reliably. In his view, the critical productions of problem solving are those that recognize general goals and conditions and translate them into a series of subgoals.

Schemata

The concepts of *chunks* and *concepts* have been of particular utility to memory theorists studying how specific units of knowledge are stored and retrieved. Theorists using such concepts as *propositions* and *productions*, however, typically have been more interested in larger-scale memory organization and how knowledge is used to interpret experience. In this latter group of theorists are individuals who could be called "schema theorists." These individuals have proposed that knowledge is organized into complex representations called **schemata** (sing., **schema**), which control the encoding, storage, and retrieval of information (Kolodner, 1984; Rumelhart, 1984; Seifert, McKoon, Abelson, & Ratcliff, 1986).

According to Rumelhart (1981) schemata are hypothesized data structures within which the knowledge stored in memory is represented. Schemata are presumed to serve as "scaffolding" (Anderson, Spiro, & Anderson, 1978; Ausubel, 1960; Rumelhart, 1981) for organizing experience. Schemata contain **slots,** which hold the contents of memory as a range of slot values. In other words, knowledge is perceived, encoded, stored, and retrieved according to the slots in which it is placed. Schemata are fundamental to information processing. Some schemata represent our knowledge about objects, and other schemata represent knowledge about events, sequences of events, actions, and sequences of actions (Rumelhart, 1981).

Whenever a particular configuration of values is linked with the representation of variables of a schema, the schema is said to be **instantiated** (Rumelhart, 1981). Much as a play is enacted whenever actors, speaking their lines, perform at a particular time and place, so schemata are instantiated by specific instances of concepts and events. Thus, one's schema for "teaching" may be instantiated by viewing a particular situation in which enough of the requisite values to activate the schema are present—some students, a teacher, and evidence for a transaction between them. Once schemata are instantiated, their traces serve as a basis of our recollections (Rumelhart, 1981).

Before 1970, the notion of schemata was an obscure one in psychology, appearing in historical perspective in the early work of Bartlett (1932) and in the work of the eighteenth-century philosopher Immanuel Kant, who referred to the "rules of the imagination" through which experience was interpreted. By the mid-1970s, however, many leading cognitive theorists and researchers (e.g., Bobrow & Norman, 1975; Minsky, 1975; Rumelhart, 1975; Rumelhart & Ortony, 1977; Schank & Abelson, 1977; Winograd, 1975) had become tremendously interested in schema theory. Why did this perspective assume such importance?

In our judgment, the reason schema theory came to the fore so rapidly had to do with its extraordinary explanatory power in accounting for memory and other cognitive phenomena. To get a better feel for the power of schemata, consider the following paragraph. Read it carefully a time or two.

Death of Piggo

The girl sat looking at her piggy bank. "Old friend," she thought, "this hurts me." A tear rolled down her cheek. She hesitated, then picked up her tap shoe by the toe and raised her arm. Crash! Pieces of Piggo—that was its name—rained in all directions. She closed her eyes for a moment to block out the sight. Then she began to do what she had to do.

Think now about some of the things you need to know in order to comprehend this passage, one with fairly simple sentence construction, no rare words, and dealing with a topic—piggy banks—familiar to most. Let's start with piggy banks. What do we know about them? A short list follows. Piggy banks:

1. are representations of pigs
2. hold money
3. usually hold coins
4. have a slot to put the money in
5. are hard to retrieve money from
6. have fat bodies
7. are not alive
8. usually are made of brittle material
9. can be shattered by dropping or a blow
10. look friendly
11. usually are smaller than real pigs
12. once broken, usually stay that way
13. etc.

Of course, this list of "piggy bank facts" could be continued almost indefinitely. Note that the list does not define the concept of *piggy bank* (a piggy bank is. . .), but rather is a partial description of our overall conception of piggy banks—how they look, work, and so on. Our overall mental representation of even a single concept like *piggy banks,* we discover, is an immensely complex array of information and its interrelationships. Within and related to this global schema, too, are embedded many other schemata—for instance, schemata for "tap shoe," for "striking something with a hard object," for "saving money," and so on.

If you turn again to "Death of Piggo" and examine it closely, you quickly will see the vital role your schemata for "piggy banks" and for many other objects and events played in comprehending this paragraph. The notions that piggy banks hold money, that they can be shattered, that shattering is necessary to retrieve their contents, that they are friendly looking—*none of this information actually is stated in the passage.* Yet, all of it must have been activated automatically as you read, or else you could not have understood what you read. You somehow "filled in" the information. In Rumelhart's terms, the slots in our schemata had **default values** assigned to them when they were activated. Although specific information actually was not presented on, say, the piggy bank containing money or its brittleness, we assumed these to be true from our general knowledge of piggy banks. Of course, the list of schemata needed for understanding even this single paragraph can be extended tremendously to include schemata for (to name only a few possibilities) "human beings," "tap dancing shoes," "gravity," "rain," and "Newton's laws of motion."

Even the simplest event or message has an infinite number of features that could be attended to. As we saw in Chapter 2, however, only a few of these actually become a part of memory. One critical function of schemata is guiding attention (Alba & Hasher, 1983; Watt, 1988). Pichert and Anderson's (1977) "home buyer" and "burglar" study (described in Chapter 1), for instance, shows this guiding function. "Home buyers" tended to recall more information relevant to that perspective, such as number of bedrooms, the presence of stone siding, newly painted rooms, and a nursery. "Burglars," however, showed significantly better recall for such details as the presence of ten-speed bicycles in the garage, a valuable painting, jewels, and a color television. Pichert and Anderson commented on their findings:

> The striking effect of perspective on which elements of a passage were learned is easily explained in terms of schema theory. A schema is an abstract description of a thing or event. It characterizes the typical relations among its components and contains a slot or placeholder for each component that can be instantiated with particular cases. Interpreting a message is a matter of matching the information in the message to the slots in a schema. The information entered into the slots is said to be subsumed by the schema.
>
> *Pichert & Anderson, 1977, p. 314*

Because "home buying" and "burglary" each represent quite different schemata, information more likely to instantiate important variables in one was less likely to instantiate the other. What individuals paid attention to and subsequently recalled was information most consistent with their currently activated schema. Thus, depending on which schemata are activated, the information selected for recall will vary.

Schemata play several other critical roles, including guiding interpretation. For example, given sentence 1 below, most people later will recall sentence 2.

1. The paratrooper leaped out the door.

2. The paratrooper *jumped out of the plane*.

Or, to take a second example, the first sentence below often is recalled as the second.

1. The student spoke to the department chair about her instructor's sexist comments.

2. The student *complained* to the department chair about her instructor's sexist comments.

Recall is transformed, often subtly, by schemata. Especially if information is general or vague, instantiation molds it into familiar form, as demonstrated by the following passage, used in early research by Bransford and Johnson (1972, 1973) and Dooling and Lachman (1971).

> The procedure is actually quite simple. First you arrange items into different groups. Of course one pile may be sufficient depending on how much there is to do. If you have to go somewhere else due to lack of facilities that is the next step; otherwise, you are pretty well set. It is important not to overdo things. That is, it is better to do too few things at once than too many. In the short run this may not seem important but complications can easily arise. A mistake can be expensive as well. At first, the whole procedure will seem complicated. Soon, however, it will become just another facet of life. It is difficult to foresee any end to the necessity for this task in the immediate future, but then, one never can tell. After the procedure is completed one arranges the materials into different groups again. Then they can be put into their appropriate places. Eventually they will be used once more and the whole cycle will then have to be repeated. However, that is part of life.
>
> *Bransford & Johnson, 1972, p. 722*

For most individuals asked to read and recall Bransford and Johnson's passage, comprehension and subsequent recall are poor. Simply adding the title "Washing Clothes," however, improves both significantly. An appropriate context for information is critical. When schemata are not or cannot be activated during learning, new knowledge cannot be assimilated easily.

Schema theory provides an explanation for a number of memory phenomena. Because the contents of memory consist of representations of knowledge, rather than exact copies of it, encoding will vary according to the schemata activated at the time of encoding. Thus, schema theory supports a constructivist view of learning and an explanation for the effect of context in memory storage (see Chapter 1). Recall is seen as a reconstructive activity (Goldman & Varnhagen, 1986; Spiro, 1980), with schemata providing frameworks that direct the recall process. Recall is not simply remembering stored information, but rather is *re-creating* information and events. Memory, in this view, is not so much reproductive as constructive and reconstructive.

Because it emphasizes the application of what learners already know, schema theory has been tremendously appealing to both cognitive theorists and educators. It helps us understand that many recall and recognition "errors" are not so much errors as they are constructions logically consistent with the mental structures learners employ. In general, schema theory portrays learners in a dynamic, interactive way. Although schema theory has been criticized for its generality and vagueness (Alba & Hasher, 1983), current cognitive research continues to strongly reflect schema-based conceptions of perception, memory, and problem solving.

EVOLVING MODELS OF MEMORY

Through the 1960s and well into the 1970s, the prominent model of memory was the modal model, exemplified by the "stage" models of Waugh and Norman (1965) and Atkinson and Shiffrin (1968). As we have seen, these models portray human cognition as computerlike and emphasize sequential steps in information processing (see Figure 3-1). Information moves from the sense receptors and sensory registers into short-term or working memory and, depending on the rehearsal that takes place, into long-term memory.

The importance of the STM-LTM distinction has diminished in recent models of memory as most models of memory have shifted from a "storage" to a "processing" emphasis (e.g., J. R. Anderson, 1976, 1983a; Collins & Loftus, 1975; Craik & Lockhart, 1972; Jenkins, 1974). This processing emphasis is retained in most current models (see Collins, Gathercole, Conway, & Morris, 1993). Rather than being conceived of as a "place" where information is held for brief periods, the concept of *STM* has been broadened into the idea of **working memory**, which better reflects the many ways in which we process and transform information. For example, J. R. Anderson's ACT* model, discussed later in this chapter, incorporates a working memory and a long-term memory. These two are not emphasized as "separate places," however, but rather as being closely interrelated. The current contents of consciousness set up a pattern of activation in LTM; this activation of LTM, in turn, "reverberates" back into working memory (J. R. Anderson, 1983b). Obviously, all of the components of memory—sensory memory, STM, and LTM—are highly interactive. Although information plainly does move through sensory memory and STM to LTM, the contents of LTM simultaneously are exerting a powerful influence on what we perceive, pay attention to, and comprehend.

The modal model has been tremendously useful in drawing our attention to important dimensions of our memory systems. It should not be taken as implying, however, that cognition is neatly separable into a set of sequential steps. The "early" process of perception, for instance, plainly is guided by semantic memory from the supposedly "later" stage of LTM. Also, many cognitive activities are highly automatic, driven by the information coming in, and seem to depend only minimally on "central processing." Thus, although the modal model captures a number of important features of memory, researchers have continued to develop new models aimed at better portraying the active, dynamic nature of cognition and its ability to interpret and restructure incoming information. Among the most prominent of these are so-called network models of memory.

Network Models

In **network models of memory**, knowledge is represented by a web or network; memory processes are defined within that network (J. R. Anderson, 1983b, 1993). In most such models, the networks are hypothesized to consist of **nodes**, which consist of **cognitive units** (usually either concepts or schemata), and **links**, which represent relations between these cognitive units.

Quillian (1968) and Collins and Quillian (1969) proposed an early network model, called the **Teachable Language Comprehender** (TLC), as a model for semantic memory. Devised as a computer program, TLC was based on the assumption that memory could be represented by a semantic network arranged into a hierarchical structure. In this hierarchy, the nodes were concepts arranged in superordinate-subordinate relationships. Properties of each concept are labeled **relational links** or pointers going from the node to other concept nodes. An example of such a network is presented in Figure 3-3.

Quillian proposed five kinds of links: (1) superordinate (ISA) and subordinate links, (2) modifier (M) links, (3) disjunctive sets of links, (4) conjunctive sets of links, and (5) a residual class of links. These links can be embedded in one another. In Figure 3-3, the links from *are fast, are agile,* and *are gentle* to *quarter horses* are modifier links; the links between *quarter horses* and *horses* and between *horses* and *mammals* are ISA links. In general, properties particular to a concept were assumed to be stored along with the concept (e.g., *are gentle* is stored with *quarter horses*). Those not unique to that concept (e.g., *have manes, have hooves*), however, are assumed to be stored with more general concepts higher in the hierarchy.

When memory is searched, activation moves along the links from the node that has been stimulated (say, by reading the word *horse*). This **spreading activation** constantly expands, first to all of the nodes directly linked with the concept (in our simple model, from *horses* to the superordinate concept of *mammal* and to the subor-

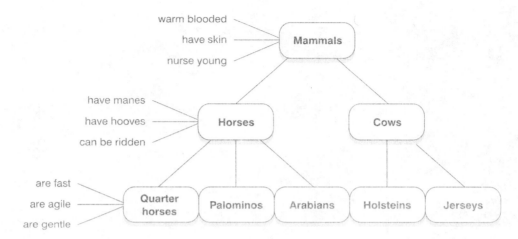

Figure 3-3
A network model of memory. This sample of a network is modeled after those developed by Collins and Quillian (1969).

dinate concept of *Arabians, palominos,* and *quarter horses*) and then to the nodes linked with these nodes, and so on (Collins & Loftus, 1975). As activation moves forward through the nodes, an activation tag is left at each. When a tag from another starting node is encountered, an *intersection* has been found. By tracing the tags backward from the intersection to their sources, the path linking the starting nodes can be reconstructed. Thus, the question *Are quarter horses mammals?* would trace a path in the network from the starting nodes *quarter horses* and *mammals* through the node for *horses*.

According to this model, language comprehension consists of path evaluation to see whether it is consistent with the constraints imposed by language. For instance, the starting point in comprehending the question *Are quarter horses mammals?* is activation of the paths from *quarter horses* to *horses* and from *horses* to *mammals.* The memory search is presumed to begin at the concepts included in the input question (*quarter horses, mammals*). Beginning with the concept of *quarter horses,* this search would arrive in one step (link) at the properties *are fast, are agile,* and *are gentle* and at the superordinate concept of *horses.* A second step takes the search to *mammals.* If the relationship between the two nodes is permitted by the syntax and context of the question, the question can be comprehended.

One assumption of the original Collins and Quillian (1969) model was that traversing these links takes a fixed amount of time. Thus, if memory search traversed only a single link, that search should take less time than a search traversing additional links. Collins and Quillian set out to verify the prediction that time required for retrieval from memory structure will depend on the number of links traversed in memory search. To test this hypothesis, they presented subjects with sentences representing relationships in simple two- or three-level hierarchies. Some sentences described modifying (M) relations; other stated superordinate (ISA) relations (as in Figure 3-3). Sentences represented the presumed number of steps in the hierarchy that would need to be traversed in order to verify the truth or nontruth of the sentence. The following are samples of the kinds of sentences Collins and Quillian used.

Number of Links	Sentences	Type of Relation
0	An oak has acorns.	M
	A maple is a maple.	ISA
1	A spruce has branches.	M
	A cedar is a tree.	ISA
2	A birch has seeds.	M
	An elm is a plant.	ISA

Subjects were given both true and false sentences. The measure taken was reaction time to make a decision about the truth of the sentence. In general, average reaction time did increase as predicted for decisions about sentences that represented a greater number of links. For instance, average reaction times for the set of M (property) sentences was just over 1,300 msec for *An oak has acorns* (0 links), close to 1,400 msec for *A spruce has branches* (1 link), and nearly 1,475 msec for *A birch has seeds* (2 links).

Like all models, however, the Collins and Quillian model had trouble accounting for some results. Although the prediction that time required to judge sentences true or false as a function of "semantic distance" usually has been borne out, there are frequency effects. For instance, it is easier to agree that a palomino is a horse than to agree that a tarpan is a horse, simply because most of us are more familiar with palominos than tarpans.

To deal with such findings, as well as with their own accumulating data from research relating to the model, Collins and Loftus (1975) extended the model, including several assumptions to make the model less "computerlike" and more "human." (Quillian's original theory was developed as a program for the computer, which imposed constraints on his theory that he thought were unrealistic.) Spreading activation remained a key assumption, but with activation decreasing over time. In addition, Collins and Loftus proposed the existence of a separate **lexical network,** in which names of concepts were stored. Links in this lexical network could serve as an alternative source of entry into memory (e.g., "words that sound like *horse*").

Collins and Loftus's revised network model now could account for results from a variety of studies and deal with many criticisms of the original model. Key concepts from their model, especially the conceptualization of memory as organized into networks of nodes and links and the idea of spreading activation, remain prominent in current theories of memory.

The ACT* Model

Perhaps the most comprehensive model of memory and cognition is J. R. Anderson's ACT* model (1976, 1983a, 1983b, 1993). Based on an early model called *human associative memory* (HAM), which Anderson and Gordon Bower developed (Anderson & Bower, 1973), ACT* is broader than those of Collins and Quillian (1969) and Collins and Loftus (1975). In formulating ACT*, Anderson's ambitious intention has been to provide a single theoretical framework for all aspects of thinking, one including principles of initial encoding of information, information storage, and information retrieval and encompassing both declarative and procedural knowledge.

Unlike the Collins and Quillian model, the basic building blocks of ACT* are propositions, not concepts. Anderson proposes a basic cognitive unit consisting of a unit node (a proposition) and a set of elements (the relation and arguments of the proposition). Cognitive units are not limited to propositions, however. Images and word strings also may be cognitive units. The size of the cognitive unit may vary, but generally the upper limit of number of elements that can be encoded with any cognitive unit is five or fewer (J. R. Anderson, 1983a). Thus, a paragraph or 24-item word list could not be encoded as a single unit, but a simple sentence or pair of associated words could. A key assumption is that all elements of a unit are encoded together. For instance, when a proposition consisting of three elements is encoded (e.g., Webster proposed a toast), all of the elements (subject, predicate, object) are encoded in the unit, not just one or two.

As in most network models, the concept of *spreading activation* is a key feature in ACT* and is seen as determining the level of activity in long-term memory. Of course, activation must begin somewhere; the points where activation begins are called **focus units**. Once focus units are activated—either externally from perception (e.g., by reading a sentence) or from working memory (e.g., by thinking about what has been read)—activation spreads to associated elements. Thus, when the word *hot* is read, elements for *cold, warm, water,* and other related items would be activated automatically. Attention determines the continued activation of the network; when the source of activation for the focus unit drops from attention, activation decays.

Because working memory and LTM overlap extensively, activation can spread from working memory to associated elements in LTM. As Anderson points out, activation can "reverberate back" to nodes in the network. If Node 1 activates Node 2, then activation from Node 2 can spread to Node 1. Retrieval occurs when focus units are reactivated. Activation is cumulative. The more units activated, the more likely an item will be retrieved. Thus, although a student may not be able to recall a fact when first questioned about it, rephrasing the question or supplying "hints" may activate additional pathways that will stimulate recall.

In ACT*, well-learned concepts are seen as producing more activation and hence more easily retrieved than less well learned concepts. Well-learned information has many associations and wide-ranging activation that permit its access through multiple routes. Also, the ACT* model implies that more activation occurs on paths leading to stronger nodes. Thus, Anderson's model would predict that students who are helped to relate new information to existing, well-learned knowledge will have superior recall.

The ACT* model has generated a great deal of research. Because of its breadth, ACT* has been adapted not only to the study of memory but also to the study of other cognitive processes, such as problem solving and decision making (J. R. Anderson, 1993). Because it can account for a wide variety of data and addresses many important aspects of cognition, this model is likely to play an important role in directing cognitive research into the foreseeable future.

Implicit Memory: Retention Without Remembering

When we think of memory, we usually think about bringing a past experience to mind. Whether the memory is voluntary (a conscious search for information) or involuntary (a thought pops into our head), we recognize it as corresponding to some past event. This kind of memory, involving conscious recall or recognition of previous experiences, is called **explicit memory.** Explicit memory has been studied for many decades by memory researchers; it usually is tested by recall and recognition tasks that require intentional information retrieval.

Often, however, the record of our earlier experience is not available to our consciousness but still affects our behavior. This kind of memory is called **implicit memory.** Implicit memory is an unintentional, nonconscious form of retention in which our actions are influenced by a previous event but without conscious awareness (Jacoby & Witherspoon, 1982). Many of our daily performances, for example, reflect prior learning but resist conscious remembering. In skills as diverse as using computers, tying shoes, and driving a car, conscious remembering seems to play little part. In fact, when a person tries to reflect on how these skills are being performed, performance often deteriorates (Roediger, 1990).

Memory researchers dating back to Ebbinghaus have recognized the phenomenon of implicit memory, but systematic research on the topic dates back only to the 1980s (Graf & Schacter, 1985; Jacoby, 1983; Jacoby & Witherspoon, 1982). In just a decade, this topic has moved from obscurity to a position of central importance in cognitive psychology (Greene, 1992; Roediger, 1990; Schacter, 1993; Schachter & Cooper, 1993).

Interest in the topic of implicit memory first developed among cognitive neuroscientists working with amnesics, individuals with certain forms of brain injury that makes them unable to remember verbal materials, such as words or names, for more than a very brief period. Other functions, such as perceptual abilities and motor skills, remain intact, however.

The early conclusion was that the inability of such individuals to transfer verbal materials from STM to LTM played a critical role in their amnesia. That view, however, proved to be too simple as researchers demonstrated that some kinds of long-term verbal memory in amnesics were not impaired at all. Instead, the crucial dimension was whether explicit or implicit memory was being tested.

A representative early experiment by Jacoby and Witherspoon (1982) comparing amnesic and normal subjects provides an excellent example of the experimental procedures that have been used to contrast explicit and implicit memory performance. They used homophones (e.g., *read/reed*) as their experimental materials. In Phase 1, all subjects were asked questions (e.g., Name a musical instrument that employs a *reed*) to bias the interpretation of the target homophones toward their less frequent interpretation. (Hearing the word in isolation, most subjects would think of *read*, not *reed*. The question prompts the less frequent choice.) In Phase 2, subjects were asked to *spell* words, a task that for the subjects seemed totally unrelated to Phase 1. The list of words to be spelled, however, contained some homophones previously presented and some not. Although the experimenters made no connection between Phases 1 and 2, how subjects chose to spell the homophones was the key measure of effects of earlier encounters with some of the homophones. If the prior presentation influenced later interpretation, the lower probability spelling (e.g., *reed*) would be more probable for the homophones encountered earlier. As Jacoby and Witherspoon pointed out, an influence of memory on spelling does not necessarily require awareness of remembering. Awareness, however, was indeed necessary in a recognition task presented in Phase 3 of the experiment, which required subjects to indicate whether they had seen words before. Words from Phase 1 were mixed into the set of words in Phase 3.

Predictably, the probability of correctly recognizing whether or not they had seen a word before (the Phase 3 measure) was much lower for amnesics (.25) than for normal controls (.76). Thus, as expected, amnesics' explicit memory was very poor. What was startling, however, was amnesics' spelling performance. It revealed very strong effects of their earlier encounters with the words primed by the questions even though they had no awareness of their impact; that is, the spellings they chose (e.g., *reed*, not *read*) reflected their implicit memory from encountering the words in the questions they had answered in Phase 1. In fact, although both groups showed the influence of implicit memory, their probability of choosing the low frequency spelling was even higher than that of normal controls (.63 vs. .59)!

Since that time, implicit memory effects have been demonstrated in both amnesic and normal subjects by using a variety of experimental methods. These have been as diverse as better performance on completion tasks, in which subjects are shown partial stimuli and asked to complete them (e.g., having seen the word *flower* before, guessing the word *FLOWER* more easily when shown _L_WER) and decision tasks, in which subjects make more favorable judgments (e.g., of liking or preference) about the member of pairs to which they earlier had been exposed. Researchers also have demonstrated that effects of implicit memory extend to nonverbal materials, such as novel visual patterns and shapes (see Schacter & Cooper, 1993).

For memory theorists, two aspects of implicit memory research have been especially intriguing. First was the emergence of unequivocal evidence that behavior can be influenced by memory of past events even when there is no conscious awareness. Second and even more exciting for many theorists was the fact that implicit and explicit memory tasks sometimes elicit **functional dissociations**, in which implicit and explicit memory performances are unrelated. In Jacoby and Witherspoon's (1982) research, for instance, explicit memory performance as demonstrated by word recognition greatly favored normal subjects, whereas implicit memory performance on the spelling task did not. Weldon and Roediger (1987; see also Roediger, 1990) similarly showed a dissociation between explicit and implicit memory tasks.

When a mixed list of pictures and words was studied and subjects' recall was tested later in explicit free recall, the names of the pictures were better recalled than the words. On an implicit word-fragment completion test (see example above), however, in which some fragments corresponded to presented words and some to names of pictures, prior study of words produced far greater effects than study of pictures.

Findings of dissociations like these are extremely interesting to memory theorists, some of whom (e.g., Squire, 1987) have proposed *distinct memory systems* to account for them. These theorists, who tend to be those working in the neuroscience tradition, argue that the declarative memory system is responsible for performance on explicit tests of retention, whereas the procedural system underlies implicit memory. Other theorists, such as Roediger and Jacoby, assert, however, the more straightforward explanation that explicit and implicit memory tasks require different cognitive *operations*. They contend there is no need to propose different memory systems. As yet, however, neither the *multiple memory systems* nor the *processing* accounts (Greene, 1992) has proven wholly satisfactory in explaining all of the experimental results.

What has been learned in the past decade nonetheless is quite remarkable. Researchers are exploring systematically a completely new class of memory tasks and have acquired much basic knowledge about how implicit memory affects behavior. The finding that implicit and explicit memory may be dissociated from each other may have important implications for understanding memory performance in special groups, such as very young children and the elderly. For instance, developmental patterns for implicit and explicit memory may differ, requiring revisions of our theories of how memory develops. Similarly, we are likely to better understand memory processes associated with aging or memory loss due to injury because of the empirical and theoretical advances in this area. Although research in this area is still in its infancy, it promises to yield rich returns into the future.

Parallel Distributed Processing: A Connectionist Perspective

Throughout much of its history, cognitive psychology has been dominated by a computer metaphor. Human cognition, cognitive scientists have argued, is computerlike. Information is taken in, processed in a single central processor of working memory, and stored in and retrieved from long-term memory. The computer metaphor has generated models of memory (e.g., Atkinson & Shiffrin, 1968), knowledge representation (e.g., Kintsch, 1986, 1988), and problem solving (e.g., Newell & Simon, 1972). Beyond providing a metaphor for cognition, computers have provided a mechanism for simulating cognition and for testing cognitive theories.

The architecture of the computers of the past three decades and of most computers today requires sequential or **serial processing**; computer programs typically are a series of instructions the computer executes very rapidly, one after the other. One serious problem in modeling cognition, however, is that this kind of serial information processing is not very "brainlike." Where digital computers are quick and precise, executing millions and even billions of operations in sequence per second, human information processing is far slower. However, it is far better suited and far more powerful than computers for many kinds of "messy" everyday cognitive tasks such as recognizing objects in natural scenes, understanding language, searching memory when given only fragmentary information, making plans, and learning from experience.

Also, in contrast to most computer programs, our cognitive systems can operate under multiple constraints. Although some cognitive processes are serial, many are **parallel**, occurring simultaneously. For instance, in the famous example from Selfridge that appears in Chapter 2, the interpretation of the middle letter in the words *THE* and *CAT* is determined by the context in which it appears. Similarly, we have little trouble identifying the words in Figure 3-4 even though parts of key letters are obscured. Our perceptual system somehow explores a number of possibilities simultaneously without committing itself to one "interpretation" until all constraints are taken into account. The identity of each letter is constrained by all the others. Most cognitive tasks, including physical performances (e.g., hitting a ball, typing, playing a piano) and language use (e.g., oral language comprehension, reading and understanding stories), involve resolving multiple constraints.

Given the characteristics of the brain and its tremendous adaptability, a number of cognitive theorists (e.g., McClelland, Rumelhart, & Hinton, 1986) have proposed replacing the "computer metaphor" with a "brain metaphor," a so-called **connectionist model of memory** or **parallel distributed processing** (PDP) model. The reason human beings are better at such tasks than conventional computers, they contend, is that the brain has an "architecture" that better fits natural information-processing tasks. What humans do so exceedingly well, far better than any computer, is to consider many pieces of information simultaneously. Processing occurs in parallel, along many dimensions at the same time. Although any single bit of information may be imprecise or ambiguous, the system's parallel processing capabilities make it possible to make judgments and decisions with a high level of confidence.

According to McClelland (1988), the major difference between a model such as PDP and other cognitive models is that in most models, knowledge is stored as a static copy of a pattern. When access is needed, the pattern is found in long-term memory and copied into working memory. In PDP, however, the units themselves are not stored. What is stored are the *connection strengths* among simple processing units. These connection strengths allow the patterns to be re-created when the system is activated.

Because processing is parallel, it can proceed simultaneously along many dimensions. In reading, for instance, the cognitive processes of reading are not portrayed

Figure 3-4
Examples of information processing with multiple constraints.

as moving through steps from "lower levels," such as decoding, to "higher levels," such as comprehension processes. Instead, processing moves ahead on many levels at once; as we read, we simultaneously depend on feature extraction processes (e.g., recognizing lines, curves, and angles in letters), on letter and word recognition processes, on syntactic assignment processes (e.g., is *feature* a noun or a verb), and on activation of schemata. These processes simultaneously trigger and inhibit one another as processing moves forward. Top-down, bottom-up, and interactive (a combination of top-down and bottom-up) processing all can occur within such a system (McClelland & Rumelhart, 1981; Rumelhart & McClelland, 1986). As we see in Chapters 10 and 11, this conception of reading seems to fit well with the data.

Another key concept in a connectionist model such as PDP is that of **distributed representation**. In PDP, as we have indicated, knowledge is stored in the strengths of connections between processing units, not in the units themselves. Thus, knowledge of any specific pattern (e.g., a letter of the alphabet, a face) does not reside in a special processing unit reserved just for that pattern, but instead is distributed over the connections among a very large number of simple processing units. Thus, our comprehension of the word *toast* in the sentence "Webster proposed a toast" arises through activation of connections among a host of processing units, including those for letter perception, word meanings, and syntactic roles, and those relating to the context in which the sentence was uttered. Thus, we comprehend automatically that the "toast" Webster proposed is something other than the whole wheat variety.

In PDP models, processing units are roughly analogous to neurons or assemblies of neurons, and the connections by which units are linked are seen as roughly analogous to synapses. When stimulated by the environment, input units cause other units to be activated via their connections. Thus, PDP models contain the familiar spreading activation dimension.

Eventually, activation spreads to those units associated with responses. In typing the word *proposed,* for example, the decision to type the word causes activation of a unit for the word. That unit, in turn, activates units corresponding to the letters in the word. The unit for the first letter inhibits the units for the other letters; the second unit inhibits the first and other letters, and so on. The patterns of activation and inhibition among the units and the responses as they are carried out activate each letter in turn. When a response begins (e.g., typing the letter *p*), a strong inhibitory signal is sent to units associated with it. Thus, it is inhibited as subsequent units (e.g., *r, o*) are activated.

Hinton, McClelland, and Rumelhart (1986) argue that it is a mistake to view distributed representations such as PDP as an alternative to semantic networks and production systems. Instead, they may help us better understand how these more abstract entities are implemented and interact with one another. PDP may represent primitives of information processing; the more abstract models usefully may describe regularities at higher levels.

"Brainlike" models of information processing now are appearing more frequently in computer hardware. In the computer world, there long has been a recognition that the conventional, single central processor design has inherent limitations. Because instructions must be operated on serially, a bottleneck eventually will occur in the central processor no matter how fast the computer. As a consequence, a number of new machines are being designed around a connectionist model.

Whether computers based on parallel distributed processing and connectionist models of cognition such as PDP are the wave of the future still is unknown. It is clear, however, that connectionist models have some intriguing qualities. Although a fair amount of work has been done in attempting to apply the PDP model to a wide variety of areas (see McClelland, 1988; Seidenberg & McClelland, 1989; also the volumes by Rumelhart, McClelland, & PDP Research Group, 1986), connectionist models of cognition still are in their infancy. Because of their higher degree of correspondence to the characteristics of the brain and their ability to match more closely certain aspects of human cognition, however, they seem likely to make a major contribution to cognitive psychology and to our understanding of human learning and memory as they are refined.

IMPLICATIONS FOR INSTRUCTION

The models of memory and the memory-related concepts we have explored provide us with several powerful conceptions about the nature of learning and memory. These have important implications for educators.

1. *Recognize that the starting point of learning is what students already know.* The models of memory we have examined in this chapter all stress the role of prior knowledge on information processing and memory. What *can* be learned depends substantially on what learners already know. In the modal model, for instance, we see knowledge from LTM affecting perception and attention. Likewise, the research based on the concept of *schema* has illustrated dramatically how knowledge structures guide information processing and influence what we learn and remember. Students understand what they read, hear, and see through the filters of their experiences in their families and cultures. Recognition of this needs to be the starting point of our instruction.

2. *Help students activate their current knowledge.* Having relevant knowledge is one thing; using it in new learning is another. From a schema theory standpoint, new information needs to be instantiated within learners' schemata. From an instructional perspective, this implies that teachers may need to ensure that students have activated relevant knowledge. Using the framework of ACT*, we can see that knowledge activation provides more and stronger links for embedding new declarative and procedural knowledge within existing networks. As teachers, we need to take maximum advantage of the powerful relationship between prior and new knowledge. Stimulating students' recall of related information, providing analogies and "schema activation," and probing both intellectual and emotional reactions to materials and activities are only a few of many ways in which what students already know can be acknowledged and used to improve instruction.

3. *Recognize the limitations of STM.* The research on STM has highlighted a number of its limitations. It can be overloaded easily. It also needs constant attention

and rehearsal and is extraordinarily vulnerable to interruption. Whenever we make a number of points in class, give a complex assignment, or ask a student to perform a sequence of activities, we need to remember that this information may exceed the capacity limitations of STM unless the student processes it in a strategic manner. For young children especially, we need to keep in mind that their ability to remember sequences of information may be even more limited than that of adults (Case, 1992).

4.   *Help students organize new information into meaningful "chunks."* Although the research on STM has highlighted its limitations, it also has pointed to a tremendous compensatory factor: our ability to "chunk." Practice leads to memory efficiency. Limitations on STM are critical only when students are unable to organize and link information. When students are helped to discover relationships, to group related concepts and ideas, and to see patterns, comprehension increases and "information overload" diminishes.

5.   *Aid students in proceduralizing their knowledge.* A frequent challenge to educators is to make their knowledge useful for students. Although it is important that we build students' declarative knowledge, particularly *organized* declarative knowledge, we usually want to go well beyond this. We hope the knowledge that students acquire will become a vital, working part of their lives. In Anderson's terminology, declarative knowledge needs to be **proceduralized**, transformed into condition-action relationships. Proceduralized knowledge can be applied rapidly and reliably across a variety of situations (J. R. Anderson, 1993). Proceduralization is a function of practice. Experiences in which students use information in solving "real-life" problems, integrate skills in complex performances, and have opportunities to practice them contribute to the development of "working knowledge" instead of "inert knowledge."

6.   *Provide opportunities for students to use both verbal and imaginal coding.* The transactions that take place in most classrooms are verbal: Teachers and students spend their days talking, listening, reading, and sometimes writing. Often neglected in classroom processes, however, are images—images generated by pictures, touch, activities, and imagination. When we concentrate solely on verbal knowledge, excluding nonverbal forms of information, we may be neglecting some of the most important goals for learning. Furthermore, we may not be taking full advantage of students' cognitive abilities for coding information in both verbal and imaginal forms. As Paivio and others have shown, imagery can be a powerful tool for increasing memorability of information students need to acquire.

SUMMARY

Memory is one of the most important concerns of cognitive psychologists. It first was studied scientifically about a century ago by Ebbinghaus, and following Ebbinghaus's tradition, early studies of memory focused on experimental investigations of rote learning. Our conception of what constitutes valid study of memory now has broadened considerably, however, as memory theorists have made immense strides in describing the encoding, storage, and retrieval of meaningful information.

The basic or modal model of memory portrays memory as comprising three major components: sensory memory, STM or working memory, and LTM. Sensory memory decays rapidly and spontaneously. STM depends heavily on repetition and rehearsal, with chunking proposed as a mechanism whereby some of STM's limitations can be overcome. LTM is the permanent repository for information and seems to have virtually unlimited capacity.

As cognitive theorists have shifted from the study of rote to meaningful learning, they have made a number of distinctions that are very useful for educators. These include contrasts between declarative and procedural knowledge, episodic and semantic memory, and verbal and imaginal representation. They also have proposed a number of cognitive units in their quest to adequately describe memory. Among the most useful have been concepts, propositions, productions, and schemata. These units are building blocks for more comprehensive models of memory, such as Anderson's ACT* model, and a connectionist model, PDP, which emphasizes parallel processing. As memory models are refined further, our understanding of human memory should continue to expand, along with our ability to enhance our students' abilities to learn, recall, and use the information they learn.

SUGGESTED READINGS

Anderson, J. R. (1993). Problem solving and learning. *American Psychologist, 48,* 35–44.

This short article is a very readable summary of J. R. Anderson's most recent views of his ACT* model and its potential for understanding the phenomenon of problem solving.

Collins, A. F., Gathercole, S. E., Conway, M. A., & Morris, P. E. (1993). *Theories of memory.* Hove, England: Lawrence Erlbaum.

A collection of papers from an international conference on memory, this volume contains scholarly papers representing many of the current issues in memory research.

CHAPTER 4

Encoding Processes

In Chapter 2, we reviewed perception and attention and noted how both were powerfully affected by people's knowledge of the world. In Chapter 3, we introduced the topic of short-term and long-term memory and how knowledge is stored. The topic of this chapter is the process involved in placing information into memory. This process usually is referred to as **encoding** (see Figure 3-1). As you might expect, encoding has a major impact on other cognitive processes, such as **storage** (how information is kept in memory) and **retrieval** (how information is gotten from memory). Chapter 5 addresses retrieval and its relationship to encoding and storage. For the present, we focus on strategies that help us encode information.

Not all of the information we want to learn is the same. Some is factual, such as the capital of Nebraska, the atomic structure of hydrogen, the names of the oceans, or even the quadratic formula. But much of what we encounter and need to learn is complex. For example, you probably will be expected to read this chapter and take a test on it. You need to know specific facts, technical terms, and perhaps some dates. More importantly, you need to understand what the chapter means in both a theoretical and an applied sense. Presumably, a theory of encoding will be presented in this chapter. Your task is to understand this theory, identify component parts of it, understand the relationships among these parts, and apply them to your everyday life.

Learning facts and learning complex information are very different tasks. Educational psychologists have identified a number of ways that students learn different types of information. Some students rely on different kinds of learning tactics to accomplish this end. Many students use a number of tactics in a highly strategic manner to regulate their learning. Surprisingly, most of these tactics are very easy to use despite the fact that few students use a wide variety of tactics. Organizing tactics into a planful sequence is more difficult. Doing so with some degree of conscious awareness is referred to as *metacognition* (an awareness of one's learning).

This section compares some of the tactics and strategies (the planful use of two or more tactics to accomplish a learning goal) that learners use to learn facts and complex information. We begin with learning facts and proceed to more complex types of learning. Virtually all of these skills are active learning processes under the direct control of the student. Students who use these tactics and strategies to construct meaning are more likely to comprehend and remember information.

ENCODING FACTUAL INFORMATION

How we process to-be-remembered information makes a difference in how well we remember it. In particular, the way we rehearse information influences the quality of our memory.

As a means of examining rehearsal more closely, let's take a look at two sixth-graders studying for a spelling test. For our purposes, we assume the two children are of equal ability, save for how they rehearse the spelling words. Susan starts at the top of the list, reads the first word, and spells it to herself over and over (*"familiar—f, a, m, i ..."*). She does this six times for each of the twenty-five words on the list and then sets it aside. Perlita also starts by reading the first word on the list, but she rehearses the information differently by breaking the words into smaller words and syllables she already knows how to spell ("familiar—fam, i, liar. That's *'fam'—f, a, m; 'i'—i;* and *'liar'—l, i, a, r"*). Perlita also cycles through her list six times for each word.

If we give Susan and Perlita a test of the spelling words after they finish studying, the odds are extremely good that Perlita will obtain a higher score than Susan. The reason for this difference is obvious to us, if not to the sixth-graders: The way the information was rehearsed influenced its memorability.

Typically, the kind of rehearsal Susan engaged in is called **maintenance rehearsal** (Craik, 1979). Maintenance rehearsal refers to the direct recycling of information in order to keep it active in short-term memory. It is the sort of rehearsal we perform when we look up a phone number and want to retain it just long enough to dial the number (e.g., repeating 555–2225 over and over until the number is dialed). The results of such maintenance rehearsal seldom are long term (McKeown & Curtis, 1987). For example, have you ever repeated a phone number to yourself until you dialed it, obtained a busy signal, and then had to look up the number two minutes later to call again?

Several studies have examined maintenance rehearsal (e.g., Schweickert & Boruff, 1986). In general, it seems that maintenance rehearsal is highly efficient for retaining information for a short time without taxing a person's cognitive resources. For example, you can cycle 555-2225 over and over while looking for a pencil and a pad of paper, picking up the phone, and thinking about what you are going to say once you reach the person at 555-2225. Maintenance rehearsal also can enhance long-term memory (Glenberg, Smith, & Green, 1977), but it is very effortful and inefficient.

In contrast to maintenance rehearsal is elaborative rehearsal. **Elaborative rehearsal** is any form of rehearsal in which the to-be-remembered information is related to other information (Craik & Lockhart, 1986). Later in this chapter, we discuss "levels of processing," which refers to the ways complex information can be elaborated. In terms of the levels-of-processing framework, elaborative rehearsal amounts to deep or elaborate encoding activities, whereas maintenance rehearsal can be seen as shallow encoding.

Perlita's rehearsal of the spelling words is a clear example of elaborative rehearsal. Rather than merely recycle the spelling words over and over, she broke them into components and elaborated (related) the to-be-remembered information to what she already knew. In contrast to Susan's, Perlita's encoding activities are much more likely to lead to high levels of recall.

Another example of elaborative rehearsal in the learning of spelling words can be seen in how the fourth-grade daughter of one of the authors learned to spell *respectfully*. While getting ready to study her spelling, she heard an old rock song in which the word *respect* is spelled out in the lyrics to a very strong beat. Later, when her father walked by, the fourth-grader had her spelling list turned out of sight and was mimicking the singer's lyric line: *r, e, s, p, e, c, t, fully*.

Research suggests that elaborative rehearsal is far superior to maintenance rehearsal for long-term recall but that it tends to use considerably more of a person's cognitive resources than maintenance rehearsal (Craik, 1979; Elmes & Bjork, 1975). It also suggests that maintenance and elaborative rehearsal need to be thought of as representing opposite ends on a continuum of rehearsal (Craik, 1979). At one extreme of the continuum would be the minimal processing needed to repeat a term over and over; at the other end would be processing activities in which the to-be-learned information was linked with several bits of information already in memory.

One implication of research on rehearsal is that different types of rehearsal are appropriate for different tasks (Palmere, Benton, Glover, & Ronning, 1983; Phifer, McNickle, Ronning, & Glover, 1983). When long-term memory is desired (e.g., when a student will be tested over content or when the information will be important for later understandings), some form of elaborative rehearsal should be employed. As you might suspect, many encoding strategies employ elaborative rehearsal, and we review several of them in the next few pages.

Mediation

One of the simplest elaborative encoding strategies is **mediation**. Mediation involves tying difficult-to-remember items to something more meaningful. The original research on mediation in memory was based on the learning of paired nonsense syllables (Montague, Adams, & Kiess, 1966). Although we hope none of what we teach is at the level of nonsense syllables (e.g., BOZ, BUH), the strategy has some implications for instruction.

In early research on mediation (Montague et al., 1966), it became apparent that subjects who used mediators in committing pairs of nonsense syllables to memory outperformed subjects who used no mediators; that is, when subjects could devise a mediator such as *race car* when faced with a pair of nonsense syllables (e.g., *ris–kir*), they were able to tie their memory for the meaningless information to something meaningful and greatly ease their memory task.

Although mediation is a very simple and easily learned technique to enhance memory for a limited range of information, it is congruent with the theme of this chapter; that is, what people do with to-be-learned information determines how it will be remembered. Mediation results in deeper, more-elaborate encodings than simple repetition of new content.

Imagery

Our emphasis up to this point has been on the encoding of verbal information. One powerful adjunct to verbal encoding is the use of imagery. (See Chapter 3 for a discussion of imagery and Paivio's dual-coding theory.) Consider the fourth-grader who conjures up an image of an emperor (complete with rich robes, a crown, and a jewel-encrusted scepter) when trying to learn the meaning of the word *czar.* Finally, think about the chemistry student who shuts her eyes and visualizes a three-dimensional picture of the bromination of benzene as she studies for a quiz. In each of these examples, imagery is an important part of the encoding of information.

As we saw in Chapter 3, imagery usually leads to better memory performance (Clark & Paivio, 1991). Some provisos should be considered, however, when we discuss the facilitative effects of imagery. One is the imagery value of various to-be-learned materials. For example, the word *car* much more easily leads to an image than does, say, the word *truth.* Similarly, the word *turban* leads easily to a clear picture, whereas the word *freedom* does not.

Easily imaged words tend to be remembered more readily than hard-to-image words, even in the absence of instructions to use imagery (Paivio, 1975). When subjects are instructed to use imagery, the difference is even more pronounced. Even subjects' memory for meaningless nonsense syllables is enhanced when they use imagery in learning.

Imagery value should not be thought of as being restricted to individual words (Paivio, 1975). The idea can be extended to the imagery value of concepts (e.g., compare internal combustion to entropy), people (e.g., compare Theodore Roosevelt to Calvin Coolidge), and whole segments of information (e.g., compare *Macbeth* with

99 percent of the situation comedies ever produced). Simply, some sets of information are easier to image than others.

A second issue to be considered when we discuss imagery is the possibility of individual differences among students in their ability to image information (Ahsen, 1987; Scruggs, Mastropieri, McLoone, Levin, & Morrison, 1987). Even though very little research has been conducted on this question, the results suggest that some students are better able to employ imagery than others and that these differences seem to lead to differences in memory performance. Unfortunately, no evidence points to whether an ability to image is learned or can be improved with practice. Still, even students who score very low on measures of ability to image do show improved memory performance when they employ imagery (Scruggs et al., 1987).

A third factor associated with imagery concerns the nature of the images people conjure up. Many memory experts have argued that the best images are bizarre, colorful, and strange. For example, if you wanted to remember that one of J. P. Morgan's characteristics was greed, you could imagine J. P. Morgan as a hog wearing a business suit with a watch fob and chomping on a large black cigar and fighting with other industrialists for a share of the spoils. Similarly, if you wanted to remember that the word *peduncle* refers to the stem bearing a flower, you could imagine a garish flower being carried by its stalk with the word *peduncle* pictured on each side of the stalk.

Research on the value of bizarre imagery, however, has been inconclusive. Early work (e.g., Collyer, Jonides, & Bevan, 1972; Wollen, Weber, & Lowry, 1972) sometimes found no advantage for bizarre imagery, as opposed to mundane imagery (e.g., trying to remember *peduncle* by picturing a daisy) and sometimes found it to be valuable (Furst, 1954). Studies that report conflicting findings continue to appear (Clark & Paivio, 1991).

As we see below, imagery is an important component of many mnemonic encoding strategies. By itself, imagery has considerable value in enhancing memory. In conjunction with some of the mnemonic techniques described below, it can be a powerful tool for improving memory performance.

Mnemonics

Mnemonics are memory strategies that help people remember information. Typically, mnemonics involve pairing to-be-learned information with well-learned information in order to make the new information more memorable. Mnemonics help us learn information by making it easier to elaborate, chunk, or retrieve it from memory (Hayes, 1988).

Mnemonic techniques include the use of rhymes ("*i* before *e* except after *c*"), sayings ("thirty days has September, April, June, and November"), gestures (the "right-hand rule" in physics is a mnemonic for determining the flow of a magnetic field around an electrical current—merely put the thumb of the right hand in the direction of the current and the curl of the fingers around the conductor will show the direction of the magnetic field), and imagery. Teachers often use mnemonics as a part of their instruction (Boltwood & Blick, 1978; Higbee & Kunihira, 1985). For example, music teachers may instruct students in the use of "*Every Good Boy Does*

Fine" to help them remember the lines of the treble clef and *FACE* to remember the spaces. Students report that they often use mnemonics without being instructed to do so (Kilpatrick, 1985; Morris & Cook, 1978; Nickerson, Perkins, & Smith, 1986). As might be expected, some mnemonics are more effective than others (J. R. Levin, 1986), and different mnemonics seem especially suited to specific forms of learning. In the remainder of this section, we examine several mnemonic techniques and see how they may be implemented in instruction.

The Peg Method.   In the **peg method**, students memorize a series of "pegs" on which to-be-learned information can be "hung," one item at a time. The pegs can be any well-learned set of items, but the most popular approach involves the use of a very simple rhyme.

> One is a bun.
>
> Two is a shoe.
>
> Three is a tree.
>
> Four is a door.
>
> Five is a hive.
>
> Six is sticks.
>
> Seven is heaven.
>
> Eight is a gate.
>
> Nine is a pine.
>
> Ten is a hen.

Students who have mastered this rhyme can use it to learn lists of items, such as the names of authors, politicians, or terms in a social studies course. The technique is simple and effective. Its use can be seen, for example, in the learning of the following grocery list: pickles, bread, milk, oranges, and lightbulbs.

If you actually were to use the rhyme, the first step is to construct a visual image of the first thing on the to-be-learned list interacting with the object named in the first line of the rhyme. For instance, to remember pickles, we could imagine a very large pickle stuffed into the center of a bun. Next, a loaf of bread could be imagined shoved into a shoe as it sits in the closet. The third item, milk, could be visualized as a milk tree—a large tree with quarts of milk, rather than fruit, hanging from it. Oranges could be remembered by picturing the knob of the door to be an orange, and, when the door is opened, it opens into a closet filled with oranges that then fall out all over the person opening the door and roll across the floor. Finally, lightbulbs readily could be seen as interacting with a beehive, such as picturing a beehive with a flashing lightbulb on its top, with additional bulbs lighting a doorway to the hive.

After each item on the list has been carefully imagined interacting with the corresponding item in the rhyme, the learner is finished until time for recall. At recall, the learner simply recites the rhyme. Each image is retrieved as the recitation proceeds, and so recall of the list follows.

When it is well learned, the peg method has been shown to be effective with word lists of various sorts (Bugelski, Kidd, & Segmen, 1968). Interestingly, the peg method can be used over and over without losing its effectiveness. It is not clear why, but previous uses of the peg method (e.g., the grocery list we gave) do not seem to diminish the effectiveness of the system when it is reused.

Beyond its use for committing various lists to memory, the peg method has been shown to be an effective means of learning written directions (Glover, Harvey, & Corkill, 1988), of learning oral directions (Glover, Timme, Deyloff, Rogers, & Dinnel, 1987), and in the learning of the steps in complex procedures (Glover, Timme, Deyloff, & Rogers, 1987). For example, Glover, Timme, Deyloff, Rogers, and Dinnel (1987) contrasted several encoding procedures with the pegword mnemonic in terms of students' ability to remember the steps in assembling office equipment. The results indicated that the pegword mnemonic was more effective than other techniques in facilitating students' recall. Indeed, an analysis of many of the procedures students learn indicated that the steps in these procedures essentially are lists to be learned and that list-learning techniques, such as the peg method, facilitate their memorability.

The Method of Loci.   One of the best-known mnemonic procedures dates back to the ancient Greeks. According to Bower (1970) and Yates (1966), the **method of loci** got its name from an event where the poet Simonides, attending a banquet, was called outside. While Simonides was outside, the roof of the banquet hall collapsed, killing everyone left inside. The disaster was especially cruel because the bodies were so badly mangled that not even the victims' loved ones could identify them. Simonides, however, was able to remember each person on the basis of where the person sat at the banquet table. Hence, the name "method of loci" came from Simonides's use of location to recall information.

Despite its longevity, the method of loci has received relatively little research attention. The method still is used widely, however, especially by memory experts (Neisser, 1982). To use the method of loci to learn new information, a very imaginable location, such as one's home or the path one walks to school, must be learned flawlessly. The location then is practiced so that the person can easily imagine various "drops" in the location, such as the sofa, coffee table, window, television, and armchair in a living room. These drops must be learned such that they are recalled in exactly the same order each time.

Once the location and its drops have been overlearned, the system is ready for use as a mnemonic. Let's suppose a student must recall five famous poets: Chaucer, Spenser, Keats, Hardy, and Eliott. We could imagine Chaucer sitting on the sofa, Spenser with his boots propped up on the coffee table, Keats looking out the window, Hardy tuning the television, and Eliott sitting in the armchair. If our list was longer, we could continue to place people in locations until we completed the list.

At the time of recall, we would take our mental walk back through the location, and each drop would lead to the image of the to-be-remembered person. As with the peg method, the method of loci can be used over and over without losing its effectiveness. In addition, it can be employed to help students remember a wide variety of information.

The method of loci and the peg method have many similarities. First, rhyme or location must be learned to perfection. Effective use of either of these mnemonics requires that their "base" be flawless. Second, each item in the to-be-learned list must be clearly pictured interacting with its appropriate "partner" in either the rhyme or the location. Third, recall depends on reciting the original rhyme or location and retrieving the appropriate image. For certain kinds of information, both methods work well indeed; they are excellent means of enhancing memory and of reducing the effort required to commit new information to memory. In addition, both methods can be used over and over with a wide variety of to-be-learned materials. Both methods, however, exact a price—the effort required to learn the original "base" on which the mnemonic depends. Students sometimes balk at giving the effort needed to develop one of these mnemonics, but they almost always report that the effort was well worth it after they begin using the mnemonics (Kilpatrick, 1985).

The Link Method.   Relatively little research has been done on the **link method** (Bellezza, 1981). Memory experts, however, report using it (Neisser, 1982), and it has the advantage over the method of loci and the peg method of not needing an external system or previously learned set of materials.

The link method is best suited for learning lists of things. In this method, a student forms an image for each item in a list of things to be learned. Each image is pictured as interacting with the next item on the list so that all of the items are linked in imagination. For example, if a student needed to remember to bring her homework, lab notebook, chemistry text, goggles, lab apron, and pencil to class tomorrow, she could imagine a scene in which the homework papers were tucked inside the lab notebook. The lab notebook then could be placed into the textbook, with her goggles stretched around it. Next, the total package could be wrapped up in the lab apron, with the ties of the apron wrapped around a pencil to make a nice bow. The next morning, when she attempted to recall what she must take to class, she would recall the image and mentally unwrap it. The interactive image makes it probable that recall of any item on the list will cue recall of the others.

Stories.   Another simple mnemonic is the use of **stories** constructed from the words to be remembered in a list (Bellezza, 1981). To use this method, the to-be-learned words in a list are put together in a story such that the to-be-learned words are highlighted. Then, at recall, the story is remembered and the to-be-remembered words are plucked from the story.

For example, let's suppose a student is expected to remember to bring a pair of scissors, a ruler, a compass, a protractor, and a sharp pencil to school. Our student could construct the following story to help him remember these items: "The king drew a *pencil* line with his *ruler* before he cut the line with *scissors.* Then he measured an angle with a *protractor* and marked the point with a *compass.*"

The story method is simple, but effective. An early study by Bower and Clark (1969) gave experimental subjects in two conditions twelve lists of ten words each.

The subjects in one condition were asked merely to learn the words in each list, as they would be tested over the words at a later point. Subjects in the other condition, however, were asked to construct stories around each list of ten words. Holding study time equal in the two conditions, Bower and Clark tested for recall after each list was presented and found no difference in recall between the two conditions. However, when they tested subjects for recall of all 120 words on completion of the entire experiment, subjects in the story condition recalled 93 percent of the words, whereas subjects in the control condition recalled only 13 percent. The story mnemonic was extremely facilitative in subjects' recall of content.

First-Letter Method.   Among all mnemonics, the one that students most often report using spontaneously is the **first-letter method** (Boltwood & Blick, 1978). This method is similar to the story mnemonic, except that it involves using the first letters of to-be-learned words to construct acronyms or words. These acronyms or words then function as the mnemonics. At recall, students recall the acronym and then, using its letters, recall the items on the list.

For example, let's suppose a high school student is trying to remember that borax is made of boron, oxygen, and sodium. The student could take the first letter of each component and construct a word, *bos,* as a mnemonic. Then, when she attempts to recall the constituents of borax on a test, she would remember the word *bos* and generate the constituents from the first letters. Similarly, if we asked you to remember a grocery list consisting of cheese, ham, eggs, radishes, razor blades, and yogurt, the word *cherry* could be constructed from the first letter of each item on the list. Then, when you visit the store, if you remember the mnemonic *cherry,* you should be able to use the letters in the word to reconstruct the items in your list.

As straightforward as their appeal might be, the results of research on first-letter mnemonics have been mixed (Bellezza, 1981; Boltwood & Blick, 1978; Carlson, Zimmer, & Glover, 1981). On the one hand, students who are already familiar with their use do seem to benefit from the strategy. On the other hand, students who have not previously used first-letter mnemonics on their own receive little benefit from using the procedure (Carlson et al., 1981). To this point, however, it is difficult to draw conclusions about first-letter mnemonics because of the sparsity of research on the technique. It would seem that students who use the procedure should be encouraged to continue, but there is no compelling evidence for teaching the method.

The Keyword Method.   Of all the mnemonic techniques, probably the most flexible and powerful is the **keyword method**. This method was developed originally to facilitate vocabulary acquisition, but it has many other uses. As in the link method, the method of loci, and the peg method, imagery is critical to the effectiveness of the keyword method. However, the use of imagery in the keyword method varies considerably from how imagery is used in the other techniques.

The keyword mnemonic consists of two separate stages: an acoustic link and an imagery link. In vocabulary learning, for example, the first stage—the acoustic link—requires the identification of a "keyword." The keyword sounds like a part of the to-be-learned vocabulary word and furnishes the acoustic link necessary to the method

(J. R. Levin, 1981, 1986). The second stage—the imagery link—requires the learner to imagine a visual image of the keyword interacting with the meaning of the to-be-learned vocabulary word. At the time of recall, the original vocabulary word on a test should evoke the interactive image in memory, which will allow for recall of the word's meaning.

An example will clarify these stages. Let's suppose a sixth-grader has the assignment of learning ten vocabulary words in a language arts unit. Among these words is *captivate.* Although our sixth-grader has a fine vocabulary, *captivate* is not in it. So he decides to use the keyword method to help remember this word. First, he searches for a keyword within the to-be-learned word and settles on *cap,* which he can picture readily in imagination. He then links his keyword with an image—in this case, his Uncle Bill, who always wears a cap and, whenever he visits, holds everyone's attention with outrageous stories. So the student's image linked with the word's meaning is of his Uncle Bill captivating him with a story. If all goes well, when he has his test and sees the word *captivate,* he will remember his keyword, *cap,* and remember his image of Uncle Bill and the word's meaning.

The keyword method does not depend on a perfect match of the keyword with the vocabulary word. For example, the word *exiguous* does not contain an easily located keyword. However, with a little Kentucky windage worked in, the keyword *exit* (rather than *exig*) can be selected. Then, if you imagine an extremely tiny exit (ours is in a darkened movie theater with red neon letters spelling out *exit* on a mouse-sized sign above it), you should have a workable interactive image. Next time you see *exiguous,* find the "exig" or "exit" and recall the image of the miniature exit. This should be all you need to remember that *exiguous* means "small."

Although it is an effective means of enhancing the learning of English-language vocabulary, the keyword method was developed originally for the acquisition of foreign-language vocabulary (Atkinson, 1975). Consider, for example, the Spanish word *caballo,* which means "horse." The keyword *ball* can be picked out easily, and an image of a horse balancing on a ball readily comes to mind. Alternatively, the keyword *cab* could be chosen, and the interactive image could be of a horse driving a cab on Chicago's Wabash Avenue.

Since 1975, an enormous amount of research has been done on the keyword method. In general, the results have been positive among students of all ages (J. R. Levin, 1986; Pressley, Levin, & Delaney, 1982) across several languages (e.g., Atkinson & Raugh, 1975; Pressley, 1977) and has been exceptionally effective in improving the learning of students with mild retardation and learning disabilities (Mastropieri & Scruggs, 1989). The method also has been an effective means of enhancing memory for facts other than vocabulary (J. R. Levin, 1986) and has been useful in increasing learning from text (Mastropieri & Scruggs, 1989; McCormick & Levin, 1984).

Even though study after study since 1975 has shown the benefits of the keyword method, recommendations for its use have not yet made their way into most teaching-method textbooks. The method is easy to teach, it is readily learned by even the youngest children, and students enjoy using it. Because students generate their own keyword and image, very little work is required of the teacher except in actually teaching students how to use the keyword method and reminding them to use it.

(Keywords and images can be generated by teachers, however—an approach some-what less effective than when students perform the method on their own [J. R. Levin, 1986; Pressley et al., 1982].)

Yodai Mnemonics.   **Yodai mnemonics** were developed in the 1920s by a Japanese educator, Masachika Nakane, but only came to the attention of Western psycholo-gists recently (Higbee & Kunihira, 1985; J. R. Levin, 1985; Pressley, 1985). Actual research on the method is scant (Pressley, 1985), especially in Western settings. How-ever, the method has achieved such widespread use in Japan that a brief review seems warranted.

The term *yodai* means "the essence of structure" (Higbee & Kunihira, 1985), and the yodai mnemonics were so named because they are designed as verbal medi-ators that attempt to spell out the essence of rules for solving problems. An example taken from Higbee and Kunihira (1985, pp. 58–59) will help describe the nature of yodai mnemonics.

> To teach kindergarten children mathematical operations with fractions, the mnemonics use familiar metaphors expressed in familiar words. Thus, a fraction is called a *bug* with a *head* and a *wing*. The head is the numerator and the wing is the denominator (words such as *fraction, numerator,* and *denominator* are not used). To add fractions with equal denominators, for example, the child is instructed to "count the heads when the wings are the same." Multiplying involves putting the heads together and putting the wings together. The multiplication sign (×) represents the bug's crossed *horns* or feelers. Dividing fractions requires turning one of the bugs upside down and then multiplying.

As you can see, a fairly complex set of skills can be taught through yodai proce-dures by putting the operations involved in the skills into concrete terms with which the students are familiar. Higbee and Kunihira reported that such methods show a higher rate of success, leading to better overall skill acquisition than traditional methods of teaching.

The major criticism of yodai techniques (the fractions example being representa-tive) has been that, used in isolation, the techniques can lead to the phenomenon of children's being able to perform skills without understanding what they are doing (see Kilpatrick, 1985). An analysis of the method indeed does suggest this is possi-ble. Kindergartners may be able to add, subtract, multiply, and divide fractions, for instance, without any sense of what they are doing or why it is being done. This is because the children are counting heads and wings, not "adding," "subtracting," "multiplying," or "dividing" in any real sense. This criticism, of course, is very similar to that leveled against the Suzuki method of teaching music, a method that also relies on yodai mnemonics (Higbee & Kunihira, 1985).

On the one hand, it seems to us there is little point in teaching skills without understanding. On the other hand, it also seems clear that yodai mnemonics can be used in conjunction with other methods of instruction; that is, mnemonics such as the bug counting used in teaching fractions could be employed as an adjunct to more traditional approaches. Certainly, fractions are difficult enough for fourth-, fifth-, and sixth-graders, so providing a mnemonic aid seems highly reasonable. Still, as promising as yodai mnemonics seem, more research is required to demonstrate their value in diverse cultural settings when used in conjunction with other teaching methods.

Summary of Mnemonics

Mnemonics are rhymes, sayings, and other procedures designed to make new material more memorable. They allow for more elaborate encodings of new materials and stronger memory traces. The peg method and the method of loci both depend on a well-learned base to which to-be-learned information is related. The link and story methods put to-be-learned items together in a list and rely on the recall of the overall image or story to facilitate recall. The first-letter mnemonic chains to-be-learned items together by forming a word or acronym from the first letters of the words in a to-be-learned list. The most powerful and flexible mnemonic is the keyword method, which employs interactive imagery to form an acoustic and a visual link. Finally, yodai mnemonics use images and terms familiar to students to describe the actions to be followed in performing skills.

Although mnemonics may be helpful used in isolation, such as employing the peg method to memorize a list of items or employing the keyword mnemonic to learn new vocabulary words, these techniques are best seen as adjuncts to instruction. In this context, teachers should provide instruction in mnemonics as a strategy for learning lists of unrelated terms or concepts. Students should be encouraged to use other methods, however, when learning complex materials.

ENCODING COMPLEX INFORMATION

Even though mnemonics have a relatively broad range of applications, they generally are limited to lists of facts, sets of vocabulary items, groups of ideas, or steps in a skill. A good deal of instruction is much broader in scope, such as when students learn about John Steinbeck's portrayal of human nature, Newton's laws of physics, or American foreign policy in the 1970s. Cognitive psychologists have given a great deal of thought to how students' encoding of such complex materials can be facilitated, and a general consensus has been emerging during the past decade.

In the following sections, we discuss a number of ways students elaborate and enrich information. The main point is that learning complex information is a highly constructive process. The sheer bulk of information we must process in a typical classroom requires us to focus selectively on what is most important, to make high-level inferences across main ideas, and to represent this information in long-term memory. A secondary point is that meaning may be constructed in many ways. Effective learners use what they know to organize, enrich, and add to new information in a variety of ways. Here, we review four approaches for improving active learning: advance organizers, schema activation, answering questions and selective attention, and levels of processing.

Advance Organizers

Advance organizers are general overviews of new information provided to learners before they actually are exposed to the new information. For example, prior to a discussion of President Franklin Roosevelt's social legislation after taking office in 1932, a high school class could be given an overview of contemporary social services available through the federal government. Ausubel (1960, 1968), who originally devised advance organizers for use with reading materials, argued that new information is learned most easily when it can be linked with well-organized information already in memory. In the example we gave earlier, even the least-knowledgeable student will have some knowledge of various social programs, if only through exposure to television. From Ausubel's perspective, advance organizers provide learners with a kind of "scaffolding" to which more detailed material can be related. Returning to our example, a discussion of Roosevelt's actions after being elected should be better encoded and remembered if students are able to relate this information to knowledge they already possess.

As we will see when we examine advance organizers in Chapter 11, the concept frequently has been criticized (e.g., Anderson, Spiro, & Anderson, 1978), primarily in terms of the theoretical basis for advance organizers (Derry, 1984) and the difficulty of exactly specifying advance organizers. More recently, however, schema theorists (e.g., Derry, 1984; Mayer, 1984) have avoided many of the problems inherent in Ausubel's (1960, 1968) early views by suggesting that advance organizers function by (1) activating relevant schemata for to-be-learned material and (2) correcting the activated schemata so that new material is assimilated to them. In this view, the interaction of students' prior knowledge and the new information form a richer, broader schema that contains both the original information (e.g., what a student knew about social services provided by the government in contemporary times) and the new information (e.g., the changes brought about by Franklin Roosevelt).

Recent work also has indicated that some of the problems of specifying the nature of advance organizers can be resolved. In general, organizers employing examples, especially concrete examples of things akin to what students will encounter later, are more effective than abstract organizers. Further, the organizers should be both familiar to learners and well learned (see Corkill, 1992). Other than the dimensions of containing an example and being concrete, familiar, and well learned, advance organizers can take many different forms: discussions, brief segments of text, schematic diagrams, drawings, and so forth.

Schema Activation

Another approach that emphasizes relating new information to students' prior knowledge as a means of enhancing learning is schema activation (Pearson, 1984). **Schema activation** refers to various methods designed to activate relevant schemata prior to a learning activity. For instance, prior to a lesson on internal combustion engines, seventh-grade students can be asked to describe the characteristics of their parents' cars or lawn mowers, their own model cars or airplanes, and city buses in order to activate relevant schemata. Similarly, high school students preparing for a lesson on the Holocaust can be asked to talk about their knowledge of prejudice, racism, and "scapegoating" in order to activate relevant schemata. Fourth-grade students, as another example, can be led in a discussion of various neighborhood animals prior to a lesson on the characteristics of mammals.

The idea underlying schema activation is that students at any age will have some relevant knowledge to which new information can be related. A class of fourth-graders we know, for example, began to learn about heat conduction and the relationship of a substance's density to its heat conductivity by first thinking of examples of objects that carried heat (the handle of a metal frying pan, the outside-facing wall of a room on a cold day, the end of a burning match) and then doing a simple but carefully supervised experiment in which several rods of different materials (e.g., iron, glass, wood) but of the same length and cross section were put into a flame. The students then discussed why some of the rods became warm rapidly, whereas others seemed to remain cool, and related the results of the experiment to their own experiences. (One girl camped out frequently and knew that a metal frying pan over a fire very quickly would become too hot to touch, whereas even a burning stick would remain comfortable to the touch at the nonburning end. One boy noted how his metal cup would burn his lips when it was filled with hot chocolate but the same hot chocolate in a ceramic cup did not make it too hot.)

With their schemata for "heat conduction" presumably activated, the students weighed the various rods on a balance scale and recorded the weights, noting next to each whether it had become hot rapidly or slowly. Then, the students were asked to guess why some of the rods conducted heat more readily than others. Finally, the teacher gave a brief lesson about density, heat conduction, and the relationship of the two.

The relationship of density to heat conduction is, of course, a fairly sophisticated concept that many adults do not clearly understand. By carefully activating her students' relevant schemata, however, the teacher in our example was able to help her students learn and remember a difficult concept.

Schema activation is a general procedure for enhancing students' encoding of new information. It can involve having students describe examples from their experiences, perform experiments, review previous learning, or use the context in which new material is presented (Pearson, 1984). Overall, any teaching procedure that helps students form conceptual bridges between what they already know and what they are to learn can be considered a form of schema activation.

Answering Questions and Selective Attention

Answering questions about a text either before, during, or after reading greatly improves comprehension for question-relevant information (see King, 1992, and Reynolds, 1993, for recent reviews). Comprehension improves largely because readers selectively focus their attention on question-relevant information. One interesting consequence of this focusing strategy is that students learn more with no more, and perhaps even less, time on-task. This result occurs because students often increase the intensity of their attention when reading question-relevant information; that is, their concentration increases. This is true especially when questions appear before or during reading.

A number of studies report very favorable improvements when students are taught to generate their own questions before or after reading (Palincsar & Brown, 1984; Raphael & McKinney, 1983) (see Chapter 11). One good case in point is when students generate questions that can be answered only by making inferences across the text or by using prior knowledge. For example, *text-explicit* questions can be answered by information presented explicitly within one sentence in the text (Raphael & McKinney, 1983). *Text-implicit* questions can be answered by information from the text that occurs across two or more sentences; in other words, an inference is required. *Script-implicit* questions require answers that depend, in part, on text-implicit inferences plus information from prior knowledge that was not included in the text. Generating and answering text- and script-implicit questions facilitate comprehension significantly.

Evidence also suggests that answering questions while performing a task is more useful than answering questions while learning about a task (Fishbein, Eckart, Lauver, Van Leeuwen, & Langmeyer, 1990). This may occur because students fail to integrate information completely or are not fully prepared for inference-type questions until they actually attempt to perform the task. Questions asked during performance appear to be most effective when they focus on salient properties of problem solving. King (1991) found that students trained to answer guided questions during problem solving solved problems more accurately, asked more strategic questions, and provided more elaborated explanations of their performance than a control group.

Asking and answering questions while studying improves learning because it helps students focus their attention. A second benefit is that questions help focus text processing on inferences that might not receive attention otherwise. Last, generating questions promotes constructivist activities that lead to greater elaboration and may help increase students' interest.

Levels of Processing

One important framework for thinking about how different kinds of encoding activities influence memory was developed by Craik and Lockhart (1972). Reacting to the mechanistic nature of computer models of human memory, Craik and Lockhart argued that memory depends on what learners do as they encode new information (see also Jenkins, 1974).

In the **levels of processing** view, memory for new information is seen as a by-product of the learner's perceptual and cognitive analyses performed on incoming information. On the one hand, if the semantic base or meaning of the new information is the focus of processing, then the information will be stored in a semantic memory code and will be well remembered. On the other hand, if only superficial or surface aspects of the new information are analyzed, the information will be less well remembered. In Craik and Lockhart's terms, memory depends on *depth* of processing. *Deep processing* is seen as that processing centered on meaning. *Shallow processing* refers to keying on superficial aspects of new material.

Two levels of processing may be seen in two common classroom assignments. In the first, students are asked to underline a set of vocabulary words in a brief essay. In the second, students are asked to read the same essay and be prepared to tell the class about it in their own words. If the students follow directions, the first assignment is a clear example of shallow processing; all they have to do is recognize the words and underline them. To perform this task, students do not have to think about the meaning of the paragraph and perhaps not even with the meaning of the words. Not surprisingly, if we tested these students for their memory of the paragraph contents, the odds are they would remember relatively little.

In contrast, if the students who were asked to explain the essay to their classmates followed instructions, we would likely see a very different outcome. To put an essay into one's own words, it is necessary to think about the meaning of the content. In so doing, the students would have had to carefully analyze and comprehend the material. If we were to surprise these students with a test, they almost certainly would remember far more of the essay's contents than could the group that underlined vocabulary words.

It can be argued that the two assignments described above were given for different instructional purposes. In fact, the vocabulary word group might remember more vocabulary words (but probably not their meanings) than the group asked to read and explain the materials. In this instance, students' recall would be appropriate to the type of processing in which they engaged (see Moeser, 1983), a topic we examine in more detail a bit later. In any event, students in the underlining group engaged in an activity almost guaranteed not to result in memory for the essay.

Another example of levels of processing can be seen in an incidental learning paradigm (one in which individuals are not directed to learn material but in which their memory for that material is unexpectedly tested). Let's suppose that one group of students is asked to count the number of i's in a list of words, and another group is asked to rate the pleasantness of the same words on a 1-to-5 scale. If, after both groups finish their tasks, we give them a surprise test and ask them to recall as many words on the list as possible, the probability is very high that the group that rated the pleasantness of the words will recall far more than the group that counted the number of i's. The reason for this difference in performance is quite simple: Rating the pleasantness of words requires students to think about their meanings. In contrast, counting the number of i's merely requires a superficial analysis (see Hyde & Jenkins, 1969).

The levels-of-processing framework is intuitively appealing and has led to a great deal of research emphasizing educationally relevant applications (see Andre, 1987b, for an extensive review). The "levels" position, however, has been criticized extensively. Essentially, these criticisms center on the absence of an independent measure of "depth" and the apparent circularity of the "depth" formulation (Baddeley, 1978; Loftus, Green, & Smith, 1980; Nelson, 1977; Postman, Thompkins, & Gray, 1978); that is, saying that something is well remembered because it was deeply processed does not tell us how we may ensure deep processing in students.

In response to these criticisms, Craik and his associates developed two variants of their original "levels" perspective: distinctiveness of encoding (Jacoby & Craik, 1979; Jacoby, Craik, & Begg, 1979) and elaboration of encoding (e.g., Craik & Tulving, 1975). By the late 1980s, the elaboration position clearly was dominant (see Walker, 1986, for a critical discussion), but both are useful in considering the applications of the "levels" framework. We examine each of these positions next, as well as an alternative position offered by Bransford and his associates.

Distinctiveness of Encoding.   The **distinctiveness of encoding** position states that the memorability of information is determined, at least in part, by its distinctiveness (Jacoby & Craik, 1979; Jacoby et al., 1979). In a series of experiments in which distinctiveness was defined by the difficulty of decisions required of students during various learning episodes (more-difficult decisions were equated with more-distinctive encoding), Jacoby et al. (1979) found that materials requiring more-difficult decisions at the time of encoding were better recalled than materials requiring less-difficult decisions.

The experiments conducted by Jacoby et al. led to a series of studies focusing on distinctiveness of encoding in reading and mastering various learning tasks (Benton, Glover, Monkowski, & Shaughnessy, 1983; Glover, Bruning, & Plake, 1982; Glover, Plake, & Zimmer, 1982). These studies were designed to determine how students' decision making during reading affected recall and to examine the possibility that an independent means of specifying "depth" of processing (or, in this case, distinctiveness) could be developed. In general, requiring students to make decisions about what they read leads to greater recall than when no decisions are required. In addition, when the Bloom, Englehart, Furst, Hill, and Krathwohl (1956) taxonomy was employed as a means of calibrating different levels of difficulty (and, hence, distinctiveness), the results showed increasing recall as students moved from decisions at the lower end of the taxonomy to the upper end.

In other words, as students make more-complex, more-difficult decisions during encoding, they remember the content better. In terms of the Bloom et al. taxonomy, materials requiring processing at the synthesis and analysis levels are recalled far better than materials processed at the knowledge or comprehension level. If we want to enhance students' recall, one important approach is to require students to make decisions during encoding. Further, recall will be greater if they are required to make decisions at the analysis and synthesis levels, rather than at lower levels of the taxonomy.

Elaboration of Processing.   The elaboration of processing perspective was outlined first by Craik and Tulving (1975) and has been specified further by J. R. Anderson and Reder (1979), J. R. Anderson (1983a), and Walker (1986). This position was articulated most clearly by Anderson and Reder (p. 388), who stated:

> The basic idea is that a memory episode is encoded as a set of propositions. This set can vary in its richness and redundancy. At the time of recall, only a subset of these propositions will be activated. The richer the original set, the richer will be the subset. Memory for any particular proposition will depend on the subjects' ability to reconstruct it from

those propositions that are active. This ability will in turn depend on the richness of the original set and hence the amount of elaboration made at study.

Considerable research on the acquisition of educationally relevant material has been performed (McDaniel, Einstein, Dunay, & Cobb, 1986; Palmere et al., 1983; Phifer et al., 1983). The results of this research generally have shown that as the elaborateness of students' encoding of information increases, so does their memory for the content (see McDaniel & Einstein, 1989, for a review). Elaborate processing is not merely reprocessing the same information, but rather it is encoding the same content in different but related ways. For example, in an explanation of how to solve a specific type of problem, students are far more likely to remember the explanation if different examples are given, than if the same example merely is restated. Similarly, when students read about a famous person, their ability to recall information about that person is strongly related to the number of details provided (Dinnel & Glover, 1985; Palmere et al., 1983).

Transfer-Appropriate Processing.   Morris, Bransford, and Franks (1977) reacted to the original "levels" perspective by offering an alternative. In their view, differences in memory are the result of what is contained in various semantic memory codes (see Glover, Rankin, Langner, Todero, & Dinnel, 1985; Moeser, 1983, for extended contrasts of the original levels position with transfer-appropriate processing). From a transfer-appropriate processing perspective, "shallow" processing leads not to the encoding of, say, the image of the letter *i* if people are seeking the number of *i*'s in a passage. Instead, a semantic memory is produced (e.g., "There were 43 *i*'s in the passage"), but one that does not contain information about the meaning of the content. In Morris et al.'s view, "deep" processing differs from "shallow" processing primarily because the semantic memories formed in deep processing contain the meaning of the content that students encounter (e.g., the main idea in a paragraph).

Transfer-appropriate processing is an interesting alternative to the original levels perspective, and it does seem clear that students' memories for to-be-learned information almost inevitably are semantic (see Bransford et al., 1982). For instance, in the example we first used to show the difference between deep and shallow processing, one group of students read to find key words and another group read to be able to explain the contents of the material. In the original levels perspective, differences in memory performance between these two groups are due to different kinds of memory codes brought about by different levels of analysis. In contrast, transfer-appropriate processing holds that both groups of children form semantic memory codes. The differences in memory are due to the contents of those memories; the vocabulary group's codes likely would contain very little more than some of the words, whereas the "explanation" group's codes would contain information about the topic of the reading passage. Finally, a recent development in this area has been the concept of *material-appropriate elaboration* (see McDaniel & Einstein, 1989). From this point of view, deep or elaborate processing activities depend on what learners do and on the type of material they encounter. In McDaniel and Einstein's view, for example, prose requires different activities for elaborate, deep processing than does poetry.

Summary of Encoding Processes

In this section, we reviewed several frameworks for encoding factual and complex information. Rehearsing, categorizing, and using special mnemonics techniques are helpful ways to encode important facts. Many of the mnemonic techniques described above rely on distinctive visual images or auditory processes.

We also considered encoding complex information. Much of the research conducted in this area is included in the levels of processing paradigm. The levels of processing framework emphasizes the importance of what students do while encoding information. To the extent that students are required to deal with the meaning of content, their memory improves. Tasks focusing on superficial or surface aspects of to-be-learned materials result in poor memory for content. Our discussion suggests a variety of ways to encode information at deeper levels. One is to relate new information to background knowledge at the time of encoding; another is to increase its distinctiveness; a third is to elaborate its meaning as much as possible.

In the next section, we turn our attention to an even broader topic—thinking about and regulating encoding, storage, and retrieval functions. Growing evidence suggests that the ability to "manage" one's thought is crucial to effective learning and intellectual growth. Being aware of one's strengths and limitations as a learner is a big part of this critical set of cognitive skills.

METACOGNITION: THINKING ABOUT THINKING

Metacognition refers to knowledge people have about their own thought processes; **metamemory** refers to knowledge people have about their own memory (Brown, Bransford, Ferrara, & Campione, 1983). An example of metamemory can be seen in the teacher who knows she does not remember names well and so has her new students wear name tags for several days. Another example can be seen in the student who listens to a teacher's explanation of how to solve a problem and takes notes only on those points she judges to be difficult. Still another example is students asking a teacher whether an upcoming test will be essay or multiple choice.

Since the term was first coined in the early 1970s, metacognition has been viewed as an essential component of skilled learning because it allows students to control a host of other cognitive skills. In a way, metacognition is like the "mission control" of the cognitive system. It enables students to coordinate the use of extensive knowledge and many separate strategies to accomplish a single goal, just as a real mission control coordinates the myriad of functions necessary for a successful space flight. This does not imply a single place in our minds where metacognition takes place; rather, we simply want to suggest that metacognition is a part of our cognition that is in charge of controlling a large number of lower-level cognitive functions, such as perception and attention.

One of the clearest descriptions of metacognition is that of Ann Brown. According to Brown (1980, 1987), metacognition includes two related dimensions: **knowledge of cognition** and **regulation of cognition**. The former refers to what we know about cognition; the latter refers to how we regulate cognition. Knowledge of cognition usually is assumed to include three components (Brown, 1987; Jacobs & Paris, 1987). The first, *declarative knowledge,* refers to knowledge about ourselves as learners and what factors influence our performance. For example, most adult learners know the limitations of their memory system and can plan accordingly for a task based on this knowledge. The second component, *procedural knowledge,* refers to knowledge about strategies. For instance, most older students possess a basic repertoire of useful strategies, such as taking notes, slowing down for important information, skimming unimportant information, using mnemonics, summarizing main ideas, and periodic self-testing. The third component, *conditional knowledge,* refers to knowing when or why to use a strategy. One case in point is when you study differently for essay versus multiple-choice tests.

Brown has argued that knowledge of cognition is usually statable and late developing. Research suggests that these assumptions are reasonable when considering the metacognitive activity of older students but do not obtain for preadolescents (Flavell, 1992; Garner & Alexander, 1989). For example, research by Paris and colleagues (Paris, Cross, & Lipon, 1984; Paris & Jacobs, 1984) found that instructional training programs enhance the development and use of metacognitive knowledge among elementary-age children. These findings indicate that metacognitive knowledge among younger students is not necessarily statable. Studies comparing expert performance among adults, however, are consistent with Brown's assumptions (cf. Glaser & Chi, 1988).

Regulation of cognition typically includes three components: planning, regulation, and evaluation (Jacobs & Paris, 1987; Kluwe, 1987). *Planning* involves the selection of appropriate strategies and the allocation of resources. Planning frequently includes setting goals, activating relevant background knowledge, and budgeting time. *Regulation* involves monitoring and self-testing skills necessary to control learning. Activities such as making predictions or pausing while reading, strategy sequencing, and selecting appropriate repair strategies also belong in the category. *Evaluation* involves appraising the products and regulatory processes of one's learning. Typical examples are reevaluating one's goals, revising predictions, and consolidating intellectual gains.

Brown has argued that regulatory processes, including planning, regulation, and evaluation, may not be conscious or statable in many learning situations. One reason is that many of these processes are highly automated, at least in adults. A second reason is that some of these processes have developed without any conscious reflection and therefore are difficult to report to others. In addition, Brown (1987) draws an important distinction about the relationship of age to metacognitive regulation and abstract reflection. She argues that regulatory mechanisms, such as planning, are independent of age, whereas reflection is not. Thus, like metacognitive knowledge, conscious use of regulatory processes may be related to limitations in one's ability to reflect, rather than in one's ability to regulate.

Research on Metacognitive Processes

Research investigating metacognition is still fairly new, though a number of important findings have appeared. One is that metacognition is late developing. In a variety of studies, children between kindergarten and sixth grade consistently show an inability to monitor accurately their comprehension and, just as important, to describe their own cognition (Baker, 1989). In one study, Markman (1979) found that even skilled readers were unable to identify information that was inconsistent with the text's meaning. Older students and adults, however, are better able to describe their own cognitive processes.

Recognizing the need to remember develops slowly throughout childhood (Johnson & Wellman, 1980; Kail, 1984) as well. Whereas preschoolers may need to be instructed to remember certain things, older children have learned that some information is likely to be important to remember (e.g., directions for where to meet a friend, tips for assembling a bicycle). By the time students reach high school, most know a great deal about what should be remembered and are very selective about what they will and will not try to remember.

Developmental trends have been found in metamemory awareness too. As adults, we understand that the sheer amount of material to be remembered makes a difference. For instance, we know that learning one phone number is considerably less demanding than committing ten new phone numbers to memory. Similarly, we know that learning, say, five new psychological terms will take less effort than memorizing thirty terms.

In contrast to adults and older children, younger children have only a rudimentary knowledge of the factors influencing task difficulty. Their diagnostic skills are immature and develop slowly (Brainerd & Pressley, 1985; Flavell, Friedrichs, & Hoyt, 1970; Kail, 1984; Yussen & Levy, 1975). Teachers still can make an important difference in children's diagnostic skills by providing instruction in how to make estimates of task difficulty, prompting children to make such estimates, and providing practice in making diagnoses.

Monitoring skills also improve as one gets older (Garner & Alexander, 1989). These changes presumably reflect important differences in *how* one monitors, as well as increased knowledge about *what* one monitors. This is not to say that adults are skilled monitors or have conscious access to metacognitive knowledge. Even college students have a great deal of difficulty monitoring their performance prior to a test (Glenberg, Sanocki, Epstein, & Morris 1987; Schraw, 1994). Although college students are better able to monitor their test performance during or after the test, it still is far from perfect (see Chapter 11).

The reason for poor monitoring among adults is becoming increasingly clear. Monitoring accuracy appears to be related to two dimensions of performance: task difficulty and prior knowledge. When a task is difficult, students are more likely to be overconfident in their performance (Schraw & Roedel, in press). Although you might expect monitoring accuracy to improve as prior knowledge increases, the opposite appears to be true. Glenberg and Epstein (1987) found that music majors monitored their performance more poorly after reading a passage about music than one about physics. A subsequent study by Morris (1990) clarified this relationship further. Prior knowledge aids performance, but it does not contribute to more-accurate monitoring. Thus, older students monitor accurately when they possess enough knowledge to perform well; in turn, performing well reduces overconfidence.

Metacognitive monitoring also appears to be unrelated to aptitude. For example, Pressley and Ghatala (1988) found that college students of different verbal ability levels monitored with similar accuracy. Swanson (1990) reported that metacognitive knowledge as measured on a verbal self-report interview was not limited by intellectual aptitude. On the contrary, metacognitive awareness sometimes compensated for lower levels of ability in that low-aptitude/high-metacognitive-knowledge students outperformed high-aptitude/low-metacognitive-knowledge students with respect to the number of moves necessary to solve pendulum and fluid combination problems. Overall, low-aptitude/high-metacognition students required 50 percent fewer moves. However, low-aptitude/high-metacognition students also used fewer domain-specific problem-solving strategies than high-aptitude/high-metacognition students, suggesting that domain-specific knowledge alone could not account for the low-aptitude/high-metacognition group's performance, a finding consistent with Morris (1990).

Several instructional studies suggest that metacognition can be improved by direct instruction and modeling of metacognitive activities. For example, Paris and colleagues' *Informal Strategies for Learning Program* (ISLP) (Paris et al., 1984; see also Jacobs & Paris, 1987) instructs children in knowledge about and the use of metacognitive reading strategies in several ways. Gains over an academic school year have been particularly impressive with respect to reading awareness and evaluating the effectiveness of reading strategies. Similar results have been reported by Kurtz and Borkowski (1987) and Palincsar and Brown (1984).

Delclos and Harrington (1991) examined fifth- and sixth-graders' ability to solve computer problems after assignment to one of three conditions. The first group received specific problem-solving training; the second group received problem-solving plus self-monitoring training; and the third group received no training. The self-monitoring problem-solving group solved more of the difficult problems than either of the remaining groups and took less time to do so.

The studies described above suggest several general conclusions about metacognition. First, younger students may have only a limited amount of metacognitive knowledge at their disposal. This knowledge improves performance; moreover, metacognitive knowledge appears to be highly trainable even in younger students. Second, aptitude and knowledge constrain metacognitive knowledge far less than one might expect. Thus, rather than reserve metacognitive training for more advanced students, teachers should make a special effort to provide training to students who appear to lack it regardless of relative achievement level. Third, evidence suggests that metacognitive awareness compensates for low ability and insufficient knowledge. Developing metacognitive skills should be particularly helpful for students attempting to learn unfamiliar content.

Becoming a Good Strategy User

Interest in strategies and metacognition has given rise to the concept of a *good strategy user*. What might such a student look like? Pressley, Borkowski, and Schneider (1987) have suggested five criteria: (1) a broad repertoire of strategies, (2) metacognitive knowledge about why, when, and where to use strategies, (3) a broad knowledge base, (4) the ability to ignore distractions, and (5) automaticity in the four components described above.

Regarding the first of these five criteria, Pressley et al. (1987) distinguish between two types of strategies. The first of these is a *domain-specific strategy* (e.g., applying the quadratic formula), which is of little or no use outside that domain. A second type of strategy is a *higher-order strategy*, which is used to control other strategies. One example is how a skilled reader *sequences* a number of strategies while reading—perhaps skimming before she begins to read, then selectively attending to important information, then monitoring, and finally reviewing. Having knowledge about how to orchestrate a number of related strategies enables good strategy users to regulate their learning efficiently.

The second criterion described by Pressley et al. (1987) corresponds closely to what we have called *conditional knowledge*. Conditional knowledge is important because knowing *how* to do something is of little practical good if you do not know *when* or *where* to use it. For example, you can study for a test for three hours and still fail it if you do not focus on the information that appears on the test. Being able to size up a test in advance, to determine what it will include and how you can best prepare, illustrates nicely the value of conditional knowledge.

By this point, we probably have convinced you that the third criterion—a broad knowledge base—is one of the most important components of learning. Pressley et al. (1987) have argued that encoding and representing new information in memory without some existing knowledge base as an anchor makes efficient learning almost impossible. But existing knowledge also is important because it promotes strategy use and, at times, compensates for lack of strategies. For example, elementary-age children have been found to learn categorizable lists without using strategies because of their ability to activate knowledge about the category (e.g., kitchen utensils include *spoons, forks,* and *knives*).

The fourth criterion of a good strategy user is what Pressley et al. refer to as *action control*. This means that students are able to motivate themselves, tune out distractions, and correctly attribute their progress to effort, rather than ability (see Chapter 7). Even very young children show signs of controlling their learning and directing their attention (DeLoache, Cassidy, & Brown, 1985), although there is steady improvement into early adulthood.

The fifth criterion is that good strategy users accomplish all of the above automatically. As we saw in Chapter 2, *automaticity* is the ability to activate knowledge or perform a task with minimum drain on our limited processing resources. Being automatic is an essential component of good strategy use because without it we are unable to allocate our resources to higher-order regulation of our learning. In fact, nonautomated students allocate most of their resources to basic cognitive tasks such as perception, attention, accessing information from long-term memory, and selecting strategies. In contrast, good strategy users accomplish these basic tasks with very little effort, freeing up valuable resources for constructing meaning and overseeing their learning.

IMPLICATIONS FOR INSTRUCTION

1. *Match encoding strategies with the material to be learned.* This chapter describes a wide variety of strategies for encoding factual and complex information. Students should match their strategy use with the materials, goals of learning, and kind of evaluation as much as possible. For example, learning a list of five recent American presidents for a recognition test should be different from learning such a list for a comparison and contrast essay about the presidents' contributions to foreign and domestic policy.

Students should be as *strategic* and *flexible* as possible when encoding information. Sometimes this means using maintenance rehearsal, rather than deep processing, though usually it means the opposite. Encouraging *material-appropriate processing* should be a goal of every teacher. Of course, to do so successfully requires students to possess a large repertoire of strategies, as well as the metacognitive knowledge to use them.

2. *Encourage students to engage in deep processing.* One consistent research finding is that the deeper the processing, the better one's memory for the meaning of to-be-learned information. One way that students can process information more deeply is to elaborate it with respect to prior knowledge and the learning context. Encouraging affective responses is a second way to promote deeper processing. A third way—answering questions about to-be-learned information or generating them yourself—clearly facilitates inferential processing of that information.

3. *Use instructional strategies that promote elaboration.* Teachers can do much in the classroom to promote elaborative encoding. Most important is that teachers encourage students to *construct* meaning based on their own knowledge, goals, and uses of information. Making students more active in this way and helping them take responsibility for their learning will do more to improve learning than anything else.

One structured technique for teachers to use is schema activation, which refers to finding ways to activate what students already know: things such as preteaching class discussions, brainstorming, and clarifying salient concepts. Another method is to use advance organizers to provide a schematic structure that students lack prior to formal instruction. This may facilitate categorizing and organizing new information.

4. *Help students become more metacognitively aware.* Having knowledge is only part of effective learning. It also is important to use one's knowledge strategically and to understand the strengths and limitations of one's knowledge. Educational psychologists became interested in metacognition because it was apparent that good learners know a lot about their own thinking and memory and use this

information to regulate their learning. One critical component is knowledge about cognition—that is, knowledge about the *how, why,* and *when* aspects of learning. Teachers should make a special effort to model their own conditional knowledge for their students. A second component is regulation of cognition. Students need to learn basic regulatory skills such as planning and monitoring and, most important, how to coordinate them.

The first step is to make students aware that metacognition is vital to good learning. Metacognitive skills should be taught and discussed in every classroom. These discussions should be between students and other students, as well as teachers. Peer tutoring or small cooperative learning groups are an especially effective way to pool metacognitive knowledge and strategies (see Chapter 6).

The second step is to develop some level of basic automaticity with metacognitive skills. One way to do so is to use *monitoring checklists* in which students check off component steps in monitoring one's learning. The checklist shown below provides an example:

1.   What is the purpose for learning this information?
2.   Do I know anything about this topic?
3.   Do I know strategies that will help me learn?
4.   Am I understanding as I proceed?
5.   How should I correct errors?
6.   Have I accomplished the goals I set myself?

Studies that have used checklists report favorable findings, especially when students are learning difficult material (Delclos & Harrington, 1991; King, 1991). We recommend that checklists be posted in the classroom and used consistently until students become automatic at using them.

   5.   *Make strategy instruction a priority.* Strategy instruction should be an integral part of every class. Research indicates that it is the *strategic use,* rather than the *mere possession* of knowledge that improves learning. Teaching students strategies not only improves their learning but also empowers them psychologically (see Chapter 7). We recommend that teachers target "age-appropriate strategies" at each grade by comparing the most and least successful students in class. The chances are good that highly successful students rely on strategies that struggling students do not use. Modeled instruction with these strategies will, no doubt, enhance students' ability to control their learning.

Teachers should consider how to sequence strategy instruction as well. We include a five-step sequence below, drawing heavily on the work of Palincsar and Brown (1984), Pressley, Harris, and Marks (1992), and Poplin (1988).

   Step 1.   Discuss and explain the value of strategies. Students should understand why they are being asked to learn strategies, what instruction will be like, and how they will use them. One reason is that strategies augment or even compensate for lack of prior knowledge and domain-specific ability. A second reason is that strategies positively affect students' self-confidence and learning expectations (see Chapters 7 and 8).

Step 2. Introduce only a few strategies at a time. Students can be overwhelmed easily. The best chance of teaching students strategies that are useful to them is to limit their number to two or three over an eight- to ten-week period of instruction. This time affords students a chance to acquire the strategy, practice, and become somewhat automatic.

Step 3. Continue practice over an extended period. Teachers should plan on six to ten weeks for instruction, modeling, and practice of a new strategy. Periodic follow-ups are helpful, as well, to ensure that the strategy has been maintained.

Step 4. Model strategies extensively. Even when students understand why they are learning a strategy and how to use it, they need to see the strategy modeled by a teacher (or other expert). Modeling should include at least two components: (1) how the strategy is used in a variety of settings to accomplish different learning objectives and (2) why the teacher uses the strategy. The former will convey declarative and procedural knowledge to the student; the latter will convey conditional knowledge.

Step 5. Provide feedback to students about strategies. One way for teachers to share their expertise with students is to provide feedback about how, why, and when to use strategies. This information helps students evaluate strategy effectiveness— that is, whether it has made a noticeable improvement on performance or has increased efficiency.

6. *Look for opportunities to transfer strategies.* One complaint many teachers have is that students do not use strategies learned in one setting in a new setting. This sometimes is referred to as **inert knowledge**. One way to combat this problem is to provide practice across the curriculum with each strategy. In our view, it is better to teach fewer strategies and have students use them in every content area than it is to bombard students with new strategies in every class. For older students, this procedure may require a high degree of coordination among different content instructors.

7. *Encourage reflection on strategy use.* The way students become metacognitively aware and, in turn, self-regulated is to think and talk about their learning. Everyone who goes to school should be encouraged to do so no matter how young. Older students should be given regular time in school to reflect on self-regulation by means of small group discussion, journals, and essays. Younger students should be helped to understand how older students and adults think about their learning. This help can be accomplished by careful teacher modeling and peer tutoring across grade levels.

SUMMARY

This chapter focused on encoding strategies and how effective learners adopt strategies relevant to the kind of information they are learning. A distinction was made between encoding strategies best suited for factual and complex information. Rehearsal, mediation, mnemonics, and the use of imagery are helpful for learning factual information.

A distinction was made between maintenance and elaborative rehearsal. *Maintenance rehearsal* refers to the recycling of information for brief periods of time to keep it ready for use, such as when a person repeats a phone number over and over while getting ready to dial the phone. *Elaborative rehearsal* is the recycling of information in ways that relate it to other, previously learned knowledge. In general, elaborative rehearsal results in superior memory performance, but both types of rehearsal have distinct uses. One form of elaborative rehearsal involves mediation, in which difficult-to-remember items are converted into something more meaningful and are easily remembered.

Mnemonics are memory aids designed to help people remember information. They include the peg method, the method of loci, the link method, the use of stories, first-letter mnemonics, the keyword method, and yodai mnemonics. The various mnemonics differ, but all share the use of familiar information to facilitate remembering unfamiliar information. Students enjoy using mnemonics, and mnemonics generally are easy to teach. In our view, mnemonics are best seen as adjuncts to regular classroom methods.

We introduced a general framework for understanding complex information— the levels of processing view. This perspective holds that what students do while encoding determines the quality of their memories. In general, activities that focus students on the meaning of to-be-learned information result in better memory performance than activities that center on superficial aspects of to-be-learned materials.

The nature of the materials that students encounter also influences memory performance. Well-organized materials tend to be better remembered than poorly organized materials. In the absence of organization, students impose their own organization on to-be-remembered information. Complex materials are best encoded by using procedures that help students relate new information to what they know already. Two general approaches for facilitating the encoding of complex information are the use of advance organizers and schema activation.

We also considered the role of metacognition in learning and saw that skilled students possess knowledge that can be used to regulate their learning. Metacognitive knowledge can help students compensate for low domain knowledge and a limited strategy repertoire. Metacognition appears to improve with instruction.

Last, we explored what it means to be a good strategy user and how strategy instruction can be improved. We observed that effective learners possess more strategies, use them more flexibly, are more automatic, and control their motivation to learn. Because all of these skills are either teachable or improve substantially with practice, all students have the potential to become good strategy users.

SUGGESTED READINGS

Pressley, M. G., & Associates. (1990). *Cognitive strategy instruction that really improves children's academic performance*. Cambridge, MA: Brookline Books.

This highly readable book outlines strategy instruction for all grades in most content areas.

Sternberg, R. J. (1986). *The triarchic mind*. New York: Penguin.

This book outlines Sternberg's theory of intelligence and explores what it means to be intelligent and how intelligence can be improved.

CHAPTER 5

Retrieval Processes

In Chapters 3 and 4, we examined the nature of memory, its structure, and the processes involved in encoding. Our description of human memory is not complete, however, until we describe the processes involved in retrieving information from memory. Our focus in this chapter is on **retrieval**, the process involved in accessing and placing into consciousness information from long-term memory (see Figure 3-1). We begin our discussion by examining some common retrieval phenomena.

Mrs. Thompson has just finished handing out her American history test. Most of the students begin writing immediately, but Ronald reads the first question and feels a cold shiver run up his spine. Not only can he not remember the answer, but he also cannot even remember that the topic was ever talked about. He gulps and proceeds to the next question.

Laura, in contrast, reads the first question and smiles to herself, remembering a joke Mrs. Thompson told on the day she covered the material. Laura starts to write her answer and finds that the words come easily. For Laura, the question is a perfect cue for remembering.

Aisha, meanwhile, writes part of the answer and then stops. She knows that she knows the rest of the answer, but somehow the words do not come to her. She raises her hand, and Mrs. Thompson drifts over to Aisha's desk. Mrs. Thompson briefly clarifies the question. After hearing just a sentence from her teacher, Aisha has a powerful "aha!" feeling, and she returns to her writing, confident that she can answer Mrs. Thompson's question.

Across the room, Scotty is having trouble remembering the answers to the test. Finally, he flips the test over and scratches out the outline he used to organize his studying the night before. Then, he uses his outline to help him remember what to say. Mrs. Thompson watches Scotty, bemused because he so often seems to provide his own cues for her tests.

The experiences of the four students in Mrs. Thompson's history class were varied, but the probability is high that we all have shared similar experiences. Sometimes, our retrieval processes seem very ineffective, and, like Ronald, we draw a blank. At other times, we marvel at our own abilities to retrieve information in great detail. At still other times, we do retrieve the information we need, but not without a struggle.

Research on human memory has focused primarily on understanding encoding and storage. Still, many important issues related to retrieval have come to light in recent years. We begin our discussion of retrieval processes by examining a phenomenon that has come to be known as *encoding specificity*.

ENCODING SPECIFICITY

In our discussion of encoding, we pointed out that the organization of material has considerable influence on how well the material is remembered. For years, psychologists have wondered whether this organization was important only at the time of encoding, only at the time of retrieval, or at both times. In an important early study, Tulving and Osler (1968) addressed this question.

Tulving and Osler divided their group of subjects into two conditions. In one condition, the subjects merely were presented a twenty-four-item word list to learn. In the second condition, the subjects received the same word list, but in this instance each of the twenty-four to-be-learned words was paired with a weak associate (e.g., boy-child; a strong associate pair would be boy-girl). Then, when the subjects were tested for their ability to remember the words, the two conditions were divided further. Half of the subjects in both of the original conditions simply were asked for free recall of the twenty-four words. The remainder also were asked to recall the twenty-four words, but these subjects were given the twenty-four weak associates that originally were given only to the subjects in the weak-associates condition. In this way, Tulving and Osler constructed four groups: (1) word list to learn without associates, test without associates; (2) word list to learn without associates, test with associates; (3) word list to learn with associates, test without associates; and (4) word list to learn with associates, test with associates.

Results of the study indicated that the weak associates or cue words facilitated memory performance only when they were available to the subjects both at encoding and at retrieval. Having cues present at encoding only or at retrieval only did not enhance memory performance. The conclusion is that cues indeed make a difference in memory performance but only when cues present at encoding are reinstated at the time of retrieval. The phenomenon Tulving and Osler observed in their experiment is known as **encoding specificity**, and it has become one of the basic principles of memory performance.

Many examples of the encoding specificity principle have been reported in the literature (see R. C. Anderson & Ortony, 1975; Tulving, 1983, 1985; Tulving & Thompson, 1973). Recently, for instance, Rabinowitz and Craik (1986) reexamined some aspects of the generation effect and found another instance of encoding specificity.

The **generation effect** refers to the finding that verbal material self-generated at the time of encoding is better remembered than material that students merely read at encoding. In Rabinowitz and Craik's Experiment 1, they presented subjects with fifty-six words to learn. Each word in the list was paired with an associated item. Half of the to-be-learned or target words merely were read by the subjects. The remaining target words had letters deleted from them that were replaced with blanks. As the subjects encoded these words, they had to generate the missing letters from memory. At the time of the test, half of the target words that subjects read were cued by the original associates, and the other half were cued by different words that rhymed with the target words. The target words that students had to generate also were split at the time of test so that half received the original cue and half got a rhyming cue.

The results were striking. As Rabinowitz and Craik had predicted from the generation effect literature (see Jacoby, 1978; McElroy & Slamecka, 1982; Slamecka & Graf, 1978; Slamecka & Katsaiti, 1987), a large generation effect was observed. Students remembered far more of the words for which they had to generate missing letters than words they merely read. The generation effect only worked, however, when the cues present at encoding also were present at recall. Apparently, even one of the most durable phenomena known to memory researchers—the generation effect—is governed by the principle of encoding specificity.

In recent years, researchers have examined whether the generation effect occurs when reading longer texts. For example, Pressley and colleagues (Martin & Pressley, 1991; Pressley, Symons, McDaniel, Snyder, & Turnure, 1988; Willoughby, Waller, Wood, & McKinnon, 1993) have investigated a phenomenon known as **elaborative interrogation,** in which students are asked to answer "why" questions about information they have just read. Studies consistently find that elaborative interrogation improves learning for text information, especially when it prompts learners to activate relevant prior knowledge they would not activate otherwise.

The research on elaborative interrogation answers a number of questions about why the generation effect occurs. One explanation is that learners are more apt to integrate new information with what they already know; thus, elaborated information is easier to store in memory. A second explanation is that elaboration helps students "enrich" incoming information by way of prior knowledge; that is, information is learned better not only because it is easier to categorize and store (as suggested above) but also because it is "reconstructed" in a way that makes it more meaningful. Not surprisingly, information learned by using elaborative interrogation is remembered better not only after studying but also after month-long delays as well.

Another instance of research on encoding specificity can be seen in a study by Corkill, Bruning, and Glover (1988) that focused on some of the factors that make for an effective advance organizer. *Advance organizers* are prefatory materials given to students prior to a reading designed to tie the to-be-learned material in an upcoming passage into what students already know. In their Experiment 3, Corkill et al. sorted students into conditions on the basis of whether or not they read an advance organizer prior to reading a chapter on astronomy. Then, at recall, Corkill et al. examined the effects of presenting advance organizers as cues for retrieval. In contrast to no cue conditions and other conditions (in which other types of cues were furnished to students at the time of retrieval), giving readers the advance organizer as a retrieval cue led to significantly greater levels of recall of the passage content. However, presenting the advance organizer as a retrieval cue worked only if the students had read the advance organizer prior to reading the chapter on astronomy. Students who merely read the chapter on astronomy without an advance organizer obtained no benefit from having the advance organizer presented to them at the time of retrieval. Apparently, even the recall of long reading passages can be facilitated when students are given cues at retrieval that were present when they first activated schemata for reading the material.

The type of cues used in studies of encoding specificity seems to make little difference, as long as the cues are present both at encoding and at retrieval. Tulving (1983; or Sloman, Hayman, Ohta, Law, & Tulving, 1988), for example, has set out a distinction between semantic and episodic elements of memory (contrast with J. R. Anderson's declarative and procedural aspects of memory discussed in Chapter 3). In Tulving's view, *semantic memory* refers to memory for general knowledge (e.g., that canaries are yellow or that Greenland has an ice cap) not tied to a specific occurrence in a person's lifetime (e.g., to remember that Pluto's moon is named Charon, it is unlikely that we remember any personal experience related to this knowledge, at least until well after we have retrieved the information). In contrast, *episodic memory* refers to our memories for specific events in our lives (e.g., once, one of the authors' daughters caught a two-pound bass; this morning, one of the authors had wheat toast for breakfast). Apparently, both semantic and episodic information may be used as effective retrieval cues. For example, a teacher could construct an item that used episodic information as a cue (e.g., "As you recall from our class demonstration in which Sharmar bent the glass tubes . . .") or an item that used semantic information (e.g., "As you recall, many historians have argued that Hoover actually laid the groundwork for recovery from the Depression. What were the . . ."). Either of these retrieval cues could facilitate retrieval as long as they were present at encoding.

One interesting aspect of encoding specificity is its generality. Researchers have discovered that retrieval is more efficient when it matches encoding conditions even when unusual affective or psychological states are involved. This phenomenon often is referred to as **state-dependent learning** (Overton, 1985). In one study, Bower (1981) found that students who learned information when they were sad recalled that information better when they were in a similar state versus when they were happy. Godden and Baddeley (1975) found similar differences when individuals learned information on land or underwater! These results suggest a very strong relationship between the conditions that exist at encoding and those at retrieval. The more these conditions match, the more likely it is that retrieval will be successful.

The results of studies focusing on encoding specificity are important for educators because they underscore the importance of context in memory. In these studies, the context of retrieval situations is varied by the presence or absence of cues available to students at encoding. However, the effects of context on retrieval go beyond the presence or absence of study cues. Smith (1986) and Smith, Vela, and Williamson (1988), for example, have shown that even the general environmental context in which encoding and retrieval occur influences memory. It turns out that students' memory for information depends not only on study cues but also on the classroom in which students study; that is, when students are tested in the same room in which they study, their memory performance is better than if they are tested in a room different from the one in which they studied.

Studies of the influence of context on retrieval and the principle of encoding specificity have become integral to our understanding of memory. Encoding specificity helps explain why some test items seem to facilitate our recall and others do not. In short, test items (whether multiple-choice, true-false, or essay) that reinstate cues that were present at the time of encoding facilitate students' retrieval of the content. Test questions that do not provide cues from encoding are less able to enhance recall.

The principle of encoding specificity is important also because it highlights the relationship between different stages of information processing. We now know that activities that improve the encoding of information will improve retrieval as well. Although it is convenient occasionally to distinguish among encoding, storage, and retrieval, it is even more important to remember that all memory functions are integrated to some extent.

Encoding specificity also helps us explain everyday memory experiences. For example, all of us have had the experience of hearing an old song on the radio and then remembering things we have not thought of in years (recall our discussion of episodic memory). Similarly, most of us have experienced a rush of memories we thought were forgotten when we met an old college roommate or a friend from our high school days. In these examples, the music or the sight of the old friend reinstates cues present when we encoded information. Without the cues, retrieval may be very difficult. With the cues, retrieval becomes much easier.

Encoding specificity once again emphasizes the importance of knowledge and context in cognition. Students' memories do not function like tape recorders or videotape machines; they cannot simply replay events at their choosing. Instead, retrieval depends on the cues they have available to call forth memory. Further, the context of a remembering event determines what will be remembered. A rich context providing multiple cues for retrieval will lead to good memory performance. A poor context with few or no retrieval cues is apt to give us a poor indication of what students really do have in memory.

One of the ways context at retrieval may be varied is by the demands we place on students at the time of testing. For instance, on the one hand, we could provide students with some information and ask them whether they *recognize* it, such as when a simple multiple-choice or true-false item is used. On the other hand, we could ask that students supply information from memory, such as when we ask them to discuss two important social consequences of the Vietnam War. In these situations, we are asking students to *recall* information. A good deal of attention has focused on how recognition and recall operate. In the following section, we briefly review each of these approaches to retrieving information from long-term memory.

RECOGNITION AND RECALL

Imagine that you are preparing to take your midterm examination for this course. The professor has announced that the test will be multiple-choice (recognition), and so you work hard readying yourself to recognize pertinent ideas on the test and to discriminate important facts from other material. You finally finish studying at four in the morning—exhausted, but happy in the knowledge that you have mastered the content. Unfortunately, your happiness lasts only until you walk into the testing room and see that the instructor has had a change of heart: The test will not be multiple-choice, but instead will be essay.

The events described above are not especially uncommon in education (even though they represent poor pedagogical practice). Even so, studies find that switching the type of test students are to take from one form to another to be upsetting (whether from multiple-choice to essay or vice versa). The reactions that students have to changing the type of test they expect would lead us to believe that significant differences exist between recall and recognition.

Further evidence for a difference between recall and recognition comes from research on how students prepare themselves for tests. In laboratory settings, students who expect recall tests tend to focus on the organization of material, whereas those who anticipate recognition tend to emphasize discriminating items from each other so that they can pick out the relevant items from the distractors on the test (Kintsch, 1977, 1986). These different methods of preparation lead to test-taking performances shaped to the type of test expected. Students who are tested in a manner consistent with their expectations for testing far outperform students who receive a type of test they did not expect (Carey & Lockhart, 1973; Glover & Corkill, 1987).

Students' actual study habits bear out the laboratory work. Typically, students prepare differently for essay tests than for recognition tests. They report that when they study for an essay examination, they emphasize organizing content, relating important ideas to each other, and practicing the recall of information. In contrast, when students prepare for a recognition test, they report focusing on becoming familiar with the material and discriminating the to-be-learned information from other materials. They also recall studying harder for essay tests than for recognition tests. This latter difference makes especially good sense because laboratory studies indicate that recognition is easier than recall. In almost all situations, students' performance is better on recognition tests than on recall tests (J. R. Anderson, 1985; Mitchell & Brown, 1988).

Despite the overwhelming array of circumstantial evidence indicating, almost certainly, important process differences in recall and recognition, the nature of these differences has been very elusive (see Nilsson, Law, & Tulving, 1988). An early hypothesis offered to account for differences in recall and recognition was put forward by McDougall in 1904. This "threshold" hypothesis held that both recognition and recall performance depend on the strength of information in memory. Further, the hypothesis held that a bit of information must have a specific strength before it can be recognized, the so-called **recognition threshold**. The threshold hypothesis also held that a greater amount of strength is necessary for information to be recalled, the **recall threshold**.

The implications of the threshold hypothesis were very clear and seemed to account for most of the data from studies that contrasted recognition and recall. This hypothesis predicted that some bits of very well learned information would be both recognized and recalled because the strength of that information in memory would be above both the recognition threshold and recall threshold. When information was poorly learned, however, it would be neither recalled nor recognized because its strength in memory was below the recall and recognition thresholds. The threshold hypothesis also predicted that some information would be recognizable, but not recallable, due to its strength being above the recognition threshold but below the recall threshold.

As appealing as the threshold hypothesis was for more than a half century, it no longer is accepted by cognitive psychologists. The threshold hypothesis was abandoned for two reasons. First, it is quite possible for some items in memory to be recalled but not recognized (Kintsch, 1970; Nilsson et al., 1988). The hypothesis, of course, would hold that this was not possible. Second, the threshold hypothesis never offered an explanation for *how* recall or recognition operated. Instead, it was a hypothesis to account for why recall seemed more difficult than recognition.

The threshold hypothesis has been replaced by more contemporary perspectives. One, typified by the work of Tulving and his colleagues (e.g., Flexser & Tulving, 1978; Nilsson et al., 1988; Tulving, 1983, 1985), argues that differences in recall and recognition are a part of larger contextual phenomena in memory akin to encoding specificity; that is, Tulving contends that it is the match of the encoding and retrieval operations that determines performance. Tulving's argument, of course, is less of an attempt to examine the processes involved in recall and recognition than it is an attempt to account for performance differences in recall and recognition. A second contemporary perspective on recall and recognition is referred to as the **dual process model of recall**. This view holds that recall and recognition essentially are the same, save that a much more extensive memory search is required in recall than in recognition (e.g., J. R. Anderson, 1983b, 1985; Rabinowitz, Mandler, & Patterson, 1977).

To understand how recall and recognition searches differ (see Chapter 3 for a detailed discussion of memory searches), we employ J. R. Anderson's (1985, 1993) model. Consider, for example, the following two questions, modeled on similar questions posed by Anderson:

1.   Who was president after Madison?

2.   Was Monroe the president after Madison?

The first question (*Who was* . . .) is a recall question; the second (*Was Monroe* . . .) is a recognition question. Figure 5-1 pictures the kind of propositional network Ander-

Figure 5-1
A propositional network. The figure illustrates a propositional network of the information that Monroe followed Madison as president of the United States. (This figure is based on a similar figure in J. R. Anderson [1985]. *Cognitive Psychology and Its Implications* [2nd ed., p. 158]. San Francisco: Freeman.)

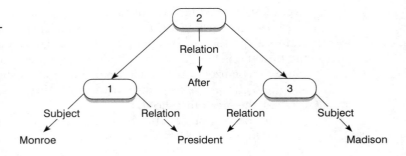

son (1983b, 1993) believes is involved in representing the information that Monroe was president after Madison.

The recall question gives students *Madison* as a point of access from which to begin a memory search. From Anderson's perspective, such a question requires that readers enter memory at *Madison* and search to *Monroe*. To accomplish this, a student first would activate the *Madison* node and have activation spread until it reached *Monroe*. If, however, the link between the second and third proposition were weak or if it could not be sufficiently activated, then recall would fail.

In contrast to the recall question, the recognition question provides two points of access in memory from which activation could spread: *Madison* and *Monroe*. Presumably, if students cannot activate the appropriate link from *Madison,* they might do so from *Monroe*. In Anderson's opinion, recognition questions typically are easier than recall questions because they offer more ways to search memory. Otherwise, however, recognition and recall essentially are the same process.

Most contemporary psychologists take a position midway between Anderson's and the context-dependent position exemplified by Tulving. Craik (1979; Craik & Lockhart, 1986), for example, argues that similar processes probably do operate in recall and recognition but that the requirements of retrieval differ; that is, Craik holds that in recognition an item is presented but information related to the item must be retrieved to allow for discrimination of the item from distractor items. For example, *Did Smith perform research on* (a) *context-dependent retrieval,* (b) *the generation effect,* or (c) *keyword mnemonics?* The item is given: *On what did Smith perform research?* To answer the question, you must retrieve information about Smith so that you can distinguish among the three alternatives. In this case, the answer is *context-dependent retrieval.* The demands of recall, in Craik's view, differ from those of recognition in that a to-be-recalled item is presented (e.g., *Who was known as "the angel of the battlefield?"*) and the person must retrieve the item (*Clara Barton*).

A full theoretical analysis of potential differences between recall and recognition is beyond the scope of this text. Our brief discussion of these processes may tend to imply that retrieval, provided that students are given the proper cues, is a matter of searching for the appropriate memory, finding it, and then just reading it off. Thus, if you were to sit down to take a test over this content, it might seem that all you need to do is find where you stored your memories and then merely read them off. This view of memory would be incorrect, however. It presumes that the entire content of a memory event (e.g., the results of studying this chapter) is stored and that it is stored in the same spot. Further, it assumes that all that must be done is to locate the memory event and read it off. If memory indeed were stored in this fashion, each of us would need a warehouse to hold our memories. We simply encounter far too much information during a lifetime to allow for such massive storage.

Reconstruction

If retrieval is not just a straightforward reading out of memory, what is it? Considerable evidence suggests that retrieval is **reconstructive memory** (e.g., Mandler, 1984; Spiro, 1977, 1980), just as encoding is constructive memory. In other words, rather than remembering the entirety of a memory event, only key elements of an episode are stored, guided by schemata (see Chapter 3). At retrieval, we bring up these key elements and put them together with general knowledge (both domain-specific and general) to reconstruct what we encountered. This process allows us to "handle" far less information than if we encoded and retrieved *all of the information* we encounter.

For example, suppose you witness an automobile accident this afternoon. Later, when a police officer asks you to tell what happened, you probably will retrieve some key elements of the event and reconstruct the rest. For instance, you can recall clearly that the pickup truck broadsided the Mercedes in the intersection. You also can recall that you were waiting for the "Walk" sign to come on. But you may not actually have been in a position to see the traffic lights. So, to describe which vehicle ran the red light, you work from what you know to conclude that the pickup must have ignored a red light. For all you know, though, the traffic lights could have been stuck so that both vehicles had green lights.

Mistakes such as which vehicle ran a light are common when we retrieve events from memory. Students make similar errors when recalling text and lecture information. They may write about George Washington having been elected the first president of the United States and note that John Adams ran with him as vice-president. In fact, Adams finished second in the race for president and so became vice-president. The election laws that set up our current system of "running mates" for president and vice-president were not formulated until well after Washington's time. In this instance, students remember who was president and who was vice-president but reconstruct how the vice-president came to office. A similar phenomenon often occurs when psychology students describe John B. Watson's famous study of Little Albert. As you know, Watson conditioned a fear response in the child Albert by pairing a loud noise with white objects until the white objects themselves elicited the fear response. However, we have seen several students who went on to state that Watson then "unconditioned" Little Albert and removed the fear response. In fact, no such thing happened. Students use their knowledge of contemporary approaches to psychology research to reconstruct a plausible ending for the story.

As can be seen from our examples, a reconstructive memory system should be far less demanding of memory "space" than a "readout" system. Only key elements

BOX 5-1
Bartlett's Story "The War of the Ghosts";
and One Student's Protocol

The War of the Ghosts

One night two young men from Egulac went down to the river to hunt seals,
and while they were there it became foggy and calm. Then they heard war cries,
and they thought: "Maybe this is a war party." They escaped to the shore, and
hid behind a log. Now canoes came up, and they heard the noise of paddles,
and saw one canoe coming up to them. There were five men in the canoe, and
they said:

"What do you think? We wish to take you along. We are going up the river
to make war on the people."

One of the young men said: "I have no arrows."

"Arrows are in the canoe," they said.

"I will not go along. I might be killed. My relatives do not know where I
have gone. But you," he said, turning to the other, "may go with them."

So one of the young men went, but the other returned home.

And the warriors went on up the river to a town on the other side of
Kalama. The people came down to the water, and they began to fight, and
many were killed. But presently the young man heard one of the warriors say:
"Quick, let us go home: that Indian has been hit." Now he thought, "Oh, they
are ghosts." He did not feel sick, but they said he had been shot.

So the canoes went back to Egulac, and the young man went ashore to his
house, and made a fire. And he told everybody and said: "Behold, I accompa-

need to be remembered about a memory event when general knowledge can be
used to reconstruct events. Of course, a reconstructive system also will be open to
far more errors that give evidence of improper reconstruction. In fact, it is errors of
just this type that have convinced many psychologists of the reconstructive nature of
memory (Mandler, 1984; Spiro, 1980).

Two classic studies performed in the 1930s have been central to arguments for
the reconstructive nature of human memory. Each has been replicated several times,
and the results remain consistent (see Schwartz & Reisberg, 1991). The better
known of the two studies was reported in Bartlett's excellent book *Remembering*
(1932). Bartlett, an English psychologist, had subjects read a very brief story titled
"The War of the Ghosts." This particular story was an abstraction of a North American Native legend that was firmly grounded in their culture. Bartlett's subjects, however, were British and had little, if any, cultural background for the story.

After the subjects read the story, Bartlett assessed their recall at differing time
intervals. Bartlett noted that recall for the passage was poor even at short intervals.

nied the ghosts, and we went to fight. Many of our fellows were killed, and many of those who attacked us were killed. They said I was hit, and I did not feel sick."

He told it all, and then he became quiet. When the sun rose he fell down. Something black came out of his mouth. His face became contorted. The people jumped up and cried. He was dead.

Student's Protocol

Two youths were standing by a river about to start seal-catching, when a boat appeared with five men in it. They were all armed for war.

The youths were at first frightened, but they were asked by the men to come and help them fight some enemies on the other bank. One youth said he could not come as his relations would be anxious about him; the other said he would go, and entered the boat.

In the evening he returned to his hut, and told his friends that he had been in a battle. A great many had been slain, and he had been wounded by an arrow; he had not felt any pain, he said. They told him that he must have been fighting in a battle of ghosts. Then he remembered that it had been queer and he became very excited.

In the morning, however, he became ill, and his friends gathered round; he fell down and his face became very pale. Then he writhed and shrieked and his friends were filled with terror. At last he became calm. Something hard and black came out of his mouth, and he lay contorted and dead.

From *Remembering: A Study in Experimental and Social Psychology* by F. C. Bartlett, 1932, Cambridge, England: Cambridge University Press. Pp. 23–26.

More importantly, Bartlett observed that subjects seemed to recall only the gist or theme of the story. From this gist, they constructed a reasonable story that made a kind of sense out of the information recalled. Not surprisingly, the reconstructed stories often contained errors and distortions that made the story fit the general cultural knowledge possessed by the British subjects (see Box 5-1).

In the same year Bartlett's book was published, Carmichael, Hogan, and Walter (1932) reported convincing evidence for reconstructive processes in subjects' memory for drawings. In their experiment, all of Carmichael et al.'s subjects were shown a set of line drawings similar to those pictured in Figure 5-2. The subjects were grouped into three conditions on the basis of the labels they received with the drawings. The subjects in the control condition received no labels; they merely were shown the drawings. The subjects in one experimental condition received the labels shown in List A in Figure 5-2. The subjects in the second experimental condition were provided the labels pictured in List B in Figure 5-2. For example, the subjects in one experimental condition saw the two circles connected by a straight line labeled

Figure 5-2

Figures similar to those used by Carmichael, Hogan, and Walter (1932). (The drawings are based on those used by Carmichael, L., Hogan, H. P., & Walter, A. A. [1932]. An experimental study of the effect of language on the reproduction of visually perceived forms. *Journal of Experimental Psychology, 15,* 73–86.)

LIST A	LIST B	
Bottle	Stirrup	
Beehive	Hat	
Eyeglasses	Dumbbell	
Ship's wheel	Sun	
Pine tree	Trowel	

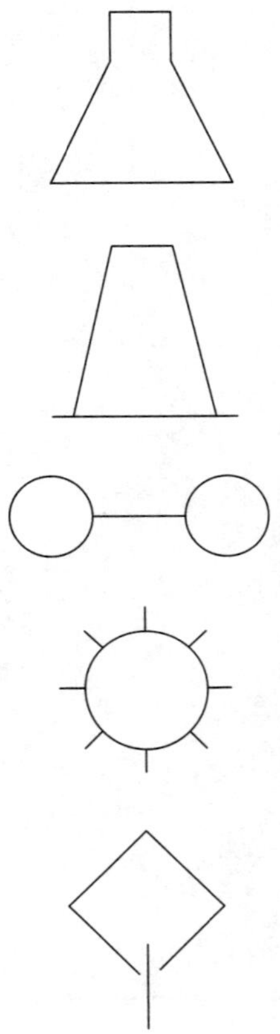

as "dumbbell," whereas the subjects in the other condition saw this drawing labeled as "eyeglasses."

When the subjects in Carmichael et al.'s study were asked to draw the figures from memory, some interesting differences among the conditions appeared. The subjects in the control condition most accurately depicted the drawings as originally shown. The experimental group given the labels in List A tended to systematically bias their drawings so that they fit the labels. In a classroom demonstration in which we repeated the Carmichael et al. experiment, one student drew nosepieces and bands on the "eyeglasses." Similarly, the subjects shown the labels in List B also biased their reproductions to fit the labels they saw. In our use of these materials, we have seen students who drew a cowboy hat for "hat" and another who put grips on the handle of the "trowel."

Although the results of Bartlett's and Carmichael et al.'s studies clearly demonstrated that memory is reconstructive, their explanations for how reconstruction operated were vague and not well accepted. It really was not until the 1970s, with the increasing acceptance of schema theory, that more sophisticated theoretical accounts of reconstructive memory began to appear. In general, the view of recon-structive processes in memory emphasizes students' assimilating new information into existing memory structures. Rather than remember all of the details in an episode, students remember the gist of an event (e.g., Washington and Adams were the first president and vice-president) and then use their general knowledge about similar events (e.g., students' schemata for "presidential elections") to reconstruct the information at the time of test. The rarity with which we see reconstructive memory in recitations of information committed to rote memory (e.g., the Pledge of Allegiance, Hamlet's soliloquy) also suggests that reconstructive memory is most likely when students learn meaningful information—information for which knowl-edge structures are readily available.

Recalling Specific Events

Our discussion above indicates that people tend to reconstruct the meaning of a story when they retrieve that information from a general knowledge store—some-thing like semantic memory described in Chapter 3. But what happens when we try to remember very specific events that have happened to us? These events probably are retrieved from a somewhat different representational schema in memory—some-thing like episodic memory.

Among the questions that researchers have studied are whether episodic events are easier to retrieve and whether they are reconstructed to the same degree as semantic information. Most of us believe we can retrieve specific events from mem-ory with a great deal of ease and accuracy. For example, many Americans remember exactly where they were and what they were doing when President John Kennedy was assassinated. Others have similar memories regarding the death of Beatle John Lennon or the space shuttle *Challenger* explosion. Highly specific events of this kind often are referred to as **flashbulb memories** (R. Brown & Kulik, 1977). Memories for a traffic accident we witnessed or for your sister's wedding also would fall into this category.

Researchers have discovered a number of startling things about flashbulb and other "less photographic" episodic memories. Flashbulb memories are not as accu-rate as one might think, and certainly they are not "photographic" memories in most cases. One example is the work of Loftus and Loftus (1980), who examined the accu-racy of eyewitness testimony. In a number of related studies, the Loftuses reported that eyewitness testimony is often highly inaccurate and, more important, that it is subject to constraints imposed at retrieval. For instance, asking a witness to recall how fast the car was traveling when it *smashed* into the other car is more likely to elicit an overestimate than a more neutral word such as *struck*. These findings strongly sug-gest that information is subject not only to serious distortion at retrieval due to learner-induced reconstruction but also to situationally induced retrieval cues as well.

Studies of flashbulb memories report similar findings. In one case, McCloskey, Wible, and Cohen (1988) asked college students to fill out a questionnaire about events surrounding the explosion of the space shuttle *Challenger* three days after the disaster. McCloskey et al. reported that most individuals had strikingly vivid memories of where they were, what they were doing, and how they felt at the time of the accident. However, an interview with the same individuals nine months later revealed a number of inaccuracies between initial and delayed memory for the event, with only about 65 percent of subjects' reports matching their original version.

These studies reveal that retrieval is not as straightforward as one might expect, even for vivid and emotionally charged information. Retrieval errors fall into two categories: those that are self-induced, as in Bartlett's study, and those that are situationally induced, such as a lawyer's "leading questions" in a courtroom. These errors occur because we try to store as little information as we need, making for a more efficient cognitive system. Most reconstructive errors are of little importance, although some may be highly important. Teachers and students must remember this fact when evaluating certain learning outcomes.

Relearning

At times, information we once knew fairly well seems forgotten forever. One of the authors, for example, had two years of high school French and twenty-some years later could not remember anything but *Je ne parle pas français*. Apparently, two years of study had disappeared somewhere, as recognition and recall of the French language seemed impossible. When the author recently visited Montreal, however, he found himself relearning basic French very rapidly—at least to the point that he was able to shop, ask simple directions, and even get the gist of the day's report on the Montreal Expos baseball team. Apparently, the knowledge of French only *seemed* to be forgotten because the relearning was far easier than the original learning had been.

The most sensitive measure of memory is not recall, recognition, or the ability to reconstruct events. Instead, it is the memory savings that people experience when relearning information (MacLeod, 1988). The relearning approach was the favorite of the pioneer memory researcher Hermann Ebbinghaus (1885). In Ebbinghaus's use of the approach, he first practiced a list of nonsense syllables until he obtained one error-free recitation. Then, after varying delays, Ebbinghaus would relearn the materials to the same criterion. Ebbinghaus determined the level of memory savings by comparing the number of trials he needed in the first and second learning sessions. The existence of any savings (if fewer trials were required on the second than on the first session), even when recognition or recall was not possible, indicated that some parts of the information had been remembered between the first and second learning sessions.

Even though psychologists are aware that the memory savings approach is the most sensitive measure of memory, the method is seldom used. A major reason is that the method often does not seem to be appropriate for complex stimulus materials. Further, a criterion of one error-free verbatim recall might seem reasonable for a list of nonsense syllables, but it hardly seems workable for the contents of a chapter on American history, a lecture on basic genetics, or a discussion of *The Grapes of Wrath*. In addition, after-the-fact attempts to measure savings in learning appear extraordinarily difficult and seldom have been attempted.

Nelson (1985) and MacLeod (1988) have developed variations on Ebbinghaus's classic procedure. In their studies, individuals learned a list of paired associates, with nouns paired with numbers. Initially, they worked until they attained one error-free pass through the list in which they elicited the nouns paired with the provided numbers. After a lengthy delay (weeks or months in Nelson's work), a second session was conducted. This second session had two phases. The first was a test of recall in which individuals were given the numerical cues and attempted to remember as many nouns as they could. In the second phase, subjects were asked to relearn the unrecalled items and an equivalent number of previously unseen items on a single trial. Differences then seen in the immediate recall of previously studied and new items were taken as indications of memory savings.

Although relearning procedures seem to hold promise for future research (see MacLeod, 1988, for a discussion), the results to this point are sketchy. What is clear is that we remember far more than we are able to recall, recognize, or even reconstruct. The form of these memories and how, exactly, relearning differs from original learning are topics of future research.

IMPLICATIONS FOR INSTRUCTION

This chapter has suggested a number of ways that information retrieval can be made more effective. One way is to provide a match between encoding and retrieval conditions. A second way is to provide relevant cues at retrieval. A third way is to use prior knowledge to reconstruct missing information. Implications of these three retrieval strategies are discussed below.

1. *Encoding and retrieval are linked.* The literature on encoding specificity clearly indicates that students' ability to remember information is related strongly to their ability to encode it in a meaningful fashion. When information is elaborated at encoding, and when information present at encoding is used to prompt retrieval, students remember more information than if "encoding-specific" information is not present.

At a broader level, encoding specificity reaffirms the highly interactive nature of our cognitive system. Learning information does not occur in isolated acts such as "encoding" or "retrieval," but rather is the result of all of these processes. Problems in one area lead to problems in another. All of us need to bear in mind the continuous, interactive nature of learning when planning instruction. This requires us to plan ahead so that our instructional goals are matched with effective review and testing.

2. *Learning always occurs in a specific context that affects encoding and retrieval.* One way to improve learning is to situate it in a context that provides useful structure to the student (see Lave & Wenger, 1991). Specifying the purpose of the learning task is one excellent means for doing so. Another useful strategy is to activate students' prior knowledge or to provide some schematic framework prior to instruction (see Chapter 4). Last, information should be presented in a way that reflects how students will be asked to use it in their everyday lives.

3. *Retrieval is state dependent.* Few teachers or students ever consider that their ability to remember information depends on their state. Nevertheless, a large body of research indicates that our ability to remember information is related to our

mood and the conditions under which we learned that information. One implication is that testing conditions should match learning conditions. Herding students into an unfamiliar room at a different time of day than their regular class may negatively affect test performance. Conducting final exams in a new time or location, as is often done at universities, may be ill-advised as well. Indeed, one way that teachers can help students is to teach them to prepare for important tests, such as the Scholastic Aptitude Test (SAT), in a "state" that closely approximates testing conditions.

4. *Memory is reconstructive.* Retrieval is more than playing back an event from memory. Students often retrieve main ideas and use them and their general knowledge to construct a reasonable response. Overall, it seems that as the richness and quantity of cues at retrieval increase, reliance on reconstruction decreases. Regardless of how well a retrieval context is provided, however, recall will vary from student to student on the basis of their world knowledge. Two students with the "same" amount of learning may write very different essays, not because one knows more than another, but because of differences in knowledge available for reconstruction.

Educators should never lose sight of the fact that learning is a highly constructive process. In Chapters 3 and 4, we saw how learners construct meaning by elaborating it with respect to their prior knowledge or processing it at a deeper level. The analog to constructive processes at encoding is reconstructive processes at retrieval. Surprisingly, some teachers look at constructive and reconstructive processes in a negative light, perhaps assuming that students should focus on explicit facts and concepts in their textbooks instead of making their own meaning. We disagree strongly with this view. Research has shown consistently that students learn more and remember it better when they are active (constructive) learners (see Chapter 11). Although constructing or reconstructing meaning may lead to more errors than a verbatim translation of to-be-learned material, these errors are usually insignificant, whereas the cost paid for learning information in a rote, nonconstructivist way is huge!

5. *Learning increases when students generate their own context for meaning.* Research on the generation effect and elaborative interrogation consistently has shown that learning improves when students *make,* rather than *take,* meaning. For example, generating an antonym to the word *stop* (e.g., *go*) will improve memory for the word *go,* compared to simply reading it from a list or seeing it paired with *stop.* Answering questions about to-be-learned information, especially when those questions are related to one's prior knowledge, also improves memory for information. One explanation is that students are more apt to remember encoding conditions when they attempt to retrieve information if they make them up themselves. Whereas student-provided cues are quite likely to be familiar and memorable, using cues provided by the text or the teacher may not be as effective.

6. *Recall and recognition are not the same.* Evidence suggests that recall and recognition tests require different retrieval processes and elicit different study patterns (Rabinowitz & Craik, 1986). Because of this, students' retrieval performance is best when the type of test is "as advertised." Students expecting a multiple-choice test will perform best on a multiple-choice test; students who have prepared for a true-false test will perform best on a true-false test; and so forth. Knowing what kind of information will be included on the test also helps students study more effectively.

7. *Retrieval is fallible.* Retrieval is subject to error under the best of circumstances. One of the main reasons for poor retrieval is that information was not encoded adequately in the first place. Errors occur in reconstruction as well. Although one might expect this to be less of a problem when retrieving specific facts or events, reconstructive errors are still common even for highly memorable events such as flashbulb memories. Some reconstructive errors are due to our desire to "bend" information to make it fit our existing knowledge (a process Piaget referred to as *assimilation*), whereas others are due to new cues not available at encoding. Thus, reconstructive errors should be more likely to occur when either the context or cues present at encoding are unavailable or changed (e.g., perhaps by a skilled attorney).

SUMMARY

The context of retrieval has a powerful influence on memory performance. Generally speaking, for cues to be effective at retrieval, they must have been present at the time of encoding. This principle of encoding specificity has direct implications for teaching so that contexts are provided for retrieval and transfer. One critical aspect of the context of retrieval is the type of test—recall or recognition—given at the time of retrieval. In general, students perform better on recognition tests, but it should be kept in mind that performance is best when there is a match between the type of test actually given and how students expected to be tested. A more important goal, however, is to make information accessible to students in a wide range of contexts by helping them encode it in many ways with a broad range of cues.

Much of recall is reconstructive. Students use their general world knowledge in conjunction with key elements of events to reconstruct information. This may lead to reconstructive errors in recall even when information appears to be "photographic," such as flashbulb memories.

SUGGESTED READINGS

Ellis, H. C., & Hunt, R. R. (1993). *Fundamentals of cognitive psychology* (5th ed.). Madison, WI: Brown & Benchmark.

Chapter 6 provides a detailed explanation of retrieval processes. Chapter 12 addresses issues pertaining to mood, emotion, and remembering.

Lave, J., & Wenger, E. (1991). *Situated learning: Legitimate peripheral participation.* New York: Cambridge University Press.

This book addresses constraints on thinking and learning within a broader context and raises many questions central to the constructivist view of memory.

PART TWO

Beliefs and Cognition

CHAPTER 6

Beliefs About Self

This chapter examines three perspectives on why students succeed and fail in the classroom: Bandura's social cognitive theory, attribution theory, and the role of student control and autonomy. The first of these theories considers how self-confidence affects academic learning. The second examines how students explain their academic success and failure to themselves. The third considers how students' and teachers' expectations create a controlling or autonomy-producing environment in the classroom.

These perspectives are by no means exhaustive, although we believe they provide a sound basis for why some students succeed while others do not. Indeed, one reason we selected these particular theories is because they appear to cover most aspects of life in the classroom; thus, they are comprehensive. We believe that most of the everyday motivational issues of special importance to teachers can be addressed by these theories.

BANDURA'S SOCIAL COGNITIVE LEARNING THEORY

Most of us realize that self-confidence is essential to success in any discipline. Few of us, however, have thought carefully about what self-confidence is, where it comes from, or how it can be improved. Albert Bandura (1977, 1986) has developed an extensive theory during the past thirty years that has examined people's self-confidence in a variety of settings, how confidence develops, and how it affects behavioral outcomes, such as persistence and effort.

At the heart of Bandura's theory is the idea of **reciprocal determinism** (Schunk, 1991). As the name implies, reciprocal determinism suggests that learning is due to a number of interacting variables. Figure 6-1 shows the relationship among three basic components described by Bandura: personal, behavioral, and environmental factors. *Personal factors* refer to beliefs and attitudes that affect learning, especially in response to behavioral and environmental stimuli. *Behavioral factors* include the responses one makes in a given situation—for example, whether one responds to a poor test score with anger or with increased effort. *Environmental factors* include the role played by parents, teachers, and peers.

The idea of reciprocal determinism suggests that personal factors, such as one's self-beliefs, affect behaviors and the interpretation of environmental cues. One way that personal factors are related to behaviors and environmental cues is through **mediated responses**—that is, how events are interpreted cognitively prior to a response. In one case, poor performance on a test may elicit anxiety in one student and increased effort in another because the same event (a poor grade) is interpreted differently.

The fact that beliefs and attitudes affect behaviors and environmental cues gives special importance to personal factors in Bandura's model. Two personal factors provide especially powerful influences on behavior. One is *self-efficacy,* or the degree to which an individual possesses confidence in his or her ability to achieve a goal. Self-efficacy has been related to many behavioral outcomes that we explore in greater detail later in this section. A second factor is an *outcome expectancy,* or the perceived relationship between performing a task successfully and receiving a specific outcome as a consequence of that performance.

Consider the plight of African American baseball players prior to 1946, the year Jackie Robinson became the first African American player to play in the major leagues. Prior to this time, two particularly talented African American players— Satchel Paige and Josh Gibson—were excluded from the all-white major leagues. Both of these players undoubtedly had a very high degree of self-efficacy concerning

Figure 6-1
Bandura's model of reciprocal determinism. (Adapted from Bandura, Albert. Copyright 1986. *Social Foundations of Thought and Action: A Social Cognitive Theory.* Adapted by permission of Prentice Hall, Englewood Cliffs, New Jersey.)

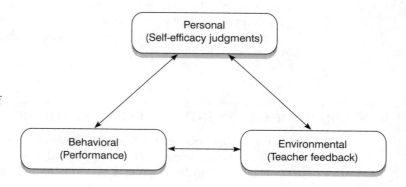

their baseball skills. In fact, both eventually were elected to the Hall of Fame long after their active careers were over. Neither, however, had high outcome expectancies for playing in the major leagues during their careers because no amount of talent would guarantee admittance due to racial bias. We return to the topic of self-efficacy in greater detail later in this section. First, however, let's examine how learning is portrayed in Bandura's model.

Enactive and Vicarious Learning

Learning occurs in two ways, according to Bandura (1986). The first—**enactive learning**—occurs when one learns a task by doing it. Bandura has argued that enactive attainments are the most important form of learning because they provide direct feedback about one's performance. Performing a task successfully over many occasions gives rise to a high level self-efficacy that is unaffected by occasional failures. The second type of learning—**vicarious learning**—occurs when one learns about a task by observing others perform or discuss it.

Both types of learning appear to be extremely important. Enactive learning enables us to develop the basic procedural knowledge necessary to perform a task, whereas vicarious learning allows us to observe the subtle nuances of expert performance long before we are capable of such performance ourselves. Vicarious learning, especially when it involves a skilled model, is useful for several reasons (Schunk, 1991). First, observing a model allows us to allocate all of our resources to learning about the task, rather than performing it. Second, vicarious learning enables us to see expert strategies performed without interruption. Third, observing others provides motivation to less-skilled observants.

Schunk (1991) has identified three influences on the effectiveness of learning and performance. One is the *developmental status* of the individual. For example, students differ with respect to reasoning skills and working memory capacity at different ages. Children also may lack the physical ability or knowledge base to perform a task modeled by a skilled adult. A second influence is the *prestige* of the model. Models with a high functional value (those judged to be more credible) exert a stronger influence on learning. The effects of model prestige also extend to other skills in which the model is not necessarily expert. For instance, some aspiring basketball players may be more apt to eat a particular breakfast cereal because Shaquille O'Neal's picture is on the front of the cereal box. A third influence is one's ability to *set an attainable goal,* often with standards provided by a model. Goals do not necessarily improve learning, but rather offer incentives to students. Goals that are specific, attainable within a limited amount of time, and of moderate difficulty appear to provide the greatest incentives.

Self-Efficacy

Self-efficacy should not be confused with general self-esteem. According to Bandura (1986), **self-efficacy** is a judgment of one's ability to perform a task *within a specific domain.* High efficacy in one setting does not guarantee high efficacy in another.

Within a specific domain, however, self-efficacy is linked reciprocally with behavioral outcomes and environmental cues (see Figure 6-1). High self-efficacy positively affects performance, whereas good performance, in turn, positively affects one's sense of self-efficacy. Self-efficacy also indirectly affects future learning by predisposing students to engage in challenging tasks and to persist longer despite initial failures.

Judgments of self-efficacy differ along three dimensions related to performance. One dimension is the *level of task difficulty*. Even students with high efficacy in a domain may be reluctant to take a challenging graduate class. One reason is that the general level of expertise in such a class is much higher than what the students are used to. Another reason is that students may lack prior knowledge or strategies necessary to do well in the class.

A second dimension is the *generality* of one's self-efficacy. Some individuals feel able to perform well in almost any academic setting. Others feel confident in only one or two settings. Still others have very little self-efficacy in any domain. Generally speaking, self-efficacy in one domain is unrelated to efficacy in another domain. This does not mean, however, that some individuals do not have high self-efficacy in general. Rather, it suggests that they have reason to believe they can perform competently in many domains. In some cases, self-efficacy may generalize from one domain to another. Shell, Murphy, and Bruning (1989) found that college students with high self-efficacy in reading also had high self-efficacy in writing.

A third dimension is the *strength* of one's efficacy judgments. Weak perceptions of efficacy are more susceptible to disconfirming evidence (observing someone else fail at a task) or to poor performance. Individuals with a strong sense of self-efficacy persevere in the face of disconfirming evidence and poor performance. Thus, two people may receive the same low grade on a chemistry test, with very different effects on their efficacy. All other things being equal, the student with the higher efficacy will be more inclined to persist and to maintain self-confidence, while the other student will not.

Research by Bandura and colleagues (see Bandura, 1993; Schunk, 1989, for reviews) indicates that self-efficacy is linked closely with initial task engagement, persistence, and successful performance. Bandura (1986) has identified four influences on the level, generality, and strength of self-efficacy. One influence is *enactive information* acquired during the performance of a task. Successful performance leads to greater self-efficacy; failure leads to lower efficacy. A second influence is *observation* of others; it often improves efficacy, especially when the model is judged to be similar in ability to the observer. Vicarious influences are strongest when observers are uncertain about the difficulty of the task or their own ability. A third influence is *verbal persuasion*. Although the effect of persuasion often is limited, it may facilitate engagement in an otherwise forbidding task that, in turn, leads to enactive feedback. Self-efficacy is judged, in part, by a fourth influence—one's *psychological state*. Sleepiness or physical fatigue often lowers efficacy even though it may be unrelated to the performance of a task. Strong emotional arousal also often reduces efficacy, chiefly by invoking fear-inducing thoughts.

Research on Teacher and Student Self-Efficacy

Bandura's social cognitive theory has attracted much attention from educational and psychological researchers. One reason is that *self-efficacy* is a concept that applies to successful task engagement and performance in any domain, whether it is math, history, waterskiing, or social events. Virtually all of this research reports the same findings; thus, we focus our attention on research most relevant to educators.

Student Efficacy.   The most important and consistent finding in the research literature is that student self-efficacy is strongly related to critical classroom variables such as task engagement, persistence, strategy use, help seeking, and task performance. High self-efficacy is associated with greater flexibility, resistance to negative feedback, and improved performance.

For example, Collins (reported in Bandura, 1993) examined the way children used math skills. She compared math performance across high-, average-, and low-ability students who exhibited either high or low self-efficacy. Students with high self-efficacy *at each level* discarded unproductive strategies more quickly than their low-efficacy counterparts. High-efficacy students also were more likely to rework problems they missed originally. High-efficacy students at each level outperformed their low-efficacy counterparts.

This study highlights two important conclusions. First, efficacy improves performance and strategy use among students even when their ability level is controlled. Second, low-ability students *may* have the same degree of self-efficacy as some high-ability students. When they do, they tend to perform as successfully as their high-ability/low-efficacy counterparts.

Bandura and Wood (1989) found that self-efficacy is related to perceived control of one's environment. Higher self-efficacy was positively related to two kinds of control. The first concerns the belief that control can be achieved through effortful use of one's skills and resources. The second addresses the degree to which the environment can be modified. Those with higher efficacy were more apt to feel greater control and, in turn, persist in the face of performance failures.

Higher levels of self-efficacy have been linked as well with the way individuals explain their success and failure in a particular situation (causal attributions). Self-efficacious individuals are more likely to attribute their failure to low effort, rather than to low ability, whereas low-efficacy individuals attribute their failure to low ability.

Research reviewed by Bandura (1993) points to other ways that self-efficacy may help students. One occurs when students have high self-efficacy for controlling their own thoughts. Students who believe they have control are less likely to experience stress, anxiety, and depression when goals have not been met. Another way occurs when students demonstrate a strong sense of self-efficacy for coping with anxiety-producing situations in the classroom or at home. Students who believe they cope well, or at least believe they can cope, are less apt to engage in avoidant behaviors.

Schunk (1989) also reviewed a number of important consequences of self-efficacy on classroom behavior and performance. One is that self-efficacious students are better goal setters, in part, because of their willingness to set "close," rather than "distant," goals. Another is that self-efficacious students are better at setting their own goals. Ironically, the ability to set one's own goals has been shown to enhance self-efficacy!

Teacher Efficacy.   Teachers' expectations and behaviors are affected by self-efficacy judgments too. Teachers appear to evaluate their performance by using two independent efficacy assessments (Woolfolk & Hoy, 1990). One is **teaching efficacy**, which refers to the belief that the process of education affects students in important ways. The second is **personal teaching efficacy**, which refers to the belief that the teacher can enact significant change in his or her students. Woolfolk and Hoy found that the relationship between teaching efficacy and controlling attitudes among teachers is negative; that is, teachers high on this dimension are more likely to value student control and autonomy. This is true especially when teachers also show high personal teaching efficacy.

A number of other studies have investigated teacher efficacy by using only a single dimension similar to what Woolfolk and Hoy refer to as "personal teaching efficacy." A review of these studies by Kagan (1992) found that self-efficacious teachers were more apt to use praise, rather than criticism, to persevere with low-achieving students, to be task oriented, to be more accepting of students, and to raise their achievement levels. In contrast, low-efficacy teachers devoted less class time to class-related activity, spent more time criticizing students, and gave up on "problem students" more quickly. Studies by Poole, Okeafor, and Sloan (1989) and Smylie (1988) also found that self-efficacious teachers were more likely to use new curriculum materials and to change instructional strategies, compared with low-efficacy teachers.

One disturbing finding, however, is that the number of years teachers spend in the classroom negatively affects their efficacy (Brousseau, Book, & Byers, 1988). Research suggests that experienced teachers are more likely to adopt a *custodial* view of classroom control in which rigid rules and standards are used to maintain discipline. In contrast, teachers with fewer years of experience or those who maintain high self-efficacy regardless of years of experience are more inclined to adopt a *humanistic* view of control in which student individuality and classroom diversity are used.

School Efficacy.   Research reviewed by Bandura (1993) also suggests that schools differ with respect to self-efficacy. School communities that collectively judge themselves powerless to improve student learning negatively affect both students and teachers. Within this context, individual teachers with low self-efficacy appear to lower the efficacy of their students, especially when students view themselves as having low ability. Factors that appear to affect school efficacy negatively are the stability of the student body and their relative socioeconomic status. The length of teaching experience of the teaching staff is negatively related to school efficacy as well, although it is positively related to students' academic achievement. Not surprisingly, students' prior academic achievement is positively related to school efficacy.

Modeling

Modeling is the demonstrating and describing of component parts of a skill to a novice. It is an extremely important component in the development of self-efficacy. Bandura (1986) proposed that positive instances of modeling are effective because they raise expectations that a new skill can be mastered, can provide motivational incentives, and can provide a great deal of information about how a skill is performed. Not all models are the same, however. Peer models are usually the most effective because they are most similar to the individual studying the model. For example, third-grade math students will not be convinced they can develop mathematical competence just by observing a teacher solve difficult math problems. Indeed, they are most likely to improve their self-efficacy vicariously when observing a student who is similar in age and especially perceived ability (Schunk, 1991).

This is not to say that teachers are not important classroom models. Often, the teacher is the only person in the classroom who can model a complex procedure adequately. One of the most effective ways to do so is through **cognitive modeling** (Meichenbaum, 1977), which includes the following six steps:

1. *Create a rationale for learning the new skill.* Explain to students why acquisition of this skill is important. Provide examples of how, when, and where this skill will be used (establish *outcome expectancies*).

2. *Model the procedure in its entirety while students observe.* For example, a piano teacher plays an entire piece of music without interruption.

3. *Model component parts of the task.* If the task can be broken into smaller parts (e.g., using the "integration by parts" method in a calculus class), model each part by using different problems or settings.

4. *Allow students to practice component steps under teacher guidance.* For example, a music student may practice only the first eight measures of a piece of music, receiving feedback on each occasion from her piano instructor.

5. *Allow students to practice the entire procedure under teacher guidance.* Component steps eventually are merged into a single, fluid procedure that is performed intact.

6. *Have the student engage in self-directed performance of the task.* Research suggests that modeling is a highly effective way to improve simple and complex skills learned in the classroom. There are many ways to model a new skill other than teacher-directed instruction. One method is **reciprocal teaching**, in which two to four students work in cooperative learning groups (Palincsar & Brown, 1984). A variety of other methods are described in Schmuck and Schmuck (1992).

Regardless of what method is used, however, feedback should be an essential part of the modeling process. Recall that Bandura's model of reciprocal determinism postulates a strong relationship between performance and environmental cues and learning. Feedback provided to students directly from the teacher improves both performance and self-efficacy. Feedback provided to students from other students appears to be equally effective in many situations. Perhaps the most effective type of feedback is *self-generated* by the student. Self-generated feedback is important because it enables students to self-regulate their performance without teacher or peer-model assistance.

Previous research indicates that different types of feedback exert different influences on performance (Hogarth, Gibbs, McKenzie, & Marquis, 1991). **Outcome feedback** provides specific information about performance and has little effect on initially correct or subsequent test performance (Lhyle & Kulhavy, 1987). **Cognitive feedback**, which stresses the relationship between performance and the nature of the task, appears to exert a more positive influence on subsequent performance by providing a deeper understanding of how to perform competently (Balzer, Doherty, & O'Connor, 1989). In a study by Schraw, Potenza, and Nebelsick-Gullet (1993), outcome feedback did little to improve students' comprehension monitoring, whereas incentives to use self-generated cognitive feedback improved both monitoring accuracy and performance.

Self-Regulated Learning Theory

During the past decade, researchers have attempted to integrate the key components of Bandura's learning theory with findings from other areas of cognitive psychology. These attempts have led to the development of self-regulated learning theory (Schunk, 1991; Zimmerman, 1990). **Self-regulated learning** refers to the ability to control all aspects of one's learning, from advance planning to how one evaluates performance afterward.

Most theories of self-regulation include three core components: metacognitive awareness, strategy use, and motivational control. In Chapter 4, we discussed how metacognition includes *knowledge about* and *regulation of* cognition. These different kinds of knowledge enable students to select the best strategy for the occasion and to monitor its effectiveness with a high degree of accuracy.

Strategies are an essential part of self-regulation because they provide the means by which learners encode, represent, and retrieve information (see Chapters 4 and 5). Skilled learners choose strategies selectively and monitor their effectiveness throughout the learning process (Zimmerman & Martinez-Pons, 1990). In turn, strategies enable skilled learners to use their limited resources as efficiently as possible.

Motivational control refers to the ability to set goals, evoke positive beliefs about one's skills and performance, and emotionally adjust to the demands of studying and learning. Skilled learners understand the role of effort and strategies in learning and are less likely than unskilled learners to attribute poor performance to uncontrollable causes, such as ability and luck. Skilled learners also are more adept at blocking out disturbances while studying (Pressley et al., 1987).

Self-regulated learning represents an important step forward in understanding how learners develop intellectual independence. To answer this question, researchers must describe complex interrelationships between cognitive and affective aspects of learning. In addition, some description must be given of how individuals introspect on their own cognition. Last, researchers must explain how internalized (e.g., self-talk) and externalized (e.g., teacher modeling) forces affect self-regulation.

Not all of these goals have been met thus far, although research continues to provide valuable insights into the self-regulation process. For example, a number of studies have found that higher levels of self-regulation are related to greater valuing of tasks, self-efficacy, strategy use, increased effort, and better performance among children and adults (Graham & Harris, 1989; Pintrich & DeGroot, 1990; Zimmerman & Martinez-Pons, 1990).

We believe the next decade will see many advances in self-regulated learning theory. New discoveries and the refinement of existing theories no doubt will improve our ability to construct educational environments that foster self-regulation. In the interim, setting "self-regulation" as a major goal of instruction may help us remember that skills and knowledge are only means to a much larger end, not ends in themselves.

Implications: Improving Self-Efficacy

Research indicates that self-efficacy is affected by self-assessments, behavioral feedback, and environmental cues. Self-efficacy strongly influences many classroom behaviors, including task engagement, performance, anxiety, stress, persistence, and use of academic or social coping strategies. Because self-efficacy is changeable, teachers and parents bear a special responsibility for providing an environment conducive to improving efficacy. Several suggestions for doing so are included below.

1. *Increase students' awareness of the self-efficacy concept.* Many teachers and students underestimate the importance of self-efficacy. Emphasizing the positive consequences of high efficacy, describing how efficacy develops and deteriorates, and promoting positive efficacy messages in the classroom are goals every teacher should adopt. Teachers may wish to communicate to parents the role of efficacy to help promote an efficacy-producing environment at home.

2. *Use expert and inexpert modeling.* Self-efficacy is domain specific. One way to improve efficacy is by exposing students to expert and intermediate-level models. The former provide examples of expert performance that are motivational and informative. The latter illustrate that expertise develops slowly and is attainable through effort and use of strategies. In many settings, peer models appear to be especially effective.

3. *Provide feedback.* Behavioral and environmental feedback are two of the most important influences on self-efficacy. Students should be helped to evaluate their own performance to enhance this function. Teachers also should provide prompt, in-depth "performance" and "cognitive" feedback. For example, teachers should emphasize not only whether a strategy succeeded or failed, but also why it did. The most effective kind of feedback relates performance outcomes to activities that cause those outcomes.

4. *Build self-efficacy, rather than reduce expectations.* Bandura (1993) has stressed the importance of improving self-efficacy by incorporating efficacy-increasing experiences in the classroom, rather than by decreasing task difficulty. Indeed,

the latter may decrease efficacy if students perceive that the teacher has little confidence in them. Teachers should consider ways in which class content is challenging yet attainable. One effective method is to incorporate small, cooperative groups. Another is to allow ample time for students to achieve mastery of the material.

5. *Encourage self-regulation.* Educators should be mindful that teaching individual skills, such as metacognitive awareness and strategies, is only one aspect of the educational process. A more important aspect is to help students integrate all of these skills in a manner that enables them to become self-regulated learners once they leave school. Doing so presents a tremendous challenge to parents, teachers, and society. Although no easy paths lead to this goal, careful planning and reflection on what it means to be self-regulated no doubt will benefit students and teachers alike.

ATTRIBUTION THEORY

Every day, events take place in our lives that can be interpreted in a number of ways. Consider two college students who receive the same mediocre score on a history test. One student becomes angry and decides to drop the class because, according to her, the professor is a poor teacher who has written an unfair test. The second student resolves to work harder to learn the material. Clearly, these students have interpreted their experiences in very different ways despite similar levels of performance.

But what separates these two students? Why does one drop the class, while the other increases her effort? One explanation is that the two students have made different attributions about their poor test performance. The first student attributes her poor showing to the teacher, although she secretly may believe it is due to low ability. The second student attributes her poor performance to lack of effort.

Attribution theory is the study of how individuals explain events that take place in their lives. An **attribution** is a causal explanation of one of those events. Attribution theory provides a framework for understanding why people respond so differently to the same outcomes. Some of these causal explanations may predispose individuals to negative emotions or decrease the likelihood of future task engagement. Other explanations may provide individuals with reasons to persist or to work even harder.

In this section, we describe some of the main assumptions of attribution theory. To do so, we must consider what causes people to make certain kinds of attributions, what are the most common attributions that people make, what kinds of affective responses attributional judgments elicit, and how attributional judgments affect our behavior. We refer to these steps as the *attributional process.* We turn now to this process.

The Attributional Process

One way to think about the attributional process is the model shown in Figure 6-2. Four components are included in this model. One is *outcome evaluation,* the process by which we assess whether an outcome (e.g., a test score) is favorable or

Figure 6-2
The attributional process.
(Adapted from Gredler, M. E.
[1992]. *Learning and Instruction: Theory into Practice* [2nd ed.]. New York: Macmillan.)

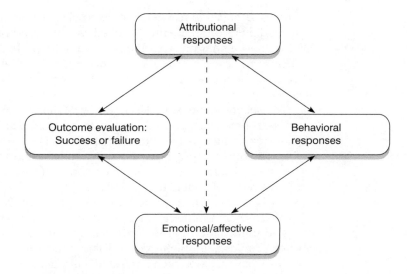

unfavorable. The second is *attributional responses,* in which we attribute this outcome to a particular cause. The third is some kind of *affective response,* in which the attributional response elicits an emotional reaction. The last is a *behavioral response,* in which we respond to the outcome in a particular way.

The key aspect of Figure 6-2 is that events do not elicit behavioral reactions *directly,* but do so only after being *mediated* by some form of cognitive interpretation. This model is similar in many regards to the basic assumptions of Bandura's social cognitive learning theory. One important difference, however, is that self-efficacy judgments pertain to future events, whereas attributional judgments pertain to past events (Graham, 1991).

Outcome Evaluation.   Outcome evaluations are made by using a number of criteria. One is the individual's prior history with similar outcomes. For example, if a student consistently performs poorly in history class, even an average grade on an essay test may seem favorable. A more important constraint, however, is performance feedback. Typically, performance that falls below a preestablished standard is viewed unfavorably. Whether an outcome is viewed favorably also depends on characteristics of the person, such as the need for achievement, the perceived importance of the task, and the expectations of others. Last, outcomes are evaluated, in large part, on the basis of cues from others. For example, students who usually do quite well in class may be chided by instructors for submitting an average paper, whereas other students performing the same level of work may be praised because instructors expect less from them.

Attributional Responses.   Attributional responses vary along three causal dimensions (Weiner, 1985, 1986). The first dimension is **locus of control**, which defines the cause of an outcome as either internal or external to the individual. Mood, for example, is an internal cause even though it may be affected by external variables. In contrast, parents and teachers are external causes of success or failure. The locus of control dimension frequently is linked with the kind of affective responses individuals experience after an outcome. For example, pride and confidence are associated with internal causes of academic success, such as ability, expert knowledge, and effort. Shame and anxiety are associated with external causes, such as unsolicited teacher help.

The second dimension described by Weiner is **stability**. Some causes of success, such as ability, usually are assumed to be stable, although there is considerable debate regarding this issue (see Chapter 7). Other causes, such as effort, are less stable. Still other external causes, such as luck, are completely unstable. The stability dimension usually is linked with a person's success expectancy. If success is attributed to a relatively stable trait, such as ability or knowledge, it seems reasonable that past success would be repeated. In contrast, if success is attributed to highly unstable causes, there is little reason to believe that success will occur again.

The third dimension is **controllability**. Some causes of success, such as effort and strategy use, are highly controllable; others, such as ability or interest, are not. Uncontrollable factors, such as task difficulty and luck, obviously fail to promote confidence in one's ability to succeed again. The controllability dimension often is related to the amount of effort and persistence an individual devotes to a task. Outcomes viewed as uncontrollable often promote anxiety and avoidance strategies, whereas those under control lead to increased effort and persistence.

The three dimensions described above can be used to create a locus × stability × controllability matrix that is shown in Table 6-1. As this table reveals, causal attributions must be categorized along all three dimensions simultaneously because two different causes, such as effort and ability, may share two common dimensions but differ along a third. According to Weiner (1985), it is the unique configuration of each attributional cause that elicits different emotional and behavioral responses in people.

Affective Responses.   Different attributional configurations give rise to different, though highly predictable, affective responses (Graham, 1991; Weiner, 1985). Posi-

Table 6-1
Three Dimensions of Weiner's Attribution Theory. (Adapted from Schunk, D. H. [1991]. *Learning Theories: An Educational Perspective.* New York: Macmillan.)

	Internal		External	
	Stable	**Unstable**	**Stable**	**Unstable**
Controllable	Typical effort	Specific effort	Teacher responses	Help
Uncontrollable	Ability	Interest	Task Difficulty	Luck

tive affective responses, such as pride and confidence, are most likely to occur when an event is attributable to an internal, controllable, and stable factor, such as general effort. This is especially true for average and low-achieving students because effort allocation is under their direct control, whereas ability and task difficulty are not. Other positive emotions, such as gratitude, are most likely to occur when an event is attributable to an external, uncontrollable, and unstable factor, such as help from individuals who are not expected to provide it.

Negative emotions, such as anger, are most likely when an event is due to external, controllable, and stable causes. In contrast, humiliating emotions, such as shame, guilt, and embarrassment, are due to internal causes that vary along other dimensions. For example, students are most likely to feel shame when an outcome (e.g., low math performance) is due to an internal, uncontrollable, and stable trait (e.g., low math ability). By the same token, pity is most apt to be elicited from others under the same conditions, wherein observers view the individual as helpless. Emotions such as guilt are most likely to occur when a cause is internal, controllable, and unstable. For instance, failing to complete one's homework or engaging in occasional inappropriate behavior produces such feelings.

Behavioral Responses.   One of the basic tenets of attribution theory is that the interpretation of an outcome (causal attribution) will determine the kind of behavioral response an individual makes. As we have seen, attributions in which stability is the critical dimension frequently give rise to higher success expectancies and, in turn, higher levels of task engagement, challenge seeking, and performance. Attributions in which controllability is the critical dimension lead to greater effort and more persistence. Attributions in which internal locus of control is critical lead to feelings of confidence, satisfaction, and pride, whereas an external locus results in positive responses, such as help seeking, as well as negative reactions, such as helplessness, avoidance, and lack of persistence (Gredler, 1992).

Attributions in the Classroom

A number of studies have examined the kind of attributions that students make and why they make them. One of the most important findings from this literature is that different students make very different kinds of attributions. Some of these differences are due to gender; others are due to students' perceptions of ability. Still others are due to the way teachers respond to students (Stipek, 1993).

A review by Peterson (1990) found that negative attributional styles (e.g., attributing failure to ability and teachers) are related to low grades, less help seeking, vaguer goals, poorer use of learning strategies, and lower performance expectations. Studies focusing on help-seeking behaviors in particular have reported that many students do not seek help because doing so provides an explicit *low-ability cue* to one's peers.

In a study by Karabenick and Knapp (1991), help seeking among college students was positively related to global self-esteem but negatively related to the perceived psychological risk of help seeking. One plausible explanation of these findings is that high-self-esteem students were more likely to attribute their success to controllable causes, including asking competent individuals for help. In addition, students who were more likely to seek help were more likely to use cognitive and metacognitive learning strategies even after the effect of perceived risk was controlled statistically.

Newman and Goldin (1990) reported similar findings in a study of elementary-age children. One interesting outcome was that children were more reluctant to seek help from peers, compared with adults (including teachers), because they were afraid to "look dumb" in the eyes of their classmates. Girls were more concerned about public appearances than boys, especially in math classes, compared with reading classes. Help seeking also was related to academic achievement in that low achievers sought *less* help. Last, the more the children thought help seeking would benefit them, the more likely they were to ask.

These studies suggest that low-achieving students are less likely to seek help because doing so provides a low-ability cue. Research by Barker and Graham (1987) and Graham and Barker (1990) has investigated low-ability cues in more detail. Barker and Graham (1987) found that teachers transmitted low-ability information to other students by way of the type and amount of praise and/or blame. Students praised for average achievement were judged by other students as having lower ability than students praised only for outstanding performances. Similar results were found when teachers blamed students for mistakes on simple versus complex tasks.

Graham and Barker (1990) extended these findings to teachers' offers of help in the classroom. Students who were quick to be helped by teachers were judged as having lower ability. The amount of teacher help also provided a low-ability cue. These cues were most apt to be detected among older (twelve-year-old) versus younger (five-year-old) students, although cues were salient at times even among the youngest students.

Together these studies suggest that teacher-student interactions provide a great deal of unintended information to other students. Several studies indicate that reluctance to seek help is due to low-ability cues provided inadvertently by teachers! Ironically, students labeled as low ability may be less likely to solicit teacher help in the future and may try to decline help even when it is offered spontaneously by teachers even though seeking help is related to improved performance and higher academic achievement.

Attributional Retraining

Attributional retraining refers to helping individuals better understand their attributional responses and develop responses that encourage task engagement. A review by Försterling (1985) found that the majority of attributional retraining programs are quite successful. The general sequence is as follows: (1) individuals are taught how to identify undesirable behaviors, such as task avoidance, (2) attributions underlying avoidant behavior are evaluated, (3) alternative attributions are explored, and (4) favorable attributional patterns are implemented.

Försterling reported that most programs emphasize a shift in "unfavorable" attributions based on ability to "favorable" attributions based on effort. Shifting attributions from ability to effort appears to be effective because effort is a controllable variable, whereas ability is not. Programs adopting this strategy frequently report an increase in task persistence and achievement levels.

In a series of studies by Schunk and colleagues (Schunk, 1983, 1987; Schunk & Cox, 1986), attributional feedback provided to students while they were engaged in a task increased self-efficacy and performance. Feedback about effort frequently improved task persistence, especially when it was given early in the learning cycle. To be effective, however, attributional feedback must be credible.

In contrast, Schunk (1984) found that sometimes feedback about ability has a stronger effect than feedback about effort. One group of students in this study received effort-only feedback, a second group received ability-only feedback, and two other groups received either effort-ability or ability-effort feedback. Schunk found that those who received ability feedback before effort feedback performed better and reported higher self-efficacy than those who received effort-only feedback or those who received effort feedback prior to ability feedback. Apparently, information regarding ability is linked more closely with one's sense of efficacy than is information about effort.

These findings suggest that attributional training should not focus exclusively on effort. In some cases, students may need to be reminded that their success is due to high ability. In other cases, especially when students lack basic skills necessary for task completion, emphasizing the role of effort may increase persistence and task performance.

In addition, attributional training programs may be more effective for some individuals than others. Perry and Penner (1990) found that college students with an external orientation (those who perceived their success as due to external causes) benefitted more from attributional retraining than students with an internal orientation. Externally oriented students receiving the training earned higher achievement scores in course work than externally oriented students without training and all internally oriented students.

Overall, the attributional retraining literature provides clear evidence that increasing students' awareness about the attributions they make and helping them make more favorable attributional responses improve self-efficacy and learning while reducing achievement-related anxiety. For this reason, we believe that teachers should discuss the role of attributions in learning and provide some degree of retraining for students who make inappropriate attributions.

Implications: Improving Student Attributions

1. *Discuss the effects of attributions with students.* Teachers can help students better understand the learning process by explaining the role that attributions play in it. Research indicates that some students struggle unnecessarily because they incorrectly attribute failure to ability, rather than to lack of effort or undirected effort.

Explaining these subtle differences to students is neither time demanding nor difficult, yet may improve learning and confidence greatly.

Studies also reveal that children younger than age ten often do not distinguish between different attributional responses to the same extent as older children, adolescents, and adults (Schunk, 1991). For this reason, younger students may need explicit instruction (retraining) to help them understand and redirect their attributional responses.

2. *Help students focus on controllable causes.* Most attributional retraining programs attempt to shift one's emphasis from ability to effort judgments. Attributing success or failure to effort is not as damaging psychologically because effort is controllable. In general, emphasizing controllable factors in the learning process increases task engagement, persistence, and performance. Emphasizing uncontrollable causes, such as ability, mood, task difficulty, luck, and characteristics of other students, increases anxiety and decreases challenge seeking.

3. *Help students understand their emotional reactions to success and failure.* Attribution theory provides a framework for understanding not only how we explain success and failure but also how we feel about it. Students who make certain types of attributions after failure experience predictable types of emotional responses. For instance, attributing failure to ability elicits some degree of humiliation in most students, whereas attributing failure to lack of effort leads to embarrassment. Clearly, some emotions are more denigrating than others. Parents and teachers can do students a great service by helping them understand their emotional reactions to success and failure. More important still, students can be shown how to change these emotions by redirecting their attributional thinking.

4. *Consider alternative causes of success and failure.* Most attributional studies investigate a core set of responses, including ability, effort, teacher help, and luck. Curiously, many students struggle in class for different reasons, but especially because they lack *prior knowledge, appropriate strategies, monitoring skills,* and *automaticity.* Fortunately, all of these factors are *controllable* (changeable) even though it may take some time to change them. Students should recognize that many difficulties in the classroom are attributable to these factors, instead of to low ability or lack of effort. Doing so may help remove blame from students for poor performance or for difficulty mastering new information.

5. *Be mindful of inadvertent low-ability cues.* Sometimes, teachers provide low-ability cues about students even when they do not intend to. Unfortunately, some of these cues are transmitted while teachers are engaged in otherwise "positive" activities, such as praising and helping students. We recommend that teachers carefully consider the kind of information they communicate to their class by the way they offer help and praise and the way they reprimand students. Offering praise or help privately or through written feedback may be more beneficial for low-achieving students or for students who are prone to low self-esteem. Similarly, praising high-achieving students privately for normatively high performance may reduce the number of performance-oriented expectations they impose on themselves.

AUTONOMY AND CONTROL

The question of student autonomy is an important one, particularly as it pertains to real and imagined success in the classroom. To examine this question in more detail, however, we first must consider what it means to be motivated and how motivation affects behavior and a student's sense of control. In this section, we review a number of important frameworks for understanding motivation, examine how motivation is related to behavior, and explore how controlling versus uncontrolling environments affect motivation.

One way to think of motivation is to distinguish between internal and external constraints on behavior. **Intrinsic motivation** refers to behaviors that are engaged in for their own sake (Deci, Vallerand, Pelletier, & Ryan, 1991). When an individual is intrinsically motivated, tasks are performed for internal reasons, such as joy and satisfaction, rather than for external reasons, such as reward, obligation, or threat of punishment. Thus, a student is intrinsically motivated when she solves unassigned math problems because they interest her. **Extrinsic motivation** refers to behaviors that are performed to achieve some externally prized consequence, not out of interest or a personal desire for mastery. Solving math problems that one does not enjoy because they were assigned as homework is one example.

A number of studies have shown that even young children distinguish between intrinsic and extrinsic sources of motivation (see Deci et al., 1991, for a review). Gottfried (1990) found that intrinsic motivation at age seven was correlated with intrinsic motivation two years later, was positively related to intellectual ability, predicted current and future academic achievement, and was positively correlated with students' grades. Vallerand, Blais, Briere, and Pelletier (1989) reported that high intrinsic motivation was related to school satisfaction and more positive emotions in the classroom.

At first glance, one might conclude that promoting intrinsic motivation would be sufficient for high levels of task engagement, persistence, and satisfaction. Unfortunately, the relationship between intrinsic motivation and classroom success is not as straightforward as it seems. Deci and Ryan (1985, 1987) have argued that a more fundamental distinction can be made between actions that are **self-determined** and **controlling**. The former actions include behaviors that individuals *choose* to engage in for intrinsic reasons. The latter are behaviors that individuals engage in due to internal or external pressure to conform to a set standard or to meet a particular expectation. For example, one student may choose to complete her homework because she enjoys the topic and takes pleasure in learning the material. Another student may chose to complete the same assignment to avoid a failing grade or because failure to complete the assignment would jeopardize his eligibility on the swim team. Although both students technically "choose" to complete the assignment, the degree of choice clearly is not the same.

According to Deci and Ryan, the distinction between autonomous and controlled actions is an important one because the degree of perceived choice determines one's behavioral response within a particular context. To be autonomous, a behavior must be both chosen without pressure and self-determined. In contrast, a controlled behavior may be chosen, but it will never be self-determined. As the example provided above illustrates, the same behavior in two individuals may be autonomous or controlling, depending on each person's understanding of why the behavior is performed and what the internal and external consequences are for performing or not performing the behavior. The subjective perception of why an action takes place is referred to as its **functional significance**. Individuals may attach different functional significance to the same event because "a person's perception of an event is an active construction influenced by all kinds of factors" (Deci & Ryan, 1987, p. 1033).

Control in the Classroom

Deci and Ryan have identified two types of environments: *autonomy supporting* and *controlling*. A growing body of research has investigated some of the factors that promote autonomy and control, as well as their effects on task engagement, persistence, and learning. The most important of these factors are the nature of the to-be-learned materials, task constraints, teacher expectations, student expectations, evaluation, and rewards. We examine in the following sections how each of these factors affects intrinsic motivation and a variety of other behavioral measures.

Materials.   One of the most important motivational characteristics of materials is their difficulty. Materials that are too difficult for students promote a controlling environment, reduce intrinsic motivation, and promote resistance to the task in many students. Materials may be difficult for several reasons, including their grammatical complexity and their relative familiarity. Information that students know little about typically will require more time and effort to learn and will be more difficult to remember due to lack of existing background knowledge.

Another important dimension is the interestingness of materials. Research suggests that students find it easier to learn and remember more when they are interested in what they are studying. This is true especially of children and adolescents (Schiefele, 1991). One reason is that interesting materials may increase intrinsic motivation to learn. A second reason is that interesting materials are more likely than uninteresting materials to be familiar to students. Not all interesting materials improve learning, however. Garner, Gillingham, and White (1989), for example, found that *seductive details* (information that was highly interesting but unrelated to the main topic of the story) interfered with learning main ideas. Wade, Schraw, Buxton, and Hayes (1993) reported that seductive details attract a great deal of readers' attention that would be spent more profitably on nonseductive main ideas.

Surprisingly, several recent studies suggest that individuals may regulate how much interest they have in materials. Sansone, Weir, Harpster, and Morgan (1992), for example, found that college students conceptually redefined boring tasks (e.g., copying information in different typefaces) that were viewed as important to complete. Whether younger students spontaneously adopt strategies to make boring tasks more exciting and intrinsically rewarding remains to be seen. In a study by Schraw and Dennison (1994), students read a story from one of two assigned perspectives. Information relevant to the assigned perspective, but not the other unassigned perspective, was judged as more interesting and was remembered better.

In general, materials are most apt to promote autonomy and to be remembered when they are student selected or generated, of moderate difficulty, personally interesting, and familiar. Research also has shown that relating newly learned material to real-life experiences increases interest in that material, facilitates learning, and promotes autonomy.

Tasks.   The nature of the task affects whether individuals perceive it to be autonomy producing or controlling. One obvious constraint frequently overlooked is whether the purpose of the task is clearly understood. A study by L. Anderson (1981) suggests that low-achieving elementary-age children often do not understand the purpose of a task. Although higher-achieving students within the same age group have a better understanding of the immediate purpose, they lack broader knowledge of the task, such as what skills the task will help them develop and how successful performance of the task is related to performance outside school.

Another factor is the task's difficulty. Tasks of moderate difficulty appear to be the most challenging and satisfying for students. For this reason, accelerating the difficulty of a task to keep abreast of student development has a beneficial effect on learning and motivation. Nonaccelerated tasks have been shown to promote within-class performance comparisons that, in turn, adversely affect intrinsic motivation.

One problem that teachers often face, however, is how to increase task difficulty in a heterogeneous group. Stipek (1993) describes several strategies for meeting this challenge. One strategy is to divide a class into smaller groups based on course achievement or task expertise. A second strategy is to use individual mastery programs in which students work at a pace comfortable for them until each has mastered the core material included in a unit. Learning centers where students work individually or in small groups provide good examples. A third strategy is that teachers may use peer tutors (including parent and volunteer aides) from either the same class or other classrooms. Research reveals that peer tutoring leads to higher motivation and learning in both tutors and tutorees.

The pace and variability of tasks is important as well. Tasks that require active student participation tend to increase intrinsic motivation and learning. Question-asking activities before, during, and after class discussions are one avenue for involving students. Similarly, encouraging students to use deeper, more elaborative strategies, such as those described in Chapter 4, leads to more active learning.

Varying the type of tasks that students are exposed to increases interest and learning. Tasks that require students to engage in problem solving, to consider unusual applications, or to think divergently about material not only encourage more active processing but also give students autonomy by allowing them to self-regulate their goals and strategy use.

Finally, research suggests that responses to different types of classroom tasks may depend on expectations established prior to beginning the task. Sansone, Sachau, and Weir (1989) found that students responded more favorably to instruction when it matched students' perceived academic goals. In one study, Sansone et al. (1989) emphasized either skill acquisition or fantasy while learning a computer game called Zork. Students in the skill-acquisition condition responded more favorably to instruction intended to facilitate skill acquisition, whereas the reverse was true of the fantasy condition. These findings suggest that responses to a learning task, as well as receptivity to instruction, depend, in part, on student- and teacher-imposed expectations.

Teacher Expectations.   Teachers create either an autonomy-producing or controlling environment in the classroom by their actions and responses to students. A number of studies have revealed some of the ways teachers intentionally or unintentionally affect student motivation. Providing enjoyable and challenging tasks, making favorable attributional responses that emphasize the role of effort and strategies while minimizing the role of ability, and evaluating in a nonthreatening manner are all ways that teachers promote intrinsic motivation and autonomy.

Research suggests that it is not so much what a teacher does, but how he or she does it, that matters most to students. For example, different "lesson-framing statements" can promote either an autonomous or a controlling environment. Statements that emphasize performance aspects of the task, such as, "I want you to learn this material so that you will do well on the test," are more apt to decrease intrinsic motivation, compared with statements that emphasize learning aspects of the task, such as, "Reading this passage will really help you understand the concept better."

Grolnick and Ryan (1987) studied different lesson-framing statements. Students in the controlling condition were told that they would take a test after reading a passage and that they were expected to do well on it. Other students read the same passage after being told to read however they wanted to. Students in the controlling group reported greater interest in the passage and outperformed the noncontrolling group on a measure of conceptual learning. These effects also were observed one week later.

In another study, Flink, Boggiano, and Barrett (1990) investigated the effect of teacher pressure on student performance. Teachers were either pressured to maximize student performance or encouraged to teach in a style comfortable to them. Students of pressured teachers also were more pressured, compared with students taught by nonpressured teachers. The nonpressured students outperformed their pressured counterparts. In addition, pressured teachers made fewer personal disclosures and laughed less.

Another way teachers promote autonomy or control in the classroom is by the type of feedback they provide to students. **Performance-oriented** feedback emphasizes how well a student has performed in relation to other students. **Information-oriented** feedback emphasizes how performance can be improved. A number of studies indicate that informational feedback leads to greater intrinsic motivation, task engagement, and persistence than performance feedback. Written informational feedback has been found to be especially effective.

In addition, teachers elicit very different student responses based on their expectations. Teachers form expectations based on a number of factors, including in-class performance and behavior, information provided by other teachers, and contact with siblings. In general, the more controlling a teacher's expectations, the more likely it is that students will have low intrinsic motivation. Ironically, performance expectations communicated to students in a controlling manner tend to lower student performance, rather than to improve it (cf. Flink et al., 1990).

Good and Brophy (1986) provide a useful framework for understanding teacher expectations. *Proactive* teachers do not allow their expectations to interfere with student interactions. Instead, they communicate beliefs and expectations openly, provide opportunities to all students, incorporate accelerated tasks, and offer genuine praise. *Reactive* teachers, however, are more likely to act on erroneous beliefs about students and to impose controlling expectations. Research surprisingly indicates that proactive teachers set performance standards that are as high or higher than those of reactive teachers even though they provide students with more choices and options for achieving those standards.

Recently, Jussim (1989) and Jussim and Eccles (1992) asked whether teachers' expectations cause students to behave in a manner consistent with those expectations. Contrary to many earlier studies (e.g., Rosenthal & Jacobson, 1968), Jussim found that teachers' expectations tended to be quite accurate and showed little evidence of creating a "self-fulfilling prophecy." Of course, this does not mitigate the effect of some teachers' controlling behaviors and expectations. Jussim and Eccles (1992), for instance, reported that teachers' expectations were unrelated to standardized test performance but were related to systematic bias in the grades they gave to students. Thus, it appears that expectations may affect teachers' views of students and influence students' motivation negatively by controlling expectations. This does not mean, however, that a teacher's expectations actually cause a student to act in accord with those expectations.

Last, teachers' expectations are shaped, in part, by ability and gender variables. Oakes (1990) reported that teachers of low-ability classes put less emphasis on basic concepts, complex problem-solving skills, and preparation for future course work in the same area. In contrast, teachers of high-ability classes attempted to provide students with more in-class control and greater autonomy. Similarly, Kimball (1989) reported that females receive less teacher contact in middle school and high school settings despite no differences in the number of student-initiated interactions. Females also received less praise and more criticism than males.

Student Expectations.   Students create their own autonomous and controlling environments by the expectations they hold for themselves. Bandura (1993) identified two ways that beliefs promote autonomy. One way concerns the strength of personal self-efficacy. As efficacy increases, individuals feel a greater sense of control, which leads to less anxiety, greater persistence, more task-related effort, and better use of feedback. A second way pertains to the modifiability of the environment. Individuals with low self-efficacy are more likely to view their environment (as well as personal traits) as fixed, rather than as changeable. This belief has been associated with a greater sense of futility, lower aspirations, and less ingenuity.

Other researchers have distinguished between a desire for control and perceived control. Desire for control among older students is related to increased effort, challenge seeking, persistence, and positive attributional response patterns, such as attributing success to effort, rather than to luck (Burger, 1985). Perceived control has been shown to be positively related to academic achievement. Skinner, Wellborn, and Connell (1990) found that beliefs of elementary school students were related to task engagement and grades. One type of belief pertained to *capacity*—that is, whether the student has the resources to accomplish a challenging goal. A second type of belief pertained to *control*—that is, whether the student could control his or her own academic progress. Skinner et al. reported that both capacity and control beliefs were significantly related to engagement and grades. In addition, teacher ratings of students' task engagement were significantly related to students' grades.

Boggiano, Main, and Katz (1988) investigated whether children's perceptions of academic control were related to academic competence and intrinsic interest. As predicted, children with a greater sense of personal control in the classroom reported more intrinsic interest in school activities, more academic competence, and a greater preference for challenge. These findings closely mirror those reported by other researchers (see Chapter 6 in Stipek, 1993, for a recent review).

A number of classroom factors increase intrinsic motivation as well. One factor is providing students with a choice of materials and in-class tasks. Students allowed to choose relevant and pleasurable tasks usually select more challenging tasks and engage in them for longer periods of time. Setting personal learning goals also has a positive effect on motivation and learning. Studies show that **proximal goals** (short-term goals that can be achieved within several learning sessions) increase intrinsic motivation, provide more feedback, and increase feelings of competence and personal control, compared with **distal goals** (long-term goals that require a great deal of time and effort to achieve).

Students also feel a greater sense of control when they are active participants in learning and classroom management. Teachers who allow students to set rules and to choose appropriate consequences for violating those rules experience fewer behavioral problems. Similarly, when students generate their own materials, select learning strategies they feel most comfortable with, and ask questions of other students and teachers, they are more likely to persist and to report greater interest in a task.

Evaluation.   One area of academic life that imposes a strong perception of control is testing and evaluation. Not all types of evaluation elicit the same reactions in students, however. **Norm-referenced evaluation** (students compete against other students) often reduces intrinsic motivation for average and low-achieving students. In contrast, **criterion-referenced evaluation** (students compete against a predetermined standard) may increase intrinsic motivation (Stipek, 1993). Achieving a preestablished standard is especially motivating when the standard is related to the student's personal goals, signifies improvement, and is reached through effort, rather than through normatively high ability. Along these lines, Covington and Omelich (1984) found that college students perceive criterion-referenced evaluation as fairer and better able to detect student effort.

Research further indicates that written evaluation serves a very useful function and frequently increases intrinsic motivation and performance. Comments that provide *formative* and/or *diagnostic* information help students identify the source of their errors, the nature of the errors, and how to correct them in subsequent assignments. In contrast, controlling feedback, such as negative remarks, excessive amount of red ink, or worst of all, a poor grade without any comments, unequivocally reduces intrinsic motivation, task engagement, and persistence.

Another aspect of evaluation that strongly affects motivation is how teachers deal with errors. In a performance-oriented class, errors reduce motivation. Emphasizing the informational value of errors through written feedback or conferences, however, increases intrinsic motivation. A number of studies indicate that errors need not undermine performance, provided that teachers believe errors are potentially useful (Poplin, 1988). Using errors to evaluate the "process," rather than the "product," components of performance is helpful. Moreover, praising correction of errors frequently increases intrinsic motivation because it rewards student effort. One helpful rule of thumb for increasing intrinsic motivation is to allow students, whenever possible, to redo work that contains errors.

In addition, teachers should consider the relative merits of private versus public evaluation. Most motivation theorists do not advocate public evaluation because it orients students to normatively high performance, rather than to improvement, and typically benefits only the top 15 percent to 20 percent of students. If public evaluation is used, teachers must ensure that all students are capable of competing with other students for high grades.

Private evaluation has a number of important advantages from a motivational perspective. One is that private evaluation does not provide ability cues to other students in the class. A second is that private evaluation is more apt to encourage students to engage in challenging assignments. It also enables students to track their progress actively by using charts and records in journals.

Rewards.   Rewards have been part of classroom life since education began. Unfortunately, from our perspective, the most commonly used type of reward has been for compliant behavior or normatively high performance. Many teachers and parents use rewards on a regular basis to motivate students. Indeed, many school programs use token economies and other sophisticated reward systems to encourage learning and good behavior. Others rely on the first cousin of rewards—some form of threat or punishment.

But how effective are rewards at motivating students and improving performance? Deci and colleagues (Deci & Ryan, 1985, 1987; Deci et al., 1991) have identified two kinds of rewards: **informational** and **controlling**. Rewards that provide useful information or feedback to students generally increase intrinsic motivation and learning, whereas rewards that attempt to shape or control student behavior and performance generally decrease it. Moreover, controlling rewards invariably lead to poorer performance, reduced task engagement, and interest *once they are terminated.*

The potentially deleterious effects of rewards have been observed in a wide variety of settings. Newby (1991) found that first year teachers' use of rewards and threats was negatively correlated with on-task behaviors, whereas confidence-building strategies, such as verbal encouragement, explicit instruction with examples, and favorable comments about mistakes, were positively correlated with the same behaviors. Hennessey and Amabile (1988) found that rewarding children for artistic performance had little immediate effect on the quality of artistic productions. When rewards were curtailed, however, students reported less interest in artistic endeavors and produced lower-quality artistic productions. Similar negative effects were found when students were given strong criticism, received controlling rather than informational feedback, or were forced to compete with other students. In many cases, mere surveillance was sufficient to reduce intrinsic motivation and to impair performance (Deci & Ryan, 1987).

The "reward withdrawal" effect described above seems universal in scope. Rewards decrease intrinsic motivation even though they do *increase* extrinsic motivation when intrinsic motivation is lacking. For this reason, rewards should be used only when individuals are not intrinsically motivated to perform a task. When rewards are used, negative effects are most likely to occur when they are expected, salient, and contingent on engagement, rather than on meeting a criterion-referenced performance standard (Deci & Ryan, 1987). Curiously, providing a reward after the fact, when it is not expected, has few negative effects on motivation and performance. Thus, it is the *anticipation* of the reward, rather than the reward itself, that impairs motivation.

For those who prefer to use limited rewards, the following tips may be helpful. First, use rewards sparingly. Rewards help motivate students, albeit extrinsically, in many tasks they would not engage in otherwise due to indifference or anxiety. Second, make sure all students are capable of meeting the criteria for earning the reward. Third, eliminate rewards once they are no longer needed, while simultaneously modeling positive, intrinsic reasons to engage in tasks (e.g., reading is relaxing and entertaining). Last, avoid threats, deadlines, and other constraints that could be construed as punishments. Often, punishments fail to elicit compliance and may impair performance and reduce intrinsic motivation.

Implications: Fostering Student Autonomy

Research reveals many ways to promote either an autonomy-producing or controlling environment. Deci et al. (1991) and Lepper (1988) are particularly good references on this topic. Below, we summarize some of the main points to consider when trying to promote student autonomy.

1. *Let students make meaningful choices.* The more options students are given, the more likely they will be to engage in, persist in, and enjoy a task. Parents and teachers should provide students with at least some choice regarding the materials, tasks, and kinds of evaluation used in the classroom. Allowing students to help select the tasks they undertake, to establish rules democratically, and to set appropriate consequences for violating rules helps promote better classroom discipline.

2. *Scrutinize teacher/student expectations.* Students often are unaware of teachers' and their own expectations. Taking some time at the beginning of the school year and periodically throughout the year to clarify expectations may be helpful. Low expectations or those that intentionally or unintentionally impose control have been shown to affect the performance of everyone in the classroom in negative ways. Teachers' expectations are especially important because students may form self-expectations based on these messages.

3. *Minimize extrinsic rewards.* Extrinsic rewards should be used thoughtfully and sparingly. Intangible rewards, such as genuine praise and attention, usually have a positive influence on students *provided* they are genuine, are not overused, and are accessible to all students. Tangible rewards, such as money, tokens, gifts, and free time, may reduce intrinsic motivation and interest in tasks while they are being performed and frequently decrease task engagement, persistence, and quality of performance once they are curtailed. Both tangible and intangible rewards, however, can promote task engagement when intrinsic motivation is low.

For these reasons, extrinsic rewards should be used only when students have no other reason to engage in the task. Using rewards as a long-term motivator may be disastrous unless the rewards are continued indefinitely. Using threats, punishment, or surveillance also is ill-advised because these methods rarely accomplish their purpose and may lower intrinsic motivation. In particular, essential academic skills, such as reading, writing, and mathematics, should never be used as punishments (e.g., writing essays after school for being late). Doing so gives students many powerful reasons *not* to be intrinsically motivated in these activities in the future.

One final point: Rewards often can be used effectively without any of the negative consequences described above, provided they are not contingent on some type of performance outcome. Rewards offered spontaneously, when they are not expected, do not reduce intrinsic motivation and performance as a rule.

4. *Incorporate criterion-referenced evaluation.* Evaluation that reduces the amount of direct competition while increasing the amount of informational/cognitive feedback to students usually increases intrinsic motivation and other task engagement variables. In most instances, criterion-referenced evaluation satisfies these constraints more readily than does norm-referenced evaluation. Examples of the former include "mastery learning," in which students work toward a preestablished standard that does not depend on the performance level of other group members, multiple-choice and essay tests that allow students to revise or justify their responses to improve their grade, portfolio assessment, and most forms of ongoing (formative) evaluation.

5. *Provide intrinsically motivating reasons to perform a task.* Providing students with an explicit or implicit rationale for engaging in an activity is a powerful instructional technique. Teachers who read more and model their own intrinsic enjoyment of reading to their students usually have students who read more inside and outside of class. Similarly, explicitly highlighting some of the positive aspects of reading may help offset feelings of low self-efficacy or anxiety in some students.

SUMMARY

This chapter described three frameworks for understanding self-beliefs and how they can affect self-determination in the classroom. Bandura's learning theory emphasizes the reciprocal relationship among self-beliefs, performance, and environmental feedback. We focused in detail on one type of belief—self-efficacy—which is related to task engagement and academic achievement. Self-efficacy is domain specific and subject to change through modeling, feedback, and self-statements.

Whereas self-efficacy beliefs are judgments about future events, attributions are judgments of past events. Attributions are causal explanations of our success and failure experiences in the classroom. Attributions vary along three dimensions: locus of control, stability, and controllability. Each dimension is associated with a particular type of emotional response. Research indicates that students' attributional patterns strongly affect their task engagement, persistence, and achievement. Undesirable attributional patterns can be changed with the help of attributional retraining programs.

We also considered the role of student autonomy in the classroom and how intrinsic motivation promotes feelings of autonomy. Students who feel a sense of control are more likely to seek challenge, to persist at difficult tasks, and to perform better than teacher-controlled students. Teachers who experience a sense of control also interact with students more favorably. A number of factors were discussed that affect students' sense of control, including classroom materials, task constraints, teacher and student expectations, evaluation strategies, and the use of rewards. Providing choices to students is an important means for increasing feelings of control and intrinsic motivation. Using extrinsic rewards, such as money or praise, generally decreases intrinsic motivation.

SUGGESTED READINGS

Bandura, A. (1993). Perceived self-efficacy in cognitive development and functioning. *Educational Psychologist, 28,* 117–148.

This review provides an up-to-date summary of self-efficacy theory.

Deci, E. L., Vallerand, R. J., Pelletier, L. G., & Ryan, R. M. (1991). Motivation and education: The self-determination perspective. *Educational Psychologist, 26,* 325–346.

This review provides a thorough discussion of intrinsic and extrinsic motivation.

Graham, S. (1991). A review of attribution theory in achievement contexts. *Educational Psychology Review, 3,* 5–39.

Graham provides a concise review of attribution theory, with a special emphasis on school achievement.

CHAPTER 7

Beliefs About Intelligence and Knowledge

This chapter examines the role that beliefs about intelligence and knowledge play in thinking and problem solving. Often, we are unaware that we hold these beliefs even though they predispose us to respond or think in a certain way. Research suggests that individuals who reflect on their beliefs are more apt to change them.

The beliefs we hold, whether they are implicit or explicit, affect our behavior in many ways. In Chapter 6, we found that individuals with high self-efficacy are more willing to try a difficult task. By the same token, people who hold certain beliefs about the changeability of intelligence are more likely to persist when faced with difficulty, and those who view knowledge as certain only within a particular context are more likely to engage in skilled reasoning than those who view knowledge as absolutely certain. Before we discuss beliefs about intelligence and knowledge in more detail, let's first look at implicit beliefs.

UNDERSTANDING IMPLICIT BELIEFS

What makes us think and act the way we do? At some point, most of us find our-selves voicing opinions we do not agree with when we reflect on them at a later time. Sometimes, we realize quite unexpectedly that we are not sure what we believe about a controversial issue; at other times, we may articulate strong beliefs about important social topics without having any conscious awareness of where these beliefs came from or why we believe them. Researchers are beginning to understand that much of our behavior is shaped by unconscious beliefs about key aspects of learning, such as intelligence and knowledge. Beliefs of this type often are referred to as **implicit beliefs** because they represent unconscious, personal beliefs about the world that evolve slowly over time (see Chapter 3 for a discussion of implicit mem-ory). No one is certain how or when these beliefs begin to develop. There is consid-erable agreement, however, that implicit beliefs have a very powerful effect on the way we view ourselves as learners and how we operate in the classroom.

Implicit beliefs often give rise to an **implicit theory**—that is, a set of *tacit* assumptions about how some phenomenon works. To illustrate, let's compare two typical students in a beginning algebra class. Imagine that both are talking after a dif-ficult test and that Akira says, "It doesn't surprise me that I'm no good in math. Nobody in my family was good at it either!" Presumably, Akira believes (at least implicitly) that success in a math class is due, in large part, to genetic inheritance; otherwise his family's math ability should have nothing to do with his own success or failure. Now, compare Akira with Alonzo, who responds, "At first I really struggled in this class, but then I went to the math lab and they really helped me improve!" Alonzo appears to believe that his success in math class is due less to ability than to effort. Of equal importance, Alonzo implicitly endorses the view that his ability to learn mathematics is changeable.

On the basis of this example, Alonzo seems to hold a very different view about his ability than does Akira about his. Their beliefs about their abilities form the basis of "theories of intelligence." These theories almost certainly are implicit. If Akira and Alonzo were asked to state their "theories of intelligence," they would find it difficult to do so (Sternberg, 1986). Moreover, the theory each actually describes may be at odds with the implicit beliefs echoed in their conversation.

Although at first glance the study of implicit theories may appear to have little to do with effective learning and teaching, a good argument can be made that understand-ing and clarifying students' implicit theories may be just as important as providing basic content knowledge or strategy instruction. One reason is that research has shown that students with differing implicit beliefs differ in their willingness to use strategies while learning (Ames & Archer, 1988). Another reason is that students with differing implicit beliefs appear to think and reason in very different ways, some of which are far more conducive to effective learning (Kitchener & King, 1981; Ryan, 1984).

At this point, you may be asking yourself what kinds of implicit theories you have and how they affect your learning. The answer to this question is that all of us have many implicit beliefs, or in some cases explicit beliefs, about all kinds of everyday intellectual phenomena. Consider your attitudes about intelligence. What is intelligence? Do you believe that your intellectual aptitude is fixed and that no amount of effort, strategy use, or metacognitive awareness will improve it, or do you believe, as does Sternberg (1986), that intelligence is changeable by improving the kind of intellectual skills that are necessary for classroom success?

Now, consider your views on creativity. Are some people born creative, whereas others are not? Is creativity teachable and, if so, to whom? Next, consider knowledge. Is there an ultimate, knowable truth in the universe that humans eventually will discover? Is knowledge relative? Does "truth" exist, and, if it does, is it fixed and certain?

These examples illustrate only too well the scope and importance of implicit beliefs on thinking and learning. The chances are good that you found these questions difficult to answer. The chances also are good that you have spent little time trying to reach definitive answers to these questions. Nevertheless, the "hidden assumptions" that underlie our thinking and behavior exert a very powerful influence. Understanding implicit beliefs is an important first step in becoming self-regulated. Let's begin by examining some specific implicit beliefs in greater detail.

BELIEFS ABOUT INTELLIGENCE

Dweck and Leggett (1988) have proposed a highly regarded social-cognitive model of motivation based, in large part, on the kinds of implicit theories people hold about intelligence. Two types of implicit theories are proposed in their framework. The first is referred to as an **incremental theory**, owing to the assumption that intelligence is changeable and improves incrementally. In contrast, individuals holding an **entity theory** of intelligence tend to assume that intelligence is fixed and unchangeable. According to Dweck and Leggett, most individuals can be characterized by one of these basic belief orientations. Individuals holding incremental and entity theories view the world in very different ways that affect how they react to challenging situations.

One interesting aspect of the Dweck and Leggett model is that incremental and entity views of intelligence seem to be independent of a person's true intellectual ability. Several studies support this view, indicating that high-ability students are no more likely to adopt incremental theories than those with lower ability (Miller, Behrens, Greene, & Newman, 1993; Schraw, Horn, Thorndike-Christ, & Bruning, 1994). This finding holds promise for educators because it suggests that students' beliefs about intelligence need not be compromised on the basis of their true ability. Even those who struggle in the classroom can change the way they think about intelligence, which, in turn, may have a positive effect on their classroom achievement.

Holding either incremental or entity views also appears to have important consequences for personal academic goals. Incremental beliefs give rise to the development of **learning goals** (also commonly referred to as **mastery goals**), in which individuals seek to *improve* their competence. Entity beliefs give rise to **performance**

goals, in which individuals seek to *prove* their competence. Research by Elliott and Dweck (1988) and Ames and Archer (1988) found that children and adolescents characterized by learning goals persist longer in the face of task difficulty; are more likely to attribute success to internal, controllable causes, such as strategy use and effort; and are characterized by an overriding concern for personal mastery. Children characterized by learning goals also show a preference for challenge and risk taking (Ames, 1992) and spend more time on-task (Butler, 1987). In contrast, individuals with performance goals are more apt to become frustrated and defensive when confronted with a challenging task; tend to attribute failure to external, uncontrollable causes, such as luck or teachers, or to internal, uncontrollable causes, such as lack of ability; and show an undue concern for demonstrating normatively high performance (Blumenfeld, 1992; Dweck, 1986).

Table 7-1 presents some of the important characteristics of individuals with learning and performance goals. Individuals with learning orientations tend to be most interested in academic improvement and, as a consequence, may be more apt to focus on the *process,* rather than on the *products,* of learning. These students enjoy learning for its own sake and feel comfortable asking for help when they do not understand something. Another important characteristic of learning-oriented students is that they enjoy intellectual challenge and usually will work harder when they encounter challenging materials. When students with learning goals fail a quiz, they correctly recognize that there are many reasons for failure and that most of these reasons are changeable. They do not tend to attribute failure to low ability, as do students with strong performance goals. This characteristic, more than any other, may give learning-oriented students a distinct advantage because academic challenge or even failure may increase their motivation.

Students with learning goals differ from those with performance goals in several other important ways. One difference is that learning-oriented students are more likely to adopt more complex strategies once they begin to fail at a task, whereas performance-oriented students resort to inappropriate strategies (Diener & Dweck, 1978). A second difference is that individuals characterized by a learning orientation are more apt to engage in adaptive behaviors, such as persistence, focusing atten-

Table 7-1
Characteristics of Learning- and Performance-Oriented Students (From Dweck, C. S., & Leggett, E. S. A social-cognitive approach to motivation and personality. *Psychological Review, 95,* 256–273. Copyright 1988 by the American Psychological Association. Adapted by permission.)

Learning Orientation	Performance Orientation
Improving competence	Proving competence
Seeks challenge	Avoids challenge
Persists	Quits
Attributes success to effort	Attributes success to ability
Positive response to failure	Negative response to failure
Uses strategies effectively	Uses inappropriate strategies
Self-regulated	Helpless

tion, and appropriate help seeking. Miller et al. (1993) found that college students characterized by a strong learning orientation were significantly more likely to persist when confronting difficult material in an introductory statistics class. One explanation of this finding is that students with learning orientations maintain a higher sense of self-efficacy while engaged in a difficult task (Bandura, 1993).

In contrast, performance-oriented students often adopt a maladaptive response pattern once they experience failure. One type of maladaptive response occurs when students assume they do not have the ability to succeed and refuse to persist at a difficult task once they begin to fail. A second maladaptive response occurs when performance-oriented students become verbally defensive after experiencing difficulty on a task: These students may change the focus of conversation unexpectedly and describe in detail their competence at skills totally unrelated to the task at hand. For example, after failing a math task, a performance-oriented student may boast about her skill at singing. A third behavior occurs when individuals refuse to engage in a task on the assumption that they will fail. In some cases, **learned helplessness** is a defense against perceived incompetence (Dweck, 1975).

In general, individuals with performance orientations often seem overly concerned with doing better than others and may show far greater concern for the grade they receive than for the amount of information they learn. These students see their success or failure as the direct consequence of their intellectual ability yet do not see their ability as controllable. Performance-oriented students do not enjoy challenge to nearly the same degree as their mastery counterparts. For this reason, they may be less likely to show interest in topics they know little about or may fail at. They also may be less willing to try new strategies or to investigate novel solutions to a problem. One particular concern is that performance-oriented students are more likely to quit when faced with a difficult task.

As you might expect, students with learning and performance goals also differ noticeably in the types of attributions they make for academic success and failure. The results of a correlational study conducted by Ames and Archer (1988) are presented in Table 7-2. In this study, approximately 200 middle school and high school students were classified according to their goal orientations. Students with learning and performance orientations were compared on a number of dimensions, including self-reported strategy use, responses to task challenge, and attributions for classroom success and failure. The results of the Ames and Archer study suggest some important and startling differences, which are summarized in Table 7-2. According to this study, students with learning goals tend to attribute their success in the classroom to effort, strategy use, and teachers.

Learning-oriented students also appear to have better relationships with teachers, compared with performance-oriented students. In fact, of all the variables considered in the Ames and Archer study, learning-oriented students considered teachers to be of greater importance to academic success than ability, effort, or strategy use! Performance-oriented students, however, saw no relationship between teacher assistance and academic success. One important consequence of these differences is that learning-oriented students may be more inclined to ask for help from teachers or other students when they begin to struggle.

Table 7-2

Attributions for Classroom Success and Failure for Students with Learning and Performance Orientations. (Numbers in parentheses indicate statistically significant correlations.)(From Ames, C., & Archer, J. Achievement in the classroom: Student learning strategies and motivational processes. *Journal of Educational Psychology, 80,* 260–267. Copyright 1988 by the American Psychological Association. Adapted by permission.)

	Learning Orientation	Performance Orientation
Reasons for success	Effort (.37) Strategy use (.22) Teacher assistance (.47)	Effort (.14) Strategy use (.24)
Reasons for failure	Teachers (–.29)	Low ability (.21) Task difficulty (.29) Lack of strategy use (.16)

A comparison of performance-oriented students reveals a rather different picture. Although these students appropriately attribute classroom success to effort and strategy use, they also view failure as the consequence of low ability, task difficulty, and poor teacher-student interactions. This pattern of attributions captures the essence of performance goals—the belief that success and failure in the classroom depend, in large part, on one's ability, rather than effort, strategy use, or teachers. Ironically, students with performance goals are more apt to quit when faced with a difficult task, on the assumption they lack the ability needed to succeed even though they do not differ in ability, compared with students with learning goals.

Constraints on Classroom Behaviors

One might ask at this point what classroom factors, if any, are known to positively affect students' goal orientations. The work of Dweck and Leggett (1988) and Ames and Archer (1988) suggest two important components: situational factors, such as classroom climate or home environment, and dispositional factors, such as basic personality makeup. Unfortunately, little is known about the relative contribution of each of these factors although many researchers working in this area believe that the type of goal orientation a student adopts depends on a complex interaction between the two (Cain & Dweck, 1989). The work of Dweck and colleagues generally places a greater emphasis on dispositional factors that the student brings to the classroom. Ames and Archer (1988), however, have argued that learning and performance orientations are largely the result of classroom structure. Classes that place normatively high emphasis on ability and performance within the classroom peer group appear to promote a performance orientation among the majority of students, whereas classes that place high value on improvement, strategy use, persistence in the face of difficulty, and effort may promote learning goals even among students who are otherwise rather performative. From a practical viewpoint, all theorists agree that goal orientations are changeable, given careful consideration on the part of the teacher and an awareness by students of the consequences of adhering to different types of goals.

Clearly, educators should think carefully about the kind of environment they create in their classrooms because situational factors are known to affect interest and motivation (Schiefele, 1991). Careful consideration should be given also to the role of ability, effort, and strategy use in successful learning. Emphasizing daily academic improvement while simultaneously de-emphasizing the importance of ability are central to establishing a learning-oriented environment. The results of Sansone et al. (1989) also suggest that instruction is most effective when skill acquisition is emphasized from the onset.

Is Intelligence Changeable?

The work of Dweck and Leggett (1988) raises a number of interesting questions about the controllability of such traits as intelligence and personality. Attributional theorists, such as Weiner (1986) and Graham (1991), suggest that intelligence is defined as an internal, stable, and uncontrollable trait, a view quite consistent with the beliefs of entity theorists (see Chapter 6). In contrast, incremental theorists believe that their intellectual ability is changeable and therefore controllable.

The idea that one's intelligence is controllable may seem foreign to some readers. Whether intelligence is controllable and, if it is, to what extent it can be changed remains a hotly debated topic. Some experts working in the area of human intelligence support the entity view (Jensen, 1992); others, such as Robert Sternberg (1986), have proposed theories consistent with an incremental theory. In Sternberg's view, individuals can improve their intellectual performance in any given situation by adapting to the demands of the situation as strategically as possible.

Ultimately, whether intelligence is fixed or changeable depends on how one defines intelligence. If *intelligence* means "the ability to adapt successfully to an environment," then surely it is changeable. In Chapter 4, for instance, we described a number of helpful learning strategies that are known to improve learning by helping individuals use their cognitive resources more efficiently. In Chapter 6, we described the many ways that academic performance and reasoning ability are improved by a concomitant change in self-efficacy (see Bandura, 1993, for a further discussion of changeable ability). Our own view is that successful learning depends far more on how one uses one's resources than on how many resources one has. Although it is unknown whether the amount of resources one has can be changed, it is well known that how effectively one uses them can be changed quite dramatically.

Guidelines for Fostering Adaptive Goals

Dweck and Leggett's (1988) theory suggests that individuals with learning orientations are more likely to feel comfortable and succeed in an academic setting. This suggestion raises the question of how teachers and parents can create an environment conducive to the development of learning goals. We offer these suggestions.

1. *Promote the view that intellectual development is controllable.* The basic distinction made in Dweck and Leggett's framework is between individuals who believe intelligence is fixed or changeable. Those who believe it is changeable report more satisfaction with school and persist longer on a difficult task without succumbing to frustration. Promoting the view that intellectual performance is controllable may lead to the kind of adaptive behaviors described above.

2. *Reward effort and improvement while de-emphasizing native ability.* Students clearly differ in ability. Basing class grades or recognition on ability, however, may promote a performance orientation, especially if carried to an extreme. In contrast, rewarding effort and improvement emphasizes the incremental nature of learning.

3. *Emphasize the process, rather than the products, of learning.* Focusing on the *process* of learning highlights its incremental nature, whereas focusing on the *products* emphasizes the outcome of that process. Research suggests that feedback acquired about the process of learning is especially important to learners.

4. *Stress that mistakes are a normal (and healthy) part of learning.* Everyone makes mistakes when learning a new skill. How teachers respond to these mistakes sends a powerful message to students. When mistakes are viewed positively, receive corrective attention, and are used to provide feedback to students, students learn more than when mistakes are viewed in a negative light (Poplin, 1988). Using mistakes constructively also highlights the incremental nature of learning, a view consistent with a learning orientation.

5. *Encourage individual, rather than group, evaluative standards.* Much of the evaluation that occurs in education, especially among high school and college students, is *norm referenced* (each student's performance is compared with the group's average performance). Group-based grading may lead to the adoption of a performance orientation, given that each student is compared directly with the group norm. In contrast, encouraging individual standards (e.g., portfolio evaluation) is more likely to promote the development of a learning orientation.

BELIEFS ABOUT KNOWLEDGE

Our discussion thus far has focused on the classroom consequences of implicit beliefs about intelligence. Researchers also have discovered that students' beliefs about the *nature of knowledge* have important consequences on academic performance and critical thinking. Historically, beliefs about the origin and nature of knowledge, or **epistemological beliefs**, have been of interest since the Greek philosophers. Recent studies of epistemological beliefs have attempted to isolate more precisely the consequences of holding particular beliefs. This research has investigated the developmental sequence individuals pass through on their way to mature reasoning about knowledge.

One of the earliest educators to investigate this phenomenon was Perry (1970), who proposed a model in which students pass through several distinct, ordered stages in the development of beliefs about knowledge. In the early stages, students adopt what Perry refers to as a *dualist* perspective, in which knowledge is viewed as either right or wrong. Students in this stage tend to view knowledge as being absolute, universally certain, and accessible only to authorities. Individuals at this level of reasoning may assume, for example, that only prominent theologians have a true understanding of life's basic truths. Rather than question this authority, dualists accept these truths on the assumption that understanding such matters is beyond their intellectual grasp and must be accepted on faith. In later stages, however, students progress beyond the dualist mode of thinking to a more relativist stage, in which knowledge is viewed as uncertain and relative. *Relativists* realize that beliefs about knowledge must be evaluated on a personal basis by using the best available evidence.

Ryan (1984) provided an experimental test of Perry's basic framework and concluded that relativists not only hold different beliefs from dualists but also approach learning in a more sophisticated way. To test the dualist-relativist distinction, Ryan first grouped college students into the two categories described above. Next, he asked them to describe the strategies they used to monitor their comprehension while reading. Finally, he tracked students through a semester-long psychology class and recorded their final grades.

The results of this study suggest a number of important findings. First, dualists do not do as well as relativists when final grades are considered. An analysis of comprehension-monitoring standards suggests why. Dualists tend to search for fact-oriented information while studying, whereas relativists tend to search for context-oriented information. Dualists generally rely on remembering information reported explicitly in the text, whereas relativists are more likely to construct a meaning from the text, to paraphrase, or to create an overall framework that summarizes the main ideas presented in the chapter. Surprisingly, these differences were found even when academic aptitude (Scholastic Aptitude Test scores) and academic experience were taken into consideration. These latter findings suggest that the performance differences observed between dualists and relativists are due to beliefs about knowledge and how these beliefs affect study strategies.

Responses to Ryan's work have been mixed, however. Schommer (1990) has argued that Ryan's dichotomous view is too simple to describe accurately the complexity of epistemological beliefs. To test this view, Schommer developed a self-report inventory in which students responded to sixty-two true-false questions on their beliefs about the nature of knowledge. Three of the questions included in this instrument are "Truth is unchanging," "Scientists can ultimately get to the truth," and "Successful students learn things quickly."

Schommer's study suggests that people hold extremely complex beliefs about knowledge that vary across four separate dimensions. The first dimension, *simple knowledge,* refers to the belief that knowledge is discrete and unambiguous. Students who score high on this dimension believe that learning is equivalent to accumulating a vast amount of factual knowledge in an encyclopedic fashion. Schommer's second dimension, *certain knowledge,* pertains to the belief that knowledge is constant: Once something is believed to be true, it remains true forever. The third dimension is *fixed ability*—that is, the belief that one's ability to learn is inborn and cannot be improved through either effort or strategy use. Like Dweck and Leggett's entity theorists, these individuals may believe that intelligence is fixed and personally uncontrollable. The final dimension, *quick learning,* refers to the belief that learning occurs quickly or not at all. Students scoring high on this dimension assume (inappropriately) that limited failure is tantamount to permanent failure. If a problem cannot be solved within ten minutes, for example, it will never be solved.

Schommer's work is unique in that it is one of the first studies to examine closely the underlying complexity of beliefs about knowledge. But Schommer's research did not stop there. After identifying the four component beliefs described above, she next investigated their relationship to socioeconomic variables and information-processing skills. One of the more interesting findings is that the amount of higher education students receive is inversely related to their belief in certain knowledge. All things being equal, the longer students attend college, the more likely they are to believe that knowledge is tentative and subject to personal interpretation. One important implication of this finding is that better-educated people may be more willing to adopt a constructivist approach to learning because believing that knowledge is certain should rarely lead one to question the legitimacy of that knowledge. This finding also suggests that encouraging individuals to further their education beyond high school may have a profound effect on their beliefs about knowledge.

Another interesting finding is that females are more likely to believe that learning is gradual, rather than quick. This belief may lead females to stick with a difficult-to-learn subject longer than males and to feel less frustrated when an answer does not occur immediately. Quick learning was related as well to a number of other socioeconomic indicators: the student's year in school, the father's educational level, and how much independent discussion was allowed at home. Those with less education were more apt to believe that acquiring new knowledge occurs in an all-or-nothing fashion; those with more college experience tended to view knowledge as tentative. Simple knowledge was related to the strictness of the home environment: Stricter standards led to the belief that knowledge is unambiguous, whereas greater tolerance led to the belief that knowledge is complex and subject to interpretation. Encouragement toward independence in the family structure also had positive effects on beliefs about simple knowledge and quick learning.

An analysis of the relationship between beliefs about knowledge and information-processing strategies showed that quick learning predicted oversimplified conclusions when students were asked to provide a written conclusion to a chapter on theories of aggression. Prior knowledge also was related to the type of conclusions students drew, in that more knowledge about the topic was associated with broader conclusions. A belief in quick learning also led to poorer performance on a summative mastery test of the material, as well as greater overestimation of understanding of the passage.

More recently, Schommer, Crouse, and Rhodes (1992) reported that beliefs in simple knowledge negatively affected complex problem solving. As beliefs in complex, incremental knowledge increased, problem solving improved. Jehng, Johnson, and Anderson (1993) found that epistemological beliefs differ across academic disciplines among college undergraduates and graduate students. Students in "soft" disciplines, such as the humanities, were more likely to believe that knowledge is uncertain than students in a "hard" discipline, such as physics. Compared with undergraduates, graduate students were more likely to believe that knowledge is uncertain and develops incrementally (they did not believe in quick learning).

Kuhn (1991, 1992) found that epistemological beliefs are related to one's ability to argue persuasively. In this study, individuals were classified as *absolutist* (one who believes that knowledge is absolutely right or wrong), *multiplist* (one who believes that knowledge is completely relative), or *evaluative* theorists (one who believes that knowledge, though relative, is constrained by situational factors such as commonly accepted rules) on the basis of their beliefs about the certainty of knowledge. Evaluative theorists were more likely than absolutists to provide legitimate evidence in support of an argument. In addition, compared with absolutists, evaluative theorists generated a greater number of plausible alternative theories and provided better counterarguments.

Elsewhere, Schoenfeld (1983) investigated some of the consequences of quick learning. Schoenfeld reported that even experienced students who were asked to solve math problems gave up after five to ten minutes on the assumption that if they failed to solve the problem during this time, the problem could not be solved. One interesting question raised by this research is whether students who are prone to quit after a brief period are more likely to hold entity theories of learning that predispose them to failure avoidance.

Together, these studies indicate that beliefs about knowledge and the knowing process affect the way one reasons, how long one persists at a difficult task, and perhaps what academic discipline one enters. They also indicate that epistemological beliefs are affected by one's home environment and, in particular, by one's educational level. More education seems to translate into a more relativist viewpoint—a fact that has not escaped the attention of some civic and religious leaders who view universities suspiciously as bastions of "secular humanism" (cf. Moshman, 1981). Ironically, when using objective criteria such as amount and kind of evidence at one's disposal, virtually all studies indicate that relativist thinking leads to better-reasoned conclusions (see Kuhn, 1991, for a comprehensive review).

Reflective Judgment

Another framework for studying beliefs about knowledge and how they affect behavior is that of Kitchener and King (Kitchener, 1983; Kitchener & King, 1981; Kitchener, King, Wood, & Davidson, 1989). The focus of this research is somewhat different from Perry's in that its emphasis is on examining differences between the way people resolve dilemmas, rather than differences in their beliefs per se. In their initial study, Kitchener and King (1981) developed a seven-stage developmental model of **reflective judgment**. Table 7-3 presents the characteristic reasoning processes and assumptions of each of these stages.

Reflective judgment is a term used by Kitchener and King (1981) to refer to one's ability to critically analyze multiple facets of a problem, reach an informed con-

Table 7-3
Stages in Kitchener and King's Reflective Judgment Model. (Adapted from Kitchener, K. S., & King, P. A. [1981]. Reflective judgment: Concepts of justification and their relationship to age and education. *Journal of Applied Developmental Psychology, 2,* 89–116.)

Stage 1: Knowledge is unchanging, absolute, and accessible
- beliefs are based on personal observation
- knowledge exists absolutely and concretely

Stage 2: Knowledge is certain but may not be accessible to everyone
- knowledge is certain
- knowledge is accessible only to authorities

Stage 3: Knowledge is certain, though it may be accessible to anyone
- knowledge exists absolutely
- no rational way to justify beliefs

Stage 4: Knowledge is uncertain and idiosyncratic
- truth varies from person to person
- knowledge is interpreted subjectively

Stage 5: Knowledge is uncertain, though contextually interpretable
- objective knowledge does not exist
- beliefs can be justified by using "rules of inquiry"

Stage 6: Knowledge is relative yet justifiable on the basis of rational arguments
- knowledge is personally constructed
- beliefs are justified by comparing evidence

Stage 7: Knowledge is relative, though some interpretations have greater truth
- knowledge is constructed
- beliefs are justified probabilistically

---

clusion, and justify one's response as systematically as possible. Previous research suggests that reflective judgment depends on a set of epistemological assumptions that develop slowly in a predictable, developmental sequence (Kitchener, 1983; Kitchener & King, 1981; Kitchener et al., 1989). For example, abandoning the belief that knowledge can be known with absolute certainty appears to improve the quality of one's reasoning (Kitchener & Fischer, 1990). A number of other studies reveal that reflective judgment develops throughout early adulthood (Kitchener & King, 1981; Kitchener et al., 1989) and is related to age and education (King, Wood, & Mines, 1990) and critical thinking ability (King et al., 1990) but is independent of measures of cognitive ability, such as verbal fluency (Kitchener et al., 1989).

Kitchener and colleagues (Kitchener & King, 1981; Kitchener et al., 1989) have identified seven developmental stages of reflective judgment that can be distinguished on the basis of three criteria. One criterion is the *certainty* of a knowledge claim (King et al., 1990). Individuals in Stages 1 through 3 of the Kitchener et al. (1989) taxonomy believe that knowledge is certain and permanent even though knowledge may be known to only a select few. Individuals in Stages 4 and 5 view knowledge as almost totally uncertain. Individuals in Stages 6 and 7 view knowledge as context dependent; some things are knowable, at least temporarily, even though one's views on a particular topic may change in light of new information or a different set of evaluative criteria.

A second criterion is *by what process* we acquire knowledge. Individuals in Stages 1, 2, and 3 emphasize the defining role of direct observation or authority figures; that is, knowledge is encoded directly from external sources. Those at Stage 4 rely chiefly on personal, idiosyncratic processes, such as personal opinion. Individuals at higher stages of reflective judgment show an increasing proclivity to rely on objective, consensual processes, such as critical debate and hypothesis testing, that are tempered by personal reflection.

A third criterion is *the type of evidence* used to justify one's views of the world. Individuals at Stage 1 typically view justification as self-evident. Thus, a Stage 1 reasoner may assert that evidence that God exists "is all around us." Those at Stages 2 and 3, in contrast, are apt to cite a specific authority, such as an eminent theologian, book, or expert. Individuals at Stages 4 and 6 tend to rely on idiosyncratic evidence. For these individuals, a belief in God would be justified on the basis of the individual's personal beliefs, whereas those in Stages 5 and 7 rely on consensual forms of evidence, such as laws, scientific facts, and the opinions of a diverse body of experts.

The work of Kitchener and colleagues suggests that two primary mechanisms affect the development of reflective judgment. One mechanism is *experience*. Previous research has found that age, education, and home environment all provide statistically significant prediction of reflective judgment skills (Kitchener & King, 1981). Related research also suggests that reflective judgment may be affected by the type of intellectual discipline one enters (King et al., 1990). A second mechanism is one's *belief system*. In this regard, Kitchener and King (1981, p. 90) state, "Differences in concepts of justification . . . are derived from different assumptions about reality and knowledge." What these assumptions are and how they differ across individuals remain unclear, however. No doubt some are related to epistemological beliefs about the certainty, complexity, and permanence of knowledge. Others may be related to a broader set of beliefs that include assumptions about the role of innate ability (Dweck & Leggett, 1988) and the legitimacy of constructivism in the knowing process (Chandler, Boyes, & Ball, 1990).

Stages in Reflective Judgment

Reflective judgment is assumed to develop in a sequential fashion; that is, individuals progress from Stage 1 to higher levels without skipping stages. This does not mean that each person reaches the highest stages or that two people progress at the same rate. Rather, development of reflective judgment is highly idiosyncratic.

Each stage is characterized by a unique set of assumptions about reasoning. These assumptions pertain to the certainty of knowledge, the processes by which one acquires knowledge, and the kinds of evidence used to evaluate one's claims about knowledge. These criteria are shown in Table 7-4.

Table 7-4

Evaluative Criteria for Each of the Seven Stages of Reflective Judgment. (Source: Dunkle, M. F., Schraw, G., & Bendixen, L. [1993, April]. *The relationship between epistemological beliefs, causal attributions, and reflective judgment.* Paper presented at the Annual Meeting of the American Educational Research Association, Atlanta, GA.)

Level	Permanence	Certainty	Justification of Conclusions
1	Fixed	Absolute; certain.	Personal beliefs that are self-evident. No justification or evidence given.
2	Fixed	Absolute; certain.	Recognized authorities. Direct observation of world.
3	Fixed	Temporarily uncertain.	Authorities or direct observation when knowledge is uncertain.
4	Changes	Permanently uncertain.	Idiosyncratic beliefs.
5	Changes	Permanently uncertain.	Rules of inquiry for a particular context (e.g., societal norms).
6	Changes	Certain in a context.	Evaluating objective evidence via personal criteria.
7	Changes	Certain in a context.	Formalized rules of inquiry (e.g., logic). Evaluation of empirical data.

Individuals in Stage 1 are characterized by the belief that knowledge is certain, absolute, and indistinguishable from one's beliefs. Beliefs are either right or wrong within this framework, but they are never ambiguous. Individuals in this stage are prone to accept apparent truths at face value, without a great deal of scrutiny. Justification of truth or knowledge is not required, owing to the close relationship between knowledge and direct observation. In many ways, Stage 1 thinkers lack the ability to make reflective judgments because they believe that knowledge is predetermined and absolute.

Stage 2 reasoners differ from those in Stage 1 in that they believe knowledge, though assumed to be absolute and predetermined, is limited to authorities and experts. Individuals at this level implicitly live by the motto, "When in doubt, ask an authority." Of course, this approach to resolving complex moral and ethical issues can have disastrous consequences because there is no reason to believe that reflective judgment will improve as long as one believes that only experts are capable of skilled reflective reasoning; that is, excessive faith in "omniscient authorities" may undermine the subsequent development of reflective judgment!

Stage 3 differs from either of the stages described above; these individuals recognize that even authorities may lack answers to difficult dilemmas. In this view of reflective judgment, individuals may come to the initially disconcerting conclusion that no one is capable of ever reaching the truth about a complex issue. Typically, however, the belief that truth ultimately will be identified empirically is still maintained. According to Kitchener and King (1981), beliefs at this level are justified by what feels right to the individual.

Stage 4 represents a dramatic change from the three earlier stages in that knowledge and beliefs now are viewed as fundamentally uncertain. Truth becomes relative within this framework because, as is often the case, different views can be supported or refuted by a variety of incompatible facts. One of the important advantages to this way of thinking is the recognition that what is true for one person will not necessarily be true for another. One of the main liabilities of this stage is that truth and knowledge must be justified on a person-to-person basis; hence, beliefs and assumptions may differ dramatically even between individuals who share otherwise similar worldviews.

Individuals in Stage 5 possess an even greater sense of epistemological uncertainty in that objective knowledge is assumed to be nonexistent. Knowledge within this framework becomes completely relative because the ultimate truth or falsity of an argument can be evaluated only within the context in which the information occurs; thus, conclusions regarding knowledge are always subject to change, given a different context to interpret the issues. According to Kitchener and King (1981), choosing between competing interpretations often is resisted during this stage, on the assumption that no single solution can ever be completely validated.

In contrast, Stage 6 reasoners recognize that some arguments are better than others and can be evaluated on their merit. A further assumption by individuals in this stage is that the basic process of evaluating arguments remains unchanged even if the context in which the argument is presented changes. Stage 6 reasoners appreciate the reciprocal relationship between the process and product of justification; that is, the conclusions one reaches are determined, in part, by the kind of argumentation one uses to reach those conclusions. Individuals in Stage 6 also recognize that multiple "constructions" of a problem are possible and indeed desirable.

Stage 7 reasoning differs still further in that although interpretations of truth and knowledge change across different contexts, some interpretations are more justifiable than others, on the basis of either evidence or the rigor of one's argumentation. Knowledge is constructed during this stage on the basis of personal inquiry into the nature of the problem and evidence that supports or refutes one's tentative conclusions. Beliefs are justified probabilistically on the basis of evidence available to the individual. In addition is the recognition that what is accepted as the most reasonable solution to a problem presently may be changed later to accommodate new information or arguments that were not considered previously.

The model of reflective judgment proposed by Kitchener and King provides a framework for understanding the development of reasoning skills by means of systematic changes in beliefs about the certainty and verifiability of knowledge. Individuals whose reasoning is typical of earlier stages (Stages 1, 2 and 3) view their world in a rather fixed and limited way, on the assumption that knowledge is certain; individuals in later stages (Stages 6 and 7) view their world in a more flexible way, on the assumption that knowledge is not fixed.

Reflective Judgment and Education

The work of Kitchener and King raises a number of important questions about the nature of teaching and learning. One question is how the classroom environment affects a student's reasoning. Does greater student autonomy lead to better reflective judgment? How do dispositional characteristics, such as one's degree of efficacy, attributional style, or personal goal orientation, affect one's willingness to engage in or improve one's reflective thinking? How are age, educational background, and home environment related to the development of reflective judgment?

Kitchener and King (1981) investigated a number of these issues and reported dramatic differences between individuals in each of the seven stages. One question concerned whether students reasoned about different problems in similar ways. The results of Kitchener and King's initial study with high school and college students revealed that most individuals reasoned about different kinds of problems in highly similar ways. Style of reasoning typically was confined to the same or adjacent stages, suggesting that people's basic assumptions about knowledge lead to predictably similar conclusions.

A second question concerned the relationship between age, educational experience, and reflective judgment. As one might expect, high school students tended to reason at lower stages (the average stage was 2.77), compared with college undergraduates (the average stage was 3.65) or graduate students (the average stage was 5.67). The difference between high school and graduate students was especially strong (three full stages), suggesting that the amount of education one receives has a clear bearing on the sophistication of one's reflective reasoning.

A number of other relationships were tested as well. Although no differences were found between males and females in any of the seven stages, students' verbal ability was highly correlated with reasoning ability. Those with better verbal skills tended to reason at higher stages than those with lower scores. Several tests of formal-operational problem solving revealed that virtually all of the sixty students participating in the study had achieved some degree of formal reasoning. Apparently, however, the ability to engage in formal-operational reasoning was not a sufficient condition for advanced reflective judgment. Many students capable of such reasoning scored at Stage 3 or lower.

In a related study, Kitchener et al. (1989) conducted a six-year analysis of change in reflective judgment. One important finding was that students progressed sequentially through adjacent stages, rather than skipping one or more stages. Another finding was that some groups progressed at a faster rate than others although differences in the rate of development were attributable, in part, to the fact that some groups started at a very high level to begin with. Over the six-year period, high school students progressed the most, moving roughly two full stages—from 2.83 to 4.99. During the same period, college undergraduates improved slightly more than one full stage—from 3.72 to 4.89. College graduate students showed little improvement at all, moving from 6.15 to 6.27.

A comparison of these stage scores reveals several interesting points. First, high school students progressed two full stages during a six-year period, reasoning at a level commensurate with college undergraduates. This finding indicates that differences in reflective judgment need not be viewed as permanent. Given adequate instruction and age-related maturation, many students can be expected to improve their reasoning abilities over time. In contrast, college undergraduates failed to bridge the gap between themselves and graduate students after a six-year follow-up even though the latter group showed no statistically significant improvement. One reason may be that better reasoners go on to graduate school, while poorer reasoners do not. An alternative explanation is that graduate school improves one's reflective judgment substantially. Unfortunately, Kitchener and King's (1981) study does not allow us to answer this question with any degree of certainty because none of the original pool of college undergraduates continued on to graduate school.

A study by Dunkle, Schraw, and Bendixen (1993) provided some insights into this problem. Dunkle et al. first measured undergraduate and graduate students' epistemological beliefs by using the instrument designed by Schommer (1990). They next asked students to respond to an open-ended dilemma ("Is truth unchanging?") and scored these responses by using Kitchener and King's Reflective Judgment Scale. The results were that students who believed more strongly in innate ability, simple knowledge, and quick learning were more likely to score in the lower stages of Kitchener and King's Reflective Judgment Scale. Most of the students scoring in Stages 5 through 7 were graduate students, whereas none of those scoring in the three lowest stages were graduate students. These findings suggest that graduate students engage in more sophisticated reasoning, in part, because of differing epistemological beliefs. Thus, increased education may improve reasoning because it enables students to change their implicit (or even explicit) beliefs about knowledge.

Education and Thinking

One question left unanswered by Kitchener and King's research is the effect that formal education has on reflective judgment. Several recent studies have provided surprising insights into this question. In a follow-up study on her earlier research, Schommer (1991) found that college undergraduates hold different epistemological beliefs, depending on their academic major. Education majors were far more likely to believe in certain knowledge and quick learning than science majors. In general, undergraduate science majors held more sophisticated beliefs about knowledge, which appeared to affect their everyday decision making. Unfortunately, Schommer's research does not allow us to determine whether students with less sophisticated beliefs chose an academic major that allows them to persist in those beliefs or whether simple beliefs are the consequence of one's academic major.

A study by Lehman, Lempert, and Nisbett (1988), however, suggests that one's academic major can shape one's way of thinking in very important ways. Lehman et al. tested graduate students in four disciplines (medicine, law, psychology, and chemistry) at the beginning of their first and third years. Participants were given four types of conceptual reasoning tests: (1) statistical reasoning applied to everyday life, (2) methodological reasoning that tested one's ability to detect flaws in an argument due to lack of a control group, (3) conditional reasoning that required students to establish necessary and sufficient conditions for an outcome to be true, and (4) verbal reasoning designed to evaluate students' ability to evaluate evidence. In one experiment, first-year graduate students were compared with third-year graduate students in the same program. In a second experiment, another group of students was compared during their first year and again two years later.

The results were similar in both cases. An analysis of first-year students across the four disciplines revealed no differences on graduate school admission tests; that is, all were of roughly the same ability level. First-year students also performed similarly on the four reasoning tests, with the exception of chemistry students, who scored significantly lower on the statistical and verbal reasoning tests. A comparison of verbal reasoning scores between the first- and third-year students revealed no important differences across the four groups. This outcome was expected because students in each of the disciplines were expected to be proficient in this skill prior to entering graduate school. The difference between beginning and advanced psychology students on the statistical reasoning test was that they improved roughly 70 percent—a rather startling gain. Medical students improved by roughly 25 percent, whereas law and chemistry students did not improve at all.

One might ask why the psychology students improved so dramatically, compared with the other groups. The answer, at least for those who have completed such a program, is rather obvious: Graduate psychology programs typically require students to complete at least three advanced level statistics classes, as well as several classes on basic research methodology. It should not be surprising that psychology students improved far more than students who are not required to take such courses.

A comparison of conditional reasoning scores led to somewhat different findings, however. In this case, the medical, law, and psychology students improved 30 percent to 40 percent during their first two years of graduate school, whereas the chemistry students did not improve. Again, the reason for such improvement can be traced to extensive use of conditional reasoning skills in these graduate programs. Students are required on a daily basis to establish the conditions under which legal, medical, or experimental evidence is necessary and/or sufficient to prove a particular hypothesis. Why chemistry students did not improve remains unclear. One likely explanation is that Lehman et al. (1988) did not include a test sensitive to the improvement made by chemists.

The results of the Lehman et al. study answer a number of important questions raised earlier. First, students' reasoning skills are affected in important ways by the intellectual training they receive. One example is that students trained in law improve conditional reasoning skills that are not improved by graduate training in chemistry. Second, students do not appear to choose an academic discipline solely on the basis of skills they already possess. None of the students differed initially on any of the reasoning tasks or on intellectual ability. In general, students seem to enter graduate programs with similar types of intellectual skills and develop greater proficiency with some of these skills only as a result of their academic training. Returning momentarily to Schommer's (1991) findings, it is probably the case that undergraduate education majors subscribe to different beliefs about knowledge, compared with science majors, for one of two reasons: Either they are never required to question these beliefs, and so they do not, or beliefs supporting simple knowledge and quick learning are reflected in the classes they take.

Summary of Beliefs About Knowledge

The research we have described indicates that people's beliefs about the certainty and complexity of knowledge profoundly affect their reasoning. The work of Perry (1970), Ryan (1984), and Schommer (1990) suggests that individuals hold many beliefs about knowledge and that these beliefs constrain information processing. Kitchener and King's (1981) research further indicates that different epistemological assumptions constrain the level of reflective judgment that individuals engage in. This conclusion is strengthened further by the research conducted by Dunkle et al. (1993). Last, the Lehman et al. (1988) study revealed that epistemological beliefs and reasoning skills are the result of one's intellectual environment, rather than determinants of what type of academic discipline one pursues.

HOPE AND ATTITUDE CHANGE

At this point, we shift our attention briefly to another kind of belief that has attracted researchers' attention—hope! Ongoing investigations by Snyder and colleagues (Harney, 1989; Langelle, 1989; Snyder et al., 1991) have reported an impressive number of statistically significant relationships between people's expressed hope and academic achievement. Hope consists of two important components that Snyder et al. (1991) refer to as *agency* and *pathways,* or more colloquially, as the "will" and the "ways." The former refers to an individual's sense of self-determination and perseverance when faced with challenges. The latter refers to how well an individual can generate workable solutions to those challenges.

To test the relationship between hope and other outcomes, Snyder et al. devised a twelve-question inventory containing a number of questions that measure a person's sense of agency and pathways. One example of an agency question is "My past experiences have prepared me well for the future." An example of a typical pathways question is "There are lots of ways around any problem." Snyder and colleagues have used this instrument in a variety of studies that compared performance on the hope inventory with frequently used measures of life orientation, life experiences, self-esteem, hopelessness, depression, stress, optimism, and sense of control. In most cases, the hope inventory is correlated with these measures to a significant degree, although none of these instruments seem to be measuring quite the same dimension as hope.

As one might expect, the two dimensions measured by the hope inventory are highly correlated, suggesting that a greater sense of self-determination usually is associated with the corresponding belief that challenges can be met and overcome. Snyder and colleagues have conducted a number of studies examining how responses to this inventory are related to specific academic and social outcomes. In a study by Yoshinobu (1989), people with high hope scores demonstrated significantly more self-determination in the light of failure. Those receiving high hope scores reported more potentially useful solutions to challenging circumstances than did those receiving low hope scores.

Subsequent studies have shown that people high on hope have a greater preference for difficult tasks that cannot be explained by differences in intellectual ability. When confronted with obstacles, high hope students showed greater self-determination and solution pathways than medium or low hope individuals. People scoring high on the hope inventory were more likely as well to have a greater number of specifiable goals across a number of domains, including job, personal relationships, health, and spiritual development. Hope also correlated with perceived academic goal attainment, indicating that those who score higher on hope expect to get higher grades in college classes. In fact, students with higher hope and academic expectations do receive higher grades even when their academic ability is taken into consideration!

A number of other important findings have been found in these studies as well. First, scores on the hope inventory appear to be independent of intellectual ability. Second, a person's tendency to score high or low on hope is unrelated to gender. Third, the degree of hope expressed by people appears to be stable over time, suggesting that some individuals seem predisposed to be more hopeful than others.

Changing Beliefs

One important question raised by Snyder et al.'s research, as well as by the work conducted by Dweck and Leggett (1988) and Schommer (1990), is how easily maladaptive beliefs can be changed. Unfortunately, little research has been conducted in this area although several preliminary investigations suggest that changing beliefs may be far more complicated than people assume. One reason is that beliefs are formed on the basis of *cognitive* and *affective* information (Breckler & Wiggins, 1989). In this view, cognitive appraisal of information is objective and rational; affective appraisal is subjective and based on emotional reactions to an object. Whether beliefs are changeable may depend, in large part, on how beliefs were formed initially. Those formed on the basis of affective responses may be resistant to change by cognitive means; those formed on the basis of cognitive responses may be resistant to affective means of persuasion.

Several recent experiments by Edwards (1990) addressed this issue. Individuals in one experiment were asked to examine a number of fictitious consumer products, such as a high-energy drink and a portable copier. Participants received information about these products in two stages: During the first stage, people received affective information (e.g., tasting the drink), followed by cognitive information (e.g., reading an advertisement for the product), or they received cognitive information first, followed by affective information. In the second stage, Edwards provided participants with additional information designed to conflict with information provided in the first stage. Half of the people received cognitive information first, followed by affective information; half received information in the reverse order. The purpose of the study was to examine whether attitudes that develop through affective and cognitive means are more resistant to change when the conflicting information is presented by using the same or a different means of persuasion.

Edwards (1990) found that beliefs acquired through affective persuasion were easier to change through affective means and that beliefs acquired through cognitive persuasion were easier to change through cognitive means. Of special interest, however, was the magnitude of change. Beliefs acquired through cognitive persuasion were more resistant to change than beliefs acquired through affective means. In addition, neither affective nor cognitive persuasion appears to be very useful when one is attempting to change beliefs that were formed by using another mode of persuasion; that is, beliefs based on affective responses show little change when individuals are presented with contradictory cognitive information.

To complicate matters more, a number of other studies suggest that affective information may alter our beliefs even when we have no conscious awareness of this information (Greenwald, Klinger, & Lui, 1989; Niedenthal, 1990). One study by Niedenthal (1990) asked college students to describe their impressions of cartoon faces after first viewing human faces that were presented below their perceptual threshold (below the level at which visual information can be consciously recognized). Some of these slides showed faces marked by disgust; others showed faces expressing joy. As expected, subjective evaluation of the cartoon faces was significantly more negative after viewing faces conveying disgust.

These studies all seem to suggest that attitudes and beliefs are acquired in complex ways and may be highly resistant to change. Appealing to students through use of well-reasoned cognitive arguments may be of little use if beliefs were formed initially by affective means. For example, consider the difficulty educators or parents face trying, through cognitive means, to dissuade teenagers from drinking alcoholic beverages when these teens are exposed to affective appeals from television showing happy, carefree young adults leading the good life on a sunny California beach, beer in hand.

From a teacher's or parent's perspective, changing beliefs about intelligence, knowledge, or any other complex phenomenon may be a slow process. Clearly, special emphasis should be placed on providing an environment wherein students are given the opportunity to reflect on their own beliefs and shift gradually to a new mode of thought.

TEACHERS' BELIEFS

Before concluding this chapter, we briefly discuss some of the recent findings on teachers' beliefs. Teachers hold many beliefs that affect their attitudes and behavior in the classroom. These beliefs, more often than not, involve tacit assumptions about students, learning, the material to be taught, and the organization of the class (Kagan, 1992) and are as diverse as perceptions of self-efficacy, subjective attitudes about content knowledge, and how it can be taught most effectively. Teachers' beliefs frequently affect student-teacher interactions and instructional planning. For example, Gibson and Dembo (1984) found that high-self-efficacy teachers provided less criticism and persisted in helping struggling students more than low-self-efficacy teachers. Ashton and Webb (1986) reported similar findings. High-efficacy teachers used more student praise, engaged in more task-oriented instruction, and ran classrooms that led to higher achievement.

Teachers' beliefs about content material also shape in-class pedagogy. Freeman and Porter (1989) found that teachers' beliefs about mathematics led to noticeable differences in how the course textbook was used. Hollon, Anderson, and Roth (1991) reported similar findings in that teachers' beliefs led to instructional practices consistent with those beliefs. Teachers' beliefs about how learning occurs also affect how they teach course content. In one study, Smith and Neale (1989) compared three teaching orientations and their effect on teacher planning and instruction. "Discovery" teachers provided interesting activities designed to invoke student curiosity and exploration. "Didactic" teachers (those who emphasize structured content, facts, and principles) were more likely to select and organize content material, give tests, and demonstrate key concepts. In contrast, "conceptual change" teachers focused on evaluation of student beliefs, restructuring of existing knowledge structures, and providing incongruent data to students.

Surprisingly, preservice teachers tend to leave teacher training programs with many of the beliefs and attitudes they held when they entered the program (Kagan, 1992). This alarming fact suggests that some teacher training programs may be ineffective at altering beliefs even though they expose students to different perspectives on pedagogy (see Chapter 14). Overall, a number of studies examining a wide range of teachers' beliefs suggest that these beliefs are quite stable and resistent to change, are associated with a congruent style of teaching, and are affected most directly by practice, rather than by continuing education.

Presently, it is unclear how to facilitate change in teachers' beliefs. Research does provide a three-pronged strategy for changing students' beliefs that may apply to older students (e.g., teachers in training) as well (Posner, Strike, Hewson, & Gertzog, 1982). First, students in teacher training programs must experience a classroom environment in which implicit beliefs become explicit. One way is to encourage open discussion and reflection on beliefs about course content and approaches to learning. Second, students should be confronted with the inconsistency of their beliefs. Third, the teacher should provide opportunities for students to weigh conflicting evidence and restructure their existing knowledge such that it can be accommodated to course content.

Generally, beliefs about three classroom factors affect teachers' behaviors the most. One factor is course content. Research indicates that teachers plan instruction in a way that is consistent with their assumptions about class material. Teachers who hold a belief in certain knowledge are more likely to focus on didactic instruction and essential course content while de-emphasizing discovery in the classroom (Rennie, 1989). A second factor is the type of student receiving instruction. Most teachers form strong opinions about students. These beliefs are based on a number of factors, including physical characteristics, test scores, class performance, social skills, parental attitudes, and student self-efficacy (Kagan, 1992). A third factor is the teacher's own explicit beliefs about teaching. One of the most consistent findings in the teacher belief literature is that teachers plan and implement instruction in a way that is consistent with their personal epistemologies.

Little is known currently about how teachers view knowledge and intelligence. We believe that many such studies will be conducted in the next decade. One important question is whether instruction and learning are facilitated when there is a match between teachers' and students' beliefs. Dweck and Leggett's (1988) theory, for instance, suggests that learning-oriented students may find it quite difficult to adjust to a classroom run by a teacher with strong performance goals. Similarly, teachers' epistemological beliefs may interfere with learning or create excessive disequilibrium when they do not match students' beliefs. This is not to say that teachers must accommodate students' beliefs; rather, a mismatch in beliefs and assumptions is apt to create disequilibrium in the classroom. As Posner et al. (1982) suggest, disequilibrium may be used productively to promote conceptual change, or it may preclude successful student-teacher interactions if handled poorly.

IMPLICATIONS

1. *Everyone holds beliefs about intelligence and knowledge.* The beliefs we hold affect the choices we make inside and outside the classroom. Many of these beliefs are implicit. Generally speaking, explicit awareness of one's beliefs makes them easier to identify and change. Beliefs about intelligence affect classroom satisfaction and persistence. Beliefs about knowledge affect reasoning skills and reflective judgment.

We believe that teachers should help students develop an awareness of their beliefs. Many younger and even older students hold implicit beliefs that nevertheless exert a profound influence on their thinking and behavior. Developing reflective awareness of these beliefs through journals and peer-based discussions gives students the opportunity to change them as they see fit.

2. *Beliefs about intelligence and knowledge affect our behaviors.* Research has demonstrated convincingly that our attitudes about intelligence and knowledge affect our learning. Individuals who believe that intelligence is fixed or who believe in simple knowledge and quick learning are less likely to persist and use helpful learning strategies. Those who adopt an entity theory are more likely to explain their success and failure in terms of different attributional responses.

3. *Beliefs about intelligence and knowledge affect the way we reason.* Thinking does not occur in an intellectual vacuum. The kind of assumptions we hold about how people think and learn determine, in part, the kind of educational opportunities we expose ourselves to and the kind of knowledge we accept as legitimate. Studies by Kitchener and King (1981), Kuhn (1991), and Lehman et al. (1988) all

illustrate this important point. For this reason, beliefs about intelligence and knowledge should be an important topic of discussion in classrooms, especially those with older students.

4. *Education affects the kinds of beliefs we hold.* Our beliefs about knowledge and intelligence are shaped by our classroom experiences. Teachers model viewpoints that echo views held at home or perhaps conflict with them. The kinds of beliefs modeled in the classroom may change the way students think. This possibility places a special responsibility on educators to analyze carefully the viewpoints they express in their classes and to provide ample time to explore the implications of these views.

5. *Educational experiences affect reasoning skills.* The study by Lehman et al. (1988) is notable in that it illustrates how environmental constraints affect the development of cognitive skills. Recall that even graduate students experienced substantial changes in reasoning skills that were linked with the specific experiences they had in graduate school. This finding suggests that the specific demands of a discipline (e.g., statistical reasoning in the social sciences) necessitate the development of certain skills. Whether the intellectual demands of different disciplines also affect the kinds of epistemological beliefs students hold is uncertain (cf. Jehng et al., 1993).

6. *Beliefs are not strongly related to ability.* This statement may seem surprising to you. We often think of "smart" people as those with the most sophisticated (or adaptive) beliefs. However, the research described in this chapter generally points to the conclusion that beliefs about intelligence and knowledge are related to home (e.g., parental beliefs) and school (e.g., performance demands) variables far more than one's measured ability. One implication of this conclusion is that adaptive beliefs (e.g., believing in incremental learning) may compensate for average or low ability (Schraw et al., 1994). We are committed to the view that high academic achievement is attainable by virtually all students, provided they develop a belief system that encourages them to use their existing skills and to cultivate more advanced thinking skills, such as metacognition. We are equally committed to the view that teachers must initiate and facilitate these changes for them to be truly successful. For a graphic portrayal of this view, we recommend that all readers view the movie *Stand and Deliver.*

SUMMARY

This chapter examined the role that beliefs about intelligence and knowledge have on academic performance. We introduced the topic of implicit theories—that is, tacit belief systems. Dweck and Leggett's theory described two kinds of theories. Entity theorists maintain a belief that intelligence is fixed; incremental theorists believe that intelligence is changeable.

Entity and incremental theories give rise to performance and learning goals, which, in turn, lead to maladaptive and adaptive behaviors, respectively. Individuals characterized by a performance orientation are less persistent, less apt to use learn-ing strategies, and attribute their failure to ability and teachers. Individuals character-ized by a learning orientation, however, are more persistent, more likely to use strategies, and attribute their success to strategy use and effort.

A number of epistemological beliefs can affect reasoning. Individuals who can be characterized by a belief that knowledge is complex and relative, that learning is incremental, and that one's ability to learn is not innately determined engage in more sophisticated forms of thinking.

We examined teachers' beliefs as well. These beliefs tend to change slowly, yet they strongly affect the attitudes teachers hold about their students. Teachers' beliefs determine what content the teachers cover and how they present this material to their students (e.g., direct lecture vs. a discovery approach). Research suggests that some teacher trainees leave education programs with the same beliefs about teach-ing they had when they entered the program. The identification and discussion of these beliefs was described as a possible belief-changing strategy.

SUGGESTED READINGS

Dweck, C. S., & Leggett, E. S. (1988). A social-cognitive approach to motivation and personal-ity. *Psychological Review, 95,* 256–273.

This review article presents Dweck and Leggett's theory in a highly readable fashion.

Kuhn, D. (1991), *The skills of argument.* New York: Cambridge University Press.

This book describes a comprehensive study examining argumentative reasoning. Chapter 7 provides an excellent discussion of the relationship between epistemological beliefs and reasoning skills.

CHAPTER 8

Problem Solving and Critical Thinking

Every day, we encounter hundreds of problems that range in difficulty from deciding what cereal to eat for breakfast to planning long-term career goals. Because we face so many types of problems, it is often difficult to say with certainty what a problem is or to know how to categorize them. In addition, the sheer range of problems we encounter makes it very difficult to approach problem solving systematically. Word problems in algebra, for example, seem to have little in common with the choices and decisions we face when buying a car.

Loosely, a problem exists when our present state differs from a desired state (Bransford & Stein, 1984). Thinking of problem solving in this way can be helpful for several reasons. First, it emphasizes the continual process of problem solving, in which we move from an initial state to a more clearly defined end state. Second, thinking about problem solving as a process of change from one state to another helps us understand that virtually every problem we encounter can be solved by using the same general strategy despite apparent surface differences.

Even though most adults possess some form of general problem-solving strategy, it is not the case that all problems are similar to one another. Rather, experts agree that problems differ with respect to how much structure they provide the problem solver (Hayes, 1988). An **ill-defined problem** has more than one acceptable solution and no universally agreed-on strategy for reaching it (Kitchener, 1983). Worldwide ecological problems, such as global warming and ozone destruction, pro-

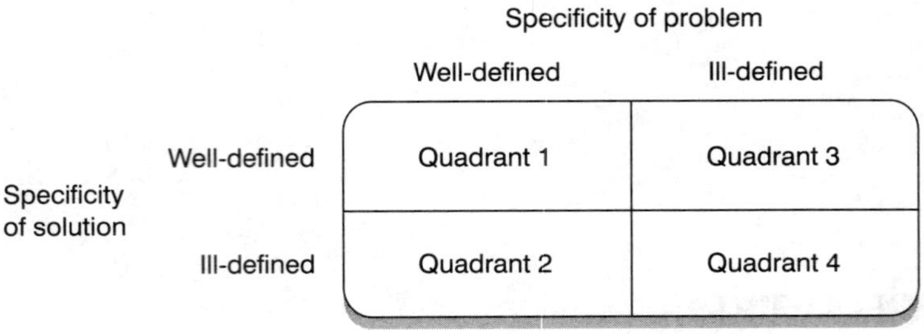

Figure 8-1
A problem evaluation matrix.

Specificity of problem

	Well-defined	Ill-defined
Well-defined	Quadrant 1	Quadrant 3
Ill-defined	Quadrant 2	Quadrant 4

Specificity of solution

vide good examples of ill-defined problems because scientists disagree about the causes and possible solutions to these problems. A **well-defined problem** has only one correct solution and a guaranteed method for finding it. Solving a quadratic equation in algebra class by using the quadratic formula is a good example of a well-defined problem because a unique solution and a guaranteed means of obtaining it always exist.

One useful way to clarify problems is to consider the specificity of the problem and the specificity of its solution simultaneously by using some form of graphic representation. Figure 8-1 illustrates what a problem evaluation matrix might look like when each dimension is divided into quadrants. Quadrant 1, in which the problem and the solution are both well defined, is typical of the minor problems we encounter in our daily lives and, to a certain extent, in the classroom. Using the quadratic formula to solve equations falls nicely into this category, as do other examples of everyday problem solving, such as finding a classmate's phone number in the telephone book or opening a savings account. But consider other problems. Writing a long essay for a midterm exam more accurately reflects the kind of activity that occurs in Quadrant 2, in which the problem is well defined but its solution is not (e.g., State whether you agree with the federal government's decision to bury nuclear waste in your state and defend your position). Even more troublesome are the problems that appear in Quadrant 4, in which neither the problem nor the solution is well defined. Many of the truly difficult decisions we face individually or collectively fall somewhere in this category. Because these problems rarely have universally agreed-on solutions, solving them takes cooperation and compromises on everyone's part.

HISTORICAL PERSPECTIVES ON PROBLEM SOLVING

Thorndike, Dewey, and the Gestalt Psychologists

Interest in problem solving among psychologists and educators developed early in the twentieth century. One of the earliest views was proposed by E. L. Thorndike (1911), who conducted a series of experiments in which he observed cats as they attempted to escape from carefully constructed wooden crates by pressing a lever.

Noting that cats typically would try a number of random behaviors prior to successfully pressing the escape lever, Thorndike concluded that problem solving consists largely of trial-and-error behaviors that eventually lead to a solution. He argued that problem solving (at least in cats) was not intentional, but rather occurred one step at a time as nonsuccessful attempts were eliminated from the cat's repertoire. Thorndike was to argue in subsequent work that human problem solving takes place in much the same way as it does with any animal: Success occurs incrementally as a function of the trial-and-error attempts to solve the problem.

In contrast to Thorndike, John Dewey (1910) viewed problem solving as a conscious, deliberate process governed by a naturally occurring sequence of steps. Dewey's model included five basic steps that he considered to be teachable skills. In Step 1, *presentation of the problem,* students (or teachers) recognize the existence of a problem. In Step 2, *defining the problem,* the problem solver identifies the nature of the problem and identifies important constraints on its solution. In Step 3, *development of hypotheses,* one or more plausible solutions are proposed. In Step 4, *testing the hypotheses,* the most feasible solution is determined. In Step 5, *selecting the best hypothesis,* the best hypothesis is determined, given the relative strengths and weaknesses of each.

A third approach to problem solving was that of the Gestalt psychologists (see Chapter 2), a group of European psychologists whose views differed widely from those of American behaviorists. One of the foremost Gestalt theorists was Wolfgang Köhler (1929), who conducted a series of studies on problem solving using chimps. The most famous of Köhler's chimps was Sultan. In one experiment, Sultan was placed in a cage in which a banana was suspended from the ceiling just beyond his reach. Köhler also placed in various parts of the cage a number of wooden crates that could be used to build a platform to reach the banana, but only if Sultan correctly grasped the concept of *using the crates in a tool-like fashion.* After several unsuccessful attempts and some apparent deliberation on Sultan's part, he succeeded in stacking the crates and reached the banana. Köhler argued that Sultan's behavior provided evidence of insight in problem solving in several ways. First, Sultan did not make numerous trial-and-error attempts to reach the banana as Thorndike would predict. Second, the crates bore no ostensible relationship to solving the problem (at least from the chimp's perspective), yet were used without prompting in a purposeful way to achieve the primary goal of reaching the banana. Köhler's findings and interpretation were considered extremely controversial at the time and continue to be debated today, in part, because researchers differ as to the nature of insight and, in part, because they suggested skilled, reflective problem solving in an animal.

Another important phenomenon introduced by a Gestalt psychologist was **functional fixedness**, a condition that arises when we lose the ability to view familiar objects in a novel way (Duncker, 1945). In one experiment, Duncker provided people with a candle, a box of matches, and some tacks. The object of the study was to attach the candle to a wooden door; the problem could be solved only by first attaching the matchbox to the door with the tacks and then using the box as a platform for the candle. Duncker added one other constraint as well; some people received the matchbox with matches inside, while others received the matchbox and matches separately. Although apparently a trivial difference, individuals who received the empty matchbox solved the problem more quickly.

Duncker concluded from this study that individuals in the empty box condition solved the problem more efficiently because they were more likely to view the box as a potential platform, rather than as a receptacle for matches. Including the matches in the box induced functional fixedness in that it activated preconceived notions (schemata) of what a matchbox is and what it can be used for. When the matchbox was perceived in a slightly different context (without matches), individuals were better able to imagine alternative uses for it. Duncker's experiment elegantly illustrated the profound impact of preexisting knowledge and how that knowledge inhibits novel solutions or uses of objects during problem solving.

Contemporary Approaches to Problem Solving

Research on problem solving has received a great deal of attention since Thorndike, Dewey, and the Gestalt psychologists. Since the 1950s, computer scientists and cognitive psychologists have attempted to develop a general problem-solving model that can be applied in domains as diverse as physics and medical diagnosis (J. R. Anderson, 1993; Hayes, 1988; Newell & Simon, 1972). These models generally emphasize two major components: the use of a general problem-solving procedure and a high degree of metacognitive monitoring by the problem solver. Although a number of models have appeared, most are quite similar to one another and can be summarized into a five-stage sequence (Bransford & Stein, 1984; Gick, 1986; Hayes, 1988).

The five stages in the sequence are *identifying the problem, representing the problem, selecting an appropriate strategy, implementing the strategy,* and *evaluating solutions.* One might note that these five stages are quite similar to the five steps described by Dewey. Within each of the five stages, a number of component subskills have been identified as well. We consider each of these stages separately and then discuss the relative merits of a general problem-solving model at the end of this section.

Identifying the Problem.   Identifying a problem is one of the most difficult and challenging aspects of problem solving because it requires creativity and persistence, yet a willingness to ponder a problem for a long period of time without committing to a solution too early in the process (Hayes, 1988). Many problems (and their solutions) that seem obvious in retrospect are not so obvious to begin with. Consider that batting helmets were not used routinely in major league baseball until the early 1950s despite the fact that several players had been killed over the years by being struck in the head by wild pitches!

A number of obstacles to effective problem finding have been identified by researchers. One obstacle is that most people are not in the habit of actively searching for problems. Usually, we let the problem "come to us," rather than seek it out. A good argument could be made, however, that virtually all great discoveries are made only after a previously unrecognized problem has been "discovered." A good case in point is the germ theory of disease. Prior to the nineteenth century, many physicians believed that illnesses originated from such sources as evil spirits, bad air (e.g., malaria), and poisoned blood. These beliefs led to a number of nonproductive treatments, such as incantations, whipping, and bloodletting. It was not until the advent of a germ theory of disease that physicians correctly identified the source of many treatable diseases.

A second obstacle to successful problem finding is the degree to which the problem solver possesses relevant background knowledge. Problems in the development of computer microchips, for instance, cannot be solved or even identified without a great deal of preexisting knowledge about computer circuitry. Similarly, consider how background knowledge affects "problem finding" in a highly familiar activity such as reading (see Chapter 11). Research indicates that prior knowledge facilitates the perception and temporary elaboration of new information. More important, prior knowledge (the use of *content schemata*) enables readers to attend selectively to important information in the text and to encode new information into an existing schematic structure with less effort.

A third obstacle to problem finding is that people do not take as much time as they need to reflect carefully on either the nature of a problem or its solution. In a landmark study of artistic creativity, Getzels and Czikszentmihalyi (1976) found that the time spent investigating objects prior to drawing a still life was a significantly better predictor of originality than was time spent making the drawing! This relationship was found even when the artist's technical ability was taken into consideration. From extensive observations and interviews, Getzels and Czikszentmihalyi concluded that artists who considered more options during the initial stages of problem finding were more original in their solutions. Most surprising of all was the finding that time spent discovering problems during the initial stages of problem solving correlated highly with artistic success seven years later!

Getzels and Czikszentmihalyi also described a number of other interesting findings in their study. One was that the majority of successful art students listed "problem finding" as the primary goal of their work. These artists were more concerned with finding and coming to terms with a perceived problem than they were in solving it. Successful artists also tended to possess three dispositional characteristics that facilitated problem finding. First, they were more open to the problem; that is, they did not allow first impressions to interfere with discovering alternative approaches to artistic expression. Second, they engaged in more exploratory activities, such as handling objects in a still life or viewing those objects from different perspectives. Third, they permitted the problem and their initial solution to evolve as they worked with it.

More recently, Moore (1990) examined the problem-finding behaviors of experienced teachers and university students studying to be teachers. One difference found between these groups was that experienced teachers spent significantly more time planning when placed in a hypothetical classroom setting. In addition, experienced teachers spent more time than novices investigating and manipulating objects found in the classroom and also provided a greater number of solutions to potential classroom problems. In many respects, experienced teachers appear to behave in much the same way as successful artists in the Getzels and Czikszentmihalyi study.

Another aspect of time spent identifying problems is the persistence of problem solvers in the face of initial difficulties. Some individuals give up too easily after only a short period of time because they view problem solving as a time-limited activity (Gick, 1986). In this regard, Schoenfeld (1983) found that students solving mathematical word problems tended to give up after five minutes, on the assumption that if the solution did not occur during this period, it would not occur at all. Research reviewed by Gick (1986) and Hayes (1988) clearly suggests that successful problem solving is related to the amount of time one spends during the initial stages of problem finding, as well as to the number of solutions that are considered. In many situations, expert problem solvers spend more time identifying problems than do novices.

Finally, effective problem finding is strongly related to **divergent thinking**. Divergent thinking occurs when a problem solver explores solutions that are novel or even inconsistent with the problem at hand. Hollowing out a brick so that it can be used as a mug is a good illustration of divergent thinking because it exemplifies one of the unusual ways an object can be used when we see it in a new light. As you might expect, divergent thinking is related to creativity and problem finding, although problem-finding ability appears to be a better predictor of creativity than does divergent thinking (Runco, 1991). The ability to find problems and to think divergently seems to enhance the evaluation of proposed solutions during problem solving. One reason is that problem solvers are better able to plan in advance, which enables them to eliminate poor potential solutions early on. Divergent thinking helps students think more broadly not only when they are generating ideas but also when they are testing them.

Representing the Problem.   Representing a problem can occur in several ways. One form of representation is simply thinking about problems abstractly, without committing one's thoughts to paper. Another is expressing the problem in some tangible form, such as a graph, picture, story problem, or equation. Representing problems on paper has a number of important advantages. One is that many problems are so complex that they impose severe demands on short-term memory unless we find a convenient way to summarize information. Think back to all of the information you needed to consider when applying to college. Some individuals find themselves trying to remember the cost of tuition and housing, distance from home, quality of institution, availability of desirable academic majors, and social opportunities. Perhaps you had to compare this information for ten to fifteen universities. Clearly, this is too much to consider at one time. Using some form of external representation can reduce greatly the amount of information that needs to be remembered in order to identify and solve a problem.

Using external representations of problems can be useful for another reason. Sometimes, problems are just too difficult to solve mentally because we consider so many possible solutions. Using a visual representation can help us keep track of these solutions or reason more clearly. Consider the Monk's Trip problem, in which a monk journeys all day on foot to the top of a mountain, meditates overnight, and then returns by foot again the following morning by way of the exact same path, making the return trip down the mountain in two-thirds of the time. The problem is to determine whether there is a spot on the trail that the monk crosses at exactly the same time each day. Take a few minutes now to solve this problem before you turn to Figure 8-2, which provides a visual representation of this problem.

As Figure 8-2 illustrates, it is impossible for the monk to make the return trip without crossing one spot on the trail at exactly the same time of day. Solving this problem pictorially seems to make this point obvious, whereas solving the problem without the benefit of a picture can be rather difficult. One reason for this difficulty is that much of our limited cognitive capacity in short-term memory is exhausted just trying to remember relevant information. Few resources are left over to actually solve the problem!

Representing problems either internally or externally can be made easier when we analyze the component parts of a problem. Most theorists distinguish among four components that are known collectively as the problem space: goal state, initial state, operators, and constraints on operators. The **problem space** refers to all of the operators and constraints on operators involved in the problem. Some problem spaces are small, such as choosing a personal computer that meets your needs and your budget; others are extremely complex, such as finding a vaccine against HIV. Problems that include a greater number of possible **solution paths** (more paths from the initial state to the goal state) have larger problem spaces than those with few paths, although the size of a problem space may vary considerably between two people, depending on the way the problem is understood by each person (Hayes, 1988).

The **goal state** refers to what we want to accomplish once the problem is solved. Goals vary in their specificity and complexity, although the clearer the goal, the easier it will be to solve the problem, all things considered. The **initial state** refers to

Figure 8-2
A graphic representation of the Monk's Trip problem. (Adapted from Hayes [1978].)

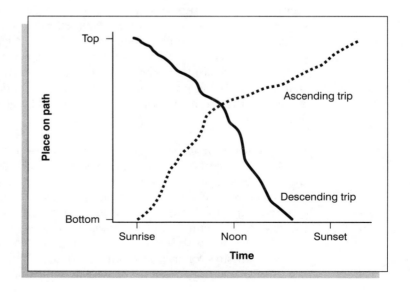

what is known about the problem before one attempts to solve it. How much information do you have about the problem? What information is most important? Is information missing that you will need to consider before proceeding? Can the problem be broken down into smaller subproblems? Have you ever solved a problem like this before? **Operators** refers to objects or concepts in the problem that can be manipulated to reach a solution. Pieces on a chessboard are operators, as are variables (e.g., x and y) in an algebraic equation. When taking a test, time and knowledge about the content of the test are operators. **Constraints on operators** refers to restrictions that limit the use of one or more operators. In a game of chess, queens can move in horizontal, vertical, or diagonal directions on the board, whereas bishops can move only diagonally. Knights are restricted to an entirely different set of moves (two spaces in a horizontal or vertical direction, then one step at a ninety-degree angle to the first). On a test, you are limited frequently to one hour or less, and you may not use books or notes.

A good deal of research has investigated the importance of operators and constraints on operators (see Hayes, 1988, for a summary). One consistent finding is that good problem solvers distinguish relevant from irrelevant constraints on a problem more efficiently than do poor problem solvers and use this information to facilitate problem solving (Kaplan & Simon, 1990; Ross & Kennedy, 1990). For example, good readers know when to slow down, rather than skim a text; that is, they identify relevant information and allocate more attention to it.

Good and poor problem solvers also differ in their ability to categorize problems. Good problem solvers tend to group problems according to "deep structure" principles, such as what kind of solution strategy is required to solve the problem. In contrast, poor problem solvers rely on "surface structure" features, such as the objects that appear in the problem (Hardiman, Dufresne, & Mestre, 1989). When novice problem solvers are taught to categorize by using deep structure principles, their performance usually improves, compared with other novices. These findings suggest two important conclusions. First, effective problem solving is due, in part, to experience; those with more practice solving a particular type of problem can categorize problems more efficiently because of their background knowledge and experience. Second, students can learn to categorize (represent) problems more efficiently by analyzing problems differently. Less attention should be given to surface features of the problem; more attention should be given to the underlying nature of the problem.

Selecting an Appropriate Strategy.   People use many kinds of strategies to solve problems. Some of these are highly structured and are referred to as **algorithms**. An algorithm is really just another name for a rule. Using algorithms or rule-based strategies can be very effective because they are guaranteed to work. Finding the roots of a quadratic equation by using the quadratic formula is a good example of a rule-based strategy. But sometimes it is not possible to use a rule-based strategy because either the rule does not exist or the student lacks proficiency at using it. In this case, people rely on **heuristics**, or "rules of thumb," to help them solve problems. Heuristics are not as efficient as algorithms because they do not always guarantee a solution; in fact, they may even make problem solving more difficult if the student uses the wrong heuristic (Tversky & Kahneman, 1974).

Two of the more common heuristics are **trial-and-error** and **means-ends analysis**. Trial-and-error is clearly the least efficient of all the methods because learners have no strategic plan whatsoever. Trial-and-error may be our only alternative when we are faced unexpectedly with an unfamiliar problem. Often, however, most people will use a trial-and-error approach at the onset of the problem and then switch to a more efficient method after some preliminary information is gained about the problem.

Means-ends analysis differs from trial-and-error in that the problem solver tries to reduce the distance to the goal by taking a sequence of steps that can be evaluated individually. In essence, means-ends analysis requires the learner to do three things: (1) formulate a goal state, (2) break down the problem into smaller subproblems, and (3) evaluate the success of one's performance at each step before proceeding to the next. One example of means-ends analysis is writing a compare-and-contrast essay on a timed test. The first step is to identify the goal state (the position you want to defend); the second step is to break down the paper into smaller problems (e.g., introduction, comparison of evidence, conclusion); and the third step is to proceed through the paper one section at a time.

Not surprisingly, good and poor problem solvers differ in the kinds of strategies they use to solve problems. Experts tend to use some form of means-ends analysis in which they first categorize the problem on the basis of the kind of solution it requires, then break down the problem into smaller parts, and finally solve each part in a sequential manner. In contrast, inexperienced or poor problem solvers often resort to trial-and-error or use a crude form of means-ends analysis based on surface features of the problem. Novice problem solvers also are more likely to break down a problem into fewer meaningful parts and to solve those parts out of sequence.

Another difference between good and poor problem solvers is the ability to plan—a skill that depends on experience, background knowledge, and one's awareness of different kinds of problem-solving strategies. Good problem solvers plan farther in advance and coordinate the entire problem-solving sequence more efficiently. Research in the area of writing suggests that some writers plan "locally," whereas others plan "globally" (Bereiter & Scardamalia, 1987). Global planning seems to contribute greatly to effective writing. As with other types of problem solving, good writing and good planning depend on declarative knowledge about how a text is structured, as well as procedural knowledge about how to compose a text.

Implementing the Strategy.   The success one has when implementing a strategy depends, in large part, on how well one identifies and represents the problem and on the type of strategy one adopts. Clear differences exist at each of these levels between good and poor problem solvers. In addition, good problem solvers coordinate the solution phase of problem solving more efficiently. One consistent finding is that experts change strategies more often (strategy shifting), consider more solutions, evaluate solutions more carefully before discarding them, and reach conclusions that are more workable than do novices.

In a recent study that compared expert and novice teachers, Swanson, O'Connor, and Cooney (1990) found that expert teachers used more strategies while solving classroom management problems than did novices. Experts placed a high priority on defining and representing the problem before deciding on a solution; novices did not. Experts also tended to classify problems at a "deeper" level by carefully evaluating the type and severity of classroom misbehavior; novices tended to categorize problems on the basis of how they would respond to them. As a consequence, experts were more likely to consider different solutions and to evaluate those solutions, given the larger context of the classroom environment. Novices were more likely to choose a single solution based on the apparent severity of the misbehavior. Another important difference between the two groups was that expert teachers were more likely to choose externally based interventions, such as physically separating children, while novices were more likely to select internally based interventions, such as counseling students.

One reason for different problem-solving strategies between expert and novice teachers is that the former possess a great deal of procedural knowledge gained from experience that allows them to focus more of their attention on defining problems, rather than on selecting a strategy to solve the problem. In contrast, novices feel a greater need to reach a solution early, often at the expense of analyzing the problem carefully. One implication of this research is that novice teachers may be poorer problem solvers because they focus too much attention on finding a solution even before they understand the problem. Presumably, novice teachers could benefit by considering problems more carefully or, if that were not possible in a busy classroom, by considering various solutions to problems before they enter the classroom.

Evaluating Solutions.   One might think that evaluating solutions is unimportant because it typically occurs after the problem has been solved. This simply is not true. Those who fail to evaluate both the products and the process of problem solving miss an excellent opportunity to improve these skills. An abundance of research in the areas of metacognition (Baker, 1989), reflective practice (Schön, 1991), and self-regulation (Zimmerman, 1990) all strongly suggest that most of the improvement we experience in learning is the result of purposeful evaluation. Evaluation helps us better understand the usefulness and applicability of a particular strategy. Considering why a strategy did not work in one context may enable a learner to use it more efficiently in another. In addition, evaluating solutions permits us to reflect at a deeper level about the process of problem solving.

For these reasons, any complex problem-solving task, such as reading, writing, studying, or learning new skills in the classroom, should be accompanied by two types of evaluation. The first is an analysis of *products*. Is the end result the best solution available? How does this solution compare with others? Are there likely to be other solutions that were not considered? The second type of evaluation examines the *process*. How well did you do? What did you do right or wrong? How could you improve? Only by asking these types of questions can students be expected to improve significantly their problem-solving skills and their understanding of how to solve problems.

Expert Knowledge in Problem Solving

In the above section, we described a general model of problem solving that can be applied to any domain. Many researchers have noted that people's ability to solve a problem usually depends on two critical factors. One is the amount of domain-specific knowledge at our disposal; another is the amount of experience we have in trying to solve a particular class of problems. Debate continues concerning the most useful way to improve problem solving in the classroom and the workplace, with some researchers emphasizing the development of domain-specific knowledge and others stressing the role of general problem-solving skills (cf. Perkins & Salomon, 1989). Before we attempt to compare the relative strengths and weaknesses of the two approaches, it may be helpful to examine the role of domain-specific knowledge and experience in greater detail.

Let's begin by considering first what it takes to become an expert. Researchers studying the development of expertise estimate it takes on the order of five years or 10,000 hours to develop true expertise in a domain regardless of intellectual aptitude (Hayes, 1988)! In many cases, it may take even longer. It may surprise (or alarm) you to know that beginning radiologists (X-ray specialists) perform far below experienced experts even after completing four years of medical school (Lesgold, 1988).

One reason why expertise develops so slowly is that much of the declarative and procedural knowledge needed to master a domain is acquired *tacitly* over a long period of time (Wagner & Sternberg, 1985). For example, most college students possess a great deal of expert knowledge about their native language. They read and write fluently, using syntactic (grammar) and semantic (meaning) knowledge to convey complex meanings. They also use language metaphorically to convey nonliteral meaning (e.g., *prisons are junkyards*). Yet, most of them find it very difficult to describe what it is they know about language or how they learned it. Indeed, we often can use what we know but cannot explain it.

Evidence suggests that much of our knowledge is acquired tacitly even when we receive a great deal of formal training in a domain. Because of this, even highly skilled experts often find it difficult to describe what it is they know about a body of knowledge and, as a consequence, may be poor decision makers when forced to reflect on their knowledge (Johnson, 1988). Typically, however, experts are better problem solvers than novices for a variety of reasons, including experience, background knowledge, and information-processing advantages that are the consequence of expert knowledge (Glaser & Chi, 1988). Table 8-1 lists seven key characteristics of experts.

Seven Characteristics of Expert Performance.   Although our intuitions may suggest otherwise, the first characteristic of experts is that they usually are no better able to solve problems in unfamiliar domains than novices; that is, expertise is domain specific. Consider a brilliant chemist whose car breaks down on a deserted highway. The chances are good that the stranded motorist will walk to the nearest gas station, rather than solve the problem herself *unless* she happens to have expert knowledge about auto repair as well. No evidence, however, suggests that expertise

Table 8-1
Seven Characteristics of Experts. (From Glaser and Chi [1988].)

1. Experts excel only in their own domain.
2. Experts process information in large units.
3. Experts are faster than novices.
4. Experts hold more information in short-term and long-term memory.
5. Experts represent problems at a deeper level.
6. Experts spend more time analyzing a problem.
7. Experts are better monitors of their performance.

in one domain readily transfers to another. Rather, expertise develops slowly, is highly labor intensive, and is confined to a particular body of knowledge.

A second characteristic of experts is that they organize information far more efficiently than do novices. Typically, this is accomplished by chunking information into larger recognizable units than a novice might use (see Chapter 4). Chase and Simon (1973a, 1973b) found that one of the main differences between expert and novice chess players was not the absolute size of their working memories (about seven pieces of information), but rather how much information they could analyze and remember in a single brief exposure (their ability to categorize information). Chess experts were able to view complex chess configurations for as little as five seconds yet remember them in remarkable detail; novices remembered very little of what they saw. Surprisingly, when the same experiment was conducted using nonmeaningful chess patterns, no difference was found between the experts and the novices!

A third characteristic is that experts are faster than novices at processing meaningful information because they search and represent problems more efficiently. If you ever have had the experience of watching an expert mathematician solve word problems, you observed how easily the expert identified relevant information and selected an appropriate strategy. Although rather disconcerting to the novice, the expert's behavior may be less impressive than it appears because he or she probably has solved hundreds or perhaps thousands of similar problems in the past. The experience gained by solving these problems enables the expert to remember similar problems and solutions and to select appropriate strategies with little effort. These differences even have been observed when comparing expert and novice figure skaters (Deakin & Allard, 1991).

A fourth characteristic that makes experts better (and faster) problem solvers is that their thoughts and actions are highly automatized. Being automatic allows experts to use their short-term memory in a more efficient way, compared with novices. Expert mathematicians, for instance, activate and implement appropriate solution strategies so efficiently that they place very few demands on their cognitive resources. These resources can be used to accomplish higher-order cognitive tasks, such as monitoring one's progress and evaluating solutions.

As a fifth characteristic, experts represent problems differently from novices. Experts usually focus more of their attention on the underlying structure of the problem, rather than on superficial surface features. Many studies show that expert physicists categorize physics problems on the basis of mechanical principles, whereas novices categorize them on the basis of objects mentioned in the problem (e.g., the angle of a shadow). Experts also are more likely to break problems into subgoals and to work forward toward the desired end state (use means-ends analysis).

A sixth characteristic is that the experts spend more time than novices analyzing the problem at the *beginning* of the problem-solving process. In a number of studies reported by Voss and Post (1988), experts were found to spend a greater proportion of their time identifying and representing the problem, compared with novices, even though they spent considerably less time choosing an appropriate solution strategy once the problem had been clarified. Experts also were more apt to rely on complex conditional strategies for reducing a problem into smaller component problems (Clancey, 1988).

The seventh characteristic is that experts are better monitors than novices in most situations *within their domain of expertise.* Experts are more likely to generate alternative hypotheses before solving a problem and are quicker to reject inappropriate solutions during problem solving. Experts also judge the difficulty of problems more accurately than novices and ask more appropriate questions at all stages of the problem-solving process.

The characteristics described above all point to one simple conclusion about the nature of expertise: Experts are faster, more efficient, and more reflective *because of the depth and breadth of their knowledge.* We do not mean to imply by this statement that extensive knowledge guarantees expert performance. Most researchers agree that true expertise represents a complex interaction between general problem-solving strategies and extensive domain-specific knowledge. These two components can best be thought of as complementary processes: Expert knowledge facilitates strategy use, whereas knowledge about general problem-solving strategies enables learners to use their expert knowledge more efficiently (cf. Perkins & Salomon, 1989).

Implications: Improving Problem Solving

Problem-solving skills can be improved in a number of ways, some of which require a long-term investment (e.g., accumulating extensive expert knowledge), and some of which lead to more rapid improvement (e.g., mimicking expert strategies). In general, we emphasize the fundamental role of expert knowledge in effective problem solving. Although it is possible to improve problem-solving skills by improving *general knowledge about problem solving,* there is no substitute for 10,000 hours worth of expert knowledge acquired through hands-on activities. With this caveat, we suggest the following steps:

1. *Facilitate the acquisition of expert knowledge.* Years of research indicate that extensive domain knowledge is clearly the most important constraint on effective problem solving. One instructional strategy is to help students acquire as much

expert knowledge as quickly as possible. Educators should give serious consideration to what constitutes an "expert" body of knowledge in their discipline and attempt to convey this information to all students. This means that teachers must make a special effort to select and organize the core body of knowledge one needs to learn to become an expert.

Another highly effective strategy, though one that is neglected too often, is for a novice to ask an expert for help when he or she does not understand a problem. One reason to do so is to acquire an expert's "way of knowing" the problem. Indeed, it could be argued that learning what kinds of strategies experts use is less important than understanding why they use them.

2. *Develop an awareness of a general problem-solving strategy.* Everyone, to some extent, can become a better problem solver by understanding the basic process of problem solving (Bransford, Sherwood, Vye, & Rieser, 1986). The five-step sequence outlined earlier provides an excellent framework for developing component skills (e.g., representing problems externally), as well as for understanding the relationship between component skills.

Studies investigating the value of teaching younger students a general problem-solving method yield impressive findings. In one study, King (1991) compared groups of fifth-grade students in which students solved problems by using or not using a problem-solving prompt card. Those using the prompts solved problems better. Delclos and Harrington (1991) compared three groups of fifth- and sixth-grade students; one group received problem-solving and monitoring training, another received problem-solving training, and a third received no training. Although the combined group (metacognitive and problem-solving training) group outperformed all others, the problem-solving-only group outperformed the control group.

Together, these studies suggest that problem-solving training has a beneficial effect on younger students. Problem-solving training also is enhanced when it is coupled with other kinds of instruction, such as question answering (King, 1991) and metacognitive training (Delclos & Harrington, 1991). Readers interested in teaching general problem-solving skills may wish to consult Bransford and Stein (1984) and Gick (1986) for further information.

3. *Focus on discovering and identifying problems.* Many studies reveal that problem discovery is the most critical stage of the problem-solving sequence. Indeed, to be a good problem finder requires one to be highly creative and motivated. Individuals should be encouraged to "linger" on a problem during this stage because there is a direct relationship between time spent conceptualizing a problem and the quality of its solution. Those wishing to promote the creative aspect of problem finding may wish to consult Dacey (1989) and Weisberg (1993).

4. *Use external representations whenever possible.* One limitation that individuals face when trying to solve problems is overloading their cognitive resources. Sensory and short-term memory are limited to about seven pieces of information at a time. Many problems greatly exceed this limitation, which results in the inability to hold all relevant pieces of a problem in working memory. Committing as much of the problem as possible to paper can reduce this cognitive overload greatly and, in turn, improve problem-solving effectiveness.

5. *Mimic expert strategies.* Sometimes, it is possible to teach individuals without expert knowledge to act like experts. Using a certain "expert" fingering technique when playing the piano may improve one's performance rapidly. At other times, expert strategies are useless without the knowledge needed to *use those strategies in a planful way.* Consider a chess novice who is taught the Sicilian Defense but who gets into trouble quickly by trying to use it against a skilled opponent. When it comes to problem solving, the old proverb "A little bit of knowledge is a dangerous thing" often rings true. Using experts' strategies may be helpful in some situations but not others. Professional discretion is advised!

CRITICAL THINKING

A great deal of debate has occurred recently about whether American schools should direct their efforts to teaching students *how* to think, rather than *what* to think (Ennis, 1987; Perkins, Jay, & Tishman, 1993). The fact that such questions are being asked at all invites us to consider what it means to "think critically." Most of us would agree that critical thinking is important, that it is complex, and that it encompasses a host of lesser skills, such as identifying and evaluating information. But how does critical thinking differ from problem solving or creativity? In this section, we examine these issues and address three related questions as well: What skills are necessary to think critically? Is critical thinking constrained by intelligence? and How should one go about designing a critical thinking program?

Toward a Definition

For most experts, critical thinking differs from problem solving in two ways. One way is that problem solving usually requires an individual to solve specialized problems in a particular domain. These problems typically are well defined and have one or perhaps two correct solutions. Solving word problems in algebra class and replicating a heat-exchange experiment in a science class provide good examples. Performance on such problems has been shown to correlate highly with the amount of domain-specific expertise that learners have.

In contrast, critical thinking usually requires us to consider general issues that cut across a number of domains. These "problems" frequently are ill-defined and have many possible solutions or even may be unsolvable. Consider some of the issues we must weigh when choosing a president: how to eliminate (or at least reduce) the national debt, the constitutionality of abortion and capital punishment, and whether financial aid should be offered to formerly hostile foreign nations.

A second way that problem solving differs from critical thinking is in the nature of what is being evaluated. Most problems are external states, whereas most critical thinking is directed toward internal states. Choosing a political affiliation, for instance, is part problem solving in that we must choose whom to vote for, but it is also part critical thinking in that we first need to clarify and evaluate our own beliefs and expectations about each of the candidates.

One definition of critical thinking is *reflective thinking focused on deciding what to believe or do* (Ennis, 1987). We believe that an analysis of some of the key terms in this definition are helpful for understanding what critical thinking entails. First, critical thinking is a *reflective* activity. Often, its goal is not to solve a problem, but rather to better understand the nature of the problem. Critical thinking also is *focused,* in that we are not just thinking, but thinking about something we wish to understand more thoroughly. The purpose of thinking critically is to weigh and evaluate information in a way that ultimately enables us to make informed *decisions*. Finally, unlike problem solving, the content of our critical thinking is often a *belief* or a motive we wish to examine more thoroughly.

A second definition of critical thinking is *better thinking* (Perkins, 1987). This view suggests that learning to think critically will improve our ability to gather, interpret, evaluate, and select information for the purpose of making informed choices. We suspect that this is the definition most teachers and parents have in mind when they say, "Students need to think more critically about their lives." Of course, statements such as these require us as parents and professional educators to think more critically about how to improve students' thinking!

A third definition of critical thinking is *distinguishing between thinking that is directed at adopting versus clarifying a goal* (Nickerson, 1987). *Adopting* is closer to problem solving because it emphasizes a "product" view of decision making, whereas *clarifying* emphasizes the "process" one uses to reach that decision. We view critical thinking as more than decision making and believe that the process of informed decision making is more important than the decision itself. Let's turn now to some of the skills involved in critical thinking.

Component Skills in Critical Thinking

Earlier, we described a number of important skills used in problem solving. We now turn our attention to an analogous set of skills used in critical thinking. Ennis (1987) has proposed the most comprehensive set of skills thus far in which he distinguishes between two major classes of critical thinking activities: *dispositions* and *abilities*. The former refers to affective and dispositional traits that each person brings to a thinking task, traits such as open-mindedness, an attempt to be well informed, and sensitivity to others' beliefs, feelings, and knowledge. The latter refers to the actual cognitive abilities necessary to think critically, including focusing, analyzing, and judging.

Table 8-2 lists twelve skills included in Ennis's taxonomy. An inspection of these skills (and selected subskills) suggests that some are appropriate for any type of thinking, whether critical or creative. Others, such as making value judgments, seem to be less important when solving physics problems than when voting for a presidential candidate. According to Ennis (1987), each subskill contributes to critical thinking in its own

Table 8-2
Twelve Critical-Thinking Abilities Described by Ennis (1987).

1. Focusing on the question
2. Analyzing arguments
3. Asking and answering questions of clarification
4. Judging the credibility of a source
5. Observing and judging observational reports
6. Deducing and judging deductions
7. Inducing and judging inductions
8. Making value judgments
9. Defining terms and judging definitions
10. Identifying assumptions
11. Deciding on an action
12. Interacting with others

unique way, helping us clarify our goals and objectives, acquire and analyze an adequate knowledge base, make inferences, and interact with others in a rational manner.

Analyzing critical thinking in terms of separate subskills can be somewhat risky, however, because we are apt to lose sight of what critical thinking entails: critical examination of beliefs and courses of action. Instead, some authors suggest that a smaller set of general skills should be used to describe critical thinking (Kurfiss, 1988; Nickerson, 1987; Quellmalz, 1987; Swartz & Perkins, 1990). These skills include knowledge, inference, evaluation, and metacognition.

Critical thinking of any kind is impossible without the first of these components—*knowledge.* Knowledge is something we use to think critically and also acquire as the result of critical thinking. As we have seen, expert knowledge enables humans to solve problems faster, better, and differently from those without such knowledge. Knowledge provides the basis for judging the credibility of new information or points of view; it also helps us critically scrutinize our goals and objectives. Knowledge in the form of strategies actively shapes the direction we take when trying to resolve a dilemma.

Inference refers to making some type of connection between two or more units of knowledge. Much of successful critical thinking draws on our ability to make simple, though insightful, inferences between otherwise unrelated facts. In Chapter 6, for example, you learned that each of us makes attributional inferences concerning our success and failure in the classroom. Some of these inferences may be inappropriate under certain circumstances (e.g., beginning algebra students attributing their failure to low ability), while others are more appropriate (e.g., poor performance in algebra may be due to lack of prior knowledge, domain-specific strategies, and automaticity). Making inferences is an essential step in critical thinking because it enables individuals to understand their situations at a deeper, more meaningful level.

Several types of inference processes seem to be especially important. One is *deduction,* the process by which we reach specific conclusions from given information. Logicians and mathematicians have identified a variety of deductive reasoning approaches that are useful when solving well-defined problems, such as syllogisms. No matter what the approach, all deductive inferences are similar in that conclusions are based only on the information provided by the problem. In the parlance of Chapter 2, deduction is a data-limited reasoning process. Thus, if Ahmed borrows his mother's car and returns with a dented fender, we can deduce that Ahmed had an accident. We cannot deduce that Ahmed was speeding, legally drunk, or watching a pedestrian while driving, which, in turn, caused the accident.

Another kind of inference process is *induction,* the process by which we reach general conclusions from given, or perhaps inferred, information. Induction is in many ways the opposite of deduction in that conclusions can be reached that go beyond the limits of the data. Inductive inferences tend to be broader and more sweeping than deductive inferences. One of the best examples of inductive reasoning is making up a theory to explain an event before it is investigated (or perhaps even happens). Darwin's theory of natural selection provides a stunning example of inductive inference because it transcends the data described in *The Origin of Species.*

The third component described above—*evaluation*—refers to a number of related subskills, including analyzing, judging, weighing, and making value judgments (Swartz & Perkins, 1990). These skills probably come closest to what we normally think of as critical thinking. *Analyzing* includes activities that enable us to identify and select relevant information. *Judging* requires us to assess the credibility of information or sources of information in an effort to eliminate bias. *Weighing* consists of comparing all information at our disposal, choosing the most appropriate information, and organizing it as logically as possible. *Making value judgments* assumes we have some moral, ethical, or emotional response to the information that affects our decision making.

The final component of critical thinking is *metacognition* (McGuinness, 1990; Swartz, 1989). As described in Chapter 4, metacognition refers to "thinking about thinking." Clearly, an important aspect of critical thinking is our ability to analyze the adequacy of our decisions. Insufficient data or conflicting beliefs and attitudes may require us to postpone an important decision and may limit our ability to construct an informed opinion on a topic. Metacognition is essential to the critical-thinking process because it allows us to monitor the adequacy of the information on which we base our opinions, as well as the reasonableness of our inferences.

Is Critical Thinking Constrained by Intelligence?

In the previous section, we described a number of skills necessary for critical thinking. One might ask whether these skills depend on intellectual aptitude. If they do, educators are faced with difficult decisions about grouping students on the basis of ability. Until recently, an ability groups model formed the backbone of the American educational system. But what if thinking skills are not strongly linked with ability? How, then, should educators go about planning instruction?

Surprisingly, not a great deal of research has been done on the relationship between intellectual ability and critical thinking skills, although the existing research does suggest that normatively high intellectual ability is neither a necessary nor sufficient condition for successful thinking (see Baron, 1988, for a further discussion). Earlier, we reported that Kitchener and King (1981) found that verbal ability (a correlate of general intellectual ability) was not related to reflective reasoning. Among children, Swanson (1990) found that metacognitive awareness was not constrained by intellectual ability.

Many contemporary researchers have adopted a broad view of what it means to be intelligent and how intellectual skills affect critical thinking (cf. Gardner, 1983; Sternberg, 1986). One view we find particularly attractive is the model of critical thinking proposed by Perkins (1987). Perkins's model addresses three distinct aspects of intelligence: power, knowledge, and tactics. *Power* refers to the basic level of intellectual aptitude that each of us brings to a task. Clearly, this potential differs from person to person and, in many cases, differs within a single person across a variety of tasks (cf. Gardner, 1983). *Knowledge* refers to the domain-specific and general knowledge at our disposal. Every intellectual activity we undertake is affected in some way by what we already know. One way in which knowledge helps us is in facilitating the organization of incoming information. Prior knowledge also enables us to construct meaning based on what we already know about a topic.

Unlike power and knowledge, tactics can be improved dramatically in only a short period of time (Perkins, 1987; Perkins & Salomon, 1989). *Tactics* refers to the mental strategies we use to make a cognitive task easier to understand or perform. Perkins and many others (cf. Pressley et al., 1990) place a high premium on tactical knowledge for one important reason: Even a modest repertoire of tactics can compensate for lack of power or knowledge. The compensatory nature of tactics has been demonstrated in many studies (King, 1991; Swanson, 1990).

The fact that a compensatory relationship exists among power, knowledge, and tactics is of tremendous importance to educators (see Figure 8-3). When developing critical-thinking skills, teachers and students alike should be encouraged to focus less attention on the role of power and more attention on knowledge and tactics. Teachers and students also should bear in mind that some tactics are "welded" to a particular body of knowledge, whereas others are not (Perkins, 1987). For example, factoring a quadratic equation to find its roots (a tactic) is difficult to separate from

Figure 8-3
Components involved in learning, problem solving, and critical thinking. (Perkins, D. N. Thinking frames: An integrated perspective on teaching cognitive skills. From: TEACHING THINKING SKILLS by Baron and Sternberg. Copyright (c) 1987 by W.H. Freeman and Company. Used with permission.)

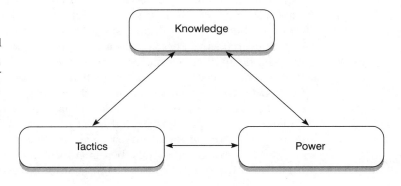

knowledge about quadratic equations because the two tend to be learned together. However, other tactics, such as monitoring one's comprehension, are not specific to any particular body of knowledge. Monitoring is as useful when learning about American history as it is when assembling a sump pump or reading a road map. Some tactics need to be taught within a specific context for knowledge to be mastered; others are far more general and may be used successfully in many domains.

Tactics need not be limited to simple strategies such as skimming a text, factoring an equation, or carrying an umbrella when it looks like rain. Perkins (1987) has described a broader tactical approach to learning that he refers to as "thinking frames." According to Perkins, a **thinking frame** is a guide or structure that organizes and supports thought processes. One example of a thinking frame is the "scientific method" commonly taught to beginning science students. Another example is the SQ3R (survey, question, read, recite, review) method of study. Other examples encountered in this text are levels of processing (a frame for understanding the depth of encoding), epistemological beliefs (a frame for explaining how individuals think about knowledge), and the general problem-solving method described above (a frame for attempting to solve any kind of well-defined problem).

One advantage to having thinking frames is that they provide an organizational structure for understanding new information and learning new skills. The Lehman et al. (1988) study described in Chapter 7 indicated that graduate students in different disciplines acquire expertise in reasoning skills that are especially important to their discipline (e.g., statistical reasoning). Acquiring these skills is one way that graduate students learn to "think like" experts. Another way is for graduate students to acquire the thinking frames a discipline holds about the phenomena it studies. For example, medical researchers assume that bacteria and viruses cause diseases; thus, the researchers search for cures for these diseases on the basis of external-agent models (they use a germ theory thinking frame).

Perkins (1987) has described three stages in frame development: acquisition, automaticity, and transfer. *Acquisition* refers to learning a thinking frame and, in turn, using a thinking frame to think and reason. Perkins is a strong proponent of teaching frames directly, including extensive modeling. *Automaticity* refers to being able to apply the frame automatically. As with other skills, using a thinking frame automatically is the result of extensive practice; the more practice one gets, the more automatic the frame becomes. *Transfer* refers to using the frame in a new context. Perkins (1987) and Perkins and Salomon (1989) have identified two kinds of transfer. The first kind of transfer, *high-road transfer,* occurs when students make a conscious, reflective effort to abstract the basic principles of the frame in a way that they can be applied in a different content area. High-road transfer requires students to be active, constructive, and reflective. In contrast, the second kind of transfer, *low-road transfer,* occurs spontaneously without awareness, given a narrow range of examples. As a consequence, students may not achieve a thorough (transferable) understanding of the frame. High-road transfer can be promoted by emphasizing reflection, self-monitoring, and extensive practice in a variety of settings.

Perkins strongly advocates the direct teaching and modeling of tactics and thinking frames for several reasons. First, he believes that power (native ability) is extremely difficult to change. Second, he assumes that developing a body of expert knowledge is too time- and labor-intensive, taking perhaps thousands of hours. In contrast, strategy instruction can be accomplished in a much shorter period of time. Although strategies cannot substitute completely for power and knowledge, they often are able to compensate for lower levels of power and knowledge.

Planning a Critical-Thinking Skills Program

Programs designed to improve thinking, reasoning, and problem-solving skills fall into one of two categories: stand-alone and embedded programs. **Stand-alone programs** focus on the development of thinking skills independent of content area material. **Embedded programs** focus on improving thinking skills within the context of a particular content area, such as history or science.

Most experts suggest that thinking skills be embedded in specific content areas at least some of the time (Beyer, 1987; Swartz & Perkins, 1990). One reason is that content material may increase students' interest in learning in a way that is not possible with stand-alone programs. A second reason is that there is little evidence to suggest that learning thinking skills is made more difficult when students are asked to learn new content material as well.

This section provides several guidelines for designing either a stand-alone or embedded thinking-skills program. These programs should include the following three goals: (1) identifying appropriate skills, (2) implementing instruction, and (3) evaluating the program. We consider each of these steps separately.

Identifying Appropriate Skills.   Program design should begin with questions about the kind of model that will guide instruction (Baron, 1988). *Descriptive models* explain how good thinking actually happens. Often, good thinkers use sophisticated rules, strategies, and heuristics to evaluate information and reach decisions. This does not mean that such thinking is free of errors or is the best way to think in a particular setting. Rather, it describes what good thinkers actually do. *Prescriptive models* explain how good thinking ought to happen. They presume that some forms of thinking are better than others. Educators sometimes design instruction based on a prescriptive model that is too complicated or time consuming to be used in most everyday settings. An alternative is to approach the teaching of thinking skills from a descriptive standpoint, emphasizing how good thinkers solve problems and reach decisions in everyday life, even if their thinking is less than optimal.

Instructors also must decide what kinds of thinking skills they wish to include in their program. Table 8-3 presents a summary of some of the component skills and assumptions involved in four kinds of thinking programs: creative thinking, critical thinking, decision making, and problem solving. It is important to recall that some of these skills may exceed students' developmental limitations. Some programs also may require more time or resources than others.

Last, instructors should consider whether *direct* or *indirect* instruction will be used. The former refers to teacher-directed instruction that focuses on clearly identified rules for good thinking. The latter refers to a student-directed approach to

Table 8-3

Characteristics of Four Thinking Skills. (Adapted from Swartz, R. J., & Perkins, D. N. [1990].
Teaching Thinking: Issues and Approaches. Pacific Grove, CA: Critical Thinking Press & Software. Formerly Midwest Publications.)

Type of Skill	Goals	Component Skills
Critical Thinking	To evaluate contrasting positions or the clarity of ideas	Identify position or idea, analyze competing views, weigh evidence, gather new information
Creative Thinking	To generate new ideas, develop new products	Establish need for idea, restructure existing view of problem, generate possibilities
Decision Making	To reach an informed decision	Consider available information, evaluate information, identify options, weigh options, make decision
Problem Solving	To reach one or more adequate solutions to a problem	Identify, represent, select a strategy, implement the strategy, evaluate progress

instruction that emphasizes the discovery of meaningful criteria for good thinking. Direct instruction appears to be most effective in situations in which an easy-to-identify strategy exists and problem solutions are limited. Indirect instruction may be most useful when attempting to develop guidelines for thinking about ill-defined problems, such as moral and ethical dilemmas faced in everyday life.

Implementing Instruction.   To be effective, teachers must present thinking skills in a clear and meaningful sequence. Instructors should identify this sequence and model it for students. The first part of this chapter described a representative five-step problem-solving sequence. An analogous decision-making sequence might include (1) generating hypotheses about the causes of an event, (2) establishing rules for what constitutes acceptable evidence, (3) accumulating evidence from internal and external sources, (4) assessing the reliability of the evidence, and (5) evaluating the reasonableness of different causal claims.

Several rules of thumb are helpful when considering sequencing. One rule is to start broadly, even in embedded programs. A second rule is to provide ample time to teach the thinking-skill sequence. In general, planning on a six-month to one-year time frame seems most reasonable. A third rule is to use what Swartz and Perkins (1990) refer to as "bridging." **Bridging** involves grafting a skill previously used in a stand-alone program onto a regular content class, such as history or biology. In essence, bridging refers to embedding previously isolated thinking skills. Bridging is important because eventually students should be able to use general thinking skills in a variety of settings and in a variety of content areas.

Students also must be helped to increase their awareness of new skills. To increase awareness, students should be encouraged to reflect on the acquisition and use of new thinking skills (see Chapter 4). One method is to include in-class discussion of these skills. Other methods are the use of small cooperative discussion groups, journals, and "think aloud" exercises in which one student explains the skill while he or she performs it.

Promoting awareness and discussion of thinking skills, including the component steps involved in each skill, is useful because students are not always as aware as we would like them to be. Along these lines, Swartz and Perkins (1990) have identified four levels of awareness. At the lower end of the scale is the *tacit use* of a skill, which is characterized by skilled performance without awareness. In comparison, *aware use* of a skill occurs when an individual is aware of using it even though the skill cannot be explained. Consider how easily we use grammatical rules and knowledge without explicit knowledge of these rules. *Strategic use* occurs when an individual possesses conscious awareness about the skill and uses this knowledge to regulate the use of the skill. *Reflective use* occurs when an individual reflects on the skill, understands how the skill works, knows how to use it strategically, and can explain it to others.

Effective instruction also must provide varied, extensive practice. The idea of practice as a means for developing automaticity is an important one. Researchers know that automaticity develops faster if a skill is practiced regularly, over a long period of time, and in a variety of settings.

Evaluating the Program.   Most experts agree that thinking-skills programs are underevaluated, rather than overevaluated (Barrel, 1991; Swartz & Perkins, 1990). Unfortunately, a number of common problems can undermine the evaluation process. One frequent problem is that teachers encounter resistance to teaching "thinking skills," as opposed to teaching "content." Some students, parents, and administrators may be suspicious of such programs. A second problem is that very few tests reliably measure improvements in thinking. A third problem is that successful thinking-skills programs may take years to achieve their aims.

Notwithstanding these concerns, instructors should evaluate three aspects of every program (Norris & Ennis, 1989; Swartz & Perkins, 1990). One aspect is the design adequacy of the program *before* it is implemented. Questions to ask at this stage include (1) Does the program include the kind of skills you want to improve, (2) is the program sustainable for long enough to achieve its goals, (3) are support systems available, (4) will the criterion skills transfer to new domains, and (5) are there plenty of opportunities to practice the new skills?

A second aspect is the need to evaluate the program *during* implementation. Questions to ask at this stage include (1) Are the criterion skills being mastered, (2) are the new skills being used inside and outside the classroom, (3) do the new skills seem to make a difference in students' thinking, (4) does the program provide sufficient feedback to students, and (5) does the instructor have access to evaluative feedback?

A third aspect is the need for evaluation *after* the program has been implemented. Questions to ask at this stage include (1) Has the program achieved its goals, (2) did the program improve students' thinking, (3) was this improvement seen in other areas of thinking or across the curriculum, (4) are provisions made for maintaining the progress made in the program, and (5) was the program the most effective use of the students' time?

Some Examples of Stand-Alone Programs

During the past two decades, a number of stand-alone programs designed to teach problem solving and critical thinking skills have appeared. Typical examples that have been studied are the Productive Thinking Program (Covington, Crutchfield, Davies, & Olton, 1974); the IDEAL Problem Solver (Bransford & Stein, 1984); the CoRT Thinking Materials (de Bono, 1973); and the Feuerstein Instrumental Enrichment (FIE) Program (Feuerstein, Rand, Hoffman, & Miller, 1980). We review each of these approaches briefly. For a discussion of other thinking-skills programs, see Bransford et al. (1986) and Vye, Delclos, Burns, and Bransford (1988).

The Productive Thinking Program.   This program includes a set of fifteen lessons designed to teach general problem-solving skills to upper-level elementary school children. Each lesson (see Covington et al., 1974, for a more complete description) consists of a booklet describing a basic lesson, accompanied by supplementary problems. The lessons describe two children who face a number of "mystery" situations requiring detectivelike activities. Under the guidance of an uncle, the children attempt to solve the mystery (the problem). Presented in a gamelike way, the lessons are grounded in a model of problem solving similar to the five-point sequence described above. Lessons deal with problem definition, getting the "facts" (knowledge), checking facts, making plans, and rerepresenting problems. The lessons are designed to be completed during a one-semester period. Evaluation suggests that students of differing abilities all show rather striking improvement on measures of problem-solving skill, compared with comparable control groups (see Mansfield, Busse, & Krepelka, 1978; Olton & Crutchfield, 1969).

The IDEAL Problem Solver.   The IDEAL Problem Solver describes five stages consistent with the IDEAL mnemonic (Bransford & Stein, 1984). The first, *Identifying Problems (I)*, asks the solver to actively seek problems requiring solution. The second step, *Defining Problems (D)*, focuses on problem representation. Emphasis is placed on obtaining a clear picture of the problem prior to any solution attempts. The third step, *Exploring Alternatives (E)*, involves generation and analysis of alternatives (operators) that might deal with the problem. The fourth step, *Acting on a Plan (A)*, is closely linked with Step 5, *Looking at the Effects (L)*.

Because it is a general stand-alone model, IDEAL can be adapted to a wide range of age and ability groups. It also can be embedded in many content domains, such as physics, history, and composition. Research on the IDEAL method and other similar programs has been quite positive, especially when the method is used to improve children's problem-solving skills (Delclos & Harrington, 1991; King, 1991; Vye et al., 1988).

The CoRT Thinking Materials.   CoRT (Cognitive Research Trust) materials consist of a two-year course for improving thinking skills (de Bono, 1973). The lessons include not only problem-solving skills but also the development of interpersonal skills and creative thinking. The lessons are presumed to be appropriate to children of a wide age range. The six units of materials include topics such as planning, generating alternatives, analyzing, comparing, selecting, and evaluating. A unit designed for a ten-week period consists of a series of leaflets, each discussing a single topic. Also included are examples, practice items, and ideas for further practice on the topic. The leaflets can be used easily in group settings. A number of games called Think Links are designed to facilitate practice with the topics. In the Gestalt tradition (see Chapter 2), de Bono stresses the perceptual aspect of problem solving and tries to teach students effective techniques for breaking loose from ineffective patterns. He also believes that thinking skills are improved by practice; thus, following a brief description of each principle in a leaflet, the bulk of instructional time is spent practicing the principle.

Feuerstein's Instrumental Enrichment.   Feuerstein's Instrumental Enrichment (FIE) system centers on what Feuerstein (Feuerstein et al., 1980) calls "mediated-learning experiences" (MLEs). *Mediated-learning experiences* provide activities that teach learners to interpret their experience. MLEs are deliberate interventions, by teachers, parents, or others, designed to help learners interpret and organize events. The basic task of the MLE is to teach the child to play an active role in critical thinking and, ultimately, to think and solve problems independently.

Instructionally FIE provides a series of exercises (called "instruments" by Feuerstein) that provide the context for learning. At present, fourteen or fifteen instruments, arranged in order of increasing complexity, are available for ten- to eighteen-year-old students. The program is designed to be taught three to five times per week for two or three years. The exercises are paper-and-pencil activities designed to help the student identify problem-solving procedures and permit the teacher to "bridge" from the activities (problems) to subject matter of interest to student and teacher. Most FIE lessons provide "practice" exercises carried out under teacher supervision to provide feedback to students in their attempts to identify and evaluate the strategies used in solution attempts. FIE also provides a language for teaching problem-solving concepts such as *planning, strategy choice, evaluation,* and the like. Each instrument is designed to have wide generality. A special feature of this program is the deliberate focus on instruction of special populations. Thus, it has been used with youngsters who have mental retardation, learning disabilities, behavioral disorders, and hearing impairment.

Bransford, Arbitman-Smith, Stein, and Vye (1985) and Savalle, Twohig, and Rachford (1986) have evaluated the effectiveness of FIE. On the basis of a wide range of evaluation studies conducted in Israel, Venezuela, the United States, and Canada, students exposed to the FIE program performed better than control groups on tests such as the Raven's Progressive Matrices and some achievement subtests, such as mathematics. The effects were found with a wide variety of student types. However, a number of studies also have shown no significant difference as a result of FIE training. In general, features of successful studies were the presence of well-trained FIE teachers and student instruction that lasted eighty hours or more.

SUMMARY

This chapter examined problem solving and critical thinking. Both types of thinking are constrained by two important factors: (1) expert knowledge within a domain and (2) knowledge about a general problem-solving (or critical-thinking) strategy.

Expert knowledge improves problem solving for a number of reasons, including faster processing, better representation, more effective use of solution strategies, and better monitoring. Knowledge of a general problem-solving strategy also improves performance, even among children. Five stages in this strategy were described: problem finding, representing problems, selecting a strategy, implementing a strategy, and evaluating the solution.

We also provided several definitions of critical thinking, a cognitive activity that is assumed to overlap with problem solving but that differs from it as well. Critical thinking is related more closely to ill-defined problems, whereas problem solving often relates to well-defined problems. We described four general skills known to influence it: knowledge, inference, evaluation, and metacognition.

We next considered whether intellectual ability constrains problem solving and critical thinking. We argued for a compensatory relationship among power, knowledge, and tactics, emphasizing that although native ability affects critical thinking, it can be compensated for through the selective use of knowledge and strategies.

A plan for identifying, implementing, and evaluating a critical-thinking program was presented as well. Basic components of such programs include defining an instructional sequence, promoting higher-order awareness of critical-thinking skills through the development and use of metacognition, and providing ample time for students to engage in extensive and varied practice of newly acquired thinking skills.

We examined several stand-alone instructional programs to improve general problem solving and critical thinking: the Productive Thinking Program, the IDEAL Problem Solver, the CoRT Thinking Materials, and the Feuerstein Instrumental Enrichment System. Research indicates that all of these programs enhance thinking skills, although each promotes a different set of skills.

SUGGESTED READINGS

Baron, J. (1988). *Thinking and deciding*. New York: Cambridge University Press.

This scholarly text considers problem solving, critical thinking, and reasoning from an in-depth perspective. Although it is highly technical and requires some knowledge of cognitive psychology, it is well written and provides a sweeping view of the field.

Chi, M., Glaser, R., & Farr, M. (Eds.). (1988). *The nature of expertise*. Hillsdale, NJ: Lawrence Erlbaum.

This is an excellent, though technical, collection of articles investigating both theoretical and applied aspects of expertise.

Perkins, D. N. (1987). Thinking frames: An integrated perspective on teaching cognitive skills. In J. Baron & R. Sternberg (Eds.), *Teaching thinking skills: Theory and practice* (pp. 41–61). San Francisco: Freeman.

This is an extremely thought-provoking chapter accessible to all readers. Must reading for any teacher.

Swartz, R. J., & Perkins, D. N. (1990). *Teaching thinking: Issues and approaches.* Pacific Grove, CA: Midwest Publications.

This book, by two highly regarded experts, is directed toward helping nonexperts design, implement, and evaluate a thinking-skills program.

Weisberg, R. W. (1993). *Creativity: Beyond the myth of genius.* San Francisco: Freeman.

This book combines a review of research with interesting case studies to dispel many of the myths about creativity. Easily accessible to readers with a limited knowledge of cognitive psychology.

Building Knowledge and Reflective Thought

In the preceding chapters, our goal has been to develop the reader's understanding of the nature of human cognition. Our approach has been to describe systematically an information processing model of cognition and its most important features (e.g., attention, memory, problem solving). In this chapter, our focus shifts away from the model itself to an emphasis on cognitive processes in the classroom. This chapter is about how the activities in classrooms can affect how knowledge is created, reflected on, and transformed. We begin the chapter by discussing the role of declarative, procedural, and metacognitive knowledge, first in content domains and then more generally. Our perspective on knowledge acquisition is derived from features we have seen in earlier chapters to be characteristic of human information processing—a system in which the learner's prior knowledge, activities, and goals provide a context for creation of new knowledge.

We adopt a *constructivist* perspective, which emphasizes the contribution of the learner to what is learned. We examine three aspects of this constructivist perspective but concentrate most strongly on one of the three—*dialectical constructivism*—which highlights the importance of social interactions in knowledge acquisition. This is the perspective we take in considering the elements that are most likely to create a "reflective classroom"—one in which teachers and students interact in ways that stimulate both knowledge construction and metacognitive growth. In the final section of the chapter, we examine how classrooms can become environments for interactions that foster knowledge acquisition. We focus particularly on the potential of well-managed classroom discourse—extended, thematic communication among classroom participants—for building knowledge and reflective thinking.

TYPES OF KNOWLEDGE

In Chapter 3, we contrasted two major types of knowledge: *declarative knowledge* ("knowing what" or factual knowledge) and *procedural knowledge* ("knowing how" to perform activities). In Chapter 4, we added another major category—*metacognition*—which includes two related dimensions: *knowledge of cognition* (the degree of awareness that learners have about their cognitive processes) and *regulation of cognition* (conditional knowledge they use to guide their cognitive processes and approaches to learning). Now, let's return briefly to the example of Kari we presented in Chapter 1. She was faced with the task of writing a short paper. To write this paper, Kari first needed to draw on her semantic memory and on other sources, such as articles and texts, for the declarative knowledge that would form the body of her paper. Second, she needed to exercise procedural skills as diverse as those needed for simply handling and looking through texts and those she needed for running her computer and preparing her final paper. Third, she needed to use metacognitive knowledge to sequence and manage a multitude of cognitive activities. Her own awareness of what she did and did not know provided a starting point for her planning. Then, at each step in this very complex process of writing a "simple" paper, she needed to decide which information to select and which to ignore, how to combine information with other information, how to express her ideas, and how to communicate with her history teacher, the primary audience for her final product.

These three categories of knowledge are fundamental to successful performance in every school task. Students must be able to (1) access a declarative network of information and comprehend relationships among its elements, drawing from external information sources and semantic memory, (2) carry out simple and complex procedural skills that move the task toward completion, and (3) use metacognitive knowledge to reflect on what is known and carry out the task. For each of these categories of knowledge, however, it is useful to make one further distinction—the distinction between *domain knowledge* and *general knowledge*.

Domain Knowledge

To write her paper, Kari needed information about the specific topic she selected. The realm of knowledge that individuals have about a particular field of study is called *domain-specific knowledge,* or simply **domain knowledge** (Alexander, 1992).

Knowledge domains typically are subject areas (e.g., mathematics, modern art) but also can represent areas of activity (e.g., bicycle mechanics, taxi driving, gardening). They encompass declarative, procedural, and metacognitive knowledge and can operate at a tacit or an explicit level. For many tasks, including school-related ones, the amount of domain knowledge required to perform successfully is very large indeed. For instance, try to visualize the amount of knowledge needed to make sense out of novels such as *The Color Purple* and *Moby Dick,* a momentum problem in physics, or a description of gene-splicing techniques.

Examples of useful domain knowledge can be seen all about us every day. Each plays a role in an individual's functioning effectively. Examples of domain knowledge that is more declarative in nature are the knowledge needed to make sense of a road map, the information required to judge what kind of home loan might be best for a person's circumstances, and knowledge of the capitals of Eastern Europe. Examples of domain knowledge that is more procedural also abound—for instance, the knowledge that an office worker reveals as he duplicates a report or runs a spreadsheet program, that a mechanic exhibits in successfully diagnosing the cause of a poorly running automobile, and the skills an athlete exercises, say, in the course of a volleyball match. Likewise, domain-related metacognitive knowledge is shown as students make the observation they are "poor in math," find main ideas in a science text, and plan their part in a class project on the Civil War.

Obviously, one of the major goals of schooling is to build all three dimensions of students' domain knowledge. By the time students finish formal schooling, we expect they all possess a large and usable body of information in each of a number of curricular fields, such as history, literature, mathematics, biology, and foreign languages. We also hope that students will have built their domain knowledge in a number of areas of everyday life, such as jobs, the environment, and community functioning.

An Example of the Role of Domain Knowledge in Cognition.   The influence of domain knowledge is very potent but is so pervasive that we may lose sight of it. Consider, for example, the role of domain knowledge in reading. Typically, we think of differences in what students comprehend and remember from reading as due to their basic abilities in reading, not to their domain knowledge. We do know, however, that good readers remember more of what they read and possess more knowledge about the world than poor readers (see Taft & Leslie, 1985). At the same time, good readers not only remember more about what they read but also read a great deal more than poor readers. This close relationship between reading ability and knowledge has made research in the area difficult. However, a study by Recht and Leslie (1988) was designed in a way that allowed them to see what effect domain knowledge had on students' memory for what they read.

Recht and Leslie searched for a topic that some good readers and some poor readers would know a great deal about, but also one that some good and some poor readers would know very little about. They settled on baseball. After identifying some junior high school students who were very good readers and some who were poor readers, Recht and Leslie tested all of them about their knowledge of baseball. This procedure allowed them to identify good readers who knew a great deal about baseball, good readers who knew very little about baseball, poor readers who knew a great deal about baseball, and poor readers who knew very little about baseball. Next, the students were asked to read a 625-word passage that described half an inning of a baseball game between a local team and a visiting rival. They then were tested in several ways for their ability to remember the passage: (1) reenacting the inning with a model field and miniature wooden players while verbally describing what happened, (2) summarizing the passage, and (3) sorting twenty-two sentences taken from the passage on the basis of how important the sentences were to the happenings of the inning.

The results of Recht and Leslie's (1988) study were striking. On each of the measures of memory, poor readers who knew a great deal about baseball greatly outperformed good readers who knew very little about baseball. In fact, they performed nearly as well as the good readers who knew a great deal about baseball. Poor readers who knew very little about baseball, however, remembered the least about the passage on all measures. Thus, knowledge in the domain of baseball had a very powerful influence on how much and what was remembered.

The influence of students' domain knowledge on new learning reaches far more broadly than baseball, of course. Remembering information in areas as diverse as chess, art, computer programming, electronics, and biology all have been shown to be related to previous knowledge. In general, the more students know about a specific topic, the easier it is for them to learn and remember new information about that topic.

Not surprisingly, domain knowledge also is related to problem-solving abilities (see Chapter 8). Experts, be they artists, mechanics, or nuclear physicists, know that problems in their field are solved most easily when they can be related to other, similar problems. Experts typically think before they act. They also understand the importance of sketches and diagrams in problem solving. Novices, in contrast, may work very hard at problem solving—even harder than experts—but their strategies are less productive because of their limited domain knowledge and the inefficient ways they go about trying to make their knowledge relevant to problems.

General Knowledge

Although domain knowledge is fundamental for comprehension and for performing day-to-day activities, another kind of knowledge—**general knowledge**—also is needed. General knowledge is broad knowledge that is not linked with a specific knowledge domain. Thinking back once again to our example of Kari, you can see she needed information, skills, and strategies beyond the specific topic of her paper. To successfully write her report, for example, she needed a declarative network of concepts and a vocabulary to express her ideas, knowledge of punctuation and grammar to guide her writing, general information about reports and their functions, and procedural skills for operating a word processor. She also needed metacognitive knowledge to organize and carry out all of these activities. None of this general knowledge is related directly to the topic she chose to write about, but it nonetheless is essential for completing this and virtually all tasks.

Because it is information that can be applied to almost any task, general knowledge can be thought of as complementary to domain knowledge. Of course, what constitutes general knowledge and what constitutes domain knowledge can shift as the task focus shifts. For students reading a novel by Willa Cather and trying to understand her use of certain literary devices, the relevant domain knowledge may be primarily in the realm of English literature. If her descriptions of the native prairie are being studied by a biology class for how they characterized prairie ecology nearly a century ago, however, and the task is to map changes that may be occurring in the prairie environment, the relevant domain knowledge now centers on the plants, animals, and environment, with literary knowledge becoming general knowledge.

Ordinarily, however, one can think of general knowledge as knowledge appropriate to a wide range of tasks but not tied to any one task. The declarative networks represented by our vocabulary, knowledge of current affairs, and historical knowledge; the procedural knowledge for speaking, for doing mathematics, and for carrying on a conversation; and the metacognitive skills we use across a variety of cognitive tasks are all examples of general knowledge that is useful for a very broad array of activities. Indeed, one can consider the almost infinite amount of general knowledge necessary for a fifteen-year-old such as Kari to function on a day-to-day basis at home, in her social world, and at school.

An Additional Comment on Metacognitive Knowledge

As we saw in Chapter 4, *metacognition* refers to the awareness of cognition and to the ability to regulate one's own cognitive functions. Researchers increasingly have recognized the importance of metacognitive knowledge to success in most school-related tasks, from completing assignments to reading effectively (e.g., Brown, Day, & Jones, 1983; Guthrie, 1993). Students' abilities to think about assignments, to search for and find relevant information, to organize their ideas into meaningful sequences, and to write in ways that consider the perspective of readers are all important types of metacognitive knowledge linked with school success. For instance, Kari well might have written her paper differently if it were to be entered in an essay contest, rather than read by her history teacher and her peers. For many educators, the goal of developing metacognitive knowledge ranks as high as or higher than the goals of developing basic declarative or procedural knowledge. For students to be successful as independent learners, they must be aware of their own cognitive processes and have self-regulatory skills to help them acquire information, determine what is important to learn, reflect on purposes of tasks, monitor the quality of their performance, and move them toward their goals.

A primary goal of education is to aid students in acquiring knowledge in a variety of content domains. Each knowledge domain, such as mathematics, literature, or science, represents an important aspect of student competence. Domain knowledge— whether a young child's expansive network of declarative knowledge about dinosaurs or an older student's proceduralized knowledge of principles of photography—is a key to expertise. Domain knowledge, however, must be embedded in a larger context of general knowledge in order for it to be used flexibly. Students also need a large array of declarative knowledge about the world in order to make sense of domain knowledge, and generalized procedural knowledge to carry out most tasks.

In both specific domains and in general, however, no category of knowledge is likely to be more important than metacognitive knowledge. We want students to be aware of what they know, to monitor their learning, and to learn strategically. Because domain and general knowledge change so rapidly, students must learn to be skillful, motivated, self-directed learners.

The challenge to teachers is to provide a social and intellectual environment in their classrooms that supports knowledge construction in all of its forms and that encourages student self-awareness and self-direction. We now turn, therefore, to a general perspective that emphasizes the role learners play in creating new knowledge and regulating their learning: the perspective of constructivism.

CONSTRUCTIVISM: THE ROLE OF THE LEARNER IN BUILDING AND TRANSFORMING KNOWLEDGE

Constructivism is a philosophical and psychological position that holds that much of what an individual learns and understands is constructed by the individual (Graves & Graves, 1994). Many constructivists also emphasize the role of social interactions (e.g., teacher with students, students with students) as heavily influencing what learners acquire. Scholars differ in the degree to which they ascribe knowledge construction solely to the learner. Some constructivists view mental structures as reflective of external realities, whereas others see no independent reality outside the mental world of the individual. The dimensions of constructivism having most influence on psychology and education, however, are ones shared by most constructivists: the ideas that learners are active in constructing their own knowledge and that social interactions are important to knowledge construction.

Many key concepts of cognitive psychology (e.g., *schema theory, levels of processing*) represent constructivist thinking. Constructivist perspectives also are shaping a number of significant changes in curriculum and instructional practices now underway across the United States. A constructivist view of learning underlies the shift to literature-based approaches to reading instruction, for instance. Likewise, the *Curriculum and Evaluation Standards for School Mathematics* (1989) of the National Council of Teachers of Mathematics, though not explicitly constructivist, have a strongly constructivist flavor, as do the recently published *Benchmarks for Science Literacy* (1993) of the American Association for the Advancement of Science.

The aim of teaching, from a constructivist perspective, is not so much to transmit information, but rather to encourage *knowledge formation* and development of the metacognitive processes for judging, organizing, and acquiring new information. A constructivist approach will manifest itself in the classroom in numerous ways: in selection of instructional materials (e.g., employing materials that children can manipulate or use to interact with their environments), in choice of activities (e.g., favoring student observations, data gathering, hypothesis testing, field trips), in the nature of classroom processes (e.g., using cooperative learning, discussions), and in attempts to integrate curricula (e.g., developing long-term thematic projects in an elementary classroom integrating math, science, reading, and writing). In "constructivist classrooms," students typically are taught to plan and direct their own learning to the greatest extent possible. Teachers serve more as coaches and facilitators than as primary sources of information, with students encouraged to take an active, not passive, role in their learning.

Types of Constructivism

Although constructivism sometimes is discussed as if it were a unified philosophical and psychological perspective, a more differentiated view is useful for understanding its implications for instruction. Moshman (1982; see also Pressley, Harris, & Marks, 1992) has distinguished among three types of constructivism: exogenous constructivism, endogenous constructivism, and dialectical constructivism. All involve knowledge construction but reflect different views of how knowledge construction occurs.

In **exogenous constructivism**, knowledge formation is basically a *re*construction of structures (e.g., cause-effect relationships, presented information, observed behavior patterns) that already exist in external reality. Mental structures reflect the organization of the world. Although they cannot be classified exclusively as examples of exogenous constructivism, a number of important concepts in cognitive psychology, such as *schemata, network models,* and *production systems,* clearly reflect this perspective. The philosophical basis of exogenous constructivism lies in the worldview of *mechanism,* of knower as machine (Pepper, 1942/1961).

Exogenous constructivism emphasizes a strong *external* influence on knowledge construction (e.g., by physical reality, presented information, social models). Knowledge is adequate or "true," from this perspective, to the extent that it accurately copies the external structures it ideally represents (Moshman, 1982).

Contrasted with exogenous constructivism is **endogenous constructivism**, which is rooted in the metaphor of knower as biological organism. In endogenous constructivism, according to Moshman, the key process is *coordination of cognitive actions.* Concepts are not mirrors of the external world; knowledge exists at a more abstract level and develops through cognitive activity. Cognitive structures are created from other, earlier structures, not directly from information provided by the environment. Structured knowledge does not evolve out of the social environment (e.g., children playing together), nor does it mirror the physical properties of manipulables (e.g., a child's learning to count with a set of checkers). Instead, new structures are abstracted from old ones and follow one another in invariant, predictable sequences. Piaget's stagewise view of cognitive development, for example, is a prominent example of endogenous constructivism. Adequacy or "truth" of such structures is more a matter of internal coherence than of match or accommodation to reality.

The third category of constructivism represents a point between the extremes of exogenous and endogenous constructivism. **Dialectical constructivism** places the source of knowledge in the *interactions* between learners and their environments. Knowledge is a "constructed synthesis" that grows out of contradictions that individuals experience during these interactions (Moshman, 1982, p. 375). Dialectical constructivism is linked with yet another philosophical point of view that has become increasingly influential in American psychology—*contextualism*—which holds that thought and experience are inextricably intertwined with the context in which they occur.

Although these types of constructivism represent three worldviews (mechanistic, organismic, and contextualist) considered irreconcilable (Pepper, 1942/1961), Moshman argues that each can be applied to some conditions of knowledge construction; that is, each is a productive metaphor for understanding the different ways in which individuals might construct knowledge. If, for instance, our primary interest is in how accurately children perceive the organization of some body of information (e.g., students' comprehension of narrative or expository structure in texts), we likely would find an exogenous view of constructivism inviting. If our interest is children's cognitive growth from naive to sophisticated scientific or mathematical concepts (see Chapters 13 and 14), however, an endogenous constructivism is more likely to be useful.

A dialectical perspective contains both elements and focuses our attention on the *interaction* between internal and external factors. For instance, if we are considering instructional interventions focused on building children's interpretations of literature or aimed at challenging children's naive conceptions in mathematics or science (see Chapters 13 and 14), we enter the realm of the dialectic.

Of the three, dialectical constructivism provides the most general perspective; exogenous and endogenous constructivism can be considered special cases of it (Moshman, 1982; Pressley, Harris, & Marks, 1992). Dialectical constructivism has become increasingly important in today's cognitive psychology, and we now turn to a closer examination of its most distinguished proponent, the Russian psychologist Lev Vygotsky. Publication of Vygotsky's *Mind in Society* in 1978 and subsequent translations of his work (e.g., Rieber & Carton, 1987) created a resurgence of interest in Vygotsky's thinking and marked the beginning of an era in which his ideas have had an enormous influence on psychology and education.

Vygotsky's Dialectical Constructivism

The core of Vygotsky's theory is its integration of "internal" and "external" aspects of learning and its emphasis on the social environment for learning (Newman, Griffin, & Cole, 1989). In Vygotsky's view, cultures externalize individual cognition in their "tools," by which he means not only the shared physical objects of a culture (e.g., a toothbrush, an auto, artwork) but also more abstract social tools (e.g., written language, social institutions). Cognitive change occurs as children use cultural tools in social interactions and internalize and transform these interactions. In Vygotsky's view, all higher human cognitive functions have their origin in each individual's social interactions in a cultural context.

Perhaps the most influential concept in Vygotsky's theory has been the *zone of proximal development*. The **zone of proximal development** can be defined as the difference between the difficulty level of a problem a child can cope with independently and the level that can be accomplished with adult help. In the zone of proximal development, a child and an adult (or novice and expert) work together on problems that the child (or novice) alone could not work on successfully.

Cognitive change takes place in the zone of proximal development or, in the clever phrase of Newman et al., (1989), in the "construction zone." Children bring a developmental history to the zone of proximal development; adults bring a support structure. As children and adults interact, they share cultural tools. This culturally mediated interaction, in Vygotsky's view, is what yields cognitive change. The interaction is internalized and becomes a new function of the individual.

Vygotsky's colleague, Leont'ev (1981), suggested the term *appropriation* to describe how learners internalize cultural knowledge from this process of interaction. Children, Leont'ev suggests, need not, and in fact should not, reinvent the artifacts of a culture. The culture has built up these artifacts over thousands of years, and children can appropriate them to their own circumstances as they learn how to use them.

Internalization of knowledge in the zone of proximal development is not an automatic reflection of external events. Children bring their own understandings to social interactions and make whatever sense they can of exchanges with adults. They can, however, participate in activities more complex than they can understand (e.g., a two-year-old "reading" a book with his or her parent) but still be affected by them. Likewise, adults may not fully understand children's perspectives but still play an important role in their cognitive change. As children and adults interact, children are exposed to adults' advanced systems of understanding, and change becomes possible.

Part of the attractiveness of Vygotsky's thinking for cognitive and educational theorists has been the stress Vygotsky has placed on social influences on cognitive change. Cognitive development, in Vygotsky's view, is not simply a matter of individual change, but rather is the result of social interactions in cultural contexts. Many educators find the emphasis on adult-child interactions in cognitive growth especially appealing. The concept of **instructional scaffolding**, for example, is closely aligned with Vygotsky's theoretical perspective. As we see in more detail later in our discussion of classroom discourse, in instructional scaffolding a teacher provides students with selective help (e.g., by asking questions, directing attention, giving hints about strategies they might consider) to enable them to do things they could not do on their own. Then, as students become more competent, the support is withdrawn gradually (see Beed, Hawkins, & Roller, 1991, for a discussion of scaffolding).

Social Constructivism: Social Factors in Knowledge Construction

Early research and theory of cognitive psychology focused on individual cognitive processes, with relatively little emphasis on the context in which individuals were functioning. Under the influence of theorists such as Vygotsky, however, cognitive theory has expanded to include a much greater recognition of social influences on cognition. As a consequence, researchers increasingly are turning their attention to children's interactions with parents, peers, and teachers in their homes, neighbor-hoods, and schools.

The perspective guiding these investigations is *social constructivism.* Closely related to dialectical constructivism, social constructivism stresses the relationships among human skill, activity, and thought and the influence of specific historical and cultural activities of the community. Social exchanges between individuals are seen as the primary source of cognitive growth. In the next sections, we examine two promi-nent social constructivist models of cognitive growth and knowledge construction: Rogoff's apprenticeships in thinking model and Schön's reflective practitioner model.

Rogoff's Apprenticeships in Thinking Model.   Barbara Rogoff (1990), following the lead of Vygotsky, has argued that cognitive development occurs when children are guided by adults in social activities that stretch their understanding of and skill in using the tools of the prevailing culture. When children are with their peers and adults, they are *apprentices in thinking.* In an apprenticeship, a novice works closely with an expert in joint problem-solving activity (Brown, Collins, & Duguid, 1989). The apprentice also typically participates in skills beyond those that he or she is capable of handling independently. In the manner of an apprenticeship, Rogoff states, development builds on "the internalization by the novice of the shared cogni-tive processes, appropriating what was carried out in collaboration to extend existing knowledge and skills" (p. 141). Rogoff argues that cognitive development is inher-ently social in nature, requiring mutual engagement with one or more partners of greater skill.

Other children form one important pool of "skilled partners." For instance, chil-dren's play and their dialogues with each other help them think collaboratively and offer a host of possibilities for considering others' perspectives. Play also involves imagination and creativity and thus helps children extend themselves into new roles, interactions, and settings. Peers are highly available and active, as Rogoff points out, providing each other with "motivation, imagination, and opportunities for creative elaboration of the activities of their community" (p. ix).

For most children, however, adults are the most reliable and important "skilled partners." Parents, relatives, and teachers, for instance, routinely play many roles with important implications for cognitive development. These include (1) stimulat-ing children's interest in cognitive tasks, (2) simplifying tasks so that children can manage them, (3) motivating children and providing direction to their activities, (4) giving feedback, (5) controlling their frustration and risk, and (6) demonstrating ide-alized versions of the acts to be performed (Rogoff, 1990).

Adults often engage in **guided participation** with children, a process by which children's efforts are structured in a social context and the responsibility for problem solving gradually is transferred to them. In guided participation, children learn to solve problems in the context of social interactions. Guided participation always involves interpersonal communication and "stage setting" to build bridges between what children already know and the new information they encounter.

Rogoff argues that mental processes are enriched in guided participation because they occur in the context of *accomplishing something;* that is, the cognitive processes direct intelligent, purposeful actions. Participants develop a sense of common purpose that grows out of extended dialogue and a shared focus of attention. Children are intrinsically motivated to come to a better understanding of their world and often initiate and guide interactions in which cognitive growth takes place.

Guided participation is not always formal or explicit, however. Events often are shared without participants being aware of efforts at guided participation or intending them to be instructional. A parent may help a child order at a restaurant, for example, without thinking of it as teaching. Similarly, a younger sibling may learn about teachers and students and their roles by playing school with an older brother or sister.

In sum, cognitive development for Rogoff is a process growing out of interactions with other children and adults. Individual cognition is built on the intellectual tools that a particular society has available. Although interactions with their peers provide support for development of structured knowledge, adults play a unique role in helping children move to new cognitive levels. Parents and teachers are reliable, expert partners with children in guided participation. These interactions help children build bridges between what they know and what they don't and provide vital support for children's efforts at acquiring new knowledge.

Schools provide an especially rich opportunity for guided participation with adults and for appropriating adults' knowledge in solving problems (e.g., acquiring a "technical" vocabulary for understanding perspective in painting, learning methods of searching for information to answer a question, applying cause-effect frameworks for understanding historical events, employing algorithms for solving word problems in mathematics, using research methods for gathering and categorizing data). Among fundamental challenges for teachers are learning how best to share their knowledge and to help students acquire an effective array of mental tools. As we discuss later in the chapter, classroom dialogue guided by the teacher can provide a number of important conditions to meet these challenges.

Schön's Reflective Practitioner Model.   Like Rogoff, Schön (1987) also has taken a dialectic constructivist perspective on cognitive development. Schön draws less explicitly from Vygotsky, however, and whereas Rogoff has concentrated on children, Schön's interests have centered mainly on teaching and learning in the professions. His perspective on cognitive development nonetheless shares several key elements with Vygotsky's theory and with Rogoff's approach: guided discovery, learning by doing, and the importance of social interactions in building knowledge and understanding. Schön has developed his system around three key concepts: *knowing-in-action, reflection-in-action,* and *reflection on reflection-in-action.*

Knowing-in-Action.   **Knowing-in-action** is *tacit knowledge,* the sort of knowledge that is unarticulated but revealed in our intelligent actions (Polanyi, 1967; see also our discussion of implicit memory in Chapter 3). We show our tacit knowledge whenever we act in reasonable ways but are not explicitly aware of the thinking underlying our actions. Knowing-in-action may be publicly observable, such as driving a car, greeting a friend, or typing a letter, or may be private and essentially unobservable, such as understanding what we are reading, following a movie's story line, or recognizing who is with whom at a party.

Much of what we know is knowing-in-action and is revealed only as we go about our daily lives. Our implicit knowledge is revealed as we perform acts in spontaneous, skillful ways. These acts may be as simple as pulling a key out of our pocket and unlocking our car or as complex as playing a Scott Joplin ragtime piece on the piano. Although it is possible to describe the implicit knowing that underlies our actions by observation and reflection, these descriptions will always be *constructions,* "attempts to put into explicit, symbolic form a kind of intelligence that begins by being tacit and spontaneous" (Schön, 1987, p. 25). By describing knowing-in-action, we convert it to **knowledge-in-action**, labeling a dimension of tacit proceduralized knowledge and making it a part of our semantic memory.

Ordinarily, however, knowing-in-action is not verbalized; our actions consist largely of spontaneous, routinized responses. We ordinarily just do it, not do it and describe it; that is, we drive to work, order a pizza, write a letter, carry on a conversation, and read text chapters. As long as the situation is "normal" (e.g., our activities yield the outcomes we intend, such as getting to work as expected, ordering the pizza) and there are no "surprises" that do not fit our knowledge-in-action categories, our scripts flow smoothly into action. Surprises—outcomes that do not fit our scripts—are not necessarily negative events, however. In fact, they are the key to triggering reflection-in-action, a mechanism Schön argues is critical for change and cognitive growth.

Reflection-in-Action.   **Reflection-in-action**, simply put, is conscious thought about our actions and about the thinking that accompanied them. Reflection-in-action is a form of metacognition in which we question both the unexpected event and the knowledge-in-action that brought on the unexpected event. We may, for example, have used our key over and over in unlocking our car, but one day we place our key in the lock and it doesn't turn. This unexpected outcome triggers a conscious consideration of what has happened and why our well-established routine might not be working. On reflection, for instance, we might find that we have pulled out a key similar in appearance to the right key, or, worse, we might discover that we have the right key but have gotten off at the wrong level in the parking garage and have been trying to unlock a car nearly identical to ours! Similarly, a child entering a new class may tug and pull at the teacher's clothing and be reprimanded by that teacher. A formerly successful routine now is not working for that child, and the "surprise" forces the child to reflect both on his actions and on the reasons for the changed circumstances.

Intellectual routines may stimulate reflection-in-action as contexts change. A sixth-grade student who in the fifth grade learned to use encyclopedias for her research may attempt to do so again. This time, however, she may find this approach blocked by a new teacher who wants students to use a variety of trade books, tables of contents, and indexes in finding information. The sixth-grader's familiar routine is interrupted, and she is forced to consider other ways of finding the information she needs.

As you can see, Schön's concept of *reflection-in-action* has a great deal in common with both of the dimensions of metacognition discussed in Chapter 4: knowledge of cognition and regulation of cognition. Reflection-in-action stimulates a kind of "on the spot" thought experiment. Depending on the extent of prior knowledge, unexpected failures and successes may lead in various directions: to *exploration,* in which the learner makes no predictions; to *testing moves,* in which different paths are tested for their feasibility; or to *hypothesis testing,* in which competing hypotheses are tested to determine which is valid.

The experience of one of the authors provides a simple example of the "on the spot" experiment. He was trying to dislodge ice cubes from a container in an ancient refrigerator and was tapping the container (a little hard, it seems) on the base of the freezer compartment. The refrigerator, perhaps in protest, began emitting a very loud, rhythmic whining noise from that area, one quite inappropriate for a well-functioning refrigerator. This unexpected "surprise" not only disrupted the author's attempt to get the ice loose but also stimulated a set of reflections aimed at (1) comprehending how the tapping might have initiated the noise and (2) terminating it. The author initially entertained two thoughts: (1) The tapping had forced the bottom of the compartment downward against a moving part (e.g., a fan), or (2) a cooling coil had been compressed by the tapping and was vibrating as the coolant flowed through it. The first hypothesis quickly gave way to the second, as the author recalled that refrigerators typically have few moving parts above the compressor, which usually is in the base. He inserted a key into a convenient gap in the aluminum, lifted it slightly, and the whining changed tone. A few more lifts and the whining ceased, much to his relief. Further attempts to dislodge the ice were carried out successfully (and more sensibly) at the kitchen sink.

Under a skilled teacher's guidance, a similar process can lead to student learning. The potential for learning lies in the constructive nature of reflection-in-action. When students are placed in situations that are uncertain and that they are motivated to change, Schön contends, they begin a process of exploration, movement, and hypothesis testing. Their primary motivation is usually just change, not necessarily understanding (just as your author's primary motivation was "solving" the problem with the refrigerator, not necessarily understanding the physics underlying the problem). Nonetheless, the feedback that learners receive allows them not only to move toward goals they find satisfactory but also to discover features that make the situation comprehensible. New questions now appear.

The power of reflection-in-action in a school setting is illustrated by the work of Guthrie (1993), who has described the semester-long activities of a group of children taking part in his Concept-Oriented Reading Instruction (CORI) program. The teacher of these fifth-grade students had begun instruction on the solar system by having students observe the daily changes in the appearance of the moon. The students' observations, combined with predictions they were asked to make, quickly led to curiosity about the solar system and to further experimentation (e.g., with models and flashlights and plastic foam balls). Working groups of students interested in particular planets soon formed. Their reading and other investigative activities were sustained not only by their growing expertise but also by their chance to communicate their findings to others. By the end of the semester, their knowledge, their ability to organize knowledge, and their skills at managing their own learning had changed fundamentally.

Reflection on Reflection-in-Action.   All of us construct and reconstruct our cognitive worlds as we experience the events of our lives and reflect on them. By assisting students in constructing new knowledge, however, skilled teachers can help learners do much more than they could do alone. Schön (1987) refers to this process as **reflection on reflection-in-action**. By reflection on reflection-in-action, Schön is speaking about the metacognitive capacity of skilled *teachers* to help students think about their own reflection-in-action. Skilled teachers, in other words, help learners to develop reflection-in-action—that is, to articulate the thoughts guiding their actions and to judge their adequacy. Consistent with Vygotsky's views of the zone of proximal development, the teacher's goal is to be literally "thought-provoking" (Schön, 1987, p. 92). Ideally, the teacher creates an interactive setting in which both the teacher and the students are co-learners, but students' self-discovery has the highest priority.

According to Schön, *students cannot be taught what they need to know,* but *they can be coached* toward self-understanding. Thus, Schön also stresses a dialectical, social constructivism and largely rejects an exogenous one. The kind of coaching Schön advocates is not the familiar pattern of observing performance, pointing out errors, and rewarding correct responses, however. Instead, he advocates creating *practice situations*—relatively low-risk events in which students can learn by doing and receive rich feedback. These situations motivate learners toward understanding and contain at least some elements the students themselves have created.

In Schön's profession—architecture—practice situations typically take the form of design problems in which students attempt to design a structure that meets multiple criteria (e.g., serves the intended purpose for the structure, is aesthetically pleasing, fits the site, is structurally sound). The goal is to create an environment in which students' actions and thoughts about design issues lead to new levels of understanding. Part of reaching that goal involves creating a climate of openness—by the teacher modeling his or her own self-reflection and by expressing thoughts and feelings usually withheld.

Students may initially strongly resist this kind of coaching approach and may become unsettled, even angry, when there seem to be "no right answers." They may demand to be told what is "correct" or become frustrated with the instructor. The teacher-coach, however, must keep in mind that he or she is managing a transaction between learners and their environment, not offering information. Uncertainty and conflict about values are inevitable. In Schön's view, this uncertainty is among the most powerful motivating forces available to teachers.

Having created a situation in which the student must act, the teacher now must help construct a "reflective conversation" (Schön, 1987, p. 78) around the student's experiences with the situation. In this conversation, the teacher reflects his or her own deepest thoughts and gives students opportunities to express theirs.

In summary, Schön reflects a constructivist point of view by portraying learning as a social-interactive process in which students are helped to create new understandings. The key goal is students' reflection-in-action, metacognitive reflection on unexpected events or variations in phenomena and the thinking that led to them. In Schön's view, students learn when they act and when they are helped to think about their actions. Learning by doing forces them to make judgments; reflection helps them recognize their assumptions and see what is important. Although students initially may perceive this kind of instruction as threatening, ambiguous, or confusing, clarification comes when students "stay with" problems and dialogue continues between the teacher-coach and the students.

Together, both Rogoff's and Schön's models reflect a social constructivist viewpoint consistent with Vygotsky's. The exchanges between teachers and students create a zone of proximal development in which students acquire habits of reflection and increased metacognitive knowledge. These exchanges with teachers and advanced peers are essential to cognitive change and growth and vital to creating useful situated knowledge and thought. Dialogue between teachers and students is not the only mechanism for building students' understanding and revealing their misunderstandings, of course, but it is among the most potent tools teachers have available. Thus, in the next section, we extend our examination of social constructivism by exploring the nature of the verbal exchanges that take place in the classroom. We consider the potential of different kinds of classroom dialogue for building knowledge and for fostering reflection.

THE ROLE OF CLASSROOM DISCOURSE IN KNOWLEDGE CONSTRUCTION

Most people's prototypical images of the classroom involve language use; teachers asking questions and students answering, classes discussing works of literature, students poring over textbooks, and students struggling with writing satisfactory answers to test questions. Language is the medium by which concepts are presented and clarified and through which students' knowledge typically is expressed and judged.

In later chapters, we focus on reading (Chapters 10 and 11) and writing (Chapter 12). Here, we examine classroom discourse. **Discourse** is a general term referring to structured, coherent sequences of language. In discourse, propositions (see Chapter 3) take on meaning in relationship to one another. Meaning is contextual. Thus, discourse has the property of **coherence**, in which references forward or backward give meaning to individual elements. A conversation is an example of discourse, as is an essay, a short story, a novel, and a classroom discussion. When researchers use the term *classroom discourse,* they ordinarily are referring to the oral exchanges of the classroom. We adopt that usage here.

Researchers increasingly are considering the quality of classroom discourse to be one of the most critical elements in effective schooling (e.g., Calfee et al., 1994; Nystrand & Gamoran, 1991; O'Flahavan, Wiencek, Marks, & Stein, 1994). Classroom discourse, they argue, is a primary vehicle by which teachers guide, organize, and direct their students' activities. Like Rogoff and Schön, these researchers view learning as a constructive process in which social exchanges with others are fundamental to students' construction of meaning. As Hull and her associates (Hull et al., 1991) have stated, "In the classroom, it is through talk that learning gets done, that knowledge gets made" (p. 318). This view is being translated into research aimed at finding the discourse structures and uses of classroom discourse that best promote learning (e.g., Calfee et al., 1994; Chinn & Waggoner, 1992; Hull et al., 1991; O'Flahavan & Stein, 1992; O'Flahavan et al., 1994).

The discourse in most classrooms today is not particularly supportive of student expression and reflection. At all levels, from primary grades through college, classroom discourse almost universally is dominated by teacher talk. Students typically talk very little, and students' questions are rare. Most classroom talk centers around a single dominant discourse pattern: a teacher asks a question, a student responds, and the teacher gives feedback (Alvermann, O'Brien, & Dillon, 1990; Cazden, 1988; Mehan, 1979). Often simply called the **IRE pattern** (initiate, respond, evaluate), the sequence in slightly more elaborated form is as follows:

1. *Teacher Initiates.* The teacher informs, directs, or asks students for information. For example:

   Teacher: Jeni, can you tell me the name of the town where they were going?

2. *A Student Responds.* Students' responses to the teacher's prompt or question can be verbal or nonverbal.

   Jeni: Uh . . . I think it was Peatwick.

3. *The Teacher Evaluates.* The teacher comments on the student's reply or reacts to it nonverbally.

   Teacher: Right. Peatwick. Good. And where were they . . .

As Cazden and others have pointed out, the IRE is the "default pattern" for classroom exchanges between teacher and student—that is, what happens unless deliberate intervention is made to achieve some alternative. Although this pattern can support a discussion of sorts, it most often is used for *recitation* in which a teacher quizzes students about content they have just studied. It often is accompanied by "mini-lectures"—periods of teacher talk that the teacher uses to elaborate on information already being discussed or to present new information. Chinn and Waggoner (1992) and others (e.g., Alvermann & Hayes, 1989; Cazden, 1988) have pointed out that it is extraordinarily difficult for teachers to move away from these patterns and their variations. It may be, as Chinn and Waggoner speculate, that teacher control and authority are at stake, or it simply may be that teachers stick to this pattern because they judge it to be useful for probing comprehension and ensuring that students are attentive.

Toward a More Reflective Classroom

We have been building the case in this chapter that student cognitive growth is best nurtured in a social environment in which students are active participants and in which they are helped to reflect on what they are learning. For teachers to create a "reflective classroom" in which students build new knowledge and learn to manage their own learning, they almost certainly need to extend classroom discourse beyond the IRE recitations and the IRE-type "discussions" in which turn-taking rotates between teacher and students.

Calfee et al. (1994) have proposed **disciplined discussion** as an alternative to the IRE. Disciplined discussion draws on the best features of both *conversation,* which ordinarily is structured informally and student generated, and *instruction,* which typically refers to a more formal and teacher-directed interaction organized around a lesson. In disciplined discussion, a classroom discussion group approaches a text or other information source strategically with a particular goal in mind. The roles and responsibilities of the participants are made explicit: Students solve problems by using interactive processes they have learned through modeling, practice, and feedback; a teacher plays several important but not dominating roles, as diverse as organizer and participant and simply being an observer or a facilitator.

But what kinds of interactions are most likely to help students build knowledge and reflect on their learning? Chinn and Waggoner suggest that teachers first need to ensure that students have sufficient knowledge to support the discussion topic, knowledge that may come from personal experience, reading, or other sources. Beyond this, however, are two fundamental criteria, both reflecting a social constructivist viewpoint: (1) that students share alternative perspectives and (2) that the discourse has an open participation structure.

When students *share alternative perspectives,* they give their personal reactions and interpretations and consider the viewpoints of other participants. A group of students reading a short story, for instance, are likely to interpret parts of it in different ways. A good discussion provides a forum for negotiating elements of meaning they agree on and for building metacognitive awareness. Likewise, children examining a picture of a snail may disagree about whether or not particular protrusions on its head are antennae or eyes. Resolution of the matter can come with discussion and the further inquiry that discussion can stimulate.

Open participation structure, which refers to the ability of students to talk freely with each other as they would in ordinary conversations, also is vital to building knowledge and reflection. In an open participation structure, students, not just the teacher, can initiate topics and ask questions (Chinn & Waggoner, 1992). When classroom discourse incorporates both of these functions, it can become **authentic** (Brown et al., 1989; Graesser, Long, & Horgan, 1988; Nystrand & Gamoran, 1991), organized around genuine questions that elicit the perspectives of the participants (Calfee et al., 1994; Sperling, in press).

What are some of the ways discussions can affect the development of knowledge and reflective thought in participating students? Calfee et al. (1994) suggest four possibilities by referring to their CORE (connecting, organizing, reflecting, and extending) model of instruction (Calfee, Chambliss, & Beretz, 1991). First, discussions provide connections for learning. Useful knowledge is contextual, grounded in what students already know. Good discussions draw on students' prior domain and general knowledge and allow them to share what they know with their discourse partners. To take part effectively in discussions, students must recall information and use their metacognitive knowledge to link and sequence their ideas. Students learn that good discussions have *coherence*. By staying on-topic and building on the ideas brought up by the participants, they together create a new body of shared information.

Second, discussions help organize knowledge. Knowledge construction is not simply a matter of accumulating particular facts or even of creating new units of information. It also involves organizing old information into new forms. Discussions are uniquely suited to serve these purposes. As participants strive to understand and contribute to discussions, they are forced to relate and organize what they know.

Third, good discussions can foster reflective thought. Discussions offer many opportunities for students to acquire greater metacognitive awareness about the quality of their thinking and to learn skills for regulating their thoughts and actions. Like all forms of discourse, discussions require participants to externalize thought. Presenting, organizing, clarifying, and defending ideas push students' cognitive processes "into the open." The reactions of their discussion partners provide feedback on whether they have been persuasive and coherent. Teachers, by coaching before and after discussions and by adopting roles that allow them to scaffold student thought as needed during discussions, can influence significantly students' abilities to reflect on their interactions and on the substance of their thinking (O'Flahavan & Stein, 1992).

Guthrie (1993) gives an example of how discussion can stimulate reflection, describing how fifth-graders in one of his project classrooms were engaged in a debate about whether there might be life on Mars. One student, "John," insisted he had read that life did exist on Mars. He was challenged immediately by the other students to identify the book that supported this belief. One student, "Patty," proposed that the book in question most likely discussed what it *might be like* to live on Mars but that it did not say life *actually* existed on Mars. After further discussion, she volunteered to return to the school library to try to find more information that would resolve the question. This information did lead to more discussion and finally to resolution of the question (she was correct). Discussions like these, involving debate and reaching a conclusion, have a strong reflective component and stimulate students' use of strategic skills (e.g., for seeking additional information).

Finally, discussions help extend knowledge. As students work on long-term projects, their discourse can lead quite naturally into new domains. Guthrie (1993) observed that student discourse on one topic (the moon and its phases) quickly extended into several related topics. Students' declarative and procedural knowledge expanded rapidly as they searched for answers to questions they had posed; metacognitive knowledge increased as they discussed strategies for acquiring information with their peers and with the teacher and as they tried to explain their findings to their classmates.

Using Classroom Discourse to Build Knowledge

It is one thing to assert that high-quality discourse is at the heart of the reflective classroom; it is another to actually create classrooms in which knowledge construction and reflective thinking are the norm. On the one hand, when the teacher retains too much involvement in discussion, the result often is the IRE pattern, in which classroom discourse more nearly resembles recitation sequences than authentic exchanges. On the other hand, a laissez-faire approach to discussion that gives up social and interpretive authority totally to student groups is an invitation to chaos and deprives students of essential contributions by the teacher (O'Flahavan et al., 1994; Rogoff, 1990; Schön, 1987).

How, then, does one best reach the goal of having students engaged in authentic, extended discourse with each other and with their teacher? O'Flahavan (O'Flahavan, personal communication, 1993; O'Flahavan & Stein, 1992; O'Flahavan et al., 1994) suggests that because discussions are highly complex, it is useful to consider them from a variety of perspectives, each involving a somewhat different form of knowledge construction. In O'Flahavan's view, optimal contexts for classroom discussions are most likely to be created when teachers and students work together from the outset to (1) construct the norms for participating in the discussions, (2) determine the interpretive agenda for a group's discussion, and (3) reflect after each discussion about the group's success in achieving both its social and interpretive goals. O'Flahavan argues that teachers can play two especially important roles in these discussions: coaching and scaffolding. Although O'Flahavan favors decentralized, student-centered discussions, he considers teacher involvement essential if students' cognitive strategies, motivation, and expertise are to develop over the long term. In addition to managing some features of the discussions themselves, teachers are responsible for other features important to their success: creating the physical context in which the discussion is to occur, including determining group size and composition; devising seating arrangements; and making texts and other materials available.

Perhaps the most basic strategy for creating productive discussion groups is helping students construct **group participation norms**. Most students understand basic social norms for interacting in groups. For instance, most students know they need to raise their hands in classroom discussions and not to interrupt. They may not, however, know how to work well with other students, particularly in decentralized groups in which the teacher is not directing their interactions. One approach would be to teach interactive skills directly (e.g., "These will be our rules. We should . . ."). It seems to be more effective, however, when students are allowed to help create their own rules for interaction. O'Flahavan and Stein (1992), for instance, had their students keep running lists of their group's participation norms, which typically included such rules as paying attention, not interrupting, taking turns, and the like. Because these were the *students'* norms, they were highly valued, probably more so than if the teacher had devised them. At the same time, however, the teacher plays an important role in helping the students reflect on whether their participation norms are effective. By serving as a *group process monitor* (O'Flahavan & Stein, 1992), for instance, the teacher can help the students periodically evaluate how well their group processes are working.

A second strategy is helping students develop **interpretive norms** for judging their progress. In effective decentralized discussions, students need to assume considerable intellectual responsibility. Assume, for instance, that a high school biology class is preparing a detailed report for local officials on the environmental threats to a nearby wetland. To meet this challenge, the class must make many decisions on how it will proceed—for example, what data it will gather and the format of the document it eventually will produce. Again, an effective teacher is likely to adopt a stance somewhere between authoritarian determination of the group's intellectual agenda (e.g., "OK, first I want you to study these maps of eastern Douglas county . . .") and laissez-faire inattention to students' attempts to grapple with this very complex and metacognitively demanding task.

A third strategy in helping students develop a reflective stance is coaching (O'Flahavan & Stein, 1992; Schön, 1987). Under a skilled teacher's guidance, discussion group participants can learn to reflect on both the group's procedural skills and its interpretive norms. In general, O'Flahavan and Stein's judgment is that students will be most productive when they are allowed to work together in their groups for significant blocks of time, say fifteen to twenty minutes, with teachers coaching at the boundaries of discussion—that is, before and after discussion blocks.

For O'Flahavan and Stein (1992), coaching takes two major forms: (1) providing students with guidance and direction and (2) helping students reflect on their interactions and achievements. For instance, in a long-term science project for middle school students (e.g., describing the status of a wetlands habitat), most students would need coaching in basic strategies for gathering information, such as determining what is important, drawing inferences from texts, and monitoring their understanding while reading about birds, plants, and insects. They also likely would need coaching in such procedural strategies as keeping reflective logs, identifying variables for observation, recording their observations, and planning simple experiments. The teacher also might want to remind students of supplies and resources they are likely to need to complete tasks and to discuss ways these might be obtained. Students who need information about, say, marsh plants and water beetles, could be coached in using indexes and tables of contents effectively to search books in the library for relevant information.

A fourth strategy is helping students articulate what they are thinking, reminding them of assumptions they are making, drawing their attention to information, and providing new perspectives. This activity, of course, qualifies as an example of *scaffolding* in the zone of proximal development. The teacher, as the more expert person, provides frames of reference and modes of interpretation that students are capable of acquiring but do not yet have. In a discussion relating to sources of information about wetlands, for instance, one teacher became aware that her students did not know how to get information about land use, and so posed an indirect question about where it might be found (e.g., "Maybe we should think about where we might find information about land uses"). Students, given this hint and an occasional suggestion, soon began to debate the merits of such sources as surveying, aerial photography, satellite images, landowner reports, and the like. Without the teacher's direction, the students likely would have been unable to continue their inquiry. With the scaffolding, however, they soon began to search library resources and initiated a series of productive contacts with landowners, agencies, and governmental units. The teacher's comment helped move them toward considering new information and frames of reference.

O'Flahavan suggests several distinct roles that can be useful for scaffolding student thought. Included among these are the role of the *framer,* in which the teacher draws attention to relevant background knowledge or helps students in interpretation; the *elicitor,* in which the teacher focuses the group's thinking on a point by bringing forth elaboration and extension from students; and the *interpretive peer,* in which the teacher is a participant in the group's inquiry.

Finally, positive motivation is critical to successful classroom discourse. Perhaps the most fundamental motivational requirement is that discussions be authentic, accessing the "real culture" of the domain (Brown et al., 1989; Calfee et al., 1994). This can be ensured if the group is engaged in purposeful communication about goals meaningful to them. For instance, if upper-level elementary students were developing a class book about their neighborhoods, writing and directing a play for presentation at Parents' Night, or creating a mural promoting school safety for younger students, they likely would find each of these activities meaningful and motivating. Besides rich topics, however, other factors important to motivation include the extent of teacher participation (not too much or too little) and the teacher's ability to value and "take up" students' ideas and incorporate them into the ongoing discussion (Nystrand & Gamoran, 1991).

IMPLICATIONS FOR TEACHING: A PORTRAIT OF THE REFLECTIVE CLASSROOM

We return now to our starting point—the goal of building student knowledge. We have seen that building knowledge is not a simple matter. First, there are several kinds of knowledge, each important in its own right. Expertise in any domain requires large networks of declarative knowledge, as well as readily available arrays of procedural skills. It requires metacognitive awareness and the regulatory knowledge of knowing how and when to apply what is known. Because the amount of knowledge we need is very large and the relationships among the knowledge elements so complex, the process of acquiring significant domain knowledge requires motivated, long-term student effort. Thus, the challenge to teachers is considerable.

If we succeed in building an "ideal reflective classroom," what might it look like? We could begin by imagining a classroom in which the teacher has placed student knowledge construction as its centerpiece. To help accomplish this goal, the teacher has organized class activities around long-term, thematic projects in which students acquire knowledge they can use in ways they find meaningful. We see a "hands-on" teacher who makes little use of the IRE pattern and who lectures infrequently. Instead, in our reflective classroom, we see a teacher who works as a partner with the students and who has organized classroom activities around student information seeking and information exchange. Our teacher's primary role is guiding and supporting students in becoming self-directed, strategic learners.

In our ideal classroom is a great deal of purposeful activity, as the teacher and the students work together to achieve the goals of their projects. This activity alternates among whole class instruction, in which students are coached on how to find and organize information; student reading and writing, in which students search for, find, and organize information and reflect on how they found it; and small group discussions, in which students report what they have learned, discuss their differing points of view, and make judgments about how well they are progressing toward their goals. We see our teacher helping students pick the goals they judge to be most important, coaching them on possible strategies for reaching their goals, and scaffolding their thinking as needed.

Over time, we see the students in our ideal classroom becoming more and more expert and self-directed. Their growing knowledge, moreover, does not consist of "inert" and isolated facts memorized from texts, but rather is organized and meaningful because it is important for their projects. Their knowledge is multidimensional and flexible. They have learned not only "what" but also "how," "why," and "when." As a consequence, they can explain readily the strategies they use to find information, why they judge it as important or not, and how it is organized.

Although our classrooms may fall short of this ideal, we still can draw on a number of basic principles as we move toward it. First, we need to take a broad perspective on knowledge. "Building student knowledge" does not mean only that we help students acquire large declarative networks of information. They also need procedural knowledge, a knowledge of doing, as well as knowing. Perhaps even more importantly, however, both declarative and procedural knowledge need to be contextualized, linked with metacognitive awareness and conditional knowledge. In the long run, the conditional or regulatory aspect of metacognition may be the most important aspect of knowledge acquisition. Because what is known changes rapidly and the amount of information available far exceeds anyone's ability to acquire it, students must develop the capacity for self-regulation in their learning and the motivation to acquire new information and skills.

New knowledge can come from a number of sources. Student observations provide rich information. The most consistent source of new knowledge for most students, however, is reading. Students can learn to search for information related to concepts they have identified, questions they have posed, and strategies they are considering trying. In the work of Guthrie and his colleagues, for instance (e.g., Guthrie, 1993; Guthrie, Bennett, & McGough, 1994), fifth-graders not only learned reading strategies that enabled them to acquire new declarative information about the planets but also simultaneously acquired multiple strategies for searching text and judging information.

Second, we need to organize our classroom instruction in ways that favor knowledge construction. One of the most useful contributions of cognitive psychology has been to remind us that learners' activities influence what is learned and determine how functional knowledge will be. We therefore must teach students to use their considerable resources for learning effectively. Rote rehearsal in which meaning is ignored tends to generate rote, listlike, fragile learning. Approaches aimed at student comprehension of the meaning of what is to be learned, in contrast, are much more likely to achieve the goals of student understanding and organized knowledge.

Effective knowledge construction almost certainly requires a classroom culture organized to support it. Early on, cognitive scientists sometimes tended to portray intellectual growth as a solitary pursuit, but social constructivist theory and research increasingly have emphasized how learning and knowledge grow out of interactions in family, school, and community. Both Rogoff's model of the child as cognitive apprentice and Schön's concept of *reflection on reflection-in-action* emphasize the social nature of cognitive growth as outlined by Vygotsky. One of the most important social resources for generating knowledge construction and reflection in classrooms is the kind of discussions in which students grapple with authentic questions and interact freely with each other and in which thinking is stimulated and scaffolded by the teacher.

Third, we need to use specific strategies for generating the kind of discourse that supports knowledge construction and reflection. One such strategy is creating open participation structures, a pattern now largely lacking in U.S. classrooms. The predominant IRE classroom discourse pattern—a stereotypic pattern of teacher queries, student responses, and teacher evaluations—offers relatively little opportunity for opinions and introduction of new ideas. Where the IRE pattern dominates, students are less likely to gain new understandings or to develop a reflective posture toward their own learning. For instance, as Rosenblatt pointed out many years ago in her classic book *Literature as Exploration* (1938), prototypical classroom discussions of literature typically converge on "the author's meaning" and analysis of literary devices the author used, with negative effects on both learning and motivation. Far better, she argued, was to encourage students to express what the work meant to them and then to use discussion to negotiate a shared understanding of its meanings. Students' initial understandings, though often immature and incomplete, nonetheless are the only legitimate starting point for learning. As students continue their exchanges with each other and with the teacher while interacting with what they are reading, understanding will deepen.

In considering the teacher's role in guiding discussions, it is useful to recall Rogoff's metaphorical reference to students as "apprentices in learning." Like the guidance provided by the master tradesperson, teachers' coaching and scaffolding are vital to building new levels of student understanding. O'Flahavan and Stein (1992) argue for concentrating coaching at the boundaries of discussions; *before* discussions teachers can help students set the agenda for discussion, and *after* discussions teachers can assist students in reflecting on their successes and failures. Scaffolding, in contrast, works effectively *within* discussions: A teacher-participant can help frame students' ideas in new ways, encourage elaboration, and help students reflect on their progress.

Teachers also should consider decentralizing discussions. Although large group discussions can be productive (Calfee et al., 1994), opportunity for individual students to participate always will be limited by group size. Also, some students are reluctant to take part in a full-class setting because of perceived lack of knowledge or shyness. O'Flahavan and his colleagues (O'Flahavan & Stein, 1992; O'Flahavan et al., 1994) have shown that groups of four to six upper-level elementary students can carry on long-term inquiry relatively independent of the teacher if they are supported periodically by teacher coaching and scaffolding. Students in such groups can learn to monitor their progress and reflect both on the quality of their interaction and on the extent to which they have achieved their goals.

A final suggestion for creating a reflective classroom is that we need to practice and coach tolerance as a fundamental rule for classroom interactions. Students do not necessarily come to our classrooms with well-refined social and cognitive skills. They often need to learn rules for classroom and small group discussion. For instance, the prevailing norms governing whole-class discussions may specify what kinds of replies to questions are considered appropriate, points at which it is acceptable to interrupt, and preferred ways to signal attention. For a variety of reasons, such as family history or ethnic background, some students' communication styles will not match those of the class. Students who interrupt frequently, for example, may have developed this style of communication in their families, had success with it in other classes, or simply may be extraordinarily eager to do well (see Hull et al., 1991).

This variation in styles and skill levels demands that both students and teachers practice basic principles of respect for others' ideas. For the long term, it seems to be useful for discussion groups to develop their own participation norms (see O'Flahavan & Stein, 1992; O'Flahavan et al., 1994). The rules students themselves generate (e.g., "Take turns," "Don't hog the discussion," "Don't put anyone on the spot") are usually less coercive and probably more effective than any the teacher might impose. Furthermore, students can be coached to reflect on whether their rules are working in creating effective, pleasant working groups or need to be modified.

SUMMARY

The chapter has described processes by which declarative, procedural, and metacognitive knowledge is created within content domains and more generally in classrooms. The position taken in this chapter is that knowledge acquisition is a constructive process in which learners build and organize knowledge. Three perspectives on a constructivist view of learning were outlined: exogenous constructivism, endogenous constructivism, and dialectical constructivism. Of these, dialectical constructivism is the most general.

Stimulated by the work of the Russian psychologist Vygotsky and his concept of *zone of proximal development,* cognitive scientists now increasingly emphasize social processes in knowledge formation. Social interactions involving guided participation with a peer or an adult build bridges between what children already know and the new information they encounter. Much of cognitive development occurs within the social environment of the child. Children are apprentices in thinking; knowledge and ways of knowing grow out of interactions with members of their culture. Learning and knowledge are embedded in their cultural context.

Classroom discourse is a significant factor in building knowledge and shaping cognitive growth. If that discourse is authentic, honors students' points of view, and has continuity, it will engage students and become a basis for knowledge construction and reflective thinking. The tenor of classroom discourse also shapes students' perceptions of self and learning; it can be supportive or threatening, uplifting or demeaning.

Authentic discussions allow alternative perspectives and have open participation structures. By providing a forum for expression and feedback, they create opportunities for extending knowledge and for developing reflective thought. Strategies for creating productive discussion groups include having the groups develop and modify their own social and interpretive norms, teacher coaching before and after discussions, and scaffolding during discussions. These approaches enhance the possibility of knowledge construction and development of self-directed, strategic, reflective approaches to learning.

Because expertise requires organized, flexible knowledge, teachers need to encourage students in habits of acquiring and judging their knowledge. Ideally, classrooms provide authentic contexts for learning—learning that builds on prior knowledge, allows expression of multiple perspectives, and is aimed at goals students find meaningful. The ideal outcome is for students not only to acquire knowledge but also to become independent, self-regulated learners. Well-managed classroom discourse, particularly discourse in which teachers function as coaches and provide scaffolding for student thought, can help us reach these objectives.

SUGGESTED READINGS

Rogoff, B. (1990). *Apprenticeship in thinking: Cognitive development in social context.* New York: Oxford University Press.

Rogoff's text provides a useful exposition of the perspective of social constructivism, especially as it applies to early child development.

Schön, D. A. (1987). *Educating the reflective practitioner.* San Francisco: Jossey-Bass.

Although it is focused on the goal of developing expertise in professionals, the conceptual framework of the book is very helpful in thinking about interactions of any kind of teacher-learner pair. Readers will be drawn into reflections on their own teaching in a variety of contexts.

PART FOUR

Cognition in the Classroom

CHAPTER 10

Learning to Read

At first glance, the act of reading seems simple. Words have meanings; reading, therefore, is a straightforward translation from symbol to thought or to speech. As we explore it more deeply, however, reading quickly reveals itself as a complex domain of knowledge in which a number of cognitive activities interact with one another. The complexity of reading, however, does not render it incomprehensible. Although the interactions among cognitive activities are certainly complicated, the underlying structure is relatively clear (Calfee & Drum, 1986). In this chapter, we describe the basic mental activities involved in beginning reading and how these activities appear to interact.

Through reading, we can make contact with the thoughts and imaginations of people removed in time and space, learn from them, and understand the meanings they have attempted to communicate. These functional qualities are the reason reading is so important at virtually all levels of formal education. We begin early by teaching first-graders to read, and reading ability soon becomes instrumental for success in other areas of study. Without the ability to read, a child's likelihood of achievement in virtually any area of the school curriculum is seriously diminished. Reading's importance extends well beyond school; reading is critical to success in most jobs and is an important source of information and pleasure for many adults.

In this chapter, we focus on beginning reading, the stage of reading called "learning to read." Learning to read marks an important transition for the child into the literate world. Its foundations, however, are built on a vast array of knowledge the child has acquired previously about language and the world. We thus look first at the linguistic and cognitive prerequisites of reading. We then examine a current view of the relatively brief period during which children make the transition to becoming readers. In this section, we look at the stages through which children pass as they consolidate their growing knowledge about language sounds and the printed word, moving from prereaders to "experts" with the skill to read unfamiliar words accurately and to understand what they have read. Finally, we end with a discussion of the world of reading instruction, highlighting prominent methods and materials used to teach reading and summarizing key issues in the sometimes heated debates over teaching methods.

THE FOUNDATIONS OF LITERACY IN LANGUAGE DEVELOPMENT

For more than a quarter century, the study of language development has proven to be an exciting and fertile area of investigation. Because this research yielded a much more complete description of language acquisition than was available earlier, researchers in literacy turned to it for insights into the processes by which children become literate, studying language-related phenomena as diverse as children's language concepts (e.g., Downing, 1979) and their awareness of print and its uses (Chaney, 1992; Hiebert, 1981; McGee, Lomax, & Head, 1988). Perhaps the most important generalization that has come out of this body of work is the recognition that learning to read is not a skill separate from a child's language experience, but rather is one growing naturally from it. Literacy builds on the child's rapidly expanding knowledge about a variety of dimensions of language (Sulzby, 1991), knowledge children acquire from encountering and using language in their homes and communities.

First-graders' expressive language has been developing rapidly since the second year of their lives; most already have extensive vocabularies of about 5,000 or 6,000 words (Chall, 1987; Chall, Jacobs, & Baldwin, 1990). They also have a basic command of the mechanics of their native language, as well as an ability to use language pragmatically in communicating with others. Part of this knowledge about language is *linguistic knowledge,* the ability to directly perceive and use language. Another part, however, is a developing metacognitive awareness about their own language use and about language in general. This *metalinguistic knowledge* not only is important to speech regulation and comprehension but, as we shall see, also underlies children's transition into literacy.

Students in most classrooms typically have wide variations in their language backgrounds, in their oral language skills, and in their linguistic and metalinguistic knowledge. Beyond differences in competence and rapid developmental changes are also large differences in the way children of different social and cultural backgrounds use language. For a growing number of children in the United States, learning to read may take place in a language different from their primary one. The diversity in students' language backgrounds is one of the greatest challenges teachers face in teaching children to read.

To better understand the nature of differences in knowledge about language and how they affect learning to read, we begin by examining the major dimensions of language. From the moment children begin to acquire knowledge in each of these dimensions, they not only are becoming a part of a language community but also are setting out on the road to literacy.

The Dimensions of Language

Human languages are immensely complex systems of conventions for linking symbols with meanings. In virtually all human languages, the primary symbols are *speech sounds* with organized patterns of sounds representing meanings. Languages are structured; they do not merely collect sounds into words, words into sentences, and sentences into larger units. Instead, at each level of structure, units combine meaningfully according to general organizational principles, rather than randomly or idiosyncratically.

Languages typically are described at three major levels of structure: (1) at the level of combinations of sounds into words—the **morphology** of the language; (2) at the level of combinations of words into phrases, clauses, and sentences—the **syntax** of the language; and (3) at the level of **discourse**—combinations of sentences into higher-order units, such as paragraphs, narratives, and expository text (see Chapter 9 for details on classroom discussions as a form of discourse). We thus begin our discussion of the dimensions of language with the topic of speech sounds and how they are combined into words.

Sounds into Meaning: The Morphology of Language.   Humans can vocalize a tremendous range of sounds: clicks and chirps, babbling, cooing, and speaking. These vocalizations, called **phones**, are the raw material of language. Among the huge range of possible sounds, however, only a very small subset—the **phonemes** of a language—are perceived as meaningful by speakers and listeners in that language. Each phoneme forms a kind of perceptual category; each is a sound—or perhaps more precisely a closely related cluster of sounds—that carries meaning (Anisfeld, 1984). English has, for instance, only about forty phonemes. Speech comprehension depends on an individual's distinguishing these phonemic categories from one another (e.g., distinguishing between /l/ and /r/ lets us tell the difference between *load* and *road*) in order to access the meaning the sounds carry.

Each of the world's languages has its own distinct set of phonemes. Although their phonemes do overlap, phonemes in one language may not be phonemes in another. For instance, the sound /v/, which is a phoneme (has meaning) in English (e.g., *viper* and *wiper* are distinctly different words), is not a phoneme in the Thai language. As a consequence, native Thai speakers attempting to learn English words containing the sound /v/ (e.g., di*v*ide) may hear the English /v/ as the familiar phoneme /w/ (/w/ is a phoneme in Thai) and perceive and pronounce such words incorrectly (e.g., as de*w*ide). They also would experience considerable difficulty in distinguishing between two words differing only in these consonants. The tables are turned, of course, when English speakers encounter other languages. For instance, English speakers often experience difficulty in perceiving phonemes that are meaningful in, say, Spanish, Chinese, or Russian—differences obvious to native speakers of those languages but initially very difficult or impossible for nonnative speakers to perceive.

By the time children enter school, most have a relatively sophisticated linguistic knowledge about their language's sound system. For any child, acquiring a basic understanding of how sounds are organized and what they mean is critical to his or her becoming a member of the language community. Although their abilities to pronounce and perceive sounds are not fully mature, most children can produce and use accurately the sound segments of their language. Their pronunciation and intonation patterns also conform closely to those of adults. Knowledge about the relationship of sounds to language symbols is equally important to becoming literate, learning to read and write.

A capability only in its beginning developmental stages when children start school, however, is a form of metalinguistic knowledge called **phonemic awareness**, the ability to recognize phonemes as individual and separable speech sounds (Ehri & Robbins, 1992; Mason, Herman, & Au, 1991). At age four, few children understand how words can be broken down into phonemic segments; by age six, however, most will show some degree of phonemic awareness (Grunwell, 1986).

In alphabetic languages, such as English and Spanish, phonemic awareness is critical to learning how to read. For instance, phonemic awareness is involved in understanding how sounds are combined to form words (e.g., Cuh-ah-tuh . . . CAT) and how specific words are similar or differ in sound structure (e.g., How are MAT and SAT alike? How are they different?). In learning to read, students need to learn not only to identify and label letters and the phonemes they represent but also to segment, rearrange, and substitute them for each other (Adams, 1990; Bryne & Fielding-Barnsley, 1991; Ehri & Robbins, 1992; Spector, 1992; Vellutino, 1991). Although the challenge of learning English spelling-sound relationships is a significant one for most children, it is not impossible. The relationship of spelling to sound in English is a complex domain of knowledge, but not an arbitrary one (Calfee & Drum, 1986).

Whereas phonemes are the minimal meaningful distinctions in the *sounds* of a language, **morphemes** are sounds or combinations of sounds that are the minimal units of *meaning* (Prideaux, 1984). Words are made up of one or more morphemes. For example, the word *cat* is a single morpheme. The word *joyfully,* in contrast, is a combination of three morphemes, *joy + ful + ly* (of course, the word *joyfully* contains multiple phonemes, corresponding to the basic sounds making up the word). Each of the three morphemes in *joyfully* conveys a dimension of meaning of the word. The root word *joy* has a meaning of itself; adding -*ful* to the noun *joy* converts it to its adjectival form; and adding -*ly* to *joyful* transforms it to its adverbial form. Only certain combinations of morphemes are possible in a given language; for instance, we know immediately that utterances such as *fuljoy, joylyful,* and *joyly* are not English. English morphology allows only a few of a near-infinite number of possibilities.

Children begin to use morphological rules soon after their speech moves beyond the single-word level, as they begin to add markers for pluralization and tense. Early on, children tend to overapply their growing morphological knowledge (e.g., two *sheepses,* she *goed* home) but gradually move to more mature forms. Like all aspects of language, morphological rules are complex, and learning them continues throughout the entire period of formal schooling.

Words Combined: The Syntax of a Language.   The second major level of language structure is **syntax**—the ordering of words into larger units, such as phrases, clauses, and sentences. The study of syntax has long been a major emphasis in linguistics, but especially so after the publication of Noam Chomsky's *Syntactic Structures* in 1957 and *Aspects of the Theory of Syntax* in 1965. These books transformed the way linguists looked at language learning, especially at how syntactical knowledge is acquired and used. Chomsky took a strongly nativist position, arguing that much syntactical knowledge is "hardwired" into the developing human and that syntactic structures are not acquired completely through processes of modeling, feedback, and the like.

Understanding the meaning of any language depends on comprehension of its syntax. Syntactic speech is closely linked with propositional thought (Anisfeld, 1984); propositions ordinarily cannot be comprehended except through their expression in the syntax of language. For instance, the information contained in the syntax of the sentence *The horse kicked Eddie* is essential to understanding what the sentence is saying—that is, to the encoding of the proposition underlying the sentence (see Chapter 4). Obviously, the sentences *Eddie kicked the horse* and *The horse kicked Eddie* carry very different meanings!

Syntactic regularity appears very early in children's speech, even earlier than morphology; children use consistent word order as soon as they begin to use two-word sequences (Anisfeld, 1984; R. Brown, 1973). Syntactic development does continue well into the middle elementary grades and beyond, however. Because most primary-level students have difficulty in comprehending sentences with complex syntax, most materials used in beginning reading instruction have simple syntactic structures.

Frameworks for Comprehension: Discourse Structure.   A final form of language knowledge that children use in learning to read is **discourse structure**. Propositions take on a meaning in relation to one another in discourse. References forward or backward affect the meaning of individual elements. We typically encounter language in the context of discourse; even for children just learning to talk, the meanings of their utterances are shaped by prior and subsequent utterances. Reading and writing typically involve extended sequences of discourse. Comprehension depends on students' abilities to tie discourse elements together. To do so, they must recognize, at least implicitly, the structure of a story or text.

Two discourse structures of particular interest to teachers of reading are narratives and exposition. **Narratives** are "stories" structured by a temporal sequence of events. Most children begin to recognize narrative structure not long after they begin to use language (Applebee, 1983; McNamee, 1987) and use this knowledge to understand stories being read or told to them. By first grade, knowledge of narrative structure is often well developed. Here, for instance, is a first-grader's narration about a set of events, which reflects her understanding of a narrative sequence.

And then she got some ice cream.

And then she put it in the cone.

And then he . . . she went outside.

And a . . . the kitty-cat scared her.

And she dropped the cone.

And she looked real mad.

Many narratives, of course, are much more complex than this child's narration; they can range from very simple recountings like this one to complex plays, novels, and historical accounts. The essential feature of all narratives, however, is a discourse structure based on the temporal sequence of events.

Expository texts, in contrast to narratives, reflect the organization of abstract thought about a topic or a body of information. Although expository texts may contain narrative elements (and vice versa), the basic structure of exposition is logical, not temporal. Textbooks, essays, and persuasive arguments typically use expository structure. Because expository structure is based more on logical relations than on directly observed temporal associations, comprehension and use of exposition develop considerably later than for narratives. For this reason, the majority of children's early reading instruction is organized around narratives, not expository texts.

Linguistic and Metalinguistic Knowledge and Reading

Although learning to read builds on children's considerable knowledge of language, it nonetheless is a significant challenge in most children's language development. In reading, children must link the oral language they already know with a new, visual system of symbols and combinations of symbols. To do so, children must draw on their basic abilities to use and comprehend language (linguistic knowledge) but also must acquire and apply metalinguistic knowledge—an awareness of the abstract properties of language that allows them to treat language as an object of analysis and to use their analysis to regulate their language-related activities. The ability to learn to read rests, therefore, not only on children's basic knowledge *of* the dimensions of language but also on their knowledge *about* language at all of its different levels: its sound system, how words are formed, how sentences are put together, and how sentences become stories.

Although learning to read involves recognizing and using multiple sources of information, in alphabetic languages, such as English, no source is more important than the relationships of letters to sounds (Adams, 1990). Thus, a basic goal in almost all methods of reading instruction is that students acquire the *alphabetic principle*—that is, understanding that individual letters and combinations of letters represent speech sounds. Researchers may differ on specific methods of instruction on this topic, but most generally are in agreement that explicit instruction in this area (generally called **phonics** instruction) makes a positive difference in long-term reading achievement (Adams, 1990; Bryne & Fielding-Barnsley, 1991; Ehri & Robbins, 1992; Foorman, Francis, Novy, & Liberman, 1991).

Explicit instruction may be required because English pronunciation, though reasonably predictable, is not wholly so. Letters are pronounced differently, depending on their role in words and syllables (e.g., the *c* in *cat* and *face*), how they are combined with other letters (e.g., the *i* in *big* and *night*), and the presence of signals to their pronunciation (e.g., the *a* in *hat* and *hate,* as signaled by the "silent e"). The challenge can be daunting to some children; they must learn to recognize these unfamiliar and highly abstract representations and to map them in reasonably reliable and rapid ways onto the language system they already possess. Table 10-1 is a summary of several linguistic and metalinguistic abilities that underlie early reading. For

Table 10-1
Some Linguistic and Metalinguistic Abilities Underlying Early Reading.

Word-Level Abilities	
Print awareness	Understanding that print carries meaning; that reading is directional, can represent objects or speech, has special words (e.g., *word, letter*) to describe it.
Graphic awareness	Recognition of letter details (e.g., difference between *d* and *b*), that words are composed of letters.
Phonemic awareness	Ability to "hear" sound units; knowledge that spoken units can be analyzed and compared (e.g., *sh* and *ch*).
Awareness of grapheme/phoneme correspondence	Knowledge that letters and sounds "go together"; ability to apply that knowledge to decoding unknown words.
Contextual-Level Abilities	
Syntactic awareness	Recognition and use of sentence-level patterns, within-sentence context of words (e.g., correctly pronouncing *read* in the sentence *The girl read the book*).
Text-structure awareness	Comprehension of relationships between parts of text, including recognition of cohesive elements in text, general knowledge of text structures (e.g., narratives).
Pragmatic awareness	Knowledge of purposes of written messages, uses of print.

Note: Word-level categories adapted from Lomax and McGee (1987).

most reading teachers, developing these abilities in their students is a major goal. Direct instruction on these and other aspects of reading as separate skills, however, does not seem to be a particularly good idea; children taught in this way can come to view reading as an incomprehensible set of fragmented tasks (Norris, 1988). A better approach is to teach skills systematically, but in the context of activities emphasizing the central purpose of reading—understanding the story or text being read.

COGNITIVE PREREQUISITES OF LEARNING TO READ

Although reading is a language-based activity, it also is a cognitive process that involves constructing meaning from text. As Mason and Au (1990) point out, reading is not word calling or "sounding out," but rather is a special form of reasoning in which both the reader and the writer contribute perspective, inference, and logic. In this section, we highlight three cognitive factors on which children's success in learning to read depends: (1) world knowledge, (2) short-term and long-term memory capabilities, and (3) the ability to focus attention. These are not discrete, separable factors, of course; when readers read successfully, all of these dimensions operate at once and interact with linguistic knowledge. In discussing the beginning reader, however, it is useful to separate them. Just as is true with children's language experience, some children may be well prepared on one factor and less well prepared on the others. These factors do not necessarily develop simultaneously. A beginning reader who has reasonably good skills overall may perform well on some kinds of reading tasks but not on others that require different knowledge or skills.

Knowledge of the World

We read to understand the meaning of written materials. This search for meaning— the process of comprehension—depends on both the writer and the reader. As we have stressed throughout this text, schema theory has had an especially important role in helping us better understand the nature of comprehension processes, including those in reading (Pressley, 1994). To illustrate, let's turn again to a "piggy bank" passage, this one considerably simpler than the one you saw in Chapter 4:

> Toby wanted to get a birthday present for Chris. He went to his piggy bank. He shook it. There was no sound.

As you now recognize, the knowledge a young reader needs in order to comprehend even a brief passage like this is very extensive. For instance, the reader must know that getting a birthday present means buying one, that Toby went to his piggy bank to get some money (the passage does not say so), that piggy banks contain money (the passage does not say so), that this money typically is in coin form, that coins in shaken piggy banks make noise, and that no rattling meant no money. For adults, comprehension comes without any special effort; all of these things are recognized automatically (and mostly without consciousness of their recognition). Many primary-level students, however, have not had experience with piggy banks, with buying and giving presents, or, for that matter, with birthday parties. With any part of this knowledge missing, the whole sequence of events in the passage can become incomprehensible. The main point of reading—getting meaning—would not be apparent to these students.

Our knowledge directs attention in reading, guides interpretations, and makes comprehension possible (R. C. Anderson, 1984; Rumelhart, 1981). The meaning that an active reader constructs, therefore, is not solely the meaning the author intended as he or she wrote the passage. Neither is it simply the reader's own mental constructions and inferences. As children read, they necessarily interpret words and events in terms of what they know. Children who have helped care for a garden by watering, cultivating, and feeding the plants and who have gathered produce from the garden, for example, would be much more likely to make sense of a story about, say, a young Chippewa girl who works with her father harvesting wild rice than children who have not had these kinds of experiences.

It is useful for teachers and parents to remind themselves that reading is a constructive process aimed at comprehension. As we see below, even when children mispronounce and misidentify words, teachers should continue to direct considerable attention to the meaning of what is being read. Although beginning readers undeniably need decoding skills, such as letter, sound, and word identification, these skills in themselves do not add up to reading. To focus solely on "skills" with beginning readers misses the main point of learning to read—getting meaning from what is read. Indeed, children even can be misled about the purposes of reading and can come to believe that "reading" consists of figuring out pronunciations, doing exercises with words, and completing worksheets (Cairney, 1988).

Short-Term and Long-Term Memory Capabilities

Because it depends on world and linguistic knowledge, reading also is an act of memory. A child fixating on a particular word, for instance, must keep that word in mind long enough to build up the more complex meaning of phrases, sentences, and whole passages. New meaning requires the continuing availability of earlier information; comprehension processes depend on the linkage between the words currently being processed and those processed earlier (Just & Carpenter, 1987; Rayner & Pollatsek, 1989; Swanson, 1992).

As many studies have shown, human short-term or working memory is limited and quite fragile. Young children's short-term memory capacity is especially restricted, most likely because they lack well-developed skills for encoding and rehearsal (e.g., Henry & Millar, 1991). For example, the number of digits a five-year-old can recall from a single presentation is only four or so (Dempster, 1981), compared with seven for an adult. If the number of digits presented exceeds this amount, the immediate memory span is exceeded, and all or most of the information will be lost.

Reading, however, consists of sequential encounters with related, not isolated, elements: Letters are clustered into meaningful words, words into phrases and sentences, and sentences into text. Thus, although it might appear that information encountered while reading would exceed almost immediately the immediate memory span (after a child has read five or six words), it ordinarily does not. If words and sentences have meaning, the reader can "chunk" information or, perhaps more accurately, convert it into propositions (see Chapter 4). Each word is part of a meaningful pattern, not a discrete, isolated unit.

Obviously, however, both short-term and long-term memory processes are fundamental to reading. Constructing meaning depends on an interaction of the two types of memory. New information must be "kept alive" in short-term memory while previously encountered information is drawn from long-term memory. With this interaction in mind, some researchers and theorists who have examined reading from a memory perspective (e.g., Breznitz, 1987; Breznitz & Share, 1992; Swanson, 1992) have argued that slower-than-normal speeds of word decoding may place higher-than-normal demands on short-term memory and interfere with meaningful reading. When words are decoded more slowly, the meaning of each must be held in memory longer in order for the reader to comprehend the meaning of a sentence or paragraph. At least some evidence has been presented in support of this position, though it would appear that conflicting demands on attention for the poor decoder (poor decoders do not comprehend as well because they must concentrate more on decoding, whereas good decoders decode more automatically, allowing more attention to meaning) also is an equally plausible explanation of poor decoders' inability to comprehend and recall what they have read (Laberge & Samuels, 1974; Samuels, 1988).

Attention

Reading requires that children's attention be focused on the materials to be read. For instance, children obviously must have a book out, be oriented toward the book, and be looking at it in order to read. Reaching this point with some children is not a trivial accomplishment. Teachers can take advantage, however, of a large array of behavioral management systems (e.g., see Axelrod, 1983; Kazdin, 1994) developed to help foster attentional skills.

Attention also is critical within the act of reading. Readers need to direct their attention to the relevant elements of text in an organized, systematic way (e.g., "Look at the first letter. What is it, Sean?"). They need to control their eye movements, focus on specific words, and, at least in English, move their eyes in a left-to-right direction. Attention must move to each word successively and back to important points in the text. Attention must shift appropriately between text and illustrations. During formal instructional periods, the problem of attention allocation becomes even more complex, as attention must be allocated, in turn, to the text, to classmates' responses, and to the teacher's directions and feedback. As we discuss in the next chapter, metacognitive skills for guiding these and related processes are vital to reading comprehension.

Summary of Cognitive Prerequisites for Reading

At first glance, reading seems simply to be a matching task in which children learn to link visual cues with their vocabulary. In fact, reading is a highly complex interaction with text, requiring orchestration of a stream of complex graphic input with several levels of linguistic and world knowledge. Reading places demands on short-term memory and requires that children draw on their long-term memory to understand what they are reading. It also necessitates involvement with books and other reading materials and attention to details of letters, words, and text.

FROM READING READINESS TO EMERGENT LITERACY

Almost everyone would agree there are developmental limits on how young children can profitably be taught to read. Today, most children in the United States learn to read during their first year in school, when they are about six or seven years old. Only a small minority of students know how to read when they enter school. For many years, our thoughts about when to begin to teach reading were shaped by the concept of **reading readiness**, the idea that a certain level of mental maturity is necessary to begin reading instruction. The concept of *reading readiness* was given considerable impetus by an early study by Morphett and Washburne (1931), who examined the relationship between general intellectual functioning and reading success. Their data, though flawed, led them to conclude that reading success was considerably greater for children who had a mental age of at least six years and six months when they started school. From their analysis, Morphett and Washburne recommended that it was prudent to postpone reading instruction until children reached this mental age, which usually occurs during the first grade.

Although the connection between teaching reading and the first grade has endured, the idea of reading readiness began to be defined more specifically as the subskills thought to underlie reading—such as letter name knowledge and visual, auditory, and perceptual readiness. A major influence in this transformation was the development of measures of reading readiness, which were attempts to measure critical factors underlying the ability to read (see Sulzby, 1991; Teale & Sulzby, 1986). The subskills view of reading readiness fits well with a conception of reading instruction as development of a carefully sequenced hierarchy of skills. This point of view also was aligned closely with the task-analysis approach to learning that dominated thinking about learning and instruction in the 1960s and 1970s (e.g., Gagne, 1965, 1970; see also Chapter 1). Hierarchical sequences of reading skills soon provided the framework for many basal reader series—the packages of texts, teacher guides, and student activities around which reading instruction still is organized.

One difficulty with the *reading readiness* concept is that children are placed into two discrete groups: readers and nonreaders. Also, reading is artificially isolated from writing and other language skills as the "real" dimension of literacy to which the extensive language experiences of early children are mere precursors. The concept of **emergent literacy**, however, provides an alternative point of view. From the perspective of emergent literacy, the most important consideration is that literacy development begins well before children actually being to read (Heath, 1986; Sulzby, 1991; Teale & Sulzby, 1986). A prereader is neither "ready to read" nor "not ready to read." Instead, literacy development, like general language development, is seen as a continuous process beginning far in advance of formal instruction. Table 10-2 is a summary of some points of comparison between the reading-readiness and emergent-literacy perspectives.

Children's movement into reading indeed does seem more continuous than discontinuous. As we saw earlier in this chapter, the kinds of metalinguistic knowledge that are so vital to reading—phonemic awareness, analysis of syntactic structure, knowledge of story structure—continue to develop throughout the preschool and primary school years. Also, although they cannot yet read, many prereaders already have discovered much about the processes of reading and writing. They know that the purposes are to get and convey meaning, that the print context often provides cues for meaning, and that reading and writing have many functional uses (Clay, 1991; McGee et al., 1988; Sulzby, 1991).

Table 10-2
Contrastive Views: Reading Readiness and Emergent Literacy.

Reading Readiness	Emergent Literacy
Focus	
Reading as a critical skill in literacy.	Broad literacy development, including reading, writing, listening, and speaking.
Prototypical view of reading	
Reading as a hierarchy of skills.	Reading as a functional activity.
Function of preschool language activity	
Preparation for reading.	Part of multifaceted language-development process.
Focus in learning to read	
Formal instruction in reading.	Engagement with literate adults, adult modeling, self-exploration, formal instruction.
Sequencing of instruction	
Read first, write later.	Simultaneous use of all language forms—writing, reading, speaking, and listening.
Nature of curriculum	
Sequenced reading instruction and hierarchical array of reading skills.	Variable language sources, language-based activities that include reading.

From the standpoint of emergent literacy, reading is not the only important language skill learned in school, but rather is one among a complementary array of critical language-based skills: reading, writing, speaking, and listening. Reading and writing are best learned from active engagement in meaningful communication activities, such as purposeful writing assignments and group projects. Although beginning reading instruction obviously needs to be planned and organized carefully so that important aspects of instruction are not neglected (Pressley, 1994), we need to remember that reading is a natural expansion of children's knowledge about language to the medium of print and to take advantage of this considerable resource.

The emergent-literacy perspective reminds us also that the goal of "learning to read" might be broadened profitably to being competent in all forms of language expression. Reading is the key to literacy, but it is not all there is to literacy. Critical literacy—linking thinking and expression through competent use of all forms of language—should be our goal, not simply functional literacy (Calfee, 1994).

THE TRANSITION TO READING

As we have seen, the ability to read rests on a wide variety of linguistic, metalinguistic, and cognitive skills, each necessary but not sufficient for learning to read. Young children display a wide array of reading and writing behaviors (e.g., looking at picture books, scribbling) that precede and develop into conventional literacy (Sulzby, 1991). From this standpoint, it seems inappropriate to label children as "readers" or "nonreaders" because literacy-related behaviors are developing on multiple dimensions. Nonetheless, it is useful to map the changes young readers go through as they move from a stage in which they have little or no facility in decoding words to one in which they can do so easily. Moving through this transition is at the heart of learning to read and is one of its primary accomplishments (Adams, 1990).

Linnea Ehri (Ehri, 1991; Ehri & Wilce, 1985, 1987a, 1987b) has presented persuasive evidence that children's decoding skills develop quite predictably and that children pass through at least four stages as they begin to learn to read. At first, children have little or no skill in decoding words. Ehri calls these children "nonreaders." Then, children typically move into what she calls visual-cue reading, on to phonetic-cue reading, and finally to "expert" status, in which they use systematic phonemic decoding. We describe each of these levels in the following sections.

Nonreaders

In Ehri's analysis, nonreaders are children who are unable to read any primer or preprimer words in isolation (Ehri, 1991). Given a list containing such words as *bat, hit, go,* and *is,* for instance, nonreaders would be unable to read any of them. However, many of these children show an emerging knowledge of literacy by being aware that print carries meaning (Chaney, 1992; McGee et al., 1988). They know, for instance, that newspapers, written advertisements, and books tell people *something.*

They even may be able to "read" in the sense of identifying the names of products or businesses from signs. What these children are reading is more context than print, however. They cannot read any print materials removed from context and pay little attention to the graphic (letter) cues.

A good example of this phenomenon can be seen in a study by Masonheimer, Drum, and Ehri (1984). Masonheimer et al. located a number of three- to five-year-olds who could identify "environmental words" (e.g., *Pepsi, Wendy's*) in their familiar context (as part of the logo). Most of these children, however, could not read these same words when they appeared in contexts other than the original ones (simply as printed words). They also were unable to detect alterations in the graphic cues (e.g., *xepsi*). Children at this stage are primarily responding to their environment, and not the print (Mason, 1980; Mason et al., 1991). To become a "real" reader, skills other than those acquired from simple exposure to the environment are needed (Ehri, 1991; Ehri & Robbins, 1992).

Visual-Cue Reading

Visual-cue reading is the first "real" reading. In this stage, children begin to rely less on the context in which words are embedded and more on the characteristics of words themselves. The word features to which many children first pay attention, however, seem to be predominantly visual ones. Examples of such cues are the "tail" at the end of the word *dog* or the "look" of the word (Ehri & Wilce, 1987a). For children attempting to read with a visual-cue strategy, reading is a kind of paired-associate task (see Chapter 4) of linking a word's look with its pronunciation and meaning. Unfortunately, because words' distinctive visual features are exhausted quickly and because of the arbitrary nature of these associations, visual-cue readers are unable to read consistently over time. The memory demands of reading in this way soon become overwhelming. In Ehri's judgment, this associative strategy soon is abandoned by most readers in favor of one relying more on generalizations based on phonetic information.

Phonetic-Cue Reading

Ehri contends that a major step toward full word reading takes place when children begin to use phonetic cues. In phonetic-cue reading, words are read by forming and storing associations between some (but not all) of the letters in words' spellings and some of their sounds in pronunciation. For instance, a child may learn to read the word *fix* by associating the letter names *f* and *x* with the word's sounds, or write the word *giraffe* as *jrf*. These associations, because they are not arbitrary, are much easier to remember and are more effective in reading than the visual cues of word and letter shape.

Systematic Phonemic Decoding

In Ehri's judgment, children become "expert" word readers and have unlocked an important key to reading when they can apply their phonemic knowledge to distinguish among similarly spelled words and read them with a reasonably high accuracy rate. These systematic phonemic decoders have learned the alphabet, can hear the separate sounds in words, and understand that spellings more or less systematically correspond to pronunciations (Ehri, 1991; Ehri & Wilce, 1987a; Gough & Hillinger, 1980). In an alphabetic language, such as English, this means they are beginning to master a cognitive mapping system linking the forty or so English phonemes with a vast array of letters and letter combinations. Of course, these children are not yet "expert readers" in the more general sense, but they are showing considerable phonemic awareness and ability to use it in decoding. As we have pointed out, however, reading is a complex, interactive process focused on comprehension, not simply on decoding. Decoding is a fundamental key to reading but not the only one and not necessarily even the first one that should be taught (Calfee & Drum, 1986). Reading places demands on the full range of a child's linguistic and world knowledge, and reading instruction needs to draw on all of its dimensions.

Knowledge and Skill in Decoding

As we have stated, virtually all authorities are in agreement that beginning readers must acquire decoding skills. Rapid and eventually automatic decoding is critical to the ability to read effectively, and context cannot substitute for the ability to identify words rapidly and accurately (Adams, 1990; Chall et al., 1990; Rayner & Pollatsek, 1989). There is less certainty, however, about where to place the emphasis in beginning reading instruction—on decoding or on the more global meaning of what is being read. What should be the focus of beginning reading instruction? Following the lead of many reading experts (e.g., Adams, 1990; Calfee & Drum, 1986; Pressley, 1994; Uhry & Shepard, 1993), we would argue that the answer to this question may be analogous to the advice for a healthy diet: varied fare combining the acquisition of decoding skills with contextual analyses in a meaningful reading activity (Samuels, 1988).

Consider, for example, the passage in Figure 10-1. Take a moment to try to make sense of it. Although the parallel to beginning reading is not exact because of your superior knowledge as an adult, we believe it is highly instructive. Think especially about the kinds of knowledge you use in reading it. If you are like most readers, reading a text like this forces you to draw on a variety of kinds of knowledge. Some letter and word decoding obviously is important. Like beginning readers, you probably made a rough correspondence between many of the letters and sounds, but not all of them. You also used your knowledge of syntax and your pragmatic knowledge that this passage probably means something, however. At the same time, as soon as you were able to decode your first word or two, your knowledge about the world—in this case, your knowledge about real estate sales—was brought into play.

Just as it was for you in this "bungalow" passage, beginning readers' word decoding is not simply a process of mapping symbols to phonemes and words. Reading is a meaning-getting activity in which all kinds of knowledge are used. Sentence and passage meaning assists in decoding, whereas decoding is the route to sentence and passage meaning. Thus, instructional methods stressing only a single approach to

dɪlʌks bʌŋəloz̧. eksepšʌnlǫ prɛstɪž lʌkšurǫ lokešʌn ɪmidiʌt akypʌnciz̧
θri larĵ bɛdrumzz̧, lɔts ʌv specz̧, atïčt gʌrɔĵˈ. əplyʌnsʌz stez̧ hy wʌnetɪzz̧,
kal čïd at ʌfɔrdəbl riʌltiž. 555-1234

Figure 10-1
A short passage from the *Chronicle*.

learning to read may handicap children who need multiple keys to unlock the meanings of words, sentences, and stories.

Skilled teachers draw on children's knowledge to help them read, interweaving
information from the text and its illustrations and from a child's own memory to
develop the ability to read. A demonstration from Norris (1988) is a case in point. It
uses an illustrated text from Wagner (1971) that describes how Tony, a friendly lion
who lives in a zoo, is approached by a bird needing some of his hair for a nest.

The teacher begins by pointing back and forth between a picture of Tony and
the lion's name in print and says, "This is Tony." The teacher then explains what the
author wants the child to know about Tony. For example, in pointing to the first sentence, which tells that Tony lived in a zoo, the teacher might say, "This tells you
where Tony lived." If the child is able to use the context cues available in the picture
and the teacher's facilitation, the sentence is very predictable without "knowing" any
of the words. The teacher points to the words as the child provides the information.
If the child is unable to make use of the context cues, more information can be provided to direct the child's attention to them.

Each line of text is treated as an extension of the idea communicated in the first
sentence so that the child views reading as a series of integrated thoughts, rather
than as a series of disconnected ideas or words. For instance:

Facilitator: Now it tells you what kind of zoo animal Tony was.

Child: Tony was a lion.

Facilitator: Oh, a lion! A lion who lives in a zoo [pointing to relevant words in
the text].

New or unpredictable words, such as *friendly,* are introduced by using them in context. Cohesive terms that tie segments of discourse together (e.g., the pronoun *he*
referring to Tony) are introduced. Similarly, the child's attention can be drawn to
specific features of words, such as suffixes, that modify their meanings. For example:

Child: He was a friend lion.

Facilitator: It's not telling you that Tony was a friend. It's telling you how he
acted. He acted friend*ly* [pointing to the word]. He was nice and did not
bite or growl. Tell me about Tony.

Child: He was a friend . . . a friendly lion!

Facilitator: I'm glad he was friendly and not mean!

Similarly, misreadings of words are pointed out by repeating previous information and providing new cues.

Child: He saw a friendly lion.

Facilitator: No, I don't think he saw a friendly lion. This is telling you about Tony: He's the one who was friendly.

Child: He was a friendly lion.

After the child has finished "reading" the ideas on the page and understood their meaning, the child can be asked to tell the story by using the words on the page—that is, by reading the words from the print. Context cues still can be provided as necessary, but the emphasis shifts strongly to decoding from the print. For instance:

Facilitator: Remember, this [pointing to the appropriate line in the text] tells you where Tony lived.

Child: Tony lived in the—zoo.

Facilitator: And this tells you what kind of animal Tony was.

Child: Tony was a lion.

Facilitator: And this tells you that he was nice.

Child: Tony was a friendly lion.

Facilitator: When we know it is Tony, this [pointing to the word *he*] is the other word we can use to talk about him.

Child: He was a friendly lion.

Ideas in unpredictable and difficult sentences can be developed within the sentence one at a time, in a logical order.

Facilitator: The bird needs to build something to keep her eggs in. I wonder what that is.

Child: A nest?

Facilitator: Oh, a nest [pointing to those words in the sentence]. And she needs something from Tony [pointing to his hair in the picture] that she can use to build her nest.

Child: Hair?

Facilitator: Oh, I see, hair . . . [rising intonation, pointing to a nest].

Child: Hair for a nest!

Facilitator: Right! But she doesn't tell him that she wants all of it, just . . . [pointing to the word *some*].

Child: Some of it.

Facilitator: So tell me [pointing to the sentence within quotes] what the bird said she needed.

Child: She needs some hair for a nest.

> *Facilitator:*   Right, but it is the bird who is talking, so she doesn't say, "She needs some," she says . . .
>
> *Child:*   I need some hair for a nest. (Norris, 1988, p. 671)

The principal skills this teacher demonstrates are drawing out the child's considerable knowledge of language while maintaining a clear focus on meaning. Although some information is provided for the child, the teacher mainly focuses the child's attention on the text and elicits text-relevant information from the child. In the preceding example, that information is as diverse as knowledge about zoos and zoo animals and information about how language is used. Included in the latter are the child's experience with sequencing of ideas, cohesiveness of text, and purpose in communication, plus specific aspects of sentence structure and vocabulary use. At the same time, the child is not allowed simply to continue to use the context. From the outset, attention is directed to the words and the need to decode their specific features (e.g., *friend/friendly, was/saw, a/the*). Reading instruction reflects a balance between meaning and decoding. Each aspect is used to create a source of information for the other. Reading is not an abstract, decontextualized "drill and practice," nor is it solely "a guessing game" in which text features can be ignored. The strategy is to help the child find the meaning expressed in print and to begin to acquire an understanding of how letters and words represent meaning. The goal of increasingly rapid and fluent decoding—translating the printed word into speech and meaning—is embedded in a meaningful context. When we help children draw on all of their available cognitive and linguistic resources, their decoding skills, sentence analysis, and text-comprehension abilities will develop simultaneously.

METHODS OF TEACHING READING

In the example above, a skillful reading teacher draws on several categories of children's knowledge in teaching reading. In the same way, teachers' overall objectives need to be broadly based, focusing on the important dimensions of reading. Calfee and Henry (1986), for instance, have identified mastery of four general dimensions of reading as vital to successful reading:

1. *Decoding.* Printed words must be translated into their pronounceable equivalents.
2. *Vocabulary.* Meaning must be assigned to words and a network of associations activated.
3. *Sentence and paragraph comprehension.* Text units need to be "fit" to their functional roles (e.g., as the subject or predicate of a sentence or as topic sentences).
4. *Text comprehension.* Complete texts need to be understood as entities—as "stories" (narratives), expositions, or dialogues, for instance.

A sensible reading curriculum must address each of these dimensions. The history of reading instruction, however, typically has not been one of balanced attention to all of the dimensions important to learning to read. Instead, proponents of one method or another often have advocated, sometimes with near-religious zeal, methods such as "systematic phonics" or "patterning." Others have favored "meaning" or "whole language" approaches with equal fervor. Over the years, numerous debates have raged about the efficacy of various methods.

One landmark event in the debate about reading instruction was Jeanne Chall's 1967 book *Learning to Read: The Great Debate*. As part of a comprehensive analysis of reading instruction, she divided reading methods into two broad categories: **code-emphasis methods** and **meaning-emphasis methods**. The former referred to approaches that initially emphasized decoding, learning the correspondence between letters and sounds. Prominent among code-emphasis methods was **phonics**, which stressed acquisition of basic letter-sound relationships and the rules for sounding out words. Contrasted with these code-emphasis methods were meaning-emphasis approaches, which Chall judged to favor meaning over decoding in beginning reading. Included in the meaning-emphasis category were the **sight word methods** (sometimes called "look-say"), which stressed the need for children to acquire at least a limited stock of familiar words they could recognize on sight. Another meaning-emphasis approach was **language experience**, a general method in which children's oral language, such as their narratives about their experiences and observations, is dictated and written down; what is written then becomes the basis for reading. Thus, skills are taught in the context of the child's own direct experience with language and the world.

Chall's analysis showed that code-emphasis approaches to beginning reading instruction generally produced superior achievement as measured by standardized tests. Many others (e.g., Carbo, 1988; K. S. Goodman, 1967; Goodman & Goodman, 1979; F. Smith, 1982; Weaver, 1988), however, have disagreed with her and have continued to advocate meaning-based instruction for beginning readers. Most current models of reading (e.g., Just & Carpenter, 1987; McClelland, 1986) and authorities on reading instruction (e.g., Adams, 1990; Calfee, 1994; Clay, 1991; Pressley, 1994) stake out a middle ground between code and meaning emphases, arguing that both emphases are necessary in learning to read. Even Rayner and Pollatsek's (1989) model of reading, described by its creators as primarily a "bottom-up" model, depicts top-down processes as interacting with bottom-up processes. These models suggest that reading is not best construed as "either-or"—that is, neither as an exclusively bottom-up, data-driven process (e.g., Gough, 1972) nor as a top-down process dominated by higher-level cognitive and language activity (e.g., K. S. Goodman, 1967; F. Smith, 1971).

In spite of the sensibility of a balanced approach, reading instruction has swung widely between methods strongly emphasizing either code- or meaning-emphasis approaches. In a climate that emphasized reading subskills and skill development, meaning-based approaches languished in the 1970s. In some instances, beginning reading instruction followed a pattern dominated by seatwork and worksheets prescribed by the basal readers. Also, in designing text materials for basals, readability formulas and restricting vocabulary were used frequently to try to simplify text. Unfortunately, in the attempt to control readability (a quantitative estimate of text difficulty typically derived from sentence length and word frequency), other critical aspects of text often were ignored. For instance, continuity, coherence, conflict, and surprise all contribute to children's interest and reading comprehension but are not captured by measures of readability (Brennan, Bridge, & Winograd, 1986). The result of modifying text on the basis of readability measures was text that, although theoretically carefully matched with the student's grade level, was often disjointed, poorly formed, and quite unreadable.

By the early 1980s, analyses of classroom instruction and the contents of basal reading materials had begun to reveal the extent to which reading comprehension and the literary value of reading materials were being neglected (e.g., see D. Durkin, 1978-1979, 1981). Also, the development of more clearly articulated theories of comprehension in cognitive psychology (e.g., R. C. Anderson & Pearson, 1984) provided developers of curriculum and materials with a theoretical basis for emphasizing comprehension. Again, however, what began as a sensible antidote to decontextualized skill-based instruction was misinterpreted by some as a call to abandon virtually all teaching of strategies and skills, including instruction in decoding. This position was represented most strongly by a number of advocates of "whole language" approaches to reading, some of whom seemed to be proposing that children would learn to read through simple exposure to good literature (see Pressley, 1994, for an interesting discussion of these issues).

In general, however, reading instruction seems now to have attained a better balance than was true a decade ago. In the mid-1990s, more reading materials with excellent literary value are available, both in trade books and in the basal reading series. The basal series more strongly emphasize comprehension, analysis, and extension. Although the status of systematic decoding instruction is somewhat unclear in some reading series, more meaningful exercises are beginning to be included. Most sexist portrayals of characters have been eliminated, and a wider range of racial and cultural backgrounds is represented in the basal literature. To us, these changes generally seem to be moving in the direction of the desired "balanced diet" of meaningful reading instruction and to reflect the development of a more coherent view of reading as an interactive, multifaceted process.

Summary of Reading Methods

Reading instruction is a highly variable and often emotion-laden enterprise representing many philosophies about how best to teach reading. Some methods strongly emphasize decoding; others stress text meaning and using general and linguistic knowledge to a much greater extent. In most schools, however, reading instruction has been dominated by an eclectic perspective represented by most basal reading series, which are packages of materials for reading instruction that include coordinated texts, teacher manuals, and student worksheets. In the past, basal reading series were criticized, appropriately, for providing a less-than-coherent view of reading; poorly structured, uninteresting, and stereotypic reading materials; and deadly "practice activities" on worksheets that were boring and meant little to children. Many basal readers now have moved toward improved literary quality, as well as toward a greater emphasis on comprehension and on embedding reading instruction in a literate context of writing, speaking, and listening. These changes are welcome from both a theoretical and a practical perspective.

IMPLICATIONS FOR READING INSTRUCTION

Whether or not reading is a "natural act," most would agree that the assistance of a skilled teacher in learning to read is important for most children. Reading rests on children's linguistic and world knowledge and depends on their ability to link written symbols with their spoken language. In alphabetic languages, such as English, children must learn a system that maps graphemes (letters and combinations of letters) to phonemes (the sounds of the language). As we have seen, however, reading is much more than decoding words; multiple levels of cognitive processes ranging from basic perception to the highest levels of cognition are involved. Thus, teaching reading cannot be a simple-minded, "by the book" activity. If success is to be achieved, it requires the orchestration of many components into a meaningful whole. The scaffolding techniques discussed in Chapter 9 are particularly critical to successful reading instruction; with the help of the teacher, students become aware of and begin to use their linguistic knowledge in meeting the challenges of learning to read. Without the teacher's scaffolding, many would not succeed. Following are themes we believe underlie successful reading instruction.

1. *Approach reading as a meaningful activity.* Reading is a meaning-making act. This fact may be lost in some kinds of reading instruction. When reading is broken down into isolated skills and subskills, for instance, the overall context of reading can be lost. Children can come to perceive learning to read as a kind of training; the purposes of reading can be obscured if they experience only isolated skills. We need to remind ourselves and our students of the basic reasons for reading—reading to learn and reading for enjoyment.

2. *Put reading into its proper context.* We believe that "critical literacy" (Calfee, 1994) is a better goal than functional literacy. Critical literacy includes not only the ability to read but also the ability to use all forms of language effectively—writing, reading, listening, and speaking. Critical literacy is achieved by allowing children to use their developing language skills in meaningful long-term projects and by the teacher's systematic attention to developing the student's overall linguistic and cognitive competence. Although reading may be the most important skill taught in the early grades, our goal is to develop individuals who can use all forms of language effectively in thinking, reasoning, and communicating.

3. *Build on children's domain and general knowledge.* Knowledge is fundamental to effective cognitive functioning (see Chapter 9). All children have some knowledge about their worlds that can be accessed and used in reading. Unless relevant knowledge is activated, however, reading can become a meaningless exercise in word calling. Evoking children's frames of reference allows them to give meaning to what they read. Helping them become aware of their own knowledge aids them in better regulating their own learning.

4. *Encourage children to develop and use their metalinguistic knowledge.* Learning to read draws on many dimensions of knowledge about language: knowledge of letter-sound relationships, vocabulary, syntax, and text structure. Some children may not yet have developed metalinguistic abilities that would enable them to detect important distinctions about letters, words, or sounds. Others who do not share a background in the English language community face even greater challenges. No matter what level of language skill the children bring, however, the teacher needs to draw their attention to language features to build their metalinguistic awareness. Becoming a more independent, self-regulated reader and moving to more advanced levels of literacy both depend on a growing metalinguistic awareness.

5. *Help young readers move toward automatic decoding.* Rapid, fluent word decoding underlies skilled reading. Although beginning readers can and should use context to help them decode words, ultimately they need to develop highly automatic word recognition to become skilled readers. Good readers eventually rely little on context for their decoding (Perfetti, 1985), although they can use it very effectively if they need to. Poor readers typically have difficulty in automatic word decoding (Rayner & Pollatsek, 1989). Although it does not follow that children therefore should be drilled extensively on decoding exercises, word analyses, phonics rules, and the like, teaching decoding skills should be an important part of any approach to reading instruction. Practice in decoding can be obtained in many ways, not the least of which is through guided meaningful reading, in which the teacher directs students' attention to relevant graphic and phonemic characteristics of words. Structured decoding practice also may be beneficial, as long as this activity is not elevated to the status of reading. Rereading passages to improve fluency (Samuels, 1988) and to attain automaticity also may be very helpful.

6. *Expect children to vary widely in their progress toward fluent reading.* Although children may struggle with learning to read, most learn to read quite well. In any given group of readers, however, as many as 10 percent to 15 percent will fall one or two years behind their peer group in reading level by third or fourth grade. From 3 percent to 5 percent will have more serious problems; these children will lag two or more grade levels behind their peers.

The origins of reading difficulties vary and are a matter of great debate. Some students simply may not be developmentally ready for reading instruction in the first grade and cannot cope with the abstract linguistic tasks of learning to read. Others will come from cultural or language backgrounds that match poorly with their experiences in reading instruction. Still others simply are poorly taught. All of these groups of children likely would have performed well if reading instruction had been delayed or improved; a significant challenge is avoiding these kinds of problems in the first place and, for those who have not yet succeeded, undoing the false concept of themselves as "poor readers."

Some students, however, have considerable difficulty in learning to read even with excellent instruction. A few of these students have low general ability; their difficulty is less with reading than with the cognitive demands of comprehension. A significant number, however, will have normal or above normal intelligence but have a specific handicap or learning disability in the area of reading. These children differ from children who are simply poor readers. Many of them have notable speech and language deficits, often coupled with difficulty in spelling and writing. In fact, the root problem for many disabled readers may well be one of language. A genetic basis seems probable for some reading disabilities: They tend to occur more among males than females, among left-handers than right-handers, and to run in families (Rayner & Pollatsek, 1989).

Poor reading skills, of course, can make school achievement very difficult. Yet, many children with severe reading disabilities do go on to high levels of accomplishment, both by using their own ingenuity to compensate for lack of reading skill and by drawing on the talents of teachers specially trained in methods designed to help disabled readers learn to read. As teachers, we need to recognize the difficulties these children face and to be prepared to help them obtain the specialized assistance they need.

SUMMARY

Learning to read is a significant linguistic and cognitive achievement, but one most children accomplish early in their primary school years. Reading superficially seems to be simply word-by-word decoding, but in fact it is a multifaceted process in which all aspects of language and cognition are orchestrated. The success of beginning readers hinges on their ability to use and analyze language, plus three cognitive dimensions: their knowledge of the world, their short-term and long-term memory, and their ability to focus their attention. Linguistic knowledge makes possible the mapping of the visual symbols of written language onto oral language and the creation of meaning; world knowledge underlies comprehension. Short-term and long-term memory are critical processes as input is processed sequentially, held in memory, and related to existing knowledge and language structures. Attention is equally important; developing readers must learn to focus strategically on the appropriate aspects of words, letters, sentences, and texts in order to read effectively.

Learning to read was seen once as depending on reading readiness. A more current view is that literacy develops out of the entire array of children's early language experiences and is only one of several important linguistic skills. Well before they begin to read, most children already know a great deal about the purposes of reading and its conventions. Some children can "read" environmental cues, such as signs and logos. True reading, however, requires attention to word and text features. As children begin to learn to read, many first seem to rely on visual cues in text, such as word shapes. Children who know the alphabet, however, can begin to use partial phonetic cues supplied by letter names. Children who "know how to read" can use the entire range of phonemic cues supplied by letters and letter combinations.

Although decoding is important, it is only part of learning to read. Full ability in reading demands competence in four main areas: letter and word decoding, vocabulary recognition, syntactic mapping, and text-feature analysis. Effective reading instruction must include all four areas. Instructional methods in reading generally involve each of these areas; some, however, place far greater emphasis on certain dimensions than on others. Some methods emphasize bottom-up processing and count on word decoding to lead to meaning. Others heavily stress meaning, with the expectation that a top-down meaning emphasis will lead to skilled decoding. Because reading is an interactive process involving simultaneous processing at multiple levels of language and cognition, however, it is unlikely that any approach in an extreme form will be effective. Each of the dimensions of reading contributes important information to the comprehension process. What seems certain is that the emphasis on reading as a meaningful process must be maintained in any successful program of reading instruction, no matter what dimension of reading is being addressed.

SUGGESTED READINGS

Adams, M. J. (1990). *Learning to read: Thinking and learning about print.* Cambridge: MIT Press.

Adams brings together much research on reading and learning to read and argues that effective instruction must combine an emphasis on meaning with an emphasis on developing decoding skills.

Pressley, M. (1994). Commentary on the ERIC whole language debate. in C. B. Smith (Moderator), *Whole language: The debate* (pp. 187–217). Bloomington, IN: ERIC/REC.

In this chapter, Pressley is highly critical of those making extravagant claims for whole language approaches to reading instruction. He argues that reading instruction should draw on the best features of whole language but not neglect explicit instruction on important skills.

CHAPTER 11

Reading to Learn

At about the third grade, when most students have acquired basic reading skills, the emphasis in many classrooms shifts from learning to read to "reading to learn." Elementary school students may read about pioneer life, for example, about the moon, or about animals and their homes. As they move toward middle school and high school, the emphasis on reading as a primary avenue to learning becomes more pronounced. Eighth-graders may be expected to learn basic principles of ecology from a general science textbook; twelfth-graders routinely are assigned essays or chapters in books in preparations for discussions. Many college teachers rely heavily on reading assignments in textbooks as part of their instructional strategies. You may, in fact, be reading this chapter as part of an assignment. The assumption, of course, is that at least part of what is important for you to learn can be acquired by reading this text.

Educational psychologists always have been intensely interested in learning from reading, and their research on this topic has generated a massive literature. Early research tended to focus on acquiring information; more recent work has emphasized *reading comprehension* and the factors affecting it. In this chapter, we examine several dimensions of "getting meaning" from texts. To provide an overall context for our discussion, we begin by describing three types of models of reading comprehension. Then we explore three aspects of comprehending texts. First, we focus on a basic but important outcome of reading—learning new words. We examine the factors that influence vocabulary acquisition during reading and their implications. Second, we shift to a more general perspective emphasizing how organized knowledge is acquired. Here, we take a schema theory perspective on comprehension processes and illustrate how readers construct and remember representations of text material. We also discuss the effect of readers' general world knowledge and strategies on comprehension. Third, in the last section of the chapter, we outline an elaborative processing model that suggests how readers give their attention to important aspects of text materials. Using this model, we describe a series of external aids to reading comprehension.

MODELS OF READING COMPREHENSION

Reading comprehension models can be clustered into three general groups: data-driven, conceptually driven, and interactive (Andre, 1987b; Rayner & Pollatsek, 1989). As we described in Chapter 3, *data-driven* (or bottom-up) *processing* refers to processing guided primarily by external stimuli, where data flow quickly and mostly automatically through the information processing system. *Conceptually driven* (or top-down) *processing,* in contrast, refers to processing guided heavily by conceptual frameworks stored in memory. *Interactive processing* refers to processing guided by an interaction between processes generated by the data a text provides, on the one hand, and by the readers' knowledge and strategies, on the other. We now turn to a closer examination of each.

Data-Driven Models

Reading comprehension models that emphasize decoding and word meanings are called **data-driven models** (Andre, 1987b; Rumelhart & McClelland, 1981). In portraying the comprehension of a passage, for instance, such models identify a starting point, such as word identification; higher-order structures, such as sentences, are built up word by word as the reader moves through the text (Rayner & Pollatsek, 1989). In this perspective, information flow is from words to syntactic structures to discourse and semantic structures. One early but particularly well developed data-driven model was formulated by Gough (1972), and we examine it as an example of data-driven models of reading comprehension.

Gough's Model.   To understand Gough's model, it is necessary to review some issues from basic research on reading. Many researchers, Gough among them, have used eye-tracking equipment to follow the movements of readers' eyes as they move across a page of printed text. Typically, readers' eye movements consist of a series of stops and starts. The eyes focus briefly on one point of text (called a **fixation**) and then move rapidly to another point. The movement is referred to as a **saccade**. Vision is limited, during fixations, to a visual span of only a few letters.

Gough used the results of eye-tracking research as a starting point for his model. According to his model, readers proceed through a sentence "letter by letter, word by word" (1972, p. 354). Reading processes begin with an eye fixation at the first segment of text, followed by a saccade, a second fixation, and so on through the text. Gough posited that each fixation places about fifteen to twenty letters in the iconic store (see Chapter 2). Once that information is in the iconic store (in raw, unprocessed form), pattern-matching processes begin, moving one letter at a time from left to right. Gough estimated that it would take about 10 to 20 msec for the identification of each letter. Gough further assumed that the information in the iconic store would last about 0.25 sec and that readers could perform about three fixations per second. On the basis of these assumptions (which were based on available data about readers' eye movements), Gough estimated that reading rates of about 300 words per minute were possible.

Gough envisioned that once pattern-matching processes on each letter were complete, a mapping response occurred in which the representations of letters' sounds were recalled and blended together to form the representation of the sound of the word. When the representation of a word's sound is complete, the word meaning is retrieved from memory and the process repeats with the next word. The decoded words are held in short-term memory, and the meaning of sentences is determined there. If a clear understanding has been gained, the gist of the meaning passes on to long-term memory.

Although no data-driven models of reading totally exclude the role of long-term memory and presume meaning to be determined completely by stimulus input, Gough's model is one of the clearest examples of a data-driven approach. It portrays each letter of each word as being processed in serial fashion, with meaning assigned to text on the basis of stored meanings in memory. Gough himself foresaw, however, some serious problems with such strict data-driven models (see Andre, 1987b, for a detailed analysis of data-driven models). Among them are the fact that information does not necessarily come from the iconic store in a serial fashion (reading off the iconic store from left to right; see Chapter 3), that strict translations of letters into their sound representations would not allow readers to comprehend homonyms (or words in which spelling-sound correspondences are irregular, such as *through, enough,* and *cough*), and that the context of words in sentences often determines their meaning (e.g., Bob admitted to the judge that he *stole* the fur *stole*).

Conceptually Driven Models

In contrast to data-driven models, **conceptually driven models** of reading comprehension place their emphasis on the guiding role of knowledge. Instead of describing reading as a sequential, detailed, letter-by-letter, word-by-word analysis of text to gain meaning, conceptually driven models are based on the premise that readers' expectations about a text and their previous knowledge determine the comprehension process. In this view, readers use their knowledge and the printed symbols on a page to construct meaning.

Just as no model of comprehension is totally data driven, none are completely top-down either. Clearly, there must be some connection between what appears on the printed page and the meaning constructed by the reader, otherwise there would be no reading. Still, models vary tremendously in emphasis. Perhaps the best-known model that has heavily emphasized conceptually driven processing is Kenneth Goodman's.

Goodman's Model.   Unlike Gough's model, which was based on analyses of eye movements during reading, Goodman's model grew out of his observations of children's errors in oral reading. Goodman's research (see 1982b, 1982c) asked children to read stories aloud, choosing stories that were somewhat difficult for them and listening as they read. His analysis of the kinds of mistakes children made indicated to him that reading was governed by processes that led readers to predict the contents of upcoming text. Further, Goodman believed that readers used the text as a means of confirming or disconfirming their predictions about what the text was going to say.

Unlike Gough's model of reading, Goodman's (1982b, 1982c) does not require a sequence of invariant steps. Instead, Goodman's model portrays four cycles of processing occurring simultaneously and interactively: *optical* (picking up the visual input), *perceptual* (identifying letters and words), *syntactic* (identifying the structure of the text), and *meaning* (constructing meaning for the input). Once a reader starts reading, an initial meaning is constructed for the text. This meaning then is a prediction against which future input is judged. If the reader's prediction is confirmed, reading continues and the constructed meaning is enriched with new information. If the reader's prediction is incorrect, however, the reader will slow down, reread, or seek additional information to construct a more accurate meaning.

Goodman's model suggests that errors, or *miscues,* as he prefers to call them, should be fairly common. They are not necessarily the result of poor reading, but instead stem from the same processes as good reading. In fact, the strongest support for Goodman's idea that constructed meanings govern reading comes from his research on reading errors (Goodman, 1982a; Goodman & Goodman, 1982). When the children Goodman observed made errors in oral reading, they spontaneously corrected errors that interfered with meaning—typically by rereading and correcting themselves. When children made errors that did not affect meaning, however, these errors seldom were noticed or corrected (e.g., reading *headlights* for *headlamps*). Generally, if words that children called out fit the meaning they had constructed for the story, they seldom saw them as errors, regardless of whether or not they were read correctly.

The strength of Goodman's model lies in its emphasis on conceptually driven processes, and its base in the analysis of children's reading errors makes it highly appealing. Andre (1987b), however, points out that the model overemphasizes conceptually driven processes; he also notes that Goodman's model has not been particularly helpful in guiding reading research or applications. The model does remind us of the importance of readers' knowledge, however, and the necessity of their understanding what they read.

Interactive Models of Reading

A purely data-driven model of reading comprehension, on the one hand, will have problems accounting for the effects of readers' knowledge and the effects of context. Conceptually driven models, on the other hand, focus directly on the role of knowledge but tend to be vague and to overlook the importance of data-driven processes in reading comprehension. Because of these apparent limitations of data-driven and conceptually driven models, several interactive models have been proposed (e.g., Adams & Collins, 1977; Kintsch, 1986; Kintsch & Van Dijk, 1978; Rumelhart & McClelland, 1981). In **interactive models** of reading, both data-driven and conceptually driven processes are present. Reading comprehension is a product of their interaction. One interactive model that has led to considerable research and applied interest is that of Just and Carpenter (1987); another is that of Kintsch and Van Dijk (1978; Kintsch, 1986). We begin by examining Just and Carpenter's model.

Just and Carpenter's Interactive Model.   Like Gough's data-driven model, Just and Carpenter's (1987) interactive model of reading comprehension evolved out of a program of eye-movement research. Unlike Gough, however, Just and Carpenter proposed an *interactive* set of processes in which readers' interactions with text result in construction of meaning. They posit processes at the level of pattern matching, working memory, and long-term memory. These processes are not sequential, but rather are highly interactive. Reading comprehension begins at the first fixation, at which visual stimuli enter the iconic store. Unlike Gough, who argued for a fixed number of letters in iconic store, Just and Carpenter suggest that the amount of input depends on several individual differences: reading ability, knowledge of the content area being read about, and the reader's purpose.

Once the visual input has been picked up in the iconic store, the next step is to extract the physical features of words. This process is largely data driven, but it interacts with reading knowledge and the context of reading. For example, the **Ħ** in **CĦT** becomes an *a,* whereas the **Ħ** in **TĦE** becomes an *b.* Meaning then is assigned, although predictions of meaning could precede and guide the extraction of physical features. For instance, when most people encounter the sentence *Sarah stroked the long, silky fur of the ⌇*, they read the word *cat* for the illegible scrawl appearing in its place. When this same scrawl appears in the following sentence, however, different features are extracted: *He ⌇ his hand on a broken bottle.* Meaning and context are important, even at the level of basic perception.

Assigning word meaning thus depends not only on the extraction of physical features and word recognition or recall but also on the meaning the reader is constructing for the current passage. Unlike most other proponents of interactive models (e.g., Kintsch, 1986), Just and Carpenter argued that almost every word in a passage is read and that the reader continuously integrates the meanings of new words with the constructed meaning in memory.

Kintsch and Van Dijk's Discourse Processing Model.   Kintsch and Van Dijk (1978; Kintsch, 1988) also have proposed an interactive model that has been highly influential in guiding researchers' thinking about how readers process text information. Their model focuses on *discourse processing* and on how meaning is constructed as readers move through written materials.

In Kintsch and Van Dijk's model, the basic meaning of sentences is represented by propositions (see Chapter 4), with a single sentence usually broken down into several propositions. In discourse, propositions are linked with one another. Kintsch and Van Dijk's model represents the meanings of texts as hierarchical networks of these propositions.

Kintsch and Van Dijk's model is organized at two basic levels: microstructure and macrostructure. The **microstructure** of the text is the basic level of discourse in which the propositions are connected with one another. It is a knowledge structure that interrelates all of the propositions in a text. The propositions are linked with one another because they share common elements or nodes. In Kintsch and Van Dijk's conception, readers constantly attempt to associate propositions by linking their common elements. Through short cycles of processing, the reader builds up a microstructure from the basic propositions of the text. Repetition of vocabulary, inferences, and limitations on short-term memory all play important roles in the nature of the microstructure a reader constructs.

At the same time readers are creating a microstructure, they also are creating a macrostructure. The **macrostructure** of the text corresponds to the *gist,* or meaning, of the text. Whereas the microstructure directly represents the propositions in text, the macrostructure is schema driven; it combines the prior knowledge of the individual with the microstructure of the text. In essence, elements of the macrostructure are "main ideas" abstracted from the microstructure.

The Kintsch and Van Dijk model has generated a number of predictions, along with a great deal of empirical research. The model predicts that propositionally complex texts should take longer to read than texts with fewer propositions, even with length held constant. They do. Another prediction of their model, based on assumptions about the nature of propositions and their importance, is that memory for higher-level propositions in microstructure and for gist will be better than memory for lower-level information. This prediction also has been supported.

Overall, Kintsch and Van Dijk's model (see also Kintsch, 1988; Van Dijk & Kintsch, 1983) and tests of its utility have provided researchers with an important theoretical tool for advancing understanding of how mental representations of text meaning might be created. The features of their model, in which overall text representation (its meaning) is a result of multiple memory traces for successive sentences being connected with the prior knowledge structures of the individual, plausibly describe a process in which meaning is "built up" out of the basic structure of the text, the structure of what a person knows, and inferences connecting the two.

Summary of Models of Reading

Although reading models continue to evolve, our judgment is that interactive models like Just and Carpenter's and Kintsch and Van Dijk's strike an appropriate balance between data-driven and conceptually driven processes. These kinds of models propose a foundation of relatively automatic processes for reading, such as the reader's fixations on words in text or converting sentences to propositions. At the same time, these automatized processes are seen as guided by the reader's general knowledge and as interacting with the meaning the reader is constructing. In common with top-down models like Goodman's and in contrast with some completely bottom-up models, they strongly emphasize the role of context (e.g., making inferences based on memory for what stories are like, interpreting word meanings based on general text meaning). Neither model, however, neglects the role of the text itself; both strongly emphasize how contact with the text drives meaning construction, with the reader's prior knowledge shaping the meaning that is constructed.

This brief description of models of reading comprehension focuses our thinking on several levels of processes that almost certainly are involved in comprehending text and learning from reading. At a basic level, we see how reading comprehension builds on automatic or near-automatic processes, such as letter perception, word recognition, and sentence understanding. At the same time, models of reading remind us of the importance of readers' knowledge and the strategies readers use as they read. They help us realize that readers construct unique representations of meaning, built out of what they already know, the strategies they select, and the texts they encounter. The various emphases of the models also remind us that the knowledge constructed can take a variety of forms, depending on readers' goals for reading. We now turn to a basic but vitally important level of knowledge constructed extensively through reading—knowledge about words.

BUILDING VOCABULARY THROUGH READING

"Words embody power, words embrace action, and words enable us to speak, read, and write with clarity, confidence, and charm" (Duin & Graves, 1987, p. 33). This statement rings true to most educators, who observe firsthand that vocabulary knowledge is linked closely with competence in many areas. Understanding words and knowing how to use them—**vocabulary knowledge**—is an important index of domain and general knowledge. Vocabulary knowledge also influences the efficiency of learning; larger vocabularies aid cognitive processing in ways as diverse as more rapid listening and reading comprehension and more precise expression of ideas in speaking and writing.

The link between vocabulary knowledge and important educational outcomes has been known for many years. For instance, Conry and Plant (1965), in an early but representative study, found correlations of .65 and .46 between vocabulary scores and high school rank and college grades, respectively. Correlations between vocabulary scores and intelligence test scores typically are quite high, often + .80 or above. Fundamental language-based skills, such as reading comprehension (e.g., Farr, 1969; Stahl & Fairbanks, 1986; Sternberg, 1987) and writing quality (e.g., Duin & Graves, 1987; Stewart & Leaman, 1983), also are linked closely with vocabulary.

Because knowing words is so important, educators have concentrated a great deal of energy on helping students acquire them. Direct instruction has been the most common approach, typically by having students memorize words and their definitions. The limitations of direct vocabulary instruction, however, have been pointed out forcefully by Nagy and his associates (Herman, Anderson, Pearson, & Nagy, 1987; Nagy, Anderson, & Herman, 1987; Nagy & Herman, 1987; Nagy, Herman, & Anderson, 1985). They argue that, for most students, *reading* is the more potent route to vocabulary growth.

Their argument for reading as the main source of vocabulary growth is as follows. First, vocabulary growth during the years children are in school is quite extraordinary. Nagy et al. (1987) have estimated, for instance, that children may add as many as 3,000 words per year to their vocabularies between the third and twelfth grades; average vocabulary size reaches 27,000 words or more by the end of high school (Mason et al., 1991).

Second, learning word meanings to a level where they can be accessed quickly and usefully takes considerable time (e.g., Wysocki & Jenkins, 1987). Because the time that can be devoted to direct vocabulary instruction is limited, only a small portion of vocabulary growth during the school years, perhaps 200 to 300 words per year, actually can be attributed to direct instruction (Mason et al., 1991; Nagy & Herman, 1987).

Nagy and his associates contend that reading is a much more compelling explanation for students' rapidly growing vocabularies, even though acquiring meanings through reading is a slow, incremental process. A single contact with a word, for instance, typically produces only partial learning, and full comprehension of a new word requires multiple encounters.

Reading does, in fact, provide ample opportunities for vocabulary learning. In a series of carefully designed studies examining how words might be learned from context, Nagy and his coworkers showed that incidental learning of word meanings does occur during normal reading and that the absolute amount of learning is quite small. The probability of acquiring significant word knowledge from reading a word once in text is not more than 10 percent or so (Nagy et al., 1987; Nagy & Herman, 1987).

This small increment in word knowledge becomes very important, however, when the amount of reading children do in and out of school is considered. R. C. Anderson, Wilson, and Fielding (1988), for instance, showed that a typical fifth-grade student reads about 300,000 words from books outside school per year; other print materials, such as newspapers and comic books, increase the total to about 600,000 words. When a conservative estimate of fifteen minutes per day of reading in school is added, the number of words read by the typical fifth-grader is upward of a million a year; avid readers read many times this amount. The strong inference from data like these is that reading is indispensable to vocabulary growth; the words students learn through reading likely represent a third or more of the words most acquire annually.

This argument that reading is a primary avenue of vocabulary growth has been strengthened further by recent work relating amount of *print exposure* to vocabulary size. Stanovich and Cunningham and their colleagues (Cunningham & Stanovich, 1991; Stanovich & Cunningham, 1993; West, Stanovich, & Mitchell, 1993) measured print exposure through checklists in which respondents indicated whether they were familiar with particular authors, book titles, magazines, and newspapers. The assumption was that the more items respondents checked, the more reading they had done. Real items on the checklists were mixed with foils so that guessing could be controlled; for instance, a list of children's book titles included titles of real books (e.g., *A Light in the Attic, Polar Express*), as well as plausible-sounding but nonexistent book titles (e.g., *The Lost Shoe, Curious Jim*).

Print exposure as measured by these scales turned out to be a potent predictor of vocabulary knowledge for fourth- and fifth-grade children (Cunningham & Stanovich, 1991), for college students (Stanovich & Cunningham, 1993), and even for a sample of adults who completed the scales in an airport waiting room (West et al., 1993). Moreover, the relationship of print exposure to vocabulary holds even when the influence of general ability (e.g., high school grade point average, mathematics ability test scores, reading ability scores) is removed statistically, which suggests that differential exposure to information through reading is the key factor in vocabulary size no matter what the individual's ability level. Print exposure is not only a unique predictor of vocabulary size but also an even better one than ability measures, which, as we saw earlier, typically relate significantly to vocabulary.

Word Knowledge: What It Means to Know a Word

It may seem from our discussion that vocabulary knowledge is an either-or thing—either a word is known or it is not. Picture for a moment, however, the answers you might get if you asked a group of college students the meaning of a relatively rare word, say, *ascetic*. Some would have no idea at all; some might venture a guess (e.g., "Is it something like 'clean'?"). Others would be more confident (e.g., "I think it means 'austere, self-denying'") and perhaps even add an instance of its use (e.g., The monk lived an *ascetic* life, denying himself all but the most basic necessities). Still others might ask for clues before they ventured a guess (e.g., "Could you use it in a sentence for me?"). Given the example "He looked much like a student, thin and *ascetic,*" some of them might propose, "Well, it has something to do with a student and how he or she looks. It's either 'pale' or 'poor,' . . . could be either!" Still others simply would be confused: "Isn't it something like 'art appreciation'?" "Knowing a word" obviously is not an all-or-none phenomenon.

Graves (1987) has pointed out that learning a word's meaning varies markedly, depending on the learner's present knowledge and the depth of understanding required. For instance, first-graders often are asked to read words they already have in their oral vocabularies (e.g., *house, car, mother*). It is a different challenge to learn a new meaning for a known word, however. Many words are *polysemous;* that is, they have multiple meanings (e.g., *run, set*). Still another demand arises when the student must learn a new word for a known meaning (e.g., a child understands the idea of "being on time" but does not understand the word *punctual* when she reads it). Finally, in some instances, a student may have neither the concept nor the word, as in reading research or text materials that contain unfamiliar concepts (e.g., *paradigm, eufunctional*). Initially, our goal is for students to understand the words they are reading. Our ultimate goal, however, is much more ambitious: We hope they learn to use the words fluently in writing and speaking.

Definitional Versus Contextual Word Knowledge.   In thinking about goals for learning new vocabulary, vocabulary researchers also have found it useful to distinguish between definitional and contextual word knowledge. **Definitional knowledge** refers to the relationship between a word and other known words, as in a dictionary definition (e.g., An octroi is a tax paid upon certain goods entering a city). When asked about vocabulary, most people envision definitional knowledge first (Johnson & Bruning, 1984). A definition places a word within a semantic network of words the learner presumably already knows and can be a way for students to acquire useful knowledge about a word.

The knowledge developed from exposure to words in context is often more useful, however. For example, a native speaker of English immediately recognizes the oddity of certain vocabulary choices in sentences like *She drove her plane to Austin, Texas; I hope I have a capable application to your program; He initiated his car's engine;* and *She despaired her hope of ever meeting him again.* Sometimes, when we consider words individually, we are tempted to think of their meanings as unrelated to their context. With rare exceptions, however, word use in natural language is highly contextual: What words mean virtually always depends to some extent on how they are combined with others. Thus, student vocabulary knowledge needs to extend well beyond words' dictionary definitions to **contextual knowledge**, understanding how words actually are used in written and spoken language.

The contextual nature of word knowledge has led many authorities (e.g., Nagy, 1988; Powell, 1988; Sternberg, 1987; Sternberg & Powell, 1983) to propose that vocabulary knowledge be viewed as organized in schemalike structures containing not only the "meaning" of the word but also a host of temporal, spatial, and grammatical cues. Look, for instance, at the following sentence:

> As the mechanic tried to tighten the bolt one last turn, the bolt _____ , and his wrench clattered to the concrete.

If we are asked to supply a word for the blank, we immediately draw on our linguistic, metalinguistic, and world knowledge. Choices such as *cried, sensitive,* and *happily* are discarded as either unboltlike or grammatically nonsensical, and we quickly move on to more acceptable possibilities.

In even a very short passage, suitable word choices typically are surprisingly constrained by the syntactic and discourse context in which the word needs to be embedded. Clues to the meaning of the word come from outside the word itself

(Sternberg, 1987). Thus, in our example, we quickly surmise from the context that the missing word must be a verb, something that might happen to a bolt when a mechanic tightened it one last time, and that, if it happened to a bolt, would result in the wrench's flying off and clattering to the floor. In this example, a word was missing, but the process is very similar when readers encounter any unknown word while reading.

With the word present, however, even an unknown one, **morphological cues** (within-word cues) also become available to the reader (Drum & Konopak, 1987; Mason et al., 1991). Consider the following example:

To his dismay, the inventor found that his automatic bed-maker was *unmarketable.*

A reader unfamiliar with, say, the word *unmarketable* also has, besides the external cues, several within-word cues available. From earlier instruction or from other experiences with prefixes and suffixes, many students are able to analyze the parts of the word and recognize *un-* as a prefix, *market* as the stem or root word, and *-able* as a suffix indicating an adjectival form of a word. From contact with an array of more frequent words beginning with *un-,* such as *unsafe, unhappy,* and *unclear,* these students should have a sense of *un-* as indicating negation. Knowledge of the root word *market* may enable them to recognize that the word *unmarketable* has to do with buying and selling.

This assortment of internal cues, coupled with those from the external context, make it possible for students to approximate word meanings as they read. Presence of both within-word and external context cues by no means ensures that students will be able to use or even recognize them as potential clues to "figuring out" words, however. The less sophisticated the readers, the fewer linguistic and metalinguistic cues they will recognize. Also, some contexts in which new words are encountered are relatively "rich," whereas others are not (Graves, 1987; Herman et al., 1987; Sternberg, 1987).

Understanding words in context does not necessarily mean consciously "figuring out the word." In ordinary reading, fixations on a word simply trigger automatized knowledge related to word recognition and use (see Chapter 3). For example, we automatically comprehend the different meanings of the word *bank* as we read the following three sentences: The river's *bank* was eroded, You can *bank* on it, and The First National *Bank* opened a new branch in Greenwich. When we speak, similarly, we almost never pay any attention to words' dictionary definitions. We just *use* words, stating confidently, for example, "The girl dropped her piggy *bank,*" or "The pilot put the plane into a steep *bank.*"

In summary, word knowledge is not a simple "either-or" matter; "knowing a word" extends far beyond dictionary definitions to subtle knowledge about words' meanings and uses in context. Vocabulary knowledge, therefore, often is tacit and unrecognized—knowing what words go with others, for instance. Much vocabulary knowledge also is highly automatized and more procedural than declarative, as in the correct recognition and use of the polysemous word *bank* in our examples. Encountering words in reading is an ideal means of acquiring this contextual knowledge about words, their meanings, and their uses.

Helping Students Use Reading to Build Vocabulary

How best do we help students increase their vocabularies? An obvious starting point is simply to encourage reading in any way possible. From the work by Nagy and his associates, we know that students acquire vocabulary as they read and that vocabulary growth is strongly related to how much students read. Over their lifetimes, students will acquire most of their vocabulary on their own, without having been taught (Graves, 1987). Reading is one of the most important gateways to this vital category of learning.

Beyond simply encouraging reading, however, teachers can do much more to stimulate vocabulary growth. Reading provides a rich context for learning vocabulary, but only if students are prepared to use this context. Learning how to use context to learn words may be even more important than learning specific words; students can be helped to acquire reading strategies for using context to figure out word meanings. Morphological, syntactical, and discourse clues (e.g., Nagy & Herman, 1987; Nagy et al., 1987; Sternberg, 1987; Wysocki & Jenkins, 1987) are potentially available for students to use, but students may need encouragement and practice in using their linguistic and world knowledge effectively.

The vocabulary knowledge that students acquire through reading should be supplemented by at least some direct vocabulary instruction. Functional vocabulary knowledge is built on a solid foundation of declarative knowledge about word meanings and their relationships to one another. When words are presented around a theme or topic (e.g., Beck, Perfetti, & McKeown, 1982; Duin & Graves, 1987; McKeown, Beck, Omanson, & Perfetti, 1983; McKeown, Beck, Omanson, & Pople, 1985), knowledge structures develop that make new vocabulary acquisition and reading comprehension more likely.

Direct instruction can be used also to encourage students to notice and learn new words as they read. In an intensive vocabulary instruction condition in Duin and Graves's (1987) study, for instance, students were asked to keep track of the times they read, spoke, or heard selected words in outside activities. Because the students were encouraged actively to notice the new words (which they did), Duin and Graves found that they also were more inclined to learn them and use them on their own.

BUILDING ORGANIZED KNOWLEDGE THROUGH READING

Recall from Chapter 3 that schemata are organized knowledge structures in memory. Schema theory holds that the meaning of reading materials is constructed by readers on the basis of the information they encounter, the information they already possess, and the way they interact with new information. Consider the following paragraph drawn from a well-known study performed by R. C. Anderson, Reynolds, Schallert, and Goetz (1977). As you read the paragraph, form some preliminary thoughts about Tony.

Tony got up slowly from the mat, planning his escape. He hesitated a moment and thought. Things were not going well. What bothered him most was being held, especially because the charge against him had been weak. He considered his present situation. The lock that held him was strong, but he thought he could break it. He knew, however, that his timing would have to be perfect. Tony was aware that it was because of his early roughness that he had been penalized so severely—much too severely, from his point of view. The situation was becoming frustrating; the pressure had been grinding on him for too long. He was being ridden unmercifully. Tony was getting angry now. He felt he was ready to make his move. He knew that his success or failure would depend on what he did in the next few seconds.

R. C. Anderson, Reynolds, Schallert, & Goetz (1977, p. 372)

On the one hand, if you are like many readers, you may have decided that Tony was a prisoner in a jail cell. Enough segments in this paragraph match up with people's "prisoner" schemata so that this decision is reasonable. On the other hand, you may be like readers who decide that Tony is a wrestler. In this instance, too, are several elements of the passage that fit "wrestler" schemata. As in the examples we gave in Chapter 3, the meanings that readers construct for passages depend on the particular schemata they activate during reading. These constructed meanings, of course, affect what individuals will remember. Indeed, we know that if we were to test people's memory for the Tony passage by giving them a free-recall test, we would find qualitative differences in recall between those people who decided Tony was a prisoner and those who decided Tony was a wrestler.

Because schema theory was discussed in depth in Chapter 3, we do not recapitulate it here. In understanding learning from reading, however, it is important to note that schemata have several important functions in reading comprehension (Andre, 1987b):

1. Providing the knowledge base for assimilating new text information

2. Guiding the ways readers allocate their attention to different parts of reading passages

3. Allowing readers to make inferences about text material

4. Facilitating organized searches of memory

5. Enhancing editing and summarizing of content

6. Permitting the reconstruction of content

How knowledge affects understanding should be clear from your recent reading of the Tony passage. Your understanding was created within the knowledge framework you activated. The ways schemata guide readers' attention during reading are more difficult to demonstrate. When we overtly attempt to activate certain schemata prior to reading, however, readers' selective allocation of attention can be seen. For instance, Glover, Dinnel, et al. (1988) performed an experiment in which "preview" sentences were embedded in an initial chapter of text. These preview sentences (e.g., "As you will see in Chapter 12 . . .") were designed to alert readers that more about a specific topic mentioned in the chapter they currently were reading would appear in a later chapter. When Glover, Dinnel, et al. later observed readers working through the subsequent chapter, they noted that readers focused more of their attention on those parts of the subsequent chapter that had been signaled. Apparently, the activation of schemata guided readers in how they allocated their attention while reading. Likewise, if we gave some people the Tony passage with the title "The Wrestler" but gave other people the same passage with the title "The Prisoner," we almost certainly would see differences in the ways readers in these two groups attended to specific elements of the passage. Probably, those people reading from the wrestler perspective would focus on elements of the passage related to wrestling, and those individuals reading from the prisoner perspective would examine most closely materials congruent with a "prisoner" schema.

The importance of schema theory for understanding reading is that text comprehension depends heavily on learner inferences. No text can list exhaustively the information required for understanding. If you remember our Piggo example in Chapter 3, you recall that we presented a brief passage about a girl breaking open a piggy bank. Not stated in that passage were such things as what Piggo was made of, what Piggo looked like, and what size Piggo was. Your knowledge (your schema) of piggy banks, however, let you infer these things almost instantly and construct a passage meaning. Which schemata readers activate and how elaborated they are guide the kinds and quality of inferences they will make.

Schemata also facilitate organized searches of memory. To use Anderson and Pearson's (1984) example, if you were reading a passage about a ship's christening, your schema for "ship christening" likely represents a cluster of related instances of knowledge. Thus, if you encountered a question related to the passage (e.g., "What kind of bottle is usually broken over a ship?" or "Where is the bottle broken on the ship?"), your search of memory would be guided by this schema.

Schemata make it possible for readers to summarize content. New information constantly is being assimilated to readers' schemata, which allows readers to edit input in an efficient manner (e.g., "That fits what I know about schema theory, I know this stuff; I'll speed up until I see something new").

To summarize a passage, readers need to select some parts of the passage as more important than others, condense materials and substitute higher-level superordinate concepts, and integrate what is being read into a coherent, accurate representation (Hidi & Anderson, 1986). Without the knowledge structures that schemata provide, none of these are possible.

Finally, as we saw in Chapter 5, evidence is compelling that human memory is more reconstructive than a "copy" of experience; schemata permit the reconstruction of content. In reading to learn, we very seldom are required to recall the entirety of passages in verbatim form. Most often, our goal is to remember the gist of a passage and to reconstruct it as needed. So, if you were asked to recall the Piggo passage from Chapter 3, the probability is high that you could do a very fine job of describing a girl's destruction of a piggy bank. It also is very likely, though, that you would reconstruct the passage on the basis of your knowledge of piggy banks—your "piggy bank" schema—rather than remember it verbatim.

The Utility of Linking New Information with Old

An important prediction from schema theory is that to the extent to-be-learned information can be linked with what readers already know, their memory for the to-be-learned information should increase. This view has led to two very useful lines of inquiry and to a widespread set of applications. In this section, we examine these two areas of research in some detail.

Advance Organizers.   Advance organizers are "appropriately relevant and inclusive introductory materials . . . introduced in advance of learning. . . . and presented at a higher level of abstraction, generality, and inclusiveness" than subsequent to-be-learned reading materials (Ausubel, 1968, p. 148). Advance organizers are designed to provide "ideational scaffolding for the stable incorporation and retention of the more detailed and differentiated material that follows" (Ausubel, 1968, p. 148). In short, they provide frameworks for materials to be learned.

The idea of *advance organizers* has been one of the most intuitively appealing concepts in research on reading comprehension. Anything that can help learners relate new information to what they already know ought to be valuable. Early research on advance organizers was, in fact, quite promising. For example, Ausubel and Fitzgerald (1961) had students read a passage about Buddhism and tested them for their mastery of the content in three conditions: (1) a condition in which subjects first read a historical introduction, (2) a condition in which the principles of Buddhism were first set forth in abstract and general terms, and (3) a condition that first used a review of Christianity as an organizer designed to relate what the students already knew about religions to the material they were being asked to learn on Buddhism. The results were clear: On the posttest, students who read the advance organizer relating Christianity to Buddhism outperformed the students in the two other conditions.

Although Ausubel and his associates (e.g., Ausubel, 1960; Ausubel & Fitzgerald, 1961, 1962; Ausubel & Youssef, 1963) continued to obtain positive results on the utility of advance organizers, other researchers encountered difficulties, and by the mid 1970s, the research on advance organizers had become quite confused. Although some studies showed effects, others did not. Careful reviews of the advance organizer literature by Barnes and Clawson (1975) and Faw and Waller (1976), however, began to clarify the area by pointing out problems in the research. Perhaps the most serious problem was that the definition of advance organizers was so vague that standardization was impossible. Text features as diverse as outlines, questions, pictures, graphs, and paragraphs were being defined in one study or another as advance organizers. Coupled with the often-severe methodological problems seen in early research (e.g., not keeping track of how long students studied material, not employing true control groups, poor development of posttests), the vagueness of what made for an effective advance organizer greatly limited research progress.

In the 1980s, however, researchers began to clear up the methodological problems and tie their work into schema theory, which then was becoming more widely known (Derry, 1984; Mayer & Bromage, 1980). In these studies, advance organizers in the form of a paragraph or two of material prefacing the to-be-learned content showed consistent, if somewhat small, beneficial effects on readers' memory for materials. Still, the problem with defining organizers remained.

A series of studies by Glover and his colleagues, however, suggested that good written organizers have a number of common characteristics. In general, organizers that give readers an analogy for upcoming content, that are concrete and use concrete examples, and that are well learned by readers are more beneficial than abstract, general, or poorly learned organizers (Corkill et al., 1988; Corkill, Glover, Bruning, & Krug, 1988; Dinnel & Glover, 1985). Thus, if properly developed, advance organizers can be effective devices for enhancing readers' comprehension of text. The same is true for a set of procedures grouped under the label *schema activation*.

Schema Activation.   As in the case of advance organizers, the concept of **schema activation** often has been loosely defined. In general, schema activation refers to an array of activities designed to activate relevant knowledge in students' memory prior to encountering new, to-be-learned information (e.g., Alvermann, Smith, & Readence, 1985; Pearson, 1985; Rowe & Rayford, 1987; Schallert, 1991). These activities typically involve having students answer questions germane to an upcoming topic, review previous learning, or develop a "schema map" of related knowledge already in memory (R. C. Anderson & Pearson, 1984; Schumacher, 1987).

In many ways, schema activation procedures attempt to accomplish the same goal as advance organizers (tying new information with what is already known) but rely on readers' generation of information from their own knowledge and experiences. The emphasis is on helping students remember and use things they already know that are relevant to a new topic. Consider, for example, an early study conducted by Peeck (1982) and his colleagues.

Peeck, Van Den Bosch, and Kruepeling (1982) had a group of Dutch fifth-graders read a brief (125 words) passage about a fictional fox. Prior to reading, half of the children activated relevant prior knowledge by generating ideas from memory about foxes. The remaining half of the children generated ideas about a topic not relevant to the fox passage—American farms. Immediately after reading, the children were tested through free recall. The results indicated that the children who had activated their knowledge about foxes remembered significantly more of the passage content than the other children. More recently, Rowe and Rayford (1987) examined the effects of a specific form of schema activation in the reading performance of first-, sixth-, and tenth-grade students. They found that "purpose" questions (questions designed to help readers understand the purpose of a passage by activating relevant background knowledge) had facilitative effects at all three grade levels.

Not all schemata are created equal, however, at least insofar as their activation assists in the learning of a particular set of information. As Schallert (1991) cautions, background knowledge needs to be relevant and well learned for its activation to be useful in new learning. Thus, a general exhortation to "teach the prior knowledge required," purportedly a schema activation technique, may make little or no sense in a given instructional setting (e.g., if children have little or no experience with a topic). Activated knowledge, to be useful in anchoring new learning, must itself be stable and well organized.

Both advance organizers and schema activation techniques share the idea that reading comprehension and recall can be improved by finding ways to help students relate new information to what they already know. The research on both topics suggests that these procedures can be effective and useful additions to one's teaching strategies. In general, the more ways teachers can find to help students relate new information to what they already know, the better the comprehension and the more that will be learned and retained.

The Utility of Strategies: Key Strategies in Reading Comprehension Instruction

A cognitive view of reading to learn has emphasized teaching students a set of adaptable strategies they can use to construct meaning and to comprehend text (Dole, Duffy, Roehler, & Pearson, 1991; Pressley, El-Dinary, et al., 1992). The goal is to help students gain metacognitive awareness and conscious control over a set of versatile and powerful strategies for comprehending text meaning. Awareness of the need to teach students reading strategies came from earlier research that identified a number of metacognitive reading skills associated with reading comprehension (Cross & Paris, 1988; Jacobs & Paris, 1987; Palincsar, Brown, & Martin, 1987; Waller, 1987). In the next few pages, we examine five key strategies that research has shown to be among the most effective in helping students comprehend what they read.

Determining Importance.   To comprehend what they are reading, readers must locate the most important ideas in reading passages. Many readers, even some who can fluently "call out" the words in a passage, have difficulty determining what is important and what is not. As a consequence, the metacognitive activity of determining importance has received a great deal of research attention over the years (e.g., Baumann, 1984; A. L. Brown, 1980; Hare & Milligan, 1984; Taylor & Beach, 1984).

Early research in determining importance focused on "finding the main idea." For instance, in an early study on teaching children to identify the main ideas in paragraphs, Glover, Zimmer, Filbeck, and Plake (1980) had students who scored below average on a reading comprehension test attempt to identify the main ideas in a series of paragraphs. Training was provided through the simple procedure of having students underline the parts of paragraphs they believed were the main ideas. After underlining, students could turn a page and compare the portion of the paragraph they thought was the main idea with one the experimenters determined was the main idea. Across a training period of twenty-five days in which praise and other positive outcomes were given for improved accuracy, students' abilities to identify the main ideas in paragraphs improved dramatically, as did their scores on a postexperiment test of reading comprehension.

Palincsar and Brown have provided a particularly useful and flexible program to teach students to judge the importance of ideas in texts (e.g., A. L. Brown & Palincsar, 1982, 1989; Palincsar & Brown, 1984; Palincsar et al., 1987). Although the focus of

Palincsar and Brown's methods is broader than just teaching students to determine importance, we review them here because they are germane to much of what we discuss in the next few pages.

In Palincsar and Brown's approach, referred to as **reciprocal teaching,** a teacher models reading comprehension strategies aloud and guides students in performing them. At the start of a lesson, the teacher engages the students in a short discussion designed to activate relevant prior knowledge (see our earlier discussion of schema activation). Both the teacher and the students then silently read a brief passage, and the teacher provides a model by summarizing the passage, developing a question about the main point, clarifying difficult ideas, and predicting what will happen next. Everyone then reads another passage, with the teacher now asking the students questions that give the teacher clues about what the students are thinking and what kind of instruction they need. As the students respond, often haltingly at first, the teacher provides guidance and support, helping them ask questions, summarize, comprehend, and predict.

Gradually, across sessions, the teacher shifts responsibility to the students so that they are the ones asking questions, summarizing, clearing up misunderstandings, and predicting future happenings. What is highlighted in the process is how the teacher and the students think as they try to comprehend. Teacher scaffolding may be fairly direct when the teacher guides the process (e.g., a teacher comments, "Try putting yourself in Juan's place for a moment") or rather informal (e.g., a comment to a student, "I like to check after each section to see if I can say what it's all about—the main idea, you know"). Reciprocal teaching also includes direct instruction on how to perform comprehension activities, as well as tips for reading more effectively.

The outcomes of research on teaching children strategies for determining the importance of ideas in passages generally have been very positive (see Dole et al., 1991; Pressley, El-Dinary, et al., 1992; Pressley, Johnson, Symons, McGoldrick, & Kurita, 1989). Students' abilities to determine importance improve with practice and feedback, especially when the instruction focuses on comprehending and regulating the metacognitive strategies that are being used.

Summarizing Information.   Summarizing requires not only determining the most important ideas in a passage but also creating a new text that represents the original one. A decade and more ago, researchers (e.g., Winograd, 1984) were reporting that one of the major deficiencies readers have is their inability to adequately summarize content (see also Le Fevre, 1988). Recent assessments show that students still lack skills in this area (NAEP, 1993). Research on teaching students to summarize, however, suggests that students can be taught this skill fairly readily. In their reciprocal teaching approach, Palincsar et al. (e.g., 1987), for example, have teachers and students practice summarizing passages. At first, the teacher models summarization but gradually shifts the responsibility to the student. By the time the student becomes the primary summarizer, the teacher's role is centered on providing feedback, prompts, and praise for good work. In Palincsar et al.'s method, the consistent emphasis is on acquiring and thinking about using the skill of summarization.

Hidi and Anderson (1986) have identified three common operations in summarization. First, some information needs to be selected, while other information is deleted. This step obviously has much in common with the strategy of determining importance. Second, some material needs to be condensed, while other, superordinate material needs to be substituted. For instance, if three sentences in a paragraph contain information about Costa Rica's warm average temperature, its location near the equator, and its high annual rainfall, a summarization sentence likely would highlight Costa Rica's tropical climate. Third, materials need to be integrated into a coherent, accurate representation. For longer texts, summaries often are a paragraph or more in length. In producing them, readers essentially are creating new *compositions* that represent the larger, original text (Hidi & Anderson, 1986).

Whether summarization training has emphasized a tutoring approach (e.g., Palincsar et al., 1987) or a more didactic approach in which rules for summarizing are taught directly (e.g., King, Biggs, & Lipsky, 1984), the results of research on teaching summarization skills also have been positive. When students learn to summarize text as they read and to use their summarization skills in studying, significant improvements in learning are likely (Dole et al., 1991; Pressley, El-Dinary, et al., 1992).

Drawing Inferences.   All texts leave some things unsaid. Text comprehension depends on readers inferring information (e.g., when a character's age is not mentioned, but his or her traits suggest immaturity). Drawing inferences from reading materials also includes the ability to infer ideas beyond the realm of a reading passage (e.g., inferences about how you could enhance the reading comprehension of your own students). As we might expect, making inferences about reading materials is a skill good readers have that tends to be absent in less-skilled readers (Dewitz, Carr, & Patberg, 1987; Le Fevre, 1988).

Several studies have shown that learning to make inferences enhances reading comprehension (Dewitz et al., 1987). Among the clearest findings on teaching inference skills are those of Raphael and her colleagues (e.g., Raphael & McKinney, 1983; Raphael & Pearson, 1982; Raphael & Wonnacott, 1985). Raphael and Wonnacott (1985), for example, contrasted fourth-graders in a control condition with students of similar ability levels who received training in finding the answers to questions about reading materials. Three types of questions were used: (1) those for which the answers were *explicit* in the text, (2) those for which the answers were *implicit* in the text (inferences were needed, much as the inference used in determining someone's age from his or her description), and (3) those for which an *integration* of the reader's background knowledge and text information was required (the inferences required were similar to those you might make in using the content of this chapter to devise methods for improving your students' reading comprehension). Students in the experimental condition received four days of training and practice in answering the three types of questions. Considerable attention was given to showing students how to answer the questions. The results indicated that the training greatly facilitated students' abilities to draw inferences about text materials and significantly improved their comprehension.

In a second experiment, Raphael and Wonnacott taught teachers in an in-service program how to train students to answer the three types of questions. The results again were highly positive. Instruction in how to answer the different kinds of questions, coupled with practice and feedback, resulted in students' significant improvements in reading comprehension.

Recently, researchers have begun to explore the technique of **elaborative interrogation** as a device for generating inferences (e.g., Pressley, McDaniel, Turnure, Wood, & Ahmad, 1987; Seifert, 1993; Wood, Pressley, & Winne, 1990). In its simplest form, learners are asked to read target sentences and then to answer a "why" question to clarify the relationship between the subject and the predicate of the sentence. For instance, if children read the sentence "Cats like to lie in the sun," they would be asked why—that is, to generate a reason why this fact might be true (e.g., because the sun makes them warm). In general, recall of facts processed in this way is increased substantially (see Seifert, 1993, for a summary of elaborative interrogation studies). Although the effect may not be as strong as it is in the learning of simpler materials, a similar effect seems to be present when elaborative interrogation is used with expository paragraphs (see Seifert, 1993). Overall, elaborative interrogation appears to have potential as a technique for enhancing readers' comprehension by stimulating their inferences about what they are reading.

Generating Questions.   Good readers frequently ask themselves questions about their comprehension, determine the utility of the information, and decide whether ideas are important. As you recall, self-questioning and clarification of content are integral parts of Palincsar et al.'s reciprocal teaching. Because self-questioning is embedded in their overall program, however, it is difficult to determine how this skill alone contributes to reading comprehension. King et al. (1984), however, reported on the results of a self-questioning condition contrasted with the control and summarizing conditions we described earlier. Students in one condition were asked to form "higher-level" questions based on the text (students first were taught what "higher-level" meant on the basis of a taxonomy of learning), to record them as notes, and then to read the passage to gain the answers. Results showed the students who used self-questioning during reading did not recall as much content as the students who summarized, but they did recall nearly 20 percent more of the passage's ideas than the control group. Taken with the results of Palincsar et al.'s (e.g., 1987) studies of reciprocal teaching and earlier work (e.g., Andre & Anderson, 1978-1979; Duell, 1978), King et al.'s results suggest that self-questioning directly enhances reading comprehension and that it is a relatively easy skill for students to learn.

Monitoring Comprehension.   One of the differences between good and poor readers is that good readers know when they are comprehending and when they are not. They also are better at controlling and adapting their strategic processes accordingly. These two parts—*being aware* of the quality and degree of comprehension and *knowing what to do and how to do it*—describe comprehension monitoring (Dole et al., 1991). As you can see, these two components parallel the two dimensions of metacognition—knowledge of cognition and regulation of cognition.

An approach used frequently to study comprehension monitoring is the **error detection task,** in which readers are asked to detect inconsistencies or anomalies in text as they are reading. The assumption is that if readers are monitoring their comprehension, they will readily detect anomalies. Researchers document the accuracy and speed of error detection.

Although readers seem to develop a nonverbal awareness of anomalies before they actually can report them, even fairly sophisticated readers struggle when they are asked to identify errors and inconsistencies in reading materials (e.g., see Baker, 1985; Baker & Wagner, 1987) and often have trouble reading critically. Research suggests, however, that students can be taught to be more critical and to do a better job of detecting errors. Grabe and Mann (1984), for instance, taught fourth-graders to detect inconsistencies through an activity they called the Master Detective game. In this approach, the children read a series of ten statements displayed on a computer screen. The statements supposedly were made by ten different suspects in a crime. Five of the statements were consistent; five contained inconsistencies. The point of the game was for the children to find the inconsistencies, such as in the sample below taken from Grabe and Mann:

> All the people that work on this ship get along very well. The people that make a lot of money and the people that don't make much are still friends. *The officers treat us like dirt.* We often eat our meals together. I guess we are just one big happy family. [Italics of the inconsistent statement added.]

> *Grabe & Mann (1984, p. 136)*

The children in Grabe and Mann's experimental condition played the game once as a pretest, four times for practice (with different sets of statements each time), and once as a posttest. The children in the control condition merely played the game twice, as a pretest and a posttest. The results showed that the children who completed the four practice sessions far outperformed the children in the control condition on the posttest. Practice with feedback in identifying inconsistent statements (in a motivating game situation) brought about significant improvement in the identification of inconsistencies, suggesting that fairly simple procedures may improve students' abilities to monitor whether texts are making sense.

Closely related to the ability to identify errors or inconsistencies in reading materials is how well students can estimate how much they have learned from reading. The correlation between what students *believe* they have learned from reading passages and their *actual* test performance is referred to as their **calibration of comprehension** (Glenberg et al., 1987).

When students set out to learn text materials, it seems reasonable that they read and study until they believe they have mastered the material and then stop. If they are studying for an exam, for example, studying too little is risky. However, studying more than is needed to master the material may be seen as a waste of time. Students have many responsibilities and must divide their time among tasks wisely.

Our day-to-day experiences as educators suggest that most students have a reasonably good sense of how well they have mastered the material they study—an accurate calibration of comprehension. After all, many students regularly succeed on tests. In contrast with this intuitively appealing belief, however, are the findings of a set of studies conducted by Glenberg and his associates (e.g., Epstein, Glenberg, & Bradley, 1984; Glenberg & Epstein, 1985; Glenberg et al., 1987; Glenberg, Wilkinson, & Epstein, 1982). In general, these studies have found that adult readers' beliefs about what they have learned from reading have little relationship to actual test performance.

Typically, studies of calibration of comprehension consist of having students read a series of brief passages, complete ratings of how confident they are in answering specific types of questions over the material, and take a posttest. In Glenberg et al.'s (1987) Experiment 1, for example, the correlation between college students' estimates of performance on an inference test and their actual test scores was nearly zero.

Although these studies show low levels of calibration of comprehension, relatively simple procedures can be used to greatly increase the accuracy of students' estimates of learning from text. For example, Pressley, Snyder, Levin, Murray, and Ghatala (1987) found that when readers have the opportunity to test their learning during reading, the accuracy of their performance estimates improves substantially. Although research on procedures to influence the calibration of comprehension is yet very limited, activities such as self-questioning, summarizing, and other metacognitive skills also should aid students in estimating how well they understand what they have read. In general, it seems that any program designed to improve reading comprehension should include a component focused on having students learn to make accurate judgments about their learning (see also Vosniadou, Pearson, & Rogers, 1988).

Building Organized Knowledge Through Reading: Summary and Applications

Cognitive theory holds that the meaning of reading materials is constructed by readers on the basis of the information they encounter, the information they already have in memory, and the ways they interact with new information. Advance organizers and schema activation are approaches designed to facilitate the construction of meanings by bringing about a more complete interaction of readers' general knowledge with the information in a reading passage.

A large body of research supports the use of techniques, such as advance organizers and schema activation, that help readers relate what they already know to what they are learning. Teachers also may want to highlight the value of already acquired task-relevant knowledge for learning new information.

Another large body of research (see Dole et al., 1991) supports the wisdom of teaching key comprehension strategies and metacognitive skills to allow readers to use them appropriately and flexibly. These strategies include determining the importance of information, summarizing what has been read, drawing inferences, self-questioning, and monitoring comprehension. Reciprocal teaching (e.g., Palincsar et al., 1987) is one highly effective approach for teaching a constellation of strategies. The research indicates, however, that each of these strategies can be taught usefully alone or in combination with other skills. In general, as students master comprehension strategies, their reading comprehension improves. Most of the strategies are reasonably simple and can be taught to most readers who are beginning to use reading for learning.

Some of the basics of reading comprehension can be acquired simply through practice with feedback. More flexible use is likely, however, if some variation of reciprocal teaching and its metacognitive orientation is employed. Beginning with direct modeling and clear explanations of how and why each skill can be implemented, teachers gradually need to shift more and more responsibility to the students. Teachers assume a position of helping students clarify their understanding and judge the effectiveness of the strategies they are using. Although teaching students how to read with comprehension is time-consuming (see Palincsar et al., 1987), it appears to be time very well spent.

REMEMBERING WHAT HAS BEEN READ: MEMORY FOR TEXT MATERIALS

Thus far, we have focused on two important outcomes of reading to learn: acquiring vocabulary from reading and acquiring organized knowledge from reading. Research in these areas has been influenced heavily by schema theory and by the concept of *metacognition* in examining how readers construct meaning and comprehend text.

Another very large body of research in educational psychology has focused on what is *retained* as a result of reading. This research, which has come to be known as "memory for text" or "memory for prose" research, represents a wide variety of theoretical frameworks. Because of this theoretical diversity, we limit our discussions primarily to studies linked with the concepts of *schema theory* and *elaboration of processing* (see Chapters 3 and 4).

Text Signals

Text signals are devices designed to improve the cohesion of reading materials or to indicate that certain elements of the text are more important than others (Britton, 1986). The assumption behind using signaling in text is that recall of expository text involves a top-down search of a text that is represented in memory in a hierarchical fashion (Lorch, Lorch, & Inman, 1993). If signals improve memory for a text's topics and its relations, then recall of text content should be improved.

Several kinds of text signals are used by writers, including *number signals* (e.g., The three most important points are [1] . . ., [2] . . ., and [3] . . .); *headings* (see the heading at the top of this section); underlined, italicized, or boldfaced text; *preview sentences* (e.g., As we will see in Chapter 15, . . .); and *recall sentences* (e.g., Recall from Chapter 4, where we . . .). The literature on text signals has implications for the construction of handouts, worksheets, and reading assignments.

One of the most common forms of text signal is the *number signal* (Lorch & Chen, 1986; Lorch, 1989). Number signals are exactly what they sound like—numbers used to enumerate a set of points, a set of steps in a process, a list of names, or other reading content. Number signals are useful for identifying important elements of a text that students are to remember (e.g., four causes of the War of the Roses, five steps in readying a lathe for operation). When students read a brief passage, such as on a handout sheet, they tend to give more of their attention to the signaled content than to the unsignaled content and better remember the signaled material (Lorch & Chen, 1986).

Similar to number signals is the use of *italic* or **boldface** print. When either of these techniques is used sparingly, students pay more attention to the highlighted material and remember it better (Crouse & Idstein, 1972; Fowler & Barker, 1974; Glynn & DiVesta, 1979). *Headings* have a somewhat different effect in that they serve to improve the cohesion and readability of text (Wilhite, 1986).

Number signals, underlining, boldface print, and headings all are useful devices in constructing study materials for students. When specific elements of reading materials are critical, they should be italicized or boldfaced. Students pay more attention to such signaled content and are more likely to remember it. When a set or series of ideas, names, or steps is to be remembered, number signals are useful. Headings break up longer text into segments of thematically related content and reduce the amount of cognitive effort required to comprehend the material (Glynn & DiVesta, 1979; Lorch & Chen, 1986; Wilhite, 1986).

Two other types of text signals are preview sentences and recall sentences. *Preview sentences* signal upcoming contents; *recall sentences* signal back to previously learned material. Preview and recall sentences often are seen in textbooks but seldom show up in brief passages. However, they can have an important use in shorter reading assignments (Glover, Dinnel, et al., 1988; Lorch, 1985).

Preview sentences placed early in a reading passage tend to focus readers' attention on the upcoming material they signal and help students better remember it (Lorch, 1989). Preview sentences also have interesting effects when they signal content in an upcoming assignment. Glover, Dinnel, et al. (1988), for example, had students read a brief assignment in which some preview sentences were embedded. These preview sentences signaled material the students would encounter in a later assignment. Then, when students read the second assignment, Glover et al. kept track of how readers allocated their attention to various parts of the material and looked at memory and organization when students were tested on the material. The results indicated that students focused more of their attention on signaled text, confirming Lorch and Chen's (1986) findings. In addition, more of the signaled content in the second assignment was recalled than unsignaled material. Students also tended to organize their recall such that the material in which the signals had been embedded and the information the preview sentences signaled were recalled together.

These results are important to teaching for three reasons: (1) Preview sentences help focus students' attention on important content, (2) information signaled by preview sentences is better recalled than unsignaled information, and (3) students tend to cluster the signaled content and the information in which the signal was embedded. For example, suppose we have for students two brief reading assignments we wish to assign on different days as classroom activities. Further suppose we want students to link together important information in the second day's assignment with some of the information given in the first day's assignment. One effective way of doing this is through the use of preview sentences. For instance, suppose at the end of a paragraph on, say, Japan's economy, we insert a preview sentence (e.g., We will examine the reasons for Japan's reliance on imported technology in tomorrow's assignment). Then, during the next day, we give the students a brief reading in which the signaled material appears. Not only are the students more likely to attend to the signaled information as a result of the preview sentences we placed in the first assignment, but they also are more likely to remember the signaled information and remember it in the context of the previous day's reading.

Preview sentences have not yet been examined in contexts other than reading materials. Logic suggests, however, that preview sentences also should be effective in lectures and demonstrations. Although simple in concept, preview sentences seem to be an effective means of influencing students' learning.

Recall sentences similarly have an interesting effect on students' processing of information. Unlike preview sentences, recall sentences signal back to previously learned material. Recall sentences are a commonly used device by textbook writers, but they also have uses in shorter assignments. Across brief assignments, recall sentences have the effect of helping students remember information relevant to the content in which the signal is embedded. Further, recall sentences help students cluster information in memory; that is, it seems that students assimilate the information in which the signals are embedded into relevant knowledge they already possess (Glover, Dinnel, et al., 1988). As with preview sentences, recall sentences have been studied only in the context of reading, but it seems reasonable that recall sentences in lectures, discussions, or demonstrations should have positive effects on students' memory for signaled information.

Adjunct Questions

More than thirty years ago, Ernst Rothkopf began a research program exploring the effects of inserted questions on readers' memory for expository text. In one of his initial studies (Rothkopf, 1966), participants read material taken from an expository text and were tested on their ability to remember the content. Some of the participants answered questions while reading (called **adjunct questions**); others did not. The positioning of the questions was varied across the conditions in which participants answered questions. In addition, the adjunct questions were relevant to only some parts of the reading materials. Much of the content was not surveyed through the adjunct questions.

After the participants in Rothkopf's study finished reading, they took a test on the material. Some of the test items were repeated versions of the adjunct questions; others covered content not related to the adjunct questions. We may think of the repeated questions as tapping *intentional learning*—learning required by the adjunct questions. The posttest questions not assessing content relevant to the adjunct questions tap *incidental learning*—learning not required by the adjunct questions.

Four major findings came from Rothkopf's (1966) pioneering study. First, adjunct questions had a powerful effect on intentional learning; that is, students' performance on the posttest questions that assessed their knowledge of content required for the adjunct questions was far superior to students' performance on questions assessing incidental learning. Second, when adjunct questions were placed *after* reading materials, they facilitated both intentional and incidental learning, although the impact on incidental learning was not large. Third, when adjunct questions prefaced reading materials, they enhanced intentional learning but did not facilitate incidental learning. Indeed, on measures of incidental learning, a control group that received no adjunct questions but that was asked to study hard and to remember the details of the passage outperformed the participants who received prefatory adjunct questions. Fourth, reading times (including the answering of adjunct questions during reading) seemed to vary directly with participants' performance on the posttest.

Rothkopf's study had an important influence, both methodologically and conceptually, on subsequent research. After his seminal paper came an explosion of research on adjunct questions (see R. C. Anderson & Biddle, 1975; Andre, 1987a; Faw & Waller, 1976; Hamaker, 1986; Hamilton, 1985; Rickards, 1979, for reviews). The results of these studies generally have painted a consistent picture. Below, we review the findings and highlight the practical applications of adjunct question research. Before proceeding, however, it is important to note that, for all practical purposes, the findings on adjunct questions are identical to those on the use of instructional objectives given to students; that is, studies that have contrasted how instructional objectives (or learning objectives) and adjunct questions influence readers have indicated little or no difference between them (Petersen, Glover, & Ronning, 1980; Zimmer, Petersen, Ronning, & Glover, 1978).

Level of Questions.   Although many different ways to classify questions used in reading materials have been proposed over the years, one widely used in research on questions (and also used extensively in the development of instructional objectives and test items) is a hierarchy of objectives created by Bloom et al. (1956). The Bloom et al. taxonomy posits six levels of learning, based on the sophistication and complexity of the learning required. The levels of learning described in the taxonomy, moving from simple to complex, are knowledge, comprehension, application, analysis, synthesis, and evaluation. We briefly describe the kind of learning required by questions at each of the levels of the Bloom et al. taxonomy.

Knowledge-level learning merely requires the retention of facts, such as names or dates. It is akin to rote learning and is the learning tapped by the level of question employed by Rothkopf in his 1966 study. *Comprehension-level* questions require more sophisticated knowledge, as they require students to paraphrase the to-be-learned material into their own words. *Application-level* learning requires the use of information in some concrete form. It differs from comprehension-level learning in requiring the implementation of knowledge, such as the distinction between when a student is able to *explain* the concept of "irony" (comprehension) and actually *use* "irony" in a segment of writing (application). *Analysis-level* learning is more complex yet, in that learners must be able to break down information into its component parts so that the relationship among all of the components is clear. For example, the request, "Compare and contrast levels of processing with schema theory," requires that students break down both schema theory and levels of processing into their component parts (encoding, storage, etc.) and relate them one to another. *Synthesis-level* learning demands that students put together old knowledge in new ways. For example, the request, "Using your knowledge of encoding specificity, construct a test over content you are teaching that will enhance students' test performance," requires the use of knowledge you already have (both how to construct tests and the concept of *encoding specificity*) in a new way. *Evaluation-level* learning involves students making judgments about the value of methods or materials, based on their knowledge. For example, if you were shown three videotapes of teachers presenting a lesson and were asked to determine how well each teacher employed the principles of cognitive psychology, you would be engaging in evaluation-level learning.

When we review the results of research on adjunct questions in terms of the level of learning required by the questions, some interesting findings emerge. Knowledge-level questions tend to facilitate only knowledge-level learning, and their effects are focused primarily on intentional learning (Andre, 1987a). Comprehension-level questions also have a strong effect on intentional learning and a limited but consistent effect on incidental learning (Hamaker, 1986; Muth, Glynn, Britton, & Graves, 1988).

Higher-order questions (at the application level or above) tend to enhance both intentional and incidental learning. Further, higher-order questions have their facilitative effect regardless of whether they preface or follow reading materials, although their greatest effect occurs when they preface text (Halpain et al., 1985). Higher-order questions also seem to enhance both lower-order (knowledge and comprehension) and higher-order learning (Andre, 1987a; Halpain et al., 1985; Hamaker, 1986).

In terms of applications, two lines of reasoning are possible. In the first line, if teachers want students to learn specific facts from a reading passage, they should employ lower-order questions prefacing text. The problem with such an approach, however, is that it tends to result in a "post hole" effect; that is, students tend to learn in depth only those segments of text specifically indicated by the questions. The remainder of the text and perhaps even the main point of the passage may receive very little elaboration and, consequently, be poorly remembered.

The second line of reasoning emerges if teachers have less interest in specific elements of knowledge, but instead are more interested in overall comprehension. In this case, teachers should use higher-order questions. Higher-order questions cannot be answered by locating a specific term or phrase in a passage. Instead, they require that large segments of a passage be attended to. Consequently, students remember the gist of passages better after answering higher-order questions than after answering lower-order questions (Benton, Glover, & Bruning, 1983; Halpain et al., 1985).

Questions Requiring Decisions.   There is no doubt that adjunct questions can have positive effects on students' memory for prose. It turns out, however, that questions requiring students to make decision are more effective than questions at the same level of the Bloom et al. (1956) taxonomy that do not require decisions. The act of making a decision (e.g., yes/no) about some content, in addition to answering the question, appears to result in considerably more elaborated processing (see Chapter 4), leading to better memory for the content (Benton, Glover, & Bruning, 1983; Benton, Glover, Monkowski, & Shaughnessy, 1983). If student decision making is a part of a teacher's instructional goals, adjunct questions should be written so that students go beyond simply writing an answer to recording a decision.

Location of Questions.   In general, the research suggests that students' overall recall of content will be best if higher-order questions precede text and lower-order questions follow it (Hamaker, 1986; Hamilton, 1985). Because higher-order questions require more extensive and elaborated processing, they result in better learning when they preface materials. In this arrangement, students must carefully search and evaluate large segments of prose to determine their relevance to the questions. When higher-order questions follow reading, however, students must rely on their memories to answer the questions. Consequently, although the effect of higher-order questions following text is still greater than that of lower-order questions in any configuration, their impact is considerably less than if they preface text.

Number of Questions.   Only a handful of studies have examined how different numbers of questions influence readers' memory for content (see Andre, 1987a). In general, it seems that only a few higher-order questions need to be employed to optimally enhance students' memory for text. Perhaps one higher-order question for every 1,000 words of text is sufficient to ensure elaborated processing of the text materials. When lower-order questions are considered, the number of questions is less critical and should be determined on the basis of specific instructional goals.

Are Higher-Order Questions Appropriate for All Students?   The kinds of thinking required by higher-order questions are not restricted to high school or even middle school students. Application, analysis, synthesis, and evaluation learning activities are well within the abilities of elementary school children if the activities are structured in ways that are meaningful to them. Glover and Zimmer (1982), for example, gave fourth-and fifth-grade students practice in devising their own analysis-level questions about current affairs readings in the newspaper. With two weeks of daily practice in their thirty-minute current affairs classes, the children were able to formulate several analysis-level questions for each of their readings and were able to answer analysis-level questions without difficulty. Elementary school children, by and large, do require practice in developing and answering higher-order questions, but it seems to us that the time taken to systematically model higher-order thinking and give children practice with feedback for application, analysis, synthesis, and evaluation is likely to be rewarded.

IMPLICATIONS FOR TEACHING

This chapter has focused on the processes of reading to learn—"getting meaning" from text materials. The importance of reading to learn is hard to overestimate; it is fundamental to learning in school, is a significant part of effective living, and provides an unparalleled source of enjoyment. As a consequence, most educators would endorse readily the goal of what Guthrie (1993) has called *engaged reading*—choosing to read frequently for a variety of reasons and having the requisite cognitive skills for comprehending the materials that are read. The chapter has highlighted a number of key dimensions of reading that are important in this quest. The following implications for teaching draw on these dimensions.

1. *Encourage reading.* Read, read, read! Teachers need to take the lead in encouraging students to read. Reading is linked strongly with success in school and in the workplace. Even in the information age, with its emphasis on a variety of media, reading remains the primary source of the information that underlies serious understanding in almost every field of endeavor. Unfortunately, a growing body of evidence shows that students today are not reading effectively; for too many students at all levels, comprehension is minimal and literal (Guthrie, 1993). Thus, we need to work hard at developing engaged readers—readers who not only are motivated to read for a variety of purposes but also have the skills to comprehend the materials they select to read. Although this is far from a trivial challenge, it is not an impossible one. For instance, teachers and schools can establish school-home reading programs that encourage reading at home and library use. Being read to by parents and reading to parents and siblings can form values and habits that last a lifetime. In school, teachers can make reading more rewarding by selecting interesting reading materials and using reading in ways that students find meaningful and functional. Teachers also can help students develop comprehension skills. By modeling comprehension skill use and teaching these skills directly, teachers can help students read more effectively. As students' skill levels improve, reading becomes a more positive and productive experience.

2. *Encourage students to be active readers.* Current models of reading portray a range of reading processes as diverse as automatized perceptual processes and activation of reader conceptual frameworks. None can be ignored if reading comprehension is the goal. The more active the reader is—asking questions about what is read, relating what is read to what the reader already knows, thinking of implications, putting ideas into the reader's own words—the more likely comprehension and learning become. Learning results from an active reader interacting with text materials.

3. *Help students become active vocabulary learners.* Reading is a major avenue to vocabulary growth. The more readers read, the larger their vocabularies and the richer the networks of knowledge that underlie these words. Voracious readers tend to have very large vocabularies; moderate readers, moderate vocabularies; and infrequent readers, small vocabularies. Although vocabulary growth from reading can occur without intervention, teachers can assist students in acquiring vocabulary from reading by teaching them strategies for using context effectively. Direct instruction also can supplement vocabulary growth, but its effects are augmented by linking it with reading; when students are encouraged to notice new words, their vocabulary learning is enhanced.

4. *Use advance activities to heighten reading comprehension.* Most reading theorists view learning as resulting from an interaction between the reader and the

materials being read. When information to be learned is linked with what readers already know, understanding will be heightened. Two prominent methods for accomplishing this linking are *advance organizers* and *schema activation.* Advance organizers are materials intended to serve as scaffolding for what is to be learned; they provide a known framework for new, unfamiliar material. Schema activation has similar functions but relies more on the readers themselves to generate frames of reference and knowledge. Because both methods tend to make reading materials more meaningful, their effect is to increase comprehension, as well as recall.

5. *Teach important strategies explicitly.* Nearly a generation of research on the role of metacognition in reading comprehension has focused our attention on the key role of a few important reading strategies. Students need, for example, to tell the difference between important and unimportant information and to summarize extended chunks of information into more manageable ones. They need to make appropriate inferences from what they read and to monitor whether or not they are comprehending. We know that students who generate questions as they read are likely to comprehend better and learn more. Each of these strategies has been shown to make an important contribution to helping students read effectively and adaptively, and research has demonstrated that students can learn to use them relatively quickly and effectively.

SUMMARY

At the outset of the chapter, we reviewed three types of models of reading comprehension: data-driven, conceptually driven, and interactive. Data-driven models emphasize serial, word-by-word processing in which the meaning of a text is deciphered by readers. Conceptually driven models emphasize the construction of meaning based on readers' background knowledge. Interactive models envision both data-driven and conceptually driven processes interacting in the construction of meaning.

One important outcome of reading is vocabulary acquisition, a process that occurs naturally as students read. Although acquisition of word meanings during reading occurs in small increments, the knowledge acquired is particularly useful because it includes information about the context of words' use. Contact with words during reading appears to be a major source of vocabulary growth, which proceeds at a phenomenal rate during the school years.

In general, the more students read, the larger their vocabularies. Students' effectiveness as vocabulary learners, however, can be enhanced by encouraging them to notice new words and by teaching them strategies for using context to figure out what words mean.

Reading is a primary means for acquiring organized knowledge, with schema theory providing a general backdrop for understanding reading comprehension. In a schema theory view, readers construct meaning from the text material, their knowledge, and their purposes for reading. Research on advance organizers, schema activation, and metacognitive reading strategies all emphasize the importance of active, strategic approaches to reading.

Advance organizers preface to-be-learned reading materials and are designed to help students tie new material to what they already know. Schema activation is a process whereby students activate relevant knowledge prior to reading. Both facilitate readers' comprehension of text. Readers also can acquire a number of strategies that improve reading comprehension. These strategies can be taught individually or together in comprehensive training programs, such as the reciprocal teaching approach of Palincsar et al. (1987).

Finally, a large body of research has been concentrated on recall of content from reading texts. Two aspects of this literature have concentrated on the influence of signals in text and the effects of adjunct questions. In general, text signals focus readers' attention on specific segments of text and help make reading materials more coherent. The effect of adjunct questions (questions inserted in text) depends on the level of the questions and where they are placed. Comprehension is best aided by a few higher-order questions prefacing text.

SUGGESTED READINGS

Dole, J. A., Duffy, G. G., Roehler, L. R., & Pearson, P. D. (1991). Moving from the old to the new: Research on reading comprehension instruction. *Review of Educational Research, 61,* 239–264.

This review article outlines key strategies for improving reading comprehension and discusses the research on which the authors' choice of strategies is based. It also describes the evolution of researchers' thinking about strategy instruction in reading to learn.

Ruddell, R. B., Ruddell, M. R., & Singer, H. (Eds.). (1994). *Theoretical models and processes of reading* (4th ed.). Newark, DE: International Reading Association.

This book is the latest revision of a classic collection of chapters by many leading authorities in reading. Sections on comprehension processes, reader response, metacognition, and theoretical models of reading relate particularly closely to the topics of reading comprehension and learning from text materials.

CHAPTER 12

Writing

Many students have difficulty using writing to state their ideas, express their feelings, and persuade others (Applebee, Langer, Jenkins, Mullis, & Foertsch, 1990; Graham & Harris, 1993). Confidence in themselves as writers also is low. Although they judge writing to be very important for such things as success in school and on the job, many plainly do not see themselves as good writers (Shell, Colvin, & Bruning, in press; Shell, Murphy, & Bruning, 1989).

One reason for this lack of student skill and confidence in writing may be that, until fairly recently, students were getting very little, if any, practice writing. Surveys and other research done in the 1980s (e.g., Applebee, 1984, 1988; Applebee, Langer, & Mullis, 1986a, 1986b) showed that most students were doing very little writing in school and that quality of writing had declined steadily.

The small amount of writing they were doing was mostly low-level activity, such as making lists, copying instructions, and taking notes. Further, on those occasions when significant writing was required, for instance in a term paper, it too often involved an arbitrary topic, inadequate preparation in how to approach the writing task, and sometimes grading based mainly on marking errors in grammar and usage.

These conditions hardly could be called ideal for developing confidence, pleasure, and skill in writing.

The past decade, however, has seen a number of positive developments in the field of writing. Both researchers and educators have begun to pay attention to concerns about the amount and quality of writing instruction. Compared with ten years ago, much more writing is occurring in our schools now, especially at the elementary levels. Writing not only is being integrated with reading and incorporated into language arts instruction but also is appearing across the curriculum in such areas as science, social studies, and even mathematics.

Research on writing and cognitive models of writing also have become more sophisticated in the past decade (e.g., Bereiter & Scardamalia, 1987; Hayes & Flower, 1986). As a consequence, we now understand a great deal more about the writing process than we did earlier. Researchers have begun applying cognitive principles to writing instruction with good effect: They have shown that such techniques as modeling writing strategies, encouraging students to plan and revise, and creating a supportive social environment for writing can significantly improve student writing and attitudes about writing (e.g., Atwell, 1987; Bereiter & Scardamalia, 1987; Calkins, 1986; Englert, Raphael, Anderson, Anthony, & Stevens, 1991; Graham & Harris, 1993; Graves, 1983; Harris & Graham, 1992).

In this chapter, we present a cognitive model of the writing process, along with applications based on what cognitive research tells us about writing. We begin by examining a model that has had a great influence in guiding research on writing—the model of Flower and Hayes. We then explore the issue of individual differences in writing, comparing the qualities of more sophisticated writers with those who are less developed. In the final major section of the chapter, we draw heavily on applied cognitive research on writing in describing the implications of a cognitive framework for writing instruction. We end with some thoughts on the topic of creative writing.

A COGNITIVE MODEL OF WRITING

Writing can take many forms. Novels, letters to the editor, poetry, and grocery lists all are forms of writing. Writing tasks also can differ dramatically in intent, length, and amount of creativity expected of the writing. Writing also varies in complexity and quality by student age (compare a third-grader's narrative about Christmas vacation with a college student's essay on the Middle-Eastern peace plan), by topic, and by the writer's goals.

One feature of a good model is that it can take variations such as these into account, highlighting components and processes that remain stable regardless of the type of activity under consideration. A good model also generates a conception of processes that helps researchers think productively about a phenomenon and guides the design of research. Probably more than any other model of writing, the model proposed by Linda Flower and John Hayes (e.g., Carey & Flower, 1989; Flower & Hayes, 1984; Hayes & Flower, 1986) has served these important purposes.

The Flower and Hayes model (see Figure 12-1) portrays writing as a problem-solving activity with three major components: the task environment, long-term memory, and working memory. Each major component contains subcomponents representing specific writing processes.

The Task Environment

The task environment, for Flower and Hayes, essentially "defines the writer's problem." It consists of two major components: the *writing assignment* (the writing task encountered by a writer) and *external storage* (the writing a writer produces and the external aids he or she may use).

The Writing Assignment.   In Flower and Hayes's model, *writing assignment* is a generic label referring to the external conditions that provide a framework for a writer's initial representation of the writing task. School writing assignments often provide such a framework. They usually describe a topic and its scope, imply an intended audience, and often contain motivating cues. Take, for instance, an assignment that asks students to write a two-page essay on the political problems involved

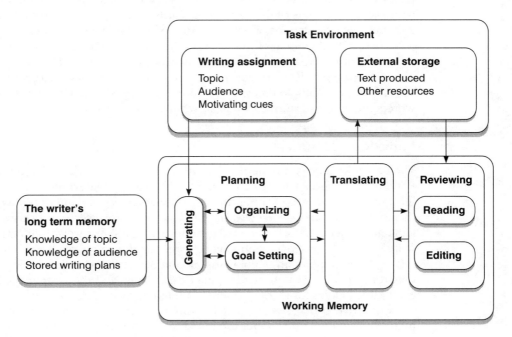

Figure 12-1
The Flower and Hayes model of writing. (Adapted from Gregg/Steinberg, *Cognitive Processes in Writing*, p. 11. New Jersey: Lawrence Erlbaum Associates, Inc. Used by permission.)

in curtailing acid rain. Such an assignment clearly specifies the topic and the scope of the essay. Although audience is not mentioned, the students typically would have this information (whether it is for the teacher's consumption, for judges in an essay contest, etc.). Motivating cues, such as grades (e.g., "This essay is worth 100 points") or other outcomes (e.g., "Five winners will receive scholarships to the university's Summer Institute of Environmental Sciences") also often are significant aspects of a writing assignment.

As with other forms of problem solving, how tasks are represented initially has a great deal to do with ultimate performance. Assignments vary in how effective they are in helping students represent their writing goals. Unclear assignments can produce poor or incomplete representations of writers' goals; likely outcomes for such assignments are low-quality writing or writing that is mismatched with its audience.

External Storage.   The second part of the task environment component of Flower and Hayes's model is *external storage*—the text the writer is creating and other materials that serve as resources to the writer. For example, a student working on an essay has the partially completed essay itself to look back on. She also may have notes she has written to herself about the assignment (e.g., "Be sure to mention acid rain damage to Germany's Black Forest"). For longer assignments, such as term papers, students often have several forms of external storage to consult as they write, including drafts of the paper, note cards, summaries of sources they have read, and their own evaluations of different parts of what they have written.

The external storage of information in writing drastically reduces memory load as the individual creates new information. Compared with speakers, for instance, for whom there typically is no external record of what they have said, writers can consult their work multiple times. The Flower and Hayes model notes this potential for writers drawing on external storage as writing is reread, evaluated, and revised.

Long-Term Memory

The second major component in Flower and Hayes's model is long-term memory. Bereiter and Scardamalia (1987) divide the knowledge that writers can access in long-term memory into two major groupings: *knowledge about content* (knowledge about the topic itself) and *knowledge about discourse processes* (e.g., knowledge about audiences, metalinguistic knowledge about structural features of different genres of writing). This knowledge continually changes as the writer reads and writes. In fact, it is useful to think of an ongoing interaction between the external environment and long-term memory, where reading materials, notes, and the writing itself constitute external resources for writing, whereas memory provides internal resources.

Cognitive processes interact continually in working memory and long-term memory as writers think about their goal, search for ideas and vocabulary, and evaluate and review text they have written. Writers do not simply check with long-term memory at the outset of their writing; rather, long-term memory is a continuing resource for writing throughout the writing process.

No matter how well developed a writer's composing abilities are, the ultimate quality of writing produced depends on the writer's ability to apply both content and discourse knowledge to a particular writing assignment (Bereiter & Scardamalia, 1987; Hayes & Flower, 1986). Lacking content knowledge, even Shakespeare might have written poorly had he been assigned an essay on, say, nuclear physics. Conversely, only a very few nuclear physicists could produce a literary work of the highest quality, at least partly because most would lack substantive knowledge about the more subtle features of literary discourse.

Working Memory

The third major component of the Flower and Hayes model is *working memory*. Flower and Hayes envision three major processes occurring in working memory: planning, translating, and reviewing. Writers do not necessarily go from planning to translating to reviewing, however. Instead, most move back and forth interactively from process to process as the need arises. For instance, a writer may shift from reviewing back to planning and then to translating. More complex arrangements, in which a writer accesses the external task environment and long-term memory, also are likely. We begin our discussion of the processes in working memory by examining the planning process more closely.

Planning.   The planning process includes three subprocesses: goal setting, generating, and organizing. These subprocesses (see Hayes & Flower, 1986) interact vigorously and may be initiated at any time during writing. *Goal setting* refers to establishing objectives for writing. Goals may be long-term (e.g., "I'll write an A+ paper," "This chapter has to fit into the rest of the book") or short-term (e.g., "Here I need to give a few examples," "I need to do a summary that sets up the next section"). Goals are a part of the writer's preparation before writing begins (e.g., "I'll use lots of metaphors. My teacher likes 'em," "I really want my mom to know how much I appreciated her doing that") but also may be set after an initial writing session has been completed (e.g., "I think I'd better add something about the Adirondacks"). As you can see, goal setting is not a one-time activity, but rather occurs many times during the course of writing.

The *generating* subprocess refers to the development of the ideas and content used in writing. Ideas may be generated from long-term memory (e.g., "Let's see, didn't we talk about that in class?") or from the external environment ("I know it's in my notes here somewhere. Oh, great, here it is"). Generation, as can be imagined, is an ongoing process influencing all other parts of the writing model. For example, suppose you are responding to an essay question about, say, presidential elections. At first, you may plan to analyze the choice of the last three vice-presidents. Soon, however, you discover you cannot remember all of their names. To continue, either you will need to consult some source for this information or your goals must be altered. Goals also may change, of course, as a result of generating unanticipated ideas, as when you hit on a good example or unexpectedly recall facts about an event.

The *organizing* subprocess of planning is closely related to both generating and setting goals. In organizing, writers create a sensible, coherent structure out of their goals and ideas. Although organizing also typically is seen as happening early in writing, writers return to it again and again as writing proceeds. Each new paragraph and new sentence requires organization. Also, any changes in goals or in the ideas available require a return to organizing.

Translating.   In Flower and Hayes's model, translating is a second process in working memory. Translating involves transforming one's ideas into written text. Translating requires accessing semantic memory, finding vocabulary to express ideas, putting words into sentences, and reading off words as they are written. Translating can put an enormous strain on the capacity of writers' working memories. As many translating activities become automatic or nearly so in good writers, however, the load is reduced greatly (Hayes & Flower, 1986).

Reviewing.   The reviewing process in working memory involves a reexamination of what has been written and a comparison of this product with the writer's internal standards for acceptable writing. Although we think of reviewing occurring when writing is finished, it happens at any time during writing, even when the initial plans for a passage are being created (Hull, 1987).

Reviewing consists of two subprocesses: evaluating and revising. *Evaluating* amounts to rereading the text and judging its quality. Obviously, evaluating what has been written depends not only on the writer's general content knowledge but also on a writer's sophistication with the particular form of writing he or she was attempting to produce (Hull, 1987; Smagorinsky & Smith, 1992).

Good and poor writers differ dramatically in how well they evaluate their writing. For example, when confronted with samples of poor writing, good writers are apt to point to flaws in the writer's construction, coherence, and choice of words. Poor writers, in contrast, tend to blame their own inability to decode the text as the source of the problem. In other words, good writers understand what good and poor samples of text are like. They further understand that good writing involves a writer's needing to blend both content and discourse knowledge. Poor writers do not readily identify these features; instead, they tend to believe that their reading is at fault. This general pattern also is seen when writers critique their own products. Good writers often identify problems in their own work, whereas poor or immature writers are less likely to see shortcomings and often are surprised when others have comprehension problems.

Revising, the second subprocess involved in reviewing, refers to the rewriting and restructuring of text. Again, depending on the sophistication of the writer, revising can vary tremendously. Less-skilled writers often have great difficulty even seeing that a first draft might benefit from additional editing (Graham & Harris, 1993). When less skilled writers do edit, editing often is limited to minor changes of wording or just adding content. More accomplished writers, however, are much more likely to revise materials they have written, viewing almost any sample of their work as preliminary and subject to editing (Bereiter & Scardamalia, 1987; Graham & Harris, 1993; Hull, 1987).

An Example of the Writing Model

Perhaps the best way to capture the full flavor of the Flower and Hayes model is to follow a hypothetical individual through the task of completing a writing assignment. Let's try to keep up with Evelyn. She is enrolled in a high school journalism class and has been assigned the task of writing an article for the school paper.

"Hmmm," reflects Evelyn, "I need to write a 250- to 275-word article describing the three candidates for senior class president. Well, I do have a file of the candidates' descriptions of themselves. It'd make sense to look at those first."

Evelyn pulls out a folder and begins flipping through it until she comes to the set of candidate descriptions. She examines them carefully, tapping her pencil on her desk. "Some of these are pretty fancy and use big words. But everybody in school has to be able to read the article. I won't try to impress anybody with my vocabulary. Also, when Mr. Barker says, 'keep it brief,' he means 'keep it brief.'"

Evelyn turns on her computer and glances at a handout Mr. Barker gave out that day. On a yellow pad, she begins to scratch together an outline and thinks, "I'll just start by putting down their names and listing the honors and awards they've won so far in high school. That should be pretty easy to do. Next, I'll take their responses to the candidate survey they filled out and try to summarize how each person feels about the 'issues,' using their own words, of course. I also need to find one special thing to say about each person. Mr. Barker will like that."

Evelyn's reaction to the assignment is not especially unusual or striking, but it does allow us to see some elements of the model in action. The initial *task environment* (the assignment, the questionnaire, and Mr. Barker himself) seemed quite clear to Evelyn. She immediately began using her long-term memory in planning at least a rough framework for the whole writing task (see Hull, 1987). Note that, in her planning, Evelyn used both content knowledge (her knowledge of the candidates) and discourse knowledge (e.g., knowledge that her audience was both Mr. Barker and the students at her school, that she was writing a journalistic-style article, and that her writing could be guided by the handout describing the candidates' responses to the issues). Evelyn's brief thoughts also allow us to see that she was busy organizing the material she was going to write as she began to form, at least loosely, her goals for writing.

Later, as we look back in on Evelyn, we see that she has begun actually writing and is working in short bursts, stopping now and again to stare at the computer screen. "Oh, what a horrible sentence!" she mutters. She erases the line and starts again. "I don't want to make it sound like Susan doesn't like sports at all," she muses, "just because she thinks sports shouldn't be so important. Instead, I'll try this: 'Susan Smith believes sports are . . .'"

Evelyn writes several more lines and then stops, leaning closer to the computer screen: ". . . believe . . . ," she mutters to herself. "No, it's 'The group *believes*,' because group is one thing—singular."

This little segment of Evelyn's thinking lets us in on the *translating* process, in which she turns her ideas into words. In addition, we can see that she is reviewing her work as she goes along. She evaluated a sentence, found that it did not convey the meaning she wanted, erased it, and revised it. She then made another attempt at translating, this time producing an appropriate sentence.

Looking back at Evelyn one last time, we find that she finally has completed her article and is rereading it, making changes as she moves along. "OK. That sounds pretty decent. But this doesn't. Wow, not so good, Evy! Gotta fix that pronto. . . . Mmm. I think a comma goes there and, well, I'd better cut out that *which*. . . . Capitalize *Kappa,* dummy! . . . Hey, this is pretty darned good, if I say so myself."

In this final observation of Evelyn, we see that her *reviewing* of her work was typical of most better writers' reactions; that is, she carefully evaluated the material and made revisions where needed, some of them fairly substantial. Further, she made a last check of the mechanics of writing (punctuation, capitalization) after the task was complete.

Even a small sample of a writer's work, such as Evelyn's, tells a great deal about the dynamics of the writing process. *What is written is linear, but the processes of writing are not.* Writers do not move from planning to translating to reviewing in a neat, orderly progression. Instead, they cycle back and forth among all of the subprocesses involved in writing. In fact, some of the most important individual differences among writers seem to be based in their abilities to shift rapidly from operation to operation.

INDIVIDUAL DIFFERENCES IN WRITING

During the past several years, much research has focused on how individual writers differ in ways other than the obvious difference in ability to write (e.g., see Benton, Glover, Kraft, & Plake, 1984; S. Brown, 1986; Dickinson & Snow, 1986; Graham & Harris, 1993). Some surprising and not so surprising differences have been documented. In terms of traditional measures, good and poor writers at the same grade level do not differ widely in measures of intelligence, academic achievement, or motivation (Benton et al., 1984). They do differ, however, in reading ability (Benton et al., 1984; S. Brown, 1986) and in the amount of writing they have been required to produce (Mazzie, 1987).

Generally, good readers are better writers than poor readers. Correlational studies have indicated that measures of reading comprehension are positively related to writing ability (+ .50 or above) and to students' beliefs about their ability as writers (Shell, Colvin, & Bruning, in press). These relationships are not surprising when we consider that frequent reading exposes students to many more samples of writing (most of which, we would assume, are of reasonably good quality). At least indirectly, reading can teach students about good writing.

Better writers also have done more writing. This fact also should not be surprising because writing is a complex cognitive skill and, like any skill, will improve with practice and feedback. In general, we would expect that as students are asked to write more and more, their ability to write will improve. As an editor put it to one of the authors several years ago: "If you want to write, you have to write, write, write. No person ever mastered writing by talking about it."

Beyond reading ability and amount of practice in writing, however, writers differ on several other dimensions. One of these is how individual writers process information.

Information-Processing Differences

Several studies have examined differences in how more and less effective writers process information (e.g., Benton et al., 1984; Daiute, 1986; Kellogg, 1984). Benton et al., for instance, contrasted better and poorer college student writers (defined on the basis of how samples of their writing were scored by a panel of judges) on a series of information-processing tasks. They found no significant differences in the students' grade point averages or achievement test scores, which confirmed earlier work. They also found no differences between the groups in the size of iconic store or short-term memory. They did find differences, however, in how individuals in the two groups manipulated information.

In one task, for instance, Benton et al. exposed subjects to a series of letters randomly generated by computer. After the last letter was presented, subjects were instructed to reorder the letters they were holding in working memory into alphabetical order. All subjects completed several trials to allow reliable estimates of their abilities to reorder the letters. The results indicated that better writers were both faster and more accurate on this task than poorer writers.

Letter reordering might be seen as a rather trivial task, one not very related to writing skills. However, other information-manipulation tasks closer to those required in actual writing activities showed comparable results. On a word-reordering task (presumed to be similar to actually forming a sentence from memory), for example, subjects were given sets of words (from nine to fourteen words in each set) in random order. Their task was to reorder the words into the one order that made a sentence for each string of words. Across several trials, the better writers again proved to be faster and more accurate than the poorer ones. They also were better on a task that required them to put sets of randomized sentences into a well-formed paragraph (presumed to be similar to the activities required in assembling a paragraph during actual writing) and on a task that necessitated the organizing of sets of twelve sentences into three different paragraphs (presumed to be akin to the kinds of activities students engage in when organizing information for writing).

Benton et al.'s (1984) first experiment then was replicated with a sample of high school students. On each of the information-manipulation tasks, better writers again were significantly more rapid and accurate than poorer ones, supporting the conclusion that better writers are superior at manipulating verbal information; that is, they can reorder letters, words, sentences, and paragraphs more efficiently than less-skilled writers.

Directly related to the information-processing differences just described are the ways different writers allocate their attention during writing. Young writers, for instance, often need to focus on the mechanics of writing, such as manipulating a pencil and forming letters. For very young writers, especially, the motor skill demands of writing often can be such that they mouth each letter and word as they write it. With practice, however, children begin to gain automatic control over the motor aspects of writing and no longer need to devote as much of their attention to making letters.

Even older writers, however, will show wide differences in attention. Less-skilled writers and writers with learning problems continue to focus on mechanical features of writing, such as grammar, punctuation, capitalization, and spelling, whereas good writers seem better able to concentrate on the meaning they intend to impart (Atwell, 1981; Bereiter & Scardamalia, 1987; Diamond, 1985; Graham & Harris, 1993; Robbins, 1986). Writers with more advanced skills perform mechanical functions, such as punctuation and spelling, automatically or put off worrying about mechanical issues until a first draft of the ideas has been put onto paper. It seems likely that many of the information-processing differences observed by Benton et al. (1984) and others may be the result of better writers having learned the skills of writing to a more automatic level. As these skills become more highly developed, writers can concentrate their attention more fully on the meaning they are trying to express.

Idea Generation

As one might suspect, considerable differences are found in the number and quality of ideas for writing that students of different ages and abilities generate (Harris & Graham, 1992; Robbins, 1986). Older children generally will have more ideas than younger ones, and adults more than either. One of the most persistent problems for young writers is finding enough to say. Development is only one of several factors affecting idea generation, however. Others are knowledge about the topic (Carey & Flower, 1989), knowledge of audience (Bates, 1984), knowledge about what makes for a good story (Root, 1985), and acquisition of metacognitive writing strategies (Englert et al., 1991; Raphael, 1986). Thus, the extent to which writers have acquired tools for idea generation seems to be at least as important as development per se.

One of the more interesting studies examining the idea-generation phenomenon in writing was conducted by Root (1985), who surveyed the idea-generation techniques of professional expository writers. The writers in this sample were professionals who wrote magazine and newspaper articles. Most focused their efforts on developing a wide range of marketable stories similar to those seen in general-interest magazines (e.g., "The Great Northern Line," a story about railroading; "Three-Mile Island Revisited," a story about the aftermath of a nuclear accident); a few emphasized book-length projects. Because these people made their living from writing, idea generation was critical.

The results of Root's survey were both commonsensical and interesting at the same time. These professional writers spent a great deal of their time reading. Although they read about specific topics primarily while working on particular stories (e.g., reading about nuclear power when preparing a story on the dangers of nuclear reactors), their general tendency was to read widely and to look for ideas in varied places. Further, these professional writers typically kept newspaper and magazine clippings, along with their own notes about ideas for later use, even when they had no idea that the notes ever would be helpful.

The results of Root's study parallel one of the major theses of this volume: Knowledge plays a key role in effective cognitive functioning. There is no substitute for knowledge if idea generation is the goal. For most young children and even for many older ones, roots of this knowledge will lie in their own direct experience. Acquiring strategies for finding and comprehending text materials, however, can greatly expand students' knowledge base for writing (Guthrie, 1993). Of course, the highest levels of creativity within any discipline, including writing, require years of practice not only because the content areas are so complex but also because of the myriad of forms writing can take.

Our students, of course, typically are novices, not experts, at writing and will not have the broad range of knowledge possessed by professional writers. We can, however, increase the number of ideas students can draw on by simple techniques in which they brainstorm vocabulary and writing topics either prior to or during writing (Glover, 1982; Harris & Graham, 1992). These kinds of strategies can be learned by students at almost any age and ability level (see Englert et al., 1991; Graham & Harris, 1993; Harris & Graham, 1992) and have significant effects on the amount and quality of writing that students will produce. With careful attention from the teacher, students will realize that idea generation is a critical part of writing effectively. If they learn strategies for generating ideas and are rewarded systematically for idea generation, their idea generation is almost certain to improve, along with their writing.

Planning Differences

Beyond information-processing and attentional differences are important differences in what writers attempt to accomplish with their writing. Effective writers, for instance, will concentrate on *expressing meaning* as their primary goal (Gagne, 1985). This is not to say they ignore grammar, spelling, punctuation, and other related dimensions, but most are concerned about mastering mechanical aspects of writing because they see errors as interfering with their communicating meaning.

In contrast, concern with mechanics and avoiding errors tend to dominate the writing and editing processes of less-effective writers (Bates, 1984; Birnbaum, 1982; Graham & Harris, 1993). Whereas comments of better writers focus on large blocks of text (e.g., an entire essay), with the emphasis on meaning, less-capable writers concentrate their attention at the level of individual words and sentences. Revision for less-capable writers often is limited to checking for mechanical errors, such as spelling, and recopying a document to make it look neater (Graham & Harris, 1993).

Writers with less-developed skills also tend to write associatively; that is, they perform mostly as *knowledge tellers* (Bereiter & Scardamalia, 1987). Faced with a writing task, these writers often will write down what they know about a topic with little apparent monitoring of the structure or coherence of what they are writing.

Some forms of associative writing, however, can be very useful, especially when employed as an antidote to students' obsession with mechanics and fear of making mistakes. In **free writing**, for instance, students may be encouraged to get out quickly as many ideas as possible, without worrying about organization, correctness, or precision. Later, on the "voyage home," students can be helped to select, organize, and revise what they have written (Elbow, 1981).

Differences in Organization

Good writing is organized. Organization in writing has a variety of dimensions (e.g., well-formed sentences, paragraphs that express ideas clearly, arguments that flow logically) and differs by type of text being created (e.g., narratives have one type of form; expository texts, another). One dimension of organization that appears in all texts and that varies considerably across writers is a property of texts called "cohesion."

Cohesion refers to writers' and speakers' use of linguistic devices to link ideas (Halliday & Hasan, 1974; Mosenthal & Tierney, 1984; Norris & Bruning, 1988). These linguistic devices, called **cohesive ties**, come in many forms. Among the most common are referential ties, conjunctive ties, and lexical ties (for a more complete discussion, consult Halliday & Hasan, 1974, or Butterfield, 1986.) Referential ties may employ pronouns (e.g., Enrique fell asleep. *He* was tired.) and definite articles (e.g., Three writers were there: a hack, a poet, and a playwright. *The* hack made the most money.). Conjunctive ties, as one might imagine, employ conjunctions to connect ideas (e.g., Kesia ate the pizza *and* Quinn's french fries), to show causation (e.g., Felicia tossed and turned all night *because* she ate too much pizza), and to show the obverse of ideas (e.g., Hiroshi had heard about pineapple pizza *but* couldn't believe anyone actually would eat such a concoction). Lexical cohesion binds together ideas through word choice. A simple form of lexical cohesion employs the same word or phrase on more than one occasion (e.g., Royce found himself a *sunny* spot in the bleachers. He thought two hours of *sun* would be perfect.).

Good writers use both more cohesive ties and more varied ties. Consider the following sample of a child's short paragraph lacking these connections:

> Lynette and Marissa went to town. She saw a store with glasses and marbles in the window. She bought some from the woman. She was happy.

The reader of this paragraph has no idea whether Lynette or Marissa saw the store or which of the items was purchased. Also, beyond not knowing who made the purchase, the reader does not know who went away happy—the buyer or the seller.

As writers develop, however, they become more sensitive to the need for cohesion in texts and begin to make their writing more "considerate." For instance, more-experienced writers often use transition sentences between paragraphs (notice how the first sentence in this paragraph cleverly tied back to previous material) and occasionally preface paragraphs with sentences that tie the upcoming content back to things discussed on previous pages (e.g., "As you recall, . . ."). Experienced writers also use text signals (see Chapter 11) to alert readers to coming content (e.g., "As you will see in the next chapter, . . .") and insert summaries of information at reasonable intervals. Thus, two important goals related to cohesion are (1) helping students learn to use cohesive devices to guide readers' attention and ensure comprehension and (2) helping them learn to monitor their writing to see whether it "hangs together."

IMPROVING STUDENTS' WRITING

In the first two major sections of this chapter, we examined the Flower and Hayes model of the writing process and then reviewed a variety of factors that underlie individual differences in writers. In this section, we turn to applied research on writing, much of it the product of the last decade. As we mentioned previously, an increasing amount of cognitive research has examined ways to help young writers improve their skills. In this section, we review methods for developing writing ability that research has shown to be effective. The foundation for most of these methods is creating an atmosphere of collaborative problem solving and mutual support in which writing occurs. We begin there.

Creating a Context for Writing: The Literacy Community

The content and quality of writing varies tremendously, depending on the context in which it is embedded and how it is used. As we saw earlier, writing was neglected in our schools for many years. On those occasions when students were asked to do extended writing, the goal often was only to test their knowledge of specific content (e.g., "Describe three factors that shaped the search for a new world order in the years immediately following World War I"). Writing of this type, unfortunately, is poorly suited to students' acquiring new writing skills (Applebee, 1984).

First, when writing is used to test content knowledge, students often need only provide information a teacher or textbook previously has organized and presented. Thus, it emphasizes *knowledge telling,* simply repeating what is known. In contrast, *knowledge transforming* is a much richer cognitive activity, with writers creating new knowledge by combining what they know about the topic with their knowledge about discourse processes and goals (Bereiter & Scardamalia, 1987). Second, when writing is solely for assessment, prewriting activities typically are minimal. They often consist of little more than instructions about topic, length, and desired form of the writing. As we know from recent research (see Graham & Harris, 1993), such prewriting activities as brainstorming, goal setting, and planning can have a substantial impact on writing quality. Third, knowledge simply written down and not transformed is likely to remain isolated and detached. When content knowledge is tested, for instance, there typically is little opportunity for students to use their own ideas, to try out new thoughts on their classmates, or even to organize what they know about a particular subject area.

Consider, however, a different kind of context for writing. Here, the teacher conceives of writing *as a tool for learning,* rather than as a way of displaying what the student already has learned. In this setting, writing is motivated by a student's desire to communicate and is valued as an expression of what he or she wants to say. Social interactions are not only desirable in this context but also fundamental; students are members of a *literacy community* consisting of their peers and the teacher. Reading, writing, speaking, and listening are the main activities of this community.

Students in the Literacy Community.   Students are full-fledged members of the literacy community. Here, students discuss writing plans, write, read their own and others' writing, and reflect on their writing. The social interactions occurring in the literacy community can create a powerful context for students' learning to use writing effectively and pleasurably (Dyson & Freedman, 1991; Englert, et al., 1991; Freedman, 1992). Two important dimensions of these interactions are students (1) engaging in dialogue with one another and (2) using each other as editors.

With increased recognition of the social bases of cognition (see Chapter 9) has come increased recognition of the importance of the first dimension of social interaction—*dialogue*—to writing. Talking with peers about writing helps students consider different perspectives, more clearly formulate their ideas, and think about audiences for their writing. In peer groups, students can give and receive advice, ask and answer questions, and learn and teach (Cazden, 1988; Freedman, 1992). Such activities are highly consistent with assumptions of a social constructivist perspective that thought is the internalization of social interactions and that social exchanges in family, school, and culture are sources of cognitive growth.

The second dimension of social interaction increasingly used to support the teaching and learning of writing is *peer editing* (see Bissex, 1980; Dyson, 1983; Graves, 1983; Harris & Graham, 1992; Lamme & Childers, 1983). In its simplest form, students are paired with a writing partner. Each student "edits" the other's writing, giving feedback on what he or she likes about the writing and talking about ways the writing might be improved. Peer editing in a classroom need not be limited to pairs of students; larger groups of up to four or five students can work together effectively.

Peer editing may be varied in many ways. It often includes "editing" prewriting activities, such as plans for writing or oral versions of a story or expository text. It also may involve reading each other's paper aloud to one another, collaborating on revisions, trading papers and revising each other's work, and so on.

Peer editing has been used successfully with writers of all ages, ranging from primary level to college age. Research on peer editing has shown positive outcomes as diverse as enhanced quality of writing and improved student attitudes toward writing (Englert et al., 1991; Hilgers, 1986; Olson, Torrance, & Hildyard, 1985).

What makes peer tutoring successful? Our analysis of the technique suggests several reasons. One reason is that students are writing for a specific audience. Unlike traditional writing assignments, peer editing puts a very real premium on audience awareness. In Englert et al.'s words, peers "silently but effectively represent the needs of the audience and make the concept of audience visible" (1991, p. 340). In reading other students' drafts, students also begin to adopt the perspective of readers. They learn quite directly how writing communicates or fails to communicate meaning to another person.

A second reason is the immediate or near-immediate feedback students receive on their planning and writing. Whereas a teacher may need several days to get through 100 or more essays, students can readily share plans for writing with their partners, write brief segments of prose, trade with their partners, and react to their partners' materials within a class period or two. It also seems that students may accept the judgments of their peers more readily than those of adults.

A third reason for the success of peer editing is that the skills generalize to the planning, evaluation, and revision of one's own writing. Improved editing leads directly to establishing and using personal standards for writing, especially when "read aloud" techniques are stressed.

Our judgment is that peer editing can be used successfully in almost every writing program. Beyond the instructional emphasis we described above, the technique also has the advantage of freeing the teacher to concentrate on coaching and motivating students to acquire the specific skills they need. In many ways, the teacher who uses peer tutoring becomes a managing editor available to mediate disagreements and teach "as-needed" lessons to individual students or groups.

The Teacher in the Literacy Community.   Teachers play a vital leadership role in the literacy community. To run a literacy community, teachers need to orchestrate an environment in which all of the dimensions of literacy—speaking and listening, as well as writing and reading—occur productively. As we have seen above, some environments and teacher activities do little to support writing growth and even may be counterproductive. Others, however, can contribute greatly to students' development as writers and to their positive attitudes toward writing (Borkowski, 1992).

An initial challenge for teachers is finding stimulating writing tasks that will challenge students to be thoughtful and inventive as they plan, write, and revise. Often, these kinds of writing tasks are found in in-depth student projects, in which students work on a topic or theme over several days or weeks.

Another challenge for teachers is the need for flexibility in adopting new teaching roles that may be quite different from traditional ones. In the environment of the literacy community, the teacher is much more likely to function as a coach and facilitator than as an authority and information source. Instruction almost always is varied and often individualized, with teachers providing collaborative support to students as they move ahead in their writing. Often, this support includes teacher-student dialogue aimed at helping the student better define the writing task, think of alternative ways to express ideas, and make decisions about revision. Although generally underused as a technique for developing students' writing (Sperling, 1990), the teacher-student conference can be an extremely useful mechanism for stimulating productive dialogue between teachers and students.

In some teacher-student conferences, interactions are dominated by the teacher, with students seeking and receiving input from the teacher. In others, however, dialogue is much more like conversation than instruction, with active negotiations between teacher and writer aimed at developing ideas and strategies for writing. Overall, teacher-student conferences are occasions for a good deal of negotiation and meaning-making, wherein students gradually acquire the cultural knowledge about what it means to be a good writer (Sperling, 1990).

In teacher-student writing conferences, the emphasis should be on the quality of the students' writing, the process by which the students arrived at their product, and the relationship between writing processes and the quality of writing (Olson et al., 1985). During such conferences, which are held with individual students, the teacher poses questions about the quality of the writing, the meaning the student wants to convey, and the cognitive processes the student is using during writing. This interaction can help the teacher single out important aspects of the writing for discussion.

Teacher-student conferences also can provide time for students to write while talking about the process. Having the students write while the teacher observes and interacts can be an effective way to teach skills in a personalized manner. Consider, for example, the following exchange drawn from a tenth-grade composition class:

Teacher: I like how you described Fiver, but let me read the sentence about Hazel aloud. You listen critically.

Student: OK.

Teacher: "Hazel was leader material but he didn't know yet."

Student: It doesn't sound so good, does it.

Teacher: No, but I think you can do much better. Here [points at note pad], write another sentence and share your thinking as you do.

Student: OK. Let's see . . . "Hazel had" I mean a word that says he didn't know about . . . "undiscovered"?

Teacher: That'd work.

Student: "Hazel had undiscovered leadership."

Teacher: OK, but not just leadership.

Student: I see. It doesn't fit just . . . Mmmm. "Hazel had undiscovered leadership abilities."

Teacher: That's a good sentence!

Student: Yeah. You don't just have it. It's like a skill or something, so you have to say "abilities."

As you can see, the teacher was acting like an editor and gently nudging the student along as he constructed a clear sentence. The teacher also was careful to praise the student's efforts when positive change occurred. Modeling can be seen in an excerpt drawn from a conference the teacher had with another student.

Student: "Sir Holger fought the followers of the evil mage."

Teacher: That's a pretty good sentence. The meaning you want to share is very clear. I don't like the structure as well as I could, though. I prefer to avoid *of* the way you've used it. I like possessives instead. They save words. For example, "Sir Holger fought the evil mage's followers." It flows a little better.

Student: It does sound better that way.

Teacher: Some teachers might disagree, but I've always thought that if you can eliminate unnecessary words, you've helped your writing. Look here [points to an assigned reading]. I thought of this last night. Instead of "Bring me the swords that are sharpest," I'd say, "Bring me the sharpest swords."

Given both positive and negative examples of writing samples, students are better able to discriminate between them and begin to internalize standards for their own writing. "Internalizing standards," of course, is a shorthand way of describing writers' growing metalinguistic awareness about writing and their increasing ability to use that knowledge to regulate their writing activities.

IMPLICATIONS FOR TEACHING: ENCOURAGING THE WRITING PROCESS AND BUILDING WRITING SKILLS

Once neglected by both researchers and educators, writing now is recognized as a window to cognitive activity and important to cognitive growth. For researchers, studies of writing have afforded many additional insights into human cognitive processes and their development. Writing has been shown to be a multifaceted process with many important cognitive elements, including those of problem solving. Writers use their goals, sense of audience, and knowledge about discourse to transform content knowledge into new forms.

Educators' primary interest in writing has been as a tool for cognitive development. When students plan their writing, try to express themselves, and examine their own and other students' writing, they are engaging in constructive processes that research has shown lead to cognitive growth. The following implications are drawn both from the basic cognitive literature on writing and from the work of applied writing researchers, most especially that of Graves (1983), Calkins (1986), Graham and Harris (1993), and Englert et al. (1991).

1. *Have students write frequently.* More than thirty years ago, McQueen, Murray, and Evans (1963) performed an impressive study of the factors that led to proficient writing performance among entering college freshmen. Their findings pointed to one factor as the most important determinant of writing skill—how much the students had written in high school.

Because of the growing recognition of the positive cognitive and social effects of writing and the discussions that surround it, educators increasingly advocate that students write as part of all their classes. Recent curriculum reform movements in mathematics and science, for instance, propose extensive use of writing as an important learning tool (e.g., see the *Curriculum and Evaluation Standards for School Mathematics* [1989] of the National Council of Teachers of Mathematics). Many teachers still do not use writing extensively, however, possibly because frequent student writing requires both an extensive commitment of time and effort and a change of their teaching style. Few school activities, however, are more productive than having students write often and receive thoughtful feedback on their writing.

2. *Create an informal, supportive climate for writing.* Traditional writing instruction, particularly at the secondary level and above, has tended to follow a teacher-centered course in which student writing is a response to teacher assignments and instructions. Until recently, most writing instruction also had been based on the view that writing is a solitary activity, with writing evaluated primarily by grades and comments from the teacher (see Sperling, 1990).

Newer conceptions of writing, however, are based on the social constructivist assumption that learning to write, like all language acquisition tasks, is a social, not a solitary, activity. If this assumption is correct, then the more productive environments for learning to write involve groups of student writers. They also are settings in which students generate a great deal of written language; in which social interactions are organized around students thinking about writing, writing, and revising;

and where students receive positive confirmation for their efforts at writing. Creating these kinds of environments is within the reach of every teacher and every school, although to establish them teachers may need to move away from some familiar roles (e.g., lecturer, presenter of information) and toward others (e.g., coach, conversation partner, facilitator of discussions).

3. *Emphasize prewriting strategies.* Of all the strategies for helping writers develop their skills, few are as important as those that take place prior to writing (Graham & Harris, 1993). Determining goals for writing, for instance, motivates writing, gives students a basis for making decisions about content and writing strategy, and allows them to determine whether they have been successful. Generating ideas for writing through brainstorming or other techniques likewise has proven value in improving the quality of writing. Thinking about audiences also shapes what writers do and helps them improve it. As Bereiter and Scardamalia (1987) recognized, the time spent in advance of writing is not only evidence of writers' levels of sophistication but also critically important to writing quality.

4. *Stress knowledge transforming, not knowledge telling.* One of the most useful distinctions made by writing researchers is Bereiter and Scardamalia's (1987) distinction between knowledge telling and knowledge transforming. As we have seen, planning and goal setting are minimal in *knowledge telling;* writers generate ideas on a topic and basically write them down until their supply is exhausted. *Knowledge transforming,* however, is a generative, problem-solving process that involves active reworking of thoughts. In knowledge transforming, thinking is affected by the composing activity itself. Instead of writing being a process of individuals telling what they know, writing transforms and develops writers' knowledge. Viewed in this way, writing clearly is closely linked with higher-level cognitive processes: elaboration of ideas, problem solving, and reflective thought.

Students of all ages can learn to become knowledge-transforming writers. Several teaching approaches have been shown to be effective in helping students use writing to transform knowledge. One approach is to directly teach strategies for planning, writing, and revision (Englert et al., 1991; Graham & Harris, 1993). Bereiter and Scardamalia (1987), for instance, noted that knowledge-transforming writers spend considerably more time planning before they begin writing than do knowledge-telling writers. During this time, they are engaged in such activities as making notes, thinking about their audience, and mentally "trying out" various discourse structures. Even very young writers can be helped to acquire variations on these skills.

Interacting with peers is an equally important second teaching approach to the development of knowledge-transforming writers. When they talk with others about their writing, students learn to envision the content, form, and creation of a text and to think about its audience. This external dialogue of the novice gradually becomes the metalinguistic awareness and self-regulation of the mature writer.

Teachers are a final important key in the third teaching approach to the development of knowledge-transforming writers. Through their assignments and discussion, teachers can provide models for high-quality writing. Providing students with excellent models of specific kinds of writing does have beneficial effects on students' writing abilities (Phillips, 1986; Smagorinsky & Smith, 1992). An obvious way of learning to write short stories is by reading and discussing short stories. Similarly, an important part of students' learning to write essays may be asking them to read essays and to use good ones as models for their own.

Teachers also provide the vital support that bridges the gap between the novice writer's ability and the level of performance required to solve the problems of writing. Teachers' scaffolded instruction helps students think of strategies for attaining their goals and supports the development of fragile new skills and abilities (Englert et al., 1991).

5.   *Encourage students to develop productive revision strategies.* One of the surest signs of novice writers is their belief that once something has been written, no change can or should be made. When these writers do make revisions, they tend to be "cosmetic," focused on such things as neatness and spelling. More expert writers, however, have learned that revision greatly improves their writing; they make editing and revising an integral part of the writing process.

Several avenues lead to improved revision strategies. First, revision strategies can be taught directly and, when learned, will produce positive effects on writing quality. Graham and Harris (1993), for instance, developed a seven-step approach to teaching strategies that results not only in students' increased use of a given strategy but also in students' understanding of how and when to apply the strategy.

Second, dialogue with peers also can lead to improved revision strategies. As Englert et al. (1991), have pointed out, peers represent an important audience for student writing and make the concept of *audience* real. Talk with peers can provide the foundation for the internal dialogue of the accomplished writer.

A third avenue to improve revision strategies is to have students set aside things they have written for a period of time before rereading and revising. Imposing a delay between the time when something is written and when it is reread allows some forgetting to occur and facilitates the possibility of fully processing the material as if it has been written by someone else (see Dellarosa & Bourne, 1985, for a discussion of this phenomenon).

A fourth avenue is to have students read their writing aloud to a peer, parent, or sibling. Tell the students to trust their ears and to revise sentences that sound awkward. Our experience has been that students often overlook mistakes when reading silently to themselves (adding missing words, deleting unneeded words, fixing tenses, etc.) but that reading their writing aloud often makes errors obvious. Children quickly find that some writing "sounds wrong" and that good writing is pleasing to the ear. Reading aloud to others also provides the students with immediate feedback on the quality of their writing. Merely reading aloud is not enough, of course; the students need to rewrite the awkward places until they "sound right."

6.   *Use computer-based technology as needed.* Although student access to computer technology in our schools is still by no means universal, more and more student writing is being done on the computer. As one might expect, a growing number of studies are focused on the value of writing on a computer and how the

computer affects students' writing quality and motivation to write (e.g., Beesley, 1986; Klein, 1988).

Some writing on the computer plainly can be impressive. Consider the following essay written by a first-grader near the end of the school year:

The Little Bear Goes Camping

Once there was a little bear. She had a mom and a dad. It was summer and little bear had nothing to do. Then her mother and father desited maybe to let little bear go camping with her big cousen. So they asked little bear if she wanted to. So they asked little bear and she said yes she thoaght that was a great idia. So little bear got all packed. Then her cousen came. So they went to the woods and started to camp. They had a wunderful time. They went fishing and they did a hole bunch of stoff When they got home they started to talk all about what they did when they went camping. They had a wunderful time. Little bear broaght back flowers for her faimly pretty ones i mean it!!!! THE! END!!!

There really is no doubt in our minds that a story of the quality and length of "The Little Bear Goes Camping" would have been less likely for this first-grader to write with paper and pencil, rather than with a computer.

Although a great deal of research still needs to be done in evaluating the utility of computers as writing tools with beginning writers, preliminary evidence suggests that the early acquisition of writing skills is enhanced when children work with computers, especially by facilitating the acquisition of editing and revising skills (Daiute, 1986; Hawisher, 1987; Sharples, 1985). The ease with which segments of text can be rearranged and saved greatly reduces the logistic efforts involved in editing and revising materials. When students can easily rearrange a text, add words, delete words, and insert whole sentences into an essay, much less effort is required than when the entire product must be rewritten by hand or retyped. Whereas writers once had to devote most of their energies to recopying their work, they now can focus their efforts on the quality of their writing (Daiute, 1986).

Computers, however, are not a miracle cure for problems in writing instruction. Students still need to write frequently and to get good feedback on their writing. Also, using a computer can place a number of limitations on students' flexibility. For instance, working on a computer can interfere with the social interactions with peers and teachers that are critical to cognitive development. Most computers today also do not easily allow incorporation of visual materials (e.g., artwork, sketches) into the writing. For young children, especially, this limits the important activity of linking verbal and imaginal realms of cognition. Also, because student access to computers in U.S. schools remains very uneven, writing instruction that relies heavily on computers will not reach many children.

7.   *Keep grammar and language mechanics in perspective.* Must a writer know that a *gerund* is not a small, white-and-brown furry animal related to hamsters in order to compose a good sentence? Is the skill of diagramming a sentence into its constituent parts important for the budding young novelist? Research designed to shed light on such questions has been done since at least 1904 (De Boer, 1959), with consistent results. Apparently, no relationship exists between knowledge of grammar

and the ability to write. What? That's right; research dating back to 1904 shows no relationship between grammatical knowledge on the one hand and an ability to write on the other (see Olson et al., 1985). The situation seems analogous to that of carpentry and structural engineering. One does not need to know the formal discipline of structural engineering in order to frame in a window.

Also, no evidence has been found that teaching students grammar improves their ability to write (De Boer, 1959; Frogner, 1939; Kraus, 1957). In fact, the literature abounds with one failure after another of teaching grammar as a means of improving writing (see Olson et al., 1985). As long ago as 1939, Frogner contrasted teaching students grammar with teaching them a "thought" method (an approach based on analyzing meaning) as a means of improving their writing. Whereas teaching grammar made no difference, an emphasis on meaning brought about a very clear change in writers' abilities. Nonetheless, many teachers continue to emphasize grammar at the expense of meaning, perhaps unaware of the overwhelming evidence showing that writers' knowledge of grammar is not critical to writing skill.

We are not suggesting that students should not be helped to acquire the morphological and syntactical skills that are fundamental to writing (punctuation, capitalization, and spelling) or that a shared vocabulary about grammar is not very helpful (e.g., student and teacher both understanding what adjectives and adverbs are). We believe, instead, that the process of encouraging and developing writing is a matter of "first things first." Students need to understand that the fundamental purpose of writing is the making of meaning—stating ideas, expressing feelings, and persuading others. Communication of meaning, not acquisition of grammar facts, is the proper focus of writing instruction.

Acquiring basic skills in using language nonetheless is very important. Writing needs to communicate effectively. Poor writing distracts, confuses, and frustrates readers. Readers, unfortunately, also judge the competence of writers on the basis of what they read; misspelled words, misplaced commas, and poor sentence structure often are judged harshly. For teachers of writing, the challenge is to direct students' attention to the mechanics of language and to develop students' skills within the framework of the meaning students are trying to convey.

A Final Note: Creative Writing

Thus far, we have emphasized using writing for expressing ideas and developing thinking and have avoided the issue of "creative" writing. The literature on creative writing is large, and of interest to many (see Carey & Flower, 1989, for a brief overview). Not much of this literature has dealt with the cognitive processes that might be involved in creative writing, and little has examined instructional procedures designed to make writing more creative. Still, some important issues are worth reviewing.

Creativity and the Evaluation of Writing.   One debate about creative writing has focused on evaluation. Some have argued that creativity in writing and evaluation of writing are antithetical; that is, writers cannot be creative if they are constrained by the possible evaluation of their work. The arguments supporting this position are based on reasoning that writers will not be willing to take risks and to explore new paths if they are worrying about evaluation. From this perspective, the way to foster creative writing is to withhold all forms of evaluation from writing and to form a safe environment in which writers feel free to express themselves.

The argument that creative writing requires an evaluation-free, judgment-free environment has led to the belief among some teachers that "creative writing" should not be graded. Many teachers gave up correcting spelling, punctuation, and grammar because they believed that correcting these elements of students' writing surely would limit creativity. A careful analysis of this approach to teaching writing, however, suggests that it not only fails to enhance creativity but also keeps students from improving the mechanics of their writing (Applebee et al., 1986b).

Encouraging creativity and evaluating writing need not be mutually exclusive. Much of the publishing enterprise, for instance, requires the expression of creativity. However, no editor will even bother to read a manuscript unless it is mechanically correct. To write creatively in the world of editors and publishers, one first must be able to write correctly. Analogous to expressing creativity in playing a musical instrument, a certain level of technical competence is necessary for creative writing.

Although teacher evaluation has not been shown to restrict creativity, care should be taken to avoid quashing new ideas or attempts to be creative. Your feedback should make it very clear that you are not trying to discourage students from being creative, but rather are helping them express themselves more effectively. We advise that teachers always provide students with feedback designed to improve the quality of their writing without being needlessly critical. Further, teachers' expectations are important. Students are far more likely to strive for creativity if teachers expect it.

Carey and Flower (1989) point out that creative writing cannot occur without a great deal of knowledge about both the topic and the processes of writing. In terms of enhancing creative writing, then, both building students' knowledge about the writing topic and teaching them about writing will increase their chances of writing creatively. Our argument is highly similar to what writers and editors long have said to beginning writers: "To write well, one must write about what one knows."

A classic example of a highly successful writer who followed the dictum of writing about things he knew is James Michener. Michener, author of *Caravans, Tales of the South Pacific, Centennial, Space,* and many other novels, spent years of his life acquiring the knowledge he needed to write. Prior to beginning each of his later volumes (*Tales of the South Pacific* was based on his wartime experiences), Michener spent months and even years learning about the areas and cultures he wanted to write about. In fact, as he became more successful, he hired an entire staff of researchers to travel with him and help him learn enough to write knowledgeably. Although one can quibble over how creative Michener has been, an examination of his habits and the results of research on other writers (e.g., Root, 1985) sheds light on a seldom-mentioned issue related to creativity: Gathering information, an important part of planning for writing, is an integral part of creative writing.

SUMMARY

Writing is the process of expressing ideas in the printed symbols of a language. Long neglected in the United States by both researchers and educators, writing now occupies an important place both in cognitive research and in educational programming. One useful model describing how thought and language are linked in writing is that developed by Linda Flower and John Hayes. This model describes writing as a problem-solving activity involving three interacting components: task environment, long-term memory, and working memory. The major cognitive processes—planning, translating, and reviewing—occur in working memory.

More-effective and less-effective writers show a number of differences. Among these are the ability to manipulate information, to generate ideas, to plan, and to organize. Creating a supportive environment for writing is a key feature of effective writing instruction. Procedures such as peer editing and teacher-student conferences can be used to create a literacy community that will enhance the quality of students' writing and their enjoyment of writing activities. Teaching grammar directly seems to have little effect on writing quality; a better approach appears to be to provide feedback on writing mechanics as students engage in meaningful writing activities. Creativity in students' writing also can be facilitated by a supportive, nonthreatening environment that helps students increase their knowledge about writing topics and gain knowledge about the processes of writing.

SUGGESTED READINGS

Bereiter, C., & Scardamalia, M. (1987). *The psychology of written composition.* Hillsdale, NJ: Lawrence Erlbaum.

This work by Carl Bereiter and Marlene Scardamalia significantly expanded our understanding of the writing process. Their research has concentrated on the distinction between knowledge telling and knowledge transforming in writing. The results of that research, summarized in this book, helped us understand the nature of writing and how it developed. It also pointed the way to the strategies educators now are beginning to use widely for developing writing ability.

Harris, K. R., & Graham, S. (1992). *Helping young writers master the craft: Strategy instruction and self-regulation in the writing process.* Cambridge, MA: Brookline.

Karen Harris and Steve Graham have conducted research for more than a decade on helping students with learning difficulties acquire writing strategies and learn to use them at the appropriate times. This volume highlights their most important findings and provides a structure educators can use in teaching students of all ability levels to improve their writing.

Cognitive Approaches to Mathematics

Teaching mathematics is a complex task involving many factors. Students need not only to acquire procedural skills for solving mathematics problems but also, more important, to understand the concepts and principles to which the skills relate. For too long, mathematics has been viewed and taught in the United States as a set of isolated skills to be learned mostly through repetitive practice. An unfortunate result is that many students today lack understanding of what they are doing; they can do math problems but have little comprehension of their meaning. Students often are unable to use knowledge about mathematics in their lives or even to use their skills on mathematics problems that are even slightly different from those they have studied.

The beliefs that many students in the United States hold about mathematics also are often negative and unproductive. Many think the mathematics learned in school has little or nothing to do with the real world. One particularly damaging and widely held belief of many American students is that skill in mathematics is innate (see

Chapter 7) and that ordinary students cannot be expected to understand what they are being asked to learn.

American students perform quite poorly on international comparisons, and dropout rates are high. Although approximately four-fifths of students in the United States will take a first algebra course, fewer than half will take Algebra 2; and fewer than one-tenth of all students enroll in calculus, an area of mathematics that is a key to entry into many occupational fields. Further, the dropout rates are disproportional by gender and ethnicity; significantly fewer girls than boys go on to advanced classes, and significantly fewer African American and Hispanic students than white students take classes beyond beginning algebra. Thus, although the data in the past ten years show some trends toward improvement, obvious difficulties still remain in the area of mathematics instruction and learning (Council of Chief State School Officers, 1993).

Like many other subject areas, however, mathematics is being "reinvented" within a cognitive and social constructivist framework. National statements of goals, such as the *Curriculum and Evaluation Standards for School Mathematics* (NCTM, 1989), *Everybody Counts* (National Research Council, 1989), and *Reshaping School Mathematics* (National Research Council, 1990), now offer a dramatically different perspective on the learning and teaching of mathematics. These goals stress helping students make sense of mathematics. The overall aim could be called "quantitative literacy," in which students are able to interpret data and use their mathematics in their everyday lives. Mathematics is envisioned as a subject of ideas and mental processes, not one of learning facts. In this new, cognitive conception of mathematics learning, students are encouraged to formulate conjectures, explore patterns, and seek solutions, not to practice repetitive exercises and memorize procedures and formulas (Carpenter et al., 1994; Fennema, Franke, Carpenter, & Carey, 1993).

The knowledge base supporting this new conception of mathematics is expanding constantly, as both researchers and practitioners use the theory and methods of cognitive science to study mathematics learning and teaching (e.g., see Hiebert & Carpenter, 1992; Jensen, 1993; Owens, 1993; Romberg, 1992; Schoenfeld, 1992; Wilson, 1993). The growing body of cognitive research in mathematics, though strongly domain specific, is built on the basic model of cognition we outlined in the early chapters of this book.

As we described in Chapter 8, a major characteristic of problem solving in any domain is acquiring specialized and organized knowledge. Mathematics is no different. Students must acquire a body of conceptual and procedural knowledge in mathematics to support an array of problem-solving strategies (Owens & Super, 1993). They need to acquire positive beliefs and attitudes about themselves and their mathematical knowledge and the self-regulatory skills to use their knowledge in flexible and adaptive ways (Schoenfeld, 1992). For students' mathematical problem solving to be useful, they need to generalize their conceptual knowledge and procedural skills across school subjects and beyond the school setting.

This expectation requires a conceptual understanding of mathematics that has sufficient flexibility to permit students to analyze "informal" problems that occur outside the boundaries of the conventional tasks presented in mathematics curricula.

Along with their mathematical understandings, students must acquire a set of procedures for the operations of mathematics. Evidence from studies of simple addition and subtraction (e.g., Carpenter, 1985; Carpenter et al., 1994; Fuson, 1992; Fuson & Fuson, 1992; Riley, Greeno, & Heller, 1983) suggests, however, that even these apparently simple procedures are much more complex and rooted in conceptual understandings than most teachers and other adults believe.

As you have seen throughout this text, cognitive research on instruction emphasizes the value of comprehension-based approaches to learning. In this chapter, we pursue in considerable depth the learning and teaching of two important and illustrative components of the mathematics curriculum: addition and subtraction, and algebra. Each topic is examined in some detail to demonstrate its complexity, as well as the usefulness of cognitive approaches for understanding the mathematical processes students acquire. In contrast with the judgments of many that arithmetic is a rote skill and algebra more "conceptual," we portray both addition/subtraction and algebra as problem-solving processes.

The thrust of much cognitive research in both areas has been to search for clearer understanding of the mental processes students use to solve mathematics problems. For instance, Riley et al. (1983) and Kintsch and Greeno (1985) proposed that representing mathematics problem solving as schemata provides a vehicle for such an understanding. A *set schema,* for instance, represents the idea of parts and a whole. To illustrate, the concept of *addition* can be understood as the presentation of two or more sets (parts) mathematically combined to form a whole (the superset). Besides a set schema, addition also requires a *change schema* to show how parts may be combined. Much of arithmetic, and potentially much of other mathematics, can be described by using these two schemata. In general, we argue that mathematics operations are not at all mechanical, but rather require the acquisition of networks of mental representations. Understanding grows as networks become larger and more organized. The class of operations we collectively call "mathematics" is built on the understanding these networks represent.

For mathematics knowledge to be functional, networks of schemata must be linked with a set of procedures. These procedures, more commonly called "algorithms," guide the actions necessary to solve problems. **Algorithms** are procedures (rules) that apply to a particular type of problem and that, if followed correctly, guarantee the correct answer. In arithmetic, for example, children use a number of counting algorithms, whereas in algebra, students learn various algorithmic routines connected with solving algebra problems. Algorithms are important to mathematics, but sometimes teachers and students have confused algorithmic skills with problem solving itself. Carrying out an algorithm is not problem solving, but a student's creating an algorithm and applying it to a set of problems is (Wilson, Fernandez, & Hadaway, 1993).

For algorithms to be flexible enough for use in problem solving, they need to be initiated and guided by conceptual knowledge. If they are run off in a rote manner based on surface features of problems, the results can be extremely poor (e.g., see Reed, 1984). Allowing students to create their own algorithms helps them link conceptual knowledge with the procedures they select. Also, as they try out various algorithms, the consequences (success or failure) of using certain procedures often will result in changes in the conceptual framework (Schoenfeld, 1992). The interactive feedback between conceptual and procedural knowledge leads to increasingly sophisticated mathematics proficiency.

HEURISTIC KNOWLEDGE

A key problem for mathematics students (and hence for their teachers) is recognizing whether particular conceptual or procedural information is appropriate to a particular problem. Mathematicians such as Polya have argued for the need to teach more general heuristic (strategic) knowledge so that flexibility in problem solution is enhanced. **Heuristics** are general problem-solving strategies learners use to match conceptual and procedural knowledge with the solution of a specific problem. Polya's classic 1973 book *How to Solve It* consisted largely of general heuristic suggestions applicable to many mathematical problems. Polya suggested, for example, that to get started on a problem, one should ask: What is the unknown? What is the condition?

Recent research (e.g., see Schoenfeld, 1992) has shown that heuristics such as Polya suggested are less likely to be effective than strategic knowledge that is carefully delineated and linked with specific problem types and specific procedures. Schoenfeld (1985, 1987) has asserted that heuristics tend to be labels for categories of related strategies and thus do not lead to specific procedures. Further, he has argued that solving many mathematics algorithms is so complex and consists of so many phases that a general strategy is likely to be ineffective. General strategies cannot substitute for the specific information necessary for mathematics problem solving. Only after considerable mathematical conceptual and procedural knowledge is acquired do heuristics about mathematical problem solving appear to generate useful strategies. Also, metacognitive training involving guided practice, self-monitoring, and self-regulation is needed to help students develop problem-solving strategies and learn to apply them at the right times (Schoenfeld, 1992).

KNOWLEDGE ACQUISITION

As students acquire a larger conceptual and procedural base in mathematics and a greater linkage among these conceptual and procedural elements, they become more efficient and flexible problem solvers (Carpenter, 1986; Carpenter et al., 1994; Hiebert & Carpenter, 1992; Schoenfeld, 1992). Expert mathematicians use the *semantic* (meaning) aspects of a problem to encode its relevant features. Many students in mathematics, however, appear to lack semantic information and therefore often rely on problem form—the *syntactic,* or surface, features of problem presentations (see Reed, 1984). Schoenfeld (1985) observed that many textbooks in arithmetic have taught a kind of "keyword" problem-solving method based heavily on syntactic structure. If this continues to be the case, children may learn a set of rote operations based on the keywords without necessarily understanding the semantic structure of the problem and being able to specify the relationships among the variables (Carpenter et al., 1994; Fennema et al., 1993; Kieran, 1992). Consider the following arithmetic word problem:

> Bill has six marbles and gives two to Joe. How many marbles does Bill have left?

If a student is reacting only to "keywords," he or she would identify the two numbers in the problem and a keyword—in this case, *left*—that elicits the schemata for "subtraction." Focusing on keywords will give the correct response for this problem. Schoenfeld (1985) observed that, in one major textbook series, the "keyword method" gave the "right" answer for virtually all problems (97 percent).

Real-life mathematical problems seldom are so neatly packaged, however. Any teaching strategy permitting students to solve a problem without requiring them to form a meaningful (semantic) representation of the problem statement seems unlikely to help students develop flexible and complex problem-solving strategies. Students need to extend the conceptual web of their mathematics knowledge by linking it with new, meaningful information. Only if this information is meaningful will students develop algorithms appropriate to a wide variety of mathematical tasks.

In the past fifteen years, empirical research in mathematics carried out from an information-processing perspective has burgeoned. The structure of mathematics provides a clear base from which to examine the development of problem solving in elementary and secondary school students. We examine this body of research by focusing on problem solving first in arithmetic and then in algebra.

ARITHMETIC PROBLEM SOLVING

At one time, mathematics educators distinguished between *computational* aspects of mathematics, which in most cases focused on learning rules such as the algorithms for addition and division, and *conceptual* aspects of mathematics, which involved problem solving and understanding. The general assumption was that basic skills were the foundation on which conceptual understandings are built. One outcome of this assumption was that beginning mathematics instruction traditionally has been aimed at mastery of arithmetic facts and computational procedures. Only after these "basics" were acquired and as students progressed through the grades could the emphasis gradually shift to the conceptual content and the methods of inquiry of mathematics. With the basic skills mastered, students were ready to learn and understand the content of such subjects as algebra, probability, and calculus.

This traditional approach of "skills first, concepts later" persists in many of our elementary schools. Arithmetic continues to be taught in many classrooms as a "drill-and-practice" activity in which arithmetic facts and computations are discrete items to be practiced and learned. As a consequence, competence in arithmetic often is weighted toward rapid, accurate performance. This view has a long history in American education. We vividly recall, for instance, "arithmetic races" from our own elementary school experiences in which expertise was demonstrated by racing to the chalkboard and solving problems (e.g., summing several three-digit numbers) before an opponent could do the same. Even today, accurate and rapid access to basic arithmetic "facts" is admired.

More and more, however, researchers and educators are arguing that the fundamental nature of all mathematics is conceptual, not procedural (Baroody & Standifer, 1993; Carpenter et al., 1994; Hiebert & Carpenter, 1992; Schoenfeld, 1992). A wealth of recent theory-driven research with young children has shown that children's knowledge about addition and subtraction, far from being algorithmic, is a succession of increasingly more complex, abstract, and efficient conceptual structures that children invent (e.g., Fuson, 1992; Fuson & Fuson, 1992). Although the computational operations for addition and subtraction are habitual for most adults and superficially seem to represent what arithmetic "is," our near-automatic performance obscures their basic problem-solving nature. The addition and subtraction algorithms that most adults employ with such ease and competence were once, for all of us, "problems" in the sense of our definition of problem solving in Chapter 8.

Whether adult or child, we need a set of highly flexible conceptual rules in order to employ algorithms effectively in the varied situations that require mathematical competence. If this conceptual understanding is rigid or lacking, algorithms will be applied in a rote manner and transfer of learning will be poor. Consequently, we take the perspective that all mathematics, perhaps most especially the early stages of children's acquiring knowledge about arithmetic, should be viewed as a problem-solving activity.

What "Bugs" Can Teach Us

The study of errors that children make in addition and subtraction has contributed greatly to our understanding of the nature of arithmetic problem solving. In their early examination of the subtraction errors of a large number of children, for instance, J. S. Brown and Burton (1978) discovered that a sizable number were using consistently one or more incorrect versions of the general subtraction algorithm. Many of the incorrect algorithms gave correct solutions part of the time but in other applications gave incorrect ones. For example, some children consistently applied a subtraction algorithm that led them to subtract smaller numbers from larger ones regardless of which number was on top:

8	23	47	52
− 3	− 16	− 35	− 17
5	13	12	45

Note that this incorrect, or "buggy," algorithm (J. S. Brown & Burton, 1978, described it and others as "bugs") does give the correct answer in the first and third problems; in fact, in those problems the child's subtraction algorithm seems correct. Yet, the algorithm used throughout these four problems—"Take the smaller number from the larger in each column"—yields the wrong answer in the second and fourth problems.

A teacher, seeing all of the problems in sequence, might well dismiss the mistake in the second problem as "carelessness" and the one in the fourth as a "difficulty with 'borrowing,'" not recognizing that the child is using the same defective subtraction algorithm for all of the problems. Failure to diagnose a consistent error like this may well prevent the teacher from isolating conceptual difficulties the child is having.

By analyzing the performance of thousands of schoolchildren, J. S. Brown and Burton (1978; Burton, 1981) identified and classified more than 300 different subtraction bugs. This impressive array of bugs in subtraction alone led to a closer examination of the processes children use in both addition and subtraction. A first step in this examination has been to classify the different types of addition and subtraction problems so that meaningful analyses of algorithm errors could be pursued.

Problem Typologies

Finding the best way of organizing the many kinds of addition and substraction situations that exist in the real world has been the subject of much research (Fuson, 1992). One organization possibility is to treat addition and subtraction problems as open "sentences." By varying the unknown, six addition and six subtraction "sentences" (e.g., $a + b = ?; a - ? = c$) can be created (Carpenter & Moser, 1983). These deceptively simple tasks, in fact, do provide the content for much of early elementary school arithmetic. For elementary school students, the numbers used in these sentences yield whole-number solutions drawn from the basic arithmetic facts. These sentence types are not of equal difficulty to early elementary school children, however. In general, subtraction sentences are more difficult than addition sentences (but see Fuson & Fuson, 1992). Sentences of the form $a + b = ?$ or $a - b = ?$ are easier than sentences of the form $a + ? = c$ or $a - ? = c$, and sentences with the operation to the right of the equal sign (e.g., $c = ? - b$) are more difficult than parallel problems with the operation to the left of the equal sign. Exactly why differences like these exist has not been determined with certainty; one plausible hypothesis is that teachers and textbooks present problems in one form much more frequently than in the others. This means that students get much more practice with $a + b = ?$ structures than those with operations on the right of the equal sign. Another possibility is that some structures map better than others on the addition and subtraction strategies that children are constructing (Fuson, 1992).

Drawing on earlier work by Carpenter and Moser (1982), Riley et al. (1983), and Fuson (1992), Baroody and Standifer (1993) have classified addition and subtraction into five basic situations: change-add-to, change-take-from, part-part-whole, equalize, and compare. Both change-add-to and change-take-from involve beginning with a single collection and changing it by adding to or removing something from it. This results in a larger or smaller collection. For instance:

CHANGE-ADD-TO: Heather had six apples. Chris gave her five more apples. How many apples does Heather have altogether?

CHANGE-TAKE-FROM: Chris has five apples. He gave away two apples. How many apples does he now have?

Part-part-whole, equalize, and compare all begin with two quantities, which are either added or subtracted to find the whole of one of the parts. Two numbers are operated on to produce a unique third number. For example:

PART-PART-WHOLE: Heather had six red apples and five green apples. How many apples does she have?

EQUALIZE: Heather has six apples. Chris has three apples. How many more apples does Chris have to buy to have as many as Heather?

COMPARE: Heather has twelve apples. Chris has five apples. How many more apples does Heather have than Chris?

Each of these problem types also can be presented in different ways; for instance, the compare problem above has an unknown *difference* but also could be stated as having an unknown second part (e.g., Heather has twelve apples. She has seven more than Chris. How many apples does Chris have?) or unknown first part (e.g., Heather has some apples. She has seven more than Chris, who has five. How many apples does Heather have?).

Because primary-grade children use counting as a primary means of adding and subtracting, determining how children solve these problems and their various forms requires an examination of counting strategies. Most children come to kindergarten with some counting skills, and many can count sets up to ten objects (Van de Walle & Watkins, 1993) because four-year-olds often are taught by parents, older siblings, or others to count to ten. In the beginning, however, children may have learned only a sequence of words (Fuson, 1992) and do not yet understand the critical idea of a one-to-one correspondence between a collection of objects and a particular number. Soon, however, they begin to integrate counting to cardinal meanings of number words (e.g., that the word *three* corresponds to three things) and can use counting strategies for solving problems.

Examination of protocols of young children solving addition problems such as those outlined above reveals three levels of counting strategies (see Carpenter & Moser, 1982) for solving problems. A description of these situations follows.

Counting All with Model

Carpenter and Moser (1982) indicate that in carrying out the simplest addition strategy, children use physical objects or their fingers to represent each number or set to be combined, after which the combination of the two sets is counted. Thus, to add 4 and 7, a child represents each addend (set to be added) with a model of blocks or other objects (4 and 7, respectively) and then counts the combination of the two (in this case, 1,2,3,4 [pause], 5,6,7,8,9,10,11).

Counting on from First

As children gain experience with numbers, their strategies change. In this somewhat more efficient addition strategy, the child recognizes that it is not necessary always to begin from 1, but rather counts with the first addend and then counts forward the extent of the second addend. Thus, in our example, the child counts: 4 (pause), 5,6,7,8,9,10,11.

Counting on from Larger

Later, an even more efficient strategy appears: The child begins with the larger addend. Hence, in the example 4 + 7, the child counts: 7 (pause), 8,9,10,11. This strategy often is used when children are asked to add numbers greater than 10, numbers difficult to represent with their fingers.

During their first four years in school, children invent a series of increasingly abbreviated and abstract strategies to solve both addition and subtraction problems (Carpenter & Moser, 1984; Fuson, 1992; Fuson & Fuson, 1992). Instruction can help students learn specific strategies in the developmental sequence. Fuson and Fuson (1992), for instance, examined students' acquisition and use of *counting on* and *counting up* strategies in a long-term project aimed at giving first- and second-graders opportunities to solve a wide range of addition and subtraction word problems. Children were taught to use a *counting up* strategy for subtraction. This strategy involves beginning with the first addend and then keeping track of the *number of words* said after the first addend word. For instance, to solve 10 – 7, a child would say "7 (pause), 8,9,10" while keeping track of the number of words after the pause. Fuson and Fuson showed that children learned to both count on and count up very accurately. Moreover, they were as accurate and fast at counting up for subtraction as they were at counting on for addition. An important benefit of using counting up for subtraction, Fuson and Fuson argued, is that counting up uses ordinary forward counting and avoids the much more difficult backward counting that is part of the usual "take away" meaning of subtraction. Thus, children acquired a reliable method for subtracting, an important developmental achievement in becoming competent in solving such problems. Perhaps even more important, however, was that children in their study acquired a broader conceptual understanding of different meanings of subtraction and the minus sign.

As Fuson and Fuson point out, counting on and counting up do eventually drop out, and children move on to other strategies. The majority of first-graders use some form of counting strategy. In second grade, about one-third of such responses appear to be based on number facts, and by the third grade, almost two-thirds of the responses are based on number facts (Carpenter & Moser, 1983). Fuson and Fuson observed, however, that many children continued using these strategies for a long time because these strategies yield reliable results. Counting methods do not appear to be crutches that interfere with more complex problem solving. In Fuson and Fuson's study, children were observed to use them productively in addition and subtraction as complex as four-digit problems with regrouping.

An early study by Lankford (1972) suggests that more than one-third of seventh-graders still may be using counting strategies, rather than stored arithmetic facts, in solving addition and subtraction problems. Careful observation of adult addition and subtraction behavior also suggests that counting strategies are not limited to children! Furthermore, all number combinations are not learned equally quickly. For example, in addition, doubles (e.g., 6 + 6, 9 + 9) and numbers that sum to 10 are learned as addition facts earlier than other combinations.

In sum, the seemingly simple behaviors of single-digit addition and subtraction mask their true complexity; we can easily imagine the extent of the conceptual knowledge and associated algorithms needed to add and subtract two-, three-, and four-digit numbers. Although most children do acquire the necessary algorithms for solving these more complex problems, the discussion thus far provides persuasive evidence that children will need a great deal of both conceptual and procedural knowledge to use their problem-solving skills flexibly. What specifically do children need to know in order to solve addition and subtraction problems?

Arithmetic Knowledge

Riley et al. (1983) analyzed arithmetic tasks, such as those we have described, and developed a theoretical model of the solution process. Their model takes the form of a computer simulation that solves problems of the change, combine (part-part-whole), compare, equalize form. In their model, the problem text (the statement of the problem) provides the basis for task comprehension, which, in turn, leads to a problem representation. This representation is drawn from a network of problem schemata stored in long-term memory. When particular problem schemata are activated, an action schema (a production) then is represented in working memory and carried out as a solution attempt. Riley et al. propose that strategic knowledge (see Chapter 3) is required to generate a sequence among the production rules that permits top-down planning for efficient and accurate problem solving. In Riley et al.'s view, every arithmetic problem requires knowledge of three sorts: (1) problem schemata (derived from the semantic structure of the problem statement), (2) action schemata (stored actions for solving problems), and (3) strategic knowledge for sequencing (planning) solutions to problems.

Problem Schemata.   Riley et al. (1983) suggest that one or more *problem schemata* (mental representations of a problem) can be applied to every problem. Consider the following change-take-from problem:

> Joe had eight marbles. Then he gave five marbles to Tom. How many marbles does Joe have now?

Riley et al. propose that the problem representation for this task consists of three components. The first component is the *start set,* the initial quantity—eight marbles. The second component, a change, must be recognized; this is called the *take-out set*—five marbles. Finally, there must be recognition that the remaining marbles form the third component, the *result set*—three marbles.

Action Schemata.   Once a problem has been represented, its solution requires knowledge of *action schemata.* In the marble problem above, beginning with an empty set, the problem statement instantiates a schema (put-in) such that the start set equals eight marbles (representing the sentence "Joe had eight marbles"). Then the action schema (take-out) indicates the change (removal of five marbles from the initial set). Finally, another action schema (count-all) counts the objects remaining—the result set, represented by the sentence "How many marbles does Joe have now?"

Strategic Knowledge.   Note that because even simple addition and subtraction problems require differing action schemata, learners need *strategic knowledge* to choose schemata appropriate to different types of problems. Besides problem and action schemata, a top-down (strategic) approach must be acquired that matches existing schemata stored in memory with problem representations and, in turn, with action schemata. For children learning addition and subtraction, a continuing difficulty is to acquire enough flexibility in the choice of schemata so that the right schema is applied to a particular problem at the right time. Learning to apply schemata appropriately, of course, involves regulation of cognition, a form of metacognitive knowledge (see Chapter 4).

Language: Another Factor

"Simple" problems in arithmetic may be more or less difficult, depending on the nature of the language used in the problem statement. Hudson (1980), for instance, gave children problems similar to that shown in Figure 13-1 and asked them one of the following questions: (1) How many more dogs than cats are there? (2) Suppose the dogs all race over and each one tries to chase a cat! Will every dog have a cat to chase? How many dogs won't have a cat to chase? Kindergarten children answered 25 percent of such problems correctly in response to the first question formulation, whereas they answered 96 percent correctly in response to the second type. Clearly, the form of the question affects the problem representation and, consequently, the application of an appropriate solution schema. Question 1, cast in a more abstract manner, seems to lead to more problem-representation errors.

The question of level of abstraction of problem statement leads naturally to an issue of long-time concern in mathematics—word problems. Most of us remember the difficulty we had with so-called "story problems" in algebra. Comprehending the text (an aspect of which Hudson's study touches on), as well as comprehending the appropriate mathematical schema, apparently makes such problems difficult. Text comprehension as it relates to arithmetic problem solving has been the topic of careful study.

Text Comprehension and Arithmetic Problem Solving

Building on work in text-processing theory by Kintsch and Van Dijk (1978; Van Dijk & Kintsch, 1983), which proposes that readers comprehend text by segmenting sentences into propositions and by relating these propositions to one another within the text structure (see discussion in Chapter 11), Kintsch and Greeno (1985) posed this general question: How does text processing (reading a word problem) interact with understanding the semantic information in the problem and the generation of appropriate mathematical schemata for problem solution? In other words, how are

Figure 13-1
Dogs and cats. Hudson (1980) used problems such as this one to determine children's difficulty with "How many more ____ than ____ are there" problems.

text comprehension and problem solving in mathematics related? They proposed that solving word problems is a two-step process. In the first step, the reader creates schemata for comprehending the text of the word problem. In the second step, these text schemata activate mathematics schemata. In other words, when students encounter a word problem, they first need to make sense out of the text of the problem. The schemata for text comprehension generate a second set of schemata for mathematics problems that lead to problem solution.

In Kintsch and Van Dijk's model, comprehending a word problem means constructing an appropriate conceptual representation from the text on which problem-solving processes can operate. For example, consider a part-part-whole arithmetic problem of the sort we described earlier:

> Jill has three marbles. Jack has five marbles. How many marbles do they have altogether?

This problem provides information about two sets of marbles (Jill's and Jack's). It has an unknown—the superset (the sum, as we learned to call it) of the two given sets. Kintsch and Greeno (1985) suggested that one useful representation of this task involves the creation of a set schema.

Table 13-1 represents a general set schema suitable for problems such as these. In the table, the *object slot* refers to a common noun labeling the sort of objects in the set. The *quantity slot* provides either the number of objects or a place holder (SOME, HOW MANY) denoting an indefinite statement or question. The *specification slot* distinguishes one set from others either by name of owner or by other description. Finally, the *role slot* provides a relational term that puts a particular set in the context or structure of the entire problem.

The slots and values given in Table 13-1 describe a set schema. Thus, for the three propositions contained in the first sentence in this problem ("Jill has three marbles"), the schema slots and values (in the same order as in Table 13-1) are *object*—marbles; *quantity*—three; *specification*—Jill. Similarly, the three propositions in the second sentence ("Jack has five marbles") take the form *object*—marbles; *quantity*—five; *specification*—Jack. The last item in the schema (role) is unknown for these two sentences until the last sentence of the problem is read. To this point, the problem solver has formed two sets: a set of three for Jill and a set of five for Jack. For the third sentence ("How many marbles do they have altogether?"), the propositions are *object*—how many (marbles); *specification*—Jill and Jack together. At this point, the *role* is determined (find the superset). This leads to an action strategy—making a superset for Jill and Jack combined.

The assignment of subset roles to both Jill's and Jack's marbles is not in the text statement, but rather is an inference the reader must make from the text; that is, the need to form these sets is not mentioned specifically in the problem. The necessity for such inferences intuitively suggests a potential source of error in correctly representing word problems. Finally, the solution to the problem is computed by a procedure such as a count-all strategy that counts the total of the two subsets taken together. The superset is formed.

This elongated description of "simple" processes—addition and subtraction—once more illustrates the underlying cognitive complexity of mathematical learning and problem solving. The language of cognitive psychology—knowledge acquisition, problem representation, schemata—provides a way to picture the task of mathematical problem representation. It seems clear that helping children achieve the schema

Table 13-1

A Schemata for Representing Sets. (From "Understanding and Solving Arithmetic Word Problems," by W. Kintsch and J. G. Greeno, 1985, *Psychological Review, 92*, p. 114. Copyright 1985 by the American Psychological Association. Adapted by permission.)

Slot	Value
Object	(noun)
Quantity	(number), SOME, HOW MANY
Specification	(owner), (location), (time)
Role	start, transfer, result; superset, subset; largest, smallest, difference

of a set is vital to success in understanding problems such as those given in the examples above. Note, however, that understanding and carrying out such an activity does not mean children must acquire the *formal* language of sets and supersets, although at some point this may well be important in mathematics instruction.

The schema-formation process we have described is especially useful for analyzing the problem solving of children having difficulty. A careful analysis of a child's schematic representations for each part of a problem may well provide a diagnosis of a "bug" in the way the schema is formed. The specificity of this process can lead to error determination and specific corrective action.

Kintsch and Greeno (1985) proposed that the propositions of the type we have discussed are created as children read or hear a problem. Whenever a proposition triggers a set-building strategy, the set is formed and stored in working memory. Kintsch and Greeno also described how this intricate process relates to working-memory capacity and the use of long-term memory. They concluded that models of text processing, coupled with the hypotheses Riley et al. (1983) suggested about understanding word problems, provide plausible descriptions of arithmetic word-problem solving.

A great deal of elaboration of these ideas will be necessary to provide a comprehensive description of addition and subtraction. Kintsch and Greeno point out, however, that it is not enough simply to have knowledge (say, of the meaning of a superset). Problem solvers must have strategies for building such structures as they read a problem. In some cases, teachers may find that arithmetic problems actually are reading problems; they may need to provide support (e.g., reading a problem to a child) so that attention may be focused on the arithmetic schemata activated by reading, rather than on reading per se.

Developmental Issues in Arithmetic Problem Solving

Before we conclude our discussion of arithmetic problem solving in elementary school children, a significant developmental issue must be addressed. The well-known work of Piaget describes a series of developmental stages through which all children pass. These stages are age related, with most children of kindergarten age in the preoperational stage, whereas children of early elementary age (grades one through three) often have reached the concrete-operations stage. One general strategy used by educators has been to look at the curriculum in terms of the cognitive demands it places on children. The traditional curriculum tends to hone children's mechanical counting skills and then move almost immediately to addition and subtraction. The abstractness of arithmetic and the need for time for children to construct a variety of number relationships suggests that formal mathematics instruction might profitably be delayed in favor of informal problem-centered approaches that help children construct their own mathematical concepts (e.g., see Carpenter et al., 1994; Van de Walle & Watkins, 1993).

The reasons why children might or might not be ready for formal mathematics are not completely clear, but one possibility is the demands that many mathematical skills place on dealing with a variety of bits of information, coupled with the short-term memory capabilities of young children. Case (1978, 1985) systematically examined the short-term memory capacity of young children, defining what he has called M-space (*Memory space*—memory capacity, in chunks). Short-term memory capacity in adults has long been estimated to be approximately seven plus or minus two chunks of information (see Chapter 3). Case's work suggests that young children are far below this adult level of performance.

Romberg and Collis (1987) carried out a systematic evaluation of short-term memory capacity in young children as a part of a larger study of mathematics competence. They proposed situations such as the following, in which a child (age six or seven) was asked to find a sum as follows:

Teacher: What number equals 2 + 4 + 3?

Child: 2 + 4 = 6, now what was the other number?

Teacher: What number equals 2 + 4 + 3?

Child: Now, 2 plus, uh, what are the numbers?

According to Romberg and Collis, this conversation reveals a short-term memory difficulty. They suggested the following explanation: The request for the other number in the first response of the child does not imply an operational failure, but rather a memory failure. The second response of the child suggests that the child's effort to remember the third number has resulted in a capacity overload that prompts the request to repeat the numbers. Using a series of memory tests, Romberg and Collis demonstrated that average M-space directly increases with grade level, although, as might be expected, with rather large within-grade variability. On their best measure of M-space, Romberg and Collis discovered that kindergarten children had M-space scores of almost exactly 1, whereas first-grader M-spaces equaled about 1.23, and the M-spaces of second-graders averaged just over 3. These data suggest a considerable difficulty with memory for younger children that might inhibit even simple abstract arithmetic problem solving.

A direct implication of these findings is that kindergarten and first-grade children are likely to face storage and processing problems in working memory when dealing with arithmetic involving abstract symbols. For the present, it seems reasonable to conclude that some apparent lack of "readiness" primary school children exhibit may be seen more precisely as a lack of short-term memory capacity. New approaches to teaching arithmetic concepts increasingly rely on manipulables (physical objects such as dice, dominos, blocks) and on children's own invented strategies for visualizing number concepts (e.g., using fingers to count) both to build comprehension and to avoid short-term memory failures (Baroody & Standifer, 1993). Most elementary school children, of course, even without formal instruction, develop and use a variety of techniques to make arithmetic tasks visual and hence reduce memory demands.

How younger children build conceptual and procedural knowledge in mathematics has dominated much of our discussion thus far. To examine these processes at a different level, we now turn to an examination of mathematical knowledge and problem solving in algebra. Understanding the cognitive processes involved in algebra also is important from a very practical standpoint: Ensuring student success in algebra is critical because it often functions as a "dividing point," beyond which many students do not venture. We focus particularly on word problems, which pose a particularly great challenge to many students.

PROBLEM SOLVING IN ALGEBRA

Most of us recall, sometimes painfully, our first experience with algebra word or story problems (e.g., "A river steamer was going upstream . . ."). Word problems in algebra typically are encountered after a brief initial period of instruction in algebra that provides basic information dealing with equations, unknowns, and so forth, and in most cases follows seven or eight years of instruction in various aspects of arithmetic. Thus, word problems would appear to be built on a substantial knowledge base of prior instruction in mathematics. It is unfortunate that the knowledge base is such that, in many cases, algebra word problems are perceived as new, rather than as growing out of and extending prior knowledge.

Apparently, the situation wherein a representation of the problem must be constructed by the reader while reading a problem is what makes algebra word problems "new" and difficult. The propositions in the text must be understood and converted into a mathematical model. Student performance with algebra word problems, coupled with their expressed dislike for such tasks, suggests that the issues raised by Kintsch and Greeno (1985) are real. The dual tasks of reading (comprehending) the text of an algebra problem and at the same time constructing the appropriate mathematics representation for problem solution pose a difficult challenge to many students. An adequate representation of a problem is critical because only a good representation will lead to a solution. In many mathematics curricula, however, students have little experience with comprehension processes such as those described by Kintsch and Greeno. Story problem solving is likely to be difficult unless algebra students have had extensive prior work with both text comprehension and mathematical problem solving.

Mayer (1981) analyzed algebra word problems in a number of high school algebra textbooks. He found more than 100 problem types, including 12 kinds of distance/rate/time problems. He also discovered that problems differed in frequency of appearance in the textbooks and that when he asked students to read and then recall a series of eight story problems, they remembered high-frequency problems more successfully (Mayer, 1982). This finding suggests that students store in long-term memory their story schemata for common types of algebra problems.

Silver (1981), in an interesting example of studies of schema development for algebra word problems, asked seventh-graders to sort sixteen story problems into piles and then compared the sorting performance of good and poor problem solvers. Good problem solvers tended to sort the stories on the basis of an underlying algebra schema structure. The poor problem solvers, however, tended to group the stories on the basis of the *surface structure* of the problems.

Thus, one may conclude from studies like these that successful problem solving is related to the formation of a wide variety of problem schemata types. However, Mayer's (1981) finding of a variety of problem types (as many as twelve) within a problem category suggests that rather than needing to learn and store perhaps six-teen to eighteen clusters of schemata, algebra problem solvers must develop and store as many schemata as there are varieties of problems within a cluster. According to Mayer (1981), this may be as many as 100 different subtypes.

Explaining Algebra Errors

The implication that students need to store a very large number of schemata seems disconcerting. If algebra problems demand a new schema for each subtype, then sheer numbers make it likely that not all will be learned. Furthermore, as the size of the pool of schemata increases, the chances of learning and storing faulty schemata also must increase. S. K. Reed's work on algebra errors suggests that this may indeed be the case.

Using Inappropriate Schemata.   Just as appropriate schemata can help a problem solver represent and solve word problems, so inappropriate schemata can hinder correct problem representation and solution. Reed and his colleagues (Reed, 1984, 1987; Reed, Dempster, & Ettinger, 1985) carried out a number of studies of students' ability to estimate answers to algebra word problems. Consider the following prob-lem from Reed (1984, p. 781):

> Flying east between two cities that are 300 miles apart, a plane's speed is 150 mph. On the return trip, it flies 300 mph. Find the average speed for the round trip. (Answer: 200 mph)

Working with college students, Reed (1984) found that 84 percent estimated 225 mph as the average speed. Only 9 percent gave the correct response. Why the high failure rate? Students' responses clearly showed that the problem elicited an "aver-age speed" schema. The overwhelming majority of students, however, saw the prob-lem as one of a *simple* average (Find the sum of the two speeds and compute the mean; 450/2 = 225 mph), rather than as a *weighted* average. In other words, for many students the problem elicited a schema ("find the average") that yields an incorrect response. Note that implied in the problem is the fact that the plane flew twice as long at the slower speed. Thus, it took 3 hours to fly the 600 miles, and hence the average speed was 200 mph. Many students, unfortunately, apparently failed to make that inference.

As the work of Kintsch and Greeno (1985) and Riley et al. (1983) suggests, the need to make inferences from the written text of the word problem may activate inappropriate schemata. To test that hypothesis, Reed (1984) gave the following ver-sion of the same problem to a group of students:

> A plane flies 150 mph for 2 hours and 300 mph for 1 hour. Find its average speed. (p. 781)

Note that, in this version, the fact that the plane flew slowly for two hours is made explicit. This time, 40 percent of the students gave the correct response in this version, and only 19 percent chose the incorrect 225-mph response. Although a substantial number still did not solve the problem correctly, making the problem more explicit apparently evoked the appropriate schema for "estimating a weighted average" in a much larger number of students.

Making Faulty Estimates.   A major question growing from Reed's (1984) research was students' ability to evaluate the reasonableness of answers. For mathematics teachers and tutors, evaluating whether an answer makes sense is almost axiomatic. Yet, Reed's data suggest that few students had adequate schemata for making useful estimates of whether an answer is correct or not. This may be illustrated more clearly with an example of a "work schema" problem, such as the following:

> It takes Bill twelve hours to cut a large lawn. Bob can cut the same lawn in eight hours. How long does it take them to cut the lawn when they both work together?

Thirty percent of students estimated the simple average—ten hours. This answer, of course, contains a serious inconsistency: The answer implies that it takes longer for the two boys to mow the lawn together than for Bob to do it alone! These students apparently lacked an intuitive schema for when and how to compute weighted averages. Furthermore, they did not seem to have an "estimation" schema for evaluating the reasonableness of their answer. Reed pointed out the value of estimation as a tool for detecting a student's intuitive "problem-solving" schema. He further argued that students develop schemata for a particular type of algebra problem that translate into an algorithm for solution. If a student does not estimate well and lacks "number sense" (e.g., Van de Walle & Watkins, 1993), then this is, at least, partial evidence that an algorithm is being applied by rote and is not based on understanding.

Failure to Use Analogies Effectively.   New learning occurs more readily if it is seen as analogous to previously mastered concepts. For instance, Gick and Holyoak (1980, 1983) used analogies to help problem solvers represent tasks. They did so by giving general problems (and solutions) to individuals who then were asked to solve related problems. Although the procedure generally was helpful, many students did not use the first problem to solve the second until they were given an explicit hint that it was valuable for solving the second problem.

Reed et al. (1985) hypothesized that in an area such as algebra word problem solution with a limited number of problem types, analogies might prove more directly useful. Thus, they predicted that solvers given a practice problem from a particular cluster of problems would use that information to solve similar problems from the same cluster. Reed et al. carried out an elaborate set of experiments to test this hypothesis, but the results were, in the main, disappointing. Students were able to use a practice problem as an analogy for solving subsequent equivalent problems, but only when the practice problem was carefully analyzed and summarized for them. When students were given problems similar, but not equivalent, to the practice problems, they failed to see them as analogous and could not solve them. Instead, most students attempted to match exactly the solution of the practice problem with the new problem. This resulted in failure, of course, because the problems were not identical.

Careful research efforts like these suggest that reducing errors in algebra word problem solving is difficult. Apparently, students' schemata often are incompletely understood or stored so specifically that they are not perceived as useful for solving other problems. Further, if a match is made with their stored schemata, solvers often appear to use it almost by rote; thus, problems not identical to stored schemata often are not solved.

To summarize, a schema-based approach to mathematics may be useful both to explain learning and as a means for diagnosing errors. Learners may or may not use schemata effectively, however. In arithmetic, schema-based approaches seem to work well. In contrast, the research in algebra suggests that although students do form schemata, the schemata by themselves often are not sufficient for problem success. One critical difference between the two subject areas may be the number of schemata that must be learned. Another difference may be the extent to which the schemata are learned meaningfully and grounded in students' informal knowledge (Ginsburg & Baron, 1993). The evidence supplied by Reed and his colleagues suggests that, in too many cases, algebra instruction produces rote acquisition of schemata that cannot be applied to problems even slightly different from those on which the schemata were based. These kinds of findings have broad implications for the need for fundamental changes in the teaching of mathematics.

COGNITIVE PSYCHOLOGY AND MATHEMATICS INSTRUCTION

As we indicated at the beginning of this chapter, new conceptions of mathematics teaching and learning and their expression in the standards of the National Council of Teachers of Mathematics (1991) emphasize the goals of building understanding and positive attitudes. Procedural skills in mathematics are not neglected—without reliable algorithms, problems cannot be solved—but they need to be grounded in a strong, flexible knowledge base containing linked conceptual, procedural, and strategic knowledge.

Our view of mathematics learning and teaching is fully in keeping with this perspective. In both arithmetic and algebra, we contend that a cognitive perspective provides useful insights into their problem-solving nature. We take the position that all of mathematics instruction might be treated as a predominantly cognitive enterprise and, in particular, as a problem-solving activity. This has not led us to include a chapter on problem solving in mathematics, but rather to recommend problem solving as the instructional orientation for all topics in the mathematics curriculum. Is this approach viable? Is it necessary?

Carpenter (1985) and others (e.g., Fuson, 1992; Van de Walle & Watkins, 1993) have asserted that prior to formal instruction in arithmetic, almost all children exhibit reasonably sophisticated and appropriate mathematics problem-solving skills, including attending, counting, modeling problems, and inventing more and more efficient procedures. Unfortunately, children's performance several years later is too often characterized by their trying to solve problems by arithmetic operations based on surface details. In other words, the traditional push toward computational skill mastery seems to cause many children to abandon earlier, more-flexible problem-solving approaches in favor of more compartmentalized numeric thinking and application of rote skills. Traditional, computation-oriented instruction can have the result of teaching children that mathematics is merely an exercise in symbol manipulation, one unrelated to problem solving. Unfortunately, acquiring that belief can create tremendous obstacles in learning mathematics. Once students divorce mathematics from problem solving, difficulties in later course work seem inevitable.

Are these scholars correct? By the eighth or ninth grade, many students do appear to apply algebra schemata in highly specific, inflexible ways, suggestive of a rote process. Furthermore, analysis of National Assessment of Educational Progress (NAEP, 1993) data for children in grades four, eight, and twelve continue to show serious deficiencies in U.S. students in tasks requiring thinking or understanding. Among seventeen-year-olds in the 1990 NAEP data, for example, only 7 percent were prepared for advanced mathematics beyond high school by meeting proficiency standards for algebra, geometry, and multistep problem solving.

At the same time, the research in arithmetic problem solving provides reasonable evidence that possession of more powerful and flexible strategies grounded in conceptual knowledge leads to improved problem solving. This knowledge, not computational skills, permits problem solving. Versatile mathematics performance requires combining conceptual, procedural, and strategic knowledge. Procedures can be taught essentially by rote, of course. The challenge for all teachers and, in the context of this chapter, the challenge to mathematics teachers especially is to help students develop the conceptual web of information and metacognitive knowledge underlying the procedures and strategies for using them flexibly. The problem-solving approaches that young children bring to the learning of mathematics must be nurtured and built on, not extinguished (see Hiebert, 1986; Hiebert & Carpenter, 1992; Van de Walle & Watkins, 1993).

In 1980, the National Council of Teachers of Mathematics (NCTM) proposed that problem solving be the focus of mathematics instruction. The growing body of research and the many changes in curriculum since then suggest that this proposal has had a great impact on mathematics research and practice. On the one hand, the view of simple addition and subtraction as problem solving, rather than algorithm memorization, is a case in point. On the other hand, the limited success that many algebra students still are having in using their knowledge flexibly suggests that the view of mathematics instruction based on student reasoning, problem solving, and creative thinking has not been translated into instruction. Too many students' mathematics knowledge has been acquired by rote, leading to learning that the students can apply only to a few of the wide variety of mathematics problems.

The bulk of mathematics instruction continues to emphasize the development of procedures, and, although procedures are necessary, a likely outcome is the development of highly specific schemata that students can apply only to a small number of problems (Maher, 1991). From this perspective, students faced with algebra problems requiring procedures slightly different from their rote-memorized ones quickly display the inadequacy of their problem-solving skills. Such inadequate problem solving is not inevitable, however. According to Reed (1984; see also Chipman, 1988), detailed analyses of the relevant semantic features of algebra word problems would help many students develop a richer, more flexible conceptual knowledge that, in turn, would lead to the formation of more-flexible problem schemata and procedures. Similarly, a study by Jones, Krouse, Feorene, and Saferstein (1985) provides evidence that instructional sequences dealing with different types of problems within clusters, coupled with emphasis on the relevant semantic features that show the similarities and differences between problems, significantly improves student problem solving.

In sum, accurate and flexible performance in algebra, like that of arithmetic performance, grows out of the acquisition of a web of conceptual understandings. This conceptual structure includes acquisition of conceptual, procedural, and conditional knowledge from which solutions can be derived. As is true for younger children's performance with arithmetic word problems, instruction in algebra word problems needs to help students develop a semantic understanding. Only when there is understanding will students be able to apply their knowledge to a wide variety of problems. More-focused approaches aimed at identifying "keywords" or memorizing solution algorithms will yield predictable results—a focus on surface features of problems and, most particularly, a failure to solve even slightly different problems.

IMPLICATIONS FOR INSTRUCTION

Cognitive approaches to learning mathematics imply a "thoughtful" approach to instruction (Maher, 1991), one that promotes learning with understanding. In learning with understanding, mental representations are built as new information is connected with old and as new relationships are constructed (Hiebert & Carpenter, 1992). The following suggestions summarize current thinking about mathematics instruction from a cognitive perspective.

1. *All mathematics should be taught from a comprehension-based, problem-solving perspective.* Specific facts and concepts, procedures, algorithms, and schemata should be learned in the framework of meaningful problem solving, not as isolated items. Just as readers construct an understanding of what they read, math students need to construct their knowledge about mathematics. They are most likely to do so when they are allowed to use mathematical knowledge in solving problems that are interesting and meaningful to them. The process of constructing meaning in mathematics is not smooth or predictable, but, over time, students can construct relationships and build understanding (Hiebert & Carpenter, 1992).

2. *Mathematics instruction should focus on processes, structures, and decisions, not on answers.* Students need to be encouraged to reflect on their own thinking and activities (see Chapter 9). Problems should be structured so that students are not simply searching for right answers, but for *reasons* why a procedure might or might not be useful in a particular situation. Flexible mathematics knowledge includes not only conceptual and procedural knowledge but also metacognitive knowledge related to using it appropriately and effectively (Schoenfeld, 1992).

3. *Build on students' informal knowledge.* In any domain, students construct meaning from their experience. Brown et al. (1989), in their discussion of situated cognition, argue that mathematics instruction should not immediately attempt to abstract mathematics concepts and procedures from the contexts that initially gave them meaning. The implication is that, at least initially, learning should be linked with authentic problem situations that students understand well (Hiebert & Carpenter, 1992). Because procedures are built on comprehension, students will be able to apply their knowledge more flexibly.

4. *Teachers need to spend time verbally modeling mathematics problem-solving behavior.* Students can benefit greatly from observing teachers make their thinking overt while solving exemplar problems "cold." Talking through solution strategies details the procedural and strategic processes that can be used to solve problems and shows their importance. Also made explicit in teacher "think-alouds" is the sequence of thinking, as well as the relationships between the information contained in the problem and the strategies the teacher is considering. "Incorrect" solutions also should be demonstrated; they show not only that errors are a natural part of mathematics reasoning but also where and how such errors can occur.

5. *Assist students in verbalizing and, if possible, visualizing processes used in solution attempts.* When mistakes occur and students "get stuck," teachers can enhance student problem solving by asking them to examine what they are doing and to look for errors or new approaches. Rather than provide the "correct" answer when students get stuck, teachers need to be coaches and facilitators.

6. *Use students' errors as a source of information on students' understanding.* How students think about mathematics problems is a source of valuable information for teachers. Errors provide especially rich information that teachers can use to search for specific misunderstandings. Close examination of student problem-solving processes may reveal errors attributable to a student's lack of conceptual, procedural, or metacognitive knowledge. Errors should not be taken lightly; superficial examination of error patterns may lead teachers to inappropriate conclusions about the nature of student problem-solving performance.

7. *Provide a mixture of problem types.* The common practice of grouping together all problems solvable with a particular approach seems ill advised. A better practice is to provide a variety of problems or, even better, a setting in which students can apply various kinds of mathematics knowledge as they attempt to solve a complex problem. Students need to have practice in recognizing different problem types; exposure to a variety of problems leads to both discrimination among problem types and better generalization of mathematical knowledge.

8. *Teachers themselves need appropriate levels of mathematics skill.* Implicit in all of the preceding suggestions is the requirement for teachers who are well prepared in mathematics and comfortable with the topic. Children enter elementary school with well-developed problem-solving skills that should be enhanced by a skilled teacher, not extinguished. Many current teachers, however, especially at the elementary level, do not have adequate levels of preparation in mathematics or understanding of new mathematics teaching methods. In recognition of this situa-

tion, teacher education institutions are increasing the level of mathematics preparation required of their teachers. Also, agencies such as the National Science Foundation (NSF) increasingly are providing in-service teachers with the opportunity to learn new teaching strategies based on cognitive approaches. This increased emphasis should produce teachers who not only are more competent and confident in their own mathematics abilities but also able to use cognitively based approaches in their teaching.

SUMMARY

A major purpose of this chapter was to demonstrate the value of a cognitive perspective for understanding how students learn mathematics. An extensive body of research on arithmetic operations, such as counting, addition, and subtraction, has shown that success in arithmetic seems to depend on the acquisition of an increasingly organized body of conceptual knowledge. Procedures (algorithms) for solving problems need to be linked closely with this conceptual knowledge. Students also need to have metacognitive knowledge for knowing when and how to apply their mathematical knowledge. Treating the content of addition and subtraction and other arithmetic operations as problems to be solved, rather than as sets of facts to be stored in memory, appears to be a productive approach to the learning of arithmetic content.

An examination of how students solve algebra word problems suggests that difficulties stem from students' failures to learn flexible and powerful strategies based in conceptual knowledge. Students often do not develop procedures adaptable to a wide range of problems, and many appear to acquire procedures applicable to only a very narrow range of problems. Consequently, faced with problems beyond that range, they have no basis for understanding the task. Some authorities have argued that traditional mathematics instruction (which is focused on content acquisition, rather than on problem solving) turns productive, problem-solving primary school children into rigid, unproductive middle school and secondary school students. Although this position may be somewhat overstated, there is little doubt that instruction focusing on developing mathematical understanding and problem solving is likely to be more effective than methods emphasizing computation and rote learning of "math facts."

SUGGESTED READINGS

Grouws, D. A. (Ed.). (1992). *Handbook of research on mathematics teaching and learning.* New York: Macmillan.

Another productive undertaking of the NCTM, this handbook contains chapters by noted authorities reviewing research on mathematics teaching and learning in their areas of specialization.

Jensen, R. J. (Ed.). (1993). *Research ideas for the classroom: Early childhood mathematics.* New York: Macmillan.

In this volume and in two companion volumes on middle grades mathematics (edited by Douglas T. Owens) and high school mathematics (edited by Patricia S. Wilson) commissioned by the NCTM, mathematics researchers and classroom teachers collaborate on reporting and interpreting research on teaching mathematics. These volumes, available in paperback, are excellent sources for those wishing research-based thinking about teaching mathematics at all levels of development.

CHAPTER 14

Cognitive Approaches to Science

The goals of science are ambitious: to understand the physical, biological, and social worlds; and to understand the methodology of science. Such complex goals present great challenges to science teachers. Helping students acquire an understanding of these three worlds and of the methodology of science is a formidable task.

To fully appreciate the methodology of science (the development and testing of hypotheses), one must learn science as a problem-solving process. Unfortunately, many elementary and secondary school science textbooks place a premium on vocabulary development, rather than on problem solving. Indeed, Carey (1986) argues that junior and senior high school science texts introduce more new vocabulary per page than foreign-language texts! She goes on to say that "science as a vocabulary lesson is a recipe for disaster, especially if understanding is the goal" (p. 1124). Understanding science is more than memorizing vocabulary. Understanding science means using its concepts to solve problems, problems not only from the science curriculum and the science laboratory but also in real life.

The recognition that domain-specific knowledge is essential to problem solving quickly led psychologists to the choice of science as a knowledge domain in which to study problem solving (Bhaskar & Simon, 1977; Shavelson, 1973; Simon & Simon, 1978). Early studies in this area involved collaboration of cognitive scientists and college science instructors, particularly in introductory college physics courses. This early research focused on several areas of classical physics (mechanics, kinematics, statics) chosen because the areas were clearly specified and the basic information, principles, and criteria for effective problem-solving performance all were well defined.

To examine the effects of differing amounts of domain-specific information on problem-solving success, researchers (e.g., Chi, Feltovich, & Glaser, 1981; Larkin, McDermott, Simon, & Simon, 1980; Simon & Simon, 1978) contrasted the performance of experts (typically, college physics instructors) and novices (undergraduate physics majors). They made the reasonable assumption that extensive physics knowledge differences existed between the two groups and, further, that this knowledge (expertise) difference would be reflected in different problem-solving processes. To test this assumption, physics problem-solving protocols (verbal reports made while solving a problem) were obtained from novices and experts. Strikingly different patterns of performance emerged after the protocols were analyzed. As expected, experts and novices differed widely in extent of knowledge, but they differed in other ways as well. One startling difference was the finding that many novices had a number of erroneous beliefs or preconceptions that made understanding basic physics principles difficult.

NAIVE SCIENCE CONCEPTIONS

McCloskey, Caramazza, and Green (1980) asked college students to respond to situations like that shown in Figure 14-1. They then used students' reactions to these situations to determine the extent to which they understood Newtonian (classic) physics. Students encountered the two drawings of a coiled tube shown in the figure. Each drawing shows a marble leaving the "exit" of a coiled tube. The students' task was to determine which line (straight or curved) better depicted what would happen if someone rolled a marble through the tube. One of the solutions (the straight line) represents what the laws of physics say will happen in the situation and, indeed, what actually happens when this experiment is conducted.

Figure 14-1
Balls leaving coiled tubes.
McCloskey et al. (1980) used figures like this one to determine students' understanding of Newtonian physics.

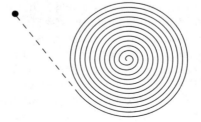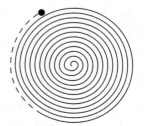

Surprisingly, McCloskey et al. found that even students who had taken a course in high school physics gave answers that showed naive conceptions of physical laws. On the coil-and-marble task shown in Figure 14-1, one-third of the students indicated that the ball would continue in a curved line. Of course, such an outcome violates Newton's first law (inertia), which states that any object continues either in a state of rest or in uniform, straight-line motion unless acted on by another force.

The errors observed by McCloskey et al. and those reported in a similar study that used gravity problems (Champagne, Klopfer, & Anderson, 1980) reveal that incorrect responses represent people's naive, "intuitive" conceptions of physics. Such **naive beliefs** are not isolated events restricted to a few unusual physics problems, however. McCloskey (1983) has argued that people develop remarkably well articulated naive theories of scientific phenomena on the basis of their everyday experiences. These theories provide people with causal explanations for how the world operates (see McCloskey, 1983).

The ordinary experiences of everyday life (even prior schooling) are a source of data that seem to support naive theories. Consequently, the presence of well-developed but incorrect theories, coupled with everyday experiences that seem consistent with these theories, leads to a set of beliefs about how the world operates that is very difficult to change. In fact, many students find their naive concepts superior to the abstract and, in many cases, seemingly counterintuitive principles of Newtonian physics.

To illustrate, Clement (1983) presented data on naive beliefs about motion involving a coin toss. In this problem, an object, such as the block in Figure 14-2, is tossed into the air and caught by the tosser. The problem solver is asked to draw a diagram and to use arrows to show the direction of the force acting on the block at any particular point. The left side of Figure 14-2 shows an expert's response; the right side shows a typical incorrect response.

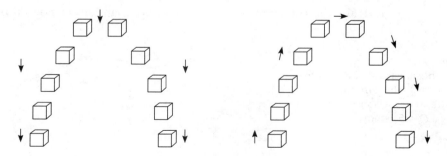

Figure 14-2

Conceptions of the force acting on a block tossed into the air (arrows indicate direction of force). An expert's conception of the force acting on a block tossed into the air is presented on the left. The right side is a novice's response. This task is similar to that used by Clement (1983).

The "simple" expert drawing (see Figure 14-2) appears to ignore (and hence contradict) the intuitive, and incorrect, "upward motion" illustrated in the right part of the figure—what students call the "force of the throw." Clement (1983) reported that only 12 percent of engineering students responded correctly to this question prior to taking a college physics course. He gave the same problem to two more-experienced groups of students. Only 28 percent of a group who had completed the introductory course in mechanics (in which motion is a prominent topic) responded correctly. Furthermore, only 30 percent of a second group, who had completed two semesters of physics (including mechanics), solved the problem correctly. Although these data suggest that instruction improves class performance somewhat, a remarkably high percentage (more than 70 percent) continued to display naive responses. Teaching effectiveness aside, these data suggest the difficulty that teachers may have in overcoming naive beliefs.

Another example of the naive concepts students have about the workings of the world can be seen in Osborne and Freyberg's (1985) study in which, among other questions related to biology, children were asked whether certain objects were plants. Amazingly, only 60 percent of the twelve- and thirteen-year-olds in the study identified carrots as plants, and only 80 percent of the fourteen- and fifteen-year-olds agreed that oak trees were plants. In fact, 10 percent of the twelve- and thirteen-year-olds thought that grass was not a plant. It was not clear from the study what the dissenting children thought carrots, oaks, and grass were, but there is no question that their conceptual systems related to plants were rudimentary.

Still another instance of poorly developed conceptual systems can be seen in an experiment reported by Osborne and Freyberg that focused on a typical elementary school science problem—electrical flow. In this case, Osborne and Freyberg presented children with a simple electrical circuit problem (see Figure 14-3) in which a battery was used to light a bulb. When the students were asked to show how the electric current flows in the circuit, about 35 percent of the ten- to fourteen-year-old participants reported that current in both wires flowed from the battery to the bulb. In fact, only 80 percent of the seventeen- to eighteen-year-old participants were able to make the correct response and indicate that current flows through the wire in

Figure 14-3
A simple electrical circuit. A figure such as this one was shown to children in Osborne and Freyberg's (1985) study.

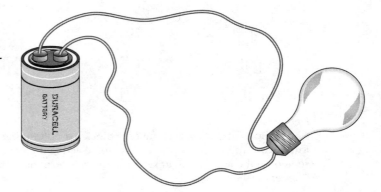

one direction, with the same current level in both wires. Further, when asked to explain the amount of current in various parts of the circuit, many students erroneously stated that because the bulb emits light and heat, some of the current is "used up." Therefore, these students concluded, less current is going back to the battery than leaving it.

A final experiment taken from Osborne and Freyberg's volume (1985) illustrates a similar problem quite nicely. In this instance (see Figure 14-4), students were asked questions about the physics concept of *force*. Stop reading at this point and indicate the forces acting on the football at points A, B, and C in Figure 14-4. The rest of our description depends on your understanding the figure.

Finished? Good. According to Osborne and Freyberg, the answers to such questions provide a basis for distinguishing between students who understand force in Newtonian terms and those who have naive conceptions of force. Of 800 thirteen- to seventeen-year-olds in their experiment, less than 22 percent at any age level chose the correct (Newtonian) response pattern (down, down, down; after the ball has been thrown up, the only force acting on it is gravity). Astonishingly, three-quarters of the high school students who participated in Osborne and Freyberg's study—even those who had completed a physics course—could not correctly identify the forces acting on such an object.

The overwhelming evidence indicates that students not only lack scientific information but also bring misinformation that affects the manner in which they try to understand problems. Students' misconceptions tend to be very powerful—in some areas, negating direct evidence they observe in experimental and classroom settings. Some researchers (see Kuhn, 1989, for a review) argue that this misinformation is more than a simple set of false beliefs. Instead, they argue that most students lack a coordinated and consistent conceptual system for understanding the world. They appear to have a set of incomplete and uncoordinated schemata that arise primarily from unguided experience—that is, *uncontrolled observation*.

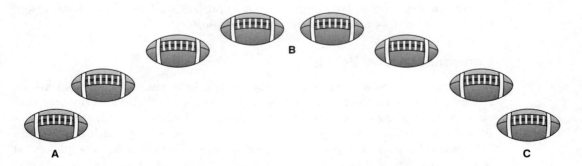

Figure 14-4
A football being thrown into the air. Osborne and Freyberg (1985) employed a figure such as this one to test students' knowledge of force. The students were asked to indicate the direction of force acting on the football at points A, B, and C.

Other researchers have taken an even stronger position, arguing that many students possess well-organized but incorrect conceptual systems. For example, Carey (1985) and Carey and Smith (1993) have argued that elementary school children have very rich conceptual frameworks. These frameworks are not simply fragmentary, unconnected false beliefs. Instead, they are coherent conceptual systems, albeit incorrect, that are consistent with many real-life observations.

Regardless of which view of children's misinformation is correct, students bring considerable erroneous information to science classes. This information must be unlearned before appropriate conceptual systems can be acquired. Unfortunately, because students' incorrect conceptual systems are the result of a life's worth of personal, unguided observations of the world, these systems may be held strongly and may be difficult to change. Teachers must expect children to have incorrect conceptions and, indeed, seek them out. Because children's beliefs have developed out of their life experiences, children are not likely to abandon them unless they are presented with instruction that shows "new" ideas are "more intelligible, more plausible, and more fruitful" than old, incorrect beliefs (Osborne & Freyberg, 1985, p. 48).

To summarize, as a consequence of long periods of informal knowledge accumulation, many, perhaps most, students have misconceptions about science that formal instruction may not always modify. The acquisition of new and more-appropriate scientific conceptual systems is likely to be slow. Moreover, the process is more than simply correcting errors. You can demonstrate the tenacity of incorrect belief systems by giving any of the examples used by McCloskey et al. (1980) or Osborne and Freyberg (1985) to naive adults (your friends in other classes). If the problems are presented in a nonauthoritarian manner, denial of Newtonian explanations will be common, and existing belief systems will be maintained in the face of evidence of the correct answers. Indeed, many naive scientists appear to trust their intuitions rather more than they do laboratory experiments that appear to contradict those intuitions. Thus, expert/novice differences are much more complex than simple differences in the amount of information people possess, and teachers must be aware of "intuitive" (and often incorrect) science knowledge that students bring with them. Substantial instructional time must be used to present students with situations that expose their naive beliefs so that they may be confronted.

Confronting Naive Beliefs

Unlike mathematics, wherein much of the content is taught first in school settings, children enter school with a wealth of science knowledge based on uncontrolled observations made as part of their daily experience. Children learn physical "laws" as they throw a ball, do a sit-up, play on a slide, turn on a lamp, and so on. These uncontrolled experiences permit the development of inadequate, incomplete, and often incorrect conceptions of how the world operates. Much of this knowledge is tacit, unarticulated information embedded in the actions of the child (Kuhn, 1989). These conceptions are stored in memory and, quite naturally, provide the basis for explanations when children are faced with science problems. Teachers not only should expect to find these naive beliefs but also must find ways of seeking them out before systematic instruction in science can begin.

The best way to eliminate naive, incorrect beliefs is to expose them and confront them directly (Pintrich, Marx, & Boyle, 1993). Such confrontation requires more than the mere teaching of basic science facts, or *cold* conceptual change, as Pintrich et al. refer to it. Instead, instruction in science must be experience-based within the context of the classroom and must provide a motivational incentive to change.

In summarizing a comprehensive review of studies in conceptual change, Pintrich et al. identified four necessary conditions for meaningful conceptual change to occur. One condition is *dissatisfaction* with current conceptions. Unless students (and teachers) have sufficient reason to abandon naive beliefs, it is unlikely that a radical change will occur. A second condition is that new conceptions must be *intelligible*. Clearly, students will feel little need to replace existing beliefs with new beliefs that have even *less* explanatory power. A third condition is that new conceptions must be *plausible*. In essence, plausibility increases the chances that new beliefs will be related meaningfully to existing knowledge structures and used during scientific problem solving. The final condition is that new frameworks must appear *fruitful* in order to facilitate further investigation.

Other researchers have investigated the extent to which conceptual restructuring is necessary (Vosniadou & Brewer, 1987). Special emphasis has been put on two kinds of conceptual change. The first is *weak restructuring,* in which existing knowledge within a specific domain, such as physics, is reorganized but not added to. This kind of conceptual change may be appropriate when students possess relevant expert knowledge that nevertheless leads to erroneous conclusions. The second kind of conceptual change is *radical restructuring,* which is appropriate when students possess naive theories that are deficient, compared with those of experts. In this case, students "do not simply have an impoverished knowledge base compared to that of an expert; the novice has a different theory, different in terms of its structure, in the domain of the phenomenon it explains, and in its individual concepts" (Vosniadou & Brewer, 1987, p. 54). Radical restructuring may be necessary when students possess relevant *knowledge* but lack relevant *conceptual structure* to that knowledge. Only by redefining what they already know (and perhaps adding new knowledge) can these students hope to understand important scientific concepts adequately.

A Model for Changing Naive Beliefs

Nussbaum and Novick (1982) have proposed a threefold strategy for changing naive beliefs: (1) reveal and understand student preconceptions, (2) create conceptual conflict with those preconceptions, and (3) encourage the development of revised or new schemata about the phenomena in question. We examine each step below.

Revealing Student Preconceptions.   Teachers first must engage students in activities that reveal their naive beliefs. Figure 14-5, based on the work of Nussbaum and Novick (1982), presents the responses of some elementary students at a laboratory school to an exposing event whose content deals with the particle theory of gases. In this event, students were shown a flask and a vacuum pump. They were told that half of the air in the flask had been drawn out of the flask with the pump. The children

Figure 14-5
Children's depictions of a science problem. These depictions are representative of those made by elementary students at a university laboratory school.

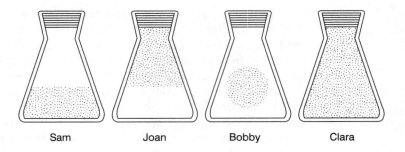

Sam   Joan   Bobby   Clara

then were asked to imagine that they possessed magic spectacles that permitted them to see the air remaining in the flask. Finally, they were asked to draw a picture on the chalkboard of the air remaining in the flask. On completion of the drawings, students were asked to describe and explain them. This class activity thus generated both verbal and pictorial accounts of student preconceptions.

Figure 14-5 shows that students hold a wide range of conceptions about the nature of gases. Obviously, all members of the class do not share the same view of the properties! During this first stage of instruction, the teacher's major role is to help students express their ideas clearly and concisely. The teacher also encourages confrontation of ideas among the students but does not judge the adequacy of students' responses. The teacher's expectation is that exchanging views with other students about student-generated ideas not only has intrinsic interest but also serves to clarify each student's own thinking. These activities serve to move the students to the next phase.

Creating Conceptual Conflict.   The drawings and explanations generated by the class are posed as alternatives to whatever view each child holds. (If it happens that the "correct" or "scientific" view is not posed by the children, the teacher may wish to supply it as one given by a student in another class.) The teacher must, of course, resist students' appeals for "which is the right one?"

Student-to-student discussion in itself may change some students' conceptions. Children with differing views may be paired and asked to choose the "best" drawing and to give a rationale for their choice. After allowing substantial time for discussion, the teacher then leads the students to see the need for an empirical test to determine the merits of the alternatives. Teacher questions such as "How can we decide which is better?" or "What can we do to decide?" may help students see the need to gather evidence for decision making. (If the teacher is very lucky, a student will spontaneously suggest such a test.)

The test must be selected so that after careful examination it will eliminate all but the scientifically correct alternative. In the example from Nussbaum and Novick, the teacher diverted the children to a different task altogether. She took a syringe, closed the opening at the end, and then drove the plunger halfway into the barrel. She asked the class to describe the nature of the contents of the apparently empty syringe, to which they responded, "Air." She then asked what happened to the air when she pushed the syringe halfway home. Students readily generated answers that included some version of "squeezing" or "compressing" the air. As a technique for generalizing the meaning of the concept of *compression,* the teacher then reminded the children of earlier work with liquids and solids that had demonstrated their relative lack of compressibility. She then asked them to speculate about the special characteristics of air that permitted it to be compressed. Following discussion of this question, she returned their attention to the "exposing event" (the partially evacuated flask) and asked the children to think about the air in the flask and the syringe. According to Nussbaum and Novick, in a number of replications of this experience, some child always made a comment such as, "Maybe the air is made up of little pieces with empty space between." The class then reviews the drawings made during the exposing event and begins to make inferences and eliminate various of the alternatives. In this process, students raise questions that lead to the final phase.

Encouraging Cognitive Accommodation.   After the empirical test has been completed and discussed, the teacher needs to give students support, new information, and elaboration of existing information that will help them restructure their ideas about the situation in question. In the gas example, prior to accepting the scientific explanation, students frequently asked such questions as, "What holds the particles apart?" This question permitted the teacher to bring in another property of gases— the inherent motion of the particles. To complete the teaching example, the teacher drove the plunger still farther into the syringe and asked the students to comment. Finally, she asked whether she could compress the air to zero volume. These additional steps permitted her to give further information about compression and to remind students that a limit of compressibility is reached when there is no space left between the particles.

We presented the air example to provide you with some sense of the complexity of obtaining student explanations of physical phenomena and how those naive explanations can, by use of the students' own questions and comments, be used to lead students toward more-scientific conceptual structures. When students' discussions are followed by empirical tests that permit students to discover a more nearly scientific explanation, many (though by no means all) students acquire more-accurate science schemata.

EXPERT-NOVICE DIFFERENCES IN SCIENCE

It goes without saying that few elementary or secondary school students will achieve the expertise of professional physicists, chemists, or biologists. Nor is it reasonable to think that they should. Still, elementary and secondary school science instruction, at a minimum, should help students progress toward content expertise and, perhaps more important, toward expert scientific problem solving. But just what are the characteristics of expert problem solvers in science?

Differences in Problem Solving

Studies of experts show that they possess substantially more information than novices (e.g., Glaser & Chi, 1988). Experts also solve problems much more quickly than novices. This finding suggests that experts, even though they have far more relevant knowledge to search in memory, are much more efficient at searching a particular solution space. Furthermore, studies of solution time reveal that experts' recall is chunked. For example, a number of equations all linked with a particular physics principle may be recalled by an expert in a single configuration or "bundle," followed by a pause, and then the recall of another bundle of equations appropriate to another relevant principle. Novices, in contrast, show no such chunking patterns. The presence of bursts of recall among experts suggests, consistent with our discussion of mathematics problem solving, the presence of meaningfully linked schemata elicited as bundles when appropriate problem demands are encountered.

Research contrasting experts and novices in science also has revealed some differences that are harder to describe. One important difference between novices and experts is experts' use of what Larkin (1977) referred to as "qualitative analysis" and what Simon and Simon (1978) called "physical intuition." In both cases, the authors were referring to the development of rather elaborate problem representations, often representations that include the construction of a sketch or other physical version of the problem. Such elaborate problem representations, whether visual or verbal or both, typically are constructed as a first (or early) step in problem solving. They apparently serve to locate ambiguity in problem descriptions and to clarify or make specific aspects of the problems that must be deduced or inferred. Once constructed, these sophisticated task representations serve to generate succeeding solution steps, such as the generation of particular solution equations.

Still another difference between experts and novices is in their choice of strategies. As described in Chapter 8, experts consistently use a *working-forward* (e.g., means-ends) strategy, whereas novices use a *working-backward* approach (Anzai, 1991). Experts appear to identify problem variables and then move forward to generate and solve equations that use existing information. Novices, in contrast, seem to begin the solution process with an equation that contains the problem unknown (the desired end product). If the equation contains a variable that was not given, novices work backward from that equation, searching for an equation that yields (they hope) the variable they need, and so on.

For example, suppose the solution to a physics problem required solving the equation $V = mgh$, where the several values in the equation are unknown but h is the unknown asked for by the question. The novice, on the one hand, typically works backward from that equation, seeking to generate other equations that will give the values of m, g, and V so that ultimately the equation can be solved for h. The expert, on the other hand, apparently understanding the problem in a more fundamental way, works forward from a set of equations generated from the problem statement, concluding the solution sequence with the equation $V = mgh$ in a fashion so that all of the relevant values are known and are placed in the equation, and the solution to h is calculated. It seems the rich network of information that experts possess is organized into schemata that use key concepts from problem statements and from their own knowledge base to instantiate forward-moving solution procedures. These science schemata seem very similar to the algebra schemata we described in Chapter 13.

Differences also exist between expert and novice scientists in terms of the structure (as well as content) of information they use to solve problems. Experts are more likely to generate necessary inferences (those essential for an adequate solution) from problem statements than are novices. Differences exist in problem representation as well; novices tend to organize their problems in knowledge around the surface structure of the explicit statements in problems, whereas experts organize their knowledge schematically around fundamental science principles (e.g., Newton's laws) that often only are implied by problem statements (Anzai, 1991).

Once schemata related to the fundamental principles are activated, experts use stored procedural knowledge to generate solution attempts that then are tested against the requirements of the problem statement. Experts possess substantially more procedural knowledge than novices. This difference in procedural knowledge may account for the differences in problem-solving strategies chosen by experts (working forward) and novices (working backward).

Differences in Understanding Theories

Profound differences exist between experts and novices with respect to their understanding of science. Kuhn, Amsel, and O'Loughlin (1988) and Kuhn (1989) examined some of these differences among children, lay adults, and practicing scientists. Kuhn and colleagues proposed that children experience more difficulty with science for two reasons. One is that they lack domain-specific knowledge and strategies used by adult experts. These differences were described above. Another reason is that children fail to understand the structure and scientific uses of a theory.

Formal scientific theories have at least two distinguishable parts: a *formal aspect* (postulates about how a phenomenon occurs) and an *empirical aspect* (a test of those postulates, usually in the form of data or mathematical proofs). Kuhn (1989) found that most children and many lay adults (e.g., young adults who did not attend college) failed to distinguish between these two aspects of a theory. As a consequence, they either "adjusted" experimental data to fit the theory or changed the theory to fit the data even when the data were ambiguous or unreliable. Both of these adjustment strategies were faulty for one important reason: They prevented children from coordinating data and theory. In contrast, educated adults and especially practicing scientists were quite skilled at coordinating data and theory.

Kuhn (1989) identified three essential skills in scientific reasoning: (1) explicit awareness of what a theory says, (2) distinguishing between evidence that supports or refutes the theory, and (3) justifying why the data support one theory but not another. It turns out that many children and lay adults often fail to understand the theories they are expected to work with and therefore find the two remaining steps impossible to complete (Carey & Smith, 1993; Kuhn et al., 1988). In addition, ample evidence suggests that children and many adults fail to distinguish between different kinds of evidence (Kuhn, 1991). For example, Kitchener and King (1981) found that many college undergraduates could not provide a detailed justification for why data support one viewpoint but not another.

Kuhn has proposed a number of strategies for improving scientific reasoning. One strategy is to help students recognize and compare alternative theories; a second is to provide practice coordinating a given set of data with competing theories; and a third is to increase metacognitive awareness of the scientific reasoning process itself. A number of studies reported that teacher modeling coupled with guided discovery improves each of these dimensions significantly (Kuhn, Schauble, & Garcia-Mila, 1992; Schauble, 1990).

Carey and Smith (1993) have suggested a fourth strategy for improving scientific reasoning that addresses the relative sophistication of students' epistemological beliefs (see Chapter 7). In this view, some children fail to distinguish between theories and to coordinate evidence within a theory because they adopt a *commonsense,* rather than a *critical,* epistemological worldview. The former assumes (often tacitly) that a theory is a collection of facts based on unequivocal data. The latter assumes that a theory is a constructed approximation to reality that may or may not be supported by the data (or rational analysis). As a consequence, students adopting a critical epistemology place a great deal more emphasis on evaluating the quality of data and coordinating it with the formal postulates of the theory.

Carey and Smith designed a scientific thinking curriculum that focused on two important skills: theory-building and explicit reflection on the theory-building process (see Chapter 9). Carey, Evans, Honda, Jay, and Unger (1989) tested this approach by asking junior high students to conduct a research program aimed at discovering why yeast, sugar, and water produced a gas when combined. Results were mixed in that awareness of scientific reasoning improved but not enough to suggest that genuine conceptual change had occurred. However, a similar study by Kuhn et al. (1992) indicated that guided discovery significantly improved scientific reasoning skills.

A MODEL FOR TEACHING SCIENCE

The differences between novices and experts described above suggest a model for science instruction. Teachers need to help students acquire both declarative and procedural science knowledge and, to a larger extent, understand the role of theories in scientific reasoning. Instruction should help students think about science problems in terms of the underlying scientific laws of the discipline. Research indicates that novices need a great deal of support in acquiring these skills and in making inferences from the context of particular problem statements. These inferences, for experts, lead to the activation of schemata that trigger procedures that move the solver toward solution. Knowledge, independent of well-organized conceptual schemata, is not sufficient to generate procedures for successful problem solving. Furthermore, because school-age students may have a large storehouse of incorrect or incomplete science schemata (Carey, 1985; Osborne & Freyberg, 1985), tasks and assignments must be chosen carefully, first to confront these naive beliefs, and then to lead students to develop and store schemata related to fundamental scientific laws.

Science instruction, according to this view, should be directed at building knowledge structures (schemata) that allow learners to react to problems with appropriate solution procedures. The trick is to help students organize their knowledge into schemata that are productive and related to fundamental scientific concepts. Such organization is critical.

The National Science Teachers Association (NSTA) has proposed a number of instructional priorities to achieve this end (Aldridge, 1992). One goal is to shift the focus of instruction to hands-on experience. Courses that rely primarily on textbooks often are perceived as boring and irrelevant to students' lives. This may explain, in part, why fewer than 50 percent of American students take a science course after the tenth grade. A second goal is to extend science instruction over many years, rather than to devote one year to chemistry and another to physics. Aldridge (1992) has argued that using a "layer cake" approach in which students study a topic, such as chemistry, and then move on to other topics without ever returning to chemistry fails to provide sufficient depth within that topic area.

A third NSTA goal is to shift instruction gradually from concrete experiences to abstractions. In particular, complex scientific theories should not be introduced until students have acquired the concepts and principles necessary to understand them. A final goal is to strive for more in-depth coverage of a topic even if it means sacrificing the breadth of coverage. One way to achieve this goal is to adopt a "spiral" approach to instruction, in which students return to important issues in chemistry or physics on a yearly basis. Achieving this goal, however, requires a far greater degree of planning than is presently the case.

Learning Strategies

Students come to instructional settings with learning strategies acquired from school experience, as well as from unstructured settings. One goal of science education is to teach students new learning strategies that help them acquire and organize information. The evidence suggests that this goal is not always met. Some students actually acquire learning strategies that interfere with learning new science material.

In one study, Roth (1985) asked middle school students to read science materials (written at their grade level) and examined how they thought about it. She identified five "learning" strategies used by the children, only one of which, unfortunately, resulted in restructuring and refining naive schemata. The five strategies are described briefly below.

Overreliance on the Sufficiency of Prior Knowledge.   Students who exhibited the strategy of overreliance on prior knowledge read the assignment and then reported they understood the text; in fact, many reported they had "known this stuff" before they even read the material. One student, after reading a passage that used milk as an example of how all food ultimately can be traced back to green plants (the food producers), reported the passage was "about milk." When pressed, he reported it was how we get milk from cows. The point of the reading—that plants make food that cows convert to milk—was missed entirely. In this student's view, he already knew the content. Instead of using the knowledge just acquired from the text to answer questions, students of this type tend to use associations of the new material with prior knowledge to report that the text simply was repetitious.

Overreliance on Text Vocabulary.   In the overreliance on vocabulary strategy, students isolated new words or phrases in the assignment, often out of context, but expressed feelings of comprehension if they could state that the text was about a specific word, for example, "photo-something" (*photosynthesis*). According to Roth, the children reported feeling confused about the text only if they could not decode the new words. For these children, answering questions about the text simply required recall of new or big terms and a phrase or sentence around them. Often the new words were not put into the context of the students' own experiences. Unfortunately, this strategy often pays off when the questions that teachers ask about text materials consist of requests for definitions or identifications of new words. This is the kind of almost mindless vocabulary acquisition we referred to in the opening of the chapter.

Overreliance on Factual Information.   Many students have adopted a view of science as the accumulation of facts (e.g., air expands when heated; water boils at 212 degrees Fahrenheit). Such students see science learning as demanding recall of facts and other natural phenomena. In Roth's study, such students displayed quite accurate recall of these bits of information. The ideas were not linked into meaningful schemata, however, nor was there differentiation of major from trivial points. These students did best from teachers who employed a vocabulary-oriented view of science. Just as some students see science as vocabulary acquisition, other students see it as mere fact acquisition.

Overreliance on Existing Beliefs.   Many students in Roth's study used this strategy. For these students, new topics were understood in terms of naive beliefs based on prior knowledge. These well-motivated students sought to link text knowledge with existing prior knowledge. However, the goal of students using this strategy was not to modify the structure of existing knowledge (their naive theory), but rather to confirm its correctness. In many cases, students distorted or even ignored information inconsistent with existing knowledge. In the light of the existence of naive beliefs in many children, this strategy poses special difficulty for teachers. Students' efforts to make new knowledge conform to existing, often incomplete or incorrect theories may well interpret the outcome of an experiment in ways very different from those anticipated by the teacher. In contrast to the overreliance on the sufficiency of prior knowledge learning strategy, these students realized that the information was new; however, they did not appear to understand that it might challenge their existing beliefs.

Conceptual-Change Students.   Conceptual-change students see text materials as a vehicle for changing existing schemata. In Roth's study, they worked to reconcile old ideas with new material. As a result, they not only identified and learned the main ideas in the text but also were able to state where the text or other materials conflicted with their existing schemata. Further, they saw the text as a source of new knowledge and were willing to revise their old schemata in the light of new information. Interestingly, but not surprisingly, this group of students was most often likely to admit to being confused or puzzled by the text.

The reason for such differences in learning strategies is unclear. Nonetheless, teachers need to anticipate them. If students report new material as "old stuff," the teacher must provide a teaching situation that shows how the new material challenges old beliefs, making it clear that the material is, in fact, new and must be accommodated by students into revised schemata. Similarly, students who see science as vocabulary or fact acquisition may be presented with situations (experiments, demonstrations, field studies) that require the linking of words and facts into schemata that help students better understand and explain the world.

Teaching Strategies

Given the range of possible student learning strategies, what instructional strategies might help students learn and understand science at more mature and scientific levels? Four of the five learning strategies we described above permit children to avoid learning new information by classifying it as already known. Simply assigning these students material to read is unlikely to lead to the sorts of accommodation new schemata require. Instead, it may be more appropriate to introduce students to new concepts by first finding out what they already believe to be true about them.

The best way to find out what students know is from individual interviews. According to Osborne and Freyberg (1985), the questions teachers use in interviews should be posed in a personal way—"Will you explain to me the way you think our eyes work?"—rather than impersonally—"How do people's eyes work?" (The second question suggests there is a correct answer the child should know and provide—an answer the child may neither fully understand nor agree with.) Further, questions should represent a balance of easy-to-answer (often factual) questions and more-penetrating ones, such as, "Why do you think that?" The point of questioning individuals is to lead them to reveal their own sense of how science works.

Many researchers interested in elementary and secondary school science believe that individual interviews are necessary to establish the beginning point for science instruction. However, because the individual interview may take more time than teachers can afford, other techniques have been proposed. Nussbaum and Novick (1982) suggested that one useful way to obtain children's conceptions (and misconceptions) is through what they call an *exposing event*—a situation or demonstration posed to a group of children that evokes personal comments. It is not enough, though, simply to expose preconceptions; means must be found to challenge the preconceptions and to help children construct new and more-adequate science schemata. These goals cannot be achieved at a national level without some general consensus among science educators, school administrators, and the public.

So what needs to be done to improve the quality of laboratory-based instruction in the schools? We recommend a three-pronged approach involving teacher-training institutions, the public schools, and the schools' relationships with the public. First and foremost, the requirements of students studying to become elementary school teachers must be revised drastically. Many colleges and universities still allow elementary education students to complete their undergraduate degrees with no more than one "real" science course. Science requirements must be increased. Elementary school teachers must attain a basic level of literacy in biological, physical, and earth sciences that will allow them to model the kind of expert conceptions science instruction requires. It may very well be that new college-level science curricula are needed as well.

A second point focuses on the schools and their relationships with their communities. Essentially, the schools, including the faculty, administration, and school boards, will have to educate their communities on science instruction matters. Such educational efforts will have to be every bit as rigorous as the changes we prescribe for higher education. The reason is economic. Laboratory-based educational experiences are expensive. The monies needed to provide laboratory experiences must come from taxpayers. The schools and those who support the schools must begin an education campaign to provide a solid base of intellectual and economic support in the community; the best-prepared teachers will come up short if they do not have the laboratory facilities and materials needed for instruction.

Our third point also has a clear school orientation: Science instruction must be given time. The most excellent teachers employing the finest methods and materials will not succeed if science is not a regular part of each child's school day. Sadly, the one area of instruction most likely to be cut from the elementary school day is science.

Benefits of Effective Instruction

Students' cognitive structures do change as a result of effective science instruction. Champagne, Klopfer, Desena, and Squires (1981) carried out an instructional sequence in which they evaluated the effects of a four-week individualized instructional sequence for changing schema structure in a junior high school geology lesson. Champagne et al. first constructed an integrated structure (a schema) for thirteen words in a unit of material on rocks. This was saved for reference and not used in the instruction. Prior to instruction, Champagne et al. (1981) gave a junior high school group the same thirteen words and asked each person to arrange them on a sheet of paper to show "how you think about the words" (p. 100). They then were asked to explain their arrangement. After the four-week period of instruction, the students were given the thirteen words and were asked to sort them a second time. A comparison of students' responses after the unit with their first responses, as well as a comparison with an expert's responses, indicated that the introduction brought about more complex, expertlike, and complete schematic structure concerning rocks. In this test of the effectiveness of instruction, eighteen of a class of thirty students achieved substantial improvement in schematic structure as an apparent result of the instructional sequence. Not only does this experiment show the effectiveness of instruction, but it also suggests an interesting technique for assessing students' schema structures before and after instruction. This sorting technique seems particularly appropriate when the subject matter is a set of concepts whose relationships are readily classified.

Kuhn et al. (1992) also reported an example of effective science instruction. In this study, Kuhn et al. asked a group of ten fifth- and sixth-grade students to investigate why some balls led to better tennis serves than others and a similar group of ten students to investigate what led to better performance among three cars. Both groups participated in seven thirty-minute discussions over a two-month period. Students were asked to generate a theory about either the balls or the cars and to support that theory by using available evidence.

The longitudinal nature of this study allowed Kuhn et al. (1992) to draw inferences about several critical behaviors. One conclusion was that scientific reasoning improved over time in similar ways even though the two groups solved different problems. This finding suggested that guided discovery improves scientific thinking at a level beyond the specific domain of the problem. A second conclusion was that strategies used to solve the problem were revised and improved over time. This finding suggested that students discover, revise, and delete solution strategies on a continuous basis, given extended experimentation on a single problem (see Siegler & Jenkins, 1989, for a similar finding). Thus, one critical aspect of scientific reasoning instruction in the schools may be that students move from problem to problem without a sufficient amount of time to discover and refine important reasoning skills.

Instructional sequences such as those described above take a great deal of classroom time. Teachers may well argue that because time available for science already is limited, it is not feasible to put such a three-phase teaching program into action, except occasionally for demonstration purposes. Clement (1983), in discussing the difficulties of tackling naive physics beliefs of college students, takes issue with this point of view and has argued that much more instructional time at the college level should be devoted to examining such preconceptions. He asserts that attempts to cover many physics topics, especially while using formal scientific/mathematical language, may make it impossible for students to gain an intuitive understanding of Newtonian concepts of physics. If Clement is correct, arguments made at the beginning of this chapter against treating science as vocabulary acquisition gain additional strength, and the use of student (rather than textbook or teacher) language to confront naive beliefs is further supported.

The three-step instructional approach described earlier is not the only teaching technique science teachers should use. Students and teachers need and value variety. Researchers generally have found that science instruction leads to important changes in the way students represent and think about science concepts when emphasis is put on *coordinating knowledge* and on *how* one thinks about science problems, rather than on *what* one thinks about (Kuhn et al., 1992). Thoughtful teachers will find many variations of this approach that serve to meet the basic goals the model described earlier: expose naive beliefs, create conceptual conflict, and encourage cognitive accommodation to more mature views of science.

A MODEL OF SCIENCE ACHIEVEMENT

One important question is what factors above and beyond expert knowledge and problem-solving strategies lead to science achievement. Reynolds and Walberg (1991, 1992) conducted several studies involving more than 5,000 students across the nation to answer this question. Their research considered a number of potential influences among middle school and high school students, including home environment, prior science achievement, motivation, instructional time, and instructional quality. The relative contribution of each variable was considered by using a complex statistical modeling procedure called LISREL. Analyses such as LISREL allow researchers to investigate the interrelationships among many different variables simultaneously. One advantage of this approach is that the *direct* and *indirect* effects of a variable can be separated. A direct effect occurs when one variable directly causes a change in another variable. For example, Reynolds and Walberg (1991) found that instructional time was related directly to science achievement in eighth grade; that is, more instructional time led to higher achievement regardless of other variables. In contrast, an indirect effect occurs when the relationship between two variables is mediated by another. In the Reynolds and Walberg studies, home environment affected prior science achievement (in seventh grade), which, in turn, affected eighth-grade science achievement. Thus, home environment did not have a direct effect on eighth-grade science achievement even though it had a substantial indirect effect.

The Reynolds and Walberg studies of middle school and high school science achievement reported similar findings; for this reason, the results of these studies are summarized in a single model of science achievement shown in Figure 14-6. The model shown in this figure is referred to as a path diagram. Measured variables are represented as boxes; the relationship between these variables are shown by

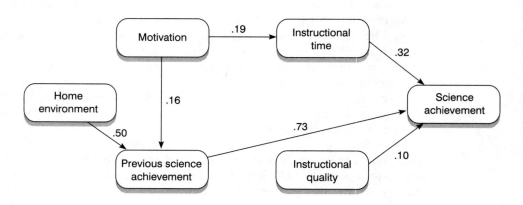

Figure 14-6
A model of science achievement. (Adapted from Reynolds and Walberg [1991].)

arrows. The number beside each arrow is the correlation between variables. The absence of an arrow indicates that a meaningful statistical relationship was not found between variables.

Figure 14-6 suggested a number of important conclusions. The most important was that prior science achievement was strongly related to current science achievement. This finding highlights the vital role of prior knowledge in learning and scientific problem solving (see Chapter 8 and the beginning of this chapter). Another finding was that the amount of instructional time was related to current science achievement. This finding indicates that the amount of science instruction makes an important contribution to learning. One possible reason is that students are given a greater diversity of training. An alternative may be that students spend more time delving into a small number of problems but do so in detail. A third finding was that home environment plays an important role in current science achievement by facilitating prior achievement. One interpretation of this outcome is that the beliefs and attitudes that parents and siblings have about science affects a student's involvement in science throughout his or her early school career.

The model shown in Figure 14-6 also is noteworthy in that several "intuitively obvious" relationships were not found. For example, no relationship was found between instructional time and instructional quality, nor was a strong relationship found between instructional quality and current science achievement. At face value, these findings suggest that the amount of instruction is far more important than the quality of instruction. Caution is needed when interpreting these results, however, because it is quite possible that instructional quality was uniformly high (or low) across this sample—a condition that would tend to reduce the observed magnitude of the correlation.

The results of these studies are consistent with the main themes of this book; namely that (1) prior knowledge and (2) time on task greatly constrain present achievement, whether it is in reading, mathematics, or science. Home environment and motivation also were found to be important determinants of science achievement, a finding that strengthens the argument for a global approach (one that involves parents and siblings) to improving science education. This does not mean that other variables included in the Reynolds and Walberg studies were unimportant, only that they affected present achievement far less than prior knowledge, instructional time, and home environment.

One other variable not included in the Reynolds and Walberg studies deserves attention—gender differences. In a recent review, Kahle, Parker, Rennie, and Riley (1993) reported that males and females differed with respect to science self-efficacy and access to equipment in science classes. These differences were compounded by the fact that teachers believe that males are more self-confident and, as a consequence, direct higher-level questions to males, compared with females. Overall, the evidence suggests that teacher expectations promote differences between males and females with respect to self-confidence and science achievement, although these differences may be ameliorated by interventions that attempt to break down stereotypes among teachers and students.

In summary, even though science achievement ends with expert conceptual knowledge, a flexible repertoire of problem solving strategies, and an understanding of the distinction between theory and data, it begins with a home environment that motivates students and a school environment that provides equal access for all students. The acquisition of knowledge and skills necessary to excel at science is a very complex process that clearly transcends the schoolroom. A very broad approach to science instruction will be needed in the future if American students are to compete worldwide in scientific endeavors.

IMPLICATIONS FOR INSTRUCTION

1. *Teach science as a complex process.* The ambitious goals that science sets for itself—understanding the physical, biological, and social worlds, as well as the methodology of science—provide great challenges to teachers. Cognitive approaches to learning science recommend that science be presented to students as a problem-solving process, rather than simply as a knowledge (vocabulary or facts) acquisition process.

2. *Identify naive beliefs.* Students bring to science a wealth of preconceptions, many of which are incomplete or incorrect. These preconceptions must be identified before effective instruction can occur. The identification process often is slow and uncertain. It requires considerable teaching time, accompanied by a careful choice of instructional materials that elicit the student's own thinking, not just verbalization of information the student thinks a teacher desires.

3. *Confront naive beliefs immediately.* Most science educators believe that science curricula should not begin with the structure of subject matter. Rather, curricula should begin with a focus on ideas that students bring with them. Curricula then are constructed to provide students with a set of experiences that ask them to confront their preconceptions in ways that lead to more-informed conceptions. The magnitude of this task should not be underestimated. Historically, science curricula have been written from the perspective of the expert, not the novice. To write materials that challenge the naive beliefs of children in productive ways and that lead them, ultimately, to more expertlike knowledge structures requires careful attention.

Techniques that effectively confront children's naive beliefs include introduction of exposing events, introduction of discrepant events, generation of a range of conceptual responses to an exposing event, and practice extending new conceptual responses to a broad range of situations. These activities are most valuable when accompanied by direct student involvement with science materials and with other students.

4. *Use hands-on demonstrations.* Because scientific schemata often appear to be in conflict with experience-based schemata (naive beliefs), experiments or demonstrations usually are necessary to challenge the preconceptions. These demonstrations must be chosen thoughtfully so that they require children to exam-

ine their own thinking (preconceptions) about concepts in ways that lead them to consider and adopt more-scientific views. Substantial teacher patience and openness are necessary so that students feel free to verbalize their own thinking and use their own language to come to grips with inconsistencies or inadequacies in their thinking. Although students can memorize correct explanations, observations of explanatory behavior following such memorization suggests that students frequently return to explanations consistent with earlier preconceptions. As we have pointed out before, knowledge alone is insufficient to change habits of thought. Students must have experience-based activities that encourage them to construct new understandings (accommodations) consistent with more-mature, expert views of science.

5. *Give students adequate time to restructure knowledge.* Conceptual change in science is a slow, long-term process. Students need opportunities to see for themselves why their scientific views of the world are inadequate. Progress in science teaching should be assessed over relatively lengthy periods of time, rather than at the close of each class period. This is not to say that teachers should not evaluate the effectiveness of their instruction frequently, but rather that expecting rapid changes in students is unrealistic. If expectations are too high, both student and teacher may become discouraged.

Some studies also suggest that restructuring and strategy development are most effective when students work through a complex problem repeatedly over time. Doing so may help students generate, test, and discard problem-solving strategies as newer, more efficient strategies are constructed to match their developing conceptions of the problem. Jumping endlessly from unit to unit may be counterproductive even though it exposes students to a wide range of materials and problems.

6. *Monitor the use of dysfunctional strategies.* Even older students rely on dysfunctional strategies when reading science texts (Roth, 1985). The most common of these are overreliance on prior knowledge, vocabulary, and factual information, rather than on relational knowledge. Students should be warned (repeatedly, if necessary) against overreliance on these strategies. Interviewing and questioning are good techniques for sounding-out students' beliefs and strategies.

7. *Help students understand the nature of scientific theories.* Research indicates that few students prior to high school have a thorough understanding of the distinction between theory and data. However, learning about the process of scientific inquiry is almost impossible without this distinction. Students must be helped to understand the properties of a theory, how a theory differs from data, and how the two are coordinated.

8. *Involve parents and siblings.* The research by Reynolds and Walberg (1991) suggests that effective long-term science instruction needs to involve parents and siblings. No doubt, views expressed about science at home are crucial. In addition, the kind of epistemological worldview (commonsense vs. critical) modeled at home may play an important role in the student's understanding of the scientific process. Teachers may need to address problems that arise between older students' views of science and opposing parental views.

SUMMARY

Science involves gathering data, making and verifying predictions, and producing explanations of scientific events. Within science, the domain of physics served as a vehicle for the initial attempts of cognitive scientists to study how people solved problems in knowledge-rich domains. Cognitive scientists used protocol analysis to examine the differences in problem-solving behavior between novices (beginning students in a science) and experts (usually Ph.D.-level practitioners). As one might expect, large differences were found in the extent of scientific knowledge, with experts revealing different strategies and conceptual frameworks from novices. An examination of these differences led to the recognition that novices bring with them naive beliefs that, in many cases, make expertlike task representations impossible.

A significant part of effective science instruction is helping students reveal their preconceptions about that domain. Students, then, need to be exposed to carefully chosen empirical and scientific events that lead them to examine the value of their preconceptions and to revise these preconceptions in the direction of more-scientific (expertlike) conceptions. The process of confronting naive beliefs and making accommodations to these beliefs that permit construction of more expertlike schemata is lengthy. Teachers not only should present challenging experiences to children but also must take care to allow students sufficient time to examine their naive beliefs. After this confrontation, children must discover means for accommodating their naive beliefs in the direction of more-scientific views.

Middle school students also exhibit a number of dysfunctional learning strategies. These include overreliance on vocabulary and prior knowledge, and learning factual information in isolation. The use of demonstrations, followed by carefully guided and constructed discussions and questions, appears to help students confront and change these misconceptions. Teachers must be cognizant of such student strategies and provide instruction that challenges these unproductive approaches to studying science.

Considerable consensus exists that confronting students' naive schemata is best accomplished by means of a threefold instructional process. Extensive opportunities (most practically in group settings) must be taken to expose naive beliefs. Then empirical events (experiments, demonstrations, field trips) must be presented to challenge these naive beliefs and lead students to change their schemata so as to incorporate more scientific (expert) schemata. Some evidence suggests that the feedback children give each other is particularly effective in leading them to confront their own naive beliefs.

Studies of expertise in science suggest not only that scientists possess more knowledge of science but also that their knowledge is represented differently. Whereas novices appear to organize their knowledge around surface features of problems, experts organize their knowledge around fundamental physics concepts that may not be present in the problem statement, but rather are inferred by the nature of the problem. Experts' schemata include procedural, as well as declarative, information, whereas most novices appear to lack useful procedural components.

Experts and novices also differ in very important ways with respect to distinguishing formal and empirical aspects of theories. Novices often "adjust" either the theory itself or the data in a way that obscures genuine scientific understanding.

Effective science instruction helps students acquire a view of science as problem solving, rather than simply as declarative knowledge acquisition. Students' naive beliefs (at all levels of instruction) need to be transformed into more expertlike schemata that permit them to accurately represent science problems and to use procedural knowledge to solve the problems.

SUGGESTED READINGS

Ericsson, K. A., & Smith, J. (1991). *Toward a general theory of expertise.* New York: Cambridge University Press.

This edited volume includes a number of science-relevant articles (e.g., Y. Anzai), as well as a more general approach to understanding expertise.

Kuhn, D. (1989). Children and adults as intuitive scientists. *Psychological Review, 96,* 674–689.

This article reviews important differences among children's, lay adults', and real scientists' thinking about theories and the process of coordinating theory with data.

Pintrich, P. R., Marx, R. W., & Boyle, R. A. (1993). Beyond cold conceptual change: The role of motivational beliefs and classroom contextual factors in the process of conceptual change. *Review of Educational Research, 63,* 167–199.

This article provides an up-to-date review of problems in identifying and changing naive beliefs.

Glossary

Action Control: Ability to control actions (e.g., motivation, concentration) that help an individual self-regulate (Ch. 4)

Adjunct Questions: Questions inserted in text materials that readers answer as they read (Ch. 11)

Advance Organizer: Brief prefatory material written at a high level of abstraction that serves as a framework for materials to be learned (Ch. 4)

Algorithm: Procedure in computer science or mathematics that applies to a particular kind of problem and that, if followed correctly, guarantees the correct answer (Ch. 8, 13)

Assignment of Meaning: Stage of perception in which meaning is given to a stimulus (Ch. 2)

Attention: Mental energy used in perception and thought; the focused allocation of resources to a stimulus (Ch. 2)

Attenuated Processing Model: Model of attention that postulates that most attention is allocated to one channel, while a small portion is allocated to the unshadowed channel (Ch. 2)

Attribute: A feature shared across the examples of a concept (e.g., water is an attribute of the concept of *ocean*). Attributes essential to defining the concept and shared across all examples of a concept are called *defining attributes*. (Ch. 3)

Attribution: Causal interpretation of an event or outcome (e.g., that academic success is due to ability) (Ch. 6)

Attributional Retraining: Programs designed to change the attributional responses individuals make in specific settings (Ch. 6)

Attribution Theory: Theory proposed by Weiner to explain the attributional process (Ch. 6)

Authentic Discourse: Discourse that is organized around genuine questions and that elicits the perspectives of participants (Ch. 9)

Automaticity: Performing of any cognitive skill automatically; automated procedures require very few resources (Ch. 2)

Bottom-Up Processing: See *data-driven processing* (Ch. 2)

Bridging: Activities designed to promote transfer of knowledge from one domain to another (Ch. 8)

Calibration of Comprehension: Relationship between what students believe they have learned and what they actually have learned. This metacognitive ability is important for gauging amount of effort required for successful performance. (Ch. 11)

Chunk: Stimulus, such as a letter, number, or word, that becomes unitized. The concept of *chunk* was proposed by Miller as a unit against which short-term memory capacity could be calibrated. (Ch. 3)

Closure (Law of): Phenomenon of incomplete figures tending to be perceived as complete (Ch. 2)

Code-Emphasis Methods: As used by Chall, beginning reading instruction methods that emphasize learning the correspondence between letters and sounds (Ch. 10)

Cognitive Centration: Tendency to pay attention to a single dimension of a problem or situation (Ch. 2)

Cognitive (Informational) Feedback: Specific information that links information about performance with the nature of the task (Ch. 6)

Cognitive Modeling: Procedure for developing students' performance that involves giving a rationale for the performance, demonstrating the performance, and providing opportunity for practice (Ch. 6)

Cognitive Unit: In network models, a concept or schema that is a node in the network (Ch. 3)

Coherence: Property of discourse in which individual elements derive their meaning from earlier or later elements (Ch. 9)

Cohesion: Relations of meaning that exist within a text and that define it as a text (Ch. 12)

Cohesive Ties: Instances of cohesion, such as repetition of words and anaphoric reference, that link a pair of cohesively related items in a text (Ch. 12)

Concept: One of the fundamental building blocks of cognition, a concept is a mental structure that represents a meaningful category and enables us to group objects or events together on the basis of perceived similarities (Ch. 3)

Conceptually Driven Model: Model of reading comprehension that stresses the guiding role of the reader's knowledge and expectations (Ch. 11)

Conceptually Driven (Top-Down) Processing: Cognitive processing guided, in large part, by prior knowledge and predictions, rather than external data (Ch. 2)

Conditional Knowledge: Knowledge about when and why to use strategies (Ch. 4)

Conjunctive Rules: In concept identification, rules for identifying concepts that require two or more attributes to be present (Ch. 3)

Connectionist Model of Memory: Memory model that represents memory as the strength of connections between units (Ch. 3)

Conservative Focusing Strategy: In concept acquisition, an approach in which learners concentrate on selecting new examples of a concept that differ in only one attribute from the first (Ch. 3)

Constraints on Operators: Restrictions that limit the use of objects or variables used to solve a problem (Ch. 8)

Constructivism: Point of view that holds that what individuals learn and understand is constructed through their mental processes and social interactions (Ch. 9)

Contextual Knowledge: In vocabulary knowledge, understanding how words actually are used in written and spoken language. See also *definitional knowledge*. (Ch. 11)

Continuity (Law of): View that perceptual organization preserves smooth continuities, rather than abrupt changes (Ch. 2)

Controllability: In attribution theory, causal dimension that defines the degree to which the cause of an outcome can be controlled (Ch. 6)

Controlling Action: Action that individuals engage in for extrinsic reasons, such as expectation, reward, or punishment (Ch. 6)

Controlling Rewards: Rewards used to control students' behavior or performance (Ch. 6)

Criterion-Referenced Evaluation: Evaluation in which an individual's performance is evaluated with respect to preestablished criteria that are unaffected by other students' performance (Ch. 6)

Data-Driven Model: Model of comprehension that emphasizes "bottom-up" processes, such as those involved in decoding and understanding word meanings (Ch. 11)

Data-Driven (Bottom-Up) Processing: Cognitive processing guided, in large part, by external information versus prior knowledge (Ch.2)

Data-Limited Task: Cognitive activity that is limited due to insufficient or degraded stimuli or information (Ch. 2)

Declarative Knowledge: Systematically organized factual knowledge; "knowing what" (Ch. 4)

Defining Attribute: Attribute of a concept that is essential to defining it (Ch. 3)

Definitional Knowledge: In vocabulary knowledge, understanding of the relationship between a word and other words, as in a dictionary definition. See also *contextual knowledge*. (Ch. 11)

Dialectical Constructivism: Form of constructivism that places the source of knowledge in the interactions between learners and their environments. Dialectical constructivism represents a midpoint between the extremes of endogenous and exogenous constructivism. (Ch. 9)

Dichotic Listening Task: Task in which a person listens to different messages in the right and left ears, usually paying special attention to only one message (Ch. 2)

Digit Span: Number of digits an individual can remember after having been given a sequence of them. The digit span for most adults is around six or seven digits. (Ch. 3)

Disciplined Discussion: Calfee's term for classroom discourse that combines the features of informal conversation and formal instruction. In disciplined discussion, students use interactive processes they have learned to reach goals they have set. (Ch. 9)

Discourse: Structured, coherent sequences of language in which sentences are combined into higher-order units, such as paragraphs, narratives, and expository texts. Conversations and extended sequences of writing are examples of discourse. (Ch. 9, 10)

Discourse Structure: Form into which discourse is organized. Common discourse structures include narratives (stories) and exposition (expository text). (Ch. 10)

Disjunctive Rules: In concept identification, rules for identifying concepts that are "either/or" in nature; that is, an object would be an example of a disjunctive concept with two defining attributes if it contained either of the two attributes (Ch. 3)

Distal Goal: Long-term goal (Ch. 6)

Distinctiveness of Encoding: View that information is memorable to the extent that it is made distinctive (Ch. 4)

Distributed Representation: Feature of connectionist models of memory in which information is stored in the connections among a very large number of simple processing units, not in the units themselves. (Ch. 3)

Divergent Thinking: Thinking characterized by the generation and testing of multiple and diverse solutions (Ch. 8)

Domain Knowledge: Knowledge that individuals have about particular fields of study, such as subject areas and areas of activity (Ch. 9)

Dual Coding Theory: Paivio's theory of memory that proposes that information is encoded within one or both of two distinct memory systems, one specialized for verbal information and the other for images (Ch. 3)

Dual Process Model of Recall: View that recall requires two steps—generation and test—whereas recognition requires only the latter (Ch. 5)

Elaborative Interrogation: Instructional method in which, in its simplest form, learners are asked to read sentences and to answer "why" questions to clarify the relationship between the subject and the predicate of the sentence (Ch. 5, 11)

Elaborative Rehearsal: Techniques, such as mnemonics, used to elaborate information in short-term memory (Ch. 4)

Embedded Program: Program that teaches critical thinking skills as part of a regular content class, such as history (Ch. 8)

Emergent Literacy: Concept that reading is only one dimension of an array of language-related skills and a natural extension of children's knowledge about language to the print medium (Ch. 10)

Enactive Learning: Learning that occurs by performing a task (Ch. 6)

Encoding: Process of transferring information from short-term to long-term memory (Ch. 4)

Encoding Specificity: Assumption that one's ability to retrieve information depends on the degree to which conditions at encoding are reinstated at retrieval (Ch. 5)

Endogenous Constructivism: Form of constructivism that portrays cognitive structures as developing out of other, earlier cognitive structures, not created directly from information provided by the environment. See also *dialectical constructivism* and *exogenous constructivism* (Ch. 9)

Entity Theory: Assumption that one's intellectual ability is fixed (Ch. 7)

Episodic Memory: The memory individuals have for events in their lives; the storage and retrieval of personal, autobiographical experiences (Ch. 3)

Epistemological Belief: Belief about the nature and acquisition of knowledge (Ch. 7)

Error Detection Task: Experimental method, used to determine whether readers are monitoring their comprehension, in which individuals are asked to detect inconsistencies or anomalies in text materials (Ch. 11)

Exogenous Constructivism: Form of constructivism in which knowledge formation is considered to be a reconstruction of structures that exist in external reality and seen as reflecting the inherent organization of the world. See also *endogenous constructivism* and *dialectical constructivism* (Ch. 9)

Explicit Memory: Memory that we recognize as corresponding to some past event. Explicit memory involves conscious recall or recognition of previous experiences. (Ch. 3)

Expository Text: Written discourse organized around abstractions about a topic or body of information. Textbooks, essays, and persuasive arguments are common examples of expository text. (Ch. 10)

Extrinsic Motivation: Motivation in which behaviors are motivated by an external reward (Ch. 6)

Feedback: See *cognitive feedback* and *performance feedback*

First-Letter Method: Mnemonic in which the first letters of to-be-learned words are used to generate an acronym, such as HOMES (for Lakes Huron, Ontario, Michigan, Erie, Superior) (Ch.4)

Fixation: In the eye movements of reading, the brief period during which eyes focus on a point in the text (Ch. 11)

Flashbulb Memory: Graphic memory about a specific, important event (Ch. 5)

Focus Gambling: Concept acquisition strategy in which learners vary more than one attribute of a stimulus at once (Ch. 3)

Focus Unit: Starting point for activation in network models (Ch. 3)

Free Writing: Method of writing instruction in which students are encouraged to write as many ideas as possible without worrying about organization or precise expression (Ch. 12)

Full Processing Model: Model of attention that postulates that full, parallel processing is allocated to two channels simultaneously (Ch. 2)

Functional Dissociation: Instance in which implicit and explicit memory performances are unrelated. To some memory theorists, functional dissociations imply separate memory systems; others propose differences in information processing. (Ch. 3)

Functional Fixedness: Inability to use familiar objects in a novel way (Ch. 8)

Functional Significance: Subjective impression of why an action or event takes place (Ch. 6)

General Knowledge: Knowledge appropriate to a wide range of tasks but not linked with a specific domain (Ch. 9)

Generation Effect: Finding that verbal material that people generate at encoding is better remembered than material merely read (Ch. 5)

Gestalt Laws: See *closure, continuity, Prägnanz, proximity, similarity* (Ch. 2)

Goal State: Terminal objective when solving a problem (Ch. 8)

Group Participation Norms: In classroom discussions, rules that students follow as they participate in the discussion. See also *interpretive norms.* (Ch. 9)

Guided Participation: Process of structuring children's efforts in a social context and gradually releasing responsibility to them. See also *instructional scaffolding* and *zone of proximal development.* (Ch. 9)

Hedge: Statement that qualifies rules for identifying concepts, required because most natural concepts are ambiguous or "fuzzy" (Ch. 3)

Heuristic: General problem-solving strategy or "rule of thumb" that often is helpful when solving a problem, but does not guarantee a solution (Ch. 8, 13)

Ill-Defined Problem: Problem with more than one acceptable solution and no guaranteed method for finding the solution (Ch. 8)

Implicit Beliefs: Beliefs that affect one's behavior without any explicit awareness of the beliefs themselves (Ch. 7)

Implicit Memory: Nonconscious, tacit form of retention in which we do not recognize the operation of memory but behave in ways that clearly show that our earlier experiences are affecting current ones (Ch. 3)

Implicit Theory: Theory about some phenomenon or set of events that has not been formalized explicitly (Ch. 7)

Incremental Theory: Assumption that one's intellectual ability is changeable (Ch. 7)

Inert Knowledge: Domain-specific knowledge that does not transfer to other domains (Ch. 4)

Informational Rewards: Rewards that provide useful feedback to students (Ch. 6)

Information-Oriented Feedback: Specific information that emphasizes how one's performance can be improved (Ch. 6)

Information Processing Model: Computerlike model of memory that portrays humans as acquiring, storing, and retrieving information (Ch. 3)

Initial State: What is known about a problem at the beginning of the problem-solving process (Ch. 8)

Instantiation: Linkage of a particular configuration of values with the representation of the variables of a schema. A schema, which is a mental structure, is instantiated by particular patterns of experience that fit the schema. (Ch. 3)

Instructional Scaffolding: Selective help provided by a teacher and gradually withdrawn that enables students to do things they could not do by themselves. See also *zone of proximal development.* (Ch. 9)

Interactive Model: Model of comprehension that blends conceptual and data-driven elements and that portrays comprehension as a product of their interaction (Ch. 11)

Interpretive norms: In classroom discussions, judgments that students make about whether they have achieved their intellectual purposes for the discussion (Ch. 9)

Intrinsic Motivation: Motivation in which behaviors are performed solely for personal satisfaction (Ch. 6)

IRE pattern: Pattern of classroom discourse in which a teacher *initiates* a discourse segment by asking a question, the student *responds* to the questions, and the teacher *evaluates* the student's response. The IRE pattern is the "default pattern" for most classroom exchanges. (Ch. 9)

Keyword Method: Mnemonic in which a distinctive sound is identified from a to-be-learned word and then that sound is associated with a distinctive image (Ch. 4)

Knowing-in-Action: In Schön's theory, implicit knowledge that is unarticulated, but is revealed in our intelligent actions (Ch. 9)

Knowledge-in-Action: Knowing-in-action that has been described and put into explicit, symbolic form (Ch. 9)

Knowledge of Cognition: Knowledge about cognitive processes and how they can be controlled (Ch. 4)

Language Experience: As used by Chall, method of reading instruction in which children's own oral language, written down, becomes the basis for their initial reading instruction (Ch. 10)

Learned Helplessness: State in which individuals have learned that any behavior they try will fail. Thus, they refuse to engage in a task because they assume they cannot succeed. (Ch. 7)

Learning Goal: Strong desire to improve one's performance and achieve mastery in a domain; also called mastery goal (Ch. 7)

Levels of Processing: View that information is processed at increasingly deeper levels of sophistication (Ch. 4)

Lexical Network: Memory network in which the names of concepts are stored (Ch. 3)

Link: In network models of memory, relations between cognitive units (Ch. 3)

Link Method: Mnemonic in which elaborative links are generated among unrelated items one must remember (Ch. 4)

Locus of Control: In attribution theory, causal dimension that defines whether the cause of an outcome is under internal or external control (Ch. 6)

Long-Term Memory (LTM): Memory over long periods of time, ranging from hours to days and years. Long-term memory is the permanent repository for the information we have acquired. (Ch. 3)

Macrostructure: In Kintsch and Van Dijk's discourse processing model, the reader's representation of the "main idea" or gist of the text. The macrostructure combines the prior knowledge of the individual with the microstructure of the text. (Ch. 11)

Maintenance Rehearsal: Techniques, such as repetition, used to hold information in short-term memory without elaborating it (Ch. 4)

Meaning-Emphasis Methods: As used by Chall, beginning reading instruction methods that favor meaning over decoding (Ch. 10)

Means-Ends Analysis: Method of learning and problem solving in which a large problem is broken into subgoals that are solved sequentially (Ch. 8)

Mediated Response: Subjective, internalized interpretation of an event prior to a response (Ch. 6)

Mediation: Encoding strategy in which to-be-learned information is related to knowledge in memory (Ch. 4)

Metacognition: Knowledge about cognition; knowledge used to regulate thinking and learning (Ch. 4)

Metamemory: Knowledge about the contents and functioning of one's memory (Ch. 4)

Method of Loci: Mnemonic in which to-be-learned information is associated with points in a familiar location (Ch. 4)

Microstructure: In Kintsch and Van Dijk's discourse processing model, knowledge structure that readers build by linking common elements in the text's propositions. The microstructure directly represents the propositions in the text. (Ch. 11)

Mnemonics: Techniques (e.g., mental images) used to elaborate factual information to make it more memorable (Ch. 4)

Modal Model: Model of memory that combines the common features of information processing models (Ch. 3)

Modeling: Demonstrating and describing the component parts of a skill to a novice (Ch. 6)

Morpheme: Sound or combination of sounds that is a minimal unit of meaning in a language. Words may be made up of one or more morphemes. (Ch. 10)

Morphological Cues: Within-word cues, such as prefixes, root words, and suffixes, that provide information on a word's meaning (Ch. 11)

Morphology: Set of principles that describe how sounds are combined into words in a given language (Ch. 10)

Naive Beliefs: Inaccurate beliefs about a phenomenon, acquired through uncontrolled observation (Ch. 14)

Narrative: Form of discourse that is structured by a temporal sequence of events; a "story" (Ch. 10)

Network Models: Models of memory, such as J. R. Anderson's ACT*, that represent memory as large networks of knowledge (Ch. 3)

Node: Cognitive unit, usually a proposition or schema, in network models of memory (Ch. 3)

Norm-Referenced Evaluation: Evaluation in which an individual's performance is evaluated with respect to the group average (Ch. 6)

Operators: Objects or variables that can be manipulated to solve a problem (Ch. 8)

Outcome Performance Feedback: Feedback that provides specific information about performance (Ch. 6)

Parallel Distributed Processing Model: Cognitive model in which there is no "central processor," only simple processing units dedicated to specific processing tasks. Stored in memory are connection strengths among these simple processing units. (Ch. 3)

Parallel Processing: Simultaneous, rather than sequential, processing of information in a cognitive system (Ch. 3)

Pattern Recognition: Identifying a perceptual stimulus (Ch. 2)

Peg Method: A mnemonic in which to-be-learned objects are associated with familiar "mental pegs," such as numbers or a rhyme (Ch. 4)

Perception: Process of sensing, holding, recognizing, and making meaning of sensory information (Ch. 2)

Perceptual Centration: Tendency to focus on only a single aspect of a stimulus or stimuli (Ch. 2)

Performance Goal: Strong desire to demonstrate one's performance and to achieve normatively high success in a domain (Ch. 7)

Performance-Oriented Feedback: Specific information about the correctness of one's performance (Ch. 6)

Personal Teaching Efficacy: Belief that a teacher can produce significant positive change in students (Ch. 6)

Phonemes: Small subset of speech sounds (phones) that are perceived as meaningful by speakers and listeners in a particular language (Ch. 10)

Phonemic Awareness: Ability to recognize phonemes as individual, separable speech sounds. This type of metalinguistic knowledge is critical to learning how to read. (Ch. 10)

Phones: Range of vocalizations of which humans are capable; the "raw material" of spoken languages (Ch. 10)

Phonics: Form of reading instruction in which letter-sound relationships are taught explicitly (Ch. 10)

Prägnanz (Law of): Phenomenon of organizational patterns taking the simplest and most stable form (Ch. 2)

Problem Space: All of the operators and constraints on operators involved in a problem (Ch. 8)

Proceduralize: Transform declarative knowledge into condition-action relationships that can be applied across a variety of situations. Proceduralization is a function of practice. (Ch. 3)

Procedural Knowledge: Knowledge that enables an individual to perform certain activities; "knowing how" (Ch. 4)

Productions: Condition-action rules in "IF/THEN" form that represent procedural knowledge. They state actions to be performed and the conditions under which the action should be taken. (Ch. 3)

Production Systems: Networks of productions. In production systems, multiple productions can be active at the same time. (Ch. 3)

Proposition: Smallest unit of knowledge that can stand as a separate assertion and be judged as true or false. Propositions are fundamental units in many network theories of memory. (Ch. 3)

Propositional Networks: Arrays of propositions in which propositions sharing one or more elements are linked with one another, often in hierarchical fashion (Ch. 3)

Prototype: "Most typical" instance of a concept that best exemplifies the concept (Ch. 3)

Proximal Goal: Short-term goal (Ch. 6)

Proximity (Law of): Phenomenon of objects close together being grouped perceptually into a meaningful relation (Ch. 2)

Reading Readiness: Idea that a given level of mental maturity is required before reading instruction can begin. Contrasted with the concept of *emergent literacy* (Ch. 10)

Recall Threshold: Minimal level of cuing needed to recall information (Ch. 5)

Reciprocal Determinism: Term used by Bandura to highlight the causal relationships among self-beliefs, experience, and external feedback (Ch. 6)

Reciprocal Teaching: Method of sequenced instruction, developed by Palincsar and Brown, in which teachers model comprehension strategies and guide students in their use. Reciprocal teaching initially relies on scaffolding students' responses; responsibility then is shifted gradually to the students. (Ch. 6, 11)

Recognition Threshold: Minimal level of cuing needed to recognize information (Ch. 5)

Reconstructive Memory: Assumption that information is reconstructed at recall on the basis of an incomplete record, rather than remembered verbatim (Ch. 5)

Reflection-in-Action: In Schön's system, conscious thought about our actions and about the thinking that accompanies our action (Ch. 9)

Reflection on Reflection-in-Action: In Schön's system, what skilled teachers do to stimulate students' reflective thinking about their actions and about the thought processes that accompanied those actions (Ch. 9)

Reflective Judgment: Degree to which one evokes epistemological assumptions and reasoning skills that lead to informed conclusions (Ch. 7)

Regulation of Cognition: Knowledge that enables one to control and regulate cognitive activities (Ch. 4)

Rehearsal: See *elaborative rehearsal* and *maintenance rehearsal* (Ch. 4)

Relational Links: In network models of memory, the connections between cognitive units (Ch. 3)

Resource-Limited Task: Cognitive activity that is limited due to insufficient attentional resources (Ch. 2)

Retrieval: Process of transferring information from long-term to short-term memory (Ch. 4, 5)

Saccade: In reading, rapid movement of the eyes from one fixation to the next (Ch. 11)

Scanning Strategy: Strategy for concept acquisition in which learners attempt to test several hypotheses at once, which can overload their ability to remember the information they are processing (Ch. 3)

Schema (pl. *Schemata*): Hypothesized mental framework that helps us organize knowledge, directs perception and attention, and guides recall. Schemata serve as scaffolding for organizing experience. (Ch. 2, 3)

Schema Activation: Instructional techniques designed to bring to mind students' relevant knowledge prior to their encountering new information (Ch. 4, 11)

Self-Determined Action: Action that individuals choose to engage in for intrinsic reasons (Ch. 6)

Self-Efficacy: Degree to which an individual feels confident that he or she can perform a task successfully (Ch. 6)

Self-Regulated Learning: Ability to control and explicitly understand all aspects of one's learning (Ch. 6)

Semantic Memory: Individuals' memories for general concepts and principles and for the relationships among them. Unlike episodic memory, semantic memory is not linked with a particular time and place. (Ch. 3)

Sensory Memory: Holding systems in memory that maintain stimuli briefly so that perceptual analysis can occur. Most is known about visual and auditory sensory memory. (Ch. 3)

Sensory Register: Buffer where perceptual information is momentarily stored until it is recognized or forgotten (Ch. 2)

Serial Processing: Information processing in which activation proceeds from one step to the next in a fixed, sequential order (Ch. 3)

Short-Term Memory (STM): Memory over short periods of time, ranging from seconds to minutes (Ch. 3)

Sight Word Methods: As used by Chall, beginning reading instruction methods that stress the need for children to acquire a stock of familiar words they can recognize on sight (Ch. 10)

Similarity (Law of): Phenomenon of similar objects tending to be perceived as related (Ch. 2)

Slot: In schema theory, informal term referring to a variable in a schema. If slots in a schema match data in the environment (e.g., a particular word problem is recognized as a subtraction problem), specific data values are assigned to appropriate slots in the schema (Ch. 3)

Solution Paths: Set of potential solutions to a specific problem (Ch. 8)

Spreading Activation: In network models, input units causing other units to be activated via their connections, with activation eventually spreading to response units (Ch. 3)

Stability: In attribution theory, causal dimension that defines whether the cause of an outcome is temporary or enduring (Ch. 6)

Stand-Alone Program: Program that teaches critical thinking skills in isolation (Ch. 8)

State-Dependent Learning: Ability to remember information only in the state (e.g., in a drug-induced condition) one learned it in (Ch. 5)

Storage: Process of holding information in long-term memory in some organized fashion (Ch. 2, 4)

Story: Mnemonic in which a meaningful story is generated from unrelated words that one must learn in order to aid recall (Ch. 4)

Syntax: Ways words in a language are grouped into larger units, such as phrases, clauses, and sentences (Ch. 10)

Teachable Language Comprehender (TLC): Collins and Quillian's early network model of semantic memory (Ch. 3)

Teaching Efficacy: Belief that the process of education affects students in positive ways (Ch. 6)

Text Base: Ordered list of propositions created by analyzing the propositional structure of an expository text (Ch. 3)

Text Signals: Words, phrases, and other devices used in reading materials to indicate that certain elements of a text are more important than others or to improve the text's cohesion (Ch. 11)

Thinking Frame: Framework for organizing knowledge and guiding thought processes. See also *schema* (Ch. 8)

Top-Down Processing: See also *conceptually driven processing* (Ch. 2)

Trial and Error: Method of learning and problem solving in which one attempts different solutions randomly (Ch. 8)

Vicarious Learning: Learning that occurs through observation of a skilled model (Ch. 6)

Vocabulary Knowledge: Understanding words and knowing how to use them (Ch. 11)

Well-defined Problem: Problem with only one acceptable solution and a guaranteed method for finding it (Ch. 8)

Working Memory: Portion of memory that contains the "current contents" of consciousness. As models of memory have shifted from an emphasis on storage to an emphasis on processing, the concept of *short-term memory* has been largely replaced by the concept of *working memory*. (Ch. 3)

Yodai Mnemonic: Memory strategy in which familiar pictorial representations are used to remember a multistage procedure (Ch. 4)

Zone of Proximal Development: In Vygotsky's theory, difference between the difficulty level of a problem a child can cope with independently and the level that can be accomplished with the help of older or more expert individuals. Interactions of children and adults in the zone of proximal development are the source of children's cognitive growth. (Ch. 9)

References

Adams, M. J. (1990). *Learning to read: Thinking and learning about print.* Cambridge: MIT Press.

Adams, M. J., & Collins, A. (1977). *A schema-theoretic view of reading* (Tech. Report No. 32). Urbana: University of Illinois, Center for the Study of Reading.

Ahsen, A. (1987). The new structuralism [Special issue]. *Journal of Mental Imagery, 11.*

Alba, J. W., & Hasher, L. (1983). Is memory schematic? *Psychological Bulletin, 93,* 203–231.

Aldridge, B. G. (1992). Project on scope, sequence, and coordination: A new synthesis for improving science education. *Journal of Science Education and Technology, 1,* 13–21.

Alexander, P. A. (1992). Domain knowledge: Evolving themes and emerging concerns. *Educational Psychologist, 27*(1), 33–51.

Alverman, D. E., & Hayes, D. A. (1989). Classroom discussion of content area reading assignments: An intervention study. *Reading Research Quarterly, 24,* 305–335.

Alvermann, D. E., O'Brien, D. G., & Dillon, D. R. (1990). What teachers do when they say they're having discussions of content area reading assignments: A qualitative analysis. *Reading Research Quarterly, 25,* 296–322.

Alvermann, D. E., Smith, L. C., & Readence, J. E. (1985). Prior knowledge activation and the comprehension of compatible and incompatible text. *Reading Research Quarterly, 20,* 420–436.

American Association for the Advancement of Science (AAAS). (1993). *Benchmarks for science literacy.* Washington, DC: Author.

Ames, C. (1992). Classrooms: Goals, structures, and student motivation. *Journal of Educational Psychology, 84,* 261–271.

Ames, C., & Archer, J. (1988). Achievement in the classroom: Student learning strategies and motivational processes. *Journal of Educational Psychology, 80,* 260–267.

Anderson, J. R. (1976). *Language, memory, and thought.* Hillsdale, NJ: Lawrence Erlbaum.

Anderson, J. R. (1983a). *The architecture of cognition.* Cambridge, MA: Harvard University Press.

Anderson, J. R. (1983b). A spreading activation theory of memory. *Journal of Verbal Learning and Verbal Behavior, 22,* 261–295.

Anderson, J. R. (1985). *Cognitive psychology and its implications* (2nd ed.). San Francisco: Freeman.

Anderson, J. R. (1987). Skill acquisition: Compilation of weak-method problem solutions. *Psychological Review, 94,* 192–210.

Anderson, J. R. (1993). Problem solving and learning. *American Psychologist, 48,* 35–44.

Anderson, J. R., & Bower, G. H. (1973). *Human associative memory.* Washington, DC: Winston.

Anderson, J. R., & Reder, L. M. (1979). An elaborative processing explanation of depth of processing. In L. S. Cermak & F.I.M. Craik (Eds.), *Levels of processing in human memory* (pp. 385–404). Hillsdale, NJ: Lawrence Erlbaum.

Anderson, L. (1981). Short-term students' responses to classroom instruction. *Elementary School Journal, 82,* 97–108.

Anderson, R. C. (1984). Role of the reader's schema in comprehension, learning, and memory. In R. C. Anderson, J. Osborn, & R. J. Tierney (Eds.), *Learning to read in American schools: Basal readers and content texts* (pp. 243–258). Hillsdale, NJ: Lawrence Erlbaum.

Anderson, R. C., & Biddle, W. B. (1975). On asking people questions about what they are reading. In G. H. Bower (Ed.), *The psychology of learning and motivation* (Vol. 9, pp. 175–199). New York: Academic Press.

Anderson, R. C., & Ortony, A. (1975). On putting apples into bottles: A problem of polysemy. *Cognitive Psychology, 7,* 167–180.

Anderson, R. C., & Pearson, P. D. (1984). A schema-theoretic view of basic processes in reading comprehension. In P. D. Pearson (Ed.), *Handbook of reading research* (pp. 255–291). New York: Longman.

Anderson, R. C., Reynolds, R. E., Schallert, D. L., & Goetz, E. T. (1977). Frameworks for comprehending discourse. *American Educational Research Journal, 14,* 376–382.

Anderson, R. C., Spiro, R., & Anderson, M. C. (1978). Schemata as scaffolding for the representation of information in connected discourse. *American Educational Research Journal, 15,* 433–440.

Anderson, R. C., Wilson, P. T., & Fielding, L. G. (1988). Growth in reading and how children spend their time outside of school. *Reading Research Quarterly, 23,* 285–303.

Andre, M.L.D.A., & Anderson, T. H. (1978-1979). The development and evaluation of a self-study technique. *Reading Research Quarterly, 14,* 605–623.

Andre, T. (1987a). Processes in reading comprehension and the teaching of reading comprehension. In J. A. Glover & R. R. Ronning (Eds.), *Historical foundations of educational psychology* (pp. 259–296). New York: Plenum.

Andre, T. (1987b). Questions and learning from reading. *Questioning Exchange, 1,* 47–86.

Anglin, J. M. (1977). *Word, object, and conceptual development.* New York: Norton.

Anisfeld, M. (1984). *Language development from birth to three.* Hillsdale, NJ: Lawrence Erlbaum.

Anzai, Y. (1991). Learning and use of representations for physics expertise. In K. A. Anders & J. Smith (Eds.), *Toward a general theory of expertise* (pp. 64–92). New York: Cambridge University Press.

Applebee, A. N. (1983). *The child's concept of story.* Chicago: University of Chicago Press.

Applebee, A. N. (1984). Writing and reasoning. *Review of Educational Research, 54,* 577–596.

Applebee, A. N. (1988, April). *The national assessment.* Paper presented to the Annual Meeting of the American Educational Research Association, New Orleans.

Applebee, A. N., Langer, J., Jenkins, L., Mullis, I., & Foertsch, M. (1990). *Learning to write in our nation's schools.* Princeton, NJ: Educational Testing Service.

Applebee, A. N., Langer, J. A., & Mullis, I.V.S. (1986a). *Writing report cards.* Princeton, NJ: The Nation's Report Card, National Assessment of Educational Progress.

Applebee, A. N., Langer, J. A., & Mullis, I.V.S. (1986b). *Writing: Trends across the decade. 1974–1984.* Princeton, NJ: National Assessment of Educational Progress. (ERIC Document Reproduction Service No. ED 273 680)

Ashton, P. T., & Webb, R. B. (1986). *Making a difference: Teachers' sense of efficacy and student achievement.* New York: Longman.

Atkinson, R. C. (1975). Mnemotechnics in second-language learning. *American Psychologist, 30,* 821-828.

Atkinson, R. C., & Raugh, M. R. (1975). An application of the mnemonic keyword method to the acquisition of a Russian vocabulary. *Journal of Experimental Psychology: Human Learning and Memory, 104,* 126-133.

Atkinson, R. C., & Shiffrin, R. M. (1968). Human memory: A proposed system and its control processes. In K. W. Spence & J. T. Spence (Eds.), *The psychology of learning and motivation: Advances in research and theory* (Vol. 2, pp. 89–195). New York: Academic Press.

Atwell, M. (1981). *The evolution of text: The interrelationship of reading and writing in the composing process.* Paper presented to the Annual Meeting of the National Council of Teachers of English, Boston.

Atwell, N. (1987). *In the middle: Writing, reading, and learning with adolescents.* Montclair, NJ: Boynton/Cook.

Ausubel, D. P. (1960). The use of advance organizers in the learning and retention of meaningful verbal material. *Journal of Educational Psychology, 51,* 267–272.

Ausubel, D. P. (1968). *Educational psychology: A cognitive view.* New York: Holt, Rinehart and Winston.

Ausubel, D. P., & Fitzgerald, D. (1961). The role of discriminability in meaningful verbal learning and retention. *Journal of Educational Psychology, 52,* 266–274.

Ausubel, D. P., & Fitzgerald, D. (1962). Organizer, general background, and antecedent learning variables in sequential learning. *Journal of Educational Psychology, 33,* 243–249.

Ausubel, D. P., & Youssef, M. (1963). Role of discriminability in meaningful parallel learning. *Journal of Educational Psychology, 54,* 331–336.

Axelrod, S. (1983). *Behavior modification for the classroom teacher.* New York: McGraw-Hill.

Baars, B. J. (1986). *The cognitive revolution in psychology.* New York: Guilford.

Baddeley, A. D. (1978). The trouble with levels: A reexamination of Craik and Lockhart's framework for memory research. *Psychology Review, 85,* 139–152.

Baer, D. M., Wolf, M. M., & Risley, T. R. (1968). Some current dimensions of applied behavior analysis. *Journal of Applied Behavior Analysis, 1,* 91–97.

Baker, L. (1985). Differences in the standards used by college students to evaluate their comprehension of expository prose. *Reading Research Quarterly, 20,* 297–313.

Baker, L. (1989). Metacognition, comprehension monitoring, and the adult reader. *Educational Psychology Review, 1,* 338.

Baker, L., & Wagner, J. L. (1987). Evaluating information for truthfulness: The effects of logical subordination. *Memory & Cognition, 15,* 279–284.

Balzer, W. K., Doherty, M. E., & O'Connor, R. (1989). Effects of cognitive feedback on performance. *Psychological Bulletin, 106,* 410–433.

Bandura, A. (1977). *Social learning theory.* Englewood Cliffs, NJ: Prentice-Hall.

Bandura, A. (1986). *Social foundations of thought and action: A social cognitive theory.* Englewood Cliffs, NJ: Prentice-Hall.

Bandura, A. (1993). Perceived self-efficacy in cognitive development and functioning. *Educational Psychologist, 28,* 117–148.

Bandura, A., & Wood, R. (1989). Effect of perceived controllability and performance standards on self-regulation of complex decision making. *Journal of Personality and Social Psychology, 56,* 805–814.

Barker, G. P., & Graham, S. (1987). Developmental study of praise and blame as attributional causes. *Journal of Educational Psychology, 79,* 62–66.

Barnes, B. R., & Clawson, E. U. (1975). Do advance organizers facilitate learning? *Review of Educational Research, 45,* 637–660.

Baron, J. (1988). *Thinking and deciding.* New York: Cambridge University Press.

Baroody, A. J., & Standifer, D. J. (1993). Addition and subtraction in the primary grades. In R. J. Jensen (Ed.), *Research ideas for the classroom: Early childhood mathematics* (pp. 72–102). New York: Macmillan.

Barrel, J. (1991). *Teaching for thoughtfulness.* New York: Longman.

Bartlett, F. C. (1932). *Remembering: A study in experimental and social psychology.* Cambridge, England: Cambridge University Press.

Bates, P. T. (1984). Writing performance and its relationship to the writing attitudes, topic knowledge, and writing goals of college freshmen. *Dissertation Abstracts International, 56,* 02A.

Baumann, J. F. (1984). The effectiveness of a direct instruction paradigm for teaching main idea comprehension. *Reading Research Quarterly, 14,* 93–112.

Beck, I. L., Perfetti, C. A., & McKeown, M. G. (1982). The effects of long-term vocabulary instruction on lexical access and reading comprehension. *Journal of Educational Psychology, 74,* 506–521.

Beed, P. L., Hawkins, E. M., & Roller, C. M. (1991). Moving learners toward independence: The power of scaffolded instruction. *The Reading Teacher, 44*(9), 648–655.

Beesley, M. S. (1986). The effects of word processing on elementary students' written compositions. *Dissertation Abstracts International, 47,* 11A. (University Microfilms No. 87–04, 015)

Bellezza, F. S. (1981). Mnemonic devices: Classification, characteristics, and criteria. *Review of Educational Research, 51,* 247–275.

Benton, S. L., Glover, J. A., & Bruning, R. H. (1983). The effect of number of decisions on prose recall. *Journal of Educational Psychology, 75,* 382–390.

Benton, S. L., Glover, J. A., Kraft, R. G., & Plake, B. S. (1984). Cognitive capacity differences among writers. *Journal of Educational Psychology, 76,* 820–834.

Benton, S. L., Glover, J. A., Monkowski, P. G., & Shaughnessy, M. (1983). Decision difficulty and recall of prose. *Journal of Educational Psychology, 75,* 727–742.

Bereiter, C., & Scardamalia, M. (1987). *The psychology of written composition.* Hillsdale, NJ: Lawrence Erlbaum.

Beyer, B. (1987). *Practical strategies for the teaching of thinking.* Boston: Allyn & Bacon.

Bhaskar, R., & Simon, H. A. (1977). Problem solving in semantically rich domains: An example from engineering thermodynamics. *Cognitive Science, 1,* 193–215.

Birnbaum, J. C. (1982). The reading and composing behavior of selected 4th- and 7th-grade students. *Research in the Teaching of English, 16,* 241–260.

Bissex, G. (1980). *GNYS AT WRK: A child learns to write and read.* Cambridge, MA: Harvard University Press.

Bloom, B. S., Englehart, M. D., Furst, E. J., Hill, W. H., & Krathwohl, D. R. (1956). *Taxonomy of educational objectives: The classification of educational goals: Handbook I. Cognitive domain.* New York: McKay.

Blumenfeld, P. C. (1992). Classroom learning and motivation: Clarifying and expanding goal theory. *Journal of Educational Psychology, 84,* 272–281.

Bobrow, D. G., & Norman, D. A. (1975). Some principles of memory schemata. In D. G. Bobrow & A. M. Collins (Eds.), *Representation and understanding: Studies in cognitive science.* New York: Academic Press.

Boggiano, A. K., Main, D. S., & Katz, P. A. (1988). Children's preference for challenge: The role of perceived competence and control. *Journal of Personality and Social Psychology, 54,* 134–141.

Boltwood, C. R., & Blick, K. A. (1978). The delineation and application of three mnemonic techniques. *Psychonomic Science, 20,* 339–341.

Borkowski, J. G. (1992). Metacognitive theory: A framework for teaching literacy, writing, and math skills. *Journal of Learning Disabilities, 25,* 253–257.

Bourne, L. E. (1982). Typicality effects in logically defined categories. *Memory & Cognition, 10,* 3–9.

Bourne, L. E., Jr. (1970). Knowing and using concepts. *Psychological Review, 77,* 546–556.

Bower, G. H. (1970). Organizational factors in memory. *Cognitive Psychology, 1,* 18–46.

Bower, G. H. (1981). Mood and memory. *American Psychologist, 36,* 129–148.

Bower, G. H., & Clark, M. C. (1969). Narrative stories as mediators for serial learning. *Psychonomic Science, 14,* 181–182.

Brainerd, C. J., & Pressley, M. (Eds.). (1985). *Basic processes in memory development.* New York: Springer Verlag.

Bransford, J., Sherwood, R., Vye, N., & Rieser, J. (1986). Teaching thinking and problem solving. *American Psychologist, 41,* 1078–1089.

Bransford, J. D., Arbitman-Smith, R., Stein, B. S., & Vye, N. J. (1985). Improving thinking and learning skills: An analysis of three approaches. In J. W. Segal, S. F. Chipman, & R. Glaser

(Eds.), *Thinking and learning skills: Relating instruction to basic research* (Vol. 1, pp. 133–206). Hillsdale, NJ: Lawrence Erlbaum.

Bransford, J. D., Barclay, J. R., & Franks, J. J. (1972). Sentence memory: A constructive versus interpretive approach. *Cognitive Psychology, 3,* 193-209.

Bransford, J. D., & Franks, J. J. (1971). The abstraction of linguistic ideas. *Cognitive Psychology, 2,* 331–350.

Bransford, J. D., & Johnson, M. K. (1972). Contextual prerequisites for understanding: Some investigations of comprehension and recall. *Journal of Verbal Learning and Verbal Behavior, 11,* 717–726.

Bransford, J. D., & Johnson, M. K. (1973). Considerations of some problems of comprehension. In W. G. Chase (Ed.), *Visual information processing.* New York: Academic Press.

Bransford, J. D., & Stein, B. S. (1984). *The IDEAL problem solver.* San Francisco: Freeman.

Bransford, J. D., Stein, B. S., Vye, N. J., Franks, J. J., Auble, P. M., Mezynski, K. J., & Perfetti, C. A. (1982). Differences in approaches to learning: An overview. *Journal of Experimental Psychology: General, 111,* 390–398.

Breckler, S. J., & Wiggins, E. C. (1989). Affect versus evaluation in the structure of attitudes. *Journal of Experimental Social Psychology, 25,* 253–271.

Brennan, A. D., Bridge, C. A., & Winograd, R. N. (1986). The effects of structural variation on children's recall of basal reader stories. *Reading Research Quarterly, 21,* 91–104.

Breznitz, Z. (1987). Increasing first graders' reading accuracy and comprehension by accelerating their reading rates. *Journal of Educational Psychology, 79,* 236–242.

Breznitz, Z., & Share, D. L. (1992). Effects of accelerated reading rate on memory for text. *Journal of Educational Psychology, 84,* 193–199.

Britton, B. K. (1986, April). *Signalled text effects on learning of six expository texts.* Paper presented at the Annual Meeting of the American Educational Research Association, San Francisco.

Broadbent, D. E. (1958). *Perception and communication.* London: Pergamon.

Brousseau, B. A., Book, C., & Byers, J. L. (1988). Teacher beliefs and the cultures of teaching. *Journal of Teacher Education, 39,* 33–39.

Brown, A. L. (1980). Metacognitive development and reading. In R. J. Spiro, B. C. Bruce, & W. F. Brewer (Eds.), *Theoretical issues in reading comprehension* (pp. 458–482). Hillsdale, NJ: Lawrence Erlbaum.

Brown, A. L. (1987). Metacognition, executive control, self-regulation, and other more mysterious mechanisms. In F. Weinert & R. Kluwe (Eds.), *Metacognition, motivation, and understanding* (pp. 65–116). Hillsdale, NJ: Lawrence Erlbaum.

Brown, A. L., Bransford, J. D., Ferrara, R. A., & Campione, J. C. (1983). Learning, remembering, and understanding. In J. H. Flavell & E. M. Markman (Eds.), *Handbook of child psychology: Vol. 3. Cognitive development* (pp. 263–340). New York: John Wiley.

Brown, A. L., Day, J. D., & Jones, R. S. (1983). The development of plans for summarizing texts. *Child Development, 54,* 968–979.

Brown, A. L., & Palincsar, A. S. (1982). Inducing strategic learning from texts by means of informed, self-control training. *Topics in Learning and Learning Disabilities, 2,* 1–18.

Brown, A. L., & Palincsar, A. S. (1989). Guided, cooperative learning and individual knowledge acquisition. In L. Resnick (Ed.), *Cognition and instruction: Issues and agendas* (pp. 117–161). Hillsdale, NJ: Lawrence Erlbaum.

Brown, J. A. (1958). Some tests of the decay theory of immediate memory. *Quarterly Journal of Experimental Psychology, 10,* 12–21.

Brown, J. S., & Burton, R. B. (1978). Diagnostic models for procedural bugs in basic mathematical skills. *Cognitive Science, 2,* 155–192.

Brown, J. S., Collins, A., & Duguid, P. (1989). Situated cognition and the culture of learning. *Educational Researcher, 18,* 32–42.

Brown, J. S., McDonald, J. L., Brown, T. L., & Carr, T. H. (1988). Adapting to processing demands in discourse production: The case of handwriting. *Journal of Experimental Psychology: Human Perception and Performance, 14,* 45–59.

Brown, R. (1973). *A first language: The early stages.* Cambridge, MA: Harvard University Press.

Brown, R., Cazden, C., & Bellugi, U. (1968). The child's grammar from 1 to 3. In J. P. Hill (Ed.), *Minnesota symposia on child psychology* (Vol. 2, pp. 70–126). Minneapolis: University of Minnesota Press.

Brown, R., & Kulik, J. (1977). Flashbulb memories. *Cognition, 5,* 73–99.

Brown, S. (1986). *Reading-writing connections: College freshman basic writers' apprehension and achievement.* (ERIC Document Reproduction Service No. ED 274 965)

Bruce, V., & Green, P. (1985). *Visual perception.* Hillsdale, NJ: Lawrence Erlbaum.

Bruner, J. S., Goodnow, J. J., & Austin, G. A. (1956). *A study of thinking.* New York: John Wiley.

Bruning, R. H. (in press). The college classroom from the perspective of cognitive psychology. In K. Prichard, R. M. Sawyer, & K. Hostetler (Eds.), *Handbook of college teaching: Theory and applications.* Westport, CT: Greenwood.

Bryne, B., & Fielding-Barnsley, R. (1991). Evaluation of a program to teach phonemic awareness to young children. *Journal of Educational Psychology, 83,* 451–455.

Bugelski, B. R., Kidd, E., & Segmen, J. (1968). Image as a mediator in one-trial paired-associate learning. *Journal of Experimental Psychology, 76,* 69–73.

Burger, J. M. (1985). Desire for control and achievement related behaviors. *Journal of Personality and Social Psychology, 48,* 1520–1533.

Burton, R. B. (1981). Debuggy: Diagnosis of errors in basic mathematical skills. In D. H. Sleeman & J. S. Brown (Eds.), *Intelligent tutoring systems* (pp. 62–81). New York: Academic Press.

Butler, R. (1987). Task-involving and ego-involving properties of evaluation: Effects of different feedback conditions on motivational perceptions, interest, and performance. *Journal of Educational Psychology, 79,* 474–482.

Butterfield, J. (Ed.). (1986). *Language, mind, and logic.* New York: Cambridge University Press.

Caelli, T., & Moraglia, G. (1986). On the detection of signals embedded in natural scenes. *Perception & Psychophysics, 39,* 87–95.

Cain, K. M., & Dweck, C. S. (1989). The development of children's conceptions of intelligence: A theoretical framework. In R. Sternberg (Ed.), *Advances in the psychology of human intelligence* (Vol. 5, pp. 47–82). Hillsdale, NJ: Lawrence Erlbaum.

Cairney, T. H. (1988). The purpose of basals: What children think. *The Reading Teacher, 41,* 420–428.

Calfee, R., Chambliss, M., & Beretz, M. (1991). Organizing for comprehension and composition. In R. Bowler & W. Ellis (Eds.), *All language and the creation of literacy* (pp. 79–93). Baltimore: Orton Dyslexia Society.

Calfee, R., & Drum, P. (1986). Research on teaching reading. In M. C. Wittrock (Ed.), *Handbook of research on teaching* (pp. 804–849). New York: Macmillan.

Calfee, R., Dunlap, K., & Wat, A. (1994). Authentic discussion of texts in middle grade schooling: An analytic-narrative approach. *Journal of Reading, 37,* 546–556.

Calfee, R. C. (1994). Critical literacy: Reading and writing for a new millennium. In N. J. Ellsworth , C. N. Hedley, & A. N. Baratta (Eds.), *Literacy: A redefinition* (pp. 19–38). Hillsdale, NJ: Lawrence Erlbaum.

Calfee, R. C., & Henry, M. K. (1986). Project READ: An inservice model for training classroom teachers in effective reading instruction. In J. V. Hoffman (Ed.), *Effective teaching of reading: Research and practice* (pp. 199–299). Newark, DE: International Reading Association.

Calkins, L. M. (1986). *The act of teaching writing.* Portsmouth, NH: Heinemann.

Campbell, D., & Stanley, J. (1963). *Experimental and quasi-experimental designs for research.* Chicago: Rand McNally.

Carbo, M. (1988). Debunking the great phonics myth. *Phi Delta Kappan, 70,* 226–240.

Carey, L., & Flower, L. (1989). Cognition and writing: The idea generation process. In J. A. Glover, R. R. Ronning, & C. R. Reynolds (Eds.), *Handbook of creativity* (pp. 305–321). New York: Plenum.

Carey, S. (1985). *Conceptual change in childhood.* Cambridge: MIT Press.

Carey, S. (1986). Cognitive science and science education. *American Psychologist, 41,* 1123–1130.

Carey, S., Evans, R., Honda, M., Jay, E., & Unger, C. M. (1989). "An experiment is when you try it and see if it works": A study of grade 7 students' understanding of the construction of scientific knowledge. *International Journal of Science Education, 11,* 514–529.

Carey, S., & Smith, C. (1993). On understanding the nature of scientific knowledge. *Educational Psychologist, 28,* 235–251.

Carey, S. T., & Lockhart, R. S. (1973). Encoding differences in recognition and recall. *Memory & Cognition, 1,* 297–300.

Carlson, L., Zimmer, J. W., & Glover, J. A. (1981). First-letter mnemonics: DAM (don't aid memory). *Journal of Genetic Psychology, 104,* 287–292.

Carmichael, L., Hogan, H. P., & Walter, A. A. (1932). An experimental study of the effect of language on the reproduction of visually perceived forms. *Journal of Experimental Psychology, 15,* 73–86.

Carpenter, T. P. (1985). Learning to add and subtract: An exercise in problem solving. In E. A. Silver (Ed.), *Teaching and learning mathematical problem solving: Multiple research perspectives* (pp. 123–161). Hillsdale, NJ: Lawrence Erlbaum.

Carpenter, T. P. (1986). Conceptual knowledge as a foundation for procedural knowledge: Implications from research on the initial learning. In J. Hiebert (Ed.), *Conceptual and procedural knowledge: The case of mathematics* (pp. 135–176). Hillsdale, NJ: Lawrence Erlbaum.

Carpenter, T. P., Fennema, E., Fuson, K., Hiebert, J., Human, P. Murray, H., Olivier, A., & Wearne, D. (1994, April). *Teaching mathematics for learning with understanding in the primary grades.* Paper presented at the Annual Meeting of the American Educational Research Association, New Orleans.

Carpenter, T. P., & Moser, J. M. (1982). The development of addition and subtraction problem-solving skills. In T. R. Carpenter, J. M. Moser, & T. A. Romberg (Eds.), *Addition and subtraction: A cognitive perspective* (pp. 42–68). Hillsdale, NJ: Lawrence Erlbaum.

Carpenter, T. P., & Moser, J. M. (1983). Acquisition of addition and subtraction concepts. In R. Lesh & M. Landau (Eds.), *Acquisition of mathematical concepts and processes* (pp. 106–113). New York: Academic Press.

Carpenter, T. P., & Moser, J. M. (1984). The acquisition of addition and subtraction concepts in grades one through three. *Journal for Research in Mathematics Education, 15,* 179–202.

Case, R. (1978). A developmentally based theory and technology of instruction. *Review of Educational Research, 48,* 439–463.

Case, R. (1985). *Intellectual development, birth to adulthood.* New York: Academic Press.

Case, R. (1992). *The mind's staircase: Exploring the conceptual underpinnings of children's thought and knowledge.* Hillsdale, NJ: Lawrence Erlbaum.

Cazden, C. (1988). *Classroom discourse: The language of teaching and learning.* Portsmouth, NH: Heinemann.

Chall, J. S. (1967). *Learning to read: The great debate.* New York: McGraw-Hill.

Chall, J. S. (1987). Two vocabularies for reading: Recognition and meaning. In M. G. McKeown & M. E. Curtis (Eds.), *The nature of vocabulary acquisition* (pp. 7–17). Hillsdale, NJ: Lawrence Erlbaum.

Chall, J. S., Jacobs, V. A., & Baldwin, L. E. (1990). *The reading crisis: Why poor children fall behind.* Cambridge, MA: Harvard University Press.

Champagne, A. B., Klopfer, L. E., & Anderson, J. H. (1980). Factors influencing the learning of classical mechanics. *American Journal of Physics, 48,* 1074–1079.

Champagne, A. B., Klopfer, L. E., Desena, A. T., & Squires, D. A. (1981). Structural representation of students' knowledge before and after science instruction. *Journal of Research in Science Teaching, 18,* 97–111.

Chandler, M., Boyes, M., & Ball, L. (1990). Relativism and stations of epistemic doubt. *Journal of Experimental Child Psychology, 50,* 370–395.

Chandler, P., & Sweller, J. (1990). Cognitive load theory and the format of instruction. *Cognition and Instruction, 8,* 293–332.

Chaney, C. (1992). Language development, metalinguistic skills, and print awareness in 3-year-old children. *Applied Psycholinguistics, 13,* 485–514.

Chase, W. G. (1987). Visual information processing. In K. R. Boff, L. Kaufman, & J. P. Thomas (Eds.), *Handbook of perception and human performance: Vol. 2. Information processing* (pp. 28–1 to 28–60). New York: John Wiley.

Chase, W. G., & Simon, H. A. (1973a). The mind's eye in chess. In W. G. Chase (Ed.), *Visual information processing* (pp. 215–281). New York: Academic Press.

Chase, W. G., & Simon, H. A. (1973b). Perception in chess. *Cognitive Psychology, 4,* 55–81.

Chi, M.T.H., Feltovich, P. J., & Glaser, R. (1981). Categorization and representation of physics problems by experts and novices. *Cognitive Science, 5,* 121–152.

Chinn, C. A., & Waggoner, M. A. (1992, April). *Dynamics of classroom discussion: An analysis of what causes segments of open discourse to begin, continue, and end.* Paper presented at the Annual Meeting of the American Educational Research Association, San Francisco.

Chipman, S. (1988, April). *Cognitive processes in mathematics.* Paper presented at the Annual Meeting of the American Educational Research Association, New Orleans.

Chomsky, N. (1957). *Syntactic structures.* The Hague, Netherlands: Mouton.

Chomsky, N. (1965). *Aspects of the theory of syntax.* Cambridge: MIT Press.

Clancey, W. J. (1988). Acquiring, representing, and evaluating a competence model of diagnostic strategy. In M. Chi, R. Glaser, & M. Farr (Eds.), *The nature of expertise* (pp. 261–287). Hillsdale, NJ: Lawrence Erlbaum.

Clark, J. M., & Paivio, A. (1991). Dual coding theory and education. *Educational Psychology Review, 3,* 149–210.

Clay, M. M. (1991). Child development. In J. Flood, J. M. Jensen, D. Lapp, & J. R. Squire (Eds.). *Handbook of research on teaching the English language arts* (pp. 40–45). New York: Macmillan.

Clement, J. (1983). A conceptual model discussed by Galileo and used intuitively by physics students. In D. Gentner & A. L. Stevens (Eds.), *Mental models* (pp. 206–251). Hillsdale, NJ: Lawrence Erlbaum.

Collins, A. F., Gathercole, S. E., Conway, M. A., & Morris, P. E. (1993). *Theories of memory.* Hove, England: Lawrence Erlbaum.

Collins, A. M., & Loftus, E. F. (1975). A spreading-activation theory of semantic processing. *Psychological Review, 82,* 407–428.

Collins, A. M., & Quillian, M. R. (1969). Retrieval time from semantic memory. *Journal of Verbal Learning and Verbal Behavior, 8,* 240–248.

Collyer, S. C., Jonides, J., & Bevan, W. (1972). Images as memory aids: Is bizarreness helpful? *American Journal of Psychology, 85,* 31–38.

Conry, R., & Plant, W. T. (1965). WAIS and group test prediction of an academic success criterion: High school and college. *Educational and Psychological Measurement, 25,* 493–500.

Corkill, A. J. (1992). Advance organizers: Facilitators of recall. *Educational Psychology Review, 4,* 33–68.

Corkill, A. J., Bruning, R. H., & Glover, J. A. (1988). Advance organizers: Concrete vs. abstract. *Journal of Educational Research, 82,* 76–81.

Corkill, A. J., Glover, J. A., Bruning, R. H., & Krug, D. (1988). Advance organizers: Retrieval context hypotheses. *Journal of Educational Psychology, 80,* 304–311.

Council of Chief State School Officers. (1993). *State indicators of science and mathematics education.* Washington, DC: Author.

Covington, M., & Omelich, C. (1984). Task-oriented versus competitive learning structures: Motivational and performance consequences. *Journal of Educational Psychology, 77,* 1038–1050.

Covington, M. C., Crutchfield, R. S., Davies, L. B., & Olton, R. M. (1974). *The productive thinking program: A course in learning to think.* New York: Merrill/Macmillan.

Craik, F.I.M. (1979). Human memory. *Annual Review of Psychology, 30,* 63–102.

Craik, F.I.M., & Lockhart, R. S. (1972). Levels of processing: A framework for memory research. *Journal of Verbal Learning and Verbal Behavior, 11,* 671–684.

Craik, F.I.M., & Lockhart, R. S. (1986). CHARM is not enough: Comments on Eich's model of cued recall. *Psychological Review, 93,* 360–364.

Craik, F.I.M., & Tulving, E. (1975). Depth of processing and the retention of words in episodic memory. *Journal of Experimental Psychology: General, 104,* 268–294.

Cross, D. R., & Paris, S. G. (1988). Developmental and instructional analyses of children's metacognition and reading comprehension. *Journal of Educational Psychology, 80,* 131–142.

Crossman, E.R.F. (1959). A theory of the acquisition of a speed-skill. *Ergonomics, 2,* 153–166.

Crouse, J. H., & Idstein, P. (1972). Effects of encoding cues on prose learning. *Journal of Educational Psychology, 63,* 309–313.

Crowder, R. G. (1976). *Principles of learning and memory.* Hillsdale, NJ: Lawrence Erlbaum.

Cunningham, A. E., & Stanovich, K. E. (1991). Tracking the unique effects of print exposure in children: Associations with vocabulary, general knowledge, and spelling. *Journal of Educational Psychology, 83,* 264–274.

Dacey, J. S. (1989). *Fundamentals of creative thinking.* Lexington, MA: D. C. Heath.

Daehler, M. W., & Bukatko, D. (1985). *Cognitive development.* New York: Knopf.

Daiute, C. (1986). Physical and cognitive factors in revising: Insights from studies with computers. *Research in the Teaching of English, 20,* 141–159.

Dansereau, D. F. (1988). Cooperative learning strategies. In C. E. Weinstein, E. T. Goetz, & P. A. Alexander (Eds.), *Learning and study strategies* (pp. 103–120). New York: Academic Press.

Darwin, G. J., & Baddeley, A. D. (1974). Acoustic memory and the perception of speech. *Cognitive Psychologist, 6,* 41–60.

Darwin, G. J., Turvey, M. T., & Crowder, R. G. (1972). An auditory analogue of the Sperling partial report procedure: Evidence for brief auditory storage. *Cognitive Psychology, 3,* 255–267.

Deakin, J. M., & Allard, F. (1991). Skilled memory in expert figure skating. *Memory & Cognition, 19,* 79–86.

De Boer, J. J. (1959). Grammar in language teaching. *Elementary English, 36,* 413–421.

de Bono, E. (1973). *CoRT thinking materials.* London: Direct Education Services.

Deci, E. L., & Ryan, R. M. (1985). *Intrinsic motivation and self-determination in human behavior.* New York: Plenum.

Deci, E. L., & Ryan, R. M. (1987). The support of autonomy and control of behavior. *Journal of Personality and Social Psychology, 53,* 1024–1037.

Deci, E. L., Vallerand, R. J., Pelletier, L. G., & Ryan, R. M. (1991). Motivation and education: The self-determination perspective. *Educational Psychologist, 26,* 325–346.

DeGroot, A. D. (1965). *Thought and choice in chess.* The Hague, Netherlands: Mouton.

Delclos, V. R., & Harrington, C. (1991). Effects of strategy monitoring and proactive instruction on children's problem-solving performance. *Journal of Educational Psychology, 83,* 35–42.

Dellarosa, D. (1988). A history of thinking. In R. J. Sternberg & E. F. Smith (Eds.), *The psychology of human thought* (pp. 1–18). New York: Cambridge University Press.

Dellarosa, D., & Bourne, L. E. (1985). Surface form and the spacing effect. *Memory & Cognition, 13,* 529–537.

DeLoache, J. S., Cassidy, D. J., & Brown, A. L. (1985). Precursors of mnemonic strategies in very young children's memory. *Child Development, 56,* 125–137.

Dempster, F. N. (1981). Memory span: Sources of individual and developmental differences. *Psychological Bulletin, 89,* 63–100.

Derry, S. J. (1984). Effects of an organizer on memory for prose. *Journal of Educational Psychology, 76,* 98–107.

Deutsch, D. (1987). Auditory pattern recognition. In K. R. Boff, L. Kaufman, & J. P. Thomas (Eds.), *Handbook of perception and human performance: Vol. 2. Information processing* (pp. 32–1 to 32–55). New York: John Wiley.

Dewey, J. (1910). *How we think.* Boston: D. C. Heath.

Dewitz, R., Carr, E. M., & Patberg, J. P. (1987). Effects of inference training on comprehension and comprehension monitoring. *Reading Research Quarterly, 22,* 99–119.

Diamond, B. J. (1985). The cognitive processes of competent third-grade writers: A descriptive study. *Dissertation Abstracts International, 46,* 05A. (University Microfilms No. DA 8513892)

Dickinson, D. K., & Snow, C. E. (1986). *Interrelationships among pre-reading and oral language skills in kindergartners from two social classes.* (ERIC Document Reproduction Services No. ED 272 860)

Diener, C. I., & Dweck, C. S. (1978). An analysis of learned helplessness: Continuous changes in performance, strategy, and achievement cognitions after failure. *Journal of Personality and Social Psychology, 36,* 451–462.

DiLollo, U., & Dixon, P. (1988). Two forms of persistence in visual information processing. *Journal of Experimental Psychology: Human Perception and Performance, 14,* 601–609.

Dinnel, D., & Glover, J. A. (1985). Advance organizers: Encoding manipulations. *Journal of Educational Psychology, 77,* 514–521.

DiVesta, F. J. (1989). Applications of cognitive psychology to education. In M. C. Wittrock & F. Farley (Eds.), *The future of educational psychology* (pp. 37–73). Hillsdale, NJ: Lawrence Erlbaum.

Dole, J. A., Duffy, G. G., Roehler, L. R., & Pearson, P. D. (1991). Moving from the old to the new: Research on reading comprehension instruction. *Review of Educational Research, 61,* 239–264.

Dooling, D. J., & Lachman, R. (1971). Effects of comprehension on retention of prose. *Journal of Experimental Psychology, 88,* 216–222.

Downing, J. (1979). *Reading and reasoning.* New York: Springer Verlag.

Drum, P. A., & Konopak, B. C. (1987). Learning word meanings from written context. In M. G. McKeown & M. E. Curtis (Eds.), *The nature of vocabulary acquisition* (pp. 7–17). Hillsdale, NJ: Lawrence Erlbaum.

Duell, O. K. (1978). Overt and covert use of different cognitive levels. *Contemporary Educational Psychology, 3,* 239–245.

Duin, A. H., & Graves, M. F. (1987). Intensive vocabulary instruction as a prewriting technique. *Reading Research Quarterly, 22,* 311–330.

Duncker, K. (1945). On problem solving (L. S. Lees, Trans.) [Special issue]. *Psychological Monographs, 58*(270).

Dunkle, M. F., Schraw, G., & Bendixen, L. (1993, April). *The relationship between epistemological beliefs, causal attributions, and reflective judgment.* Paper presented at the Annual Meeting of the American Educational Research Association. Atlanta, GA.

Durkin, D. (1978-1979). What classroom observations reveal about reading comprehension instruction. *Reading Research Quarterly, 14,* 481–533.

Durkin, D. (1981). Reading comprehension instruction in five basal reading series. *Reading Research Quarterly, 16,* 515–544.

Dweck, C. S. (1975). The role of expectations and attributions in the alleviation of learned helplessness. *Journal of Personality and Social Psychology, 31,* 674–685.

Dweck, C. S. (1986). Motivational processes affecting learning. *American Psychologist, 41,* 1040–1048.

Dweck, C. S., & Leggett, E. S. (1988). A social-cognitive approach to motivation and personality. *Psychological Review, 95,* 256–273.

Dyson, A. (1983). The role of oral language in early writing processes. *Research in the Teaching of English, 17,* 1–30.

Dyson, A. H., & Freedman, S. W. (1991). Writing. In J. Flood, J. M. Jensen, D. Lapp, & J. R. Squire (Eds.), *Handbook of research on teaching the English language arts* (pp. 754–774). New York: Macmillan.

Ebbinghaus, H. (1885). *Uber das Gedachtnis* [Memory]. Leipzig, Germany: Duncker & Humblot.

Edwards, K. (1990). The interplay of affect and cognition in attitude formation and change. *Journal of Personality and Social Psychology, 59,* 202–216.

Ehri, L. (1991). Development of the ability to read words. In P. D. Pearson (Ed.), *Handbook of reading research* (2nd ed., pp. 395–419). New York: Longman.

Ehri, L., & Robbins, C. (1992). Beginners need some decoding skill to read words by analogy. *Reading Research Quarterly, 27,* 12–26.

Ehri, L. C., & Wilce, L. S. (1985). Movement into reading: Is the first stage of printed word learning visual or phonetic? *Reading Research Quarterly, 20,* 163–179.

Ehri, L. C., & Wilce, L. S. (1987a). Cipher versus cue reading: An experiment in decoding acquisition. *Journal of Educational Psychology, 79,* 3–13.

Ehri, L. C., & Wilce, L. S. (1987b). Does learning to spell help beginners learn to read words? *Reading Research Quarterly, 22,* 47–65.

Elbow, P. (1981). *Writing with power: Techniques for mastering the writing process.* New York: Oxford University Press.

Elliott, E. S., & Dweck, C. S. (1988). An approach to motivation and achievement. *Journal of Personality and Social Psychology, 54,* 5–12.

Elmes, D. G., & Bjork, R. A. (1975). The interaction of encoding and rehearsal processes in the recall of repeated and nonrepeated items. *Journal of Verbal Learning and Verbal Behavior, 14,* 30–42.

Englert, C. S., Raphael, T. E., Anderson, L. M., Anthony, H. M., & Stevens, D. D. (1991). Making strategies and self-talk visible: Writing instruction in regular and special education classrooms. *American Educational Research Journal, 28,* 337–372.

Ennis, R. H. (1987). A taxonomy of critical thinking dispositions and abilities. In J. Baron & R. Sternberg (Eds.), *Teaching thinking skills: Theory and practice* (pp. 9–26). San Francisco: Freeman.

Epstein, W., Glenberg, A. M., & Bradley, M. M. (1984). Coactivation and comprehension: Contribution of text variables to the illusion of knowing. *Memory & Cognition, 12,* 355–360.

Ericsson, K. A., Chase, W. G., & Faloon, S. (1980). Acquisition of a memory skill. *Science, 208,* 1181–1182.

Ervin, S. M. (1964). Imitation and structural change in children's language. In E. H. Lenneberg (Ed.), *New directions in the study of language* (pp. 163–189). Cambridge: MIT Press.

Eysenck, M. W., & Keane, M. K. (1990). *Cognitive psychology: A student's handbook.* Hillsdale, NJ: Lawrence Erlbaum.

Farr, R. (1969). *Reading: What can be measured?* Newark, DE: International Reading Association.

Faw, H. W., & Waller, T. G. (1976). Mathemagenic behaviors and efficiency in learning from prose materials. Review, critique, and recommendations. *Review of Educational Research, 46,* 691–720.

Fennema, E., Franke, M. L., Carpenter, T. P., & Carey, D. A. (1993). Using children's mathematical knowledge in instruction. *American Educational Research Journal, 30,* 555–583.

Ferster, C. B., & Skinner, B. F. (1957). *Schedules of reinforcement.* New York: Appleton-Century-Crofts.

Feuerstein, R., Rand, Y., Hoffman, M. B., & Miller, R. (1980). *Instrumental enrichment: An intervention program for cognitive modifiability.* Baltimore: University Park Press.

Fishbein, H. D., Eckart, T., Lauver, E., Van Leeuwen, R., & Langmeyer, D. (1990). Learners' questions and comprehension in a tutoring setting. *Journal of Educational Psychology, 82,* 163–170.

Fisher, D. L., Duffy, S. A., Young, C., & Pollatsek, A. (1988). Understanding the central processing limit in consistent-mapping visual search tasks. *Journal of Experimental Psychology: Human Perception and Performance, 14,* 253–266.

Flavell, J. H. (1992). Perspectives on perspective taking. In H. Beilin & P. Pufall (Eds.), *Piaget's theory: Prospects and possibilities* (pp. 107–139). Hillsdale, NJ: Lawrence Erlbaum.

Flavell, J. H., Friedrichs, A. G., & Hoyt, J. P. (1970). Developmental changes in memorization processes. *Cognitive Psychology, 1,* 324–340.

Flexser, A. J., & Tulving, E. (1978). Retrieval independence in recognition and recall. *Psychological Review, 85,* 153–171.

Flink, C., Boggiano, A. K., & Barrett, M. (1990). Controlling teaching strategies: Undermining children's self-determination and performance. *Journal of Personality and Social Psychology, 59,* 916–924.

Flower, L., & Hayes, J. R. (1984). The representation of meaning in writing. *Written Communication, 1,* 120–160.

Foorman, B. R., Francis, D. J., Novy, D. M., & Liberman, D. (1991). How letter-sound instruction mediates progress in first-grade reading and spelling. *Journal of Educational Psychology, 83,* 456–469.

Försterling, F. (1985). Attributional retraining: A review. *Psychological Bulletin, 98,* 495–512.

Fowler, R. L., & Barker, A. S. (1974). Effectiveness of highlighting for retention of text material. *Journal of Applied Psychology, 59,* 358–364.

Frederiksen, C. H. (1975). Representing logical and semantic structure of knowledge acquired from discourse. *Cognitive Psychology, 7,* 371–458.

Freedman, S. W. (1992). Outside-in and inside-out: Peer response groups in two ninth-grade classes. *Research in the Teaching of English, 26,* 71–107.

Freeman, D. J., & Porter, A. C. (1989). Do textbooks dictate the content of mathematics instruction in elementary schools? *American Educational Research Journal, 6,* 207–226.

Friedman, A., Polson, M. C., & Dafoe, C. G. (1988). Dividing attention between the hands and the head: Performance trade-offs between rapid finger tapping and verbal memory. *Journal of Experimental Psychology: Human Perception and Performance, 14,* 60–68.

Frogner, E. (1939). Grammar approach vs. thought approach in teaching sentence structure. *English Journal, 28,* 518–526.

Furst, B. (1954). *Stop forgetting.* New York: Garden City Press.

Fuson, K. C. (1992). Research on whole number addition and subtraction. In D. A. Grouws (Ed.), *Handbook of research on mathematics teaching and learning* (pp. 243–275). New York: Macmillan.

Fuson, K. C., & Fuson, A. M. (1992). Instruction supporting children's counting on for addition and counting up for subtraction. *Journal for Research in Mathematics Education, 23,* 72–78.

Gagne, E. D. (1985). *The cognitive psychology of school learning.* Boston: Little, Brown.

Gagne, R. M. (1965). The analysis of instructional objectives for the design of instruction. In R. Glaser (Ed.), *Teaching machines and programmed learning: Vol. 2. Data and direction* (pp. 32–41). Washington, DC: National Education Association.

Gagne, R. M. (1970). *The conditions of learning* (2nd ed.). New York: Holt, Rinehart & Winston.

Gardner, H. (1983). *Frames of mind: The theory of multiple intelligences.* New York: Basic Books.

Garner, R., & Alexander, P. A. (1989). Metacognition: Answered and unanswered questions. *Educational Psychologists, 24,* 143–158.

Garner, R., Gillingham, M. G., & White, C. S. (1989). Effects of "seductive details" on macroprocessing and microprocessing in adults and children. *Cognition and Instruction, 6,* 41–57.

Getzels, J., & Czikszentmihalyi, M. (1976). *The creative vision: A longitudinal study of problem finding in art.* New York: John Wiley.

Gibson, E. J., & Spelke, E. S. (1983). The development of perception. In J. H. Flavell & E. M. Markman (Eds.), *Handbook of child psychology: Vol. 3. Development* (pp. 1–76). New York: John Wiley.

Gibson, S., & Dembo, M. H. (1984). Teacher efficacy: A construct validation. *Journal of Educational Psychology, 76,* 569–582.

Gick, M. L. (1986). Problem-solving strategies. *Educational Psychologist, 21,* 99–120.

Gick, M. L., & Holyoak, K. J. (1980). Analogical problem solving. *Cognitive Psychology, 12,* 306–355.

Gick, M. L., & Holyoak, K. J. (1983). Schema induction and analogical transfer. *Cognitive Psychology, 15,* 1–38.

Gillespie, D. (1992). *The mind's we: Contextualism in cognitive psychology.* Carbondale: Southern Illinois University Press.

Ginsburg, H. P., & Baron, J. (1993). Cognition: Young children's construction of mathematics. In R. J. Jensen (Ed.), *Research ideas for the classroom: Early childhood mathematics* (pp. 3–21). New York: Macmillan.

Glaser, R., & Chi, M. T. (1988). Overview. In M. Chi, R. Glaser, & M. Farr (Eds.), *The nature of expertise* (pp. xv–xxviii). Hillsdale, NJ: Lawrence Erlbaum.

Glaze, J. A. (1928). The association value of non-sense syllables. *Journal of Genetic Psychology, 35,* 255–269.

Glenberg, A. M., & Epstein, W. (1985). Calibration of comprehension. *Journal of Experimental Psychology: Learning, Memory, and Cognition, 11,* 702–718.

Glenberg, A. M., & Epstein, W. (1987). Inexpert calibration of comprehension. *Memory & Cognition, 15,* 84–93.

Glenberg, A. M., Sanocki, T., Epstein, W., & Morris, C. (1987). Enhancing calibration of comprehension. *Journal of Experimental Psychology: General, 116,* 119–136.

Glenberg, A. M., Smith, S. M., & Green, C. (1977). Type I rehearsal: Maintenance and more. *Journal of Verbal Learning and Verbal Behavior, 16,* 339–352.

Glenberg, A. M., Wilkinson, A. C., & Epstein, W. (1982). The illusion of knowing: Failure in the self-assessment of comprehension. *Memory & Cognition, 10,* 597–602.

Glover, J. A. (1982). Implementing creativity training of students through teacher inservice training. *Educational Research Quarterly, 6,* 13–19.

Glover, J. A., Bruning, R. H., & Plake, B. S. (1982). Distinctiveness of encoding and recall of text materials. *Journal of Educational Psychology, 74,* 522–534.

Glover, J. A., & Corkill, A. (1987). The spacing effect in memory for prose. *Journal of Educational Psychology, 79,* 198–200.

Glover, J. A., Dinnel, D. L., Halpain, D., McKee, T., Corkill A. J., & Wise, S. (1988). Effects of across-chapter signals on recall of text. *Journal of Educational Psychology, 80,* 3–15.

Glover, J. A., Harvey, A. L., & Corkill, A. J. (1988). Remembering written instructions: Tab A goes into Slot C, or does it? *British Journal of Educational Psychology, 58,* 191–200.

Glover, J. A., Plake, B. S., & Zimmer, J. W. (1982). Distinctiveness of encoding and memory for learning tasks. *Journal of Educational Psychology, 74,* 189–198.

Glover, J. A., Rankin, J., Langner, N., Todero, C., & Dinnel, D. (1985). Memory for sentences and prose: Levels-of-processing or transfer-appropriate processing? *Journal of Reading Behavior, 17,* 215–234.

Glover, J. A., & Ronning, R. R. (Eds.). (1987). *Historical foundations of educational psychology.* New York: Plenum.

Glover, J. A., Timme, V., Deyloff, D., & Rogers, M. (1987). Memory for student-performed tasks. *Journal of Educational Psychology, 79,* 445–452.

Glover, J. A., Timme, V., Deyloff, D., Rogers, M., & Dinnel, D. (1987). Oral directions: Remembering what to do when. *Journal of Educational Research* 33–53.

Glover, J. A., & Zimmer, J. W. (1982). Procedures to influence levels of questions asked by students. *Journal of General Psychology, 107,* 267–276.

Glover, J. A., Zimmer, J. W., Filbeck, R. W., & Plake, B. S. (1980). Effects of training students to identify the semantic base of prose material. *Journal of Applied Behavior Analysis, 13,* 655–667.

Glynn, S. M., & DiVesta, E. J. (1979). Control of prose processing via instructional and typographical cues. *Journal of Educational Psychology, 71,* 595–603.

Godden, D. R., & Baddeley, A. D. (1975). Context-dependent memory in two natural environments: On land and underwater. *British Journal of Psychology, 66,* 325–332.

Goldman, S. R., & Varnhagen, C. K. (1986). Improving comprehension: Causal relations instruction for learning among handicapped learners. *The Reading Teacher, 39,* 898–904.

Goldstein, E. B. (1988). Geometry or not geometry? Perceived orientation and spatial layout in pictures viewed at an angle. *Journal of Experimental Psychology: Human Perception and Performance, 14,* 312–314.

Good, T., & Brophy, J. (1986). *Educational psychology* (3rd ed.). New York: Longman.

Goodman, K. S. (1967). Reading: A psycholinguistic guessing game. *Journal of the Reading Specialist, 6,* 126–135.

Goodman, K. S. (1982a). Miscues: Windows on the reading process. In F. V. Gollasch (Ed.), *Language and literacy* (Vol. 1, pp. 64–79). Boston: Routledge & Kegan Paul.

Goodman, K. S. (1982b). Reading: A psycholinguistic guessing game. In E. V. Gollasch (Ed.), *Language and literacy* (Vol. 1, pp. 19–31). Boston: Routledge & Kegan Paul.

Goodman, K. S. (1982c). The reading process: Theory and practice. In F. V. Gollasch (Ed.), *Language and literacy* (Vol. 1, pp. 33–43). Boston: Routledge & Kegan Paul.

Goodman, K. S., & Goodman, Y. (1979). Learning to read is natural. In L. B. Resnick & R. A. Weaver (Eds.), *Theory and practice of early reading* (pp. 51–94). Hillsdale, NJ: Lawrence Erlbaum.

Goodman, K. S., & Goodman, Y. M. (1982). Learning about psycholinguistic processes by analyzing oral reading. In F. V. Gollasch (Ed.), *Language and literacy* (Vol. 1, pp. 149–168). Boston: Routledge & Kegan Paul.

Goss, A. E. (1961). Verbal mediating response and concept formation. *Psychological Review, 68,* 248–274.

Gottfried, A. (1990). Academic intrinsic motivation in young elementary school children. *Journal of Educational Psychology, 82,* 525–538.

Gough, P. B. (1972). One second of reading. In E. Kavanagh & I. G. Mattingly (Eds.), *Language by ear and by eye* (pp. 331–358). Cambridge: MIT Press.

Gough, P. B., & Hillinger, M. L. (1980). Learning to read: An unnatural act. *Bulletin of the Orton Society, 30,* 180–196.

Grabe, M., & Mann, S. (1984). A technique for the assessment and training of comprehension monitoring skills. *Journal of Reading Behavior, 16,* 131–144.

Graesser, A. C., Long, K., & Horgan, D. (1988). A taxonomy for question generation. *Questioning Exchange, 2,* 3–16.

Graf, P., & Schacter, D. A. (1985). Implicit and explicit memory for new associations in normal and amnesic subjects. *Journal of Experimental Psychology: Learning, Memory, and Cognition, 11,* 501–518.

Graham, S. (1991). A review of attribution theory in achievement contexts. *Educational Psychology Review, 3,* 5–39.

Graham, S., & Barker, G. P. (1990). The down side of help: An attributional-developmental analysis of helping behavior as a low-ability cue. *Journal of Educational Psychology, 82,* 7–14.

Graham, S., & Harris, K. R. (1989). Components analysis of cognitive strategy instruction: Effects on learning disabled students' compositions and self-efficacy. *Journal of Educational Psychology, 81,* 353–361.

Graham, S., & Harris, K. R. (1993). Self-regulated strategy development: Helping students with learning problems develop as writers. *Elementary School Journal, 94,* 160–181.

Graves, D. H. (1983). *Writing: Teachers and children at work.* Portsmouth, NH: Heinemann.

Graves, M., & Graves, B. (1994). *Scaffolding reading experiences: Designs for student success.* Norwood, MA: Christopher-Gordon.

Graves, M. E. (1987). The roles of instruction in fostering vocabulary development. In M. G. McKeown & M. E. Curtis (Eds.), *The nature of vocabulary acquisition* (pp. 165–181). Hillsdale, NJ: Lawrence Erlbaum.

Gredler, M. E. (1992). *Learning and instruction: Theory into practice* (2nd ed.). New York: Macmillan.

Greene, R. L. (1992). *Human memory: Paradigms and paradoxes.* Hillsdale, NJ: Lawrence Erlbaum.

Greenwald, A. G., Klinger, M. R., & Lui, T. J. (1989). Unconscious processing of dichoptically masked words. *Memory & Cognition, 17,* 35–47.

Grolnick, W. S., & Ryan, R. M. (1987). Autonomy in children's learning: An experimental and individual difference investigation. *Journal of Personality and Social Psychology, 52,* 890–898.

Grossberg, S. (1986). The adaptive self-organization of serial order in behavior: Speech, language, and motor control. In E. C. Schwab & H. C. Nusbaum (Eds.), *Pattern recognition by humans and machines* (pp. 1–42). New York: Academic Press.

Grunwell, R. (1986). Aspects of phonological development in later childhood. In K. Durkin (Ed.), *Language development in the school years* (pp. 34–56). Cambridge, MA: Brookline.

Guthrie, J. T. (1993, August). *An instructional framework for developing motivational and cognitive aspects of reading.* Division 15 Invited Address at the Annual Convention of the American Psychological Association, Toronto.

Guthrie, J. T., Bennett, L., & McGough, K. (1994). *Concept-oriented reading instruction: An integrated curriculum to develop motivations and strategies for reading* (Reading Research Report No. 10). College Park, MD: National Reading Research Center.

Halliday, M., & Hasan, R. (1974). *Cohesion in English.* London: Longman.

Halpain, D., Glover, J. A., & Harvey, A. L. (1985). Differential effects of higher- and lower-order questions: Attention hypotheses. *Journal of Educational Psychology, 71,* 703–715.

Hamaker, C. (1986). The effects of adjunct questions on prose learning. *Review of Educational Research, 56,* 212–242.

Hamilton, R. J. (1985). A framework for the evaluation of the effectiveness of adjunct questions and objectives. *Review of Educational Research, 55,* 47–85.

Handel, S. (1988). Space is to time as vision is to audition: Seductive but misleading. *Journal of Experimental Psychology: Human Perception and Performance, 14,* 315–317.

Hardiman, P. T., Dufresne, R., & Mestre, J. P. (1989). The relation between problem categorization and problem solving among experts and novices. *Memory & Cognition, 17,* 627–638.

Hare, V. C., & Milligan, B. (1984). Main idea identification: Instructional explanations in four basal reader series. *Journal of Reading Behavior, 16,* 169–203.

Harney, P. (1989). *The Hope Scale: Exploration of construct validity and its influence on health.* Unpublished master's thesis, University of Kansas, Lawrence.

Harris, K. R., & Graham, S. (1992). *Helping young writers master the craft: Strategy instruction and self-regulation in the writing process.* Cambridge, MA: Brookline.

Hawisher, G. E. (1987). The effects of word processing on the revision strategies of college freshmen. *Research in the Teaching of English, 21,* 145–159.

Hawkins, H. L., & Presson, J. C. (1987). Auditory information processing. In K. R. Boff, L. Kaufman, & J. P. Thomas (Eds.), *Handbook of perception and human performance: Vol. 2. Information processing* (pp. 26–1 to 26–48). New York: John Wiley.

Hayes, J. R. (1978). *Cognitive psychology.* Homewood, IL: Dorsey.

Hayes, J. R. (1988). *The complete problem solver* (2nd ed.). Hillsdale, NJ: Lawrence Erlbaum.

Hayes, J. R., & Flower, L. S. (1986). Writing research and the writer. *American Psychologist, 41,* 1106–1113.

Haygood, R. C., & Bourne, L. E., Jr. (1965). Attribute- and rule-learning aspects of conceptual behavior. *Psychological Review, 72,* 175–196.

Heath, S. B. (1986). Separating "things of the imagination" from life: Learning to read and write. In W. H. Teale & E. Sulzby (Eds.), *Emergent literacy* (pp. 156–172). Norwood, NJ: Ablex.

Hennessey, B. A., & Amabile, T. M. (1988). The role of the environment in creativity. In R. Sternberg (Ed.), *The nature of creativity: Contemporary psychological perspectives* (pp. 11–38). New York: Cambridge University Press.

Henry, L. A., & Millar, S. (1991). Memory span increase with age: A test of two hypotheses. *Journal of Experimental Child Psychology, 51,* 459–484.

Herman, P. A., Anderson, R. C., Pearson, P. D., & Nagy, W. E. (1987). Incidental acquisition of word meaning from expositions with varied text features. *Reading Research Quarterly, 22,* 263–284.

Hidi, S., & Anderson, V. (1986). Producing written summaries: Task demands, cognitive operations, and implications for instruction. *Review of Educational Research, 56,* 473–493.

Hiebert, E. H. (1981). Developmental patterns and interrelationship of preschool children's print awareness. *Reading Research Quarterly, 16,* 236–260.

Hiebert, J. (Ed.). (1986). *Conceptual and procedural knowledge: The case of mathematics.* Hillsdale, NJ: Lawrence Erlbaum.

Hiebert, J., & Carpenter, T. P. (1992). Learning and teaching with understanding. In D. A. Grouws (Ed.), *Handbook of research on mathematics teaching and learning* (pp. 65–97). New York: Macmillan.

Higbee, K. L., & Kunihira, S. (1985). Cross-cultural applications of yodai mnemonics in education. *Educational Psychologist, 20,* 57–64.

Hilgers, T. C. (1986). How children change as critical evaluators of writing. Four three-year care studies. *Research in the Teaching of English, 20,* 36–55.

Hinton, G. E., McClelland, J. L., & Rumelhart, D. E. (1986). Distributed representations. In D. E. Rumelhart & J. L. McClelland (Eds.), *Parallel distributed processing: Explanations in the microstructure of cognition: Vol. 1. Foundations* (pp. 77–109). Cambridge: MIT Press.

Hogarth, R. M., Gibbs, B. J., McKenzie, C.R.M., & Marquis, M. A. (1991). Learning from feedback: Exactingness and incentives. *Journal of Experimental Psychology: Learning, Memory, and Cognition, 17,* 734–752.

Holland, J., & Skinner, B. F. (1961). *The analysis of behavior.* New York: McGraw-Hill.

Hollon, R. E., Anderson, C. W., & Roth, K. J. (1991). Science teachers' conceptions of teaching and learning. In J. Brophy (Ed.), *Advances in research on teaching* (Vol. 2, pp. 145–186). Greenwich, CT: JAI.

Homme, L., Csanyi, A. P., Gonzales, M. A., & Rechs, J. R. (1968). *How to use contingency contracting in the classroom.* Champaign, IL: Research Press.

Hudson, T. (1980, July). *Young children's difficulty with "How many more ____ than ____ are there?" questions* (Doctoral dissertation, Indiana University, 1980). *Dissertation Abstracts International, 41.*

Hull, C. L. (1934). The concept of the habit-family hierarchy and maze learning: Part 1. *Psychological Review, 34,* 33–54.

Hull, C. L. (1952). *A behavior system: An introduction to behavior theory concerning the individual organism.* New Haven, CT: Yale University Press.

Hull, G. (1987). The editing process in writing: A performance study of more skilled and less skilled college writers. *Research in the Teaching of English, 21,* 829.

Hull, G., Rose, M., Fraser, K. L., & Castellano, M. (1991). Remediation as social construct: Perspectives from an analysis of classroom discourse. *College Composition and Communication, 42,* 299–329.

Hunt, E. (1987). Science, technology, and intelligence. In R. R. Ronning, J. A. Glover, & J. Conoley (Eds.), *The impact of cognitive psychology on measurement* (pp. 156–178). Hillsdale, NJ: Lawrence Erlbaum.

Hyde, T. S., & Jenkins, J. J. (1969). Recall for words as a function of semantic, graphic, and syntactic orienting tasks. *Journal of Verbal Learning and Verbal Behavior, 12,* 471–480.

Intons-Peterson, M. J. (1993). Imagery and classification. In A. F. Collins, S. E. Gathercole, M. A. Conway, & P. E. Morris (Eds.), *Theories of memory* (pp. 211–240). Hove, England: Lawrence Erlbaum.

Jacobs, J. E., & Paris, S. G. (1987). Children's metacognition about reading: Issues in definition, measurement, and instruction. *Educational Psychologist, 22,* 255–278.

Jacoby, L. L. (1978). On interpreting the effects of repetition: Solving a problem versus remembering a solution. *Journal of Verbal Learning and Verbal Behavior, 17,* 649–667.

Jacoby, L. L. (1983). Remembering the date: Analyzing interactive processes in reading. *Journal of Verbal Learning and Verbal Behavior, 22,* 485–508.

Jacoby, L. L., & Craik, F.I.M. (1979). Effects of elaboration of processing at encoding and retrieval: Trace distinctiveness and recovery of initial context. In L. S. Cermak & F.I.M. Craik (Eds.), *Levels of processing in human memory* (pp. 1–22). Hillsdale, NJ: Lawrence Erlbaum.

Jacoby, L. L., Craik, F.I.M., & Begg, I. (1979). Effects of decision difficulty on recognition and recall. *Journal of Verbal Learning and Verbal Behavior, 18,* 585–600.

Jacoby, L. L., & Witherspoon, D. (1982). Remembering without awareness. *Canadian Journal of Psychology, 36,* 300–324.

Jehng, J. J., Johnson, S. D., & Anderson, R. C. (1993). Schooling and students' epistemological beliefs about learning. *Contemporary Educational Psychology, 18,* 23–35.

Jenkins, J. J. (1974). Remember that old theory of memory? Well, forget it! *American Psychologist, 25,* 785–795.

Jensen, A. R. (1992). Understanding *g* in terms of information processing. *Educational Psychology Review, 4,* 271–308.

Jensen, R. J. (Ed.). (1993). *Research ideas for the classroom: Early childhood mathematics.* New York: Macmillan.

Johnson, C. N., & Wellman, H. M. (1980). Children's developing understanding of mental verbs: Remember, know, and guess. *Child Development, 51,* 1095–1102.

Johnson, C. W., & Bruning, R. H. (1984). Keywords and vocabulary acquisition: Some words of caution about words of assistance. *Educational Communications and Technology, 33,* 125–138.

Johnson, E. J. (1988). Expertise and decision under uncertainty: Performance and process. In M. Chi, R. Glaser, & M. Farr (Eds.), *The nature of expertise* (pp. 209–228). Hillsdale, NJ: Lawrence Erlbaum.

Jonassen, D. (1991). Objectivism versus constructivism: Do we need a new philosophical paradigm? *Educational Technology, Research, and Development, 34,* 5–14.

Jones, E. D., Krouse, J. P., Feorene, D., & Saferstein, C. A. (1985). A comparison of concurrent and sequential instruction of four types of verbal math problems. *Remedial and Special Education, 6,* 25–31.

Jusczyk, P. W. (1987). Speech perception. In K. R. Boff, L. Kaufman, & J. P. Thomas (Eds.), *Handbook of perception and human performance: Vol. 2. Information processing* (pp. 27–1 to 27–66). New York: John Wiley.

Jussim, L. (1989). Teacher expectations: Self-fulfilling prophecies, perceptual biases, and accuracy. *Journal of Personality and Social Psychology, 57,* 469–480.

Jussim, L., & Eccles, J. S. (1992). Teacher expectations II: Construction and reflection of student achievement. *Journal of Personality and Social Psychology, 63,* 947–961.

Just, M. A., & Carpenter, P. A. (1987). *The psychology of reading and language comprehension.* Boston: Allyn & Bacon.

Kagan, D. M. (1992). Implications of research on teacher belief. *Educational Psychologist, 27,* 65–90.

Kahle, J. B., Parker, L. H., Rennie, L. J., & Riley, D. (1993). Gender differences in science education: Building a model. *Educational Psychologist, 28,* 379–404.

Kail, R. V., Jr. (1984). *The development of memory in children* (2nd ed.). San Francisco: Freeman.

Kaplan, C. A., & Simon, H. A. (1990). In search of insight. *Cognitive Psychology, 22,* 374–419.

Karabenick, S. A., & Knapp, J. R. (1991). Relationship of academic help seeking to the use of learning strategies and other instrumental achievement behavior in college students. *Journal of Educational Psychology, 83,* 221–230.

Kazdin, A. E. (1994). *Behavior modification in applied settings.* Belmont, CA: Brooks/Cole.

Kellas, G., Ferraro, E. R., & Simpson, G. B. (1988). Lexical ambiguity and the timecourse of attentional allocation in word recognition. *Journal of Experimental Psychology: Human Perception and Performance, 14,* 601–609.

Kellogg, R. T. (1984). *Cognitive strategies in writing.* (ERIC Document Reproduction Service No. ED 262 425)

Kieran, C. (1992). The learning and teaching of school algebra. In D. A. Grouws (Ed.), *Handbook of research on mathematics teaching and learning* (pp. 390–419). New York: Macmillan.

Kilpatrick, J. (1985). Doing mathematics without understanding it: A commentary on Higbee and Kunihira. *Educational Psychologist, 20,* 65–68.

Kimball, M. M. (1989). A new perspective on women's math achievement. *Psychological Bulletin, 105,* 198–214.

King, A. (1991). Effects of training in strategic questioning on children's problem-solving performance. *Journal of Educational Psychology, 83,* 307–317.

King, A. (1992). Facilitating elaborative learning through guided student-generated questioning. *Educational Psychologist, 27,* 111–126.

King, J. R., Biggs, S., & Lipsky, S. (1984). Students' self-questioning and summarizing as reading study strategies. *Journal of Reading Behavior, 16,* 205–218.

King, P. M., Wood, P. K., & Mines, R. A. (1990). Critical thinking among college and graduate students. *Review of Higher Education, 13,* 167–186.

Kintsch, W. (1970). Models for free recall and recognition. In D. A. Norman (Ed.), *Models of human memory* (pp. 177–236). New York: Academic Press.

Kintsch, W. (1974). *The representation of meaning in memory.* Hillsdale, NJ: Lawrence Erlbaum.

Kintsch, W. (1977). *Memory and cognition* (2nd ed.). New York: John Wiley.

Kintsch, W. (1986). Learning from text. *Cognition and Instruction, 3,* 87–108.

Kintsch, W. (1988). The role of knowledge in discourse comprehension: A construction-integration model. *Psychology Review, 95,* 163–182.

Kintsch, W., & Greeno, J. G. (1985). Understanding and solving arithmetic word problems. *Psychological Review, 92,* 109–129.

Kintsch, W., & Van Dijk, T. A. (1978). Toward a model of text comprehension and production. *Psychological Review, 85,* 363–394.

Kitchener, K. S. (1983). Cognition, metacognition, and epistemic cognition: A three-level model of cognitive processing. *Human Development, 4,* 222–232.

Kitchener, K. S., & Fischer, K. W. (1990). A skill approach to the development of reflective thinking. In D. Kuhn (Ed.), *Developmental perspectives on teaching and learning thinking skills* (pp. 48–62). Basel: Karger.

Kitchener, K. S., & King, P. A. (1981). Reflective judgment: Concepts of justification and their relationship to age and education. *Journal of Applied Developmental Psychology, 2,* 89–116.

Kitchener, K. S., King, P. A., Wood, P. A., & Davidson, M. L. (1989). Sequentiality and consistency in development of reflective judgment: A six-year longitudinal study. *Journal of Applied Developmental Psychology, 10,* 73–95.

Klein, E. (1988, April). *The potential utilization of microelectronic technology in accomplishing the major goals of schooling.* Paper presented at the Annual Meeting of the American Educational Research Association, New Orleans.

Kluwe, R. H. (1987). Executive decisions and regulation of problem solving. In F. Weinert & R. Kluwe (Eds.), *Metacognition, motivation, and understanding* (pp. 31–64). Hillsdale, NJ: Lawrence Erlbaum.

Koffka, K. (1933). *Principles of Gestalt psychology.* New York: Harcourt, Brace, and World.

Köhler, W. (1929). *Gestalt psychology.* New York: Liveright.

Kolers, P. A. (1975). Memorial consequences of automatized encoding. *Journal of Experimental Psychology: Human Learning and Memory, 1,* 689–701.

Kolodner, J. L. (1984). *Retrieval and organizational strategies in conceptual memory.* Hillsdale, NJ: Lawrence Erlbaum.

Kosslyn, S. M. (1987). Seeing and imagining in the cerebral hemispheres: A computational approach. *Psychological Review, 94,* 148–175.

Kraus, S. (1957). A comparison of three methods of teaching sentence structure. *English Journal, 46,* 275–281.

Kuhn, D. (1989). Children and adults as intuitive scientists. *Psychological Review, 96,* 674–689.

Kuhn, D. (1991). *The skills of argument.* New York: Cambridge University Press.

Kuhn, D. (1992). Thinking as argument. *Harvard Educational Review, 62,* 155–178.

Kuhn, D., Amsel, E., & O'Loughlin, M. (1988). *The development of scientific reasoning skills.* New York: Academic Press.

Kuhn, D., Schauble, L., & Garcia-Mila, M. (1992). Cross-domain development of scientific reasoning. *Cognition and Instruction, 9,* 285–327.

Kurfiss, J. G. (1988). *Critical thinking* (ASHE-ERIC Higher Education Report #2).

Kurtz, B. E., & Borkowski, J. G. (1987). Development of strategic skills in impulsive and reflective children: A longitudinal study of metacognition. *Journal of Experimental Child Psychology, 43,* 129–148.

Laberge, D., & Samuels, S. J. (1974). Toward a theory of automatic information processing in reading. *Cognitive Psychology, 6,* 283–323.

Lamme, L., & Childers, N. (1983). The composing processes of three young children. *Research in the Teaching of English, 17,* 31-50.

Langelle, C. (1989). *An assessment of hope in a community sample.* Unpublished master's thesis, University of Kansas, Lawrence.

Lankford, F. G. (1972). *Some computational strategies of seventh-grade pupils* (U.S.O.E. Project No. 2-C-013).

Larkin, J., McDermott, J., Simon, D. P., & Simon, H. A. (1980). Expert and novice performance in solving physics problems. *Science, 208,* 1335-1442.

Larkin, J. H. (1977). *Skilled problem solving in experts* (Tech. Report). Berkeley: University of California, Group in Science and Mathematics Education.

Lave, J., & Wenger, E. (1991). *Situated learning: Legitimate peripheral participation.* New York: Cambridge University Press.

Le Fevre, J. (1988). Reading skill as a source of individual differences in the processing of instructional texts. *Journal of Educational Psychology, 80,* 312–314.

Lehman, D. R., Lempert, R. O., & Nisbett, R. E. (1988). The effects of graduate training on reasoning. *American Psychologist, 43,* 431–442.

Leont'ev, A. N. (1981). *Problems in the development of mind.* Moscow: Progress.

Lepper, M. R. (1988). Motivational considerations in the study of instruction. *Cognition and Instruction, 5,* 289–309.

Lesgold, A. (1988). Problem solving. In R. Sternberg & E. Smith (Eds.), *The psychology of human thought* (pp. 188–213). New York: Cambridge University Press.

Levin, E. M. (1966). Hypothesis behavior by humans during discrimination learning. *Journal of Experimental Psychology, 71,* 331-338.

Levin, J. R. (1981). The mnemonic '80s: Keywords in the classroom. *Educational Psychologist, 16,* 65-82.

Levin, J. R. (1985). Yodai features = mnemonic procedures: A commentary on Higbee and Kunihira. *Educational Psychologist, 20,* 73-77.

Levin, J. R. (1986). Educational applications of mnemonic pictures: Possibilities beyond your wildest imagination. In A. A. Sheikh (Ed.), *Imagery in the educational process* (pp. 202-265). Farmingdale, NY: Baywood.

Lhyle, K. G., & Kulhavy, R. W. (1987). Feedback processing and error correction. *Journal of Educational Psychology, 79,* 320–322.

Loftus, E. R., & Loftus, G. R. (1980). On the permanence of stored information in the human brain. *American Psychologist, 35,* 409–420.

Loftus, E. T., Green, E. E., & Smith, R. H. (1980). How deep is the meaning of life? *Bulletin of the Psychonomic Society, 15,* 282-284.

Lomax, R. G., & McGee, L. M. (1987). Young children's concepts about print and reading: Toward a model of word reading acquisition. *Reading Research Quarterly, 22,* 237-256.

Lorch, R. E. (1985). Effects on recall of signals to text organization. *Bulletin of the Psychonomic Society, 23,* 374-376.

Lorch, R. E., & Chen, A. H. (1986). Effect of number signals on reading and recall. *Journal of Educational Psychology, 78,* 263-270.

Lorch, R. F., Jr. (1989). Text-signaling devices and their effects on reading and memory processes. *Educational Psychology Review, 1,* 209–234.

Lorch, R. F., Jr., Lorch, E. P., & Inman, W. E. (1993). Effects of signaling topic structure on text recall. *Journal of Educational Psychology, 85,* 281–290.

MacLeod, C. M. (1988). Forgotten but not gone: Savings for pictures and words in long-term memory. *Journal of Experimental Psychology: Learning, Memory, and Cognition, 14,* 195-212.

Maher, C. A. (1991). Is dealing with mathematics as a thought subject compatible with maintaining satisfactory test scores?: A nine-year study. *Journal of Mathematical Behavior, 10,* 225–248.

Mandler, J. M. (1984). *Stories, scripts, and scenes: Aspects of schema theory.* Hillsdale, NJ: Lawrence Erlbaum.

Mansfield, R. S., Busse, T. V., & Krepelka, E. J. (1978). The effectiveness of creativity training. *Review of Educational Research, 48,* 517-536.

Markman, E. M. (1979). Realizing that you don't understand: Elementary school children's awareness of inconsistencies. *Child Development, 50,* 643–655.

Marr, D. (1982). *Vision.* San Francisco: Freeman.

Marr, D. (1985). Vision: The philosophy and the approach. In A. M. Aitkenhead (Ed.), *Issues in cognitive modeling* (pp. 26-61). Hillsdale, NJ: Lawrence Erlbaum.

Martin, V., & Pressley, M. (1991). Elaborative integration effects depend on the nature of the question. *Journal of Educational Psychology, 83,* 253–263.

Mason, J. (1980). When do children begin to read? An exploration of four-year-olds' letter and word reading competencies. *Reading Research Quarterly, 15,* 203-227.

Mason, J. M., & Au, K. H. (1990). *Reading instruction for today* (2nd ed.). Glenview, IL: Scott, Foresman.

Mason, J. M., Herman, P. A., & Au, K. H. (1991). Children's developing knowledge of words. In J. Flood, J. M. Jensen, D. Lapp, & J. R. Squire (Eds.), *Handbook of research on teaching the English language arts* (pp. 721–731). New York: Macmillan.

Masonheimer, R. E., Drum, P. A., & Ehri, L. C. (1984). Does environmental print identification lead children into word reading? *Journal of Reading Behavior, 16,* 257-271.

Mastropieri, M., & Scruggs, T. (1989). Constructing more meaningful relationships: Mnemonic instruction for special populations. *Educational Psychology Review, 1,* 83–111.

Mayer, R. E. (1981). Frequency norms and structural analysis of algebra word problems into families, categories, and templates. *Instructional Science, 10,* 135-175.

Mayer, R. E. (1982). Memory for algebra story problems. *Journal of Educational Psychology, 74,* 199-216.

Mayer, R. E. (1984). Twenty-five years of research on advance organizers. *Instructional Science, 8,* 133-169.

Mayer, R. E., & Bromage, B. K. (1980). Different recall protocols for technical texts due to advance organizers. *Journal of Educational Psychology, 72,* 209-225.

Mazzie, C. A. (1987). An experimental investigation of the determinants of implicitness in spoken and written discourse. *Discourse Processes, 10,* 31-42.

McCann, R. S., Besner, D., & Davelaar, E. (1988). Word recognition and identification: Do word-frequency effects reflect lexical access? *Journal of Experimental Psychology: Human Perception and Performance, 14,* 693-706.

McClelland, J. L. (1986). The programmable blackboard model of reading. In D. E. Rumelhart & J. L. McClelland (Eds.), *Parallel distributed process: Explorations in the microstructure of cognition: Vol. 2. Psychological and biological models* (pp. 122-169). Cambridge: MIT Press.

McClelland, J. L. (1988). Connectionist models and psychological evidence. *Journal of Memory and Language, 27,* 107-123.

McClelland, J. L., & Rumelhart, D. E. (1981). An interactive activation model of context effects in letter perception: Part 1. An account of basic findings. *Psychological Review, 88,* 375–407.

McClelland, J. L., Rumelhart, D. E., & Hinton, G. E. (1986). The appeal of parallel distributed processing. In D. E. Rumelhart, J. L. McClelland, & PDP Research Group (Eds.), *Parallel distributed processing: Explorations in the microstructures of cognition: Vol. 1. Foundations* (pp. 3-44). Cambridge: MIT Press.

McCloskey, M. (1983). Naive theories of motion. In D. Gentner & A. L. Stevens (Eds.), *Mental models* (pp. 71-94). Hillsdale, NJ: Lawrence Erlbaum.

McCloskey, M., Caramazza, A., & Green, B. (1980). Curvilinear motion in the absence of external forces: Naive beliefs about the motion of objects. *Science, 210,* 1139-1141.

McCloskey, M., Wible, C. G., & Cohen, N. J. (1988). Is there a special flashbulb-memory mechanism? *Journal of Experimental Psychology: General, 117,* 171–181.

McCormick, C. B., & Levin, J. R. (1984). A comparison of different prose learning variations of the mnemonic keyword method. *American Educational Research Journal, 21,* 379-398.

McDaniel, M. A., & Einstein, G. O. (1989). Material appropriate processing. *Educational Psychology Review, 1,* 113–145.

McDaniel, M. A., Einstein, G. O., Dunay, P. K., & Cobb, R. S. (1986). Encoding difficulty and memory: Toward a unifying theory. *Journal of Memory and Language, 25,* 645-656.

McDougall, R. (1904). Recognition and recall. *Journal of Philosophical and Scientific Methods, 1,* 229-233.

McElroy, L. A., & Slamecka, N. J. (1982). Memorial consequences of generating nonwords: Implications for semantic memory interpretations of the generation effect. *Journal of Verbal Learning and Verbal Behavior, 21,* 249-259.

McGee, L. M., Lomax, R. G., & Head, M. H. (1988). Young children's written language knowledge: What environmental and functional print reading reveals. *Journal of Reading Behavior, 20,* 99-118.

McGuinness, C. (1990). Talking about thinking: The role of metacognition in teaching thinking. In K. Gilhooly, M. Keane, & G. Erdos (Eds.), *Lines of thinking* (Vol. 2, pp. 301–312). New York: Academic Press.

McKeown, M. G., Beck, I. L., Omanson, R. C., & Perfetti, C. A. (1983). The effects of long-term vocabulary instruction on reading comprehension: A replication. *Journal of Reading Behavior, 15,* 3-18.

McKeown, M. G., Beck, I. L., Omanson, R. C., & Pople, M. T. (1985). Some effects of the nature and frequency of vocabulary instruction on the knowledge and use of words. *Reading Research Quarterly, 20,* 522-535.

McKeown, M. G., & Curtis, M. E. (1987). *The nature of vocabulary acquisition.* Hillsdale, NJ: Lawrence Erlbaum.

McKoon, G., & Ratcliff, R. (1986). Inferences about predictable events. *Journal of Experimental Psychology: Learning, Memory, and Cognition, 12,* 82-91.

McNamee, G. D. (1987). The social origins of narrative skills. In M. Hickmann (Ed.), *Social and functional approaches to language and thought* (pp. 287-304). New York: Academic Press.

McQueen, R., Murray, A. K., & Evans, E. (1963). Relationships between writing required in high school and English proficiency in college. *Journal of Experimental Education, 31,* 419-423.

Medin, D. L., Wattenmaker, W. D., & Hampson, S. E. (1987). Family resemblance, conceptual cohesiveness, and category construction. *Cognitive Psychology, 19,* 242-278.

Mehan, H. (1979). *Learning lessons: Social organization in the classroom.* Cambridge, MA: Harvard University Press.

Meichenbaum, D. (1977). *Cognitive behavior modification: An integrative approach.* New York: Plenum.

Melton, A. W. (1963). Implications of short-term memory for a general theory of memory. *Journal of Verbal Learning and Verbal Behavior, 2,* 1-21.

Mewhort, D.J.K., Butler, B. E., Feldman-Stewart, D., & Tramer, S. (1988). "Iconic memory," location information, and the bar-probe task: A reply to Chow. *Journal of Experimental Psychology: Human Perception and Performance, 14,* 729-736.

Meyer, B.J.F, & Rice, G. E. (1984). The structure of text. In P. D. Pearson (Ed.), *Handbook of reading research* (pp. 316-342). New York: Longman.

Meyer, D. E., & Schvaneveldt, R. W. (1976). Meaning, memory structure, and mental processes. *Science, 192,* 27–33.

Miller, G. A. (1956a). Information and memory. *Scientific American, 195,* 42–46.

Miller, G. A. (1956b). The magical number seven, plus-or-minus two: Some limits on our capacity for processing information. *Psychological Review, 63,* 81-97.

Miller, R. B., Behrens, J. T., Greene, B. A., & Newman, D. (1993). Goals and perceived ability: Impact on student valuing, self-regulation, and persistence. *Contemporary Educational Psychology, 18,* 2–14.

Minsky, M. (1975). A framework for representing knowledge. In P. H. Winston (Ed.), *The psychology of computer vision* (pp. 211–277). New York: McGraw-Hill.

Mitchell, D. B., & Brown, A. S. (1988). Persistent repetition priming in picture naming and its disassociation from recognition memory. *Journal of Experimental Psychology: Learning, Memory, and Cognition, 14,* 213-222.

Moeser, S. D. (1983). Levels-of-processing: Qualitative differences or task-demand hypotheses? *Memory & Cognition, 11,* 316-323.

Montague, W. E., Adams, J. A., & Kiess, H. D. (1966). Forgetting and natural language mediation. *Journal of Experimental Psychology, 72,* 829-833.

Moore, M. T. (1990). Problem finding and teacher experience. *Journal of Creative Behavior, 24,* 39–58.

Morphett, M. V., & Washburne, C. (1931). When should children begin to read? *Elementary School Journal, 31,* 496-503.

Morris, C. C. (1990). Retrieval processes underlying confidence in comprehension judgments. *Journal of Experimental Psychology: Learning, Memory, and Cognition, 16,* 223–232.

Morris, C. D., Bransford, J. D., & Franks, J. J. (1977). Levels of processing versus transfer appropriate processing. *Journal of Verbal Learning and Verbal Behavior, 16,* 519-533.

Morris, P. E., & Cook, N. (1978). When do first letter mnemonics aid recall? *British Journal of Educational Psychology, 48,* 22-28.

Mosenthal, J. M., & Tierney, R. J. (1984). Cohesion: Problems with talking about text. *Reading Research Quarterly, 24,* 240-244.

Moshman, D. (1981). Jean Piaget meets Jerry Falwell: Genetic epistemology and the anti-humanist movement in education. *The Genetic Epistemologist, 10,* 10–13.

Moshman, D. (1982). Exogenous, endogenous, and dialectical constructivism. *Developmental Review, 2,* 371–384.

Murdock, B. B., Jr. (1961). The retention of individual items. *Journal of Experimental Psychology, 62,* 618-625.

Muth, K. D., Glynn, S. M., Britton, B. K., & Graves, M. E. (1988). Thinking out loud while studying text: Rehearsing key ideas. *Journal of Educational Psychology, 80,* 315-318.

Nagy, W. E. (1988, April). *Some components of a model of word-learning ability.* Paper presented at the Annual Meeting of the American Educational Research Association, New Orleans.

Nagy, W. E., Anderson, R. C., & Herman, P. A. (1987). Learning word meanings from context during normal reading. *American Educational Research Journal, 24,* 237-270.

Nagy, W. E., & Herman, P. A. (1987). Breadth and depth of vocabulary knowledge: Implications for acquisition and instruction. In M. G. McKeown & M. E. Curtis (Eds.), *The nature of vocabulary acquisition* (pp. 19-35). Hillsdale, NJ: Lawrence Erlbaum.

Nagy, W. E., Herman, P. A., & Anderson, R. C. (1985). Learning words from context. *Reading Research Quarterly, 20,* 233-253.

National Assessment of Educational Progress (NAEP). (1993). *The Third National Mathematics Assessment: Results, trends, and issues* (Report ED 1.118-13-MA-01). Washington, DC: National Institute of Education.

National Council of Teachers of Mathematics (NCTM). (1980). *An agenda for action: Recommendations for school mathematics of the 1980s.* Reston, VA: Author.

National Council of Teachers of Mathematics (NCTM). (1989). *Curriculum and evaluation standards for school mathematics.* Reston, VA: Author.

National Council of Teachers of Mathematics (NCTM). (1991). *Professional standards for teaching mathematics.* Reston, VA: Author.

National Research Council (NRC). (1989). *Everybody counts: A report to the nation on the future of mathematics education.* Washington, DC: National Academy of Sciences.

National Research Council (NRC). (1990). *Reshaping school mathematics.* Washington, DC: National Academy of Sciences.

Neisser, U. (1967). *Cognitive psychology.* New York: Appleton-Century-Crofts.

Neisser, U. (1982). *Memory observed.* San Francisco: Freeman.

Neisser, U., & Weene, P. (1962). Hierarchies in concept attainment. *Journal of Experimental Psychology, 64,* 640-645.

Nelson, T. O. (1977). Repetition and depth of processing. *Journal of Verbal Learning and Verbal Behavior, 16,* 151-171.

Nelson, T. O. (1985). Ebbinghaus's contribution to the measurement of retention: Savings during relearning. *Journal of Experimental Psychology: Learning, Memory, and Cognition, 11,* 472-479.

Neves, D. M., & Anderson, J. R. (1981). Knowledge compilation: Mechanisms for the automatization of cognitive skills. In J. R. Anderson (Ed.), *Cognitive skills and their acquisition* (pp. 86-102). Hillsdale, NJ: Lawrence Erlbaum.

Newby, T. J. (1991). Classroom motivation: Strategies for first year teachers. *Journal of Educational Psychology, 83,* 195–200.

Newell, A., & Simon, H. A. (1972). *Human problem solving.* Englewood Cliffs, NJ: Prentice-Hall.

Newman, D., Griffin, P., & Cole, M. (1989). *The construction zone: Working for cognitive change in school.* Cambridge, England: Cambridge University Press.

Newman, R. S., & Goldin, L. (1990). Children's reluctance to seek help with schoolwork. *Journal of Educational Psychology, 82,* 92–100.

Nickerson, R. S. (1987). Why teach thinking? In J. Baron & R. Sternberg (Eds.), *Teaching thinking skills: Theory and practice* (pp. 27–38). San Francisco: Freeman.

Nickerson, R. S., Perkins, D. N., & Smith, E. E. (1986). *The teaching of thinking.* Hillsdale, NJ: Lawrence Erlbaum.

Niedenthal, P. M. (1990). Implicit perception of affective information. *Journal of Experimental Social Psychology, 26,* 505–527.

Nilsson, L., Law, J., & Tulving, E. (1988). Recognition failure of recallable unique names: Evidence for an empirical law of memory and learning. *Journal of Experimental Psychology: Learning, Memory, and Cognition, 14,* 266-277.

Noble, C. E. (1952). An analysis of meaning. *Psychological Review, 59,* 421-430.

Norman, D. A. (1976). *Memory and attention* (2nd ed.). New York: John Wiley.

Norman, D. A., & Bobrow, D. G. (1976). On the role of active memory processes in perception and cognition. In C. N. Cofer (Ed.), *The structure of human memory* (pp. 123-156). San Francisco: Freeman.

Norris, J. A. (1988). Using communication strategies to enhance reading acquisition. *The Reading Teacher, 41,* 668–673.

Norris, J. A., & Bruning, R. H. (1988). Cohesion in the narratives of good and poor readers. *Journal of Speech and Hearing Disorders, 53,* 416-424.

Norris, S., & Ennis, R. (1989). *Evaluating critical thinking.* Pacific Grove, CA: Midwest.

Nusbaum, H. C., & Schwab, E. C. (1986). The role of attention and active processing in speech perception. In E. C. Schwab & H. C. Nusbaum (Eds.), *Pattern recognition by humans and machines* (pp. 113-157). New York: Academic Press.

Nussbaum, J., & Novick, N. (1982). Alternative frameworks, conceptual conflict, and accommodation: Toward a principled teaching strategy. *Instructional Science, 11,* 183-200.

Nystrand, M., & Gamoran, A. (1991). Instructional discourse, student engagement, and literature achievement. *Research in the Teaching of English, 25,* 261–290.

Oakes, J. (1990). *Multiplying inequalities: The effects of race, social class, and tracking on opportunities to learn math and science.* Chicago: Rand McNally.

O'Flahavan, J. F., & Stein, C. (1992). In search of the teacher's role in peer discussions about literature. *Reading in Virginia, 17,* 34–42.

O'Flahavan, J. F., Wiencek, J., Marks, T., & Stein, C. (1994). *Interpretive development in peer discussions about literature: An exploration of the teacher's role.* Manuscript submitted for publication.

Olson, D. R., Torrance, N., & Hildyard, A. (1985). *Literacy, language, and learning.* New York: Cambridge University Press.

Olton, R. M., & Crutchfield, R. S. (1969). Developing the skills of productive thinking. In P. Mussen, J. Langer, & M. Covington (Eds.), *Trends and issues in developmental psychology.* New York: Holt, Rinehart & Winston.

Osborne, R., & Freyberg, R. (1985). *Learning science.* Portsmouth, NH: Heinemann.

Overton, D. A. (1985). Contextual stimulus effects of drugs and internal states. In P. D. Balsam & A. Tomie (Eds.), *Context and learning* (pp. 357–384). Hillsdale, NJ: Lawrence Erlbaum.

Owens, D. T. (1993). Introduction. In D. T. Owens (Ed.), *Research ideas for the classroom: Middle grades mathematics* (pp. xi–xvii). New York: Macmillan.

Owens, D. T., & Super, D. B. (1993). Teaching and learning decimal fractions. In D. T. Owens (Ed.), *Research ideas for the classroom: Middle grades mathematics* (pp. 179–198). New York: Macmillan.

Paivio, A. (1971). *Imagery and verbal processes.* New York: Holt, Rinehart & Winston.

Paivio, A. (1975). Imagery and long-term memory. In A. Kennedy & A. Wilkes (Eds.), *Studies in long-term memory* (pp. 64-110). New York: John Wiley.

Paivio, A. (1986a). Dual coding and episodic memory: Subjective and objective sources of memory trace components. In F. Klix & H. Hafgendorf (Eds.), *Human memory and cognitive capabilities: Mechanisms and performances* (Part A, pp. 225-236). Amsterdam: North-Holland.

Paivio, A. (1986b). *Mental representations: A dual coding approach.* New York: Oxford University Press.

Paivio, A., Clark, J. M., & Lambert, W. E. (1988). Bilingual dual-coding theory and semantic repetition effect on recall. *Journal of Experimental Psychology: Learning, Memory, and Cognition, 14,* 163-172.

Paivio, A., & Csapo, K. (1975). Picture superiority in free recall: Imagery or dual coding? *Cognitive Psychology, 5,* 176-206.

Paivio, A., Yuille, J. D., & Madigan, S. A. (1968). Concreteness, imagery, and meaningfulness values for 925 nouns. *Journal of Experimental Psychology, 76*(Suppl), 1-25.

Palincsar, A. S., & Brown, A. L. (1984). Reciprocal teaching of comprehension-fostering and comprehension-monitoring activities. *Cognition and Instruction, 1,* 117-175.

Palincsar, A. S., Brown, A. L., & Martin, S. (1987). Peer interaction in reading comprehension instruction. *Educational Psychologist, 22,* 231-254.

Palmere, M., Benton, S. L., Glover, J. A., & Ronning, R. R. (1983). Elaboration and recall of main ideas in prose. *Journal of Educational Psychology, 75,* 898-907.

Paris, S. G., Cross, D. R., & Lipon, M. Y. (1984). Informal strategies for learning: A program to improve children's reading awareness and comprehension. *Journal of Educational Psychology, 76,* 1239-1252.

Paris, S. G., & Jacobs, J. E. (1984). The benefits of informed instruction for children's reading and comprehension. *Child Development, 55,* 2083–2093.

Pearson, P. D. (1984). Guided reading: A response to Isabel Beck. In R. C. Anderson, J. Osborn, & R. J. Tierney (Eds.), *Learning to read in American schools* (pp. 21-28). Hillsdale, NJ: Lawrence Erlbaum.

Pearson, P. D. (1985). *The comprehension revolution: A twenty-year history of process and practice related to reading comprehension* (Reading Education Report No. 57). Urbana: University of Illinois, Center for the Study of Reading.

Peeck, J. (1982). Effects of mobilization of knowledge on free recall. *Journal of Experimental Psychology: Learning, Memory, and Cognition, 8,* 608-612.

Peeck, J., Van Den Bosch, A. B., & Kruepeling, W. (1982). The effect of mobilizing prior knowledge on learning from text. *Journal of Educational Psychology, 74,* 771-777.

Pepper, S. C. (1961). *World hypotheses: A study in evidence.* Berkeley: University of California Press. (Original work published 1942)

Perfetti, C. A. (1985). *Reading ability.* New York: Oxford University Press.

Perkins, D., Jay, E., & Tishman, S. (1993). Introduction: New conceptions of thinking. *Educational Psychologist, 28,* 1–5.

Perkins, D. N. (1987). Thinking frames: An integrated perspective on teaching cognitive skills. In J. Baron & R. Sternberg (Eds.), *Teaching thinking skills: Theory and practice* (pp. 41–61). San Francisco: Freeman.

Perkins, D. N., & Salomon, G. (1989). Are cognitive skills context bound? *Educational Researcher, 18,* 16–25.

Perry, R. P., & Penner, K. S. (1990). Enhancing academic achievement in college students through attributional retraining and instruction. *Journal of Educational Psychology, 82,* 262–271.

Perry, W. G., Jr. (1970). *Forms of intellectual and ethical development in the college years.* New York: Academic Press.

Petersen, C. H., Glover, J. A., & Ronning, R. R. (1980). An examination of three prose learning strategies on reading comprehension. *Journal of General Psychology, 102,* 39-52.

Peterson, C. (1990). Explanatory style in the classroom and on the playing field. In S. Graham & V. Folkes (Eds.), *Attribution theory: Applications to achievement, mental health, and interpersonal conflict* (pp. 53–75). Hillsdale, NJ: Lawrence Erlbaum.

Peterson, L. R., & Peterson, M. J. (1959). Short-term retention of individual verbal items. *Journal of Experimental Psychology, 58,* 193-198.

Phifer, S. J., McNickle, B., Ronning, R. R., & Glover, J. A. (1983). The effect of details on the recall of major ideas in text. *Journal of Reading Behavior, 15,* 19-29.

Phillips, L. M. (1986). *Using children's literature to foster written language development.* (ERIC Document Reproduction Service No. ED 276 027)

Piaget, J. (1969). *The mechanisms of perception.* New York: Basic Books.

Pichert, J. W., & Anderson, R. C. (1977). Taking different perspectives on a story. *Journal of Educational Psychology, 69,* 309-315.

Pintrich, P. R., & DeGroot, E. V. (1990). Motivational and self-regulated learning components of classroom academic performance. *Journal of Educational Psychology, 82,* 33–40.

Pintrich, P. R., Marx, R. W., & Boyle, R. A. (1993). Beyond cold conceptual change: The role of motivational beliefs and classroom contextual factors in the process of conceptual change. *Review of Educational Research, 63,* 167–199.

Pisoni, D. B., & Luce, P. A. (1986). Speech perception: Research, theory, and the principal issues. In E. C. Schwab & H. C. Nusbaum (Eds.), *Pattern recognition by humans and machines* (pp. 1-42). New York: Academic Press.

Polanyi, M. (1967). *The tacit dimension.* London: Routledge & Kegan Paul.

Polya, G. (1973). *How to solve it* (2nd ed.). Garden City, NY: Doubleday.

Pomerantz, J. R. (1985). Perceptual organization in information processing. In A. M. Aitkenhead & J. M. Slack (Eds.), *Issues in cognitive modeling* (pp. 157–188). Hillsdale, NJ: Lawrence Erlbaum.

Poole, M.B.G., Okeafor, K., & Sloan, E. C. (1989, April). *Teachers' interactions, personal efficacy, and change implementation.* Paper presented at the Annual Meeting of the American Educational Research Association, San Francisco.

Poplin, M. S. (1988). Holistic/constructivist principles of the teaching/learning process: Implications for the field of learning disabilities. *Journal of Learning Disabilities, 21,* 401–416.

Posner, G. J., Strike, K. A., Hewson, P. W., & Gertzog, W. A. (1982). Accommodation of a scientific conception: Toward a theory of conceptual change. *Scientific Education, 66,* 211–228.

Posner, M. I., & Boies, S. J. (1971). Components of attention. *Psychological Review, 78,* 391-408.

Posner, M. I., & Keele, S. W. (1968). On the genesis of abstract ideas. *Journal of Experimental Psychology, 77,* 353-363.

Posner, M. I., & Keele, S. W. (1970). Retention of abstract ideas. *Journal of Experimental Psychology, 83,* 304-308.

Postman, L., Thompkins, B. S., & Gray, W. D. (1978). The interpretation of encoding effects in retention. *Journal of Verbal Learning and Verbal Behavior, 17,* 681-706.

Powell, J. S. (1988, April). *Defining words from context: Is helpfulness in the eyes of the beholder?* Paper presented at the Annual Meeting of the American Educational Research Association, New Orleans.

Pressley, M. (1977). Children's use of the keyword method to learn simple Spanish vocabulary words. *Journal of Educational Psychology, 69,* 465-472.

Pressley, M. (1985). More about yodai mnemonics: A commentary on Higbee and Kunihira. *Educational Psychologist, 20,* 69-73.

Pressley, M. (1994). Commentary on the ERIC whole language debate. In C. B. Smith (Moderator), *Whole language: The debate* (pp. 187–217). Bloomington, IN: ERIC/REC.

Pressley, M., Borkowski, J. G., & Schneider, W. (1987). Cognitive strategies: Good strategies users coordinate metacognition and knowledge. In R. Vasta & G. Whitehurst (Eds.), *Annals of Child Development* (Vol. 5, pp. 89–129). Greenwich, CT: JAI.

Pressley, M., El-Dinary, P. B., Gaskins, I., Schuder, T., Bergman, J. L., Almasi, J., & Brown, R. (1992). Beyond direct explanation: Transactional instruction of reading comprehension strategies. *Elementary School Journal, 92,* 511–554.

Pressley, M., & Ghatala, E. S. (1988). Delusions about performance on multiple-choice comprehension tests items. *Reading Research Quarterly, 23,* 454–464.

Pressley, M., Harris, K. R., & Marks, M. B. (1992). But good strategy instructors are constructivists! *Educational Psychology Review, 4,* 3–31.

Pressley, M., Johnson, C. J., Symons, S., McGoldrick, J. A., & Kurita, J. A. (1989). Strategies that improve children's memory and comprehension of text. *Elementary School Journal, 90,* 3–32.

Pressley, M., Levin, J. R., & Delaney, H. D. (1982). The mnemonic keyword method. *Review of Educational Research, 52,* 61-92.

Pressley, M., McDaniel, M. A., Turnure, J. E., Wood, E., & Ahmad M. (1987). Generation and precision of elaboration: Effects on intentional and incidental learning. *Journal of Experimental Psychology: Learning, Memory, and Cognition, 13,* 291–300.

Pressley, M., Snyder, B. L., Levin, J. R., Murray, H. G., & Ghatala, E. S. (1987). Perceived readiness for examination performance (PREP) produced by initial reading of text and text containing adjunct questions. *Reading Research Quarterly, 22,* 219-235.

Pressley, M., Symons, S., McDaniel, M. A., Snyder, B. L., & Turnure, J. E. (1988). Elaborative integration facilitates acquisition of confusing facts. *Journal of Educational Psychology, 80,* 268–278.

Pressley, M., Woloshyn, V., Lysynchuk, L., Martin, V., Wood, E., & Willoughby, T. (1990). Cognitive strategy instruction: The important issues and how to address them. *Educational Psychology Review, 2,* 1–58.

Prideaux, G. D. (1984). *Psycholinguistics: The experimental study of language.* London: Croom Helm.

Pylyshyn, Z. W. (1981). The imagery debate: Analogue media versus tacit knowledge. *Psychological Review, 88,* 16-45.

Quellmalz, E. S. (1987). Developing reasoning skills. In J. Baron & R. Sternberg (Eds.), *Teaching thinking skills: Theory and practice* (pp. 86–105). San Francisco: Freeman.

Quillian, M. R. (1968). Semantic memory. In M. Minsky (Ed.), *Semantic information processing* (pp. 21-56). Cambridge: MIT Press.

Rabinowitz, J. C., & Craik, F.I.M. (1986). Specific enhancement effects associated with word generation. *Journal of Memory and Language, 25,* 226-237.

Rabinowitz, J. C., Mandler, G., & Patterson, K. E. (1977). Determinants of recognition and recall: Accessibility and generation. *Journal of Experimental Psychology: General, 106,* 302-329.

Raphael, T. E. (1986). *Students' metacognitive knowledge about writing.* Research Series No. 176. (ERIC Document Reproduction Service No. ED 274 999)

Raphael, T. E., & McKinney, J. (1983). An examination of fifth- and eighth-grade children's question answering behavior: An instruction study in metacognition. *Journal of Reading Behavior, 15,* 67-86.

Raphael, T. E., & Pearson, P. D. (1982). *The effects of metacognitive strategy awareness training on students' question answering behavior* (Tech. Report No. 238). Urbana: University of Illinois, Center for the Study of Reading.

Raphael, T. E., & Wonnacott, C. A. (1985). Heightening fourth-grade students' sensitivity to sources of information for answering comprehension questions. *Reading Research Quarterly, 16,* 301-321.

Rayner, K., & Pollatsek, A. (1989). *The psychology of reading.* Englewood Cliffs, NJ: Prentice-Hall.

Recht, D. R., & Leslie, L. (1988). Effect of prior knowledge on good and poor readers' memory of text. *Journal of Educational Psychology, 80,* 16-20.

Reed, S. K. (1972). Pattern recognition and categorization. *Cognitive Psychology, 3,* 382-407.

Reed, S. K. (1984). Estimating answers to algebra word problems. *Journal of Experimental Psychology: Learning, Memory, and Cognition, 10,* 778-790.

Reed, S. K. (1987). A structure-mapping model for word problems. *Journal of Experimental Psychology: Learning, Memory, and Cognition, 13,* 124-139.

Reed, S. K., Dempster, A., & Ettinger, M. (1985). Usefulness of analogous solutions for solving algebra word problems. *Journal of Experimental Psychology: Learning, Memory, and Cognition, 11,* 106-125.

Rennie, L. J. (1989, April). *The relationship between teacher beliefs, management and organizational processes, and student participation in individualized classrooms.* Paper presented at the Annual Meeting of the American Educational Research Association. San Francisco.

Reynolds, A. J., & Walberg, H. J. (1991). A structural model of science achievement. *Journal of Educational Psychology, 83,* 97–107.

Reynolds, A. J., & Walberg, H. J. (1992). A structural model of science achievement and attitude: An extension to high school. *Journal of Educational Psychology, 84,* 371–382.

Reynolds, R. E. (1993). Selective attention and prose learning: Theoretical and empirical research. *Educational Psychology Review, 4,* 345–391.

Rickards, J. (1979). Adjunct postquestions in text: A critical review of methods and processes. *Review of Educational Research, 49,* 181-196.

Rieber, R. W., & Carton, A. S. (Eds.). (1987). *The collected works of L. S. Vygotsky* (N. Minick, Trans.). New York: Plenum.

Riley, M. S., Greeno, J. G., & Heller, J. I. (1983). Development of children's problem-solving ability in arithmetic. In H. P. Ginsburg (Ed.), *The development of mathematical thinking* (pp. 62-71). New York: Academic Press.

Robbins, J. T. (1986). A study of the effect of the writing process on the development of verbal skills among elementary school children. *Dissertation Abstracts International, 47,* 08A. (University Microfilms No. 86–87, 505)

Roediger III, H. L. (1990). Implicit memory: Retention without remembering. *American Psychologist, 45,* 1043–1056.

Rogoff, B. (1990). *Apprenticeship in thinking: Cognitive development in social context.* New York: Oxford University Press.

Romberg, T. A. (1992). Perspectives on scholarship and research methods. In D. A. Grouws (Ed.), *Handbook of research on mathematics teaching and learning* (pp. 49–64). New York: Macmillan.

Romberg, T. A., & Collis, K. E. (1987). Different ways children learn to add and subtract. *Journal for Research in Mathematics Education Monograph, 2.*

Root, R. L. (1985). *Assiduous string-savers: The idea generating strategies of professional expository writers.* Paper presented at the Annual Meeting of the Conference of College Composition and Communication. (ERIC Document Reproduction Service No. ED 258 205)

Rosch, E. (1978). Principles of categorization. In E. Rosch & B. B. Lloyd (Eds.), *Cognition and categorization* (pp. 28–48). Hillsdale, NJ: Lawrence Erlbaum.

Rosch, E., & Mervis, C. B. (1975). Family resemblance: Studies in the internal structure of categories. *Cognitive Psychology, 7,* 573-605.

Rosenblatt, L. (1938). *Literature as exploration.* New York: Noble & Noble.

Rosenthal, R., & Jacobson, L. (1968). *Pygmalion in the classroom: Teacher expectation and pupils' intellectual development.* New York: Holt, Rinehart & Winston.

Ross, B. H., & Kennedy, P. T. (1990). Generalizing from the use of earlier examples in problem solving. *Journal of Experimental Psychology: Learning, Memory and Cognition, 16,* 42–55.

Roth, I., & Frisby, J. P. (1986). *Perception and representation.* Philadelphia: Open Press.

Roth, K. J. (1985, April). *Conceptual change learning and student processing of science texts.* Paper presented at the Annual Meeting of the American Educational Research Association, Chicago.

Rothkopf, E. Z. (1966). Learning from written instructional materials: An exploration of the control of inspectional behaviors by test-like events. *American Educational Research Journal, 3,* 241-249.

Rowe, D. W., & Rayford, L. (1987). Activating background knowledge in reading comprehension. *Reading Research Quarterly, 22,* 160-176.

Rumelhart, D. E. (1975). Notes on a schema for stories. In D. C. Bobrow & A. M. Collins (Eds.), *Representation and understanding: Studies in cognitive science* (pp. 268-281). New York: Academic Press.

Rumelhart, D. E. (1980). *An introduction to human information processing.* New York: John Wiley.

Rumelhart, D. E. (1981). Schemata: The building blocks of cognition. In J. T. Guthrie (Ed.), *Comprehension and teaching: Research reviews* (pp. 3-26). Newark, DE: International Reading Association.

Rumelhart, D. E. (1984). Schemata and the cognitive system. In R. S. Wyer & T. K. Srull (Eds.), *Handbook of social cognition* (Vol. 1, pp. 161-188). Hillsdale, NJ: Lawrence Erlbaum.

Rumelhart, D. E., & McClelland, J. L. (1981). Interactive processing through spreading activation. In A. M. Lesgold & C. A. Perfetti (Eds.), *Interactive processes in reading* (pp. 37-60). Hillsdale, NJ: Lawrence Erlbaum.

Rumelhart, D. E., & McClelland, J. L. (1986). PDP models and general issues in cognitive science. In D. E. Rumelhart, J. L. McClelland, & PDP Research Group (Eds.), *Parallel distributed processing: Explorations in the microstructures of cognition: Vol 1. Foundations* (pp. 110–149). Cambridge: MIT Press.

Rumelhart, D. E., McClelland, J. L., & PDP Research Group (Eds.). (1986). *Parallel distributed processing: Explorations in the microstructure of cognition: Vol. 1. Foundations.* Cambridge: MIT Press.

Rumelhart, D. E., & Norman, D. A. (1978). Accretion, tuning, and restructuring: Three modes of learning. In J. W. Cotton & R. Klatzky (Eds.), *Semantic factors in cognition* (pp. 161-184). Hillsdale, NJ: Lawrence Erlbaum.

Rumelhart, D. E., & Ortony, A. (1977). The representation of knowledge in memory. In R. C. Anderson, R. J. Spiro, & W. E. Montague (Eds.), *Schooling and the acquisition of knowledge* (pp. 99–135). Hillsdale, NJ: Lawrence Erlbaum.

Runco, M. (1991). Creativity and the finding and solving of real-world problems. *Journal of Psychoeducational Assessment, 9,* 45–53.

Ryan, M. P. (1984). Monitoring test comprehension: Individual differences in epistemological standards. *Journal of Educational Psychology, 76,* 248–258.

Salomon, G., & Perkins, D. N. (1989). Rocky road to transfer: Rethinking mechanisms of a neglected phenomenon. *Educational Psychologist, 24,* 113–142.

Samuels, S. J. (1988). Decoding and automaticity: Helping poor readers become automatic at word recognition. *The Reading Teacher, 41,* 756-760.

Sansone, C., Sachau, D. A., & Weir, C. (1989). Effects of instruction on intrinsic interest: An examination of process and context. *Journal of Personality and Social Psychology, 57,* 819–829.

Sansone, C., Weir, C., Harpster, L., & Morgan, C. (1992). Once a boring task, always a boring task? Interest as a self-regulatory mechanism. *Journal of Personality and Social Psychology, 63,* 379–390.

Savalle, J. M., Twohig, P. T., & Rachford, D. L. (1986). Empirical status of Feuerstein's "instrumental enrichments" (FIE) technique as a method of teaching thinking skills. *Review of Educational Research, 56,* 381-409.

Schacter, D. L. (1993). Understanding implicit memory: A cognitive neuroscience approach. In A. F. Collins, S. E. Gathercole, M. A. Conway, & P. E. Morris (Eds.), *Theories of memory* (pp. 387–412). Hove, England: Lawrence Erlbaum.

Schacter, D. L., & Cooper, L. A. (1993). Implicit and explicit memory for novel visual objects: Structure and function. *Journal of Experimental Psychology: Learning, Memory, and Cognition, 19,* 995–1009.

Schallert, D. L. (1991). The contribution of psychology to teaching the language arts. In J. Flood, J. M. Jensen, D. Lapp, & J. R. Squire (Eds.), *Handbook of research on teaching the English language arts* (pp. 30–39). New York: Macmillan.

Schank, R. C., & Abelson, R. (1977). *Scripts, plans, goals, and understanding.* Hillsdale, NJ: Lawrence Erlbaum.

Scharf, B., & Buss, S. (1986). Audition I: Stimulus, physiology, thresholds. In K. R. Boff, L. Kaufman, & J. P. Thomas (Eds.), *Handbook of perception and human performance: Vol 1. Sensory perception and human performance* (pp. 14–1 to 14–71). New York: John Wiley.

Scharf, B., & Houtsma, A.J.M. (1986). Audition II: Loudness, pitch, localization, aural distortion, pathology. In K. R. Boff, L. Kaufman, & J. P. Thomas (Eds.), *Handbook of perception and human performance: Vol. 2. Sensory processes and perception* (pp. 15–1 to 15–60). New York: John Wiley.

Schauble, L. (1990). Belief revision in children: The role of prior knowledge and strategies for generating evidence. *Journal of Experimental Child Psychology, 49,* 31–57.

Schiefele, U. (1991). Interest, learning, and motivation. *Educational Psychologist, 26,* 299–324.

Schmuck, R. A., & Schmuck, P. A. (1992). *Group processes in the classroom* (6th ed.). Dubuque, IA: William C. Brown.

Schoenfeld, A. (1983). Beyond the purely cognitive: Belief systems, social cognitions, and metacognitions as driving forces in intellectual performance. *Cognitive Science, 7,* 329–363.

Schoenfeld, A. H. (1985). *Mathematical problem solving.* New York: Academic Press.

Schoenfeld, A. H. (1987). *Cognitive science and mathematics education.* Hillsdale, NJ: Lawrence Erlbaum.

Schoenfeld, A. H. (1992). Learning to think mathematically: Problem solving, metacognition, and sense making in mathematics. In D. A. Grouws (Ed.). *Handbook of research on mathematics teaching and learning* (pp. 334–370). New York: Macmillan.

Schommer, M. (1990). Effects of beliefs about the nature of knowledge on comprehension. *Journal of Educational Psychology, 82,* 498–504.

Schommer, M. (1991, April). *The relationship between students' beliefs about the nature of knowledge and academic experiences.* Paper presented at the Annual Meeting of the Midwestern Educational Research Association, Chicago.

Schommer, M., Crouse, A., & Rhodes, N. (1992). Epistemological beliefs and mathematical text comprehension: Believing it is simple does not make it so. *Journal of Educational Psychology, 84,* 435–443.

Schön, D. (1991). *Educating the reflective practitioner.* San Francisco: Jossey-Bass.

Schön, D. A. (1987). *The reflective practitioner: How professionals think in action.* New York: Basic Books.

Schraw, G. (1994). The effect of metacognitive knowledge on local and global monitoring. *Contemporary Educational Psychology, 19,* 143–154.

Schraw, G., & Dennison, R. S. (1994). The effect of reader purpose on interest and recall. *Journal of Reading Behavior: A Journal of Literacy, 26,* 1–18.

Schraw, G., Horn, C., Thorndike-Christ, T., & Bruning, R. H. (1994, April). *An investigation of academic goal orientations and course achievement.* Paper presented at the American Educational Research Association, New Orleans.

Schraw, G., Potenza, M., & Nebelsick-Gullet, L. (1993). Constraints on the calibration of performance. *Contemporary Educational Psychology, 18,* 455–463.

Schraw, G., & Roedel, T. D. (in press). Test difficulty and judgment bias. *Memory & Cognition.*

Schumacher, G. M. (1987). Executive control in studying. In B. R. Britton & S. M. Glynn (Eds.), *Executive control processes in reading* (pp. 202-244). Hillsdale, NJ: Lawrence Erlbaum.

Schunk, D. H. (1983). Ability versus effort attributional feedback: Differential effects on self-efficacy and achievement. *Journal of Educational Psychology, 75,* 848–856.

Schunk, D. H. (1984). Sequential attributional feedback and children's achievement behaviors. *Journal of Educational Psychology, 76,* 1156–1169.

Schunk, D. H. (1987). Peer models and children's behavioral change. *Review of Educational Research, 57,* 149–174.

Schunk, D. H. (1989). Self-efficacy and achievement behaviors. *Educational Psychology Review, 1,* 173–208.

Schunk, D. H. (1991). *Learning theories: An educational perspective.* New York: Macmillan.

Schunk, D. H., & Cox, P. D. (1986). Strategy training and attributional feedback with learning-disabled students. *Journal of Educational Psychology, 78,* 201–209.

Schwab, E. C., & Nusbaum, H. C. (1986). *Pattern recognition by humans and machines: Vol. 1. Speech perception.* New York: Academic Press.

Schwanenflugel, P. J., & Rey, M. (1986). Interlingual semantic facilitation: Evidence for a common representational system in the bilingual lexicon. *Journal of Memory and Language, 26,* 505-518.

Schwartz, B., & Reisberg, D. (1991). *Learning and memory.* New York: Norton.

Schweikert, R., & Boruff, B. (1986). Short-term memory capacity: Magic number or magic spell? *Journal of Experimental Psychology: Learning, Memory, and Cognition, 12,* 419-425.

Scruggs, T. E., Mastropieri, M. A., McLoone, B. B., Levin, J. R., & Morrison, C. R. (1987). Mnemonic facilitation of learning disabled students' memory for expository prose. *Journal of Educational Psychology, 79,* 27-34.

Seidenberg, M. S., & McClelland, J. L. (1989). A distributed, developmental model of word recognition and naming. *Psychological Review, 96,* 523–568.

Seifert, C. M., McKoon, G., Abelson, R. P., & Ratcliff, R. (1986). Memory connections between thematically similar episodes. *Journal of Experimental Psychology: Learning, Memory, and Cognition, 12,* 220-231.

Seifert, T. L. (1993). Effects of elaborative interrogation with prose passages. *Journal of Educational Psychology, 85,* 642–651.

Selfridge, O. G. (1959). Pandemonium: A paradigm for learning. In *Symposium on the mechanization of thought processes* (pp. 32-88). London: H. M. Stationery Office.

Sharples, M. (1985). *Cognition, computers, and creative writing.* West Sussex, England: Ellis Norwood.

Shavelson, R. J. (1973). Learning from physics instruction. *Journal of Research in Science Teaching, 10,* 101–111.

Shell, D. F., Colvin, C., & Bruning, R. H. (in press). Self-efficacy and outcome expectancy mechanisms in reading and writing achievement. *Journal of Educational Psychology.*

Shell, D. F., Murphy, C. C., & Bruning, R. H. (1989). Self-efficacy and outcome expectancy mechanisms in reading and writing performance. *Journal of Educational Psychology, 81,* 91–100.

Shiffrin, R. M. (1976). Capacity limitations in information processing, attention, and memory. In W. K. Estes (Ed.), *Handbook of learning and cognitive processes* (pp. 64-92). Hillsdale, NJ: Lawrence Erlbaum.

Shiffrin, R. M., & Gardner, G. T. (1972). Visual processing capacity and attentional control. *Journal of Experimental Psychology, 93,* 72-82.

Shiffrin, R. M., Pisoni, D. B., & Castaneda-Mendez, K. (1974). Is attention shared between the ears? *Cognitive Psychology, 6,* 190-215.

Shiffrin, R. M., & Schneider, W. (1977). Controlled and automatic information processing, II: Perceptual learning, automatic attending, and a general theory. *Psychological Review, 84,* 127-190.

Shimojo, S., & Richards, W. (1986). "Seeing" shapes that are almost totally occluded: A new look at Park's canal. *Perception & Psychophysics, 39,* 418-426.

Siegler, R. S., & Jenkins, E. (1989). *How children discover new strategies.* Hillsdale, NJ: Lawrence Erlbaum.

Silver, E. A. (1981). Recall of mathematical problem information: Solving related problems. *Journal for Research in Mathematics Education, 12,* 55-64.

Simon, D. P., & Simon, H. A. (1978). Individual differences in solving physics problems. In R. R. Siegler (Ed.), *Children's thinking: What develops?* (pp. 40–74). Hillsdale, NJ: Lawrence Erlbaum.

Simon, H. A. (1986). The parameters of human memory. In F. Klix & H. Hagendorf (Eds.), *Human memory and cognitive capabilities: Mechanisms and performances* (Part A, pp. 299-309). Amsterdam: North-Holland.

Skinner, B. F. (1938). *The behavior of organisms.* New York: Appleton-Century-Crofts.

Skinner, B. F. (1953). *Science and human behavior.* New York: Macmillan.

Skinner, B. F. (1957). *Verbal behavior.* New York: Appleton-Century-Crofts.

Skinner, B. F. (1968). *The technology of teaching.* New York: Appleton-Century-Crofts.

Skinner, E. A., Wellborn, J. G., & Connell, J. P. (1990). What it takes to do well in school and whether I've got it: A process model of perceived control and children's engagement and achievement in school. *Journal of Educational Psychology, 82,* 22–32.

Slamecka, N. J., & Graf, P. (1978). The generation effect: Delineation of a phenomenon. *Journal of Experimental Psychology: Human Learning and Memory, 4,* 592-604.

Slamecka, N. J., & Katsaiti, L. T. (1987). The generation effect as an artifact of selective displaced rehearsal. *Journal of Memory and Language, 26,* 589-602.

Sloman, S. A., Hayman, C.A.G., Ohta, N., Law, J., & Tulving, E. (1988). Forgetting in primed fragment completion. *Journal of Experimental Psychology: Learning, Memory, and Cognition, 14,* 223-239.

Smagorinsky, P., & Smith, M. W. (1992). The nature of knowledge in composition and literary understanding: The question of specificity. *Review of Educational Research, 62,* 279–305.

Smith, D., & Neale, D. C. (1989). The construction of subject matter knowledge in primary science teaching. *Teacher and Teacher Education, 5,* 1–20.

Smith, F. (1971). *Understanding reading.* Hillsdale, NJ: Lawrence Erlbaum.

Smith, F. (1982). *Understanding reading: A psycholinguistic analysis of reading and learning to read* (3rd ed.). New York: Holt, Rinehart & Winston.

Smith, S. M. (1986). Environmental context-dependent recognition memory using a short-term memory task for input. *Memory & Cognition, 14,* 347-354.

Smith, S. M., Vela, E., & Williamson, S. E. (1988). Shallow input processing does not induce environmental context dependent recognition. *Bulletin of the Psychonomic Society, 26,* 537-540.

Smylie, M. A. (1988). The enhancement function of staff development: Organizational and psychological antecedents to individual teacher change. *American Educational Research Journal, 25,* 1–30.

Snyder, C. R., Harris, C., Anderson, J. R., Holleran, S. A., Irving, L. M., Sigmon, S. T., Yoshinobu, L., Gibb, J., Langelle, C., & Harney, P. (1991). The will and the ways: Development and validation of an individual differences measure of hope. *Journal of Personality and Social Psychology, 60,* 570–585.

Solso, R. L. (1988). *Cognitive psychology* (2nd ed.). Boston: Allyn & Bacon.

Sorkin, R. D., & Pohlman, L. D. (1973). Some models of observer behavior in two channel auditory signal detection. *Perception & Psychophysics, 14,* 101-109.

Spector, J. E. (1992). Predicting progress in beginning reading: Dynamic assessment of phonemic awareness. *Journal of Educational Psychology, 84,* 353–363.

Spence, K. W. (1936). The nature of discrimination learning in animals. *Psychological Review, 43,* 427-449.

Spence, K. W. (1956). *Behavior theory and conditioning.* New Haven, CT: Yale University Press.

Sperling, G. (1960). The information available in brief visual presentations [Special issue]. *Psychological Monographs, 74*(498).

Sperling, G. (1983). *Unified theory of attention and signal detection. Mathematical studies in perception and cognition* (No. 83-3). New York: New York University, Department of Psychology.

Sperling, G., & Dosher, B. A. (1986). Strategy and optimization in human information processing. In K. R. Boff, L. Kaufman, & J. P. Thomas (Eds.), *Handbook of perception and human performance: Vol. 1. Sensory processes and perception* (pp. 2-1 to 2-65). New York: John Wiley.

Sperling, M. (1990). I want to talk to each of you: Collaboration and the teacher-student writing conference. *Research in the Teaching of English, 24,* 279–321.

Sperling, M. (in press). Discourse analysis of teacher-student writing conferences: Finding the message in the medium. In P. Smagorinsky (Ed.), *Verbal reports in the study of writing: Problems and potentials.* Thousand Oaks, CA: Sage.

Spiro, R. J. (1977). Remembering information from text: The "State of Schema" approach. In R. C. Anderson, R. J. Spiro, & W. E. Montague (Eds.), *Schooling and the acquisition of knowledge* (pp. 336-351). Hillsdale, NJ: Lawrence Erlbaum.

Spiro, R. J. (1980). Constructive processes in prose comprehension and recall. In R. J. Spiro, B. C. Bruce, & W. E. Brewer (Eds.), *Theoretical issues in reading comprehension* (pp. 245-278). Hillsdale, NJ: Lawrence Erlbaum.

Squire, L. R. (1987). *Memory and brain.* New York: Oxford University Press.

Stahl, S. A., & Fairbanks, M. M. (1986). The effects of vocabulary instruction: A model-based meta-analysis. *Review of Reading Research, 56,* 72-110.

Standing, L. (1973). Learning 10,000 pictures. *Quarterly Journal of Experimental Psychology, 25,* 207-222.

Standing, L., Conezio, J., & Haber, R. N. (1970). Perception and memory for pictures: Single trial learning of 2500 visual stimuli. *Psychonomic Science, 19,* 73-74.

Stanovich, K. E. (1990). Concepts in developmental theories of reading skill: Cognitive resources, automaticity, and modularity. *Developmental Review, 10,* 72–100.

Stanovich, K. E., & Cunningham, A. E. (1993). Where does knowledge come from? Specific associations between print exposure and information acquisition. *Journal of Educational Psychology, 85,* 211–229.

Sternberg, R. J. (1986). *The triarchic mind: A new theory of human intelligence.* New York: Penguin.

Sternberg, R. J. (1987). Most vocabulary is learned from context. In M. G. McKeown & M. E. Curtis (Eds.), *The nature of vocabulary acquisition* (pp. 89–105). Hillsdale, NJ: Lawrence Erlbaum.

Sternberg, R. J., & Detterman, D. K. (1986). *What is intelligence?* Norwood, NJ: Ablex.

Sternberg, R. J., & Powell, J. S. (1983). Comprehending verbal comprehension. *American Psychologist, 38,* 878-893.

Stewart, M. E., & Leaman, H. L. (1983). Teachers' writing assessments across the high school curriculum. *Research in the Teaching of English, 17,* 113-125.

Stipek, D. J. (1993). *Motivation to learn* (2nd ed.). Boston: Allyn & Bacon.

Sulzby, E. (1991). The development of the young child and the emergence of literacy. In J. Flood, J. M. Jensen, D. Lapp, & J. R. Squire (Eds.), *Handbook of research on teaching the English language arts* (pp. 273–285). New York: Macmillan.

Svengas, A. G., & Johnson, M. K. (1988). Qualitative effects of rehearsal on memories for perceived and imagined complex events. *Journal of Experimental Psychology: Educational Psychologist, 24,* 113–142.

Swanson, H. L. (1990). Influence of metacognitive knowledge and aptitude on problem solving. *Journal of Educational Psychology, 82,* 306–314.

Swanson, H. L. (1992). Generality and modifiability of working memory among skilled and less skilled readers. *Journal of Educational Psychology, 84,* 473–488.

Swanson, H. L., O'Connor, J. E., & Cooney, J. B. (1990). An information processing analysis of expert and novice teachers' problem solving. *American Educational Research Journal, 27,* 533–556.

Swartz, R. J. (1989). Making good thinking stick: The role of metacognition, extended practice, and teacher modeling in the teaching of thinking. In D. Topping, D. Crowell, & V. Kobayashi (Eds.), *Thinking across cultures: The Third International Conference on Thinking* (pp. 417–436). Hillsdale, NJ: Lawrence Erlbaum.

Swartz, R. J., & Perkins, D. N. (1990). *Teaching thinking: Issues and approaches.* Pacific Grove, CA: Midwest.

Taft, M. L., & Leslie, L. (1985). The effects of prior knowledge and oral reading accuracy on miscues and comprehension. *Journal of Reading Behavior, 17,* 163-179.

Taylor, B. M., & Beach, R. W. (1984). The effects of text structure instruction on middle-grade students' comprehension and production of expository text. *Reading Research Quarterly, 14,* 134-146.

Teale, W. H., & Sulzby, E. (1986). *Emergent literacy.* Norwood, NJ: Ablex.

Thorndike, E. L. (1911). *Animal intelligence: Experimental studies.* New York: Macmillan.

Triesman, A. M. (1964). Selective attention in man. *British Medical Journal, 20,* 12-16.

Triesman, A. M. (1969). Strategies and models of selective attention. *Psychological Review, 76,* 282-299.

Triesman, A. M., & Geffen, G. (1967). Selective attention: Perception or response? *Quarterly Journal of Experimental Psychology, 19,* 1-17.

Triesman, A. M., & Gelade, G. (1980). A feature integration theory of attention. *Cognitive Psychology, 12,* 97-136.

Triesman, A. M., & Riley, J.G.A. (1969). Is selective attention selective perception or selective response? A further test. *Journal of Experimental Psychology, 79,* 27-34.

Triesman, A. M., & Schmidt, H. (1982). Illusory conjunctions in the perception of objects. *Cognitive Psychology, 14,* 107-141.

Triesman, A. M., Squire, R., & Green, J. (1974). Semantic processing in dichotic listening? A replication. *Memory & Cognition, 2,* 641-646.

Tulving, E. (1972). Episodic and semantic memory. In E. Tulving & W. Donaldson (Eds.), *Organization of memory* (pp. 381-403). New York: Academic Press.

Tulving, E. (1983). *Elements of episodic memory.* Oxford, England: Oxford University Press.

Tulving, E. (1985). On the classification problem in learning and memory. In L. Nilsson & T. Archer (Eds.), *Perspectives on learning and memory* (pp. 73-101). Hillsdale, NJ: Lawrence Erlbaum.

Tulving, E., & Osler, S. (1968). Effectiveness of retrieval cues in memory for words. *Journal of Experimental Psychology, 77,* 593-601.

Tulving, E., & Thompson, D. M. (1973). Encoding specificity and retrieval processes in episodic memory. *Psychological Review, 80,* 352-373.

Tversky, A. (1977). Features of similarity. *Psychological Review, 84,* 327–352.

Tversky, A., & Kahneman, D. (1974). Judgments under uncertainty: Heuristics and biases. *Science, 185,* 1124–1131.

Uhry, J. K., & Shepard, M. J. (1993). Segmentation/spelling instruction as part of a first-grade reading program: Effects of several measures of reading. *Reading Research Quarterly, 28,* 218–233.

Underwood, B. J., & Schultz, R. W. (1960). *Meaningfulness and verbal learning.* Philadelphia: J. B. Lippincott.

Van de Walle, J. A., & Watkins, K. B. (1993). Early development of number sense. In R. J. Jensen (Ed.), *Research ideas for the classroom: Early childhood mathematics* (pp. 127–150). New York: Macmillan.

Van Dijk, T. A., & Kintsch, W. (1983). *Strategies of discourse comprehension.* New York: Academic Press.

Vallerand, R. J., Blais, M. R., Briere, N. M., & Pelletier, L. G. (1989). Construction et validation de l'Echelle de Motivation en Education [Construction and validation of the Motivation in Education Scale]. *Canadian Journal of Behavioral Sciences, 21,* 323–349.

Vellutino, F. R. (1991). Introduction to three studies on reading acquisition: Convergent findings on theoretical foundations of code-oriented versus whole-language approaches to reading instruction. *Journal of Educational Psychology, 83,* 437–443.

Von Wright, J. M. (1972). On the problem of selection in iconic memory. *Scandinavian Journal of Psychology, 13,* 159-171.

Vosniadou, S., & Brewer, W. F. (1987). Theories of knowledge restructuring in development. *Review of Educational Research, 57,* 51–67.

Vosniadou, S., Pearson, R. D., & Rogers, T. (1988). What causes children's failures to detect inconsistencies in text? Representation versus comparison difficulties. *Journal of Educational Psychology, 80,* 27-39.

Voss, J. E., & Post, T. A. (1988). On the solving of ill-structured problems. In M. Chi, R. Glaser, & M. Farr (Eds.), *The nature of expertise* (pp. 261–287). Hillsdale, NJ: Lawrence Erlbaum.

Vye, N. J., Delclos, V. R., Burns, M. S., & Bransford, J. D. (1988). Teaching thinking and problem solving: Illustrations and issues. In R. Sternberg & E. Smith (Eds.), *The psychology of human thought* (pp. 337–365). New York: Cambridge University Press.

Vygotsky, L. (1978). *Mind in society: The development of higher psychological processes.* Cambridge, MA: Harvard University Press.

Wade, S. E., Schraw, G., Buxton, W. M., & Hayes, M. T. (1993). Seduction of the strategic reader: Effects of interest on strategies and recall. *Reading Research Quarterly, 28,* 3–24.

Wade, S. E., Trathen, W., & Schraw, G. (1990). An analysis of spontaneous study strategies. *Reading Research Quarterly, 25,* 147–166.

Wagner, K. (1971). Tony and his friends. In L. B. Jacobs (Ed.), *The read-it yourself storybook.* New York: Western.

Wagner, R. K., & Sternberg, R. J. (1985). Practical intelligence in real-world pursuits: The role of tacit knowledge. *Journal of Personality and Social Psychology, 52,* 1236–1247.

Walker, N. (1986). Direct retrieval from elaborated memory traces. *Memory & Cognition, 74,* 321-328.

Waller, T. G. (1987). *Reading research: Advances in theory and practice* (Vol. 5). New York: Academic Press.

Watson, J. B. (1924). *Behaviorism.* New York: Norton.

Watt, E. (1988). *Visual processing research.* Hillsdale, NJ: Lawrence Erlbaum.

Wattenmaker, W. D., Dewey, G. I., Murphy, T. D., & Medin, D. L. (1986). Linear separability and concept learning: Context, relational properties, and concept naturalness. *Cognitive Psychology, 18,* 158-194.

Waugh, N. C., & Norman, D. A. (1965). Primary memory. *Psychological Review, 72,* 89-104.

Weaver, C. (1988). *Reading process and practice.* Portsmouth, NH: Heinemann.

Weiner, B. (1985). An attributional theory of achievement motivation and emotion. *Psychological Review, 92,* 548–573.

Weiner, B. (1986). *An attributional theory of motivation and emotion.* New York: Springer Verlag.

Weisberg, R. W. (1993). *Creativity: Beyond the myth of genius.* San Francisco: Freeman.

Weldon, M. S., & Roediger, H. L. (1987). Altering retrieval demands reverses the picture superiority effect. *Memory and Cognition, 15,* 269–280.

West, R. F., Stanovich, K. E., & Mitchell, H. (1993). Reading in the real world and its correlates. *Reading Research Quarterly, 28,* 34–50.

Wickens, D. D. (1980). The structure of attentional resources. In R. S. Nickerson (Ed.), *Attention and performance VIII* (pp. 260-304). Hillsdale, NJ: Lawrence Erlbaum.

Wilhite, S. C. (1986, April). *Multiple-choice test performance: Effects of headings, questions, motivation, and type of retention test question.* Paper presented at the Annual Meeting of the American Educational Research Association, San Francisco.

Willoughby, T., Waller, T. G., Wood, E., & McKinnon, G. E. (1993). The effect of prior knowledge on an immediate and delayed associative learning task following elaborative integration. *Contemporary Educational Psychology, 18,* 36–46.

Wilson, P. S. (1993). Introduction: Becoming involved with research. In P. S. Wilson (Ed.), *Research ideas for the classroom: High school mathematics.* New York: Macmillan.

Wilson, J. W., Fernandez, M. L., & Hadaway, N. (1993). Mathematical problem solving. In P. S. Wilson (Ed.), *Research ideas for the classroom: High school mathematics.* New York: Macmillan.

Winograd, R. N. (1984). Strategic difficulties in summarizing texts. *Reading Research Quarterly, 14,* 404-424.

Winograd, T. (1975). Frame representations and the declarative-procedural controversy. In D. G. Bobrow & A. M. Collins (Eds.), *Representation and understanding: Studies in cognitive science* (pp. 185–210). New York: Academic Press.

Wollen, K. A., Weber, A., & Lowry, D. H. (1972). Bizarreness versus interaction of mental images as determinants of learning. *Cognitive Psychology, 3,* 518-523.

Woltz, D. J. (1988). An investigation of the role of working memory in procedural skill acquisition. *Journal of Experimental Psychology: General, 117,* 319–331.

Wood, E., Pressley, M., & Winne, P. H. (1990). Elaborative interrogation effects on children's learning of factual content. *Journal of Educational Psychology, 82,* 741–748.

Woolfolk, A. E., & Hoy, W. K. (1990). Prospective teachers' sense of efficacy and beliefs about control. *Journal of Educational Psychology, 82,* 81–91.

Wysocki, K., & Jenkins, J. (1987). Deriving word meanings through morphological generalization. *Reading Research Quarterly, 22,* 66-81.

Yates, E. A. (1966). *The art of memory.* Chicago: University of Chicago Press.

Yoshinobu, L. R. (1989). *Construct validation of the Hope Scale: Agency and pathways components.* Unpublished master's thesis, University of Kansas, Lawrence.

Yussen, S. R., & Levy, V. M., Jr. (1975). Developmental changes in predicting one's own span of short-term memory. *Journal of Experimental Child Psychology, 19,* 502-508.

Zimmer, J. W., Petersen, C. H., Ronning, R. R., & Glover, J. A. (1978). The effect of adjunct aids on prose processing. *Journal of Instructional Psychology, 5,* 27-34.

Zimmerman, B. J. (1990). Self-regulated academic learning and achievement: The emergence of a social cognitive perspective. *Educational Psychology Review, 2,* 173–201.

Zimmerman, B. J., & Martinez-Pons, M. (1990). Student differences in self-regulated learning: Relating grade, sex, and giftedness to self-efficacy and strategy use. *Journal of Educational Psychology, 82,* 51–59.

Subject Index

Name Index

THE LIBRARY
CENTRAL COLLEGE OF COMMERCE
300 CATHEDRAL STREET
GLASGOW
G1 2TA